Education and Politics in India

Contributors

Paul R. Brass, *Associate Professor of Political Science, University of Washington, Seattle, Washington*

Carolyn M. Elliott, *Assistant Professor of Politics, University of California, Santa Cruz, California*

Joan Landy Erdman, *Hanover, New Hampshire*

Irene A. Gilbert, *Assistant Professor, Department of Government, Simmons College, Boston, Massachusetts*

Harold Gould, *Professor of Anthropology, University of Illinois, Champaign-Urbana, Illinois*

Janet Guthrie, *Department of Sociology, University of Chicago, Chicago, Illinois*

B. G. Halbar, *Lecturer in Social Anthropology, Karnatak University, Mysore*

T. N. Madan, *Senior Fellow (Sociology) and Head of the Asian Research Centre at the Institute of Economic Growth, Delhi University, Delhi*

Iqbal Narain, *Professor of Political Science, University of Rajasthan, Jaipur, Rajasthan*

Lloyd I. Rudolph, *Professor of Political Science, and the Social Sciences, University of Chicago, Chicago, Illinois*

Susanne Hoeber Rudolph, *Professor of Political Science and the Social Sciences, University of Chicago, Chicago, Illinois*

Education and Politics in India

Studies in Organization, Society, and Policy

*Edited by Susanne Hoeber Rudolph
and Lloyd I. Rudolph*

Harvard University Press
Cambridge, Massachusetts
1972

To J. P. Naik and David Riesman,
unconventional educators

Contents

Preface

Our concern in studying the politics of education is to identify and analyze the institutions and processes that shape educational policy and performance. The rapid and dramatic expansion of higher education in India and elsewhere has helped to generate research in educational sociology, economics, finance, manpower planning, and administration. The politics of education, however, remains a relatively neglected field. So talented and comprehensive a survey as the Indian *Report of the Education Commission, 1964–1966,* although evidently written with sensitivity to political constraints, neither specifies nor confronts them. With a few recent exceptions, the same is true of the burgeoning literature on the public responsibilities and internal government of universities in America and Europe.

This volume makes two contributions to the study of the politics of education. The first is to identify critical problems in the relationship between politics and education generally and to explore concepts and methods for their investigation. The second is to make a specific contribution to our understanding of the relationship between politics and education in India.

Governments are relying increasingly on the educational system to promote economic and political development and, more generally, to approach the moving frontier of modernity. Politicians are responding increasingly to the demands of their constituents that education be made available so that they can improve their economic and social circumstances. One result of these processes is the concentration of ever larger resources and personnel in the educational system. Another result is heightened competition between politicians and educators for control of the people, resources, and goals involved.

It is difficult to assess abstractly the kinds of demands public authorities, including politicians, can legitimately make on education in the name of social needs and how much autonomy educational institutions should have to choose and implement their policies. At the extreme, the appropriation of educational resources for primarily political purposes threatens or destroys educational effectiveness. At the same time, the political system must have sufficient influence in the educational system to shape educational policy and the use of educational resources in ways that are socially responsive. Also, educators must have political influence to command necessary resources and to make and implement educational policy. Informed judgments about the proper relationship between politics and education must rely on detailed studies that clarify the values and interests involved as politics and education contend for influence in particular settings. The studies developed in this volume provide some basis for such judgments.

Since September 1966, a number of Indian and American scholars of various social science disciplines have been corresponding and conferring on methods of investigating the relationship between the educational and political systems in India. The concerns of the various participants in these discussions crystallized in a conference held at the India International Centre in New Delhi, June 28–30, 1967. The conference was supported by the American Institute of Indian Studies.

Since then, most of the participants in the conference have continued to work on the papers circulated and discussed at the New Delhi conference. Five of them participated in a panel at the Association for Asian Studies in Philadelphia on March 24, 1968, and several more in a similar panel in San Francisco, April 3–5, 1970. Their combined effort is represented in this volume.

The book sets the educational system in its environment, particularly its political environment. Education is treated aggregatively and disaggregatively, as the educational system on the one hand and as educational institutions on the other. In analyzing educational institutions, more attention is devoted to higher education than to school and primary education, although Part II is largely devoted to the latter two levels. The educational system is disaggregated not only by educational institutions and levels of education, but also by regions.

In the six chapters of Part I, "The Political System and the Educational System; An Analysis of Their Interaction," we provide a general framework for the eight chapters of Parts II, III, and IV, which explore various facets of the relationship between education and politics in India. The framework presented in Part I has three principal dimensions; conceptual, methodological, and informational. Complementing Part I are the introductions to Parts II, III, and IV. They highlight each author's findings and methods, relate them to other chapters in the Part and connect them to the general themes of the book.

The editors are grateful to the American Institute of Indian Studies (A.I.I.S.) for making possible our research in India in 1966 and 1967 and to the Committee on Southern Asian Studies, the Social Sciences Research Committee, and the College, all of the University of Chicago, for their support of the editorial work. We owe a great debt to J. P. Naik, member-secretary of the Education Commission, 1964–1966, member-secretary of the Indian Council for Social Science Research and educational advisor in the ministry of education, for facilitating access to the materials relevant to this study, and for making available his wise counsel on the evaluation and judgment of policy issues. Needless to say, he is not responsible for the views we express. John Simon, formerly director of the A.I.I.S. in India, and D. D. Karve, formerly its executive officer, were most helpful in supporting the conference which launched this work. P. R. Mehendiratta, who managed most of the logistics of the conference, assured it a fruitful setting. We appreciate the interest taken in this book by Harold Howe II and Fred Harrington of the Ford Foundation.

Mrs. Suzanne W. Ronneau, our secretary and research assistant throughout most of the course of this book, was a model of care, efficiency, and tact.

L.I.R.
S.H.R.

Part I / The Political System and the Educational System:
An Analysis of Their Interaction

Susanne Hoeber Rudolph / Lloyd I. Rudolph

1 / Studying Education and Politics

Institutional Transfer: The University in an Indian Environment[1]

Modern universities in India began in 1858 as institutional transplants from Great Britain. Since then they have undergone a steady process of adaptation to their indigenous environment. In the last twenty years, this process has accelerated considerably. Until independence in 1947, Indian universities were relatively insulated from the influence of their Indian setting by the effects of British rule and an educational policy which protected their elite standing and the exotic quality of their alien culture.

The functions of universities under British rule were intellectual, cultural, and political: to connect Indian education to European knowledge; to transmit the cultural values specific to Britain and Europe; and to make available to the *raj* a class of clerks, bureaucrats, and political collaborators. These functions were so tightly interwoven that it is difficult to disentangle the university's role as an institution for modernizing intellectual activity from its role as an instrument of British cultural and political domination. Until 1828, the English tended to prize Indian learning and attempted to master it through Indian languages and thought forms; to rationalize and modernize it; and to introduce modern scientific ideas within its framework. Indians in turn revived, revitalized, and modernized their traditional learning and literary expression, while taking account of European knowledge. The consequence of Thomas Macaulay's cultural Ludditism was to ignore and destroy these developments, and to preempt a history that might have been. The cultural *hubris* that insisted that "a single shelf of a good European library was worth the whole native literature of India and Arabia" marked the onset of an educational policy that replaced Oriental with English learning. The resources of the *raj* were placed primarily at the disposal of English language educational institutions. As long as Indians could stand within the framework of their traditional culture, they were free to choose, reject, or selectively emulate what British learning had to offer. Macaulay's policy symbolized the rise of radical asymmetry in British-Indian cultural relations, and made copying the dominator a compulsory condition of higher education. Indian universities were shaped and limited by the fundamental cultural decision expressed in Macaulay's minute of 1835.[2]

Universities and colleges modernized Indian intellectual life by introducing European versions of the organization of knowledge and the academic specialization and disciplines associated with such knowledge. Specialization of knowledge was not new to India, but both the content and organization of knowledge associated with English higher education were different from and went beyond traditional Hindu and Muslim scholarship. English higher education encouraged scientific thinking by stressing the relationship of theory and "truth" to empirical and experimental methods. It encouraged the use of "rational" principles in nonscientific fields. (In retrospect, the rationality invoked is difficult to disentangle from the specific cultural assumptions and preferences of eighteenth and nineteenth century European civilization.) It routinized the canons of scholarly craftsmanship in line with nineteenth century ideas of research and established in a rudimentary fashion disciplinary professionalism. It created bureaucratic structures to administer the examination system and to assure compliance with the newly imported standards in curriculum and appointments. Mastery of the cultural aspects of English education — a good command of the language and literature and the right manners and style — was a condition for access to opportunities in the public services and private firms of the *raj* even as a Persian education had been a condition for access to opportunities under Moghul rule. English education introduced yet another civilizational element into the multicivilizational syncretism that is Indian culture.

British efforts to protect the cultural purity and political usefulness of the transplant checked the modernizing potentialities of the university in certain crucial areas. University attention and energies were directed away from problems in the immediate environment and toward those in an alien, distant, and often unknown environment. Englishmen and assimilated Indians often mistook Anglicization for the development and transmission of modern knowledge and skills. The university's elite bias (at the time, characteristic of universities elsewhere) and its English cultural bias not only insulated it from its Indian environment but also limited its impact on that environment. At the same time, the university's class and cultural insulation from its immediate environment shielded it from certain challenges that might have been overwhelming. Although university administrators already complained in the 1880's of too rapid expansion, the problems of scale remained in human and resource terms within manageable proportions. Colleges were small and teachers had time to teach, as well as to converse and reflect (conditions which may or may not be conducive to scholarly productivity, depending on whether one takes a nineteenth century English or a twentieth century American view of the matter). And within the confines of the exotic transplant's cultural definition, insulation not infrequently produced the learning, character, and style of expression that counted as high standards in nineteenth century British university circles.

Independence in 1947 marked something of a watershed in the development of higher education in India, as Indian school and higher education lost its elite character and took on an increasingly popular one. The establishment of political democracy after independence legitimized and accelerated demands that higher education be available to all who could qualify for it. This commitment to equality of opportunity has put tremendous pressure on government to allocate resources in sufficient measure to meet the growing demand and upon educational authorities to adjust standards for admission and the granting of degrees. State governments, which have primary constitutional responsibility for education, are closer and more responsive to popular pressures. They have continuously widened educational opportunity by sanctioning the creation of new universities and colleges and, to a lesser extent, by allocating resources. The central government is more removed from demands for education and less responsible for it because of the effects of federalism on the electoral process and the distribution of constitutional authority for education. It has used the authority it does have to try to maintain standards, and has allocated resources in ways that have had a restraining but hardly a governing effect on the size and shape of higher education in India. The escalating demand by citizens and voters for school and higher education has been intensified by the activities of territorial and social communities who found new educational institutions that qualify for university recognition or government subventions or both.

The ascendency of nationalism and democracy has increasingly deprived higher education of the exotic and elite qualities that helped to insulate it from popular and indigenous influences. Since independence educational policy and educational institutions have been increasingly forced to confront and adjust to their social and political environment. As universities have become more socially and culturally representative, they have been penetrated and shaped by democratic as against elite, by indigenous as against anglicized, norms and behavior. The many universities founded since independence have been less emulative of British ways than the few existing before it. They know less and care less about imported definitions of curriculum, university government, and educational goals. In these ways education in India has become more indigenous, that is, more like its environment and less like an exotic transplant from an alien culture. This does not mean that the structure of higher education has changed substantially. The affiliating university and the examination system adapted from the University of London in 1858 remain largely intact. But the substance of education has changed both in form — language — and in content. Although all the consequences of this transformation are difficult to assess, one is clear enough: in their constituencies and in their modes of communication, if not necessarily in their formal structures or curriculum content, Indian universities have become more connected with and relevant to their environment.

Because of these processes of change, a somewhat paradoxical situation has arisen. Universities as modern structures are becoming more parochial at the same time that traditional structures such as villages and castes are becoming more cosmopolitan. And the two processes of change seem to be interrelated. Villages and castes are experiencing an expansion of territorial and reference group boundaries that connects them to structures, roles, and values that arise out of industrial, urban, and international contexts. Those who still live within the framework of the village and the caste community are experiencing a dispersal of affect, a broadening of economic options, and an enlargement of imagination that connects them with groups, experiences, and aspirations that transcend the formal boundaries of their social settings.

As universities become more socially and culturally representative, as they are penetrated and shaped by indigenous democratic forces, their territorial and reference group boundaries also expand, but in the opposite direction from that of the boundary expansion being experienced by castes and villages. They move from reference groups and relevancies in international, industrial, and urban environments to those in rural and agricultural environments. As they do so their attention is increasingly diverted, whether they like it or not, from their international commitments and colleagues to their commitments and colleagues at home, in India, in their region, and in their university and to those leaders of organized political and social forces that affect the well-being and policies of their university. The university's expansion of reference groups, then, is in a direction which draws its attention away from the world of scholarship and learning and toward the interests and preoccupations of the *mofussil* (or locality). At the same time, villagers brought within the ambit of the university experience ideas and symbols that transcend their locality and primary group.

It is in this qualified sense of a two-way flow that we speak of the "parochialization" of the university. Parochialization is part of the price that is being paid for the cosmopolitanization and decompression of villages, castes, and other traditional structures. The demand for higher education from those whose horizons until recently have been bounded by the village and the primary group has fostered university parochialization, the drawing in of the university's symbolic and physical boundaries. It is difficult at this stage, when the curve of indigenous demand for higher education has yet to peak, to judge what the longer run consequences of parochialization will be for universities in India. Will universities be so overwhelmed by the effects of becoming more socially and culturally representative that they will lose their cosmopolitan dimension and their capacity to be connected with and to contribute to world knowledge? Or can they, as they are penetrated by new constituencies, induct those constituencies into world knowledge while making that knowledge relevant to local needs?

The Public Interest, Politicization, and Political Influence

During the nineteenth century education became one of the recognized responsibilities of most modern states. On the one hand, children were compelled to attend school; on the other, education became what T. H. Marshall has called a "social right." [3]

In the industrial and postindustrial experiences of various countries, education came to replace military prowess, land ownership, and ownership of the means of industrial production as a key determinant of wealth, status, and power. Today, in the more advanced countries particularly but also to an increasing degree in developing countries, those who have higher educational degrees can expect to help exercise a controlling influence in society and the polity.

Education became a matter of primary concern to the state not only because educated citizens could provide better manpower for conscript armies (a leading concern in Napoleonic France, which provided a model for European countries) [4] but also because, after a time, it became clear that education could lead, as in France, [5] to national integration of the elite, and because education was seen as the best available means to "civilize" and to rule the industrial classes. [6]

For a considerable time, economists failed to take into account the contributions that education could and did make to economic (as well as social and political) development by conceptualizing it as a consumer good or a welfare function. Of late, however, education has increasingly been conceptualized as a factor that promotes economic growth and, in this sense, as an important area for investment. [7] As more nations have recognized the responsibility of the state for economic growth (as well as for stability and employment), the importance of education for the collective good has grown accordingly. In industrial and industrializing economies alike investment in education is increasingly seen as investment for economic growth, as a means to improve "human quality," to enhance human resources, and to create new knowledge, new technologies, and new ways of managing the environment.

As a result of these cumulating concerns for education on the part of the state and the citizen, education receives an ever larger share of public resources. In many countries it is the single largest expenditure and in others it is second only to defense. [8] For these good, substantial reasons education today is deeply involved with the articulation and realization of the public interest.

In the face of limited resources and intense public competition for them, the idea that school and higher education is a social right to be provided or at least paid for in part by the state has become widespread and has achieved a certain legitimacy. Simultaneously, the demand for education has preceded and outpaced rather than followed and lagged behind the ability of the economy to generate resources to meet this demand. The concurrent growth of demand for school and higher education, the use of public authority and resources to meet most of this demand, and the considerable influence of democratic politics on public policy for education has multiplied the points of interaction between the political and educational systems. To assist in the analysis of the boundaries and interdigitations of these systems we have distinguished three relationships between them: politicization of educational structures; political influence exercised by educational structures; and assertion by the state of a public interest in education. These three relationships are not always easy to distinguish in concrete empirical situations but distinguishing between them has proved extremely useful in analyzing such situations. The propensity we encountered in India among those concerned with education to believe that the politics of education meant *only* politicization provides another, and quite different, reason for making and using these distinctions.

Politicization, as we use the term, involves the appropriation of educational structures and resources and the displacement of educational goals by organized political and community (religion, caste, locality) interests. The effect of politicization is to subsume the educational goals and processes of particular educational institutions to those of organized extraeducational interests.

The politicization of educational institutions is part of a larger process of politicization in India in which an increasing number of actors in various political arenas attempt to maximize political resources and through them political influence and power. The result threatens not only to raise the level of political participation and mobilization to pathological levels (that is, levels that burden the institutions and processes of the political system with more demands and conflicts than they can effectively handle) but also to bring into the competition and decision-making of the political system institutions (such as schools, colleges, and universities) that are not appropriate to it.

For example, as Harold Gould suggests below, in Uttar Pradesh, a state with relatively low levels of economic development and governmental performance, decision-making in schools, colleges, and universities is closely linked to intramural and extramural political connections and conflicts.[9] For the past fifteen years, the pervasive local, district, and state level factionalism within the ruling (until 1967) Congress party in Uttar Pradesh[10] and that party's competition with other parties has penetrated deeply into the state's educational system. Factions and parties, as well as social and territorial paracommunities that use and are used by them, find it to their advantage to control the resources and patronage of educational structures. At the higher education level, vice-chancellor appointments are merely the most important visible prizes; academic posts (professorships and readerships, as well as lesser academic posts, of which there are a large number under looser controls) are often also drawn into the vortex of political and community competition.[11] Iqbal Narain's account of the politicization of primary education in Rajasthan re-enforces the general picture Gould offers for secondary and higher education.

We distinguish between politicization and the use of political influence by universities and colleges. Educational institutions, particularly higher educational institutions, whether private or public, need political influence to pursue their goals and to protect and enhance their interests and independence. They live in particular political and social environments from which they require sustenance and sympathetic understanding. Without political influence they cannot command the resources and the autonomy essential for their intellectual and material well-being.

Political influence in the context of the relationship between the educational and political systems refers, in a sense, to the reverse of the process of politicization; it is the use of political skills, influence, and strategies to insure public decisions and allocations that are favorable to education generally and to the needs and interests of particular institutions.

Many Indian vice-chancellors have been politically influential. In this volume Irene Gilbert examines some of the accomplishments of Sir Asutosh Mukherji, perhaps the most successful among Indian vice-chancellors in the preindependence period. Two of India's four presidents, Dr. S. Radhakrishna and Dr. Zakir Husain, were eminent educators and vice-chancellors. Triguna Sen built an outstanding university at Jadavpur and was attempting the thankless task of restoring Banaras Hindu University at the time of his appointment as minister for education. In the postindependence period Hansa Mehta (discussed in our Baroda study, below); D. C. Pavate (Karnatak); J. C. Joshi (Punjab); and P. N. Thapar (Punjab Agricultural University) stand out among the vice-chancellors who quickly built newly founded institutions into outstanding universities.[12] They each used their special skills, connections, and political resources to great advantage in the state and national environments that facilitated or constrained their particular activities.

A striking example of building a new university in the postindependence period is the work at the University of Rajasthan of Mohan Sinha Mehta, a former princely state bureaucrat, educator, and postindependence diplomat. Situated in the heart of princely India, the University of Rajasthan was hindered in its growth by the limited level of educational development that characterized princely India, but at the same time was aided by the lack of vested interests and bureaucratic rigidities that often hampered educational innovation in former British India. Imaginative, skillful, and open to advice, Mehta used his position as a native and notable of Rajasthan, and more specifically of the former princely state of Udaipur, to gain a sympathetic hearing from the state chief minister (an Udaipurian), the state chief secretary (an Udaipurian), the union government education minister (an Udaipurian) and the head of the University Grants Commission (an Udaipurian) for his plans to build the University of Rajasthan (founded in 1947) into one of India's stronger institutions.

It is difficult to define the public interest in education, or to identify its articulation and assertion by public authorities. Asserting the public interest in higher education has always posed a more delicate problem than doing so in primary and even secondary education. Intellectuals believe, and most publics share their belief to a greater or lesser extent, that judging scholarly work and controlling its transmission are functions requiring expertise beyond the reach of lay opinion, and must be vested in a community of professional scholars. However, where state and federal governments, particularly democratic ones, finance education, the expenditure of public money becomes increasingly subject to public opinion and must be justified against the claims of competing expenditure. Under these circumstances, the legitimate assertion of the public interest in higher education by state and federal governments is not always easy to distinguish from politicization. The ambiguities of the distinction are highlighted in Carolyn Elliott's study. The government of Andhra considered its attempt to strengthen government control over the Andhra universities and their vice-chancellors an assertion of the public interest, a way of controlling nepotism in one university and advancing the regional language in another. Osmania's vice-chancellor and faculty saw it as an attempt to subvert university autonomy and annex the university to the political interests of the state's chief minister by assuring the appointment of compliant vice-chancellors.

Largely because the distinctions between politicization, political influence, and government assertion of public interest involve differences of degree that become differences of kind only at the extremes, it may be difficult to classify particular actions and processes in these terms. These concepts do however help to organize and clarify the evidence that is becoming available about the relationship between the educational and political systems.

Notes on Method: Comparison and Disaggregation

Accounts of higher education in India, whether or not they intend to, perforce assume comparative standards. Identifying relevant comparisons, both of institutions and of their contexts, is perhaps the most difficult aspect of a study of education. Comparisons must be specific if one hopes to avoid judging educational developments in India against some generalized, quasi-platonic idea of an educational system. Imaginative constructs of qualities one believes should characterize educational systems are only marginally useful; the constraints of particular contexts, whether Indian, American, or European, have never allowed institutions to become more than approximations of such ideas. It is the approximations, not metaphysical or metaempirical constructs, that must serve as our standard.

Specifying comparative referents may be essential; yet deciding which comparisons are relevant is by no means easy. History, culture, and society deny us perfect simulations. Our comparisons arise from at least three contexts: comparing India with herself over time; comparing India with other countries at the present moment; and comparing India with other countries at other historical moments that, for one specific reason or another, appear more relevant than the present. In each case, our criterion for selecting comparative situations has been to throw light on what other nations have done under comparable historical conditions. Such comparative self-consciousness obliges us to specify rather than assume standards, and obliges our readers to consider what the range of empirical possibilities has been in concrete historical instances.

Comparing India with herself over time, as she was rather than as she was presumed to be, sheds light on the propensity of both Indian and foreign observers to characterize the present as a decline from some postulated golden age. The belief in such a golden age, captured in the universal but unexamined use of the verb "deteriorate," (as in "standards have deteriorated," "education has deteriorated") is indeed metaempirical. It is essential to investigate the past concretely and to ask not only what it achieved in terms of its own goals — for example, did elite education achieve as much as romantic reconstruction claims? — but also whether these goals are relevant in the light of contemporary conditions and needs — how elite can higher education be in a democracy? Comparing India with other countries synchronically provides some sense of the possible range of goals, arrangements, and achievements, and is relevant because world standards in education are both known and taken into account by Indian educational policy makers. And finally, comparing India with other countries at other historical moments allows for India's embodiment of social and technological conditions of multiple historical periods, those which other countries have left behind and those which other countries are now experiencing.

A mark of the development of new nations is the skipping of "stages" which characterized the political, economic, or educational "developing" of old nations. New nations can and do directly import advanced institutional structures which elsewhere emerged only after a long period of scientific or social invention and experimentation. Insofar as new nations can and do benefit from such institutional transfer, their institutional development becomes subject to comparison with the most recent institutional developments of the west. On the other hand, to the extent that institutional development in new nations also takes place under technological, economic, or cultural circumstances characteristic of western history at an earlier stage, their institutional development is properly subject to comparisons with institutional developments at an earlier stage of western history. We have tried throughout to keep such a dual standard in mind.

Finally, it has not seemed wise to treat India or other countries, notably America, as a single unit for comparative purposes. It is now generally appreciated that a leading fault of aggregative comparison among countries has been that "global" measures severely understate the internal differences within categories, producing misleading comparisons. This is strikingly true in the realm of education. Leading metropolitan universities in America represent a different reality, professionally, intellectually, and politically, from small, rural, denominational colleges. The same is true in India, where there are not only differences among institutions, but also among regions, a fact which we shall have more occasion to discuss below. It becomes important, therefore, to disaggregate the Indian educational scene, to specify whether one is talking about the Indian Institutes of Technology with their good financing, their strong protection against regional politics, and their exceptionally severe entrance standards, or a small private college founded by a local philanthropist and political entrepreneur, catering to rural first generation B.A. aspirants. The phrase "Indian education" misleads by making homogeneous what is heterogeneous, and by overemphasizing the mean, which may cloud the understanding of future possibilities by obscuring the difference between leading sectors and lagging (or "dragging") ones.

2 / Historical Legacies:
The Genetic Imprint in Education

Universities everywhere are increasingly affected by certain common forces. The democratic demand for access to higher education, the post-industrial demand that universities meet the requirements of technological society, and the consequences of dependence on public finance are reducing the differences that once distinguished higher education within and among national environments. If all education is becoming in certain significant respects more alike, is there any point in investigating the historical origins of various educational systems? A positive answer depends on the assumption that historical traditions and experience create values, culturally defined norms, and modes of behavior that survive even when the original conditions that give rise to them fade into the past. The origins of educational institutions impress upon them certain forms and traditions that function rather like a genetic imprint, which dictates the further evolution of their institutional arrangement, not with the exactitude it exercises in a biological organism, but with a certain dependability.

The varied origins of educational institutions in Europe, America, and India have had differential effects on traditions of self-government and patterns of politicization. In Europe, the original agencies for founding institutions of higher learning were typically autonomous self-governing guilds; in America, private, usually sectarian, boards; in India, government and private boards made up of European or Indian sectarians and philanthropists.

The European guilds, the legal core of the university, were autonomous corporate bodies either of students — as at Bologna, where they employed masters — or of masters, as at Paris. Italian, Spanish, and Portuguese universities came to follow the pattern of Bologna, while the German and English frequently followed Paris. Still others represented some mixture of the two types.[1] Like other medieval guilds, the universities were self-governing bodies that elected officers and set rules. Each faculty was a deliberative body that elected its own head and participated in the government of the university as a whole.

The genetic imprint of the guild founding has affected traditions of university autonomy, just as medieval political institutions have affected the traditions of liberty and constitutional government.[2] The self-government of European universities (often now exercised, to be sure, within a framework of state supervision) is a residue of medieval liberty.[3] Detached from its original setting in medieval Europe, the idea of guild autonomy has traveled abroad and contributed to the model that has influenced university development everywhere.

The distinguishing characteristic of the founding of higher education in the United States has been what Richard Hofstadter has called "lay government," a government not by the faculty of colleges and universities, but by lay boards of trustees. They have the legal power to operate institutions of higher learning, including the power to hire and fire faculty and to determine issues of educational policy.[4] The term "lay government" suggests that Americans, coming out of the institutional traditions and political experiences of dissenting Protestant Christianity, brought with them a belief in lay or community control of church institutions and extended this principle to colleges and universities. (This distinguishing feature of American educational institutions, however, is often more formal than real. The conventional constitution of American colleges and universities usually diverged from the formal one, as faculties increasingly grasped control of their own affairs.)[5]

The Indian pattern differs significantly from both the European and the American. Four characteristics contributed to the special quality of the genetic imprint on Indian higher education: government from the beginning played a powerful role in the creation and government of universities; a bureaucratic culture markedly influenced university procedures; private management was preponderant in higher education; cooperation rather than conflict characterized relations between private and public sectors of education.

The Role of Government and the Effect of Bureaucratic Culture

Government initiative has been responsible for the founding of almost all universities and many colleges in India. A strong assertion of government influence in the management of higher education flowed from this initiative, and from the concern to protect the political interests of the *raj*. The basic distinction in American educational culture and policy between private and public founding and support had little historical meaning in India, where public financing of private institutions began early.[6] The earliest institutions relevant for present higher education were seminaries, sometimes called colleges but, like American institutions of the early nineteenth century, resembling preparatory institutions.[7] Some of these illustrate the permeable boundaries between public and private auspices that have remained characteristic of the higher educational scene.

Elphinstone College and Presidency College are examples. In 1824 Mountstuart Elphinstone, then governor of Bombay, authorized the Bombay Native School Book and School Society, a semiautonomous committee founded and dominated by the government, to open an English school in Bombay.[8] This was the origin of the Elphinstone Native Education Institution out of which Elphinstone College grew in 1834. The opening of the college was made possible to a great extent by the Rs. 200,000 raised in 1827 by the people of Bombay to commemorate Elphinstone's service. The college was administered under the general superintendence of the government, and located in the town hall. At Calcutta, the Indian reformer Raja Ram Mohan Roy and an English businessman, David Hare, with the support of Sir Edward Hyde East, chief justice of the supreme court of Bengal, in 1816 persuaded prosperous Bengalis to form themselves into an association that would found a seminary for their sons. The seminary subsequently became Hindu College, and eventually the government-operated Presidency College in the University of Calcutta. Though the original school was a private endeavor, and privately financed, East's correspondence makes it plain that in the imperial capital signs of government approval, such as his sponsorship, were essential to open private purses. In 1823, the manager's appeal for government assistance brought government influence as well.[9]

These early foundings reveal a blurring between private and public auspices. Elphinstone College had considerable private funds, though it was quickly placed under government supervision; the society responsible for its founding was itself founded with government money, though it was intended to be autonomous. Similar collaboration marked the Hindu College effort, the first private venture by Indians in modern higher education. This alliance of public and private effort, notably in financing, became a firm part of government policy at midcentury with the adoption of grant-in-aid procedures. In nineteenth century England, secondary education was the responsibility of private bodies aided by state grants. This pattern provided the model for both secondary and higher education in India. In 1854, the directors of the East India Company wrote: "The most effectual method of providing for the wants of India . . . will be to combine with the agency of the government the aid which may be derived from the exertions and liberality of the educated and wealthy natives of India. . . . We have, therefore, resolved to adopt in India the system of grants-in-aid which have been carried out in this country [England] with very great success." [10] This policy produced an enormous flowering of private venture schools after 1854, schools which became colleges toward the end of the century.[11]

The significance of these developments is that they led to a large private sector in Indian higher education (whose size and role is not always appreciated) and to a lack of faith in the notion that private and government interests in higher education ought to be kept separate. On the contrary, collaborative arrangements between the two sectors have been broadly accepted. This collaboration accounts for the expectations of private educational entrepreneurs that government will aid them, and the expectation of government that it will invariably have a voice in the affairs of private institutions. Because of these relationships, the context for judging the politicization of education in India differs from the context in a system in which private and public sectors have been separated by historical experience, interest, and ideology.

The educational objectives of the early schools and colleges that thrived under the grant-in-aid policy were in part instrumental and in part cultural and characterological. The government of Bombay aimed at a purpose of higher education from the middle ages onward, to meet manpower requirements — then for priests, jurists, *clercs* — of the occupational structure of the time. It hoped that Elphinstone College would raise "a class of persons qualified by their intelligence and morality for high employment in the civil administration of India." [12] Private institutions founded by Indians intended to qualify young men similarly. But focusing solely on the intention to train *clercs* would slight the strongly moralistic aspirations Englishmen had for education. Englishmen governing India were deeply concerned with the development of character, a function dear to many nineteenth century educators in Anglo-Saxon countries. If the English public school and "Oxbridge" intended to create Christian gentlemen, and if American sectarian institutions hoped to produce at least Christians if not gentlemen, the government of India was deeply concerned to produce Christian virtues, if not Christians. It considered the transfer of English culture and learning indispensable to this objective. [13]

The first Indian universities, created in 1857 at Calcutta, Madras, and Bombay, were mainly bureaucratic devices for controlling the quality of collegiate education. They were not, nor were they meant to be, communities of scholars, graduate departments, or physical agglomerations containing museums, libraries, laboratories, and other real estate normally associated with the continental idea of a university. Like the University of London, which served as the model, the Indian university was, as Abraham Flexner put it, "a line drawn about an enormous number of different institutions," and designed to establish and maintain minimum standards for faculties and in teaching and examining. [14] Like London, the first universities introduced a new administrative layer to control and coordinate already established institutions. Unlike the unified German university after Humboldt, they were the central core of a federal structure. Nor did they, like Humboldt's university, pursue and impart advanced learning. [15] Postgraduate departments and the advancement of learning developed only in the twentieth century. The Education Act of 1904 empowered universities to set up postgraduate teaching departments, but these powers were not used until 1916. At that time, Sir Asutosh Mukherji, India's first great university builder, and comparable to Daniel Coit Gilman at Johns Hopkins University or William Raney Harper at the University of Chicago, created postgraduate teaching departments and research programs, giving Calcutta University a new definition and function. [16]

In India government not only founded universities but maintained a strong voice in their affairs. The basis for government influence was laid at the time of founding. At the University of London, the senate, although initially appointed by the Crown, was empowered to fill vacancies by election. Sir Charles Wood, president of the Board of Control of the East India Company, whose dispatch of 1854 justified the creation of universities, was inclined initially to follow the London model in this respect. Fears that such independence might in time "introduce a body apart from & independent of the government" led the Board of Directors to question the suitability of an independent senate in India. "Should not," one educational policy maker inquired, "a majority of the Senate be for the present at least appointed by Govt.? Otherwise may you not have Religious and Political feuds?" [17]

In the event, official influence in the new universities was assured. At the University of Calcutta, the governor general served as chancellor; the governor general and council (that is, government) nominated the vice-chancellor and appointed and could dismiss all but the *ex officio* fellows of the university senate. The governor general and council approved the making of by-laws and regulations, controlled the fee fund, and received annual statements of accounts. Provincial governors at Bombay and Madras had similar powers.[18]

After a period in which government relaxed its control of universities, Lord Curzon as governor general moved boldly in the Indian Universities Act of 1904 to stop what he believed to be the degeneration of Indian universities. The act, which strongly reasserted government influence, prescribed that up to four-fifths of the senate should be nominees of the chancellor (the governor general in Calcutta and the governors in Bombay and Madras), and that the government could not only approve but also add to or alter the body of regulations which the university was required to submit.[19] Curzon's reforms would have been, as Sir Eric Ashby observes, "anathema to British civic universities, which by that time had established robust traditions of autonomy and freedom from state intervention." [20]

Lord Curzon and his secretariat did not see themselves invading university autonomy. Quite the reverse. They believed they were protecting the educational role of the university against the baleful influence of ambitious and politically interested Indians. By the end of the century, the senate and syndicate of the University of Calcutta were beginning to be strongly dominated by Indians, a large number of them lawyers. In 1890 the elective principle had been introduced into the Calcutta University senate, and Bengalis had responded to this opportunity with great enthusiasm and political skill, as Curzon noted. "Lists are kept up by the Vakils [lawyers] of the electors who, having taken their degrees, have dispersed throughout India. Agents are employed to hunt them out and canvass them; and very considerable expense is incurred. No candidate has a chance of being returned who does not resort to these methods and who is not supported by the Vakil party." [21]

The reasons which led persons to aspire to senate membership were probably the same then as now. The Indians hoped to open university admission to a greater number than English administrators thought wise and prudent. The university had the power to affiliate not only colleges, as it does today, but also schools. The ability to affect affiliation was of considerable interest to those seeking local influence. A man who could soften administrative stringency in admissions or in affiliation thought himself a good servant of his constituency.[22]

By 1900, 110 of the fellows on the senate were Indians and 77 were Europeans, a circumstance that made it possible for the senate of the University of Calcutta to serve, along with the Calcutta municipal corporation, as the first significant representative body for Indian opinion.[23] Because the senate did so, Curzon's move to reduce the role of independent Indian opinion on it exacerbated Bengali nationalist sentiment. The origin of an active political interest in Indian universities is probably to be found in this struggle between Indians (Bengalis, in this case) who sought to enhance the representation of Indian opinion and interests in the Calcutta University senate and the government of India (Curzon, as viceroy and governor general) which sought to curtail it.

Curzon viewed his use of public authority as nonpolitical, dedicated solely to realizing educational goals. His strengthening of government control was based on the view that Indian influence in education did not serve public purposes, while government policy did. But that policy was the assertion of a contrary political interest, that of the *raj,* and in this sense by no means free of "politics." [24]

The existence of a powerful official voice in university affairs was an important part of the *raj's* genetic imprint on Indian higher education. It is an imprint that facilitates politicization by not establishing a clear demarcation between educational and governmental spheres. Yet it would be wrong to say that strong government influence in higher education is necessarily asserted at the expense of university autonomy. If autonomy is understood as the freedom to determine and to realize educational goals, it may also on occasion be threatened from within the institution by administrators, faculty members, or students, and from without by organized political forces that appropriate what should be educational goals and resources to serve partisan, self-interested, or ideological ends.[25] When the threat to university autonomy comes from these sources, the assertion of government influence may strengthen educational goals. Autonomy must be judged in its social and political contexts as well as in terms of institutional arrangements and relationships.[26]

If the medieval guild served as a sort of template, a guide to molding the materials, for European university organization, and the lay congregation did the same for American collegiate government, the idea of administrative rationality molded the culture of higher education in India.

The concern for uniform and regular procedures, predictability, and orderliness, as well as the emphasis on hierarchy and official career ladders, exercised a disproportionate effect. The needs of the administrative services increased the influence of administrative culture on higher education. Discussions of university programs and problems were carried on simultaneously with discussions of training and testing for the services. Dr. F. J. Mouat, secretary for the council of education in Bengal, welcomed the idea of an examining university because it "would meet the difficulty of devising a suitable examination for entry into government service and provide a superior type of public servant." [27]

The administrative system shaped higher education by analogy. The organization of the Indian Educational Service, formed to provide a predictable supply of teachers in government colleges, was conceived along the lines of a merit system of hierarchy and qualification corresponding to that of the civil bureaucracy. The universities approved degree programs and set uniform syllabi and examinations not in some general fashion but quite specifically, designating the books required to meet standards. The concern for uniformity and specificity was increased by the intellectual problems attending cultural transfer. This concern arose from the perception that many college principals and teachers neither appreciated nor comprehended the cultural assumptions underlying the syllabi and the degree programs. The virtue of such specificity, as in other instances of bureaucratic precision, was to assure minimal standards through uniform requirements. Its vice was to suppress that openness and leeway which can facilitate creativity and innovation in higher education and which should characterize intellectual communities.

Private Foundings: Nationalist, Sectarian, and Caste

Private entrepreneurship, which was responsible for the founding of the majority of Indian schools and colleges and continues to be responsible for the management of 69 percent of the schools and 65 percent of the colleges,[28] has been important in shaping Indian higher education. Three types of private entrepreneurship have played a role in Indian educational history — nationalist, sectarian movement, and caste community. In addition, scores of individual philanthropists and local notables have helped establish or maintain private educational institutions.

The nationalist Deccan Education Society, formed and led by such eminent Bombay nationalists as B. G. Tilak and G. K. Gokhale, founded several educational institutions. The first, Fergusson College, was established in 1885 and grew out of a desire to educate young men who would serve India.[29] In the first decade of the century, Shri Aurobindo, while vice-chancellor of Baroda College, was instrumental in founding a nationalist institution, the Ganganath Vidyalaya at Baroda.[30]

In Bengal, the *swadeshi* (literally, "own country") movement's nationalist institutions became gathering points for students involved in Bengal oppositional politics. Shri Aurobindo acted as principal of Bengal National College, established by the National Council of Education in 1906 "to impart education, literary and scientific, as well as technical and professional on national lines and exclusively under national control, designed to incorporate with the best oriental ideals of life and thought the best assimilable ideals of the West." [31]

A series of "national universities" were founded after Gandhi assumed leadership of the nationalist movement in the early 1920's. They included Gujarat Vidyapith, Kashi Vidyapith in Uttar Pradesh, Bihar Vidyapith, and Tilak Maharashtra Vidyapith.[32] The Muslim leaders who joined with Gandhi in the early 1920's encouraged Muslim students at Aligarh to leave that university and establish a new one, Jamia Millia Islamia. Gandhi himself was closely associated with and acted as chancellor for the "national university" in Gujarat. A number of major Uttar Pradesh nationalists came out of Kashi Vidyapith. Sampurnanand, former chief minister of Uttar Pradesh, was a professor of philosophy there. Among the teachers or graduates who held powerful political posts subsequently were Acharya Narendra Dev, a socialist leader; Sri Prakasa, a state governor; Lal Bahadur Shastri, former prime minister of India; Dr. B. V. Keskar, former central minister for information; T. N. Singh, former planning commission member; and Kamalapathi Tripathi, chief minister of Uttar Pradesh.[33] Zakir Husain, former vice-president and president of India, was principal of Jamia Millia.

Gandhi's advocacy of *sarvodaya,* service to society, led many of his followers, who were in any case inclined in a schoolmasterly direction by caste culture and occupation, to spend their time out of jail in founding primary and secondary educational institutions.[34] Some of the educational institutions founded under nationalist auspices, such as those founded by the moderate Deccan Education Society, put intellectual concerns uppermost, but in many others staff and students were more concerned with building the nationalist movement and fighting the *raj* than with cultivating the intellect. As Harold Gould makes clear, when political goals changed from the achievement of independence to the competitive pursuit of power, the previous connection between politicians and educational institutions remained intact but the motives of postindependence politicians changed. Motives shifted from the pursuit of ideal goals — imparting a nationalist perspective and a national life style — to the pursuit of politics as a profession more oriented toward material rewards, power, and prestige. Under these changed circumstances, founding and managing educational institutions took on a more narrow and partisan meaning.[35]

The two other types of private entrepreneurship, that of sects and that of caste communities, were part of the cultural reform and group social mobility movements of the nineteenth and twentieth centuries. Hindus and

Muslims responded to each other and to the western and Christian impact in part by founding educational institutions that propagated their cultural message and identity. Caste communities too found that they could maintain group solidarity and preserve or improve their social status and economic opportunities by founding educational institutions. Vaishya (merchant caste), Kayasth (scribe caste), Rajput and Nair (warrior castes) institutions helped these castes maintain their traditional high status by facilitating access to modern educational opportunities. Mobile castes entered the field as well. Jat and Ahir colleges in Uttar Pradesh and Punjab, Ezhava colleges in Kerala, Nadar colleges in Madras, Mahar colleges in Maharasthra, and Lingayat colleges in Mysore, bear witness to the capacity of peasant and untouchable communities for self-mobilization and organization.[36]

The educational activities of the Arya Samaj, a militant Hindu reform organization, illustrate how social reform movements within Hinduism used education to express their cultural norms and identity. The Arya Samaj sought to strengthen Hinduism against its Christian and Muslim competitors by emphasizing the unity of Hinduism found in early Vedic materials. Both the "college section" and the "*gurukula* section" — which differ in their orientation to modern values and life styles — have been significant in the founding of educational institutions in Punjab, Uttar Pradesh, and Gujarat.[37] The *gurukula* section confined itself initially to opening *gurukulas* patterned on the ancient educational institutions of the same name, and laid great stress on the study of ancient Hindu literature. Recently it has founded more conventional colleges. The college section founded Dayanand Anglo-Vedic (DAV) College, a leading college formerly in Lahore and now in Jullundur.[38] Other DAV colleges have been founded in Punjab, Uttar Pradesh, and Delhi. In 1947, the Arya Samaj operated forty *gurukulas* and fifteen DAV colleges.[39] The Arya Samaj maintains close liaisons with its institutions. In 1967, the president of the college section's supreme body, Mr. Behal, was also principal of the DAV college in Jullundur. The Samaj's great social and political influence in the Punjab has given it a significant voice in educational bodies outside its organizational sphere. The appointment of Suraj Bhan as vice-chancellor of Kurukshetra University, now in Pipli, Haryana, may have been due to efforts by the late Punjab chief minister, Sardar Kairon Singh, to overcome Hindu-Sikh rivalries by conciliating the Arya Samaj, the most articulate and organized section of the Hindu community in the Punjab. Subsequently, Suraj Bhan was appointed vice-chancellor of the larger and more prestigious Punjab University, Chandigarh. A prominent leader of the *gurukula* section, Professor Sher Singh, became minister of state for education in the union (national) government after the 1967 election, an appointment which suggested that sympathy for Vedic education (based on ancient Hindu texts) continues to be entertained in the union government.

The Sanathan Dharma movement too has created a substantial number of educational institutions in Punjab and Uttar Pradesh. The Sanathanists originally intended to protect Hinduism against the reforming zeal of the Arya Samaj and others, but moved closer to the Arya Samaj as the latter grew more conservative; both found common ground in opposing secularism and Islam.[40] Among the most prominent institutions to emerge from the various nineteenth century reform movements was the Mohammedan Anglo-Oriental College, later the Muslim University at Aligarh.[41] Christian colleges, which benefitted from the imperial presence, also reflected the tendency of social and religious movements to express themselves in educational terms. (Indeed, many nationalist and sectarian institutions were meant to be "answers" to them.) Today they constitute 5 percent of all arts and science colleges in India.[42]

A macroaggregative picture of sectarian and caste community educational institutions would reflect the varied and complex social structure and history of India's regional cultures. The distribution of management among colleges affiliated with the Universities of Punjab, Agra (Uttar Pradesh), and Kerala suggests this complexity and variety.[43] Of 139 colleges in Punjab University, 43 were identifiable as being associated with organized caste or sectarian communities. Of these, 10 were associated with castes, notably peasant communities such as the Jats and Ahirs, and 33 were associated with sectarian groups, including Sikhs (13 colleges), Arya Samaj (11 colleges), and Sanathan Dharma (4 colleges). Of the 127 colleges in Agra University, 36 could be associated with a caste or sect. Thirteen were founded by caste communities (again, as in Punjab, mostly by Jats). Twelve of the 23 sectarian colleges were founded by the Arya Samaj. In Kerala the pattern shifts, reflecting the characteristic social segmentation of that state, in which Christians, mobile lower caste Ezhavas, dominant caste Nairs, and Muslims almost exhaust the social spectrum. In the University of Kerala, 42 of 89 colleges can be associated with one or another of these communities: 28 Christian colleges; 5 Ezhava colleges; and 4 Muslim colleges.

The genetic imprint on Indian education has endowed it with certain features that affect the interaction between politics and education. Indian universities were created by the state (the British *raj*) and subsequently continued to be subject to its legislation and supported in considerable measure by public funds. Their historical evolution in close relationship with government created certain presumptions in favor of a strong official interest in university affairs. The state's assertion of the public interest in education can range from fostering educational goals to subverting them; in India the legacy of state influence has tended to strengthen the presumption in favor of the government's view of the public interest in education and to create somewhat precarious conditions for the university's ability to define its autonomy. Since independence, higher education has been increasingly regarded as a social right and the effectiveness of political demand for higher education has increased. These two elements in the university's political environment have also affected its ability to define the meaning of autonomy.

The private character and management of a high proportion of colleges in India is apt to create the misleading impression that colleges, unlike universities, are at a sufficient distance from public authority and political arenas to be insulated from them. Behind the private managing boards, however, lie the grant-in-aid relationships with government and the controls over curriculum and faculties that university affiliation entails. The consequences of these relationships are by no means clear. The public interest in private education may not be articulated in public policy or, if it is, it may not be effectively administered. Glynn Wood's work on education in Mysore makes clear that arts colleges multiplied at the expense of technical ones despite an explicit policy commitment on the part of the state government to favor technical over arts education at the college level. The failure to articulate a public policy may have desirable results, for example when generalized support for private colleges protects high standard elite colleges against the consequences of a democratic demand for virtually open admissions. Articulating a policy may also have undesirable consequences, such as the exaggerated priority given to engineering college "seats" by manpower planners in the national government and in many state governments which, in 1968–69, produced a glut of engineer graduates.

If the grant-in-aid relationship places private colleges within reach of public authority and its definition of the public interest, it also creates conditions under which private interests may capture public resources for private ends. Privately managed colleges reflect the sectarian and partisan organization of their localities. Some have produced the best education in India; others have been vehicles for the politicization of education. Both directly, as a political resource for party cadres, supporters, and patronage, and indirectly, as an instrument of partisan prestige, benefaction, and influence, private colleges have played an important role in local politics. This is not surprising when competitive politics are carried on in an environment in which there is a severe scarcity of means for expressing political preferences and for mobilizing political resources and support. Private colleges may provide, as Gould's analysis makes clear, the framework for a district party organization. They may, as Madan and Halbar's study indicates, provide an institutionalized means for strengthening private community organizations by channeling grant-in-aid funds to private educational institutions and associations. Grants to a Lingayat college or a Nair school, even when admission is open to all, the contents of education is secular and modern, and students are not obliged to participate in or to honor the rituals and symbolism of the sect or community that manages the school, allocate resources to sects and communities as well as to education. By doing so they raise certain classical questions about public support of "private" and sectarian education that continue to agitate the political life of American and European nations.[44]

The most obvious and dramatic change in Indian higher education since
independence in 1947 has been the transformation from a relatively small,
elite system to a large, popular one. The mutually reinforcing consequences
of this shift from elite to popular higher education have been massive and
profound. They include a strengthening of the conditions favorable to the
politicization of educational institutions, a reordering of the symbols and
distribution of authority within educational institutions in favor of administration, and a probable decline in standards in the middle and lower
reaches of the educational pyramid (to be examined in the next chapter).

The Expansion of Higher Education

The expansion of higher education accelerated markedly after independence in 1947. Starting with a base of 423,000 enrolled students in
1950–51, the number increased over 400 percent to 2,218,972 in 1966–
67, an average annual increase of approximately 11 percent.[1] The number
of universities increased from 20 at independence (1947) to 82 (including
10 agricultural universities), 91, or 100 in 1970, depending on how they are
counted.[2] Some sense of distribution over time of the rate of growth can
be gained from figure 1; in the nine decades prior to independence 19 universities were established, while in the twenty-three years since independence 63 were established.[3] The number of university and affiliated colleges
grew at an even faster rate between 1947 and 1968 than did the number
of universities, 663 percent as against 270 percent. In 1947, there were
437 university and affiliated colleges and 20 universities; in 1967–68 the
figures were 2899 and 74.[4]

There is every reason to believe that under the present political circumstances the expansion of higher education will proceed, although perhaps
at a somewhat slower rate.[5] Political democracy in India has intensified the
powerful demand for modern education evident during the last century
of British rule; for over a century colleges, despite rapid expansion, have
had an excess of applicants.[6] Today, collegiate education is no longer confined to those sons of the rich and wellborn who choose to broaden their
minds, improve their manners or enhance their opportunities.[7] With the
exception of a few highly selective prestige institutions, Indian college students today not only come from modest social and economic backgrounds
but also are not likely to improve them radically. In 1961, Kerala Uni-

versity drew almost 60 percent of its students from families whose incomes were less than Rs. 200 per month — about $43 per month at the 1961 official exchange rates (but considerably more than that in buying power if the consumer "basket" is filled with Indian produced goods purchased to satisfy "Indian" wants).[8] Most of those receiving a first degree become white collar workers at modest salaries.[9]

In the context of this burgeoning popular demand, the prospect of various official efforts to stem the tide of expansion of school and higher education appears dim. In June 1967, just a few months after the Education Commission, 1964–1966, had asked that an "open door access" policy for admissions to colleges be replaced by a "selective" one, a working group of the ministry of education called for the opening of seven additional colleges under the University of Delhi to accommodate at least 5,000 of the 14,279 applicants without "seats" for the academic year beginning in July;[10] by 1970, the number of colleges "needed" had risen to fourteen. In the south, the *Hindu* observed editorially that "the demand for admission is at least five times the available number of seats in the schools and in the reputed ones the proportion is larger." [11]

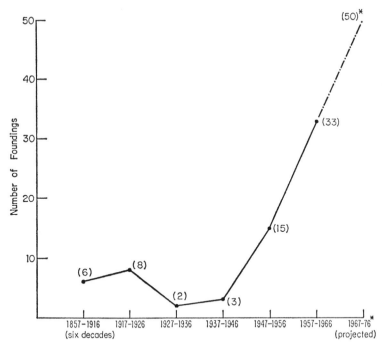

Figure 1. Indian university foundings, by decades.
       N = 82*

Source: Inter University Board of India and Ceylon, *Universities Handbook; India and Ceylon* (New Delhi, 1971).

* In the three years 1967–1970, 15 universities were founded. At the rate of 5 per year, the decade 1967–76 could experience 50 foundings.

The expansion of the educational system in India, particularly the growth of secondary and higher education, is as much a response to political demands on all levels of government as it is a result of policy decisions taken on grounds independent of political representation and pressure, such as economic growth or welfare. Political participation has climbed from 45 to over 61 percent over the four general elections held between 1952 and 1967, and now compares favorably with recent levels in U.S. presidential and congressional elections.[12] The views and demands of organized political forces are represented in the national parliament, state legislative assemblies, and local governments, through access to legislative and administrative decision-making processes, and by various forms of symbolic, agitational, and coercive politics such as fasts, strikes and *gheraos* (encirclements). Popular demands are heard and acted upon, not least with respect to education. The Congress party government of Gujarat nearly fell in 1967 because of its reluctance to found two universities rather than one. Those who have benefitted from the expansion and democratization of power and status since independence have found that access to education is vital if their children are to build on their achievements. Their pressures have strengthened the position of education in the political competition for symbolic and material resources.

The demand for higher education is also related to the failure of the educational system to provide effective and attractive terminal vocational and technical education.[13] At present, high cost vocational and technical training (about five times costlier than general education at comparable levels)[14] is characterized by low status, high levels of wastage, and too limited a relationship to job requirements and employment opportunities. Perhaps most significantly, such training is being widely used as a "back door" to higher levels of education.[15] The relative failure of vocational and technical education to lead to jobs and status has heightened pressure on higher education and led to mounting "overqualification" of employees. Forty-three percent of the bachelor of commerce graduates in an all-India sample of degree holders were working in clerical or related jobs and many graduate engineers work as technicians.[16]

College degrees may overqualify their recipients for some jobs but for many jobs it may be a fallacy of misplaced concreteness to believe that they do. Many of those working as senior "clerks" in government hold what in America would be considered administrative or executive posts, supervising contracts, work flows, and numerous personnel. Nor should expectations of Indian students be confused with those held by Americans with nominally similar degrees. Indian students with a bachelor of commerce expect to take clerical positions, not something more elevated, and graduate engineers from many colleges expect to be technicians.

The drive for college admission and college degrees is heightened by the rational propensity of employers, notably government, to value educational qualifications independently of job qualifications narrowly defined. Even if education does not add specific qualifications, it is a rough screening process. Its latent aspects insure that those who finish higher levels are disciplined and motivated in ways that are job-relevant. A degree is an indicator of job qualifications and skill.[17] Therefore, socially mobile young men and women seek B.A.'s to qualify for government jobs which offer them the status, income, and security that most of them prize highly. Almost 70 percent of the degree holders in an all-India sample were working in the public sector (central government, 17.2 percent; state government, 32.6 percent; quasi-government, 10.9 percent; local bodies, 5.2 percent).[18]

Contrary to some conventional wisdom, the propensity of Indians to seek degrees so that they can enter white collar occupations is not merely a result of an unfortunate flaw in the nation's character — a lack of ambition or a status-connected disdain for technical or agricultural work. Given the prevailing opportunities, the decision to seek a degree is mainly economically rational rather than culturally constrained. Most of those whose education was made possible by family saving and sacrifice continue to recognize joint family responsibilities. If they have been unable to qualify for professional education or a job in a modern business bureaucracy, if they lack "capital" beyond their degrees, or if agriculture is not a profitable investment sector, the income and security of government service generally represent an optimum economic choice. There is reason to believe that if the opportunity structure shifted, individuals would shift their choices from white collar to technical and agricultural employment.[19]

The Public Interest and Politicization

Expansion has prepared the ground for a more forceful assertion of the public interest in education and for politicization of the education system. It has greatly increased the proportion of national resources absorbed in this sector, making education both more visible and more vulnerable. Over the fifteen years between 1950–51 and 1965–66, per capita expenditure on education almost quadrupled. Education's proportion of national income rose from 1.2 percent to 2.9 percent in the same period,[20] and the education ministry in 1968 was trying — unsuccessfully — to double education's share to 6 percent.[21] Education was the single largest revenue item in all but three of sixteen states, representing 20 percent of aggregated state revenue budgets (in Kerala, 35 percent).[22] As education's share of national income has grown, higher education has captured an increasingly large proportion of it. Between 1950–51 and 1965–66, higher education's share of direct and indirect[23] expenditure on education grew from 24.5 to 32.6 percent.[24] India in 1961 may have spent a higher proportion of total educational expenditure on higher education than any other country.[25]

Not only has the increased expenditure made education more visible, but also the movement toward public financing has made it more vulnerable to political pressures. The percentage of educational expenditure accounted for by public funds (state and union government) increased from 57 percent in 1950–51 to 71 percent in 1965–66.[26] (These proportions do not take account of what is undoubtedly a large but at present un-estimated — much less measured — dimension of educational expendi-ture, the private tuitions [discussed in chapter 11] that are so pervasive a feature of Indian education.) Although the trend toward higher propor-tions of public funds supporting higher education parallels contemporary developments in all countries intent on strengthening their educational systems,[27] in India, which lacks the British and American experience with substantial private funding of higher education, this trend has built on and reinforced already established high levels of financial dependence on gov-ernment.

From at least the middle of the nineteenth century, when (in 1857) the first three universities were founded by government initiative and at gov-ernment expense, Indian higher education has had substantial public finan-cial support even though most of the colleges affiliated to universities are (and were) privately founded and managed. As we have already sug-gested, the distinction between and separation of private and public edu-cational institutions and finance, for so long central to the ideological and policy controversies that marked the history of education in America,[28] never developed in India. The British, willing to encourage education but reluctant to play a significant entrepreneurial role and eager to generate some financial support from the classes clamoring for western education, adopted the system of grants-in-aid already prevalent in England.[29]

The grants-in-aid policy, which was continued after independence by the governments of the various states, had resulted by 1960–61 in a one-third to two-thirds ratio of private- to government-managed educational institutions (taking all types of educational institutions together, from preprimary through higher education). The variation among states and levels was extremely wide. The percentage of privately managed educa-tional institutions in the state of Kerala was 65.3, while in Rajasthan and in Jammu and Kashmir the percentages were 3.5 and 1.7. Twenty-two percent of lower primary schools (by far the most numerous educational institutions), 69.2 percent of secondary schools and 65 percent of affiliated colleges were managed by nongovernment voluntary organizations.[30] It is also relevant to the question of dependence on government that approxi-mately 45 percent of the income of privately managed affiliated colleges comes from government sources.[31] Universities and government-managed colleges are even more dependent on government funds.

Increased financial dependence on government and the historical legacy of government influence have combined to make universities vulnerable to political pressure, penetration, and intervention. Politicians have noticed these developments and adjusted their behavior accordingly. Powerful men and those wishing to be powerful have been attracted to education ministry portfolios. Ten years ago the position of education minister in a state gov-ernment was unimportant; today it is a position of considerable prestige, influence, and power commanding the means to serve important political interests. For example, in the (non-Congress) coalition government formed in Bihar after the 1967 general elections, Kapuri Thakur, leader of the Samyukta Socialist party (SSP), the largest party in that government, became education minister and deputy chief minister. In Madras State V. R. Nedunchezhian, who ranked number two in the ruling DMK (Dravida Munnetra Kazhagam) party hierarchy, became minister for education (and industries).

The interest of politicians is related, on the one hand, to the prospect of helping define and realize the public interest in education, and, on the other, to the prospect for politicization, that is, the conversion of material, human, and symbolic educational resources into political resources that can be used in political competition for power. Defining the public interest is an immediate task in connection with government colleges, whose staffs are under the ministry of education of each state, a somewhat less immediate task with respect to universities, which are more or less autonomously governed but which are financed largely by public funds, and a more remote, though still real, responsibility with regard to private colleges, which are managed by private boards but receive large government subventions. In Bihar, where Kapuri Thakur was education minister, constituents pressed him to define the public interest in a way that would further ease the admission requirements laid down by the University of Bihar, as well as the standards for the B.A. In Madras, more Tamil-language education in government colleges was part of the DMK's definition of the public interest.

Politicization has been particularly significant in connection with private secondary and higher education. Managed by private boards operating largely beyond the scrutiny of government, private high schools and colleges have lent themselves to use as political resources by members of their managements.[32] But government too can influence employees of government colleges — principals and faculty — either to strengthen its view of the public interest or for politicization — subsuming educational institutions to its partisan and factional interests. Principals of government colleges may be under an obligation to respond to directives from the state director of education not only with respect to policy in their colleges but also with respect to their role in formulating university policy. This obligation may be variously used or exploited. One Madhya Pradesh university's senate consists of 120 persons, 88 of whom are principals of government colleges. These persons make decisions which are politically as well as academically relevant, such as whether a newly founded college will be affiliated by the university. The affiliation of colleges that do not meet the minimum conditions laid down by the university has been managed through these bureaucratic channels. According to J. P. Naik, its member-secretary, the Education Commission, 1964–1966, found that "when the question of affiliation of a new Government college comes up, the Director of Education sends a circular to those principals that they must vote for the affiliation." [33] In 1967 the government of Gujarat used its statutory authority to veto a decision of the Gujarat University senate refusing affiliation to Shri Prabhudas Thakkar Commerce and Science College (which planned to teach courses leading to the first year B.Sc. examination in the faculty of science). All six Gujarat vice-chancellors joined in a statement asking the government of Gujarat to respect the decision of the Gujarat University senate and to amend the various university acts to vest the right of affiliation exclusively with the universities. Vice-Chancellor Umashanker Joshi of Gujarat University declared that "the most fundamental issue involved in this matter is the autonomy of the university [which is] one of the most important bedrocks of a democracy." [34]

Delhi University too has become increasingly wary of the effect of affiliated colleges on its autonomy. In September 1970 it refused to accept the nominations influenced by the Jan Sangh party-controlled Delhi Metropolitan Council to fill seats on governing bodies of five colleges for whom the Delhi government acts as a trust. (There are now over twelve such colleges in the Delhi area.) The formal reason for the university's action was that too many officials had been nominated. Whether official or nonofficial, those nominated for partisan sympathies or purposes are more likely to support partisan than academic interests and values. In Delhi in 1970, they were likely to favor Jan Sangh policies with respect to language of instruction (pro-Hindi, anti-English) and admissions (more "open" admissions). Vice-chancellor Swarup Singh and his immediate predecessor, K. N. Raj, recognized the threat such appointments and policies posed for the university's colleges, first-rank postgraduate departments, and governing bodies. By May 1971, amendments to the university statutes empowered the Executive Council to dismiss any member of a college governing body if it felt his presence there was not in the best interests of the institution.[35] Control over college managing bodies is an important path to influence over university policies. For the moment, Delhi University seemed to have preserved the form and perhaps the substance of university autonomy.

At the same time that politicians and the public generally have become more interested in higher education, its capacity to defend itself against incursions has declined. The enormous demand for higher education has removed the limited seclusion that characterized such education in less democratic times. Requests for public funds required by expansion make higher education vulnerable to political demands, and the lower average quality of staff, facilities, and students weakens the case for higher education's claim to special intellectual standing and the independent decision-making authority such standing gives to universities. These developments have been exacerbated by the fact that approximately 40 percent of the Indian university student population consists of Pre-University Course (PUC) and intermediate students, functional equivalents of American high school students. This high percentage tends to place Indian colleges in the political status of high schools, which have been legitimately regarded as more subject than colleges and universities to lay (including public) decisions about goals, programs, and personnel.[36]

The logistical and personnel needs of expansion have another consequence favoring politicization. Expansion requires entrepreneurial and administrative talent of a sort that may not be compatible with intellectual and academic values. The capacity to deal with legislators, ministers, and civil servants, to arrange for funding and real estate, and to negotiate with the communities at the forefront of the expansion demand is crucial to the leadership of universities during periods of rapid expansion and democratization. The skills associated with these activities are exercised by administrators, who are likely to increase their authority at the expense of academics. (Such developments are not confined to India. The advent of open admissions in City University of New York system means that New York colleges will also perform quasi-high school functions while expanding rapidly — conditions that foster the growth of administrative authority at the expense of academic.)[37]

Indian educators have been alive to the problems of politicization and the assertion of the public interest in education. At the first conference of vice-chancellors, convened by the union (national) government in 1957, Sir C. P. Ramaswami Aiyer, formerly vice-chancellor of Banaras Hindu University observed: "The main problems in some of our universities . . . are those of autonomy and the intrusion of politics. . . . Political and public pressure is brought to bear directly on the Vice-Chancellor and indirectly upon . . . university bodies. . . . The way the fundamental features of education should be organised and developed are within the jurisdiction of the legislatures. Nevertheless, there is a great deal more than this which is sought to be done, not so much by the legislatures, as by those who are their spearpoints, viz., the executives of the ministries of the various governments." [38] Most of the educators at the conference recognized that, given the legal position of universities, political interest in them was inevitable. As K. G. Saiyidain, then education secretary to the government of India, noted: "There is not the remotest likelihood of an edict being issued one fine morning that henceforward politics will not be allowed to intrude into the universities." B. N. Jha, former vice-chancellor of Allahabad University (Uttar Pradesh) agreed: "In this democratic age, the universities cannot exist in isolation and politics must have its impact on university life. . . . There will be political parties and they will even be influencing the [student] Union elections . . . there will be [teachers] with different ideologies. . . . Political parties are represented among teachers and students."

The educators worried about where the limits on political direction should be placed. Jha feared that "government [can interfere] to such extent that it is impossible for the Vice-Chancellor to function independently." And D. C. Pavate, then vice-chancellor of Karnatak University (Mysore) reminded his fellow vice-chancellors that "if a person [were] nominated by the chancellor [usually the governor of the state], which effectively means the State Government . . . the inevitable result would be for the Vice-Chancellor to look to the government concerned for inspiration; and, as such, the political pressure of which there has been so much talk [would] persist."

Although the educators inquired into the limits on political direction, they conceded to the government a significant role in defending and asserting the public interest. "We have heard something of the interference of the Government in university matters," H. N. Kunzru told the vice-chancellors at their second meeting in June, 1960. "But we have to see whether that interference is justified or not. . . . The Government itself, whatever irregularity it may commit, is in theory [electorally] responsible. . . . If the Government does not intervene to control universities the universities become helpless. Then there is no one to control. . . . The interference of the Government may be justified in some cases. I do not think, Sir, that this is contrary to the theory of democracy." [39]

Within the plurality of internal and external interests and of priorities attached to the allocation of funds by the states and various agencies of the union government,[40] particularly the University Grants Commission (UGC), university administrators and faculties can maneuver to strengthen educational as against more manifestly political goals. For example, on the one hand the UGC was concerned to foster professional excellence through a major development program in support of Centers of Advanced Study;[41] the Education Commission, 1964–1966, proposed to establish "major universities" "comparable to the best institutions of their type in any part of the world"; and the 1967 conference of vice-chancellors endorsed "the suggestion of the [Education] Commission that the support of post-graduate education and research should become a central responsibility." [42] On the other hand, the state governments are concerned to satisfy demands for increased enrollments, to provide seats for state residents and "backward classes" and to have teaching conducted in the regional language (rather than in English). A talented vice-chancellor, dean, principal or department head intent on strengthening his institution educationally must operate within the field of force created by the conflicting pressures of state and national government and contradictory political forces, winning his victories as often in the interstices as in the open ground of institutional decision-making. If he is to win victories on behalf of educational goals and values, he will have to influence not only the academic bodies of the university but also the University Grants Commission, his professional colleagues, other intellectuals, and the state secretariat and legislature.

The conditions conducive to continued, even accelerating, politicization increase with the satisfaction of the rising demand for higher education and the shift in the center of power in the Indian federal system (particularly marked after the 1967 general elections) from the union to the state governments. Colleges and universities have become the object of massive popular attention and concern. Territorial, caste, and religious communities want colleges (and found them), and regions within states want universities (and get them).[43] Those whose role it is to represent (as well as govern) the people know that their political fate rests in part on satisfying the desires for status, wealth, and power that much of the demand for higher education expresses. The ordinary legislator, even the ordinary minister, is not inclined to examine too closely how the demand for higher education is satisfied or to examine the quality and consequences of what is provided if doing so will hinder the generation of political resources, influence, and support. The shift in the balance of power toward the states enhances these developments: not only is education constitutionally subject to state authority, but also the union government's constitutional responsibility for the maintenance and coordination of educational standards becomes more formal than efficient as the states play a larger role in policy formation and decision-making at the center.

At the same time that expanding resources, attention, and energy create conditions conducive to politicization and to an assertion of the public interest potentially in conflict with academic goals, they also create conditions conducive to educational improvement. More means are not necessarily or always subject to the laws of distributive justice. They can, and have, contributed to leveling up, to continued differentiation and variety, and to experiments that succeed (as well as fail). And there are administrators and politicians who see that education has a meaning beyond its contribution to national development, important as that is. In the very process of demanding and getting education for strictly instrumental reasons, the public, or at least a critical minority of it, comes to understand, to appreciate, and to protect educational values and interests.

4 / Outputs:
"Standards" in Democratized Higher Education

A major consequence of the vast expansion in education since independence, according to most commentators on the Indian educational scene, has been a decline in standards. The decline has been loudly and frequently lamented but less frequently analyzed empirically. The conventional argument, and it is a persuasive one, goes as follows. The universities are expanding faster than adequate secondary education, with the result that those who enter colleges are increasingly ill-prepared. The poor quality of secondary education is compounded by the increasing proportion of first generation literates who enter college each year. As a result, higher education in India is being swamped by a flood of what in America are called the culturally underprivileged. Their number is expanding faster than the supply of properly trained college and postgraduate teachers and scholars. Old, much less new, universities and colleges cannot fill sanctioned posts at all, or can do so only by lowering standards for faculty recruitment and selection. The logistical burdens caused by the large number of classes dilute the attention and resources even of good teachers and well-administered institutions. The lack of adequate facilities — books, laboratories, study space, hostels, extracurricular facilities — aggravates the unsatisfactory learning environment and helps breed the discontents that eventuate in "student unrest." [1] The remedial and custodial aspects of "higher education" in India have increased at an alarming rate.

Although there is a great deal in this line of argument, it is at best one-sided, and at worst inadequately informed about either the past or the present. To those who were excluded from higher education in the pre-independence period by the limited number of seats in colleges and by high fees and admission standards, the present, whatever its inadequacies, appears as a net improvement, although the mounting levels of student unrest suggest that many sense they are getting inferior educations.

Second, research on the quality of higher education in the "old days" suggests that there has been a nostalgic distortion of the past by more senior generations. More precise criteria or measures are needed to shape judgements about a "decline" in Indian higher education. In this volume Irene Gilbert discusses the high quality elite education that was offered by Presidency College, Calcutta; Muir Central College, Allahabad; and the Muslim Anglo-Oriental College, Aligarh. In an era of limited enrollments, they represented the best, not an average. The Calcutta University Commission of 1917–1919 indicated that university admission processes then were not notably discriminating. It found that "more than three-quarters of the successful matriculates [under the university's area of jurisdiction] . . . proceed to the university course," [2] and an Indian headmaster testifying before the commission thought "the majority . . . unfit to receive university training." [3] Intermediate students (those in programs preparatory for first degree courses) were, according to the commission, unable to "understand the simplest spoken English" or to "write four or five simple sentences in coherent English" [4] — a finding similar to those heard often in the 1950's and 1960's.

The problem of comparison is further complicated by the rapid obsolescence of many established curricula as the knowledge explosion accelerates. The standards reasonable for many subjects in 1947 may no longer be so today. Access to new subjects, as well as to new knowledge in old subjects, can make an enormous difference in the quality of education. Yet such considerations are seldom in the minds of writers who deplore a decline in standards. Instead, they deplore the failure of later generations to acquire the skills or knowledge they themselves acquired, even when such skills or knowledge may have been rendered obsolete by the knowledge explosion and changing times.

These observations about the changes in access to higher education, the actual quality of education in a putative golden age, and the meaning of quality given the knowledge explosion must be considered in evaluating standards in postindependence India. A careful examination of the available educational statistics makes such evaluation even more difficult. The statistics suggest that standards have improved in some sectors and declined in others. In still other areas, conclusions are impossible because of the inadequacy of the data. The confidence with which it has become fashionable to speak of a decline in standards is most certainly misplaced. Although the statistics that we cite and analyze below introduce an empirical dimension into a public policy and social science controversy hitherto characterized by not altogether reliable impressions or by logical deductions from doubtful premises, our "hard data" may also introduce a spurious precision into these discussions. As our cautionary notes suggest, the statistics raise almost as many problems as they solve; each table has to be received with the level of skepticism appropriate to its source and difficulties.

Disaggregating Growth by Level and Subject

One way to judge what is happening to standards in India is to examine changes in the structure of higher education, notably changes in the relative significance of more and less demanding degree programs by level and subject. One might anticipate that the increase of less qualified students would result in the swamping of advanced higher education (second and third degrees) by enrollments at the entering (first) degree level

(B.A., B.Sc., B. Comm., etc.). If, as the Education Commission, 1964–1966, argues, the second degree (postgraduate master's) level in India often corresponds to a European or American first degree (bachelor's) level, such a development would imply a kind of Gresham's law in which school education drives out higher education.[5] The data, however, indicate that the postgraduate sector, in the face of a 250 percent expansion of all higher education since 1952,[6] has held its own, not only maintaining its proportion of total enrollment in the last few years but increasing it slightly. As table 1 demonstrates, postgraduate and research levels have

Table 1. Changing structure of Indian education — level.

| Level | Students enrolled in all higher education (percent) | | Net change |
	1952–53	1964–65	
Preuniversity and intermediate	58.0	37.0	−21.0[a]
Graduate (bachelor's degrees)	35.4	54.7	+19.3
Postgraduate and research	4.9	6.0	+1.1[b]
Diploma, certificate and preprofessional	1.7	2.3	+0.6
	100.0	100.0	

Sources: Government of India, University Grants Commission, *University Development in India; Basic Facts and Figures, 1962–63* (New Delhi, 1963), p. 74; idem, *University Development in India; Basic Facts and Figures, 1964–65* (New Delhi, 1966), table 21(a), p. 63.

[a] In part an artifact of the structural reform that substituted a one year preuniversity program for the two year intermediate qualification.

[b] In 1963–64, the percent was 5.9, suggesting a rising trend to 6.0 percent in 1963–64, but this measure has to be laid against a measure of 6.3 percent in 1961–62. For the latter figure see University Grants Commission, *University Development in India; Basic Facts and Figures* (New Delhi, 1966), p. 21. The figures for 1966–67 and 1967–68 were 5.7 and 5.8 respectively. University Grants Commission, *University Development in India; Basic Facts and Figures* (Delhi, 1971), p. 145.

gained 1.1 percent. This modest proportionate increase represents a great absolute increase, from approximately 30,000 to approximately 91,000 students.[7]

The importance of the increase in enrollment at the first degree level and the decline in enrollment at the PUC (Pre-University Course)-intermediate level is difficult to assess.[8] In large part, these changes are accounted for by the consequences of reorganization of the educational structure (generally effective in all states except Uttar Pradesh and in the Bombay area of Maharashtra) from a two-year intermediate course and a two-year B.A. course to a one-year preuniversity course and a three-year B.A. course.[9] The preuniversity courses still occupy a large proportion of college enrollments (about 40 percent) and their effect is to strengthen the high school, remedial, and administrative orientations of "higher" education. The placing of intermediate or PUC levels in colleges, by contrast with the previous separation, may be a mixed blessing.

That the postgraduate and research level has maintained its share of enrollment in a rapidly expanding system of higher education suggests that Indian universities have at least formally recognized and mean to pursue under democratic conditions that function of the university which they took up in the second decade of the present century — research and the advancement of knowledge. There has been a growth in Ph.D.'s awarded (table 2). During a recent four-year period for which data was available (1960–61 through 1963–64), the annual number of Ph.D.'s awarded rose from 796 to 975, an 18 percent rise over four years. During this four-year period, twelve universities (17 percent of the total number of universities) produced a substantial number of Ph.D.'s (100 or more each), and over half produced a significant number (40 to 99). Quantity, however, tells nothing about quality. One would need to examine with some care, for example, the 412 Ph.D.'s granted in these four years at Agra (the second highest Ph.D. producer). Eighty-eight of these Ph.D.'s (21 percent) were in Hindi,[10] a subject that does not ordinarily attract top flight faculty or students. That Agra produces more Ph.D.'s in economics than the University of Delhi does not prove that its standards are higher or its academic culture livelier. (Delhi economics professors have taught at, and had offers from, leading foreign universities. Former faculty and graduates hold professorships at London, M.I.T., and Harvard.) Many of the Agra Ph.D.'s were produced at affiliated colleges. The Education Commission, 1964–1966, took a dim view of most advanced work completed at colleges because they rarely have staff or facilities adequate for advanced research.[11] Some universities, including a few older ones such as Mysore, Nagpur, Annamalai, and Kerala, as well as many recently founded ones, have given few or no Ph.D.'s. This indicates that those universities are not making the contributions to knowledge that would qualify them to be counted among India's "modern" universities.[12] (See table 6.)

Another structural change relevant to standards is the movement from arts degrees to scientific, professional, and agricultural degrees. Table 3 shows that, since 1952, arts degrees have declined by 6 percent, while degrees granted in science, professional, and agricultural subjects have gained by 3, 1, and 1 percent each. Observers were wont to believe that Indian students and educational authorities were unsympathetic to scientific and professional education and indifferent to India's need for more education in such subjects. Table 3 gives some basis for that view, notably the long-term secular rise in the proportion of arts degrees granted from 1916 to the early 1950's, and the accompanying modest decline in the proportion of science and professional degrees. The pattern may not, however, reflect what student or official preferences were. The relatively modest costs associated with establishing and maintaining B.A. colleges by comparison with professional and scientific education, even at the first degree level, have always made arts colleges the cheapest way of responding to expanding demands for higher education. Data over the last ten years,

Table 2. Rank order[a] of universities accepting more than forty arts[b] and science theses, 1960–61 through 1963–64.

University	Year of Founding	All theses (N = 3116)			Arts (N = 1382)			Science (N = 1734)		
		No.	%	Rank	No.	%	Rank	No.	%	Rank
Calcutta (W. Bengal)	1857	449	14	1	107	8	2	342	20	1
Agra (Uttar Pradesh)	1927	412	13	2	290	21	1	122	7	3
Bombay (Maharashtra)	1857	239	8	3	96	7	4	143	8	2
Lucknow (Uttar Pradesh)	1921	183	6	4	104	7	3	79	5	7
Delhi (Delhi)	1922	174	6	5	92	7	5	82	5	6
Allahabad (Uttar Pradesh)	1887	158	5	6	53	4	9	105	6	5
Saugar (Madhya Pradesh)	1946	144	5	7	80	6	6	64	5	9
Banaras Hindu (Uttar Pradesh)	1916	140	5	8	71	5	7	69	4	8
Rajasthan (Rajasthan)	1947	125	4	9	66	5	8	59	3	11
Madras (Madras)	1857	123	4	10	15	1	19	108	6	4
Poona (Maharashtra)	1949	112	4	11	52	4	11	60	3	10
Punjab (Punjab)	1947	90	3	12	39	3	13	51	3	12
Aligarh Muslim (Uttar Pradesh)	1921	81	3	13	32	2	14	49	3	13
Andhra (Andhra)	1926	68	2	14	8	1	22	60	3	10
Patna (Bihar)	1917	68	2	15	50	4	12	18	1	20
Baroda (Gujarat)	1949	61	2	16	28	2	15	33	2	15
Indian Institute of Science (Mysore)	1909	49	2	17	–	–	–	49	3	13
Osmania (Andhra)	1918	45	1	18	21	1	16	24	1	18
Gujarat (Gujarat)	1950	44	1	19	19	1	18	25	1	17
Bihar (Bihar)	1952	41	1	20	32	2	14	9	1	19
Jadavpur (W. Bengal)	1955	41	1	20	5	0	24	36	2	14
All other universities		269	8		122	9		147	9	
			100			100			100	

Source: Government of India, University Grants Commission, *University Development in India, Basic Facts and Figures 1964–65* (New Delhi, 1966), pp. 152–153.

[a] Ph.D. theses were accepted in fields other than arts and science during this period but the numbers are small and do not affect substantially the rank order given here. See table 4.

[b] Includes social sciences.

Table 3. Changing structure of Indian higher education — subject.

Subject	Students enrolled in all higher education (percentage, to nearest percentage point)							Net change 1952–53/1964–65
	1916–17 (N = 61)[a]	1926–27 (N = 92)[a]	1936–37 (N = 126)[a]	1946–47 (N = 266)[a]	1952–53 (N = 513)[a]	1964–65 (N = 1528)[a]	1967–68 (N = 2219)[a]	
Arts[b]	49	50	50	55	58	52	52	−6
Science	36	32	33	32	29	31	33	+3
Professional[c]	15	18	16	12	12	14	13	+1
Agricultural	0	0	1	1	1	3	2	+1
	100	100	100	100	100	100	100	

Sources: Government of India, University Grants Commission, *Report on Standards of University Education* (New Delhi, 1965), appendix 3; idem, *University Development in India; Basic Facts and Figures 1962–63* (New Delhi, 1963), p. 73; idem, *University Development in India; Basic Facts and Figures, 1964–65* (New Delhi, 1966), p. 35; and idem, *University Development in India; Basic Facts and Figures* (New Delhi, 1971), p. 40.

Note: In 1964–65 there was a slight reversal in the trends depicted in this table. For example, the percentage of arts (including commerce) students enrolled increased by 0.5, the percentage of enrolled students in engineering and technology declined by 0.2 (in the face of an incipient glut on the job market for engineers), and the percentage of students enrolled in agriculture declined by 0.1, all compared to the previous year, 1963–64.

[a] Thousands.
[b] Includes commerce.
[c] Includes engineering and technology; medicine, including veterinary medicine; law; education; and others.

however, suggest a decline of such resistance to professional and scientific education as there may have been. Differential applications for B.A. and B.Sc. seats suggest that student choices were (and are) primarily a result of perceived occupational opportunities and the costs associated with qualifying for them. In recent times the mushrooming of capitation-fee-based private medical and engineering institutions indicate that many more would have studied these subjects if the less costly seats in government institutions had been available.

In fact, by 1970 overproduction of engineers and doctors (relative to employment opportunities) was considered a major problem. Applications at the five Indian Institutes of Technology (IIT's), prime producers of engineers, showed great sensitivity to the professional opportunities of engineers, rising from 17,995 in 1963 to 35,216 in 1966 — at the height of the demand for engineers — and declining to 12,641 after a glut became apparent.[13]

Trends at the Ph.D. level confirm the drift away from arts degrees. Between 1960–61 and 1963–64, arts Ph.D.'s dropped from 41 to 36 percent of all Ph.D.'s while Ph.D.'s in science rose from 47 to 49 percent and in agriculture from 5 to 7 percent.[14]

The structural proportions reported in table 3 do not reveal the absolute increases in the scientific and professional fields. When Britain departed the subcontinent, approximately 5,000 students were studying engineering and technology, 9,000 medicine, and 4,000 agriculture. The number of students studying these subjects has increased ten-fold, four-fold, and six-fold, respectively, over fifteen years.[15] Such trends reflect government efforts not only to train domestically in high quality institutions those who were previously trained abroad but also to increase substantially the quality and quantity of scientific and technical education. The five IIT's (developed in collaboration with outstanding institutions in Russia, Germany, Britain, and America), which recruit and select students on the basis of all-India competitive examinations, and the regional engineering colleges, upgraded by special grants from the ministry of education, represent such efforts in technology and science. The All-India Institute of Medical Science and postgraduate training and research programs in a few medical colleges contribute to India's increasing self-sufficiency in the training of doctors and medical specialists. (Indeed, India has become a major exporter of them.)

Of the two nationwide meritocratic competitions, that conducted by the IIT's ranks with or above that for the national civil services as a prestigious competition attracting the talented and ambitious. The old Indian Civil Service exams gave intellectual prestige to the humanist generalist and the subjects that he cultivated. The IIT exams have helped give science and math subjects a similar prestige.[16]

The effect of the increase in professional training on standards, notably in technology and medicine, is ambiguous. On the one hand, these fields are highly competitive and have, until recently, paid high rewards, thereby recruiting good students and being able to press them rather hard. On the other hand, the applied professions everywhere tend to take an instrumental view of knowledge, viewing with skepticism the ornamental or abstract nature of studies that are not "useful." An institution such as the University of Baroda (see chapter 11), which has high standing in part because of its good professional schools, may not necessarily provide a hospitable environment for the standards and concerns of postgraduate education that aims to make additions to knowledge and is pursued for its own sake.

Differentiation and the Growth of New Disciplines

The graduate and postgraduate shift since the mid-1950's to science and technology represents an emphasis which is surely in line with India's social and economic requirements. But the declining prestige of arts degrees, their failure to attract the best students, and their identification with low paying clerical jobs raise other problems. The education of those who can provide the cultural formulations and social science knowledge and skills that give direction, purpose, and meaning to the uses of science and technology within the framework of Indian society and government is important. There is evidence of developments in the higher (postgraduate) levels of the arts field that can help India to meet its needs for such education.

Arts as well as science categories are being internally differentiated by the emergence and growth of new postgraduate fields. The first Ph.D.'s in such subjects as veterinary science, oriental studies, Chinese, international relations, mathematical physics, spectroscopy, marine biology, and

Table 4. Doctoral theses accepted by faculties other than arts or science, 1960–61 through 1963–64.

Subject	Universities accepting theses	Theses accepted	Rank order
Agriculture	12	185	1
Engineering/technology	12	78	2
Commerce	14	69	3
Medicine	13	57	4
Education	14	40	5
Oriental studies	2	3	6
Law	3	3	6
Veterinary science	1	2	7
Fine Arts	1	2	7
		439	

Source: Government of India, University Grants Commission, *University Development in India; Basic Facts and Figures* (New Delhi, 1966).

Table 5. Doctoral theses accepted by arts (social sciences and allied subjects) faculties, 1960–61 through 1963–64.

Subject	Number	Rank order
Economics	165	1
Political science	112	2
History	96	3
Sociology	50	4
Psychology	45	5
Geography	28	6
Mathematics[a]	24	7
Archaeology[a]	21	8
Linguistics[a]	15	9
Statistics[a]	5	10
Anthropology	4	11
International relations	2	12
Social work[a]	2	12
Applied mathematics	1	13
Public administration	1	13
	571	

Source: Government of India, University Grants Commission, *University Development in India; Basic Facts and Figures* (New Delhi, 1966).

[a] Allied subjects.

a number of Indian languages and literatures were recently completed.[17] (See tables 4 and 5.)

Within arts, the social science category is probably becoming stronger and more differentiated, again notably at the postgraduate level. Although

Table 6. Pre-1959 universities accepting less than forty Ph.D theses in arts and science, 1960–61 through 1963–64.

Name	Year founded	Name	Year founded
Mysore (Mysore)	1916	Sri Venkateswara (Andhra)	1954
Nagpur (Maharashtra)	1923	S. V. Vidyapith (Gujarat)	1955
Annamalai (Madras)	1929	Kurukshetra (Haryana)	1956
Kerala (Kerala)	1937	Indira Kala Sangit	
Utkal (Orissa)	1943	Vishvavidyalaya	
Gauhati (Assam)	1948	(Madhya Pradesh)	1956
Jammu and Kashmir	1948	Vikram (Madhya Pradesh)	1957
Roorkee (Uttar Pradesh)	1949	Gorakhpur (Uttar Pradesh)	1957
Karnatak (Mysore)	1949	Jabalpur (Madhya Pradesh)	1957
S.N.D.T. Women's		Varanaseya Sanskrit	
(Maharashtra)	1951	Vishvavidyalaya	
Viswa-Bharati		(Uttar Pradesh)	1958
(West Bengal)	1951	Marathwada (Maharashtra)	1958

Source: Government of India, University Grants Commission, *University Development in India; Basic Facts and Figures* (New Delhi, 1966).

we have no time series data to support this observation, certain historical developments suggest it. Today, social science Ph.D.'s represent 14 percent of all Ph.D.'s and 36 percent of those in the arts.[18] Social science education under the *raj* was probably more modest in size and certainly poorer in comprehensiveness. India has had a tradition of creativity in economics (Dadabhai Naoroji and R. C. Dutt are two of the most prominent, if not necessarily the most durable, of India's outstanding economists), but today she has substantial economics and economic history professions whose leaders command international reputations. Economics heads the social sciences in Ph.D. production, with 165 Ph.D.'s in the 1960–61 to 1963–64 period. Political science, also a respectable subject under the *raj,* now has outstanding practitioners with both domestic and international reputations, although some of the best are, to the detriment of postgraduate education, situated in independent research institutions.[19]

Sociology under the *raj* suffered from British biases against the social sciences, but began to develop after independence. "Academic tradition generally in Britain and especially in such ancient centers of learning as Oxford and Cambridge," a committee of Indian sociologists observed, "has not been friendly until recently to sociology . . . [which has been] associated with French (and foreign) radical thought." [20] The University of Bombay was a conspicuous exception to such unfriendliness, thanks to the maverick creativity and leadership of Patrick Geddes. He founded the sociology department in 1919 and remained its chairman until 1924, when G. S. Ghurye began a long tenure noted for its originality and productivity. Mysore University began sociology in 1928–29, but in the philosophy department. Most sociology departments were established after independence.[21] Although in the period from 1960–61 to 1963–64 sociology produced 50 Ph.D.'s and ranked fourth — after history — among the social sciences in Ph.D. production, it had not yet fully overcome the cleavages and parochialisms associated with the domination of the field by a few professors, their "schools," and their students. The UGC designation of the Delhi University sociology department as a center for advanced study and the sanctioning in 1968 of three additional professors, however, marked sociology's new significance in India.[22]

Preindependence anthropology suffered from British and Indian biases. Educated nationalists distrusted it as a discipline that served the purposes of British rule and portrayed the country as primitive.[23] Despite these biases, anthropological research (primarily ethnology and archaeology) under the *raj* was often of a high standard, carried on by British or Indian administrators who tended to practice it on the side as an avocation. The bias against anthropology declined after independence as social and cultural anthropology, often in close conjunction with sociology, came into their own as academic disciplines.

The propensity, noted by Edward Shils in 1961,[24] for Indian intellectuals, including social scientists, to orient themselves to the foreign professional reference groups of the metropole (London, New York, etc.) is now less in evidence. Indian reference groups have gained in competence and stature in the decades since independence, and foreign reference groups, particularly American ones, have become suspect in some circles as carriers of "academic colonialism." [25]

The humanities side of the arts at the postgraduate level is accounted for mainly by Indian languages and literatures. Of the 742 humanities degrees granted between 1960–61 and 1963–64, 613 were in these subjects. This latter figure represented 45 percent of all arts degrees. (See table 7.) Hindi and Sanskrit degrees alone account for 34 percent of all arts Ph.D.'s. A frequent view in India is that many of these language and literature Ph.D.'s represent "cheap" degrees which require a minimum of new concepts, skills, or imagination. Since independence, however, new creativity and new levels of excellence in some regional languages and literatures have been achieved (beyond the considerable growth that already accompanied nationalism). At least some of the language and literature Ph.D.'s reflect this pattern.[26]

Indicators of Resource Allocation and Performance

Student-staff ratios, which are another index of the fate of standards, have predictably risen, but the rise has been moderate. (See tables 8 and

Table 7. Doctoral theses accepted by arts (humanities) faculties, 1960–61 through 1963–64.

Subject	Number	Rank order	Subject	Number	Rank order
Hindi	329	1	Punjabi	5	14
Sanskrit	143	2	Comparative		
Philosophy	76	3	philology	3	15
English	61	4	Oriya	3	15
Bengali	40	5	Philology and		
Ancient Indian			linguistics	3	15
history and			Ardhmagadhi	2	16
culture	18	6	Art and		
Urdu	17	7	architecture	2	16
Gujarati	16	8	Arabian culture		
Marathi	13	9	and civilization	2	16
Telugu	12	10	Indian philology		
Arabic	10	11	and religion	2	16
Arabic/Persian/			Prakit/Pali	2	16
Urdu	10	11	Tamil	2	16
Kannada	7	12	Assamese	1	17
Persian	6	13	Chinese	1	17
Islamic studies	5	14	Malayalam	1	17

Source: Government of India, University Grants Commission, *University Development in India; Basic Facts and Figures* (New Delhi, 1966).

Table 8. Staff [a] — student ratio.[b]

Year	Mean	Median
1960–61 [c]	1:17.5	1:16.3
1961–62 [d]	1:17.9	1:16.5
1962–63 [e]	1:19.1	1:17.6
1963–64 [f]	1:19.7	1:18.2
1964–65 [g]	1:20.3	1:19.5

Sources: Government of India, University Grants Commission, *University Development in India, 1961–62* (New Delhi, 1962), pp. 21–22; idem, *University Development in India, 1962–63* (New Delhi, 1963), pp. 36–37; idem, *University Development in India, 1963–64* (New Delhi, 1964), pp. 45–46; and idem, *University Development in India, 1964–65* (New Delhi, 1966), pp. 139–140.

[a] Excludes tutors and demonstrators.
[b] Affiliated colleges only.
[c] Forty-two of forty-six universities reported.
[d] Forty-seven of fifty-four universities reported.
[e] Fifty-four of fifty-five universities reported.
[f] The number of universities reporting in 1963–64 not available.
[g] Forty-three of sixty-two universities reported.

9.) Table 8 shows only slightly less favorable student-staff ratios in 1964–65 than in 1961–62. A more extended time series than that in table 8, however, might show a steeper increase in the ratios. The staffing patterns reported in table 10 suggest the broad differences in quality between low cost arts, science, and commerce colleges on the one hand (twenty-to-one student-staff ratios) and high cost professional colleges on the other (eleven-to-one student-staff ratios). However, the ratio in law (a relatively low cost and low opportunity professional field) is worse than in any other subject except commerce at the B.A. level (table 11, both columns). Law, commerce, and arts have much higher ratios than new or high opportunity

Table 9. Staff — student ratio.[a]

Year	Colleges (percent)			
	Less than 1:10	Between 1:10 and 1:20	Between 1:20 and 1:30	More than 1:30
1961–62	24.8	42.7	20.8	11.7
1962–63	22.7	38.2	24.7	14.4
1963–64	19.2	40.8	24.6	15.4
1964–65	17.5	39.5	28.0	15.0
Net Change 61–62/64–65	−7.3	−3.2	+7.2	+3.3

Sources: Government of India, University Grants Commission, *University Development in India, for 1961–62* (New Delhi, 1962), p. 22; idem, *University Development in India, 1962–63* (New Delhi, 1963), p. 38; idem, *University Development in India, 1963–64* (New Delhi, 1964), p. 47; and idem, *University Development in India, 1964–65* (New Delhi, 1966), p. 92.

[a] Affiliated colleges only.

Table 10. Staff — student ratio, arts/science/commerce colleges and professional colleges, 1962–63 and 1964–65.

Type of college	1962–63	1964–65	Net change over three years
Arts/Science/Commerce[a]	1:22.5 [b]	1:19.8 [c]	−2.7
Professional[a]	1:11.4 [d]	1:11.5 [e]	+0.1

Sources: Government of India, University Grants Commission, *University Development in India, 1962–63* (New Delhi, 1963), p. 38; and idem, *University Development in India, 1964–65* (New Delhi, 1966), p. 93.

[a] Does not include staff and students of university departments.
[b] Number of students was 781,981.
[c] Number of students was 948,966.
[d] Number of students was 137,192.
[e] Number of students was 178,772.

fields such as veterinary science and medicine. Since the arts, science, and commerce colleges have by far the largest part of total enrollment (781,981 students as against 137,192 students for the professional colleges), most students in Indian higher education experience the higher ratios. A low student-staff ratio, however, is not always indicative of high standards. Many new colleges, notably in rural areas, have few students (less than 100) and low student-staff ratios but are, according to the Education Commission, 1964–1966, usually of limited or poor quality.[27]

The figures in table 12, without bearing directly on the question of standards, suggest a trend in one ancillary facility, hostels. Between 1960–

Table 11. Staff — student ratio, university departments and affiliated colleges (by subject), 1964–65.

Subject	University departments[a]	Rank order	Affiliated colleges[b]	Rank order
Other	1:4.7	1	1:8.8	3
Veterinary science	1:6.9	2	1:7.1	1
Agriculture	1:8.2	3	1:12.5	4
Medicine	1:9.6	4	1:8.0	2
Education	1:11.0	5	1:13.6	5
Science	1:11.2	6	1:19.2	8
Engineering/technology	1:13.7	7	1:13.7	6
All departments	1:14.0	–	–	–
All colleges	–	–	1:17.8	–
Arts	1:16.1	8	1:18.2	7
Commerce	1:29.4	9	1:35.4	10
Law	1:43.9	10	1:32.5	9

Source: Government of India, University Grants Commission, *University Development in India, 1964–65* (New Delhi, 1966), table 26, p. 87.

[a] Total enrollment in university departments was 190,489 and the total staff available, including tutors and demonstrators, was 13,637.
[b] Total enrollment in affiliated colleges was 1,127,738 and the total staff available, including tutors and demonstrators, was 63,483.

Table 12. Students resident in hostels.

Year	Number (thousands)	Percentage
1960–61 [a]	n.a.	17.6
1961–62 [b]	178	18.2
1962–63 [c]	196	18.1
1963–64 [d]	219	18.5
1964–65 [e]	250	19.0

Sources: Government of India, University Grants Commission, *University Development in India, 1961–62* (New Delhi, 1962), pp. 23–25; idem, *University Development in India, 1962–63* (New Delhi, 1963), pp. 41–42; idem, *University Development in India, 1963–64* (New Delhi, 1964), pp. 49–50; and idem, *University Development in India, 1964–65* (New Delhi, 1966), pp. 96–97.
[a] Forty-two of forty-six universities reported.
[b] Forty-seven of fifty-four universities reported.
[c] Fifty-two of fifty-five universities reported.
[d] Fifty-three of fifty-five universities reported.
[e] Fifty-nine of sixty-two universities reported.

61 and 1964–65, in the face of a rapidly expanding number of students, the proportion of students accommodated in hostels increased. Because the impact of hostels is unclear — sometimes bad hostel facilities are worse than none, concentrating discontented students and adding new dimensions to their sense of grievance, injustice, or alienation[28] — this increase is not necessarily an indication of improvement in standards. However, the data do suggest that educational authorities are somehow keeping up with the increased demand for hostels that follows from the influx of new students, particularly from rural areas.

Finally, there are some data on student performance, data which are subject to so many caveats and cautions that it is tempting not to use them at all. The main purpose in using them is to suggest that the data on performance neither confirm nor deny any assertions about trends in standards. Table 13 gives the percentages of first, second, and third class

Table 13. First, second, and third class degrees, 1959 and 1962.

Degree	First class degrees			Second class degrees			Third class degrees		
	1959 (%)	1962 (%)	Net change	1959 (%)	1962 (%)	Net change	1959 (%)	1962 (%)	Net change
B.A.	1.8	1.1	−0.7	21.2	28.4	+7.2	77.0	70.5	−6.5
B.Sc.	13.3	15.0	+1.7	43.8	42.5	−1.3	42.9	42.5	−0.4
B.Comm.	0.7	0.9	+0.2	16.2	22.5	+6.3	83.1	76.6	−6.5
M.A.	4.5	4.4	−0.1	41.9	45.3	+3.4	53.6	50.3	−3.3
M.Sc.	26.7	26.7	0.0	54.7	57.8	+3.1	18.6	15.5	−3.1
M.Comm.	7.4	5.4	−2.0	45.7	53.9	+8.2	46.9	40.7	−6.2

Source: Government of India, University Grants Commission, *University Development in India, 1963–64* (New Delhi, 1964), p. 94.

degrees in 1959 and 1962. Table 14, which reports the percentage passing various degree examinations in 1949 and 1962, shows a decline in passes in ten of fourteen degrees, the exceptions being M.A., B.Sc., Engineering, and M.B.B.S. (medical). If, for the moment, we assume that a pass in 1962 measures approximately the same performance as it did in 1949, we may conclude that the quality of students has declined in the ordinary fields (where larger proportions are failing) but has improved in some high opportunity fields (where larger proportions are passing), a con-

Table 14. Students passing, 1949–1962.

| | 1949 | | 1962 | | Net change, |
Subject	Per-centage	Num-ber	Per-centage	Num-ber	1949–1962, (%)
B.A.	50.8	17,228	46.1	65,004	−4.7
B.A. (Honors)	77.2	2,157	57.7	3,690	−19.5
M.A.	78.0	3,632	83.3	21,003	+5.3
B.Sc.	44.0	7,002	45.6	25,563	+1.6
B.Sc. (Honors)	64.7	652	60.3	1,367	−4.4
B.Comm./B.Comm. (Honors)	50.3	2,549	48.2	14,358	−2.1
M.Comm.	95.8	361	74.9	2,229	−20.9
B.Sc. (Engineering)	71.4	1,277	75.0	6,459	+3.6
B.Sc. (Agriculture)	88.8	947	69.4	2,609	−19.4
B.V.Sc.	71.1	59	64.5	774	−6.6
B.L./LL.B.	68.2	3,367	55.9	6,999	−12.3
B.Ed.	85.4	2,262	80.8	16,310	−4.6
M.Ed.	89.2	74	76.1	501	−13.1
M.B.B.S.	45.9	1,601	57.9	3,567	+12.0

Source: Government of India, University Grants Commission, *University Development in India, 1963–64* (New Delhi, 1964), Appendix 7, "Examination Results (All-India Figures) 1948–49 to 1961–62," and "University Examination Results (All Universities Combined)," pp. 81–93.

clusion which corresponds to the view that the high opportunity fields attract high quality students and can afford to exclude others. Such an interpretation implies that the canons of judgment are being held steady ("standards are being upheld") in the face of a growing and less qualified constituency. But can we assume that a 1962 pass is equivalent to a 1949 pass? That the "traditional" failure rate of 50 percent at the B.A. level has been exceeded by five percentage points in the face of massive expassion may or may not mean that standards have declined. Both interpretations must remain tentative.[29]

Our analysis has stressed the importance of disaggregating the field of education regionally and sectorally as a preliminary to higher level generalizations. This method yields a differentiated view of the fate of standards. It suggests that, statistically speaking at least, the expansion of higher education has not resulted in a swamping of the postgraduate sector by the first degree or preuniversity levels. On the contrary, the structure of higher education has been somewhat upgraded: the proportion of students at the B.A. level has increased at the expense of the proportion at the intermediate and PUC levels, and the postgraduate level has made a modest proportionate advance. The statistics also suggest a shift from arts to science, technology, and the professions, while the founding of new technological and scientific institutions of high quality suggests the upgrading of leading sectors for economic development. In the social sciences, new fields have been added and old ones strengthened since independence, and a few outstanding men in a variety of fields are, and are perceived to be, peers of internationally outstanding professionals.

Although postgraduate education has improved since independence, the ordinary B.A.-B.Sc. education has probably suffered in the aggregate. Prior to independence, when the B.A. was still the route to membership in a national elite, arts education, particularly at premier colleges, received considerable special attention and recruited a relatively limited number of well-trained students. B.A. education has now for the most part lost what elite qualities it may have had; the special attention it used to attract has been increasingly diverted to professional and postgraduate (second and especially third degree) education. First degree student-staff ratios compare badly with those in most professional and engineering colleges (law colleges excepted). It is probably safe to conclude that the head of the academic procession has improved over its counterpart at independence, while its much larger tail has suffered from the enormous expansion in education. But even here, the statistical indexes do not permit a confident assertion of "decline." The evidence concerning standards remains ambiguous.[30]

The propensity to see Indian education as a whole and to analyze and evaluate it in global terms must be tempered by an appreciation and understanding of state and regional differences. Because primary responsibility for education in the federal system lies with the states and because Indian states differ as much or more than European nations do with respect to language, historical legacies, economic development, administrative capability, and political effectiveness, their educational systems vary in a number of important dimensions. British rule in the nineteenth and twentieth centuries, particularly in its differential effects on the coastal rimland as against the interior heartland, accentuated existing differences and introduced new ones that were highly salient for education. The introduction of English education was especially important in sharpening regional differences.[1]

We begin our examination of regional differences by aggregating the states into two large subnational categories, which we term "rimland" and "heartland." We then examine indicators of their differences and analyze some explanations and consequences of such differences. Disaggregating education further, we analyze variations in state resource allocation and in enrollment patterns to further underscore the importance of viewing Indian education as a series of educational systems with varying capabilities, policies, and outputs.

Education and Development in Rimland and Heartland

The two areal aggregates, rimland and heartland, are differentiated by the degree of their exposure to external cultural, political, and economic influences and by their responses to such influences. Table 15 identifies the states of the areal aggregates and uses regional language and English language literacy as intercorrelated indicators of the differences between rimland and heartland.

The rimland includes the three former presidencies where the British impact was most marked, Bombay, Tamil Nadu (formerly called Madras), and West Bengal. Bengal and Bombay experienced higher rates of economic development in the nineteenth century than Tamil Nadu (with its lower levels of industrial investment and commercial modernization) but in all three presidencies the levels of education early pulled ahead of levels in their respective hinterlands. In Calcutta in 1886–87 10 percent of school-

Table 15. Rimland — Heartland differences: literacy.

State	Literates (1961) (%)	English literates (1951)[a] (%)
Rimland		
Kerala	46.2	1.75
Bombay (Maharashtra, Gujarat)[b]	30.0	1.27
Madras[c]	30.0	1.00[d]
West Bengal	29.1	2.41
Punjab	23.7	2.56
Heartland		
Bihar	18.2	0.65
Uttar Pradesh	17.5	0.82
Madhya Pradesh	16.9	0.66
Rajasthan	14.7	0.44

Source: Government of India, Ministry of Information, *India, 1962* (Delhi, 1962), p. 78; and Government of India, *Report of the Official Language Commission* (Delhi, 1956), appendix 12, p. 468. Grouping by present authors.

[a] These figures were computed by taking the numbers receiving the School Leaving Certificate or equivalent.

[b] The 1961 literacy figure includes the figure for Maharashtra (29.7 percent) and Gujarat (30 percent); the figure for 1951 is for pre-reorganization Bombay.

[c] The figure for English literates in 1951 combines Madras and Andhra because Andhra was still part of Madras; the figure was almost certainly much higher — approaching 2 percent — for Madras alone.

[d] This rate was mistakenly given as .1 percent instead of 1 percent in the *Report of the Official Language Commission*, a "mistake" not unhelpful to the commission's conclusions.

age males were receiving collegiate and secondary education; in the adjacent Bengal districts the figure was 5 to 9 percent; but in Bihar and Orissa, then part of Bengal presidency, the figure was only 2.5 percent or less.[2] The Tamil districts that now make up the present state of Tamil Nadu were well ahead of the Telugu districts, now the present state of Andhra but then (1886–87) the hinterland of Madras presidency.[3]

Kerala's high literacy rates cannot be attributed to the effect of British educational policy since this state, unlike others in the rimland, is made up primarily of the former princely states of Tranvancore and Cochin (plus Malabar in the north, an area formerly under the Madras presidency). These rates are related, rather, to the effect of a variety of earlier influences going back to the pre-Christian era. Not least among these influences is that of Christianity, which claims almost a fourth of Kerala's population as adherents. Punjab lies inland, but it is on the "rim" between India and the northwest invasion routes. From Alexander to Babar and Nadir Shah the Punjab has been penetrated by cultural and commercial as well as by military forces. The need for writers and clerks in Delhi, imperial capital not only of the Moghuls but also, after 1922, of the British, helps account for the Punjab's high literacy rates.

The heartland areas coincide with areas where Hindi is spoken — Rajasthan, Uttar Pradesh, Madhya Pradesh, Bihar. These areas were less

penetrated than the coastal presidencies by British or earlier extraconti-
nental influences (although merchant and associated communities in Gujarat and Rajasthan, which lie on traditional trade routes, were exposed
and affected). Their gross educational situation is considerably inferior to
that of the rimland.

Not all cases fit into the rimland-heartland distinction. Mysore, a progressive former princely state which lies inland, "fits" statistically with the
rimland states (25.3 percent; 1.44 percent on the two indicators); Assam
does not fall neatly into either rim or heartland, straddling the indicators;
Orissa, on the rim geographically but functionally inland because of its
historical isolation and low level of exposure to external influences, fits
with the heartland. So does Jammu and Kashmir and, to a lesser extent
Andhra. (We have excluded them from tables 15 and 16, but see table 23.)

The rimland-heartland distinction with respect to education runs parallel to the distinction between the states with respect to gross indicators of
development. The top five states with respect to per capita income (Maharashtra, West Bengal, Punjab, Gujarat, Tamil Nadu) comprise the high
literacy rimland group except for Kerala — which is seventh — while the
four states with the lowest per capita income, Bihar, Rajasthan, Madhya
Pradesh, and Uttar Pradesh, make up the low literacy heartland. A similar
relationship holds for level of development. These differences are summarized in table 16.

These data indicate that education and development are closely related,
although it is unclear which is the dependent and which the independent
variable. Below we examine efforts by several states to break out of this
relationship between low developmental and low educational levels by acts

Table 16. Rimland — Heartland differences: development, income.

State	Proportion of population living in districts falling in the top two quartiles of levels of development (%)	Annual per capita income (Rs.)
Rimland		
Madras	100	334
Kerala	89	314
Gujarat	88	393
Punjab	86	451
Maharashtra	73	469
West Bengal	62	465
Heartland		
Rajasthan	45	267
Uttar Pradesh	41	297
Madhya Pradesh	33	285
Bihar	22	221

Sources: tables 20 and 23.

of public policy and purposeful resource allocation. These efforts deserve special emphasis because they represent attempts to transcend the cumulative effects of historical and socioeconomic variables.

The Language of Instruction: Differential Legacies and National Trends

The educational situations of different states are the result of the intersection of certain common national trends by features specific to the particular states. Different historical legacies, administrative capabilities, and political effectiveness shape educational policy and implementation in each state. We may illustrate this generalization by reference to a particular aspect of education, the language of instruction.[4] Two competing national trends are at work here. On the one hand, regional nationalism and the decline in the quality of English teaching with the expansion of secondary enrollments are strengthening the demand for regional languages in higher education. On the other hand, increasing interest in access to the opportunity occupations, based mainly on professional, scientific, and postgraduate education in which English is still required or desirable, have sustained a continued demand for English. (Professional and postgraduate education have expanded their share of an expanding enrollment — see tables 1 and 3 in chapter 4.) Table 17, based on a special study we conducted in 1967 of a 10 percent stratified random sample of all affiliated colleges, shows the relation of language of instruction to type of degree program and level of education, with regional languages more represented among preuniversity and B.A. programs than among B.Sc., professional, and postgraduate programs.

These competing national trends are crosscut by the historical legacies of different states and regions. As the rimland-heartland discussion suggested, English education began to affect the Indian states at different points in time, and penetrated them with different rates of intensity. To use Weber's suggestive analogy, the dice of educational history have been cumulatively loaded in the direction of the original throw. What this means specifically is that in those areas which have had a strong basis of English education, cultural predilections and specific vested interests in that education have tended to press for its perpetuation. In areas possessing a weaker English educational heritage, both the cultural predispositions and the structure of vested interests are different.

Tamil Nadu's strong continuing emphasis on English language education is explained at least in part by the earlier strength of such education, especially in the Tamil districts[5] but also in the entire province previously comprised of the areas that have now become Tamil Nadu and Andhra. In the 1880's, Tamil Nadu had a higher level of literacy than any other province. Between 1864 and 1886, 61,124 candidates in Tamil Nadu sat for university entrance exams, which were in English, compared to 37,790

Table 17. Percentage of different types of college courses offered in English, regional language, or both.

| | | Type of course | | | | |
| | | | First degree level | | | |
Language of examination	Preuniversity (PUC, intermediate) (N = 19)	B.A., B.Com. (Arts) (N = 131)	B.Sc. (Science) (N = 51)	M.B.B.S., B.E. (Professional) (N = 38)	Post-graduate (N = 54)	Total (N = 293)
English (N = 178)	36.8	45.0	76.5	94.7	69.4	60.7
English and regional (N = 52)	31.6	21.4	15.7	2.6	16.7	17.0
Regional (N = 43)	15.8	23.7	5.9	–	11.1	14.7
English, regional, Hindi, etc. (N = 20)	15.8	9.9	2.0	–	3.7	6.8
Total (N = 293)	100	100	100	100	100	100

Note: For the basis of this table, see table 19, *note*. Table 19 counts the number of responding colleges (205). In this table we have, where a college offers different courses in different media, counted the number of options available. Thus if a particular college offers a B.A. in regional and English language and a B.Sc. in English, we would count that college twice. We have used language of examination rather than language of instruction (as in table 19) as the basis of this table because the answers about language of examination discriminated more sharply among courses (see table 19, *note*).

in Bengal and 24,857 in Bombay.[6] This early history is reflected in the contemporary interest structure of Tamil Nadu. The English teachers in the colleges under Madras University have been, until recently at least, a significant force in the syndicate (governing body) of the university, and have helped produce one of Tamil Nadu's most important exports, the well-educated English speakers who play a disproportionate role in the nationally recruited Indian Administrative Service (IAS) (in which Tamil Nadu represented 24 percent of the total among competitively recruited entrants between 1951 and 1961),[7] in the modern professions, and in the upper, highly skilled levels of clerical and stenographic occupations in major commercial centers like Bombay, Calcutta, and Delhi. The existence of this particular occupational opportunity structure continues to influence the aspirations of new groups and classes seeking to enter higher education in Tamil Nadu. Among such classes, the regionalist demand for Tamil language education is strong (a symbolic, collective good), but it is crosscut by the demand for English language opportunity-oriented education (an instrumental, individual good). There is reason to suppose that students and parents who, as regional nationalists, call for Tamil language, as education consumers call for English language.[8] Both Congress and DMK governments in Tamil Nadu have been caught in this dilemma. Tamil Nadu's success as an exporter of English speakers has powerfully affected regional (Maharashtrian) and national politics. The Shiv Sena movement in Bombay, which seeks, *inter alia,* to substitute Maharashtrians for Tamils in the occupational system of the city, as well as those demanding that Hindi be placed on an equal or superior footing with English in the annual Indian Administrative Service examination, are motivated in part by a desire to prevent Tamil Nadu from capitalizing on her English language advantage.[9]

In Uttar Pradesh and Bihar, by contrast, historical legacies have produced a different demand structure. English education came to these states relatively late and with lower intensity than to the presidencies. Muir Central College (1872), the premier college of the northwest provinces, was not founded until well after the other premier colleges, Elphinstone at Bombay (1834), Presidency at Calcutta (1817), and Presidency at Madras (1840). As Irene Gilbert's account suggests (chapter 10), after its founding Muir produced scholars at a more modest rate than Presidency, Calcutta. Universities in the heartland came even later than the colleges. The first, the University of Allahabad, was founded in 1888, thirty years after the three presidency universities established in 1857. In the 1920's, Uttar Pradesh still lagged behind Tamil Nadu in the absolute numbers of enrolled students at all levels of education, although it had a larger population. By 1939–40 Uttar Pradesh had moved ahead in the number of enrolled scholars in arts colleges and in secondary schools, but at the primary level Tamil Nadu continued to enroll more than twice as many pupils as Uttar Pradesh.[10]

At independence, the role of English was much less important in the heartland than in the rest of the country. In the heartland in the 1950's English was usually an optional subject for study at the middle school stage, classes V–VIII, while in non-Hindi areas it was compulsory.[11] In Uttar Pradesh and Bihar English was an optional subject at the high school stage, while everywhere else it was compulsory.[12] In Uttar Pradesh English was an optional subject even at the intermediate level (equivalent to the first two years of college).

These disparities in regional histories are strikingly reflected in the present differences in language of instruction. Table 18 suggests these differ-

Table 18. Rimland — Heartland differences: percentage of colleges using English, regional language, or both.

Region	Language of instruction				
	English	English and regional	Regional	English, regional, and Hindi	Total
Heartland [a] (N = 46)	15.2	45.7	34.8	4.3	100
Other [b] (N = 159)	68.6	16.4	7.1	8.2	100

Note: For the basis of this table, see table 19, *note.*
[a] Bihar, Uttar Pradesh, Madhya Pradesh, Rajasthan.
[b] We have included all states other than those in the heartland in this category. The English figures for this category would be higher if Orissa, Assam, Andhra, and Jammu were excluded from the "Other" category.

ences. Fifteen percent of colleges in the heartland area taught in English only, while 68.9 percent of colleges in all other areas taught in English only. This percentage is higher in the south, where 91 percent of colleges in 1967 were still using English only. (See table 19.) These figures suggest that common national trends are filtered through quite different regional legacies and cultures, producing a considerable variety of patterns in so critical an area as language of instruction.

The Impact of Administrative and Political Differentials

State government policy-making in higher education is not merely a reflection of demands coming from below. It is also a product of the government's own formulations in which the constraints of existing institutional structures, expert bureaucratic assessments, and the government's capability to implement its own formulations are all elements. Administrative traditions differ among states. States that have a history of good administration not only have greater administrative capabilities but also tend to give greater weight in policy formulation and implementation to expert and administrative authority than states with weak administrative

Table 19. Regional differences: percentage of colleges using English, regional language, or both.

| Region | English | Medium of instruction | | | Total |
		English and regional	Regional	English, regional and Hindi	
Central (N = 46)	15.2	45.7	34.8	4.3	100
South (N = 48)	91.7	–	8.3	–	100
West (N = 45)	55.6	20.0	15.6	8.9	100
East (N = 42)	64.3	35.7	–	–	100
North (N = 24)	54.2	8.3	–	37.5	100
All regions (N = 205)	56.6	22.9	13.2	7.3	100

Note: This table is based on a special study conducted by us in 1967 to determine actual practice with respect to language of instruction. We formulated a special questionnaire to colleges, which was sent out with the cooperation of the ministry of education. We acknowledge the interest and help of Mr. J. P. Naik, who had been member-secretary of the Education Commission, 1964–66 and was in 1966–67 adviser to government in the education ministry. The questionnaire was sent to 246 colleges, which we selected by a stratified random sample of India's 2,500 affiliated colleges. Two hundred and five colleges responded. The questionnaire inquired about language of instruction and language of examination. It requested colleges to specify what language was used in different subjects and at different levels, that is, for each degree program. We grouped the colleges by region: central (Uttar Pradesh, Bihar, Madhya Pradesh, Rajasthan), south (Madras, Andhra, Mysore, Kerala), west (Gujarat, Maharashtra), east (Bengal, Orissa, Assam), and north (Punjab, Delhi, Jammu and Kashmir). Mrs. Karuna Ahmad prepared this table and table 17 from the questionnaires.

legacies. As the member-secretary of the Education Commission, 1964–1966, noted: "When the [Education] Commission was in Madhya Pradesh, we found that Government Colleges did not even satisfy the minimum conditions for affiliation laid down by the University! In Bombay or in Madras if the Government starts a college which does not fulfil the minimum condition, it will never get affiliation. The University will have the courage to say we will not affiliate, and the State Government will fulfil the conditions." [13]

Governments with stable legislative majorities are in a better position to balance immediate popular demands against more long range considerations concerning the educational structure than are governments based on precarious legislative majorities or dependent on uncertain coalition arrangements. The latter are more likely to yield to demands that jeopardize educational goals and resources. Conversely, politically secure state governments are in a better position to effectuate policy, enforce rules,

the authors clearly are biased toward the urban middle class interests in ed.

and maintain boundaries between politics and education than those that are politically insecure.

Education and Development in the States

The most striking finding of a systematic state-by-state comparison of education is the great range of difference between particular states already anticipated in the rimland-heartland comparison. This range underscores the importance of viewing Indian education as a series of educational systems. Table 20 reports several indicators of resource allocation to education by states. The range of difference for each is quite striking. There is a 112 percent difference between the per capita income of Maharashtra (Rs. 469) and Bihar (Rs. 221), the first and the last ranked states. Kerala, which stands first in the percentage of state income spent on education (3.64) and in the percentage of state revenue spent on education (34.88) leads Orissa (1.54 percent of state income) and Uttar Pradesh (12.49 percent of state revenue), the low states on these indicators, by 136 percent and 183 percent respectively. The range of differences between Maharashtra, which spends Rs. 12.4 per capita on education, and Orissa, which spends Rs. 4.3 per capita, is even larger — 188 percent.

Kerala and Tamil Nadu, located in the middle third of the per capita income range, allocated the highest proportion of their state incomes to education, while Orissa and Uttar Pradesh, ninth and tenth in per capita income, allocated the lowest proportions. Kerala allocated almost 16 percent more than the national average (18.96 percent) of its state revenue to education, while Uttar Pradesh, with the lowest proportion, allocated 6.47 percent less than the national average.

Column 10 of Table 20, which shows the difference between a state's rank order for per capita income and for per capita expenditure on education, gives a rough index of educational concern and effort. Kerala and Rajasthan show the largest positive differences (+5 and +4 respectively), indicating energetic effort; Uttar Pradesh shows the largest negative difference (−4) indicating little effort.

Some explanations for these varying levels of effort can be suggested. In Kerala, more than in any other state, educational institutions are the expression of powerful private vested interests and communities (the Nair Service Society or N.S.S.; the Shree Narayana Paripalna Yogam — an association of the Ezhava community — and the Syrian Christian Church).[14] Kerala is notable for having the highest percentage of all education in the private sector, 65.3 percent.[15] These organized educational interests by themselves or under the direction of organized communities help account for Kerala devoting over one-third of its revenue budget (see table 20, column 6), a proportion more than 11 percent above the next highest state, Maharashtra. Kerala's high literacy rate — at 46.2 percent it ranks higher

Table 20. State allocation of resources to education, 1960–61.

1	2	3	4	5	6	7	8	9	10
State	Rank order by per capita income	Per capita income[a] (Rs.)	Expenditure (public and private)[b] on education as percentage of state income[c]	Rank order	State revenue spent on education[d] (%)	Rank order	Per capita expenditure on education[e] (Rs.)	Rank order	Difference between rank order for per capita income and rank order for per capita expenditure on education
Maharashtra	1	469	2.64	3	23.43	2	12.4	1	0
West Bengal	2	465	2.10	11	19.12	8	9.8	3	−1
Punjab	3	451	2.05	12	18.89	9	9.3	5	−2
Gujarat	4	393	2.34	7	20.94	5	9.2	6	−2
Madras	5	334	2.82	2	19.78	6	9.4	4	+1
Assam	6	333	2.26	8	15.89	11	7.6	7	−1
Kerala	7	314	3.64	1	34.88	1	11.5	2	+5
Mysore	8	305	2.46	5	13.14	13	7.5	8	0
Uttar Pradesh	9	297	1.81	14	12.49	15	5.4	13	−4
Jammu and Kashmir	10	289	1.99	13	13.08	14	5.7	12	−2
Andhra	11	287	2.49	4	17.98	10	7.1	9	+2
Madhya Pradesh	12	285	2.19	10	22.03	4	6.2	11	+1
Orissa	13	276	1.54	15	14.20	12	4.3	15	−2
Rajasthan	14	267	2.35	6	23.16	3	6.3	10	+4
Bihar	15	221	2.20	9	19.49	7	4.9	14	+1

Source: Education Commission, Government of India, 1964–66, "Inequalities in Educational Development (States and Districts)," mimeo (New Delhi, 1966). Arrangement and ranking by present authors.

Note: Here and on the other tables in this chapter we have not computed rank correlations of variables because the data are not all that they should be (e.g. there are discrepancies between the Education Commission's and the National Council for Educational Research and Training's figures for state per capita expenditure on education). More important, we wish to avoid a false impression of scientific accuracy or truth when all that is indicated are certain relationships and relative positions, a goal adequately realized by the methods employed.

[a] India's per capita income in 1960–61 was Rs. 335. Median state per capita income was Rs. 305. The highest state per capita income was 112 percent greater than the lowest state per capita income.

[b] "Private" expenditure presumably includes fees, tuition, endowment income, gifts, etc., but is not likely to catch expenditures on private tuitions, that is, payments by students or pupils to teachers for private instruction designed to prepare them for examinations. This is thought to be a considerable sum but it remains invisible and unmeasured.

[c] For India as a whole, in 1960–61 expenditure (public and private) on education was 2.35 percent of total national income. The median percentage of state income spent (publicly and privately) on education was 2.46. The percentage in the state spending the highest proportion of total state income on education was 136 percent greater than the percentage in the state with the smallest proportion.

[d] For India as a whole, in 1960–61 the average state expenditure on education as a percentage of state revenue was 18.96 percent. The median was 19.12 percent. The percentage in the state spending the greatest proportion of its revenue on education was 183 percent greater than the percentage in the state spending the smallest proportion.

[e] India's per capita expenditure on education in 1960–61 was Rs. 7.8. Median state per capita expenditure was Rs. 7.5. The highest state per capita expenditure on education was 188 percent greater than the lowest state per capita expenditure on education.

than any other state — is both a result of previous educational effort and an explanation of the continuing high level of effort.[16] In Kerala, it seems that the historical dice, having been loaded positively, are likely to continue falling in the direction of the original throw.

Rajasthan represents an opposite instance of a state historically weak in education that has made an explicit public policy effort to overcome its historical disadvantage. Ranking fourteenth of fifteen states with respect to per capita income, it has been able to improve its relative standing with respect to per capita expenditure on education (tenth of fifteen) by spending a high proportion of its "national income" (sixth of fifteen) and of its state revenue (third of fifteen) on education. With the conspicuous exception of Kerala and perhaps of Mysore, much of princely India, of which Rajasthan was a part, was markedly behind British India in the number of educational institutions established before independence and in the allocation of resources to education through provincial and local governments, fees, and endowments. Thus Rajasthan's relatively high rank with respect to percentage of income spent on education and per capita expenditure on education reflects, presumably, not only governmental effort as expressed in the proportion of state revenue spent on education, but also considerable recent effort on the part of local authorities or private allocations (via fees, endowments, etc.) or both. Other states that have improved their rank order over that established by their level of per capita income include Andhra, Tamil Nadu, Madhya Pradesh (another predominately princely state area), and Bihar.

There are problems in interpreting efforts such as Rajasthan's to break out of the close relationship between low developmental and low educational levels. For example, Rajasthan's investment in education may represent government effort to promote economic development by improving the quality and capabilities of the work force and to improve the quality of life by raising cultural levels (public or collective goods). Yet we do not know enough about the policy process for education in Rajasthan to be sure either that these considerations were among the intentions of policy makers; that the educational outputs coincided with intentions; or that education will under some or all circumstances positively influence economic indicators. Educational policy in Rajasthan is affected by, among other things, the demands on politicians from those constituents who see education as a personal benefit, and the demands of those politicians who may view additional educational institutions as potential political resources (private and individual goods).

The difficulty of interpreting the data on output parallels the difficulty in unraveling policy intentions. Rajasthan's substantial allocation of resources to education has not been reflected in an improvement in the state's enrollment ranking but has raised significantly its position with respect to per capita expenditure (tables 21 and 22). We are left with a variety of options in interpreting its high rank with respect to per capita expenditure on education (Table 20, column 9). Such expenditure may be accounted for by high quality and high cost education, at least in some areas or in some respects; by high cost education (such as technological) that may or may not be high quality; or, at least partially, by "hidden" transfers from the educational to the political system.

Despite these various caveats and qualifications, it is of considerable significance that, for a time at least, the investment in education was paralleled by economic growth: between 1949–50 and 1958–59 Rajasthan's rate of growth in total and in per capita income was the highest in India, and between 1960–61 and 1967–68, it ranked fifth in percentage gain in per capita income.[17]

An opposite pattern seems to characterize Uttar Pradesh, where the negative load on the historical dice has not been challenged by policy efforts in an opposite direction. Ninth in per capita income, it is fifteenth in percentage of state revenue spent on education, fourteenth in percentage of state income spent in education, and thirteenth in per capita expenditure on education. At the heart of the heartland, Uttar Pradesh experienced relatively less penetration by modern forces than the presidencies. But the rankings just cited suggest that Uttar Pradesh has not mounted a policy effort to improve its position comparable to the effort mounted by Rajasthan (and reflected in its rankings).

Resource expenditure provides one measure of state education efforts, enrollment provides another. Columns 2, 4, 6, and 10 in table 21 describe the range and distribution of students enrolled in primary, middle, and high schools and in higher education, showing enrollment as a percentage of state population. Column 8 relates technical school to high school enrollment by showing the first as a percentage of the second. The sum of each state's rank orders (columns 3, 5, 7, 9, and 11), given in column 12, provides another rough overall indicator (column 13) of state concern for and effort in education. The results in column 13 (table 21) are grouped in table 22.

Table 21 not only shows enrollment, but also disaggregates the supply of education by comparing differences between and within each state with respect to levels and types of education provided. Because of history, policy, and the incidence and effectiveness of group pressures, the educational pyramids of various states differ greatly. Some are relatively large at the bottom, others at the top, and still others in the middle ranges, depending upon the degree to which primary, school, or higher education has established priority in private and public allocations to education.

The states that ranked "very high" in overall enrollment, Kerala and Maharashtra, exhibit markedly different patterns in producing a similar aggregate outcome. Kerala leads in enrollment at the primary, secondary, and middle school levels and is third in higher education, but it drops to seventh in the percentage of school pupils enrolled in technical or vocational programs. Maharashtra's pattern is more uniform: second in pri-

Table 21. Level and type of enrollment, by state.

1	Primary education		Middle school		High/higher secondary classes (IX–XI/XII)		Secondary technical/ vocational		Higher education		12	13
	2	3	4	5	6	7	8	9	10	11		
State	Enrollment as percentage of population	Rank order	Enrollment as percentage of population	Rank order	Enrollment as percentage of population	Rank order	Percentage enrolled in secondary classes	Rank order	Enrollment per thousand of population	Rank order	Rank orders summed	Rank order scores grouped into five categories
Andhra Pradesh	8.3	5	1.1	11	0.5	6	5.2	8	1.6	8	38	4
Assam	9.5	4	1.8	5	1.1	1	3.8	11	2.3	5	26	3
Bihar	6.9	8	1.2	9	0.7	4	4.9	9	1.9	7	37	4
Gujarat	10.0	2	1.9	4	0.8	3	9.6	6	2.4	4	19	2
Jammu and Kashmir	6.0	9	1.7	6	0.5	6	NA	–	2.3	5	NA	–
Kerala	14.1	1	4.1	1	1.1	1	5.8	7	2.6	3	13	1
Madhya Pradesh	6.2	9	1.0	11	0.4	8	4.0	10	1.5	9	47	5
Madras	9.9	3	2.0	3	0.8	3	16.1	4	2.1	6	19	2
Maharashtra	10.0	2	1.9	4	0.9	2	16.4	3	2.8	2	13	1
Mysore	7.3	7	1.3	8	0.7	4	17.8	2	2.3	5	26	3
Orissa	8.0	6	0.6	12	0.2	9	9.7	5	0.8	10	42	5
Rajasthan	5.5	10	1.0	11	0.4	7	3.1	13	1.6	8	49	5
Uttar Pradesh	5.5	10	1.1	10	0.7	4	3.4	12	1.5	9	45	5
W. Bengal	8.3	5	1.5	7	0.6	5	19.3	1	4.0	1	19	2

Source: Government of India, National Council of Educational Research and Training, Educational Statistics Districtwise, 1960–61 (New Delhi, 1966). Punjab omitted because column 8 data unavailable.   Arrangement and ranking by present authors.

Table 22. Aggregate state enrollment performance, 1960–61.

Rank		State
Very high	(1)	Kerala
		Maharashtra
High	(2)	Gujarat
		Madras
		West Bengal
Middle range	(3)	Assam
		Mysore
Low	(4)	Andhra Pradesh
		Bihar
Very low	(5)	Madhya Pradesh
		Orissa
		Rajasthan
		Uttar Pradesh

Source: Table 21. Punjab omitted. See table 21, *note.*

mary, secondary, and higher education enrollment, third in technical or vocational, and fourth in middle school.

Again, among the states ranked "high" in aggregate enrollments, there are marked differences. Gujarat and Tamil Nadu exhibit a fairly uniform effort, their "lows" being technical or vocational, where Gujarat ranks sixth, and higher education, where Tamil Nadu ranks sixth. Punjab drops from second in higher education enrollment to seventh in primary school enrollment, while West Bengal ranks first in technical or vocational and higher education but slips to fifth, seventh, and fifth in primary, middle, and high school enrollment respectively.

Although it is not surprising to find highly industrialized states such as West Bengal and Maharashtra, with their great cities of Calcutta and Bombay, first and third on a measure of technical or vocational enrollment, it may be surprising to find Mysore second, Tamil Nadu fourth, and Orissa fifth. Tamil Nadu under Industries Minister R. Venkataraman pursued a self-conscious policy during the second and third plan periods of making industrial investment and location in Tamil Nadu attractive and worthwhile by trying to insure adequate supplies of trained manpower along with electricity and other overheads and amenities. Mysore, particularly the Bangalore area, has attracted a substantial number of large central industrial projects in the public sector, only partly because of the attractive climate. Here, as elsewhere, industrial needs can generate a demand which may be reflected in enrollments.[18] Most surprising, perhaps, in the rank order of enrollment in technical or vocational education is Orissa's position at fifth. This is remarkable for a state that ranks thirteenth in per capita income (table 20, col. 1) and fifteenth in level of development (table 23). The explanation of Orissa's high ranking lies to a considerable extent in the policy pursued by former Congress chief minister Biju Patnaik, who believed that technical and vocational training was a

Table 23. Rank order of states by proportion of their districts and of their populations falling within the top two quartiles of levels of development.

State	Proportion of districts falling in top two quartiles (%)	Rank order	Proportion of population living in districts falling within the top two quartiles (%)	Rank order
Rimland				
Madras	100	1	100	1
Kerala	89	2	89	2
Gujarat	82	3	88	3
Punjab	79	4	86	4
(Mysore)[a]	72	5	65	6
Maharashtra	68	6	73	5
(Andhra)[a]	55	7	56	9
West Bengal	53	8	62	7
Heartland				
(Assam)[a]	45	9	58	8
Rajasthan	38	10	45	10
Uttar Pradesh	37	11	41	11
Madhya Pradesh	32	12	33	12
Bihar	29	13	22	13
(Jammu and Kashmir)[a]	11	14	15	14
(Orissa)[a]	8	15	4	15

Source: Government of India, *Census of India 1961,* "Levels of Regional Development in India (Being Part I of General Report on India)," vol. 1, pt. 1-A(i), Text [Prepared under the supervision of A. Mitra, Indian Civil Service, Registrar General and ex-officio Census Commissioner for India], chap. 2, The Ranking Device, pp. 9–49, and Appendix 22, pp. 46–49.

Mitra advances a number of caveats: "The degree of reliability of the data varies not only from one item to another but from one geographical area to another for any particular item. [The technique used] . . . oversimplifies the scoring and loads the dice in favour of those indicators which are positively associated.

[a] State does not "fit" the Heartland — Rimland distinction advanced in the text.

"leading sector" and could spur industrialization in the face of the state's overall backwardness. Also, this high ranking is explained to a lesser extent by the biases of Orissa's leading civil servants, who, like their counterparts elsewhere, show a marked preference for "modern" industry-related programs and a marked dislike for programs related to agriculture, villages, and their needs.[19]

Some of the more backward states as measured by per capita income (table 20, column 1) and level of development (table 23) rank quite high with respect to secondary school enrollment. For example, Uttar Pradesh and Bihar, which rank ninth and fifteenth in per capita income and eleventh and thirteenth with respect to level of development, tie for fourth place in secondary school enrollment. It is likely that this pattern is related to Harold Gould's finding (below, chapter 7) that secondary schools are a

favorite object of educational entrepreneurs interested in building up political resources.

The existence of large differentials in past educational history and present
educational policy and performance between rimland and heartland on the
one hand and among states on the other suggests that education in India
can usefully and productively be conceptualized in terms of disaggregated
systems. At the same time, some measure of uniformity is created by national trends — sometimes contradictory — such as the populist pressure
for regional language teaching and the demand by economic planners and
the socially mobile for professional and technical education. Another source
of uniformity, the effort to create and implement national educational
policy, has to make its uncertain way through the tangle of competing and
varying state systems and to cope with the national spokesmen for political
demands that affect educational policy.

6 / National Educational Policy in a Federal Context: A Proximate Goal

The Indian Central Government finds it very difficult to formulate, coordinate, or implement national educational policy. Among the principal reasons for this difficulty are a federal system that places authority for educational matters in the hands of the states, and marked differentials among the states with respect to the nature and level of their educational development.

Among levels of education, the central government's authority over and resource allocations to education are most marked in the field of higher education (and research). This chapter looks to the central government's efforts to establish national policies for higher education and examines the nature and effectiveness of higher education programs in the national (as opposed to the state) sector.

The government of India has not been markedly more successful in creating or stimulating uniform national policies in education than it has been in other policy areas where formal authority and the command of resources lie in state hands. In some respects this is regrettable. Uniformity for its own sake, however, may not be desirable. On the contrary, academic values and interests often can be better and more efficiently realized through variety and diversity, sometimes constrained by uniform general rules, sometimes not, depending on needs and circumstances. It should be clear from our analysis of particular policies which values and interests are being served by uniformity and which by diversity.

National policy is shaped by three types of instrumentalities. First, there are national coordinating bodies that bring together representatives of the states or universities or both (and rely on those units for the implementation of their "decisions"). These include the Central Advisory Board of Education, conferences of state chief ministers or education ministers, conferences of vice-chancellors, the planning commission, national commissions, committees that report to the cabinet or parliament or both, and, at an unofficial level, the Inter-University Board. Second, there are agencies of the federal government armed with direct executive or financial powers to affect education in the states. These include the University Grants Commission, the ministry of education, the ministry of agriculture, and the ministry of health. Third, there is a "central sector" in education, consisting of educational and research institutions directly controlled and financed by federal agencies. We shall explore these instrumentalities in turn.

The constitutional framework assigning responsibility for education provides the parameters within which national policy is formulated and implemented. Under the Indian Constitution, the states have primary responsibility for education. Article 246 divides legislative authority between the states and the national government by creating lists of powers to be exercised by the union, the states, or both concurrently.[1] Item 11 of the state list gives the states legislative responsibility for "education including universities," subject to certain exceptions provided for in the union and concurrent lists. These exceptions include exclusive central authority over national universities (Banaras, Aligarh, Delhi, and Visva-Bharati) and other institutions "declared by Parliament by law to be institutions of national importance." [2] The union (national) government also has exclusive responsibility for "institutions for scientific or technical education financed by the Government of India wholly or in part and declared by Parliament by law to be institutions of national importance." [3] Under this provision the education ministry of the central government, by an Act of Parliament in 1961, took responsibility for the five Indian Institutes of Technology, at Kharagpur (West Bengal), Kanpur (Uttar Pradesh), Madras, Delhi, and Bombay.[4] The union government also has constitutional responsibility for "professional, vocational or technical training"; "the promotion of special studies or research"; and "coordination and determination of standards in institutions for higher education or research and scientific and technical institutions." [5] These responsibilities are carried out by the Indian Council of Medical Research, the Indian Council of Agricultural Research, the Council of Scientific and Industrial Research, the All-India Council for Technical Education, and the Atomic Energy Commission, together with their various research and teaching institutes and laboratories.[6]

Entry 66 of the Union List, Seventh Schedule, which empowers the union government to coordinate and determine standards in institutions of higher education, is potentially important to the government's role in education. In *State of Gujarat v. Shri Krishna* the Indian supreme court interpreted the entry to mean that under the Gujarat University Act of 1949 as amended Gujarat University could not compel its affiliated colleges to replace English with Gujarati or Hindi as the language of instruction because it would prejudicially affect the national government's responsibility for standards.[7] This leading case suggests that despite the general authority over education vested in the states, the union government can exercise considerable control of state action in the area of higher education.[8] The court's opinion in *State of Gujarat v. Shri Krishna* not only found state legislation that affected standards to be *ultra vires,* but also made clear that only the central government could act legislatively to coordinate and determine standards in institutions of higher education.[9]

Some educational leaders have pressed for an educational amendment to increase national government authority over education. A parliamentary committee on higher education (Sapru Committee) argued that responsibility for higher education be shifted from the state list of powers to the list conferring powers concurrently on the state and the center.[10] M. C. Chagla, a former minister for education, and two dissenting members of the Education Commission, 1964–1966, Dr. V. S. Joshi and Mr. P. Kirpal, the latter for many years secretary of the education ministry, have argued that unless the whole of education were put on the concurrent list the central government would continue to lack adequate authority to implement national policy. (One of the means favored to strengthen national policy was a revived all-India Indian Educational Service.)

The Education Commission, 1964–1966, rejected these arguments, opting instead for more effective use of the powers presently available to the central government, more vigorous central leadership, and the marked expansion of the central and central-sponsored sectors. "We are not in favour," the commission argued in response to the Sapru Committee recommendation concerning higher education, "of fragmenting education and putting one part in the concurrent and the other in the State list — education should, under any circumstances, be treated as a whole." In "a vast country like ours, the present constitutional allocations of functions and powers is probably best because it provides for a Central leadership of a stimulating but non-coercive character." To put education on the concurrent list would be to risk "undesirable centralization and greater rigidity in a situation where the greatest need is for elasticity and freedom to experiment." The commission then went on to call for a "workable" center-state "partnership within the present constitutional framework" and for "an intensive effort . . . to exploit fully existing provisions of the Constitution for the development of education and evolution of a national educational policy." [11]

Coordination in the Federal System

The proximate nature of central government efforts to formulate and implement national educational policy by coordinating federal units can be illustrated by the activities of Central Advisory Board on Education (CABE) in a few notable policy areas. CABE, which was founded under the *raj* in 1921 to bring about union-state coordination in education,[12] is made up of the union minister for education, the state ministers for education, a few experts nominated by the union government, and representatives of educational interests. It is the principal federal forum for formulating and reviewing on a continuous basis national educational policy. The recommendations of the Sargent Plan of 1944, the report of the University Education Commission of 1948, and the report of the Education Commission, 1964–1966 (the most comprehensive effort to date to articulate and effect national educational policy), all came before CABE's committee on higher education.[13]

CABE lacks legislative authority and financial means. But, like the *ad hoc* conferences of state ministers for education, chief ministers, and vice-chancellors, it provides a context in which the national government can persuade and be persuaded by the state governments and by the universities. CABE recommendations are circulated to state education ministries and to universities for information, and, hopefully, compliance. The responses to CABE recommendations, both compliant and resistant, are recorded in reports of CABE proceedings.

The fate of a major federal policy endeavor such as the three-language formula for secondary schools can be traced in CABE proceedings and records. The formula was "agreed upon" by a conference of state chief ministers and rhetorically consented to by all the states, but not implemented or even partially implemented by most state governments. CABE called for reports on the degree of compliance. The state education secretaries' equivocal responses to CABE injunctions suggest that rhetorical agreements among state chief ministers, or state ministers for education, while possibly productive of a feeling of national consensus — and the importance of such a feeling is not to be underestimated — are not necessarily productive of action, much less of uniform action.[14]

In other policy areas — for example, the adoption of a three-year first degree university course or a five-year engineering degree — national policy has been somewhat easier to formulate than in the highly controversial area of language. But here too, even though the issues are less charged with potentially explosive and divisive political implications, compliance has fallen short of the goal of creating uniform national frameworks for first degrees.[15]

Another important instrument for coordination in the federal system is the Inter-University Board of India and Ceylon (IUB), an unofficial body that operates outside the realm of public authority and resources. A "club" for vice-chancellors, it provides a convenient context for them to exchange views, canvass problems, and, on occasion, take common positions. The IUB is the main national forum for university opinion and the representation of university interests. Its conferences and its publications provide the ministries and agencies of the government of India, particularly the University Grants Commission, with an identifiable organization for purposes of mutual persuasion and bargaining. The IUB's public intervention on the side of the Osmania University vice-chancellor, D. S. Reddi, in his struggle with the Government of Andhra over the "autonomy" of the university (see chapter 12) is a recent, important example of the IUB's activity. Unlike the University Grants Commission, which feels obliged to provide material support for all universities, the IUB is selective, withholding honorific resources (recognition and membership) from universities that do not meet its academic standards.[16]

Agencies of the Union: The University Grants Commission

The agencies of the federal government which have the power or the finances (or both) to affect higher education include (but are not exhausted by) the University Grants Commission, the ministry of education, the ministry of agriculture, and the ministry of health. The University Grants Commission, an autonomous, statutory body with primary responsibility for standards and innovation in higher education, is by far the most important influence at the national level on higher education. In 1966 its policies and programs affected sixty-four universities and nine institutions deemed universities, the 2565 colleges affiliated with universities, and approximately 90,000 teachers and 1.8 million students.[17] The UGC complains that much of the financing and control of higher education escapes it, being vested in the other ministries just cited.[18] Each of these ministries, through corresponding research advisory bodies (the All-India Council of Technical Education; the Indian Council of Agricultural Research; the Indian Council of Medical Research), finance technical, medical, and agricultural education — the first two fields comprising the most prestigious sectors of higher professional education. The resulting dispersal of authority and resources makes the formulation, coordination, and implementation of national policies for education difficult. The University Education Commission of 1948 (Radhakrishna Report) and the Education Commission, 1964–1966, deplored this dispersal. The latter observed that "fragmentation unaccompanied by any effort at effective coordination [was] a serious weakness in [the] present pattern of higher education" and recommended that the "entire spectrum" of higher education be brought under the aegis of the UGC. The commission also expressed apprehension that university autonomy might be adversely affected when ministries have too close and direct a relationship to university teaching and research. "It is not desirable that Government should deal directly with the universities. It is always a great advantage to interpose, between the Government and the university, a committee of persons selected for their knowledge and study rather than for their political affiliation or official status." [19]

This may be a correct reading. On the other hand, it may be that dispersal of authority advances standards and innovation by allowing the development of different approaches to education. The technical orientation of the substantive ministries that have responsibility for education may encourage a more professional concern for university programs.

The UGC's developmental (as contrasted to maintenance) expenditures in 1960–61 represented 27 percent of the union government's expenditure on higher education and 9.7 percent of the total (union, state, local, and private) expenditure on higher education that year.[20] However, because UGC resources, although proportionately significant, are in absolute terms quite small — about seven million dollars in 1961 — and because the UGC relies on persuasion rather than on its financial sanctions, its potential to effect policy for higher education has not been fully realized.

The original UGC act of 1956 was amended in 1968 to expand the commission from nine to twelve persons — two officers of the central government, five university teachers, five others representing industry, commerce, agriculture, and the learned professions (in recognition of the more technical nature of higher education) — plus a chairman who plays a leading role in policy formulation and day-to-day administration.[21] University officers — including sitting vice-chancellors and principals of colleges — were excluded under the 1968 legislation out of a concern that they could use the office to benefit their home institutions. (It is not clear why professors, who may sit, are presumed to be less partial to their institutions.) The commission functions "in close collaboration with" the ministry of education which "invariably" accepts advice on matters of academic interest relating to universities.[22] The UGC has been, in the main, independent of government. As William Richter has pointed out elsewhere,[23] it has resembled American independent regulatory commissions in regarding itself responsible especially to its clientele — the universities. It discharges its responsibility to coordinate and determine standards mainly through visiting committees that examine the present status and needs of particular universities and report their findings to the commission. The UGC also appoints expert committees from time to time to look into particular problems, such as the creation of new programs and departments and to advise the commission on the feasibility of and the resources required for such projects.

The UGC controls universities through use of negative sanctions and positive incentives. The possible sanctions — a negative verdict on founding, the denial of funds, and the withdrawal of funds — are either ineffectual or not used. The incentives, mainly financial, on the other hand, have more significance, but they can only be used within certain limits.

Until 1968, the University Grants Commission was unable to control the establishment of new universities, in part because it lacked statutory power to do so. Then, in 1968, new legislation stipulated that the commission henceforth refuse grants to any university established without its previous approval and the approval of the central government. Prior to 1968, it could merely "advise any authority, if such advice was asked for, on the establishment of a new university."[24] State governments did not always consult the UGC with respect to university foundings, and even when they did, they did not always pay attention to the advice proffered. At least seventeen of the forty-seven universities founded or recognized by being deemed universities between 1947 and 1966 were established without or against UGC advice.[25]

In the sixties, the commission began to press state governments to prepare, in consultation with it, prospective plans for a five- or ten-year period before they attempted to establish any new universities.[26] However, a combination of political interests — towns and districts striving for the prestige and trade a university brings; college faculties and administrators hoping for university status and pay; students and parents demanding a "neighborhood university" to reduce the travel and boarding costs of higher degrees; cabinet ministers seeking universities located in their districts — often persuade state governments, closer to popular pressures than the University Grants Commission, to ignore these prudent warnings.[27]

UGC and education ministry officials do not think the new legislation is likely to make much difference. It does not prevent states from founding universities. It will strengthen the UGC slightly in that it can now insist that the universities meet certain criteria before they qualify for grants. But UGC officials feel it would be unwise to use the power vigorously. If a new university were to affiliate some colleges of an older one, it would not be fair, they believe, to penalize the students by virtue of the new affiliation, as withholding of funds would do.

Once universities came into existence, even against UGC advice, the commission rarely withheld funds even though it has always had the authority to do so.[28] As a commission spokesman told the Estimates Committee of parliament: "If they are establishing universities under the Act, they can ask for grants from the University Grants Commission because they are established by the state legislature. To that extent we have to give grants, because we have to think of the students. They should not be at a disadvantage compared with students of other universities, so we have to think of the teachers, and salaries, and standards." [29]

The University Grants Commission has power to inspect grant receiving universities and withhold funds if any university fails to comply within a reasonable time with its recommendations. But this authority, like the authority to deny grants to unsanctioned universities, has not been used. The UGC representative told the estimates committee: "We consider that it is an extreme step and it will cause quite a lot of flutter and heart burning among the students and teachers." The UGC only once threatened to withhold funds. "In only one case so far the Commission told the University that if their University's certificates on the progress was not forthcoming regularly, it would be difficult for us to give the further installments of the grant. They were willing to send whatever material they had and so no further action was taken." [30]

The Estimates Committee of the third *lok sabha* (parliament), which examined the functioning of the UGC, noted the following. "The University Grants Commission has neither so far carried out any inspection of any department . . . of any university . . . nor has the power conferred on the University Grants Commission for withholding of grants . . . been exercised so far. The Committee are surprised to note the lenient attitude of the University Grants Commission in this matter." [31] The lack of vigor in UGC inspection is part of a general reluctance on the part of public authorities that deal with higher education to use inspection, recognition, or funding as means to gain compliance with standards and directives. A similar lack of vigor characterizes the way universities enforce minimum standards in affiliating colleges. In 1966–67, 8 of more than 2500 colleges were disaffiliated, a modest number considering conditions in many institutions.[32] The reluctance to use negative sanctions is not a new development that postdates independence. In 1917 the Calcutta University Commission noted that the university syndicate was reluctant to withdraw recognition from secondary schools (at that time under the jurisdiction of the university) that failed to comply with school inspectors' recommendations to increase expenditures substantially.[33]

The Education Commission, 1964–1966, which had a close relationship with the UGC — D. S. Kothari, chairman of the UGC, also chaired the commission — supported the UGC's restrained interpretation of its role. It did not "think [the Estimates Committee's comment] to be entirely a fair criticism" but went on to suggest more frequent and more probing visitations. The power to withhold grants, the commission report observed, "is an extreme power which is not to be lightly exercised." [34] The views of the UGC and the Education Commission, 1964–1966, are in accordance with a more general pattern of policy formation by the Indian government, most of whose ministries prefer to rely on incentives and persuasion rather than sanctions to achieve administrative and policy compliance. Whether this preference reflects weakness in the face of pressures or a prudent apprehension of the limits of the Indian government's authority in the context of Indian federalism is a larger question which is only skirted here. The Education Commission, 1964–1966, observed on this point that ". . . the relationship between universities and the U.G.C. is a very delicate one . . . the U.G.C. can become an effective instrument for upgrading the standards only if it follows the method of persuasion rather than coercion." [35]

The UGC's positive incentives have been exercised on behalf of developing new departments, staff, libraries, laboratories, and other facilities in a manner resembling the "seed money" programs of American foundations. The comparison suggests both the strengths and weaknesses of UGC incentives. Under succeeding five-year plans, the UGC has made grants to meet the new needs of universities on the basis of discussions between university authorities and visiting committees of professionals appointed by the commission. The process by which leading American universities formulate a consolidated foundation proposal, and foundations vet them, is similar. Like some foundations, until 1968 the UGC has not been empowered to grant moneys beyond a limited "developmental" period, usually the five years of a five-year plan (except to the four central universities which come under its special care). Thereafter, the university has had to find the means to finance the activity;[36] ordinarily this has meant that the state government has to pick up most of the tab. Such state support has not always been forthcoming. States have sometimes simply allowed a UGC initiated activity to expire. When the UGC recommended enhanced pay scales for university and college faculties under the third five-year plan, and offered to cover 80 percent of the increase, universities and states were not always willing to raise salaries. In the short run the salary increases would have cost them little; in the long run the full amount. Some took the proffered money for this and other UGC programs, but failed to continue them once the UGC left the field. The Estimates Committee urged the UGC to counter this practice by eliciting assurances from the state governments as well as from the universities.[37] The disadvantage of this system is that it would cancel the freedoms universities gain from having a source of support other than the states.

Since 1968, the UGC had had authority to give "maintenance" grants — recurring rather than "seed money" payments — in special cases to universities other than the four central ones. The UGC sought this legislation mainly to allow it to fund for more than the five year developmental period the special centers for advanced studies which it has supported in many universities.

Most UGC programs involve matching funds, which again makes UGC initiatives dependent on a fiscal response from the state. The procedure has been sufficiently unsatisfactory that a conference of state education ministers in 1964 suggested that matching-fund arrangements be dropped in favor of a system that divided expenditures on higher education into central and state supported programs.[38] The UGC's new power to make maintenance grants is a small step in this direction. The five-year developmental grant and matching-fund arrangements, which are disliked by the universities (if not by the states), are also not clearly in the interests of the UGC either. UGC dependence on the states for matching funds and for the permanent maintenance of its initial experiments constrains its options and influence with universities by making the state a key bargaining partner and limits the effectiveness with which it can employ incentives to further the realization of its policy objectives.

It is tempting to suggest that the UGC use its negative sanctions more energetically. The suggestion, however, encounters two difficulties: the realities of the federal system and the requirements of university autonomy. So long as education remains a state subject; so long as the UGC's activities are mainly developmental and matching; and so long as universities are mainly dependent on state governments for their funds, the universities will always take the demands of state governments more seriously than UGC programs and advice. The UGC may well be right in believing that persuasion and incentives, which educate and lure on universities and state governments and strengthen the professional and intellectual elements within both, are more durable instruments of upgrading than abrupt punitive measures. Universities that care only for the ceremonial name "university" can in any case negate punitive measures by relying exclusively on the state government.

Too energetic a use of UGC authority also raises problems of university autonomy. As the discussion of historical legacies in Indian education suggested, it was partly in the name of "autonomy" and "standards" that Curzon justified strong government control over Indian universities. Strong official control in the guise of governmental effort to realize a policy it defines as in the public interest (such as "social integration" by substituting regional language for English) can be a means of politicization. A minister for education may serve the interests of certain deserving regions and classes, just as Curzon served the interests of the *raj*. UGC authority and resources probably can best be used to support education and scholarship within the universities. Given these qualifications and caveats, more emphatic enforcement of minimum standards still remains a viable strategy for the UGC.[39]

The National Sector in Education

In contrast to the states, which must respond more directly to democratic pressures, the central government has been able to act more effectively to foster quality as against quantity and national as against regional recruitment. There is no guarantee, however, that all national sector institutions are of a high quality or have a national composition. Some institutions have been placed under central authority because of special claims that arise out of their relationship to the nationalist movement. As a group, the four central universities, Delhi, Aligarh, Banaras, and Visva-Bharati, are no better or more "national" than other universities. Ecology and history are more important than jurisdiction, management, and source of funds in determining the quality and the composition of student body and faculty of these four universities. Delhi University has been a strong national university in part because its location in the capital city with its cosmopolitan population helped able vice-chancellors to build strong intellectual and professional communities by attracting a diverse student body and a talented faculty. Recent changes in its environment may alter those conditions. In contrast, even able vice-chancellors have found it difficult to overcome the regional parochialism and erosion of standards that arise from Banaras' location in the most backward area of a backward state. Of the nine institutions that qualify for central support by being "deemed" universities, four are legacies of the nationalist period and have been given such recognition as much for their historical contributions as for their educational merit. The four are: Gujarat Vidyapith (Ahmedabad), established by Gandhi; the Arya Samaj's Gurukul at Hardwar; Kashi Vidyapith (Banaras); and Jamia Millia Islamia (Delhi) — the latter two established like their Gujarat counterpart to give a national education outside the confines of "imperialist universities."

With these qualifications in mind, it is possible to observe that the national sector institutions *are* notable for their ability to provide advanced professional training and quality research. The Indian School of International Studies, the Indian Institute of Science, the Indian Agricultural Research Institute, the Birla Institute of Science and Technology, the Tata Institute of Social Science, the All-India Institute of Medical Science, the Indian Statistical Institute, and the Calcutta and Ahmedabad Institutes of Management are all notable for the high quality of their students, staff, and research.

The national government's most significant achievements in establishing academic excellence have been the five Indian Institutes of Technology and the centers for advanced study. Developed in collaboration with technology institutes from a variety of countries, well equipped and ably staffed, the IIT's are eagerly sought after by young men of talent. They recruit and select students through a common national examination that attracts a large number of able and highly qualified candidates. The creation of the centers for advanced study is the UGC's principal program for strengthening postgraduate teaching and research. A limited number of departments (twenty-seven in 1968) whose work already meets "international standards" or is within striking distance of doing so were selected for special financial support under this program.[40] The centers represent a democratic and distributive alternative to a bolder idea, that the union government should take responsibility for and support the growth of a few universities whose standards could become a model of excellence not only in all or most departments, but also as a community of scholars and students. This idea has been mooted on and off since the fifties. The most recent version is the scheme for six "major universities" proposed in 1966 by the Education Commission, 1964–1966. Such universities were conceived of as places to concentrate scarce human and other resources in order to create a "critical mass" of faculty and students that would make possible "first class post graduate work and research." The universities would be "comparable to the best institutions of their type in any part of the world." [41]

The idea has encountered resistance from all quarters (except those few universities who suspect that they might be brought into the scheme) on the grounds that resources allocated to such institutions would be at the expense of those available for all higher education and that it would create, by fiat rather than achievement, a formal elite among universities by designating some as "major" and others, by implication, as "minor." In rejecting the "major university" idea, the parliamentary committee on education of 1967 took a distributive view: "We believe that better results can be obtained if we strive to maintain at least the minimum standards in all institutions." [42]

India's vice-chancellors, at their conference in 1967, also recommended rejection of the "major universities" scheme. They preferred, they said, more advanced centers and exclusive national government responsibility (particularly financial responsibility) for postgraduate education. In rejecting one policy option and advocating others they were in their own way being political on behalf of the interests with which they were associated, the universities and states from which they came. The vice-chancellors were convinced that the "major universities" scheme would expand and upgrade the national sector at the expense of their universities and of state jurisdiction over higher education. These concerns were made explicit in recommendation 46 of the 1967 conference: "It would be better to provide liberal assistance to the State universities rather than to set up new central universities." [43] The sixty-seven vice-chancellors of state universities felt that national government assistance in the form of exclusive financial responsibility for postgraduate education was preferable to national government participation in higher education through centrally supervised and financed "major universities." The first policy option leaves most of the authority and resources for higher education in the hands of the universities and state governments, the second shifts a substantial increment of both to the national sector and does so in a way that is designed to make that sector into a "vanguard" of quality and elite (as against quantity and popular) higher education.

The "advanced centers" scheme benefits more institutions than the "major universities" scheme would have and is a less conspicuous target for equalizing pressure, although even here the Estimates Committee suggested that distributive rather than merit considerations should be used when it warned that "as far as possible one university should not initially have more than two centers of advanced study." [44]

Although the advanced centers represent a step in the direction of excellence, they also represent democratic and bureaucratic rather than intellectual conceptions of academic organization. Scientific and scholarly advances might come from isolated high quality departments, but they are more likely where enough good departments are concentrated to facilitate professional and interdisciplinary communication. Where good biology, good chemistry, and good physics exist side by side and influence one another, biophysical or biochemical theory may grow. Where good departments are "equitably" distributed to meet the democratic pressures of the federal system, such innovation on the boundaries of disciplines may be inhibited. However, it may be that the advanced centers will become a more gradual and less vulnerable vehicle for the "major university" idea. The Education Commission, 1964–1966, suggested, and the parliamentary committee on education of 1967 accepted, the idea that "clusters" of advanced centers be established which would strengthen and support one another. [45]

The formulation and implementation of national policy for higher education in a federal system that places primary responsibility for education in the hands of the states, in the face of very limited resources, and in the context of traditions and laws that protect academic freedom and university autonomy, has been difficult, extremely complex, and tenuous in its result. Bargaining and persuasion within and between levels of public authority and between public authorities and educational authorities has given some direction and coherence to higher education. At the same time it must be recognized that the growth and content of higher education have been more the result of a massive set of political demands and private initiatives than of authoritative decisions and allocations from government based on clear priorities and strategies. It is in this sense that we speak of national educational policy as at best a constant approximation, a struggle to insure that the number and size of the increments that promote national goals and serve national needs outweigh those that seem to detract from them.

Part II / Educational Institutions in Their Social and Political Environment

Introduction to Part II

The chapters in this section relate educational institutions to specific social and political environments located at various governmental levels and comprehending educational undertakings that range from primary school through college. Two of the chapters provide ethnographic accounts of the respective environments and thus of actors and their motives. Each highlights crucial processes that involve conflicting values and interests: politicians capturing educational resources to advance personal or partisan fortunes (Gould); communities appropriating educational resources to advance the fortunes of castes and religions (Madan and Halbar); the advocates of decentralized, popular control and the advocates of more centralized, professional control of primary education attempting to organize public authority in ways that favor their respective views (Narain). Such problems affect democratic educational systems in many countries. The study of the management of these problems in the Indian context helps to generate concepts and insights that can be used in relevant and comparable settings elsewhere.

Harold Gould's study of the politicization of secondary institutions and intermediate colleges (inter-colleges) in Faizabad District, Uttar Pradesh, provides a striking illustration of the extent to which the political system is capable of converting educational institutions into political resources. Secondary and intermediate institutions, characterized as they are by less professional educational standards, are more vulnerable to politicization than are colleges and universities. But the account of the method of institutional takeover by politicians is useful for understanding a similar process when it does affect colleges or universities.

It is not accidental that all the institutions in Gould's study are privately controlled. Education under private management as a whole has been more vulnerable to politicization than has education managed by government. Although government-managed education lies nearer the hand of the politician — and in some states such control may be used to subject administrators and professionals to political manipulation — government-managed educational institutions are under closer supervision and scrutiny by administrators and professional educators. Such professional and bureaucratic controls, which make innovation and imaginative education less likely, also inhibit government-managed colleges and schools from declining below a modest minimum in their standards and place some limits on politicization.

Private institutions, which constitute 69 percent of all secondary institutions,[1] offer some of the best and some of the worst education in India. The best secondary schools are mostly private, embodying legacies of the

English public school tradition and of missionary efforts. On the other hand, the tremendous demand for education has encouraged a wave of private entrepreneurs to create institutions for profit and power. Many of these are physically and intellectually jerry-built structures, Indian equivalents of the deplorable private institutions that were extensively chronicled in dour English memoirs of sordid nineteenth-century education.[2] Conditions in many private schools — terms of service, conditions of teachers, facilities, and adherence to bureaucratic norms — are well below the modest level in government schools and colleges.

Harold Gould did not come to Faizabad district to study education. As an anthropologist interested in political processes at the village, *tehsil* (subdistrict), and district level, he soon found that secondary schools and inter-colleges were among the resources Uttar Pradesh politicians utilize to build the political organizations and to generate the influence and support required to affect policy and to win elections. He collected information on the forty-four private schools and fifty-four higher secondary schools and inter-colleges located in the district. The managing committees of forty-one of these institutions are "politicized and attempt to use the institutions they control to support a specific political philosophy, party or faction." Half of the managing committees are controlled by the Congress party and the other half by other partisan interests. Gould establishes a relationship between areas of the district controlled by a party or faction and that party's domination of managing committees. He sees the private educational institutions as both an input and an output of the political system; as a force, on the one hand, for gaining and consolidating political control and as a reflection, on the other hand, of control already achieved.

Politicization of education in Uttar Pradesh has to be seen in the context of social, economic, and educational backwardness. As tables 20 and 21 of chapter 5 suggest, Uttar Pradesh ranks low with respect to most criteria of educational and economic development. Faizabad district, the location of Gould's study, is a backward district in a backward state, falling in the bottom quartile of districts ranked by level of development.[3] Although we have not established that the economic, political, and historical context of educational institutions influences levels of politicization, it seems a plausible hypothesis that high indicators of development, administrative strength, and political stability would measure conditions under which politicization is more difficult and less likely.[4]

The reputation of Uttar Pradesh's administration is not as high among administrative professionals as is the reputation of the administrations of such states as Maharashtra and Tamil Nadu. Weak administration means that in Uttar Pradesh it is difficult to protect educational institutions against political penetration and appropriation. Gould's account suggests that minimal legal conditions for foundings and grants-in-aid are not very stringent, and are laxly enforced. Although more evidence would be needed to substantiate their view, knowledgeable educationalists consider legislative constraints in Tamil Nadu and Maharashtra to be more severe, and enforcement more effectual. In addition, Uttar Pradesh's high level of factional politics not only weakens the effectiveness of government but also, as Gould shows, provides incentives to use institutions as ploys in factional infighting. Educational conditions in Faizabad district probably represent one end of a continuum measuring the vulnerability of educational institutions to political penetration and appropriation.

Secondary education in Uttar Pradesh has a number of problematic features. It has retained the inter-college, which is responsible for the eleventh and twelfth year of education. Like the preuniversity course in colleges, the intermediate curriculum (and the age and maturity of the students) more closely approximates high school than college education. The report of the Education Commission, 1964–1966, reaffirmed the recommendations of the Secondary Education Commission, 1953, that intermediate colleges be dropped in favor of upgraded high schools (classes IX, X and XI) and a three-year first degree course in the universities. When the Education Commission, 1964–1966, reported in 1966, only five states had implemented the higher secondary school proposal (relying for the most part on a preuniversity year at the university or college for the eleventh class), but all universities except those under the authority of the Uttar Pradesh government and the University of Bombay had complied with the three-year first degree policy.[5]

The reluctance of Uttar Pradesh to fall into line with these national policies is a result not only of the resistance of teachers reluctant to surrender the status and perquisites of being college teachers, a factor that was operative in other states, but also to the more strongly entrenched connection between education and politics in that state. The state of Uttar Pradesh likes to count its inter-colleges as "higher education," even though national authorities such as the Education Commission, 1964–1966, and the University Grants Commission do not always do so.[6] Gould has, quite rightly, chosen to group inter-colleges with secondary schools.

Some of the problems connected with secondary education in Uttar Pradesh probably arise from the disproportionate number of schools relative to other levels of education in its educational system. Compared to the educational pyramids in other states, that in Uttar Pradesh is top-heavy. Uttar Pradesh has stressed primary education less than secondary and higher, providing a smaller pool of prepared students from which higher levels may draw. Although the state ranks eleventh with respect to primary and tenth with respect to middle school enrollments, it ranks fourth in secondary and higher secondary, including inter-college enrollments. As in Mysore and Bihar, where the rank order position of enrollments for high and higher secondary is also conspicuously above the positions for lower levels of education, this relationship may well be related to a strong surge of private entrepreneurship in secondary education, unrestrained by legislative specification of criteria or by administrative enforcement of those criteria. Such entrepreneurship may be due to sectarian and community energy, as Madan and Halbar suggest is the case in Mysore; or it may be due to the hope of constructing a political organization and generating political support — the motive which Gould finds significant in Uttar Pradesh.

There is, in any case, some question whether such a relationship between the secondary sector and primary and lower schools is as good for education and for economic growth as it is for politics.

Gould suggests that private entrepreneurship provides the administrative energy and local support that lead to new foundings in a state in which the supply of secondary education does not yet correspond to demand. This defense raises the more general question of the justification for private entrepreneurship in secondary education. As Madan and Halbar suggest, private entrepreneurship generates only marginal financial resources for education. The Education Commission, 1964–1966, estimated that government grants supplied 48 percent and fees 36 percent of the expenditure of privately managed schools. "Voluntary organization contributed only a little more than one-eighth of the total expenditure of the private institutions." [7]

Is an eighth worth it? Private talent and local community enthusiasm can and do supplement the limited pool of administrative and financial resources. Privately founded or managed institutions, like those under close community control, may connect education to the interests and culture of publics that need or want it, a result to be weighed against the educational performance engendered (under somewhat different conditions) by more centralized bureaucratic management or trade union domination, or both (as in New York City or other large metropolitan centers in the United States). According to the Education Commission, 1964–1966, most of the expenditure of privately managed educational institutions "comes from government grants and fees; and where fees have been abolished, they depend almost exclusively on government funds. Their main assets are: strong ties with the local community on whom they depend for support; a fair measure of freedom, although this is disappearing rapidly under increasing departmental control; and the loyalty of teachers who are recruited, unlike in government or local authority service, to the individual institutions. Their main weaknesses are two: a precarious financial position, due partly to the uncertainty of government grants, and partly to their own increasing incapacity to raise funds; and very often, a bad and even unscrupulous management." [8] To these putative benefits and their associated costs has to be added the further cost of the laxity of private schools in conforming to minimum standards; the potential use of public authority and resources for private goods (individual and collective); the problematic nature of the relationship of private education to universalistic values, as the Madan and Halbar chapter and the trends in the United States toward white separatism in the south and black separatism in the north remind us; and the susceptibility of private schools to appropriation for political purposes.

The Education Commission, 1964–1966, confronted this benefit-cost syndrome by recommending the imposition of certain general administrative controls which would assure adherence to minimum criteria, even while proposing that governments discriminate among private schools and colleges — identifying and providing more freedom for those private institutions that have high standards and educational traditions that can help sustain them. The proposal to strengthen administrative controls does not, however, confront the circular relationship between the educational and political sectors. Men who, as politicians, value the private school as a political resource that supports their power may not, as cabinet ministers, be inclined to subject privately managed educational institutions to stringent controls.

Sometimes, however, rather than being potential or actual political resources, privately managed educational institutions may be arrayed against a party and its government, as in Kerala during the first Namboodiripad-led Communist government of 1957–1959. The government's educational bill, ostensibly designed to correct a variety of broadly recognized abuses in some privately managed schools, fell afoul of the constitutional guarantee expressed in Article 30(1) that "all minorities, whether based on religion or language, shall have the right to establish and administer educational institutions of their choice." It also aroused widespread opposition from politically powerful organized communities (for example, Nairs and Christians) which operated extensive school systems, from school managers and staffs, and from a broad spectrum of opposition parties. The bill, which gave the government sweeping regulatory and takeover powers, was referred by the governor to the president of India under constitutionally prescribed procedures designed to protect fundamental rights from legislative encroachments. The president, in turn, failed to give his assent after utilizing his constitutional prerogative to consult the supreme court. Article 30(1), the court held, while allowing for "reasonable regulations" (for example, concerning health, minimum qualifications for teachers, and the content and standard of instruction) "to ensure the excellence of the institution to be aided" by government, did not permit direct interference with the management of educational institutions or their replacement by government, nor was government permitted to do indirectly or under cover of the interest of education what it could not do directly.[9] The constitutional guarantee embodied in Article 30(1) together with the supreme court's interpretation of it stand as a considerable barrier to (or protection from) government action with respect to privately managed educational institutions.

Even after the state governments assume virtually the entire bill for secondary education, as they will if present proposals in many states to abolish all fees are realized, privately managed secondary education will probably survive because of the strength of the historical traditions and community interests that lie behind it; because of the vested interests of private management; because of the (often related) vested interests of politicians; and because of the effective learning that can result from community involvement and commitment, which lowers the level of alienation and conflict between teachers and administrators on the one hand and pupils and parents on the other.

We have defined politicization of education as the propensity to subordinate educational goals to those of political groups on the one hand and to those of private and community groups on the other. Harold

Gould's account illustrates the first aspect of politicization; Madan and Halbar's study of sectarian and caste control of education in the state of Mysore focuses on the second possibility. Although private foundings may supplement public effort and further the public interest, they may also, through grants-in-aid, divert public resources to narrow private goals and interests. Madan and Halbar raise two questions relevant to this problem: whether sectarian and caste institutions foster modernization, and whether they ought to be supported by state subsidy.

The authors, both sociologists at Karnatak University in Mysore at the time the research for the study was done, collected data on the social composition, notably caste and religion, of management, staff, and students of 210 private and public institutions at all levels of education in three districts of Mysore. Among private institutions, those of the Brahmans, Christians, Lingayats, and Muslims are the most conspicuous. The authors' enquiry into whether private educational bodies are modernizing structures rests less on an examination of the content of education than on whether the social composition of the schools is such as to provide a heterogeneous social experience for their students. Their findings contrast the social composition of management, staff, and students in private and public institutions. They show that in private institutions, the social composition of all three categories reflects the community of the controlling group, except in the case of small or underprivileged communities whose size or social backwardness may limit the supply of available teachers and students. In public institutions, management, faculty, and students more nearly reflect the social composition of the territorially defined community of the school district, though this reflection usually is modified by a stronger representation for socially and economically advanced castes and communities. On the basis of this data, the authors conclude that public education, due to its greater demographic representativeness, is more conducive to the promotion of universalistic values and equality, while the particularistic "favoritism" of private institutions detracts from both.

The study assumes that students will learn as much or more from the human situation in which they find themselves as from the formal learning that is transmitted to them, and that the "modern" value of egalitarian behavior will be transmitted more by socially heterogeneous institutions than by the curriculum. Although the first assumption is probably true, the second would require further investigation to be accepted. And it may be that what students learn from their human situation with respect to "universalism" and equality may be counterproductive; familiarity can breed contempt as well as affection. Heterogeneous education both in America and India has sometimes led to intra-institutional segregation: the regional, religious, or caste groups in heterogeneous Indian colleges; the ethnic and color groups in American high schools. The difficulties, often failures, of desegregation (integration) in urban America suggest that extreme class and cultural differences cannot easily be bridged.

Because sectarian and caste-founded education is important for minority interests underrepresented in the state-managed school system, and because private education provides important financial and management resources, the authors do not favor abolition of the government grants-in-aid program. However, they believe that the allocation of government resources should be dependent on more representative managing committees, teaching staffs, and student populations in sectarian and caste-managed institutions.

Popular control of primary education in the state of Rajasthan, analyzed in chapter 9 by Iqbal Narain, is associated with the neo-Gandhian movement for the reform of local government in India. *Panchayati raj* (government by locally elected councils) was inaugurated first in Rajasthan in 1959 soon after the release of the Balvantray Mehta Report on community projects and national extension services, and took its lead from the political ideas and practical suggestions of that document.[10] The objective of *panchayati raj* is to radically decentralize and democratize control of many local government functions, including primary education. It was expected that popular participation and leadership at the local level would make education more meaningful and effective, release energies and resources, and reduce the self-serving behavior and indifference to local needs and conditions that seem to plague centralized educational (and other) bureaucracies.[11] Iqbal Narain found that in practice these benefits have been unevenly and differentially realized and that the mounting cost to education of the political appropriation of educational resources and processes outweigh the benefits.

In 1954, five years before Rajasthan became the first state in India to introduce *panchayati raj,* a committee of the ministry of education went well beyond the Sargent Committee report of 1948 favoring the establishment of school boards on a more decentralized and local basis. It did not, however, recommend that authority over the appointment, promotion, transfer, and dismissal of teachers be vested in rural local authorities, that is, village *panchayats* (elected councils), although it was prepared to have major municipalities and district boards given authority (subject to specific procedures) to recruit and control teaching staffs.[12]

Panchayati raj changed this system of authority by establishing democratic political control over staff and a wide range of functions at the block level (the block is an administrative creation of an earlier community development program) and over a narrower range of functions at the village level. Inaugurated on a selective and experimental basis in 1952, the community development program had become by 1959 a national scheme that provided for a new level of administration, the block, between the district (of which there are 352, distributed over sixteen states) and the village.[13] At the village level the school, the *panchayat,* and the cooperative became the basic institutions for carrying out development programs. In 1954, the ministry of education committee had left control in administrative and professional hands by preserving state education department control of recruitment, appointment, and transfer; in 1959, *panchayati raj* began a radical change, at least in Rajasthan, by leaving the education department with authority over "technical matters" only. Primary schools in Rajasthan are now managed by 232 autonomous *panchayat samitis* (block level political bodies) with authority aggregatively over 42,000 teachers and 1,860,000 students (1966 figures), a system roughly comparable in size to New York City's, where over 1,000,000 students (between kindergarten and high school) are taught by about 50,000 teachers.

Panchayati raj control of primary education in Rajasthan is a more radical form of popular decentralization than that realized in New York City in 1970 when the state legislature, following in some measure the recommendations of the Bundy Report to Mayor Lindsay, created 30 units controlled by school committees elected from specially qualified local electorates. With almost twice as many students and almost as many teachers, the Rajasthan system has 232 units; gives more authority to the local bodies to recruit, discipline, and post teachers than does the New York arrangement; and vests the choice of local educational authorities (albeit indirectly) in all voters rather than in a specially qualified electorate. This degree of decentralized, lay control has been established in Rajasthan in the context of much more weakly established professional standards and more limited bargaining capacity on the part of the organized teachers. The situation of the teacher in Rajasthan seems in some respects to be the opposite of that of his counterpart in New York City: teachers in Rajasthan are subject to being used or appropriated by community or partisan interests, while teachers in New York, often drawn from the city's large and politically effective Jewish population, seem to have appropriated the educational system for their own benefit.

These developments in Rajasthan and New York City may be viewed as variations in the world-wide experience with educational populism. The extensive history of that experience ranges from the original expression, that of Jacobins of the Mountain in France, to later ones such as the common school movement in pre-Civil War America and the contemporary efforts of Mao Tse-tung in China and McGeorge Bundy in New York City.[14] Like Mao Tse-tung and Bundy, the architects of popular control of education in India believe that putting power and resources in the hands of the people of local communities will promote responsible and informed participation, and that bringing the curriculum and teachers closer to the needs, interests, and knowledge of the people will promote useful learning and citizenship. Iqbal Narain argues, as have several other recent reporters on education in Rajasthan, that the present arrangements, by being unable to prevent politicians from abusing popular community control for partisan and personal advantage, have gone too far and need corrective amendments in the direction of restoring some professional and administrative authority.[15]

There are substantial and instructive American analogies for the developments in Rajasthan that Iqbal Narain analyzes. The pre-Civil War movement in America for universal public education in common schools (associated with the name of Horace Mann and the leadership of Massachusetts), also sought to make universal education a reality and to vest the management of the institutions involved in the hands of the people. In state legislatures and local boards of education, popularly elected representatives were to set the goals, provide the resources, and recruit and supervise the personnel required. By 1860, a majority of the states had established public school systems, perhaps half of the nation's children were getting some formal education (somewhere between two-thirds and three-fourths are doing so in India today), and in a few states (Massachusetts, New York, Pennsylvania) free public education was beginning to include secondary schools (about 20 percent of the fourteen- to seventeen-year-old age group is attending high school in India today).

The corruption of this system — its capture by local politicians who bought and sold teaching and administrative posts, dabbled in the assignment of text book contracts and the appointments of school superintendents, and used kickbacks from school building construction to finance political activities and line their own pockets — contributed to the rise of the progressive education movement. It was antipopulist in its attempt to isolate education from politics but propopulist in its effort to replace the formalism of academic education with a diverse range of practical subjects and motivationally oriented teaching suitable to the ethnic and occupational diversity of an increasingly urban and industrial America.

At the end of World War II the stage was set for two new waves of reform, one attacking the life-adjustment, philistinism, or misguided pragmatism of progressive education, the other attacking the domination of education by bureaucratic professionals cut off from their students' culture and aspirations, from knowledge (as opposed to "method"), and from the communities they ostensibly served.[16] By the mid-sixties, after sputnik, American education seemed to have come full circle. The muckraking of the progessives in education cured local popular control of political corruption but at the price of turning education over to self-serving bureaucratic professionals.

Rajasthan has not experienced a politically effective reaction against popular control of primary education, nor is it attempting as yet to strengthen the hand of the professional educational bureaucracy. Such a reaction or attempt may not be advantageous, however, because neither centralized professionalism nor decentralized populism necessarily offers lasting solutions. America's experience suggests that educational policy will alternate in response to changing historical conditions and needs, including the impact of national security and international emulation. The persistence of the dialectic in the relationship of centralized professionalism and decentralized populism was being illustrated in the mid- and late-sixties by the struggle against centralized and professional control of primary and secondary education in America's big cities where the poor, particularly the black, Puerto Rican and chicano poor, are alienated from public school systems. Marilyn Gittell, one of a group of policy-oriented scholars attacking the structure and performance of the New York City school system, sees the problem as domination of the schools by self-serving bureaucratic professionals incapable of educating underprivileged urban populations.[17] Another reformer has observed, in a vein reminiscent of the Balvantray Mehta Report, that "once upon a time, the people created the public schools, and the schools belonged to them." Today, "control of public education in our large cities has passed over almost exclusively to management . . . increasingly distant from the public. From . . . parent groups in middle class suburbs to angry rump boards of education in New York City's ghettos, the public is seeking to repossess its schools. . . . For a long time, a few thoughtful educators have argued that education can be strengthened by linking schools intimately to a system of political accountability." [18]

It is difficult to say precisely how representative of India the politicization of primary education control that Iqbal Narain analyzes is. As chapter 5 (tables 15, 16, and 20) suggests, Rajasthan is one of India's more backward states (tenth of fifteen) in terms of the indicators used to measure level of development. At the same time, it was first among India's states in rate of economic growth between 1949–50 and 1958–59.[19] Its relative backwardness is related to its history. Made up of twenty-two former princely states, only a few of which had governments able and willing to foster even a modest amount of social change and economic growth, Rajasthan had an educational record prior to independence and the integration of the princely states that lagged well behind the record in British India or that in some other princely states such as Baroda. The princely states of Rajasthan were relatively free of the kind of ethic and performance that the Indian Civil Service brought to British India. Nor did they share in British India's experience of the nationalist movement or provincial self government. New to modern administration and popular, competitive politics in 1947, Rajasthan's political life adapted remarkably quickly to the radically changed circumstances that followed the introduction of democratic rule. Today it shares some qualities of preindustrial rural America, where localities (townships and their school districts) hired and fired locally recruited and modestly qualified teachers who could be put out the door by the bigger boys if they could not command them.[20]

These circumstances have contributed in some measure to the Jacksonian-like populism that has characterized Rajasthan's politics since the first general election of 1951–52. The politics have been Jacksonian in their emphasis on spoils, on decentralization, and on the pragmatic virtues and capabilities of the common man. Rajasthan's political leadership has shown great energy in building up educational institutions. Iqbal Narain argues that the association of local bodies with primary education has been a significant force in popularizing it. It is likely that the rapid build-up of educational institutions in Rajasthan took place in part because the administrators and the politicians were less constrained than those in some of the states of former British India by a too fastidious regard for the proprieties of public law and administration.[21]

In Rajasthan, the *panchayat samiti* (block-level council), acting through the Block Development Officer (BDO) and the *pradhan* (chairman and political executive of the *samiti*) appoint, transfer, and discipline teachers. It is these arrangements that have, in many instances, been politicized, as the Narain chapter demonstrates (partly through the use of survey data, partly through the use of legislative debates and administrative reports).[22] At the same time, the politicization has been accompanied by some use of political influence to strengthen educational resources and processes.

As Iqbal Narain observes in chapter 9, "it may not be correct to say that teachers are dragged into politics; in the view of officials, they are, more often than not, drawn into it on their own." The attempted mass transfer of primary school teachers by the Akali Dal (Sikh nationalist) government in the Punjab soon after Mrs. Gandhi's Congress party victory in the 1971 parliamentary election (the Congress party won eight of nine seats in the Punjab) suggests that teachers can act independently of the governments they serve.

If some teachers enter the political arena for partisan purposes or to secure personal advantages or to cover irregularities, others do so to pursue policies or secure resources that they believe will promote educational goals or enhance the educational experience. Thus, teacher-initiated participation in the political process is not limited to pursuing personal or partisan goals. Such participation can also strengthen local community control and management if the result is to encourage the use of administrative discretion in ways that defend or benefit particular local educational authorities. Table 45, chapter 9, "Effect of Political Involvement on Teachers' Performance," indicates that the second most frequently mentioned effect of political involvement was on grants of money and equipment by the *samitis* to primary schools. If, as Narain observes "once a teacher enters the arena [of local politics], he is constantly taken as a participant, sharing in the political rewards and the punishments, at times even in spite of himself," it is also difficult, as the Gould and the Madan and Halbar chapters suggest, to distinguish between politicization that appropriates educational resources and goals to the political sector, and the use of political influence by actors within educational institutions to strengthen educational performance.

7 / Educational Structures and Political Processes in Faizabad District, Uttar Pradesh

Harold Gould

In Uttar Pradesh they have a phrase, "The Congress has abolished the Zamindari in land and has created a Zamindari in education." Such Zamindars [land owners] are managers of colleges, who are well fed, well clothed, and maintain their own cars, all on the profits from the institutions which they run. It is now recognised that running an educational institution can be an important means of economic and political power.

J. P. Naik, Member-Secretary, Education Commission, 1964–1966 [1]

The general relationship between education and politics in India has been discussed and analyzed at great length over the years by both Indian and foreign scholars. The manner in which schools are used by working politicians to abet their efforts to gain and hold public office, however, has received less scholarly attention. The following is an attempt to get at this important and interesting dimension of political behavior. The data are drawn from the district of Faizabad in eastern Uttar Pradesh, where I have conducted a variety of anthropological investigations over the past several years.

The premise from which this study proceeds is that political penetration of the educational system has gone far in Uttar Pradesh. In this respect the province is probably not unique in India, but it stands out when compared with many others. The high degree of political penetration helps account for certain patterns of educational investment and features of the distribution of student populations which are otherwise difficult to understand. The data suggest that, within limits, faculties and student bodies

My field work in India began in 1954, on a Fulbright Scholarship and continued in the summer of 1959 with a postdoctoral fellowship from the National Science Foundation. From 1960 to 1962, I remained in India under concurrent postdoctoral fellowships from the National Institute of Mental Health, returning in 1966–67 as a faculty research fellow of the American Institute of Indian Studies. There are many persons and institutions I wish to thank for making this essay possible: At Faizabad, Mr. Brij Nandan Prasad, currently principal of K.P. Intercollege at Allahabad; Mr. Ram Harsh Singh, teacher (now retired), Government Intercollege in Faizabad, whose help and friendship have extended over thirteen years; Mr. Ram Krishna Pandey, teacher at R.D. Intercollege (Sohowal) and journalist; Mr. S. P. Arren, I.A.S. (Indian Administrative Service), district magistrate and deputy commissioner (now transferred); Mr. Avadhesh Pratap Singh, president (adhyaksha) of the Faizabad district board (zila parishad) and former member of the legislative assembly; Mr. B. S. Shukla, I.A.S., city magistrate and election officer of Faizabad district; and Mr. K. N. Shukla, district inspector of schools and religous scholar.

have frequently been created in order to generate political resources rather than for the primary purpose of fostering education and modernization per se.

Such a state of affairs seems loathsome to professional educators and idealistic laymen who ordinarily see an inverse relationship between politicization and quality in an educational system. There is another side to the question, however. In a country with India's specific complex of historical experiences, the instrumental role of politicians in establishing educational institutions may well have a positive value even in those instances where their motives for doing so are largely self-aggrandizing. An important consequence of their enterprise is that schools have been brought into being in places where, given the poverty and apathy of local populations, their existence would otherwise have been unlikely.

In a general sense, major political involvement in educational processes is inevitable in India. The cynicism and despair Indians so often manifest over the ethical conduct of their politicians make it hard for many to accept the premise that in all modern, complex societies the establishment, perpetuation, expansion, and regulation of educational systems has to be primarily the responsibility of the state acting through its political leadership. A mass service of these proportions cannot be left to haphazard individual decision-making, for too much of the society's resources and cultural goals are invested in it. But the fact that education is a vast commitment of a country's organizational energies, whose purpose ultimately affects the uses to which the human mind itself can be put, makes its management and control a political prize as well as a responsibility. In all modern societies, therefore, continuous debate and competition occurs over who shall control education and for what purposes. The question, in other words, is not whether politics and politicians shall influence educational processes, but how and to what degree they will do so. This is the real issue in India today. Susanne Rudolph has stated the matter in a way which aptly sets the keynote for what follows here: "We do not assume, as is often assumed [in India], that there is such a thing as an educational system free of political intervention; nor do we assume that such a thing would be good. In a democratic society and in educational institutions which receive government funds, there will be political influence. . . . The real questions focus on distinguishing what type of political pressure and politicization is benign and what not, . . . whether educational purposes are subsumed by the political system, or whether politics become a means for strengthening or redefining educational goals." [2]

The conditions in Faizabad district are by no means benign, as has already been suggested. They reveal a clear need for a profound upgrading of the professional quality of the Uttar Pradesh educational system. Criticisms and proposed reforms such as those contained in the recent *Report of the Educational Commission, 1964–66,*[3] reveal that Indian leaders are aware of the problems and dangers inherent in the present course. That improvements are slow should surprise no one who is aware of how difficult it is to root out old habits and institutions in any human society.[4]

The Rise of Educational Entrepreneurship

The conditions prevailing in India prior to independence have had a bearing on the contemporary relationship between politics and education in Uttar Pradesh. Western contact and the achievement of British paramountcy in the subcontinent were generally most responsible for what followed. The new culture and technology which the English spread had a profound, often shattering, impact on the traditional societies of India. Eventually the shock and confusion began giving way to a conviction that one of the chief ways out of the humiliation of colonial servitude was modern education; that the westerner's knowledge would have to be mastered and, to some extent, turned against him. The shock and confusion also gave way to a realization that the quest for modernity had a political dimension. Indian society mobilized for the purpose of terminating British rule and supplanting it with some kind of popular government.

The names of men like Raja Ram Mohun Roy and Dwarkanath Tagore are synonymous with early Indian efforts to gain access to the new knowledge and to promulgate it among their own people. These efforts began in Bengal because British administration and culture struck its deepest roots there in the early days of East India Company suzerainty. But as British administration spread across the subcontinent in the wake of successful British arms, the passion to spread western education followed. Both Indians and Europeans began founding educational institutions. Whereas originally the British responded to Indian demands for western education with efforts to provide it, the raj backed away from promulgating such education officially on a large scale when it discovered that the effort would prove expensive. Educational policy was then rationalized in terms of "nineteenth century orthodoxy," to quote Anil Seal.[5] The Indian Educational Commission of 1882 argued "the merits of private enterprise in public education, recommending that government aid to higher education should be cut down, and private education encouraged to take its place." In 1888, that policy went into effect with the declaration that the government "pioneers the way, but having shown the way, it recognizes no responsibility to do for the people what they can do for themselves." [6]

Animated by the challenge which this new government policy helped create, over the decades "educational entrepreneurs" established schools of every variety, in the remote recesses of India as well as in the more accessible cities and towns. As Seal has so aptly put it, "If the aim of the policy was to discourage the growth of higher education, it was a flat failure; but if government meant what it said about wanting to stimulate private Indian enterprise, the policy was successful beyond all expectations." [7] As one travels about Faizabad district today he frequently encounters the modest-sized brick structures, in adulterated Victorian style, which these early benefactors of knowledge erected. In many cases the buildings are still doing the job for which their founders intended them, though under different management and operating in a considerably changed socio-political environment.

It is doubtful that the educational entrepreneurs of that period (the century before independence) were primarily politically inspired. The Kayastha Pathshala Intercollege of Allahabad is a good illustration of the kind of socially conscious educational entrepreneurship that gave rise to a host of schools and colleges throughout India in an era when the government did not see mass education as one of its chief responsibilities. Its founder was a highly successful Kayastha (traditionally a caste of scribes) lawyer of Allahabad who invested most of his wealth in basic education for the youth of his own community and for worthy Indians of all classes. The creation of the Kayastha Pathshala Intercollege was his crowning achievement, for he not only provided an impressive physical plant but saw to it that the school obtained consistently good administrators and faculty. Through a trust which its founder established for this purpose, the school carries on in that tradition today, still successfully recruiting managing committees that are remarkably free of political, caste, or communal partisanship.

The founder of schools whose purpose was the propagation of learning on the western model, the "educational entrepreneur," had become an important public man in India by the second half of the nineteenth century. The educational entrepreneur might be the benefactor of strictly local institutions that served to spread his fame no farther than a *tehsil* [8] or a district, or he might be a man of the stature of Sir Syed Ahmed Khan, famed as the founder of Aligarh Muslim University. Whatever his fame, he was honored and enjoyed public gratitude and respect.

By the beginning of the twentieth century, another type of public man had emerged — the nationalist politician, who was committed to freeing his country from colonial servitude, to introducing parliamentary government, and to giving India modern institutions through national planning. Gandhi and Nehru symbolized different facets of the nationalist politician. Gandhi symbolized the method (*satyagraha,* withholding participation in political evil) of getting free of British control, while Nehru symbolized the way (the secular, democratic society with economic planning) of bringing India to the level of prosperity enjoyed by the great industrial nations. Thus, the ideal politician, like the ideal educational entrepreneur, was a benefactor of society, one who proposed to liberate India from foreign domination and endow her with the institutions and the will required to become modern.

Both types of men converged in the freedom movement, and in many instances their identities dissolved into each other. The techniques of resistance to British domination adopted by the Indian nationalists in many ways strongly abetted this process. The Congress party decisively committed itself to the promotion of mass education as the means by which the individual Indian could take advantage of the new opportunities that independent India would offer to its citizens. This commitment struck a responsive chord in the popular imagination, and has become one of the touchstones of the revolution of expectations which the government must in some measure satisfy.

Other factors were contributing to the fusion of political ambition with educational entrepreneurship. Prime among these was the nature of the Congress movement as it had been shaped by the influence of Mahatma Gandhi. The Gandhian style was a politics of renunciation, noncooperation with established authority, and service designed to bring about changes within the man, in the character structure of both self and adversary. And although it cannot be said that Gandhi succeeded in transforming every Congress party member, or even a majority of them, he set examples which most Congress party workers endeavored to follow at least in some measure. Thus Congress party workers sought ways in their home districts to be of service to their fellow Indians. Many became educational entrepreneurs. Congress party leaders of every stature became identified with the work of founding, administering, or teaching in schools in their local area as a response to Gandhi's concept of a politician as a man who renders service to others. In Faizabad district the leaders of both of the Congress party factions had become identified with educational entrepreneurship early in their political careers, one as a teacher who eventually founded a school of good quality in his ancestral village, and the other as the benefactor of several schools in his home city of Faizabad.

Courting arrest and spending long periods in prison as political *détenus* also played a role in the Congressman's attitude toward the relationship between politics and education. As a special class of prisoner, the political offender was kept apart from the ordinary criminal, exempted from menial labor, and allowed time to commiserate with his fellow political *détenus*. Congress leaders in the jails took advantage of this idle time to formulate the party's ideology, to educate its workers to enable them to be more effective and dedicated revolutionaries when they gained their release. This education not only maintained the political prisoners' morale during months and sometimes years of incarceration, but also supplemented the education of young prisoners who had been expelled from school for political activities or who had simply ceased attending in obedience to the boycott of educational institutions which the Congress party periodically enjoined on its members as part of a general policy of withholding participation in the legal, political, and educational life of the country. The experience of losing years of formal education and receiving some ex officio education through classes organized in jail sharpened many Congress party members' awareness of the value of education. Their experiences also provided a vivid demonstration of how potent a political weapon the control of educational institutions could be.

The founding of Kashi Vidyapith at Banaras in the early years of the freedom struggle was a direct by-product of these experiences and commitments. The idea of a university which would both serve the educational requirements of political prisoners and propagate a socialist version of nationalism was conceived by Acharya Narendra Deo, Sampurnanand, and other leaders of the old Congress Socialist party, while they were in prison. They organized classes in political philosophy and in the major European languages. This degree of academic scope and organization was facilitated by the scholarly and pedagogical qualifications of men like Acharya Narendra Deo and Sampurnanand (the former, it is said, enjoyed fluency in as many as a dozen languages). Kashi Vidyapith was, therefore, an institutionalized manifestation of experiences garnered from years spent in Agra prison for political crimes.[9]

In these ways the educational entrepreneur and the nationalist politician in many instances became one. As they did, numerous primary, secondary, and higher educational institutions were brought into being throughout the country whose aims were simultaneously pedagogical and ideological. Educationists became politicians, politicians became educationists, and students became political. The vast bulk of educationists and politicians in Uttar Pradesh was affected by this trend, grew together, and formed a highly complex set of interrelationships.

Postindependence Transformation

After India achieved independence from Great Britain, she embarked upon the task of erecting institutions of popular government. Her constitutional democracy, resting upon universal franchise, revealed and mobilized the complex groupings of Indian social organization, divided vertically and horizontally into myriad caste, communal, and cultural-linguistic segments. These segments became the basis for elaborate and intense political competition in every state and national assembly constituency and within and among political parties. This competitive quality in the Indian body politic was further heightened by the pattern of political dominance achieved by the Congress party, which enjoyed the overwhelming prestige and public favor of having been not only the political party of Gandhi, Nehru, and Patel, the great architects of India's successful revolt against British imperialism, but also the embodiment of the freedom movement itself. The aggregate strength of the other political parties was incapable of matching and challenging the power of Congress, which for a time developed into an organizational behemoth preoccupied with perpetuating its dominance. With its dominance established, Congress became absorbed in internal strife, probably disproportionately so in Uttar Pradesh. The lack of any outside threat to Congress dominance meant that the real struggle for power would occur among the segments that had formed within the organization. These segments had their roots in the personal antagonisms, ideological divergences, and social differences spawned by Congress' long history of being an omnibus coalition held together by little beyond common opposition to the British.

As the focus of political competition shifted from nationalist revolution to factional warfare among segments of the dominant political party (and, reflexively, to a similar type of warfare within the minority parties of both the right and the left), each district, each constituency, each municipal and town area board, and each new political body which came into being (such as *zila parishads, kshettra samitis, gram panchayats,* cooperative societies) became an arena for the expression of these personally, socially, and ideologically motivated enmities. Provinces like Uttar Pradesh became veritable jungles of ethnic style politics. The great turning point came with the advent of the first general election in 1952, when all the simmering rivalries within Congress and the other organized parties at last had a chance to come out into the open.

A statistical comparison of the 1946 and 1952 elections illustrates the shift from superficial unanimity to pervasive political competition. In Faizabad district there were six constituencies with a total of ten candidates in 1946. In four of the six, Congressmen were unopposed. In 1952, the number of constituencies had been increased to ten, eight for the legislative assembly and two for parliament. The number of candidates for the ten constituencies was sixty-eight. There were no unopposed candidates. With the change in the spirit and goals of political behavior, all the organizational talents of the politicians and all of the resources at their command were turned in the new directions.

Politics became highly personalistic and "ethnic" in character. That is, the political party, and most particularly Congress, which monopolized the sources of real power became an avenue through which men of certain temperaments and degrees of ambition sought access to the scarce supplies of jobs, commodities, and social recognition which the inadequate resources of an underdeveloped society could provide. The competition for these scarce but prized objects grew increasingly intense, bitter, and ruthless, and shaped itself around caste, religion, language and culture, and differentials in wealth and education. (In this sense the political rivalry was ethnic in style, reminiscent in many respects — though certainly not in all — of the melting pot politics of America, especially from the turn of the century to the end of World War II.) Ideology, by contrast, became less important. It occupied an important place on the political stage provided by Congress only when a man of Mr. Nehru's stature chose to make it do so (as with the declaration at Nagpur of a "Socialist pattern of society").

Gradually, then, new kinds of politics and politicians emerged in the arenas of power. The politicians utilized the old forms and idioms evolved in the halcyon days of nationalist struggle, but they applied them to new ends and filled them with new contents. The opponents were far less often oppressors of the downtrodden and far more often competitors for control of the party apparatus or officials who refused to be as pliant as a local politician or labor leader might desire. And what was occurring in the political realm was also occurring in the realm of education. Educational entrepreneurship, which had fused in an earlier period with political ambition, became an aspect of the intense political competition for position and advantage.

The Politics of Education

Because modern education had become a universal aspiration in independent India, the amount of resources invested in it, and the vested interests which could be established in it, increased greatly. Since I propose to deal with empirical data from only a single district in a single province, I shall confine my measurement of the magnitude of public investment in education to statistics compiled for Uttar Pradesh. Tables 24 and 25 show

Table 24. Growth of educational institutions in Uttar Pradesh, 1945 to 1965.

Type of institution	1945–46	1964–65	Increase, 1945 to 1965 (%)
Government	1,512	2,626	73.7
District board	24,161	53,083	120.0
Municipal board	1,332	4,275	296.0
Private aided	3,956	6,003	51.8
Private unaided accredited	505	1,808	256.0
Private unaccredited	1,387	249	−457.0

Source: Government of Uttar Pradesh, Ministry of Education, Department of Educational Statistics, *Shiksha Ki Pravti, 1965–66* [Education statistics, 1965–66] (Allahabad, 1967), statistical appendix.

that between 1945–46 and 1964–65 there was a large increase in the number of educational institutions and in the numbers attending school. In 1966, Faizabad district, which had a population of around 1.5 million, had 1,173 lower primary schools (I–IV), 50 higher primary schools (V–VII) and 54 higher secondary schools (VIII–X) and intercolleges (XI–XII) (the latter teach up to the equivalent of junior college in the U.S.).

Since independence, two kinds of educational entrepreneurship have been at work in Uttar Pradesh. On the one hand, the Congress government has directly and through local bodies fostered the widespread establishment of all types of schools in response to public demand for them. On the other hand, private individuals and groups have continued to found

Table 25. Growth of student populations in Uttar Pradesh, 1945 to 1965.

Level	1945–46	1964–65	Increase, 1945 to 1965 (%)
Higher primary (V–VII)	1,370,694	8,130,245	493.0
Lower secondary (VIII–X)	232,081	868,645	274.6
Intermediate (XI–XII)	179,443	1,385,475	670.0

Source: Government of Uttar Pradesh, Ministry of Education, Department of Educational Statistics, *Shiksha Ki Pravti, 1965–66* [Educational statistics, 1965–66] (Allahabad, 1967), statistical appendix.

educational institutions which receive accreditation and grants-in-aid of various kinds from the department of education when they fulfill certain criteria of performance. It is among the private institutions that groups and individuals with political aspirations have found the most fertile ground for exploiting the resources of mass education.

Why these institutions provide a congenial context for political entrepreneurs is better understood when it is realized how these private institutions are constituted, what sort of links they establish with the government, and at what level of education they are most inclined to operate.

A private educational institution comes into being after it forms a "general body" of subscribers who raise sufficient capital to establish the kind of school they want. The general body elects a managing committee (usually ten persons), a president, a manager (often the president and manager are the same person), and a secretary. This managing committee is the *de facto* authority in the institution; it is responsible for hiring the principal and the teaching and maintenance staff, for purchasing necessary equipment, and for administration. Private educational institutions can receive grants-in-aid of various kinds from the department of education if they prove they have the capacity to perform their purported educational functions. An institution of this kind is made to order for educational entrepreneurship, and the relationship of the institution to sources of government assistance is made to order for the encouragement of political bargaining.

Most private educational institutions are secondary schools (higher secondary schools and intercolleges), which is very nearly the ideal educational unit to be employed as a base for political operations. The number of secondary schools in Uttar Pradesh is high in relation to the levels of literacy and economic well-being in the province.[10] Table 25 shows that the greatest increase in student enrollments (670 percent) in the years since independence has been at the intermediate level.[11] An editorial in the *National Herald* of Lucknow, 12 December 1966, raised questions about the surprisingly large number of students who go on to university, and the proportionately large number of universities in backward, largely illiterate provinces like Uttar Pradesh.

Among factors which contribute to unrest and violence, one interesting point has been brought out by a study of figures of admission to universities. It is noted that in few countries does such a high percentage of secondary school boys go up to universities as in some states in India. While in the United Kingdom only 3½ percent of secondary school boys move up to universities, in Japan only 7½ percent, and France 11½ percent, the percentage is 13 in West Bengal and 21 in U.P. . . .

The number of universities too seem to bear no relation to general literacy standards. States like Madras, Kerala, Mysore, Andhra Pradesh which account for 30 percent of the country's total literate population, had between them only a sixth of the total number of universities in the country in 1961. On the other hand, U.P., Bihar, Madhya Pradesh and West Bengal which together had about the same 30 percent of the total literate population had in their territory half the total number of universities.

The *National Herald* called for remedies to this anomaly, pointing out that "uncontrolled proliferation of universities and indiscriminate enrollment for higher education exist in parts of the country where student unrest seems specially virulent."

The politicization of educational institutions make the maintenance of academic standards and promotions based on merit very difficult because institutions that use their facilities and students for political ends *owe* these students and their patrons something in exchange for the political services they have rendered. Because the purpose of modern mass education is primarily social mobility, attested by certificates of graduation, the politicized educational institution is obliged to promote its students as a kind of reimbursement for their political services. Educational entrepreneurship wedded to political entrepreneurship produces the raw material for political action. There is, so to speak, a conveyer belt which commences with secondary school membership. The successful products of the secondary school move up to the universities for more professional exploitation by higher echelon politicians. From the universities come the successors to the older political elites themselves. The real costs of such a system are the sacrifice of academic standards and the violence and chaos sometimes produced by attempts to discipline student bodies or, notably in Uttar Pradesh and Bihar, to compel honesty in examinations. Why should a student who is conditioned to believe that the political services he renders are his most important academic contribution accept the verdict of such a nonpolitical criterion of performance as marks?

Faizabad District

Faizabad district provides a substantive case of the relationship between politics and education. I discuss Faizabad district not because it typifies that relationship but because I know that district best. Nevertheless, it is of value that Faizabad has a rich and complex history of involvement in the politics of Uttar Pradesh and that all the major trials and crises that have marked the contemporary Uttar Pradesh political scene have been faithfully reflected in the district's political life. For example, one-fifth of the legislators who in 1967 crossed the floor with Charan Singh (the former Congress faction leader who twice headed Uttar Pradesh governments after the 1967 general election)[12] to form the Jan Congress party (later the Bhartiya Kranti Dal or BKD) and bring to an end twenty years of Congress party rule in Uttar Pradesh were elected from Faizabad constituencies.

Of the fifty-four higher secondary schools and intercolleges in Faizabad, forty-four are private institutions run by managing committees elected by general bodies. The remainder are managed by the government, the district board, municipal boards, and missionary organizations. To understand how they play political roles, it is necessary to describe their nature and operation in greater detail.

Politicians of all parties attempt to found as many secondary institutions as they can, and where they cannot found them they try to join the managing committees of as many as possible. In either case, the motive is the same: to develop a majority in their favor among the general body of any institution so that they can in turn get a majority of their supporters elected to the managing committee. When the latter majority is achieved, the resources of the institution are henceforth available to the politician for use in enhancing his political ambitions in the district. The group controlling the majority on the managing committee is ordinarily in a position to engage a principal of its choosing and to pursue policies with respect to hiring, firing, and promotion of the teaching staff which assure a substantial number of teachers loyal to its interests. The group in the majority controls the purse strings of the institution; it decides whom to patronize in the purchase of supplies and equipment for the school — a decision often conditioned by how much commission various suppliers are willing to pay influential members of the managing committee.

An educational entrepreneur prefers to found his own educational institution in an area where he has political ambitions, rather than gain control of an already extant one because in his own institution he can develop a general body, managing committee, and teaching staff that is overwhelmingly loyal to him. The western observer, accustomed to large and costly institutions, has difficulty imagining an obscure district politician with limited means becoming the founder of a higher secondary school. The difficulty vanishes, however, when it is realized what order of investment is actually required to establish such an enterprise in Uttar Pradesh.

It is usually possible to find space to erect a school on land owned by one's kin group. If that is not possible, one can usually find a philanthropically inclined follower who is willing to make the necessary donation. Forming a "general body" is usually easy, as is raising from among them the small amount of capital (Rs. 2,500 to Rs. 3,000)[13] necessary to construct a four room building with *kuchha* (clay) walls and thatched roof. Getting authorization to operate a school can be done by anyone who has good political contacts. Because of high white-collar unemployment, there is always an abundance of young university students or graduates who are willing to accept employment as teachers. And once the school begins operating, fees paid by the students are a basic source of revenue which is augmented by the grants-in-aid supplied by the Uttar Pradesh government to private institutions to encourage their operation. These grants-in-aid are technically conditional upon the maintenance of certain academic and administrative standards, but in reality an educational entrepreneur who enjoys political favor has little difficulty establishing his institution's qualifications.[14]

To illustrate how the Uttar Pradesh educational entrepreneur makes his calculations, I present an excerpt from my field notes. " 'X' has often said that he awaits the day when his constituency will no longer be a Scheduled Caste constituency so that he can run for the Legislative Assembly from there. Meanwhile, he plans to begin enhancing his public image in the constituency by founding a higher secondary school within the year. He will erect it on some vacant land near his village which will be donated by an admirer. He says that founding a school is not such an expensive proposition, really. You start with a *kuchha* or *pukka* building of about four rooms; you put up the four walls and for the time being lay a thatched roof over them. You are principal and you go and hire yourself a teaching staff. This immediately puts under your control and obligation a small group of educated young men who are willing to work for you. By establishing a higher secondary school you get as students young men who are old enough to be converted to your political philosophy and who can then be enlisted to function as political workers at election time. What you aim for is a 'politically conscious' school which can be 'turned into a politically active organization.' " [15]

In the same constituency is the Sri Ram Ballabha Bhagwant Vidyapith Intercollege. A brahman lawyer who has for years been active in Faizabad politics founded this institution in his natal village. As his political ambitions have grown, he has been thinking of someday obtaining a position on the Congress ticket for the legislative assembly. He has spread his influence through several constituencies of the district by his law practice and his fraternization with the religious personalities of the holy city of Ayodhya. As this scheduled caste constituency is the site of his ancestral home, the "pandit," as he is called, understandably dreams of running for election from there someday. Like "X," however, the pandit has no chance of doing this until the constituency is declared a general constituency. Meanwhile, like "X," the pandit has invested in the future by establishing himself as a benefactor of education.

His problems, however, have been rather different from those of "X." "X" is a young man with a political science degree. A teacher and a journalist, he has been active for several years in the non-Communist left of the district. He joined the Congress party prior to the 1967 general election and won recognition as a capable field worker by enabling the Congress parliamentary candidate to carry the scheduled caste constituency (one of five comprising the parliamentary constituency) against formidable odds.

The pandit, on the other hand, is getting on in years and has had to overcome the stigma of alleged misdeeds in his home community which led to his ostracism and which could prove a fatal liability to his political aspirations. To regain the respect and acceptance of his kinsmen and caste brethren, the pandit has held a very large *Brahman Bhoj* (feast for Brahmans) every year for the last several years. In order to redeem himself in the eyes of the wider public, he founded the Ram Ballabha Bhagwant Vidyapith Intercollege, which provides education and jobs to the local citizenry. These gestures have borne the desired fruit up to a point, although political observers feel that he still lacks sufficient political stature to obtain a ticket and undertake a successful campaign for the legislative assembly.

The proliferation of political parties and rival factions or segments within the parties has become one of the most significant features of post-independence Indian politics. This phenomenon has quite naturally been reflected in the forms political behavior has assumed within educational institutions. It is rare today to find a single party or faction incontestably in control of the managing committee of an educational institution. Such control usually exists only in the early stages of the life of a managing committee. As time passes and institutions grow in size and complexity, factions form within the general body or outside political forces infiltrate it. When a school is small, it provides a maximally efficient political base which is easy to discipline and control. As the school's founder succeeds politically, and gets funds to expand his school, the problem of internal control grows more difficult until at some point, instead of sitting atop a monolithic "political organization" he finds himself maneuvering to maintain a dominant faction among the staff and administration of the school through which he can utilize the lion's share of its human and economic resources. But at the point where the school becomes big enough to contain multiple factions, it becomes *penetrable* by his political opponents. They can seize control of an opposing faction and start maneuvering to erode the dominance of the founder's faction in the hope of achieving enough power to deny him the use of the institution's resources.

In Faizabad district, Congress has been the dominant political party since independence, but it has been beset by the internal dissension characteristic of the Uttar Pradesh Congress party. The old cleavages of the state Congress party have always been reflected in Faizabad as in most

other districts in the province. Since 1952, the internecine rivalries have
tended to polarize the party into two camps. One group, more or less
rooted in the two eastern *tehsils* of the district, has been led by Jai Ram
Verma, Kurmi[16] by caste, and has been allied with the Kamlapati Tripathi[17] group at the state level. The other, concentrated in the two western
tehsils and the municipality of Faizabad-cum-Ayodhya was led by the former speaker of the Uttar Pradesh legislative assembly, the late Madan
Mohan Varma, Khatri[18] by caste, and has been allied at the state level with
the C. B. Gupta group.[19] These groups have been rivals for every political
position of consequence in Faizabad for the past fifteen years; their rivalry
has been bitter and ruthless and has not changed its basic complexion even
though Jai Ram Varma's group has become the local arm of the BKD
party led by Charan Singh. This rivalry runs through the general bodies
and managing committees of several educational institutions in Faizabad.

A perhaps classic instance of the involvement of an educational institution in a political rivalry can be found in the Baldeo Vidyapith Higher
Secondary School in the small town of Milkipur. Milkipur is the center of
the Milkipur legislative assembly constituency, situated near the western
border of Faizabad district. (See figure 2.) The Congress candidate there
in the 1967 election was Ram Lal Mishra (known as Ram Lal Bai), a
member of the Madan Mohan Varma-C. B. Gupta group and an energetic
founder of public institutions. Officially, therefore, it was the duty of all
Congress party members in Milkipur constituency to work for Ram Lal
Bai's candidacy.

The Congress party's position in private education in Milkipur is not as
strong as it could be. The constituency has two intercolleges and two
higher secondary schools, but one of each is controlled by the Communist
party. Of the remaining two, one is in the hands of the Gupta faction while

Figure 2. Faizabad district, legislative assembly constituencies.

the other, Baldeo Vidyapith, is allied with the opposing Jai Ram Varma faction. Its principal is Dhorey Ram Yadav,[20] an able educator with strong political ambitions of his own.

Because Jai Ram Varma was a member of the Congress party at the time of the 1967 general elections, he was bound by party discipline to support its candidates. On the surface, therefore, Jai Ram's supporters in Milkipur endorsed and worked for Ram Lal Bai. But covertly, Dhorey Ram Yadav worked against the official party candidate. In doing so, he revealed how in many instances factional loyalties, rooted in personalistic ethnic ties, take precedence over loyalty to the party.

The immediate train of events which led to Ram Lal Bai's loss of the political use of Baldeo Vidyapith was set in motion by the District Congress Committee (DCC) when it nominated principal Dhorey Ram as the candidate for the Milkipur legislative assembly seat for the 1967 general elections. This was possible because the Jai Ram Varma group enjoyed overwhelming dominance in the DCC and used that dominance to recommend an entire slate of its own members for all ten legislative assembly and parliamentary constituencies. This was essentially a bargaining device, employed in the full knowledge that at least half of these nominations would be overturned at the Provincial Congress Committee level where the C. B. Gupta faction, to which Madan Mohan Varma and his followers were allied locally, was predominant, or at the All-India Congress Committee level, where the most intractable factional impasses are ultimately resolved by men removed from and therefore less influenced by the subtleties of local political antipathies.[21]

Dhorey Ram's candidacy was one of the casualties in this higher level political bargaining. Ram Lal Bai, a C. B. Gupta faction member, had to be accepted by the Jai Ram group in exchange for the retention of their nominees in other constituencies more crucial to their general political survival in the district. However, principal Dhorey Ram simply formed a fifth column within the Milkipur Congress organization, using Baldeo Vidyapith as its base, and worked to defeat the official party candidate both because this was what Jai Ram Varma desired him to do and because the defeat of Ram Lal Bai in 1967 might pave the way for Dhorey Ram's candidacy in 1972.

In this instance the strategy failed. Ram Lal Bai won the election despite his inability to use Baldeo Vidyapith facilities and despite much other internal sabotage. His success was due partly to the influence he enjoys in the *Gandhi Ashram* movement, which provided him with alternative bases in the *Gandhi Ashram* stores that dot the district. This indicates that the capacity to utilize the resources of educational institutions or to neutralize another's capacity to use such resources does not in itself guarantee victory or defeat. The resources of educational institutions must be combined with a host of others to be effective. But they are valuable resources, and both

Dhorey Ram and Ram Lal Bai sought to put Baldeo Vidyapith to work for their political ambitions.

Another illustration of factional rivalry for control of educational institutions is the case of R.B.N. Intercollege situated at Goshainganj, a town in the eastern part of Faizabad district, where Jai Ram Varma's power is greatest. Jai Ram founded this institution many years ago with money obtained from supporters of the Backward Classes Movement in Kanpur. He is president of the managing committee, and one of his chief protégés, fellow-Kurmi Mahadeo Prasad Varma, a two-term MLA (member of the legislative assembly) until defeated in 1967, is principal. Three other Kurmis are members of the thirteen-member managing committee, as is Hira Singh, MLC (member of the legislative council),[22] Jai Ram's ally among the important Thakur (landowner caste) party of Faizabad district.

The town of Goshainganj is in the constituency of Maya but has the special value of being situated near the juncture of three legislative assembly constituencies: Maya, Jalalpur, and Bikapur. In the 1952, 1957, and 1962 general elections, Jalalpur constituency was contested by another important Faizabad area politician, Ram Narain Tripathi. A member of the old Congress Socialist party, he resigned from the Congress party in 1948 when the Socialists separated from the parent organization, and was awarded a place on the Socialist ticket from Jalalpur in 1952.[23] He won the election and won re-election in 1957. During his second term, Tripathi was elected deputy speaker of the Uttar Pradesh state legislature. By 1962, Tripathi had rejoined Congress and received that party's nomination for Jalalpur. But as a Congress party member, Tripathi now constituted a threat to Jai Ram Varma's control over the eastern half of the district and has dominance of the DCC. Tripathi was a threat not only because he was politically active in Jai Ram Varma's stronghold but also because his previous affiliation with the Socialist group made him the natural antagonist of Jai Ram Varma, who had been identified with the Gandhians.[24] Furthermore, Tripathi had political magnetism and could possibly have risen higher than Jai Ram Varma in the Congress organization once successfully ensconced in the legislative assembly. Finally, Tripathi was a highly independent man who would not readily subordinate himself to anyone else's interests.

For these reasons, Jai Ram Varma surreptitiously engineered Tripathi's defeat in the 1962 election by encouraging one of his fellow Kurmis, Ram Aseray Varma, to run on the Socialist (Lohia) ticket. This drew Kurmi votes away from Tripathi, votes that would have normally gone to a Congress candidate; and the loss of these votes was decisive, given the other forces that were at work in the constituency. The election results show the closeness of Jai Ram Varma's political calculations. Jagdamba Prasad Singh (Ind.), allied with the Thakur party, received 11,959 votes; Bhagwati Prasad Singh (PSP), a Lohia opponent, received 11,712; Ram Narain

Tripathi (Congress), allied with the ex-Congress socialist group, received 11,153; and Ram Aseray Varma (Socialist), a Jai Ram supporter pretending to be pro-Lohia, received 6,939.

As a defeated MLA who wished to regain his seat in the next election, Tripathi cast about for new means of sustaining his power and public image in the constituency for five years. He turned to educational entrepreneurship. R.B.N. Intercollege had been the key base from which Jai Ram Varma's organization had quietly aided Ram Aseray's "spoiling operation" against Tripathi in 1962. Consequently, Tripathi set himself the task of penetrating the institution. His technique was, and is, to turn sentiment against the principal, Mahadeo Prasad Varma. A Jai Ram Varma lieutenant and former legislator, Mahadeo Prasad Varma is aging. Tripathi's strategy has been to convince people in the general body and on the managing committee that the "old man" should retire. Tripathi has hoped to precipitate and capitalize on a crisis over this issue.

Similarly, he sought to infiltrate a college in which socialist influence dominated. Following the withdrawal of the Socialists from the Congress party in 1948, the Socialist leaders in Faizabad chose Jalalpur town as the site of their major venture in educational entrepreneurship. They founded the Acharya Narendra Deo Intercollege and began to develop organizational and philosophical roots in the southeastern quadrant of the district. Their basic strategy, which was to use the school as a base for gaining control of the town area board and then the town area board as a base for gaining control of the constituency, was sound. When Tripathi was defeated in 1962 he sought to perpetuate his influence through Acharya Narendra Deo Intercollege at Jalalpur. For a time his efforts there bore fruit.

When Jagdamba Prasad Singh, *taluqdar* and symbol of the old landowning order, defeated Tripathi in 1962, Tripathi moved a petition against him in the courts charging election malpractices. Tripathi's attempt to take control of Archarya Narendra Deo Intercollege was given an unexpected boost by the decision of Babu Sarvjit Lal Varma, one of the "old socialists" of Faizabad district, to choose professional over ideological interests by agreeing to be Jagdamba Prasad's legal counsel in the election malpractices suit. As founder of the Acharya Narendra Deo Intercollege, Sarvjit Lal had always dominated its affairs. Sarvjit Lal's legal defense of a man who in socialist eyes epitomized reaction and feudalism infuriated many of his supporters among the general body of Acharaya Narendra Deo Intercollege. Seizing advantage of this situation, Tripathi sought to exploit a clause in the school's constitution which declared that persons of public eminence can be made members of the general body without paying the Rs. 250 fee and following the other formalities stipulated for the attainment of such status. Tripathi appeared at a meeting of the general body at which the manager was to be chosen and claimed to be an "eminent person" entitled to membership and, therefore, to be a candidate for manager. Sarvjit Lal and his followers were able to block this maneuver. The following year Tripathi appeared again as a candidate, this time after a friend had paid the Rs. 250 in his behalf and had him made a regular member in the usual way. But the effort again failed. The third year, however, Tripathi achieved success when his supporters lulled Sarvjit Lal into believing his own candidacy was so secure that he need not attend the meeting. In Sarvjit Lal's absence, Tripathi was able to defeat him and become manager of the institution. Once its dominance was established, Tripathi's group secured the appointment of a principal who belonged to the Tripathi group. For a time Tripathi had a key base for sustaining his political image and conducting his campaign for the legislative assembly seat in 1967.

Sarvjit Lal, however, proved to be far from politically dead. He legally challenged the qualifications of several of Tripathi's followers in the general body, had them disqualified, and restored his majority on the managing committee. Tripathi fought back by endeavoring to have his disqualified followers reinstated. Sarvjit Lal tried to dismiss the principal installed during Tripathi's regime. However, this maneuver was overruled by the district inspector of schools. When Sarvjit Lal appealed the decision, it was upheld by the deputy director of education. The result is that the managing committee is once more under Sarvjit Lal's control while the principal remains loyal to Tripathi.

At Subhash Rashtriya Intercollege in another part of Jalalpur constituency, Tripathi's entrepreneurship has been a more unqualified success. He has been able to achieve a stable regime by maintaining strong support within its general body. Thus, his educational entrepreneurship has yielded him only one secure operational base in the district's network of secondary schools and junior colleges.

The Communists and Educational Entrepreneurship

The Communists in Faizabad district have also made extensive efforts to establish and gain control of secondary educational institutions. A driving force behind Communist educational entrepreneurship is Mata Prasad Singh, a lawyer. At one time or another Mata Prasad has stood for almost every elective office in the district as an overt or covert candidate of the Communist Party of India. Deciding long ago that the propagation of Communism required points of entry into the minds of the young, he embarked upon an extensive program of founding private secondary institutions, called *Vidya Mandirs* (Temples of Wisdom), throughout the district. As these institutions have flourished, they have provided the Communist movement in Faizabad with numerous organizational focuses replete with platoons of students and teachers available for canvassing during elections.

Not all Communist-controlled institutions are equally effective as political instruments, but in two constituencies, Maya and Milkipur (both in the western half of the district), there does appear to be some measure of correlation between Communist strength and their operation of higher secondary schools and intercolleges.

In Maya, there has been a steady growth of Communist voting strength since the first general election, culminating in 1967 in the first Communist victory ever in Faizabad district in a legislative assembly election. The Communist candidate in 1957 received 40 percent as many votes as the winner (Congress); in 1962, the Communist candidate received 79 percent as many votes as the winner (Congress); and in 1967, the Communist candidate, Rajbali Yadav, defeated the Congress candidate by more than 8,000 votes. In Milkipur, the Communists have not done as spectacularly, but their candidates have consistently received 40 percent as many votes as the winning candidates. (There was every possibility that the Communists would have done far better in Milkipur in 1967 had their leaders there not been implicated in an ugly murder case which diminished their public image and resulted in the imprisonment of some of their key field workers.)

In Maya and Milkipur together there are three politically active Communist institutions — two of them *Vidya Mandirs*. The third, Indrabali Adarsh Higher Secondary School, is located in Maya, in the strategic town of Goshainganj, site of Jai Ram Varma's institution, the R.B.N. Intercollege. The head of the school's managing committee is Shambhoo Narain Singh, one of Faizabad's original Communists and the Communist candidate for MLA in 1962, when he gained 79 percent as many votes as the winning Congress party candidate. The principal is R. D. Tiwari, who is also principal of the two institutions under Communist control in Milkipur. This degree of operational integration among several schools appears to be a hallmark of Communist organization. No other political group practices it.

The two private institutions in Milkipur where the Communists have a majority on the managing committees are the Deo Vidyalaya Intercollege at Tarauli and the Vidya Mandir Higher Secondary School in Milkipur proper. The manager of the latter school is Bindhyachal Singh, the Communist candidate for MLA in 1967. Mata Prasad Singh and a number of Communist notables from the Milkipur area are also on the managing committee. The Deo Vidyalaya is controlled by Mata Prasad Singh, and both institutions, as we noted, have the same principal, R. D. Tiwari.

Mata Prasad Singh also controls the M.L.M.L. Vidya Mandir Higher Secondary School in Faizabad city, which was helpful to Mata Prasad in 1957 when he stood for MLA from the city constituency and in 1967 when the constituency was a component of the parliamentary constituency which Mata Prasad contested. Near Mata Prasad's ancestral home (in Jalalpur constituency) is the M.L.V. Higher Secondary School. He also has considerable influence here, influence which came in handy in 1967 when the Communists achieved a great coup by inducing a former PSP (Praja Socialist Party) leader there, Bhagwati Prasad Singh, to join the Communist party and run for MLA on its ticket.

The Faizabad general constituency in which Mata Prasad Singh ran for parliament in 1967 includes the five legislative assembly constituencies comprising the western half of the district. It is interesting to compare his performance in each. He compiled his largest vote in Maya, where Rajbali Yadav, the Communist candidate for MLA, won and where the Indrabali Adarsh Higher Secondary School is located. Mata Prasad's second highest total came from Ayodhya constituency, containing the city of Faizabad, where he controlled one school, the M.L.M.L. Vidya Mandir Higher Secondary School, and where he was the beneficiary of much Muslim support.[25] His third greatest total was in Bikapur, a constituency south of the city, which is heavily populated by thakurs, ex-taluqdars, and ex-zamindars. Here Mata Prasad had no educational institutions under his wing, but he is a thakur and the thakurs of the constituency generally tend to oppose Congress unless one of their own is on the Congress ticket. Mata Prasad's fourth highest total was in Milkipur, where he had control of two private institutions, the Deo Vidyalaya Intercollege and the Vidya Mandir Higher Secondary School. Most significant about Mata Prasad's performance in Milkipur is that he recorded 2,000 votes more than Bindhyachal Singh, the Communist's MLA candidate, who was more directly associated in the public's mind with the local scandal surrounding the party. Mata Prasad's poorest performance was in Sohowal, where, as in Bikapur (but without the compensating factors), he had no influence in educational institutions.

From the evidence presently at hand we cannot establish a certain correlation between Mata Prasad's educational entrepreneurship and his electoral performance. Bikapur constituency clearly shows that variables of many kinds can and do operate and that controlling the managing committees of educational institutions may have little bearing on an election's outcome. Nevertheless, the evidence suggests that sometimes there is a relationship between the two. Perhaps the number of managing committees under a politician's control is less significant than the quality of political organization that managers and principals are able to achieve in behalf of their patron. The two Communist institutions in Milkipur and the one in Maya are effectively organized for political support activities and seem to have an impact on the outcome of elections. The M.L.M.L. Vidya Mandir Higher Secondary School in Faizabad city, on the other hand, is much less skillfully organized and consequently plays a far weaker role in the political life of Ayodhya constituency. More research is clearly called for in this matter.

Political Allegiances Among Managing Committees

Table 26 contains a summary of the pattern of political control of managing committees in Faizabad by parliamentary and legislative assembly constituencies. Of the forty-four private institutions with managing committees in the district, only two are definitely not identified with any po-

Table 26. Political control in the higher secondary schools and intercolleges of Faizabad district, differentiated by legislative assembly and parliamentary constituencies.

Constituencies	Party of sitting member	Con[a]		CPI/CPM[b]		Socialist		Jan Sn[c]	Thakur	Muslim	Indep.	None or unknown
		MMV[d]	JRV[e]	MPS[f]	Other	PSP[g]	SSP[h]		APS[i]			
Faizabad parliamentary												
Legislative assembly seat	(Con)											
Maya	CPI	–	1	–	1	–	–	–	1	–	–	–
Ayodhya	JS	5	–	1	–	–	–	–	–	1	3	1
Bikapur	Con (jrv)	–	1	–	–	–	–	–	3	–	–	–
Milkipur	Con (mmv)	1	1	2	–	–	–	–	–	–	–	–
Sohowal	Con (mmv)	1	1	–	–	–	–	–	–	–	–	–
Total		7	4	3	1	–	–	–	4	1	3	1
Akbarpur (SC) parliamentary												
Legislative assembly seat	(RPI)[j]											
Jehangirganj	SSP	1	1	–	–	1	–	–	–	–	–	1
Kateri	Con (jrv)[k]	1	–	1	–	1	–	–	–	–	–	–
Jalalpur	Ind[l]	1	1[m]	–	–	1	–	–	–	–	–	–
Akbarpur	Con (jrv)	1	2	–	–	–	–	–	–	1	–	–
Tanda	Con (jrv)	–	2	–	–	–	–	1	1	1	–	1
Total		4	6	1	–	3	–	1	1	2	–	2
Grand total		11	10	4	1	3	–	1	5	3	3	3

[a] Con—Congress party.
[b] CPI—Communist Party of India (Moscow wing), CPM—Communist Party of India, Marxist (Peking wing).
[c] Jan Sn—Jan Sangh (also abbreviated JS).
[d] MMV—Madan Mohan Varma/C. B. Gupta faction.
[e] JRV—Jai Ram Varma/Kamla Tripathi faction.
[f] MPS—Mata Prasad Singh.
[g] PSP—Praja Socialist Party.
[h] SSP—Samyukt Socialist Party.
[i] APS—Avadesh Pratap Singh.
[j] RPI—Republican Party of India.
[k] Ram Narain Tripathi, who was technically in the Jai Ram Varma faction of the Congress party.
[l] Raja of Tighra, who joined the C. B. Gupta faction.
[m] This is Subhash Rashtriya Intercollege, which is controlled by Ram Narain Tripathi and therefore loyal to Jai Ram Varma only to the extent Ram Narain is.

litical group. One other may not be, but the data do not permit a positive judgment about it. The remaining forty-one managing committees are politicized and attempt to utilize the institutions they control to support a specific political philosophy, party, or faction. More than half (twenty-one) of the politicized managing committees are dominated by the Congress party, a legacy of its long organizational history reaching back to the twenties. But it is significant, on the other hand, that despite that long history nearly half of the politicized institutions are under the control of other parties and groups. In addition, because of the dissension within Congress, the allegiance of the Congress-oriented managing committees is divided virtually equally between the two rival factions in the party.

There is a distinct relationship between areas of the district where a party or faction enjoys general political predominance and the ability to dominate the managing committees of private secondary institutions. The Kamlapati Tripathi-Jai Ram Varma faction of Congress controls six of ten Congress-dominated managing committees in the Akbarpur Scheduled Caste parliamentary constituency embracing the eastern half of Faizabad district, where that group has always been dominant. The C. B. Gupta-Madan Mohan Varma group, on the other hand, controls seven of eleven Congress-dominated managing committees in the Faizabad general parliamentary constituency, which lies in the western half of the district, where they have always been uppermost organizationally. The Communists have power over managing committees in legislative assembly constituencies where they have shown the greatest strength at the polls and have a history of organizational success. The socialist parties and factions have always shown their greatest vitality in the Jalalpur, Kateri, and Akbarpur constituencies lying in the southeast corner of Faizabad but rarely elsewhere in the district.

The pattern for the so-called Thakur party, which table 26 indicates has control of five managing committees, is the same. Even though they do not really comprise an official party, the ex-*zamindars* and taluqdars of Faizabad, who are mainly of the Rajput caste, have formed an interest group which seeks as much political and economic advantage for the thakurs and their supporters as can be garnered by bargaining and competing with the other political groups in the district. Three of the five managing committees in thakur hands are in Bikapur legislative assembly constituency, which is the political base of Avadhesh Pratap Singh, the leader of this political bloc. He is the ex-raja of a former *taluqa* (landed estate) called Khajurahat, which had been a major force in the affairs of the area now embraced by Bikapur constituency. In the first two general elections, Raja Singh ran for the provincial assembly from Bikapur and won in the face of determined Congress opposition. When in the third general election Congress finally succeeded in besting him (by casting a rival ex-raja from the same area against him), Raja Singh, through alliance with the Gupta-Varma faction of Congress, was elected president (*adhyaksha*) of the Faizabad district board (*zila parishad*) and thus gained control of one of the most lucrative patronage structures in the district.

Although, for the time being, Raja Avadesh Pratap's political activities are largely focused outside Bikapur, the constituency where his traditional ties are strongest, he continues to work hard maintaining his ties there. He does everything possible to preserve his control of two of the four managing committees running private institutions near his ancestral *taluqa* because he considers the area the locus of his strength in the district, which he can fall back upon whenever his political fortunes ebb elsewhere. Essentially, this is the logic governing the organizational thinking of all political groups in Faizabad and is revealed in the distribution of their power over educational institutions.

An important question which these observations raise, however, is the causal relationship between control of managing committees and political power. Does such control facilitate political success or does political success facilitate control of managing committees?

It is impossible at the present time to provide a final answer to this question because enough studies are not available. However, it seems likely that control of managing committees is both a factor in political success and a measure of it. The political use of educational institutions is affected by a combination of local conditions and the specific talents and predilections of local political leaders. In Jalalpur constituency, for example, the socialists' strategy involved the use of the Acharya Narendra Deo Intercollege as the focal point of a projected organizational effort designed to culminate in control of an entire constituency. Evidently the causal role of politicized managing committees is different, if not more important, for the Jalalpur socialists than it was for the Congress party in Milkipur constituency during the last election, where Ram Lal Bai, with alternative political resources at his command, won decisively. The fact that all private educational institutions but one were in the hands of his political rivals was compensated for by his ability to use the *Gandhi Ashram* depots for political purposes.

Despite difficulty in specifying the precise value of controlling managing committees, we can accept the empirical findings of this study as evidence that local politicians themselves regard such control as a political resource that vitally affects political fortunes. Every managing committee in Faizabad district capable of being politicized has been seized by some group, faction, or party. Control of managing committees is sufficiently prized that attempts are constantly being made by political rivals to seize such control.

The Prospect for Educational Goals

In the private higher secondary schools and intercolleges of Faizabad district the managing committee is the ideal context for the fusion of educational entrepreneurship and political ambition. Where government is more directly involved in the management of educational institutions, the convergence of politics and education occurs but to a lesser degree as well as in a different manner. The private managing committee is autonomous, while the control of the department of education is indirect and largely, it would appear, perfunctory. In this kind of setting, the interests of the professional educator can be subordinated to the interests of the professional politician. This need not be the case, and sometimes is not; nor was it as much the case before independence as afterward. The motives for creating the managing-committee approach were noble ones — to encourage nonofficial groups to invest in the educational process, and to create educational institutions where otherwise there would be none. But the scramble for differential access to scarce resources through the instrumentalities of politics has become such a pervasive impulse that all social structures which can serve this impulse have been mobilized to do so. Educational institutions are only part of a whole range of institutions (cooperative banks, charitable trusts, the Arya Samaj) which have been coopted by the politically ambitious in search of ways of providing patronage and special advantages to their clienteles. The present situation is a bane to the men in Indian education who see their responsibility to be mainly educational. These men often find that managing committees assess their value to the educational institution in inverse ratio to the zeal they display as educators.

Brij Nandan Prasad, for example, found this to be true when he was principal of S.S.V. Intercollege of Faizabad. Early in his career as a teacher, Prasad became the protégé of an old landlord politician whose support enabled him to acquire considerable prestige in district education and to become closely identified with the C. B. Gupta-Madan Mohan Varma faction of Congress in Faizabad. The post of principal of S.S.V. Intercollege was made possible by Madam Mohan Varma, who was president of the school's managing committee. Temperamentally, Brij Nandan Prasad is not a politician. Although he has associated with politicians and helped them in their elections, his real interest lies in utilizing their favor to secure support for his educational schemes. He believes, for example, that insufficient emphasis is placed in India on the leisure-time activities of youth. Consequently, for years he endeavored to convince his political sponsors in Faizabad that they should enable him to found a youth center. But persuasion failed because the politicians were primarily interested in the political uses of the educational institutions which they controlled.

S.S.V. Intercollege is a Khatri-dominated institution which long served the political interests of Madan Mohan Varma. From Madan Mohan Varma's point of view, Prasad's political affinities made him a highly desirable appointee to the school's principalship. But Prasad, primarily concerned about educational goals and processes, eventually found conditions at S.S.V. Intercollege so bad that he accepted a position as princi-

pal of the Kayastha Pathshala Intercollege at Allahabad, where he was free
to give first priority to educational purposes.

In one sense, the seeds of Prasad's departure from S.S.V Intercollege
were inadvertently sown by the U.S. government. In 1957–58, Prasad received a Fulbright teacher's grant for six months' study and observation
of the American secondary school system. When he returned to his job as
principal in Faizabad, he was brimming with ideas for improving the curriculum and standards of teaching at S.S.V. These efforts very quickly
brought him into conflict with both his teaching staff and managing committee. The teachers accused him of being a martinet because he wanted
to reform the institution in the light of standards which he saw being maintained in the United States. The teachers through their representatives and
contacts took their complaints to the managing committee.

Prasad also collided with a member of the committee who was in charge
of acquiring supplies for the school and whom he believed to be corrupt.
This was the confrontation that precipitated his decision to leave. The allegedly corrupt committee member was a close associate of one of Madan
Mohan Varma's chief political lieutenants. When Prasad encountered opposition to his desire that the member be removed, he put his own authority in the institution on the line. Either he or the corrupt member of the
committee must go. Madan Mohan Varma, though one of the more enlightened men in Faizabad politics, was above all a politician fighting for
his survival against powerful enemies. Faced with a choice between a
capable professional educator or a trusted political lieutenant, Madan
Mohan chose to dispense with the former. He allowed Brij Nandan Prasad
to resign and take up his new position in Allahabad.

The managing committee of the Kayastha Pathshala Intercollege is dominated by Kayasthas. The president is a Kayastha, as are forty-eight of the
fifty-five faculty members. In this sense, the institution is more dominated
by a single community than is the Khatri S.S.V. Intercollege of Faizabad.
Yet when Brij Nandan Prasad transferred his administrative talents to this
institution, no efforts were made to subordinate his educational efforts to
community or political interests. He says he found conditions at Kayastha
Pathshala slack. Teachers and staff were doing their jobs lackadaisically,
not attending classes on time and not fulfilling other duties in a diligent
manner. When Prasad imposed discipline, some members of his teaching
staff went to the manager and complained against him just as some at
S.S.V. had done. In this instance the manager brusquely turned the delegation away with the remark, "If he is guilty of these things then he is
doing the job that we hired him to do." Thus, Prasad had found an educational institution where the talents of the professional educator mattered
more than the talents of the professional politician.

Prasad's experience suggests that the line between educational and political entrepreneurship is not firm and absolute, but a matter of degree
depending on varying conditions of management. The line can be deter-

mined only by examining decisions actually made by the managing committees when the chips are down. What do they defend and what do they reject, in the last analysis?

Concluding Observations

To reduce political influence in private educational institutions to a "benign" level, as Susanne Rudolph has put it, it would be necessary to reform the manner in which general bodies are selected and can be manipulated. This may not prove so easy to achieve or so unmixed a blessing as it at first might seem, however. The present system of selecting and manipulating managing committees is an important source of educational motivation. As things stand today, the noneducated layman and the politician not identified with the missionary dedication of the professional educator have reasons for turning their organizational talents to the founding or running of educational institutions.

These reasons include mobility aspirations and demand for access to scarce resources. In this sense Faizabad is India writ large. It is subdivided into a multitude of social compartments whose boundaries have been determined by the rules of endogamy, by the conceptions of hierarchy and caste inherent in the Hindu social order, and by allegiance to the country's various religions. The promulgation of a democratic constitution following independence widened the scope of popular political participation. In sociological terms this meant that the multitude of social compartments whose traditional meanings had arisen from essentially religious considerations became the focuses of political organization. The "ethnic" characteristics of the people in these compartments came progressively to the fore, while their "ritual" or orthodox characteristics became more and more secondary or residual. The castes (and other endogamous communities), in other words, have emerged as frameworks for the pursuit of group interests through political action.

Educational development has, on the one hand, helped to promote the "ethnicization" and politicization of the caste system and its structural extensions and, on the other, become one of the chief preoccupations of ethnicized groupings acting in the domain of politics. Educational development has "brought with it a movement towards a more literate population, open to new sources of influence and information."[26] People have learned what there is to ask for and how to ask for it (or *demand* it). The asking has come from groups which politicization has activated and converted into interest groups, each one of which makes demands conditioned by its particular vantage on the competitive process. Thus the demand has not been for education in the general and abstract sense, but education "for us," that is, educational institutions accessible to the children of each ethnicized social compartment and, wherever possible, under the administrative control of its own leaders.[27] One meaning of ethnicized education is that so long as group mobility through political representation remains a central preoccupation in India, educational institutions and processes (as one of the chief instrumentalities of social mobility) can hardly be kept insulated from political intervention. The temptation for a politician to divert educational resources to his constituents (who almost always include at least one ethnic community in which he has a powerful political base) in a manner which assures him a measure of political profit is irresistible, just as is the inclination of any segment of the public to support a politician whose educational entrepreneurship appears to offer them a chance to gain ground in the fierce competition for status and its economic rewards. As Joseph Gusfield puts it: "The school functions not only as a homogenizer. It also serves to intensify political and group struggles." [28]

The relationship between politics and education in Faizabad district shows how accurately Gusfield has perceived the situation. But it also shows that general discussions of Indian education, however excellent, often have not perceived the full extent to which instrumental attitudes toward education and the social structures in which it is propagated have taken hold of both the public and the politicians alike. An investigation of what the system of education does must explore dimensions of its operation which range far afield from what the more pedantic observer would care to mean by "education."

8 / Caste and Community in the Private and Public Education of Mysore State

T. N. Madan / B. G. Halbar

The preeminence of education as an instrument of modernization is widely assumed in the contemporary literature on the so-called traditional societies or developing nations. Thus, we are advised that, "the progress of modernization will . . . be directly related to the pace of educational advance and the one sure way to modernize quickly is to spread education, to produce educated and skilled citizens and train an adequate and competent intelligentsia." [1]

Statements like the foregoing are uncritical, and therefore misleading, in their excessive faith in the modernizing power of the content of education; they fail to pay sufficient attention to the organizational aspects of educational institutions and to the wider social and political environment. Anderson rightly complains "that over much of the world we are witnessing a modernization *of* education that is not matched by an equal modernization *by* education." [2]

The claims made for education, therefore, have to be qualified. The effectiveness of education varies according to the degree of underdevelopment. The introduction of literacy and inauguration of schools in the so-called nonliterate folk societies is a revolutionary turning (or starting) point in their modernization. These societies are not totally lacking in extradomestic institutions for socialization, but such institutions (for example, the dormitory among some Indian tribes) [3] are never exclusively educational.

The condition of peasant societies is essentially different from that of nonliterate societies in that the former have a tradition of literacy and formal instruction. [4] Although this tradition may generally make bigger achievements possible, it may also impede the modernizing role of education in certain cases. Conflicts may develop between the traditional and the modern content of education, and, more importantly, between modern education and traditional social structure.

The educational system interacts with the social and political systems and does not enjoy such autonomy within society that its modernizing influence can operate without check or hindrance. The goals of the edu-

Thanks are hereby expressed to the National Council of Educational Research and Training, New Delhi, for financial assistance between February 1965 and April 1966 to prepare a report ("Caste and Educational Institutions in Mysore State," 215 pp., 1966); to Karnatak University, Dharwar, for sponsoring the research; and to Shri D. C. Pavate, then the vice-chancellor of the University, for his keen interest in the project. P. C. Verma helped condense detailed tables.

cational system, and the policies and decisions regarding their implementation, emanate at least partly from the social and political systems. What
is more, traditional social structures may not prove to be wholly suitable
environments for modern education. The policy of putting new wine in old
bottles may generally help in overcoming resistance to innovations, but
sometimes only new bottles are good enough for new wine. Thus, although
the content of traditional education and old methods of teaching may be
easily displaced by new curricula and trained teachers (particularly in
state-controlled institutions), the narrow social base of privately managed
institutions and the particularistic[5] policies of their sponsors pose special
problems. Such institutions often discriminate in student admissions, staff
recruitment, and distribution of various types of patronage and facilities,
and although they do adopt modern curricula, the environment they create
may not be modern. If educational institutions fail to bring together in a
common setting the classes, castes and religious communities of neighbor-
hoods or localities, they do not help promote social and national integration. The sociocultural environment which spawns such institutions thus
acquires crucial importance in the success of educational programs.

This chapter discusses the role which caste and communal loyalties play
in the private educational institutions of the state of Mysore. More specifically, it shows that the constraints of traditional social structure, and
the attitudes and values associated with it, limit the role of educational
institutions as agents of modernization and as supporters of universalistic
as against particularistic (communal, caste, or sectarian) values.

The content of education (subjects, curricula, methods of teaching) is
not discussed in this chapter. The reasonable assumption, supported by
some general inquiries of our own, is that the content is modern. What we
are concerned with is the social composition of private educational societies
and of the institutions managed by them. In this context a comparison
between private and public educational institutions will be instructive because the latter, being under the control of the state or local authorities,
may be expected to be more demographically representative in their social
composition than those that are privately managed.

Historical Background

India has had a long and continuous tradition of literacy and of formal
educational instruction in the home of the teacher (Brahman, Buddhist,
or Muslim) or in institutions supported by the king or private bodies like
monasteries.[6] During the British period of Indian history, the variety and
number of public and private educational institutions increased considerably.

Education was included among the duties of the chaplains of the East
India Company as early as 1698, and the first "charity school" (modeled
on similar English schools) was founded in 1715 at Madras. These schools,

however, did not cater to the needs of Indian children. Education of the latter in the new schools began only with the arrival of European missionaries sent out specially for this purpose early in the eighteenth century. The company declared its interest in the education of the "natives" in the First Education Despatch of 1814. But it "proposed to do little beyond (i) leaving the learned natives of India to their old-time methods of instruction and encouraging them in their literary pursuits and (ii) encouraging its own officers to study Sanskrit with a view to improving the efficiency of its administration." [7]

The Despatch granted recognition and gave a fillip to private educational institutions. Between the first Despatch in 1814 and the second Despatch in 1854, three types of private educational institutions flourished in the country: those run by missionaries, by officials of the Company in their individual capacity or nonofficial Englishmen resident in India, and by Indians themselves. The last category included traditional as well as modern institutions.[8]

The second Despatch (also known as Wood's Despatch) "laid the foundations on which Indian education has since been built." [9] Proclaiming "that no subject could have a stronger claim to their attention than that of education," the directors of the Company recommended "that indigenous schools should, by wise encouragement . . . be made capable of imparting correct elementary knowledge to the great mass of the people," and "that in consideration of the impossibility of Government alone doing all that must be done to provide adequately for the education of the people of India they resolved to adopt, in India, the system of grant-in-aid . . . , the system being based on an entire abstinence from interference with the religious instruction conveyed in the school assisted; that no government colleges or schools should, therefore, be founded in future in any district which had a sufficient number of institutions capable, with Government grant, of supplying the local demand for education; and that they looked forward to the time when any general system of education entirely provided by Government might be discontinued with the gradual advance of the system of grant-in-aid and when many of the existing Government institutions, especially those of the higher order, might be safely closed or transferred to the management of local bodies under the control of, or aided by, the State." [10]

The "withdrawal" of the state from the field of mass education was motivated partly by financial stringency[11] and partly by the policy of patronizing missionary enterprise. Between 1854 and 1902, however, neither the missionaries nor the government expanded their institutions to any notable degree. In consequence, private Indian enterprise became the most important force in meeting the growing demand for education. "In 1854, the modern educational institutions conducted by Indians were so few that *private enterprise* really meant *missionary enterprise*. But as early as 1882, the position was considerably changed," (italics in the original) with

56,018 institutions (primary, secondary, and collegiate) run by Indians as against 2,635 by non-Indians.[12]

In the closing years of the century, private enterprise in the field of education became a prominent part of various social and religious reform movements, and in the twentieth century, of the national movement.

Table 27. Nongovernmental educational institutions as a percentage of all educational institutions in India (1960–61) (by state and by stage or sector).

State	Percentage	Stage or sector	Percentage
Andhra Pradesh	8.0	Preprimary	70.9
Assam	19.1	Lower primary	22.2
Bihar	74.0	Higher primary	27.1
Gujarat	36.0	Secondary	69.2
Jammu and Kashmir	1.7	Vocational schools	57.4
Kerala	61.6	Special schools	79.0
Madhya Pradesh	4.6	Institutions for higher general education (B.A., B.Sc., B.Comm. Colleges)	78.8
Madras	33.0	Colleges for professional education (engineering, medicine, law, etc.)	49.8
Maharashtra	48.0	Colleges for special education	74.9
Mysore	34.3		
Orissa	65.3		
Punjab	7.4		
Rajasthan	3.5		
Uttar Pradesh	14.5		
West Bengal	36.3		
Total for India	33.2	Total for all sectors	33.2

Source: Government of India, Ministry of Education, Report of the Education Commission, 1964–1966 (New Delhi, 1966), p. 446.

Table 27 suggests a great variation among states in the growth of private education, depending on particular state histories. In some states under the control of the princes, Jammu and Kashmir, Rajasthan, and the large areas of Madhya Pradesh that were princely, there was very little private effort of the sort which government aid and encouragement produced in many states under direct British control. On the other hand, the British India-princely India distinction was not decisive. The strong Christian influence in Travancore and Cochin princely states produced a large number of private institutions. Also, the states under direct British control too differed among themselves, their governments being by no means uniform either in respect to policy or administrative vigor. Finally, the percentages of nongovernmental educational institutions vary depending on idiosyncracies of local history.

Table 27 also shows that state enterprise has been more marked in primary education than in higher sectors. In the postindependence period, a policy of greater state investment, notably in primary education but also in other sectors, has led to a decline in private enterprise growth rates.[13] The policy in Mysore, however, may run counter to this national trend in view of the interest in that state in pressing private education.

Scope

The data on which this chapter is based pertain to three districts in Mysore state — Dharwar and Belgaum in the north and Mysore in the south. The former two districts were transferred to the new state of Mysore following the reorganization of the states of the Indian Union in 1956, while the third district, Mysore, was inherited from the princely state of that name. We studied these districts because, among other reasons,[14] we hoped thus to cover both the areas of active private enterprise in education (represented by the districts transferred to Mysore from Bombay and Madras) and the areas in which government and local authority institutions predominate (as in the areas formerly falling within the princely states of Hyderabad, Mysore, and Coorg).

Under private enterprise we include organizations like educational co-operative societies with limited liability, educational trusts registered under the Public Trusts Act, and educational societies registered under the Societies Act. In the residual category of local authority institutions we have grouped together schools managed by local self-governing agencies such as district school boards, municipal school boards, *taluka* (subdivision) development boards, and *panchayats* (village self-government). For the sake of convenience, schools managed by universities also have been included in this category.

All the recognized major sectors of education (general, professional, and technical) at all levels but the postgraduate[15] (that is, nursery, primary, secondary, and collegiate) were studied. Also included in the study were five special institutions (Shankarcharya Sanskrit Pathshala of Dharwar, Tontadarya Sanskrit Pathshala of Gadag, Maharaja's Sanskrit College of Mysore, Shivarathreshwara Gurukula of Mysore, and the United Theological College of Bangalore) that provide literary and religious instruction to preserve the cultural traditions of various communities. Moreover, we made intensive inquiries into the history and present educational activities of three prominent private educational societies: the Karnatak Liberal Education Society of Belgaum and the Jagadguru Shivarathreshwar Mahavidyapeeth of Mysore (both managed by Lingayats)[16] and the Janata Shikshana Samiti of Dharwar (managed by Brahmans). We also inquired into the educational programs of the Roman Catholic Diocese of Belgaum and the Anjuman-e-Islam of Hubli.

Data were collected [17] from 210 educational institutions. Table 28 gives the district, level of education, and type of management of these institutions.

Table 28. Distribution of institutions studied in Mysore state, by management, district, and level, 1965–66.

Level	Government management				Local authority management			Private management				Total
	DWa	BMb	MYc	Total	DWa	MYb	Total	DWa	BMb	MYc	Total	
	(District)				(District)			(District)				
Primary	3	–	–	3	–	–	–	13	–	9	22	25
Secondary	6	–	5	11	9	16	25	81	1	24	106	142
Collegiate	5	1	4	10	3	2	5	10	8	10	28	43
Total	14	1	9	24	12	18	30	104	9	43	156	210

a Dharwar district.
b Belgaum district.
c Mysore district.

The guiding principle in deciding the number of institutions to study was the relative importance of private enterprise, which was found to increase progressively from the primary to the collegiate levels and also to predominate at the preprimary (nursery) level. (For details see the following section.) Therefore, only 17 percent of the preprimary and less than 1 percent of the primary schools were chosen for study from the districts of Dharwar and Mysore. For secondary schools, however, the percentage chosen was 77 in Dharwar and 50 in Mysore. At the collegiate level, all the institutions in Dharwar, 90 percent of those in Belgaum, and 80 percent of those in Mysore were studied. The choice of institutions was the outcome of several considerations, of which cooperation of the respondents and our own convenience were probably the most decisive.

Private Enterprise and State Policy

The limitation of space precludes us from going into the history of private educational institutions in the areas which now comprise the state of Mysore or into the history of educational policy in the former states or provinces.[18] As table 29 suggests, Mysore is following a policy of encouragement of private enterprise in education.

Of the 156 private educational institutions studied, 23 were founded over seven decades of the 19th century (1830–1899), and another 39 over the four decades preceding World War II, but by far the largest proportion, 70 percent, have been founded in the two and a half decades since 1940.

The data on degree colleges are a good index of the increasing importance of educational societies. Of the sixteen (out of twenty) colleges studied in Mysore, four are government and two local authority colleges, while ten are privately managed. Four of these ten colleges were started after 1960, while no colleges have been started since that date in the other two sectors. In Belgaum, of the nine (out of ten) colleges studied, eight are privately managed, and two of the latter were started after 1960.

The data from Dharwar are particularly instructive, first, because we covered all the colleges in our study, and second, because the government

Table 29. Educational institutions established in Mysore state, by decade.

Decade	Government management						Local authority management				Private management						Total
	Dharwar		Belgaum	Mysore			Dharwar		Mysore		Dharwar		Belgaum		Mysore		
	P/S[a]	C[b]	C[b]	P/S[a]	C[b]		P/S[a]	C[b]	P/S[a]	C[b]	P/S[a]	C[b]	P/S[a]	C[b]	P/S[a]	C[b]	
1830–1899 (seven decades)	5	–	–	–	1		3	–	–	1	8	–	–	–	5	–	23
1900–1939 (four decades)	–	1	1	2	1		5	–	–	1	17	–	–	3	6	2	39
1940–1949	–	2	–	–	2		–	–	9	–	15	3	1	1	6	4	41
1950–1959	4	2	–	2	2		1	–	3	–	27	4	–	2	7	–	54
1960–1965 (half decade)	–	1	–	1	–		–	2	4	–	27	3	–	2	9	4	53
Total	9	6	1	5	4		9	2	16	2	94	10	1	8	33	10	210

Source: Government of Mysore, *Report of the Educational Survey in Mysore State, 1958*, pt. 1 (Bangalore, 1961); Government of Mysore, *Handbook on Education, 1964–65* (Bangalore, 1965).

[a] Primary/secondary schools.
[b] Collegiate institutions.

policy of encouragement of private enterprise in the Dharwar and Belgaum districts before the reorganization of states has been adopted by the new state of Mysore throughout its territories. There are eighteen colleges in the district, and of these ten are privately managed, five are run by the government, and three by local authorities. More significant is the distribution of the founding dates of these institutions. The first college in the district was the Karnatak College in Dharwar town. It was started in 1917 by the Bombay government in response to public demand, and came under the administration of the Mysore government in 1956 following the reorganization of states. The Mysore government in turn handed it over to the Karnatak University in 1958 to be run as a "model institution." The College is a famous institution. Among its distinguished alumni are P. B. Gajendragadkar, former chief justice of India, and D. C. Pavate, governor of Punjab and former vice-chancellor of Karnatak University. In the decade 1940–1949, three private and two government colleges were started, and in the following decade, four private and two government colleges were begun. Between 1960 and 1965, one government, two local authority, and three private colleges were started.

Private and local authority institutions anywhere in India would find it difficult to survive without government financial support. In India, government funds account for 48.2 percent of the finances of privately managed schools.[19] The dependence of private institutions on the state is particularly heavy in Mysore, where no tuition fees may be charged, under government orders, for preprimary, primary, and (since 1966) secondary school students. Public donations, contributions from members of educational societies, and student fees do not meet the financial requirements of these institutions in full. Support of the government thus becomes crucial.

The proportion of the total income of private institutions coming from government grants will, therefore, provide a significant clue to state policy. In Mysore, this proportion is high, reflecting the policy of encouragement of private enterprise. Table 30 gives the percentage share of government grants and student fees in 1964–65 in the total income of the 156 institutions studied. The balance of the income accrued from other sources; notably, bank deposits, securities, and donations. Note that the government proportion is lowest for colleges and highest for secondary schools.[20]

Grants-in-aid have been employed by the various Congress party ministries of the state of Mysore to encourage educational societies. In order to maintain uniformity in the standards of education and to prevent maladministration and misuse of funds, the government has exercised supervision and control over such institutions by establishing criteria for "recognition" of an institution as eligible for grants-in-aid. Periodic inspection has been employed as a means of determining whether recognition and the grants-in-aid are to be continued or withdrawn. Our inquiries revealed several instances where recognition was refused or withdrawn. Recognition of the Andhra primary school of Hubli was withdrawn by the deputy di-

Table 30. Government grants and student fees as percentage of total income in 156 private institutions in Mysore state, 1964–65.

Level	Belgaum district			Dharwar district			Mysore district		
	Government grants	Student fees	Total	Government grants	Student fees	Total	Government grants	Student fees	Total
Preprimary[a]	–[b]	–[b]	–[b]	17.38	42.72	60.1	15.86	23.04	38.90
Primary[c]	–[b]	–[b]	–[b]	28.73	33.17	61.9	39.63	9.47	49.10
Secondary[d]	0	13.7	13.7	60.63	22.97	83.6	61.00	17.03	78.03
Collegiate[e]	7.8	67.2	75.0	14.90	65.40	80.3	8.80	44.20	53.00

Source: Government of Mysore, *Handbook on Education 1964–65* (Bangalore, 1965).

Note: The figures regarding government grants are less than what might be expected in the light of the rules governing grants-in-aid. The reason for this is that government grants are calculated at different rates for different purposes and for different periods. Thus, maintenance receives the greatest support. General colleges are not eligible for grants during the first three years of their existence, technical institutions during the first five years and medical colleges during the first ten years. Moreover, educational institutions often spend more than what is "admissible" for the purpose of calculating government grants. Finally, part of the expenditure is met from special fees (such as games fees, reading room fees, annual day fee, and so forth) for none of which there is a corresponding government grant.

[a] Ten schools, seven in Dharwar district and three in Mysore district.
[b] No school studied.
[c] Twelve schools, six in Dharwar district and six in Mysore district.
[d] One hundred and six schools, one in Belgaum district, eighty-one in Dharwar district, and twenty-four in Mysore district.
[e] Twenty-eight colleges, eight in Belgaum district, ten in Dharwar district, and ten in Mysore district.

rector of public instruction, and the Shankar College of Yadgir was dis-affiliated by the Karnatak University in 1966, in both instances because of charges of mismanagement. Similarly, grants were withheld from the Municipal High School of Nipani (Belgaum district) and the Janata English High School of Kalghatgi (Dharwar district), but the grants were subsequently restored when the institutions mended their ways. The government and university authorities whom we interviewed on this subject, however, pointed out that the occasions for such drastic action are infrequent and that most of the lapses are usually rectified by less stern measures.

Mysore education corresponds to the national pattern in which private management dominates all except the primary school sector. This correspondence is indicated by the following facts and figures relating to the total number of institutions and the amount of grants-in-aid payable to them by the government.[21] Preprimary education is not the direct responsibility of the state government; therefore, liberal grants are advanced to private bodies at the rate of 70 percent of the authorized expenditure for rural schools and 50 percent of that for urban schools. Of the total of 465 preprimary schools in the state controlled by the department of education during 1964–65, all but 7, or 98 percent, were run by private bodies. Of these 7, 5 were government and 2 local authority schools.

Primary schools, however, are mainly a government responsibility. In 1964–65 there were 30,539 primary schools in the whole of Mysore. Of these, 21,021 (69 percent) were government institutions. Most of the remaining 9,518 schools were managed by district school boards and municipal school boards in ex-Bombay and ex-Madras areas, thus leaving only a small number in the hands of private managements. As for the finances of district school boards, almost the whole of the expenditure is met by government, the only other source being the boards' share in the local fund cess which is realized from the public along with land revenue. Municipal school boards receive 50 percent of their total expenditure as grants-in-aid from government. This overwhelming dominance of government in the field of primary education suggests that government takes seriously Article 45 of the Constitution, which places the responsibility for primary education on state governments.

In secondary education, the pattern is again reversed. During 1964–65, 910 of the 1,331 secondary schools, representing 69 percent of the total, were privately managed. Government schools numbered 164 and local authority schools, 257. The grants-in-aid code for these schools defines their main objective as the extension and improvement of secular education in the state.[22] Grants-in-aid provided 80 percent of the total expenditure on maintenance for urban high schools, and 85 percent for rural high schools. Secondary schools also received miscellaneous grants.

College education also is mainly private. Of the total of 141 degree colleges in the state in 1964–65, 68 percent were privately managed, 27 percent were the responsibility of the government, and 4 percent were run as "model colleges" by the two universities at Dharwar and Mysore.[23] The importance of private enterprise in the area of collegiate education is clearly indicated in table 31 which shows that private colleges are not only to be found in all but four subsectors, but also outnumber government colleges in all but one of the subsectors in which they operate. The ex-

Table 31. Degree colleges in Mysore state, 1964–65, classified according to management.

Institution	Management			Total
	Government	University	Private	
General education colleges (B.A.; B.Sc.; B.Comm.)	15	3	53	71
Professional and technical colleges				
Medical colleges	6	–	4	10
Commerce colleges	1	–	6	7
Engineering colleges	2	1	12	15
Law colleges	1	1	9	11
Veterinary colleges	1	–	–	1
Agriculture colleges	2	–	–	2
Educational training colleges	7	1	8	16
Physical education colleges	1	–	–	1
Technology colleges	1	–	–	1
Oriental (Sanskrit) colleges	2	–	4	6
Total	39	6	96	141

Source: Government of Mysore, *Handbook on Education 1964–65* (Bangalore, 1965).

ception is the medical college subsector, medical colleges being high cost. It is of some significance that despite their high cost, engineering colleges in these districts are predominantly private.

Private enterprise in collegiate education receives ample support from government. According to the grants-in-aid code in force in 1964–65, government was obliged to pay two-thirds of the deficit in the maintenance expenses of the private colleges, while also providing miscellaneous grants.

Support for private education is likely to be part of future state policy. Several high ranking officials, including the secretary in charge of the department of education of Mysore, were interviewed by us in December 1965. They agreed with us that private institutions suffer from various drawbacks, such as communal bias in the distribution of patronage.[24] But they also pointed out that so long as the Constitution of India permits private organizations to form educational societies, the communal orientation of private institutions must be accepted as inevitable and put up with unless it assumes flagrant proportions. To prevent such developments, one of the basic conditions laid down for an institution to fulfil, before any grants to it can be sanctioned, is that no student should be refused admission "on the ground of the caste or community to which he belongs" (quoted from Rule 10(iii) of the code governing grants-in-aid to private colleges).

Further, it was emphasized by the officials interviewed that many private institutions had high reputations not only for prolonged public service in the field of education, but also for the excellence of teaching standards. They attracted wide public patronage because of their reputations, and government had to recognize this. In providing educational facilities to the people, the government felt hamstrung by limited financial resources. The government was, on the whole, appreciative of the role of educational societies and satisfied with their working. It was said to be seriously considering whether it should not limit its own role in education to financial support and supervision and control of the standards of education, and withdraw from the direct administration of schools and colleges. (No final decision had been taken by the middle of 1967, however. According to informed circles, the government was examining the feasibility of constituting district education boards for both primary and secondary schools. These boards would be statutory local authority bodies on the model of the district school boards that are functioning in Belgaum, Dharwar, and other districts which formerly formed part of Bombay state. It is likely that the new boards may be entrusted with the supervision of private educational institutions as well.)

Community Control of Private Institutions

The importance of private educational institutions is only part of the story. We also studied the manner in which these institutions are influenced by and interact with the social environment. To do this, we examined the composition of the managements of educational societies and related that composition to other structural and functional aspects of private educational institutions as well as to some characteristics of the wider society.

The history of private enterprise in education in modern India is an aspect of a more general adaptive process through which castes, sects, and communities have tried to meet the challenge of changing times and to exploit new opportunities for their own social and political advancement. Caste associations[25] and educational societies are expressions of this general process of "decompression" of traditional institutions. Such bodies performed highly important secular functions and did not try to conceal their caste- or communal-based organization. Many educational institutions were originally, and proudly, given caste or communal names, but the practice had to be abandoned after independence because of the government's decision not to support nonsecular institutions. For example, the famous and powerful Karnatak Liberal Education Society of Belgaum, which had twenty-three institutions — eleven of them colleges — spread over four districts in the two states of Mysore and Maharashtra under its management in 1966, was formerly known as the Karnatak Lingayat Education Society. In spite of the new name, the president, the four vice-presidents, and the fifteen members of its management are Lingayats. (What is more, the society continues to be popularly known by its unchanged initials — the K.L.E. Society. The substitution of "Liberal" for "Lingayat" cleverly succeeds in preserving the identity of the Society.)

Similarly, the president, the two vice-presidents and eight out of the nine members of the governing body of the Janata Shikshana Samiti of Dharwar are Brahmans, and all the seven members of the management of Sri Shivarathreshwar Mahavidyapeeth of Mysore are Lingayats. The Roman Catholic Diocese of Belgaum and the Anjuman-e-Islam of Hubli also are under the exclusive control of their respective communities.

We have designated educational institutions by the name of the caste group or religious community whose representatives either constitute the majority of the members of the management or, failing that, occupy key management positions because of their financial and social entrepreneurship.[26]

The data on community management of educational institutions are presented in table 32.

This table indicates that Lingayats, Brahmans, and Christians are most active in educational private enterprise. Since Brahmans and Christians are minority communities, educational entrepreneurship is not explained by community size. This conclusion is supported by the fact that, although Vokkaligas are the largest single community in the state and Mysore district is one of their strongholds, they are quite inactive in educational private enterprise, even in the area where their population is most concentrated. Similarly, Marathas, who constitute almost 20 percent of the population of Belgaum, have been comparatively inactive. It may be parenthetically added here that the Christian institutions derive their financial support partly from a non-local, and extra-national, source — international missionary societies.

Of the other minorities, Muslims are the most enterprising in the districts studied. Not only do they run their own institutions, but, as we will show later, also avail themselves of the facilities offered by other private institutions.

Important data which would be relevant to an analysis of the composition of managements, namely, a breakdown by caste of the population in the state, unfortunately is unavailable after the 1931 census. Though more than three decades old, the 1931 figures (see table 33) may reasonably be expected to reflect the present distribution of castes, as there have been no recent major demographic upheavals in the concerned areas.

While Brahmans are more or less uniformly distributed in all three districts, Lingayats, Christians, and Muslims predominate in the two northern districts of Belgaum and Dharwar, and Vokkaligas in the southern district of Mysore. It would be erroneous, however, to expect an exact corre-

Table 32. Private educational institutions in Mysore state, 1965–66, classified according to managing community.

Managing community	Primary			Secondary				Collegiate				Total
	DWa	MYb	Total	DWa	BMc	MYb	Total	DWa	BMc	MYb	Total	
Lingayat	1	2	3	33	–	11	44	6	5	2	13	60
Brahman	5	1	6	28	–	5	33	3	3	4	10	49
Christian	6	6	12	13	1	5	19	1	–	3	4	35
Muslim	–	–	–	4	–	1	5	–	–	–	–	5
Vokkaliga	1	–	1	–	–	1	1	–	–	–	–	1
Reddy	–	–	–	1	–	–	1	–	–	–	–	2
Kuruba	–	–	–	1	–	–	1	–	–	–	–	1
Maratha	–	–	–	1	–	–	1	–	–	–	–	1
Kunchatiga	–	–	–	–	–	1	1	–	–	1	1	2
Total	13	9	22	81	1	24	106	10	8	10	28	156

Source: Field data collected by the authors.
a Dharwar district.
b Mysore district.
c Belgaum district.

Table 33. Number and proportion of selected castes and communities in Mysore state, by district, 1931.

Caste or community	Belgaum district		Dharwar district		Mysore district	
	No.	%[a]	No.	%[a]	No.	%[a]
Brahman	33,521	3.11	39,231	3.56	34,228	2.44
Christian	7,887	0.73	8,409	0.76	3,375	0.24
Lingayat	292,942	27.21	374,981	34.00	199,730	14.22
Maratha	212,713	19.70	52,843	4.80	4,919	0.40
Muslim	93,224	8.66	158,431	14.36	43,485	3.10
Vokkaliga	0	–	0	–	382,352	27.23
Total population[b]	1,076,701	–	1,102,677	–	1,403,984	–

Source: Government of India, *Census of India, 1931: Bombay Presidency*, vol. 8, pt. 2, table 5; *Mysore State*, vol. 25, pt. 2, table 17.

[a] Percentage of the total population of the district belonging to the caste or community.

[b] Of the district.

spondence between the population of a caste or community and its position in the field of education because of the difference in their educational traditions, Brahmans and Christians having relatively old traditions compared to the Vokkaligas. The differences are reflected in the 1931 figures for literacy in what was then Mysore state. The percentage of literacy for Brahmans was 57.3; for Christians, 43.2; for Muslims, 21.2; for Lingayats, 16.4; for Marathas, 14.7; and for Vokkaligas, only 6.5.[27]

The composition of managements can now be examined in the light of the above demographic data. Table 34 shows that one of the two major communities of the state, the Lingayats, and the minority communities of

Table 34. Composition of management of private institutions in Mysore state, 1965–66 (percentage).

Institution, by managing community	Caste or community of members of managing boards				
	Brahman	Christian	Lingayat	Other	Total
Brahman (N = 49)	73.8	1.4	11.0	13.8	100.0
	(322)	(6)	(48)	(60)	(436)
Christian (N = 35)	–	94.5	0.5	5.0	100.0
	(0)	(206)	(1)	(11)	(218)
Lingayat (N = 60)	9.3	0.2	75.0	15.5	100.0
	(52)	(1)	(421)	(87)	(561)
Muslim (N = 5)	–	–	3.1	96.9	100.0
	(0)	(0)	(2)	(63)[a]	(65)
Other (N = 7)	12.9	–	16.1	71.0	100.0
	(8)	(0)	(10)	(44)	(62)

Note: Numbers in parentheses are numbers of caste or community members on each managing board.

[a] All these 63 persons are Muslims. There are eight and six Muslims respectively on the managements of Brahman and Lingayat institutions.

Brahmans, Christians, and Muslims invariably dominate the management of their own educational institutions. The second major community, the Vokkaligas, and other minorities, the Kunchatigas and Kurubas, are often compelled to seek the cooperation of politically, socially, and educationally advanced communities, and even, in extreme cases, to yield managerial control to them. The mutual acceptance or rejection of the various communities is indicated in the accommodation of "outsiders" on the management. Thus, no "untouchable" is a member of a private management; but five such persons sit on the managements of *taluka* board high schools in Mysore district and a few on primary school boards in Belgaum and Dharwar districts. The inclusion of scheduled caste representatives on such boards is, of course, a statutory requirement.

There is contrast between the managements of local authority institutions and of private institutions. Beginning with the district and municipal school boards, which play a dominant role in primary education in the northern districts, we find that the five boards studied in the districts of Belgaum and Dharwar had seventy-one members. There were thirty-six Lingayats, eight Muslims, seven Marathas, five Brahmans, five scheduled castes, three Christians, and seven others. Lingayats predominate over the others on four boards, but in the fifth — the municipal school board of Belgaum — Marathas are in a majority.[28] Also, the important post of board chairman is occupied by a member of the dominant community in each case. The correspondence between the positions of the various castes and communities on the boards and in the general population (see table 33) is remarkable, as is the presence of representatives of scheduled castes. We were told that, ever since the inception of the boards in the 1920's, their membership has never been dominated by Brahmans. Involvement of these boards in local and caste politics has been noted by Pavate,[29] who came to know them intimately, and may be expected because the principle of elective membership exposes them to communal and political pressures. In consequence, the social composition of these boards is more representative than that of the private managements.

So far as secondary schools and colleges are concerned, it will be seen in table 35 that Lingayats, who are the largest community in Dharwar district, dominate the managements of local authority institutions. Brahmans displace Muslims from the second position, which they, in view of their larger population, might have occupied but for their educational backwardness. Similarly, and for the same reasons, Vokkaligas in Mysore district occupy the second place after Brahmans, who are fewer in number than Vokkaligas, Lingayats, and Muslims (in that order). It is particularly noteworthy that the latter three communities occupy positions in the managements of secondary schools which exactly reproduce their relative positions in the population: this correspondence indicates that the communities are democratically represented.

The above data show that in the management of local authority institu-

Table 35. Composition of management of local authority institutions in Mysore state, by district, 1965–66.

| | Caste or community of members of managing boards | | | | | | | | | |
| | Dharwar district | | | | | Mysore district | | | | |
Institution	Brah-man	Linga-yat	Vokka-liga	Mus-lim	Other	Brah-man	Linga-yat	Vokka-liga	Mus-lim	Other
Secondary school[a]	4	30	0	3	12	21	16	17	5	30
College[b]	1	12	0	0	0	–	–	–	–	–

[a] There were twenty-five secondary schools, nine in Dharwar district and sixteen in Mysore district.

[b] There were five colleges, three in Dharwar district and two in Mysore district. The two colleges in Mysore district were managed by Mysore University, a stronghold of Brahmans.

tions educationally and socially advantaged minority communities lose their importance and the principle of representation based on numerical size emerges as decisive, or nearly so. Political power related to numerical dominance replaces or competes with economic and cultural advantage. It may be noted, however, that Brahmans seem to be able to hold their own better when their competitors are really backward communities such as Vokkaligas.

Social Composition of Staff and Students

The control of an educational institution by a society or management, all or most of whose members belong to a single caste or religious community, may not by itself represent a situation inimical to the sociopolitical ideal of equality of educational opportunity. But if it can be shown that the majority on the management dictates a policy of discrimination, favoring its community or caste in the appointment of teachers, admission of students, and distribution of scholarships and other resources, then a serious problem exists. The argument that equality of opportunity is guaranteed by the freedom which all communities enjoy to run their own educational institutions is fallacious. First, only the economically powerful or culturally advanced communities seem to be able to operate effectively as managers of educational institutions. Second, the activity of many communities in fostering particularistic values and communal attitudes, and in practicing discrimination within their institutions, does not improve the situation, but actually worsens it. Third, the fact that government foots most of the bill for both public and private institutions makes this a problem of public policy as well as of private initiative.

The data on the composition of teaching staff and students are crucial to our analysis but in view of their bulk, have to be presented in a condensed form. Table 36 deals with the composition of staff and table 37 contains the data on the composition of students.[30]

Table 36 shows that the teaching staff among the institutions run by Brahmans, Christians, Lingayats, and Muslims is dominated by the manag-

Table 36. Composition of staff of private institutions in Mysore state, by district, 1965-66.

Institution, by management	Caste or community of staff														
	Belgaum district					Dharwar district					Mysore district				
	Brahman	Christian	Lingayat	Other	Total	Brahman	Christian	Lingayat	Other	Total	Brahman	Christian	Lingayat	Other	Total
Brahman	54.2 (64)	0.9 (1)	5.1 (6)	39.8 (47)	100.0 (118)	68.0 (402)	1.0 (6)	11.3 (67)	19.7 (116)	100.0 (591)	74.0 (279)	– (0)	1.6 (6)	24.4 (92)	100.0 (377)
Christian	25.0 (1)	75.0 (3)	– (0)	– (0)	100.0 (4)	31.3 (98)	46.0 (144)	9.4 (29)	13.3 (42)	100.0 (313)	31.1 (103)	58.0 (192)	0.3 (1)	10.6 (35)	100.0 (331)
Lingayat	16.1 (40)	2.4 (6)	55.6 (138)	25.9 (64)	100.0 (248)	13.3 (121)	1.3 (12)	60.4 (548)	25.0 (227)	100.0 (908)	46.9 (119)	2.3 (6)	31.1 (79)	19.7 (50)	100.0 (254)
Muslim	–	–	–	–	–	–	–	5.8 (4)	94.2 (65)[a]	100.0 (69)	–	–	–	100.0 (30)[b]	100.0 (30)
Other	– (0)	– (0)	– (0)	– (0)	– (0)	23.0 (6)	– (0)	42.3 (11)	34.7 (9)	100.0 (26)	60.6 (54)	2.3 (2)	9.0 (8)	28.1 (25)	100.0 (89)

Note: Numbers in parentheses are numbers of caste or community members on staff.
[a] Includes sixty-three Muslims (96.9 percent).
[b] Includes twenty-eight Muslims (93.3 percent).

ing community itself. Thus, Brahmans constitute 54.2 to 74.0 percent of the teaching staff in Brahman institutions; Christians, 46 to 75 percent in Christian institutions; and Muslims, 91 to 93 percent in Muslim institutions. Lingayats account for 55.6 and 60.4 percent respectively of the teachers in their institutions in Belgaum and Dharwar. In their Mysore institutions, however, they have fewer teachers (31.3 percent) than the Brahmans (46.9 percent). This situation and similar situations in the various minority community institutions are due to the lack of enough trained personnel from the managing community.

The conclusion that recruitment of staff in private institutions takes place on a communal basis is borne out by the outstanding fact that, irrespective of the social structure of population in each district, each community is better represented in its own institutions than in those managed by other communities. (This tendency is more pronounced in urban areas than in rural areas.)[31]

Other considerations besides communal loyalty — especially kinship ties, linguistic affinities, economic motives (for example, donations), and political pressures — may be responsible for various appointments. But judging from the results, these other considerations generally operate within the framework of communal interests.

Appointments are made according to government rules, but ways to circumvent the rules are found whenever necessary in the interests of the managing community. The usual justification offered is that people with common interests and aims contribute to harmony and that such a community of interests is natural among members of the same caste. Further, the managers argue, since private institutions are the fruit of the combined efforts of a particular community, so-called favoritism in appointments is justified so long as the eligibility conditions are fulfilled. These considerations represent an excellent example of the traditional particularistic point of view.

Discriminatory appointment is a vicious circle. Managements maintain that they make appointments out of the available applicants, and usually more applications are received from candidates belonging to the managing community. The reason for this is the disinclination of people from other communities to apply because they discount their chances of being selected. Informants from numerically or socially weak communities maintain that in a struggle with strong communities the former are ignored.

Among teachers, the head master or principal obviously occupies a pre-eminent position. The data on heads of institutions conform to the familiar pattern. Seventeen of the 22 heads of preprimary and primary schools, 85 of the 106 heads of secondary schools, and 24 of the 28 college principals belong to the managing community of their respective institutions. Our inquiries reveal a similar picture with regard to key administrative posts such as superintendent, accountant, and head clerk.

In the composition of students, one would expect demographic factors

Table 37. Composition of students of private institutions in Mysore state, by district, 1965–66.

Institution, by management	Caste or community of students														
	Belgaum district					Dharwar district					Mysore district				
	Brah-man	Chris-tian	Linga-yat	Other[a]	Total	Brah-man	Chris-tian	Linga-yat	Other[a]	Total	Brah-man	Chris-tian	Linga-yat	Other[a]	Total
Brahman	27.0 (444)	1.7 (29)	4.6 (75)	66.7 (1,098)	100.0 (1,646)	41.3 (4,889)	2.2 (257)	26.0 (3,083)	30.5 (3,612)	100.0 (11,841)	54.3 (2,653)	1.1 (55)	8.3 (408)	36.3 (1,768)	100.0 (4,884)
Christian	9.7 (3)	90.3 (29)	– (0)	–	100.0 (32)	27.1 (2,016)	15.6 (1,165)	20.0 (1,488)	37.3 (2,773)	100.0 (7,442)	31.8 (1,983)	12.0 (748)	9.5 (594)	46.7 (2,920)	100.0 (6,245)
Lingayat	18.1 (545)	4.6 (138)	35.7 (1,078)	41.6 (1,254)	100.0 (3,015)	14.8 (2,220)	1.1 (174)	52.9 (7,938)	31.2 (4,686)	100.0 (15,018)	22.1 (184)	0.8 (27)	31.9 (1,135)	45.2 (1,607)	100.0 (3,553)
Muslim	– (0)	– (0)	– (0)	–	– (0)	1.0 (12)	0.3 (4)	0.7 (9)	98.0 (1,248)[b]	100.0 (1,273)	0.2 (1)	– (0)	–	99.8 (527)[c]	100.0 (528)
Other	– (0)	– (0)	– (0)	–	– (0)	2.5 (7)	– (0)	28.5 (77)	69.0 (187)	100.0 (271)	33.4 (639)	1.3 (25)	7.9 (152)	57.4 (1,099)	100.0 (1,915)

Note: Numbers in parentheses are numbers of caste or community members who are students in each type of institution.

[a] Includes students whose caste could not be ascertained.
[b] Includes 1,235 Muslims (97.0 percent).
[c] All Muslims.

to be decisive, but the enrollments in private educational institutions reveal a mixed picture of communal loyalty, social and educational backwardness, and the compulsion of numbers. Table 37 shows that among Brahman institutions, Brahman students are the single largest group in all the three districts, rising up to 54.3 percent of the total student population of Brahman-managed institutions in Mysore. Lingayat schools and colleges present a similar picture.

Hardly any other community sends its children to Muslim institutions. (The principal reason seems to be that Muslim institutions use Urdu as the language of instruction, while other institutions use Kannada or, in some cases, English.) In all the other private institutions, however, students belonging to the managing community are not even the single largest group. In Christian institutions Brahman students are the dominant group, in Vokkaliga schools, Muslims, and in Kunchatiga, Kuruba, and Reddy institutions, Lingayats. Among Christians, the lack of numbers is the reason for this phenomenon, but among the other minority communities the relative absence of an educational tradition seems to be an additional factor. (The Kunchatiga college in Mysore is the creation of a single individual of the community, and not of any collective effort.) Why, then, do such communities sponsor educational institutions? Social service, prestige in society, political power, and even, in some cases, monetary gain, seem to be the principal reasons.[32]

There is a contrast between the composition of staff and students in government and local authority institutions on the one hand, and in private institutions on the other. The data are presented in condensed form in tables 38 and 39.

The data on staff (table 38) in government institutions show that, whereas in the two northern districts numerical preponderance and social advantage emerge as competing determinants of recruitment, in Mysore the numerically preponderant Vokkaligas fall behind Brahmans and Lingayats. In the local authority institutions of both Dharwar and Mysore, with the sole exception of Brahmans, staff composition reflects the relative numerical strength of the various communities in the district population. This implies that the more local the control, the more faithfully staff will reflect population distribution. So far as the social composition of the students is concerned, table 39 shows that, while in Belgaum and Dharwar all the communities with the exception of Brahmans hold their own position in the schools, in Mysore social advantage is still more important than numerical strength. The impressive presence of other students, representing backward communities such as the Adi-Karnatakas in Mysore, among others, however, is a noteworthy indicator of the inclusiveness of public institutions.

The above data confirm our earlier conclusions: first, that compared to private institutions, public (government and local authority) institutions tend to be more representative of the population; second, that the process

Table 38. Composition of staff of public institutions in Mysore state, by district, 1965–66.

Institution, by management	Belgaum district						Dharwar district							Mysore district						
	Brah-man	Linga-yat	Mara-tha	Mus-lim	Other	Total	Brah-man	Chris-tian	Linga-yat	Mara-tha	Mus-lim	Other	Total	Brah-man	Chris-tian	Linga-yat	Mus-lim	Vok-kaliga	Other	Total
State government (N = 24)	25 (6)	12 (3)	39 (9)	12 (3)	12 (3)	100 (24)	20 (97)	3 (12)	27 (132)	11 (52)	6 (29)	33 (158)	100 (480)	30 (123)	3 (13)	13 (52)	7 (28)	8 (32)	39 (157)	100 (405)
Local authority (N = 30)	– (0)	– (0)	– (0)	– (0)	– (0)	– (0)	21 (125)	2 (14)	45 (278)	6 (39)	9 (53)	17 (101)	100 (610)	38 (158)	1 (6)	10 (40)	6 (26)	16 (64)	29 (118)	100 (412)

Note: Numbers in parentheses are numbers of caste or community members on staff.

Table 39. Composition of students of public institutions in Mysore state, by district, 1965–66.

	Caste or community of students																					
Institution, by management	Belgaum district						Dharwar district							Mysore district								
	Brahman	Linga-yat	Mara-tha	Mus-lim	Other	Total	Brahman	Chris-tian	Linga-yat	Mara-tha	Mus-lim	Other	Total	Brahman	Chris-tian	Linga-yat	Mara-tha	Mus-lim	Vok-kaliga	Other	Total
State government (N = 24)	31 (32)	26 (27)	15 (15)	10 (10)	18 (18)[a]	100 (102)	23 (788)	2 (62)	34 (1,154)	6 (198)	8 (287)	27 (929)	100 (3,418)	24 (1,049)	2 (101)	15 (675)	2 (73)	6 (252)	9 (412)	42 (1,894)[b]	100 (4,456)
Local authority (N = 30)	– (0)	– (0)	– (0)	– (0)	– (0)	– (0)	16 (1,634)	1 (102)	42 (4,284)	3 (329)	4 (423)	34 (3,412)	100 (10,184)	20 (1,473)	2 (168)	20 (1,470)	1 (67)	5 (425)	17 (1,283)	35 (2,648)[c]	100 (7,534)

Note: Numbers in parentheses are numbers of caste or community members who are students in each type of institution.

[a] Includes one Christian student.

[b] Includes 587 Adi-Karnataka students who constitute 13.1 percent of the total number of all students.

[c] Includes 585 Adi-Karnataka students who constitute 7.8 percent of the total number of all students.

of representativeness seems to have made greater headway in the northern districts than in Mysore and more in local than in state government institutions; and third, that Brahmans are still a force to reckon with in the field of education all over the state of Mysore, despite the fact that the reservation of seats for backward castes has diminished the number of seats they can occupy in government educational institutions.

Student Facilities

Educational societies make student facilities available to their pupils in a discriminatory manner. Pupils belonging to the managing community have either exclusive or preferential claims to these facilities.

Lodging and board facilities almost equal in importance such requisites as classrooms, libraries, laboratories, play grounds, and so forth. In India, such facilities become increasingly indispensable as one moves from the primary to the secondary and collegiate levels, and from rural to urban areas. The number of students studying away from home at urban, upper level institutions is considerable.

In Mysore lodging and board facilities are provided mainly by two types of agencies, hostels and boarding houses attached to the institutions themselves, and those maintained by philanthropic individuals or organizations. The latter are mostly free and quite prominent in this part of the country, and the practice of starting boarding houses was an important feature of the efforts of various community leaders to educationally uplift their people. Consequently almost all the free boarding houses which started in the early years of this century were exclusively meant for particular communities. Among these, the hostels started by the Lingayats in the north Karnatak area and by the Vokkaligas in the princely state of Mysore are particularly noteworthy. In the Vokkaliga-dominated regions each landowner had to give several measures of paddy at harvest time to the hostels run by the community.[33]

It is only recently that a few students of other communities have been taken into these boarding houses. We made a close study of four free boarding houses (one Lingayat, one Jain, and one Kuruba in Belgaum, and one Lingayat in Dharwar). Two of these are still exclusive and do not admit boarders from other communities. It also came to our notice that some boarding houses which admit lodgers from more than one community do not permit mixed dining; low caste boarders are made to sit for their meals at a distance from the others. This is a pity because such institutions could work effectively in eradicating caste and communal differences, since they deal with children in their formative years.

Financial concessions (freeships) and assistance (scholarships) for students are important educational facilities in public institutions. There are several bases for award, notably financially underprivileged position, merit, community or caste, sex, region, language, and area of academic specialization. In addition to government scholarships and freeships (special and merit-based), there are endowments created by philanthropic donations. Usually such endowments are administered by trust committees appointed for the purpose, and the benefits are bestowed according to the wishes of the donors. As may be expected, such sources of financial assistance have often been applied restrictively. Since the middle of the last century a common grievance of the non-Brahman castes has been that they have been denied the privilege of education and thus left behind in the race for highly prized government appointments. Hence the special efforts of the leaders of these communities to help their own people. There are, however, instances of enlightened donors who have stipulated merit as the basis for award.

The Mysore University Calendar for 1956–57 (university endowments and aids) shows that, of the total of 171 endowments and prizes for undergraduate students accepted between 1916 (when the university was founded) and 1957, 45 were restricted to a particular caste, community, or sect. The Karnatak University does not accept such offers of endowments for restricted distribution of awards, but its constituent colleges do. Thus, the prospectus for the Karnatak University Arts and Science Colleges for 1967–68 lists three awards for specified communities, while others are reserved on the basis of residential area, parental occupation, or sex.

Concluding Remarks

This paper opened on a skeptical note, doubtful that a mere increase in literacy and in modern educational institutions in a country such as India could be regarded as a sufficient condition of the modernization of the educational system as a whole. Similar reservations have been expressed regarding the effectiveness of programs of educational expansion in some other developing countries, and the widespread view of education as "a magic medicine that can by itself transform a society," [34] or as "the master determinant of all aspects of change," [35] is now being questioned. It has been found that modern education in developing countries has not always succeeded in playing the same role in social and occupational mobility and in the emergence of a less rigid system of social stratification as it has in the western countries.[36]

Our concern in this study has been primarily with the role of private educational societies in the state of Mysore. There can be no denying that they have been a powerful progressive force wherever they have been active during the last hundred years or more. They have not only provided modern education in regions where government or local authority institutions were conspicuous by their small numbers, or total absence, but have also provided new areas for the operation of traditional communal or sectarian organizations, bringing about a certain degree of "decompression" of these organizations in the process. Srinivas has commented that "the processes of secularization and politicization have also affected . . . pre-British monasteries such as those of Smarthas, Sri Vaishnavas, Madhavas [all three are Brahman castes], and Lingayats. Gradually the feeling has grown among the Hindus that the wealth and prestige of these organizations should be used for promoting educational and social welfare of the people. . . . The Lingayats, a highly organized sect, have shown much sensitivity to this new demand, and Lingayat monasteries operate their own hostels, schools and colleges." [37]

Although this is also what we have found in the course of our inquiries, it represents only one side of the picture. In our view, modern curricula, modern methods of teaching, modern buildings and laboratories, well-trained teachers with Indian and foreign qualifications, and so forth do not guarantee that traditional particularistic values and communal loyalties will not persist in such a seemingly uncongenial environment. The main basis of our contention is the data on the composition of the management, staff, and students of private educational institutions, which does not correspond to the relative numerical strength of the various communities in district population. Unequal demand for education may partly explain these disparities in public educational institutions, but their nature and extent in private educational institutions clearly points to the existence of communal discrimination. Reference was also made, though briefly, to the discriminate distribution of various student facilities. In the course of our inquiries we also heard allegations of favoritism on communal lines in examinations, but could not verify them.

There are two ways in which the persistence of traditional particularistic values and communal loyalties in educational institutions may be related to the process of modernization. If we proclaim universalistic values and complete social equality as necessary conditions of modernization, we can dismiss the claims of private educational institutions (including engineering, medical, and science colleges) to being modern in any sense whatsoever. This seems to us too harsh a judgment. The very fact that private educational institutions do bring together people from different castes and communities, though not without discrimination in favor of a particular community, is itself a departure from the social exclusiveness of the vertically organized traditional society. Private educational institutions may not be as inclusive as public institutions are, but, being horizontal structures, they are certainly less particularistic than the traditional social structure.[38]

The alternative is to treat the discriminatory practices prevalent in private educational institutions as evidence of the tenacity of particularistic values and of the gradual nature of modernization. This does not mean, however, that we retreat from our earlier position that these institutions fail in a crucial manner to advance the modernization of the educational system and society. What seems to be indicated, therefore, is that the powers of the state must be used more vigorously to control private educational societies so that they may become better instruments of modernization. In view of the substantial public funds that are allocated to private educational institutions, the state has a responsibility to ensure that such funds are used in ways that visibly benefit all communities — not only the communities managing such institutions — and to guard against the use of public funds to subsidize narrow communal interests.

In this connection it is important to note that a private educational society by its very nature is committed to a policy of discrimination, and the social and educational advancement of communities other than the one managing it does not concern it. By contrast, government and local authority institutions are in principle equally open to all social groups, although a particular community may be able to benefit more from them and even gain control of the management of some of them. But such control need not prove permanent. Thus, there are already signs that the Brahman domination of the government and local authority educational institutions in Mysore district will weaken considerably in the foreseeable future.[39] We cannot say the same for private institutions, including Brahman institutions, in the same district that will continue to be run by caste or sectarian communities, primarily for the benefit of those communities.

At present government's ability to exercise effective control of private educational societies is limited and the provisions of the grants-in-aid code can be easily circumvented. Further, as already stated, the Constitution does not forbid the formation of such societies, and rightly so, because they protect the special interests of small minorities, which would otherwise be completely neglected. (For example, instruction in the Urdu language, which Muslims regard as their mother tongue, is provided in Mysore only in Muslim schools.) Private educational institutions, however, also foster antidemocratic, antiequalitarian, and nonsecular values. The dilemma of the situation is obvious.[40] The vast financial and administrative resources which a state takeover of private educational institutions and the consequent responsibility to meet all future demand for education would require are just not available.[41] Aided by the state policy of withdrawal from direct responsibility for providing the educational requirements of the people,[42] private educational institutions are bound to continue to exist and prosper as the demand for education from all sections of society gathers momentum. Hence the urgency of the need for well-defined and strict state control of private enterprise in the field of education in India.

Iqbal Narain

This chapter[1] explores how far the effort to maintain a depoliticized zone for education is empirically vindicated in the light of the experience of the management of primary schools under *panchayati raj* (PR), an institutionalized mechanism of decentralized and democratic local government in rural India.[2] The exploration proceeds by focusing on rural local politics as a factor in the management of primary schools. It is being increasingly realized that association of local leaders with the management of primary schools is desirable for recognizing local conditions and aspirations and for on-the-spot supervision and control. It is also being recognized that if such association tends to involve the teachers in local politics, it may do more harm than good. Thus the possibility of a depoliticized zone seems to require association of local political leaders with the management of primary schools on the one hand and protection of the schools against appropriation by local politicians on the other.

The Experiment in Local Control of Primary Education

Before their management was transferred to PR institutions, primary schools in Rajasthan were managed by the education department of the government of Rajasthan, which was responsible for administrative control and technical supervision. As a result of the transfer, administrative control is now vested in PR institutions, mainly 232 *panchayat samitis,* elected bodies paralleling the development block, a subunit of Rajasthan state's twenty-five districts. Technical supervision and guidance continue to be the obligation of the education department. Thus there is now a pattern of dual control and supervision.

Teachers are recruited and transferred by the concurrent action of the BDO (block development officer), an administrative officer attached to the *panchayat samiti,* and the elected *pradhan* (chairman) of the *panchayat samiti.* Disciplinary action against the *panchayat samiti* teacher can be taken by the district establishment committee, one administrative and political layer above the *panchayat samiti,* of which the district education officer is a member. All the subdeputy inspectors of schools (SDI) have

My associates in the research for this study were: K. C. Pandey, senior research associate, Election Research Project, Political Science Department, University of Rajasthan, Jaipur; and Mohan Lal Sharma, research scholar, Department of Political Science, University of Rajasthan, Jaipur.

been transferred on deputation to *panchayat samitis* for inspection and supervision of the primary schools and are designated as extension officers, education (E.O.'s, education). They are under the administrative control of the BDO and under the technical control of the education department. The E.O.'s, education, write the confidential report on the primary school teacher. The *panchayat samitis* get grants-in-aid on a 100 percent basis for salaries and allowances of teachers. In regard to other items of expenditure, aid is provided on a 50 percent matching basis. There are about 19,000 schools, 45,000 teachers, and 2,000,000 students under the 232 *panchayat samitis* in Rajasthan.[3]

The Naik Committee, which reported on Rajasthan primary education in 1963–64, and which was otherwise fairly critical of the management of primary schools under PR, found that PR helped to expand and improve primary education in Rajasthan. The state education minister gave the following summary of the committee's verdict. "Attendance of the teachers has improved. The disbursement of the salaries has been more regular. There is awakening among the rural population to get primary education. A new leadership has to emerge in the rural areas in the development of primary education. In addition, there are certain areas where development has taken place only because of the efforts of the individual Pradhan and the B.D.O." [4]

Table 40. Progress of primary education in Rajasthan.

Year	Primary schools	Students Male	Students Female	Teachers	Trained teachers (%)
1950–51	4,336	245,000	55,000	8,733	30.2
1965–66	18,600	1,460,000	400,000	42,400	60.0

Source: Statement of Nathu Ram Mirdha, education minister, in the Rajasthan legislative assembly. *Rajasthan Legislative Assembly Proceedings*, vol. 7, no. 12 (21 March 1965), p. 4308.

An overview of progress from 1950 to 1966 can be obtained from table 40. The governor's address of 4 May 1967 noted continued strides (though somewhat less than in 1966) in primary education. Although Rajasthan had started with one of the lowest primary school attendance records among the states of independent India, 50 percent of the children in the age group of six to eleven years, he stated, were now enrolled (against a national average in 1965–66 of 78.59 percent).[5] Although the growth in primary school enrollment has not been due exclusively to PR, even the most severe critics of PR management of primary schools admit that it has played an important part in popularizing primary education in the villages. Other measures of progress under PR management include a jump from Rs. 500 to Rs. 1,300 between 1950–51 and 1965–66 in the average amount spent per primary school teacher, and an increase in the total amount spent on primary education, from Rs. 8,400,000 in 1950–51 to Rs. 60,800,000 in 1965.[6]

PR institutions may not, however, have fully succeeded in enrolling children from the weaker (poorer) sections in primary education. In 1966, Bhairon Singh, Jan Sangh state legislator, made the following allegation. "To-day only 8.5% and 5% of the total primary students belong in scheduled castes and scheduled tribes respectively whereas it should have been 16% and 17% respectively in accordance with their population." [7] Nor have standards in primary education kept pace with the increase in numbers of students and teachers and the growth of available resources. Some allege that they have even fallen. The failure of standards to keep pace with growth cannot be entirely attributed to the management of primary schools by PR institutions, however. It is also due in part to the emphasis on quantitative growth irrespective of quality considerations, the laxity in technical supervision and control, want of equipment in schools, financial cuts in educational expenses, a too heavy work load for teachers, the phenomenon of single teacher schools, and the lack of adequate training and training facilities for teachers. Yet the PR institutions cannot be entirely absolved of responsibility; according to the Naik Committee there has been a "general demoralization in the ranks of the teachers because of transfer of primary schools to *panchayati raj* institutions" [8] where, according to an opposition MLA (member of the legislative assembly), "they are used as footballs in the game of politics." [9]

The disillusionment with the management of primary schools by PR institutions seems to have started rather early. Hardly one year after the launching of the experiment, the leader of the opposition Jan Sangh party moved the following unofficial resolution. "In the opinion of the house the powers of appointments and transfers of the teachers of primary schools given to the *panchayat samitis* should be withdrawn." [10] In the eyes of the teachers, the situation has become more grave with the passage of time. By July 1968, the Rajasthan teachers association had decided to start a statewide agitation to press the state government to take over control of primary education from the *panchayat samitis*.[11]

The politicization of primary education must be viewed in the light of the emerging nature of rural politics under *panchayati raj*. PR politics has, in contrast to the personalized politics of the traditional past, an institutionalized and, relatively speaking, impersonal character. The pull and swing of politics is largely built around the institutionalized power structure of PR rather than around the personal rivalries and family feuds of the past, though the latter still sometimes play at least a marginal role in village politics under PR.

PR politics also has a distinct orientation toward material benefits, and its elected leaders are the media for channeling the material benefits.[12] In addition, PR politics is democratic, competitive, and bargaining. As a corollary to its democratic character, politics under PR has assumed pronounced partisan overtones. The politics of PR institutions are at once a manifestation of the pulls and pressures of the social infrastructure of village life and a catalytic agent of change in relation to that infrastructure.[13] Thus one can suggest, by way of a descriptive hypothesis, that politics under PR may ultimately turn out to be a modernizing agent.

Finally, politics under PR should also be treated as a case of "link politics" [14] built on vertical alliances that serve as the proverbial hyphen that joins and the buckle that fastens the state level and rural local politicians. If one were to treat this development as legitimate, one should also accept as its logical corollary the entry of political parties in the arena of local politics.

Legislative Perceptions of Local Control

It is with this perspective that we turn to the perceptions and images that members of the Rajasthan legislative assembly have of PR management of primary schools. These can be summarized under five headings: partisan involvement of teachers; politically motivated personnel actions; teacher participation in election politics; the deterioration of educational standards and administration; and partisan distribution of benefits.

Partisan involvement of teachers

It has often been argued on the floor of the assembly that primary school teachers have no option but to involve themselves in partisan local politics if they wish to escape victimization and protect their jobs and their schools. The Jan Sangh leader described the situation in the followlowing words.

To-day democratic decentralization has generated instead of initiative, a struggle for power. And in the wake of struggle no personnel can live happily. And one can observe how the teachers, whose interests and loyalties are in clash with the competition for power, have been greatly victimized by the local politicians.

In this struggle every party tries to build up its strength and for that seeks help from the teachers, because they are directly in touch with the people. The tragedy is that even if they remain neutral and do not support this or that faction they are harassed and transferred to distant places. This is all aimed at strengthening one's own factional group.[15]

Politically motivated personnel actions

The charge that appointments and placement are politically motivated has been made in the assembly by many members, irrespective of party alignment. A Congress party MLA alleged in 1963 that "since the teachers are selected by the *samitis,* the appointments are not impartial. The B.D.O.'s and the *pradhans* can easily be influenced by relations, money, or recommendations." [16]

Transfers appear to be the most common method of political reward or victimization; those transferred against their wishes suffer expense, inconvenience, and psychological upset. "By the threat of transfers the teachers are made to propagate for and distribute the posters on behalf of the party in power. Many who dare to refuse are transferred or their salaries are not paid," alleged the Jan Sangh leader.[17] Illustrating statistically the "abuse of authority to transfer teachers," the Naik Committee cited figures from 184 of 232 *panchayat samitis* (table 41) that showed that one out of

Table 41. Frequency of transfers of primary school teachers.[a]

| | Number of transfers | | | | Teachers transferred (percentage) |
Year	Within 1 year	Within 2 years	After 2 years	Total	
1960–61	1,354	1,511	1,466	4,331	26.6
1961–62	2,008	1,599	1,909	5,516	27.0

Source: Government of Rajasthan, *The Report of Rajasthan State Primary Education Committee* (Jaipur, 1965), p. 61.
[a] Teachers in 184 *panchayat samitis* (blocks).

four teachers are transferred in any one year and that a substantial proportion of the transfers occur contrary to education department regulations; that is, before the teacher has served two years in one post.[18]

According to Mahendra Singh (Jan Sangh) it is a teacher's political connections, not his performance, that affects his chances of being transferred against his wishes. "All the villagers may be dissatisfied with a school teacher, yet if he is in the good books of the *sarpanch* [chairman of a village *panchayat*] and *pradhan* he is not transferred. But the honest teachers who do not side with any party are transferred to distant places even if they are liked by all." [19] According to Jai Narain Salodia (Swatantra), speaking in 1966, transfers are often made in midsession, regardless of the cost to students.[20] The Naik Committee report concluded: "The transfers are frequent and excessive. In several instances, they have been also absolutely unjustified. We came across the case of a teacher who was transferred ten times in one year." [21]

The merits of these allegations could be more easily ascertained if comparative figures were available on transfers of teachers by the education department before management of primary schools was shifted to PR institutions. It is generally believed that transfers are more frequent under PR than under the management of the education department, and that this is rooted in personal whim and caprice. These transfers violate the rules. The education department has laid down that no teacher should be transferred before he has put in two years of service at a particular place, a standard that the data in table 41 indicate is not taken seriously. Transfers of teachers in the middle of a session and more especially when the session is about to close are also against the rules. Education department and teacher association spokesmen indicate that these rules are honored more in the breach than in the observance by the authorities managing primary education under PR.[22]

It has also been alleged that politics has vitiated the process of disciplinary action. A somewhat exceptional case gleaned from the question hour in the Rajasthan legislative assembly throws light on this allegation.[23]

Shri Natthi Singh (Independent):

1. Is it true that Shri Raghunath Singh, head master of primary school, Helak, has been dismissed by the *panchayat samiti,* Kumher, without the prior consent of the district establishment committee? If yes, when?
2. Is it true that after the countermanding of the orders of the Kumher *samiti* by the state government, the teacher was again dismissed? If yes, what action has been taken against such arbitrary use of powers by the Officials?
3. Is it true that the teacher was suspended under the charge of 342 T.H.? [24]
4. Is it true that the court had dismissed the charges as allegedly made out of political considerations?
5. Is it also true that still the teacher is under suspension?

Panchayat Minister (Shri Bheeka Bhai):

1. Yes Sir. On 21-2-1962.
2. Yes Sir. The second dismissal order of the standing committee has also been countermanded by the government. However, there are not enough reasons to take disciplinary action against the members of the standing committee.
3. Yes Sir.
4. Yes Sir.
5. Yes Sir. The enquiry into the charges alleged by the *panchayat samiti* is still going on.

Shri Natthi Singh:

Since when is the enquiry going on and in what stage is it?

Shri Bheeka Bhai:

Since 12-2-1964. There is no information in regard to the stage of enquiry.

Shri Natthi Singh:

Is it true that the B.D.O. had submitted an enquiry report by September 1964 and he had asked the standing committee six times to arrive at a decision, but the committee had taken no decision till now in spite of the fact that the teacher has been found innocent?

Shri Bheeka Bhai:

The committee seems prejudiced against the teacher. But since no legal action can be taken in the matter, some administrative measures will be taken.

Shri Natthi Singh:

On the ground that the teacher was dismissed out of political motives, two times the dismissal orders were countermanded. The vigilance commission[25] was approached. That too proved of no help. This is because the *sarpanch* of the same *panchayat* is also the chairman of the standing committee. And consequently the teacher is under suspension from 17-5-1962. The court, government orders, all have proved helpless. The teacher should be paid for the period.

Shri Murli Dhar Vyas (Praja Socialist Party):

Please state the reason.

Shri Bheeka Bhai:

As far as the orders are concerned, they have been cancelled. Our sympathies are with the teacher.

Shri Raghunath Singh Vishnoi (Congress):

Why is the committee not dissolved?

Shri Jai Narain Salodia (Swatantra):

For three years the government have taken no decision in regard to that *samiti*.

Shri Bheeka Bhai:

The government have tried and will try to do everything to ensure that justice is done.

Shri Umrao Singh (Samyukta Socialist Party):

The administrative powers lie with the B.D.O. The standing committee cannot even transfer a teacher without the consent of the B.D.O. How could that happen then?

Shri Bheeka Bhai:

The standing committee is empowered to give minor punishment. For major punishment the case is referred to the district establishment committee. In this case the standing committee acted at its own discretion. Therefore the orders were cancelled.

Politics, like bureaucratic rules and powerful unions, can serve as a protective umbrella for negligent teachers, enabling them to be apathetic and indifferent to their teaching obligations. Another case which was noticed on the floor of the assembly in the question hour illustrates this point.[26]

Shri Hari Prasad Sharma (Jan Sangh):

1. Is it true that Shri Nemi Chand Jain of village Roteda (district Bundi) is a teacher in the same village?
2. If yes, for how many years?
3. Is it true that his behavior with the villagers is rude and many cases of abuse and beating are pending against him?
4. Is it also true that the gentleman lives 15 days in a month out of the village on account of fighting cases and other work and yet he is marked present?
5. Is it true that the school is a centre of one party and on duty hours the teacher remains looking after his farm?
6. Is it also true that many complaints have been made against the teacher and he had been suspended too, and that still he has not been transferred?
7. Is there any obstacle in the way of government transferring such teachers?
8. Has the *zila parishad* [district committee] also recommended to transfer the teacher and to investigate into the complaints?
9. Why have the recommendations of the *zila parishad* been neglected in favour of one teacher?

(Congress):[27]

---

1. Yes Sir.
2. For seven years.
3. Partially true.
4. The enquiry is being held in that matter.
5. No complaint of that type has been received.
6. Yes Sir.
7. The transfers are to be made by the *panchayat samiti* or Rajasthan Panchayat Samiti and Zila Parishad Service Selection Commission. The government cannot help in the matter.
8. The *zila parishad* has recommended an enquiry which is being held.
9. It does not appear that the directives from the *zila parishad* have been neglected.

The teacher's position is made more difficult because of the multiple control by the BDO's and the extension officer, education (E.O., education), on the official side and the *pradhan,* the *sarpanch,* and the *panchas* (elected members of the *panchayat*) on the unofficial side.[28] When the official and nonofficial wings conspire or stand at daggers drawn,[29] his plight becomes pathetic.

Teacher participation in election politics

A charge has been made rather frequently, though often without corroboration, that teachers are drawn into election politics. "The teachers are continuously taking part in politics, propagating in elections," asserted a Congress MLA as early as 1960.[30] The trend appears to have gained strength and momentum in the last three general elections.[31] After the 1967 elections, an independent MLA asserted on the floor of the assembly that "the primary schools have become the centre of politics. The teacher actively participates in the election. He thus has the upper hand over the *panchas* who abide by his instructions." [32]

This charge suggests primary school teachers are not passive instruments in the local political process but use local politicians for ends of their choosing, such as improvement of the local primary school or enhancement of their careers.

The deterioration of educational standards and administration

It has also been alleged on the floor of the assembly, though not very frequently, that educational standards suffer as a result of politico-administrative interference. Participating in the debate on budget demands for community development projects, a Jan Sangh MLA cited an exceptional case in which a BDO is said to have manipulated a promotion by misuse of his authority, and in which a subdeputy inspector had been involved.[33] A Congress MLA believed the parties encouraged such interference.[34] "The political parties themselves are responsible for falling standards. They have let politics intrude there. Many teachers are R.S.S. minded [35] and join the *Shakhas*. Many students are misguided and when they are checked they beat the authorities. Who is responsible for that?"

Politico-administrative interference, together with other factors, has also tended to weaken the span and quality of technical supervision and control.[36] The *Report of the Fourth National Seminar on Compulsory Primary Education*[37] in 1964 summarized the situation in the specific context of Rajasthan. "Primary education has been transferred to the Panchayat Samitis. The recruitment of the teachers is made by the B.D.O. and the Pradhan of the Panchayat Samiti. Education department is not represented at the time of recruitment. There is no member of the education department associated with the transfers of primary school teachers either at the block level or at the district level. Disciplinary action against the Panchayat Samiti teacher can be taken by the District Establishment Committee where the District Education Inspector is a member. But at no time is the District Education Inspector consulted while inflicting punishment against the Panchayat Samiti teacher. All the sub-deputy Inspectors of schools have been transferred on deputation to the Panchayat Samitis for inspection and supervision of the primary schools. They are under the administrative control of the B.D.O. It is pointed out that the sub-deputy Inspectors of schools . . . carry out the duties other than education and, therefore, it is felt that the primary education is suffering at the hands of Panchayat Samitis. . . . The standard of education has deteriorated because the loyalty of the teacher is shifted more towards the Education department [sic]. The sub-deputy Inspector of schools has the power to write a confidential report of the primary school teacher. But the sub-inspector of schools does not write it faithfully because he himself is under the control of the Panchayat Samiti and he does not feel safe."

Partisan distribution of benefits

The interplay of politics and management of primary schools has also resulted in partisan distribution of benefits insofar as political connections have become a factor in the opening of new schools and the upgrading of old ones. It is not clear, however, whether state or *samiti* level forces are the dominating influence. The charge made by a PSP legislator, who in his speech on budgetary demands in 1962 said, "Political motives get undue weight while opening new primary schools," [38] has been frequently repeated. MLA's have charged that the population criteria for locating schools are violated.[39] It is also alleged that state level political decisions, which are discriminatory, supercede block level decisions. "The *samitis* are not more than post-men conveying to the school what is sent by the education department. . . . Experience gained as *pradhan* tells that in regard to opening of new schools the recommendations of *samitis* are not paid heed. The schools are opened by the educational department in the villages which have returned Congress Sarpanchas." [40] There are also allegations of state level discrimination in favor of the district in which the chief minister's constituency falls.[41]

In sum, many opposition members of the legislature believe that politics has thoroughly demoralized the primary school teacher,[42] whose status and prestige stands eroded,[43] and who often has to put up with the maltreatment and misbehavior of nonofficial PR leaders.[44] The situation has been summed up in a pointed manner by an independent MLA. "The handing over of primary schools to the *samitis* is like putting a child before a wolf. The uneducated village leaders and *sarpanchas* guide the teachers and take the attendance of teachers like a sub-inspector taking attendance of a *kanjar*." [45]

The foregoing analysis of the interaction of politics and the management of primary schools tends to support the view of Bhairon Singh (Jan Sangh), a leading opposition figure in the assembly, that "the primary school teachers . . . are merely political agents. . . . They are under too many masters from *panchas,* S.D.I.'s, B.D.O.'s and even V.L.W.'s [Village Level Workers]. Politically motivated interference makes them apathetic in regard to the discharge of their duties. Their pay scale is very low. Through transfers, sanction of leave, and suspension, they are victimized if they remain aloof from politics." [46] This overview of the situation is qualified by the elements of bias and exaggeration natural in the rhetoric of partisan observations on the floor of a legislative assembly, and by the tendency to emphasize politicization at the expense of effective use of political influence by teachers. Yet the evidence marshalled in the foregoing analysis and the near unanimity among all parties in the Rajasthan assembly about most of the problem areas identified above justifies taking Bhairon Singh's characterization seriously. The Rajasthan teachers' union, in July 1968, agreed with this "legislative" view — that *panchayat samitis* harassed teachers, particularly by abusing the authority to transfer. They seemed equally concerned, however, that teachers were being overworked, made to take up adult literacy classes in the evenings, compelled to make deposits in a small savings scheme, and often not paid on schedule because *panchayat samitis* were short of funds.[47] These grievances were not necessarily related to or the result of local political control of primary education.

Local Officials' Perceptions of Local Control

Further empirical exploration of the effects of local control on primary school management was made with the help of an opinion survey in two *panchayat samitis* of Jhalawar district in Rajasthan, where primary school teachers, officials, and elected PR leaders were interviewed about their reactions to PR management of primary schools.[48] Two separate questionnaires were used, one for teachers and the other for the officials and the elected leaders. Because of the small total number of teachers and PR officials, the findings are suggestive rather than conclusive. The more important findings of the survey are summarized here.

Teachers' involvement in politics

Table 42 shows the responses to the question of whether primary school teachers took part in politics.

Table 42. Response to question: "Do primary school teachers take part in politics?" (by position of respondent).

Position	Yes		No		Non-response		Total	
	%	No.	%	No.	%	No.	%	No.
Elected PR representatives	42.6	23	42.6	23	14.8	8	100.0	54
PR officials	69.2	9	23.1	3	7.7	1	100.0	13
Teachers	50.0	9	33.3	6	16.7	3	100.0	18
Average	48.2	41	37.7	32	14.1	12	100.0	85

Forty-eight percent of the teachers answered affirmatively, 38 percent negatively, and the rest did not answer. The elected representatives seemed evenly divided on the issue, with twenty-three affirming the phenomenon and an equal number denying it. Some of the elected representatives who denied it seemed to think that they themselves were in the dock, and as such, must deny the involvement of teachers in politics.[49] Among the officials, nine gave an affirmative answer, three replied in the negative, and one was not sure. It is interesting to note that the teachers' response[50] seems broadly to correspond with that of the officials, with nine teachers agreeing, six denying, and three not answering.

Reasons for involvement

A follow-up question about the reasons for teacher participation in politics yielded the responses shown in table 43. Most of the teachers (55 percent) and elected PR officials (65 percent) seemed unwilling or unable to give reasons for teacher involvement in politics. What responses there were to this question suggest that teacher involvement is a two-way rather than a one-way street; teachers involve themselves in politics in order to protect or advance their own needs and interests or "to secure better facilities" for local schools. Political activity by teachers is more frequently explained by such motives than by "pressure from *panchas*" or by the desire "to please *sarpanchas*." The response to this question also throws a rather different light on the reasons for a high rate of transfers — teachers may get involved in politics "to secure transfer to desired place" (or to improve the local school).

One interesting finding that emerges from table 43 is that it may not be correct to say that teachers are dragged into politics; in the view of officials, they are, more often than not, drawn to it on their own with a view to securing personal or local advantages. Political involvement is not so much the pursuit of self-interest as it is a means of self-protection. The line between the two is rather thin, however, and one could well argue that teachers are not as apolitical as their normative image postulates.[51]

Ways and forms of participation

A question relating to the ways and forms of teacher participation in politics evoked the responses shown in table 44.[52] As in the previous question, most (57 percent) of the elected PR officials were unwilling or unable to respond. The response that teacher participation in politics was largely confined to elections should not lead one to conclude that such involvement in politics begins and ends with the election period. Rural politics is a continuing process; once a teacher enters the political arena, he is constantly taken as a participant, sharing in the political rewards and the punishments, at times even in spite of himself.

Teachers' involvement in politics and their performance

The questionnaire also asked whether teachers' involvement in politics adversely affected their performance as teachers. (See table 45.) Of the twenty-three elected PR representatives who thought teachers were in fact involved in politics, sixteen believed that this involvement had a negative effect on performance, four thought it did not have a negative effect and three did not answer. Of the nine PR officials who thought teachers were involved in politics, eight thought their involvement had a negative effect

Table 43. Reasons given for teachers' involvement in politics (by position of respondent).

Position	Pressure from Panchas, etc.		To please sarpanchas		To secure transfer to desired place		To secure better facilities		Alliance with group in native village		Political appointments		Other		Non-response		Total	
	%	No.	%	No.	%	No.	%	No.	%	No.	%	No.	%	No.	%	No.	%	No.
Elected PR representatives	7.4	4	–	–	5.5	3	14.8	8	1.9	1	1.9	1	3.7	2	64.8	35	100.0	54
PR officials	15.4	2	–	–	23.0	3	30.8	4	7.7	1	–	–	15.4	2	7.7	1	100.0	13
Teachers	16.7	3	16.7	3	11.1	2	–	–	–	–	–	–	–	–	55.5	10	100.0	18
Average	10.6		3.5		9.4		14.1		2.4		1.2		4.7		54.1		100.0	85

Table 44. Ways in which primary teachers take part in politics (by position of respondent).[a]

Position	Canvassing openly in PR elections		Canvassing indirectly in PR elections		Participation in general elections only		Participation in PR and general elections		Other		Non-response		Total	
	%	No.	%	No.	%	No.	%	No.	%	No.	%	No.	%	No.
Elected PR representatives	7.6	4	22.2	12	–	–	11.1	6	1.7	1	57.4	31	100.0	54
PR officials	15.4	2	15.4	2	–	–	23.0	3	7.7	1	38.5	5	100.0	13
Average	9.0		20.9				13.4		3.0		53.7		100.0	67

[a] Teachers were not asked this question. See chapter 9, note 52.

and one did not. Finally, of the nine teachers who thought teachers were involved in politics six thought involvement had an adverse effect on performance, one thought it made no difference and two did not respond.

The generally negative view of the effect of teachers' political involvement on their performance was qualified, however, by responses to a question about the effect of politics on the management of primary schools. Although respondents were given an opportunity to list two effects, most cited only one and some failed to respond. In all, there were sixty-nine responses. Thirty-three percent of the responses mentioned the effect of politics on transfers; 23 percent mentioned the effect on grants of money and equipment by the *samitis* to primary schools; 16 percent mentioned the effect on disposal of complaints against primary school teachers; 13 percent mentioned the effect on appointments and dismissals; and 15 percent identified other miscellaneous effects, including more favorable responses to requests for teachers allied with PR politicians. These responses suggest that teachers' political involvement can be important in

Table 45. Estimated effect of political involvement on teachers' performance (by position of respondent).

Position	Distribution of opinion among those who believe teachers are politically involved[a]							
	Adverse effect		No effect		Non-response		Total	
	%	No.	%	No.	%	No.	%	No.
Elected PR representatives	69.6	16	17.4	4	13.0	3	100.0	23
PR officials	88.9	8	11.1	1	–	–	100.0	9
Teachers	66.7	6	11.1	1	22.2	2	100.0	9
Average	73.2		14.6		12.2		100.0	–

[a] See table 42.

furthering the interest of particular primary schools. Particularly significant in this regard is the 23 percent of the responses that found that good political connections enhanced a school's bargaining position with respect to resource allocation.

The observations of the legislative elite and the survey data from local teachers, officials, and politicians both suggest that PR has infused politics into the management of primary schools. The quest for more depoliticized managerial systems which could enlist the support, enthusiasm, and vigilance of elected representatives in the management of primary schools without heavily involving teachers and their institutions in rural local politics is, therefore, not a mere academic pastime but a useful exercise in policy-oriented social research. Policy-makers are not inclined to abandon local control of primary education, but would like to improve administration and implementation. Thus, the joint director of primary and secondary education in Rajasthan wrote to the honorary joint secretary, All-India Federation of Educational Associations that his own feeling was "that instead of pressing for transfer of control it might be better to think of ways to redress the harassment being meted out to teachers in Panchayati Samitis." [53]

The Naik Committee reached a similar conclusion. "On a very careful consideration of the problem, we find that the negative results of the experiment are neither inherent in the system nor irremediable. They have crept in mainly because the careful planning and preparation essential for this important experiment was not done. We, therefore, recommend that the experiment of the administration of primary schools by Panchayati Raj Institutions should be continued with modifications which are essential to overcome the weaknesses which have been so far noticed in actual practice." [54]

Suggestions of modifications have not been wanting. The "Jaipur District Report" (1967) recommended autonomous school management, separate from the *samitis,* which would be an adaptation of the American autonomous school board;[55] that is, a separate political authority and process to govern primary education in which teachers and government-nominated experts would have a two-to-one majority over elected members. A few years earlier, J. P. Naik, member and secretary of the Education Commission, 1964–66, and chairman of the Rajasthan State Primary Education Committee which reported in 1964, suggested in a book on elementary education that control of primary school teachers should rest in a body further removed from the immediate village community. "If association of local bodies at any level higher than the local community is wished at all, the lowest level at which it should be attempted would be the district. The Block is too close to the village and the leadership now available at that level is of a low calibre. Consequently, the teacher's position is most weakened when control over him is vested at the block level. At the district level, there is generally a great distance between him and the members of the local body and the adverse results on his morale are not so great. Even in this case, however, I would very strongly urge that control over the services of the teacher should be vested in officers of the government who should be loaned to local bodies as chief executive officers and not in the local bodies themselves. This will ensure justice and maintenance of order." [56]

In 1965, the Naik Committee, presumably reflecting the views of its chairman, recommended that control of primary education be moved up the administrative hierarchy from the block to the district and that the elective principle be balanced by government nomination of experts.

> For administration of primary education in rural areas, a District Education Committee of the Zila Parishad should be constituted in each district by a suitable amendment of the Rajasthan Panchayat Samitis and Zila Parishads Act. This Committee should consist of twelve persons, of whom not more than half, would be elected members of the Zila Parishad (including the Pramukh who should be an ex-officio Chairman). Among the remaining six members, the District Inspector of Schools, should be nominated ex-officio and the remaining five should be persons interested in education on the lines we have suggested for the bigger Municipal Committee.[57]
>
> A whole-time officer of the status of Deputy Inspector of Schools should be appointed in each district as the Secretary of the District Education Committee. He should be a government official whose services are given on deputation to the Zila Parishad but who should draw his salary and allowances from Government. He should be under the technical control and supervision of the Director of Education. The strength of the Rajasthan Education Service would have to be increased suitably to include these posts.
>
> Relations between the Zila Parishads and the District Education Committee should be defined precisely and in detail. The broad policy should be to leave only financial matters and broad policy questions to the Zila Parishads. The day-to-day administration of primary education should be carried on by the District Education Committee as an autonomous body.[58]

The problem is not so much constructing models of management, which are forthcoming in several reports, as it is convincing politicians that there are good reasons to surrender to government-nominated experts and administrators a substantial portion of the authority they now possess over the personnel, policy, and resources of primary education. The need for depoliticization has to be established before they will support any of these models. Local political leadership helps to create, and is supported by, vested interests that operate through a network of linkages more parochial than enlightened. Rural local politics in India is no exception. There is a built-in resistance to depoliticization in the political process itself. This resistance, however, can arise not only out of a concern on the part of local leaders to protect new-found political resources but also out of a realization on their part that the original goals of panchayati raj — to adjust the goals and operation of local government to local conditions, needs and interests — cannot be realized if, in the name of depoliticization, primary schools are managed by experts, teachers, and administrators. If state level political leaders were to opt for depoliticization (more evenly balancing popular and professional authority in the management of primary education), it would signal the emerging autonomy of the political process. This process tends to mature, not through breaking linkages, but through developing strength and capability to live with them and yet to act independently of them in the larger interests of the community.

The collegiate education discussed in the first chapter of this section — three premier colleges at the end of the nineteenth century — is passing away in India as it is in the rest of the world. The college as community, even as "happy family," shaped by visions elaborated at the top by dedicated and competent teachers and willingly accepted by admiring and devoted students, is a paradigm of elite education as it existed prior to the democratic demand for expansion of higher education; prior to the revolution in generational relations that makes the acceptance of visions from the top more difficult; prior to the class and cultural diversity and the press of numbers that make "community" increasingly difficult to perceive, much less to realize.

College or university autonomy takes its meaning from the settings in which these institutions exist and from the goals they pursue. Like the meaning of values such as justice and freedom, that of autonomy varies with the society, institutional complex, and goals that give it meaning. For example, in India colleges function within the constraints of a university system that prescribes the content of education through its control of syllabi and examinations. Autonomy under such circumstances has a different meaning than in the United States where such a system of outside control would itself be regarded as a limitation on autonomy. The meaning of autonomy varies too with the expectations of those most critically involved with higher education. In the United States, the meaning of autonomy differs for private sectarian colleges and universities such as Notre Dame, Southern Baptist, or Haverford, governed by boards representative of church or sect, and broadly responsive to their purposes; for private secular institutions, such as Columbia or Chicago, whose governing bodies are composed largely of wealthy laymen with greater or lesser propensities or capacities to influence top administrators or interfere with faculty decision making; and for state colleges and universities affected by the actions of state legislatures and politically appointed or elected regents. The meaning of autonomy is related too to the purposes of colleges or universities — to produce character regarded as virtuous by Methodists, or to produce the knowledge, technology, and skills appropriate to an agricultural state. Autonomy, then, cannot be discussed apart from context and purpose, from the identity of the founders, from the composition and authority of governing boards, from the sources of funds, and from the publics and clients that take an interest in or are served by the college or university.

Irene Gilbert shows how, in India, the issues of autonomy were posed differently in government colleges and in privately managed institutions. Not only was the source of directives different — the official bureaucracy of the provincial education ministry as against private trustees — but so too was their content. Government intervention at Presidency College, Calcutta, a government college, was mainly in the interest of larger political considerations. Even though the provincial government was not subject to democratic controls, it acted with concern for the political context, responding to the interests of the educated Indian community in Calcutta. Trustee intervention at Aligarh, a private Muslim college, while partly related to the general concerns of liberal Muslims, reflected attempts by various trustee factions to build bases of political influence in the Muslim community. Although both the public and private colleges discussed in chapter 10 were affected by political considerations, the differences between them are significant. The government college was sensitive to the general demands of the political community, while private educational management was more attuned to influential groups and individuals within the community or communities represented on governing boards.

When the various publics and clients relevant to an educational institution are in agreement on its goals, the issue of autonomy is not apt to arise. "The members of the small educated Indian public, who were also the potential political class, [Irene Gilbert writes] were grateful to the Presidency professors for the educational opportunities and results they provided. In consequence, they tended to respect their opinions on the senate and boards of the university. And so long as Presidency was producing a body of competent professionals loyal to the empire, the British authorities too were content to leave professors to themselves and to allow them to manage and to reform the internal life of the college."

It is when those concerned with the university, both inside and outside it, begin to differ with respect to its goals, and come into conflict with one another, that autonomy becomes problematic. The president and faculty of an American sectarian college may feel quite "autonomous" under a fundamentalist sectarian board until they begin to believe that secular scientific views in social and physical sciences are an essential part of their roles as teachers, scientists, and scholars. So long as the Aligarh professors and the Aligarh trustees were broadly in agreement, the trustees' guidance fell lightly on the college and was willingly accepted inside. When their goals began to diverge, trustee guidance began to be felt as intervention. The same was true at Presidency, where the internal and external definitions of the college's role began to diverge, leading to a belief inside the college that undue intervention had been exercised. By focusing on the breakdown of consensus, Irene Gilbert has suggested a perspective that allows us to anticipate the point at which autonomy is likely to become an issue.

If the history of higher education in the second half of the nineteenth century makes clear that the problems of autonomy and politicization were not novel to postindependence India, the crises of the late 1950's marked the beginning of a new era for these problems. In these years, the universities discussed in this section, Osmania (Andhra Pradesh) and Baroda (Gujarat), as well as many others, began to experience the double impact of demand from below as aspirants for college education doubled, and pressures from above, as state governments sought to satisfy the popular demand for education, to consolidate support by educational allocations

and policies, and to satisfy developmental and welfare goals through educational means.

Carolyn Elliott demonstrates that autonomy becomes an issue when
authorities inside and outside the university cease to agree on goals and
what had been a consensus ceases to be one. In India as elsewhere, one
reason for the breakdown of consensus seems to be the movement from
elite to democratic higher education. When Osmania University was controlled by the princely state of Hyderabad, government influence was as
great or greater than it was after independence and the formation of
Andhra Pradesh, but because the government of the princely state and
the university community were in general agreement, this control was not
felt as a threat to or a diminution of autonomy. Since the incorporation of
Hyderabad with Andhra Pradesh in 1957 this consensus has been eroded
and challenged. Rather than being a small haven in which Urdu culture
could be protected and nurtured, Osmania University began to conceive of
itself as a cosmopolitan institution capable of encompassing a wide variety
of teachers, students, and educational programs. But the government of
Andhra, responsible to a democratic electorate and committed to promote
the development of the backward Telengana region, came to view the university as capable of serving a wider variety of uses, some of which were
extraacademic if not extraeducational. The university was to be responsive
to government's conception of goals. The unfolding visions of the meaning
and uses of the university held by government on the one hand and that
of the new leadership of the university on the other came into conflict.
These circumstances are not unlike situations in the United States where
state or city universities that have transcended more populist beginnings
by upgrading themselves into major intellectual centers have been confronted with demands for open admissions and for relevant curriculum by
constituencies, such as blacks, chicanos, and Puerto Ricans, left out of the
earlier popular waves of demand for higher education.

In Andhra, the divergence of goals between government and university
has been accentuated by emerging differentials in the social composition
of political and intellectual elites. The rural-oriented *kulaks* controlling
the government of Andhra have not always gotten on well with academic
intellectuals drawn from the remnants of an old Hyderabad courtly culture
or from among modern educated and sometimes foreign educated academics recruited outside Andhra Pradesh. Andhra's *kulak* class politicians
would prefer to see Andhra people manning an Andhra university, and
resent "aristocratic" pretensions based on class, culture, or professional
knowledge. If there is a declining consensus at Baroda, the pressures producing dissension come more from the city of Baroda than from the state
government speaking for the mobility aspirations of a democratic electorate. Baroda political and lay interests want more service from the university
— meaning both more admissions and a greater responsiveness to municipal and industrial needs. Baroda administrators and some of Baroda's
faculty have differed with respect to such city-university collaboration.

Three factors: low levels of internal factionalism and its correlate, high
levels of "collegiality"; maintenance of professional, scholarly, and in-

tellectual authority; and government self-restraint based on a broad consensus on goals have been the immediate conditions for a sense of autonomy. One or another of these conditions has given way at Osmania; at Baroda all three were still intact, if precariously so, at the time of our study. In some Uttar Pradesh and Bihar universities, a growing degree of external control has been related to rising levels of internal conflict that have so weakened self-government as to invite legislative, judicial, and executive intervention. Declining levels of professional and intellectual authority have resulted in shifting the criteria in faculty appointments and promotions from professional to bureaucratic considerations, and in locating the source of judgment increasingly in outside, nonprofessional, authority (courts). In those universities where going to court has become common, professional academic authority has evidently lost or failed to achieve the capacity to command respect, much less compliance. Reliance on the courts advances the trend of which it is a reflection, pressing universities toward a bureaucratic model in which faculty can be judged by a nonprofessional authority (such as a court) on the basis of paper criteria, at the expense of the professional model, in which professional colleagues, in the light of their knowledge, consider whether a candidate not only commands the learning in their field but also can add to it. As a result of the growing willingness of government to exercise authority and wield influence within the university, many universities have become another arena in which the party or factional struggles of state politics are conducted.

At Osmania, levels of internal conflict were low in the era of vice-chancellor D. S. Reddi; the influence of academic and professional authority over university processes was strong and on the increase with the recruitment of outstanding scholars from throughout India and abroad. The key factor in the struggle over autonomy at Osmania was the lack of self-restraint on the part of the government of Andhra. Legislation designed to correct malpractices and the decline of professional and academic authority at another state university was extended to Osmania, not because Osmania was suffering from similar difficulties, but rather because of a propensity to impose bureaucratic uniformity for its own sake.

At Baroda, the conditions for autonomy — low levels of factionalism, the hold of professional authority, and self-restraint by the state government (if not by the city) — are being maintained, but not without considerable difficulty. Professional authority is difficult to establish and maintain when teachers are needed to man preuniversity and some first degree production lines rather than to push forward the frontiers of knowledge, and when the nonacademic skills and culture of the educational entrepreneur-administrator, who is required to manage the logistics and politics of expansion, challenge those of the academic. The government of Gujarat continues to support academic excellence at Baroda and to respect its autonomy even though there are pressures to deprive the university of some of the elite characteristics that distinguish it from other Gujarat universities. It remains to be seen whether the Gujarat state commission, established to draft uniform legislation for all universities, will respect or ignore Baroda's distinguishing characteristics.

In the light of traditions of government intervention laid down in the days of the *raj,* the strengthening of the Andhra government's authority through the universities amending acts of 1965 and 1966 does not appear very extraordinary. The acts in Andhra reduced the number of academics in the university senate; reduced, after first trying to eliminate, the number of academics in the syndicate (supreme governing body of the university); increased the number of politicians and officials of the education ministry in both bodies; replaced a university-influenced system of selecting vice-chancellors by a system of government appointment; and removed from government directives, which could previously be issued to the university, some safeguards and consultative procedures that had previously surrounded them. These measures are less severe than similar ones instituted by Lord Curzon in his university acts, discussed in chapter 2. Furthermore, the Andhra measures were justified in part on grounds similar to those cited by Englishmen at the beginning of the century, that is, that the appropriation by university authorities of educational resources for political or private purposes should be reduced. As in Curzon's time, there was in Andhra some justification for such corrective action; government was not persuaded that university independence from government administrative control was essential for the successful performance of its function. The vice-chancellor of Andhra University had conspicuously misused his discretion to favor caste and kin, giving the state "cause" to intervene. The state's remedy included strengthening its control over a worthy institution in order to regulate one that was not. The case illustrates one way in which the genetic imprint of bureaucratic culture and control, discussed in chapter 2, continues to have an ambiguous influence on Indian university administration, restricting creative variety in order to control undesirable deviance.

If bureaucratic uniformity is an important aspect of the genetic imprint that was impressed on the Indian educational system, democracy has served to reinforce the propensity to uniformity. Andhra officials, like officials in other states, are likely to think uniformity a self-evident virtue. The union ministry of education, in establishing a national committee to formulate a "model act" for all universities, reflected India's educational heritage. The committee's charge contained bureaucratic notions that uniform rules might "neaten up" the confusion and conflict and perhaps "cure" the diseases that seemed to afflict academia. That the committee refused its charge, framing suggestions but avoiding an act, was a credit to its understanding of the virtue of diversity. But democratic notions of equality in India today may well strengthen bureaucratic notions concerning uniformity. Differences suggest the possibility of privilege and invite uniformity as a possible cure.

10 / Autonomy and Consensus under the Raj: Presidency (Calcutta); Muir (Allahabad); M.A.-O. (Aligarh)

Irene A. Gilbert

The efforts of professors at three Indian colleges, the Presidency College in Calcutta, the Muir Central College in Allahabad, and the Mohammedan Anglo-Oriental College in Aligarh, to approximate the autonomy of the British college system provide the subject matter for this chapter. Autonomy was easier to achieve in the nineteenth century, when British professors were left relatively free in their colleges, than in the twentieth, when the bases of Indian politics were changing, and the educated public was pushing the Indian university system toward new definitions. The emergence of new publics affected both a private college such as M.A.-O. and a government one such as Presidency, constraining principals and teachers alike by the more complex demands of multiplying constituencies. So long as there was a consensus about collegiate functions among faculty, college sponsors (public or private), and the educated public, as there was throughout much of the nineteenth century, autonomy was no issue. It became one when this consensus faded.

In 1857, universities were established at Calcutta, Bombay, and Madras; some years later, two more were established, at Lahore in 1882 and Allahabad in 1888. These were the only universities in India until 1916.[1] The provincial governors, or in the instance of Calcutta, the governor-general, were the chancellors of the five universities, and through their powers, the institutions were legislatively enabled and reformed over time.[2] The government of the university was vested in the senate to which the chancellor belonged. It was a large public body designed to facilitate discussions of educational policy and university requirements. From among its membership were elected the members of the smaller university bodies, the syndicate (supreme governing body of the university), the faculties, and the

There were many persons in India and England who gave generously of their time, materials, and facilities, but I should especially like to thank those who made available to me materials and facilities not usually requested by visiting research scholars. In Uttar Pradesh, the director of education kindly permitted me to see the records in his office at Allahabad, as did the authorities at the university there. In the same state, Mr. Muzaffer Ali, the librarian at the Azad Library, Aligarh Muslim University, displayed the same generosity in making available the materials in the library's own collection. In Calcutta, my special thanks are due to Justice A. N. Ray, president of the governing body of Presidency College, Principal Bose, Professor A. Tripathi, as well as the librarian and his staff, for making available to me the principals' reports upon which I have drawn so freely. The authorities and the librarian of Calcutta University displayed the same generosity, and thanks are due to them. They are not responsible for the uses to which I have put the materials, and many would probably disagree.

boards of study. The senate, however, always retained the right to pass on the decisions of these executive and academic bodies. Significantly, the senate had no authority to determine the composition of its own membership: a number of government offices were specified in the original enabling legislation and their incumbents appointed fellows of the university in their ex-officio capacities, while the majority of fellows were the lifetime nominees of the chancellor. Succeeding chancellors used their powers responsibly, and missionary educators, Indian notables, and professional men joined government college professors, high court justices, civil surgeons, and chief engineers on the four faculties of arts and sciences, law, medicine, and engineering into which the senate was divided.

The executive arm of the university was the smaller syndicate. Some of its members were elected by the senate, and the rest were appointed in their ex-officio capacities, as was the senior educational official of the provincial government, the director of public instruction. Its chairman was the vice-chancellor of the university, whose position was honorific, without salary, and often filled by the chief justice of the provincial high court. The syndicate was primarily responsible for the organization and coordination of the university degree examinations. It also had the power to initiate major changes in university policy, subject to the senate's approval.

The colleges in the university were not research institutions, but vehicles for the diffusion of modern knowledge in India. Their purpose was to create a class of Indian professionals qualified to serve in the administration and modern professions. From the 1840's, college certificates were preferred for entrance to the public services, and after 1857, university degrees were required for admission to the law and medical colleges.[3] In consequence, many Indian managers were content to operate arts colleges merely to prepare boys for the university degree examinations and for the later vocations which required them. Other colleges, however, were maintained for special purposes. The missionaries maintained colleges in order to infuse a Christian morality into Indian society. The provincial governments maintained special colleges in the districts to supply local educational needs. They also maintained special colleges at the seat of the university, to serve as model or "premier" colleges setting standards and equipped on the whole with the finest teaching facilities to be had in the province. And some Indian leaders maintained colleges in order to regenerate the vitality of their religious communities.

British professors were often employed at these Indian colleges. They were members of their respective colleges rather than the university because Indian universities were not teaching institutions; they were merely affiliating bodies with the power to grant degrees and conduct examinations. The boards of study (into which the faculties were divided) stipulated curricula, courses, and books. After receiving the sanction of the appropriate faculty, the syndicate, and the senate, professors in the affiliated colleges were required to teach the stipulated courses. Professors were also expected to prepare their students for the university-wide first arts,[4] bachelors, and masters first degree examinations. Although individual professors belonged to the senate and served on the boards of study and examination, the majority of college professors in India were obliged to teach and to prepare their students for examinations on the basis of academic decisions taken elsewhere.[5] Furthermore, these British professors were subject to the conditions of service laid down by their employers: the government on the one hand or Indian managers on the other. The efforts of the professors to secure autonomy in this new environment and to preserve it amidst the changes of the early twentieth century, will be explored in this chapter.

Presidency College, Calcutta

The most famed, and certainly the oldest, of the government arts colleges in India was Presidency College, Calcutta. It began as the Hindu College, founded in 1817 by the first generation of Hindu reformers in Bengal. They raised the necessary funds, joined the managing committee, and sent their sons to the new institution.[6] Their purpose was to diffuse modern knowledge among the Hindu community by encouraging the study of the English language, European history, and science.[7] Within three months of its founding, there were some sixty-nine students attending classes at the Hindu College, and in 1824, it employed its first British professor.[8]

But the managers soon had financial difficulties and turned to the British government for aid. The government helped financially, and increasingly granted funds to the college, enabling it to move to new quarters, appoint additional European professors to the staff, and extend the number of student scholarships.[9] By 1841, the Hindu College with its attached high school had grown to more than twelve times its original size, and the government's interest, as well as investment, in the institution had increased.[10] In the early 1850's, when the authorities decided that they should maintain a college of their own, open to all religious communities in India, their attention turned to the Hindu College as a likely possibility. The government entered into a long series of negotiations with the institution's managers, and in 1854 the transfer was consummated. One year later, the Bengal government's premier Presidency College opened its doors for the first time.[11]

With the founding of Calcutta University in 1857, Presidency soon became the only affiliated college in the province capable of teaching up to the full requirements of the university curriculum, and remained so. As the senate legislated new degree requirements, succeeding principals constantly approached the Bengal government for the increased budget allocations necessary for the expansion of staff, or the purchase of new equipment. The government usually responded generously. In 1874, the college was moved to expensive new quarters — which it still occupies today — and in 1910, the size of its physical plant was doubled with the opening of the Baker science laboratories.[12] From a staff of sixteen and a student body of 430 in 1884 (teaching up to the newly formed masters degree level in English, history, mental and moral philosophy, and natural and physical science), Presidency had grown in 1916 to include a staff of nearly sixty instructors and a student body of over 950.[13] Furthermore, it was in that year the only college in the university offering courses in all postgraduate subjects — English, history, political economy, mixed mathematics, physics, chemistry, and physiology.[14] In 1919, the members of the Calcutta University Commission found the college unrivaled in eastern India: its facilities, the strengths of its staff, and the quality of its students all compared favorably with the finer collegiate institutions of Europe and America.[15]

Because of its staff, facilities, and reputation, Presidency attracted the best students in the province from shortly after its founding. James Sutcliffe, the first principal, noted that the college had grown from 285 students in 1866 to 338 in 1869, and that these were "the picked students of Bengal." [16] These students were not drawn from the landowning groups made rich by the permanent settlement, as the government had hoped. They came, instead, from a newly rising professional class of lawyers and doctors, government servants, and poorer zamindars (land owners).[17] And they were, as the director of public instruction, William S. Atkinson, noted, from the only class that seemed to be taking effective advantage of the opportunity for higher education in Bengal. He might have gone on to add that they were the only students who would have to earn their living by using that education.[18]

Presidency continued to draw its students from these "middle classes," as the principals termed them.[19] In what became an accepted educational pattern, the brighter boys from the districts and middle class Calcutta tended to seek admission to Presidency after gaining a first in their matriculation examinations or the later intermediate examinations (taken at the end of the second postschool year), and the college experienced a steady but controlled growth. By 1872, there were some 440 students on its rolls, most from the middle classes; in 1832, their number had expanded by only ten, but by 1896, student numbers had swelled to 620. Twenty years later, the student body had grown to nearly 1,000.[20] In consequence, the principal was able to use his discretion in admissions to advantage. By the turn of the century, it was known that the Presidency principal admitted "firsts" first, and others second — and tuition fees were never set so high as to keep these students away.[21]

At Presidency, students received the finest education, mainly because of the efforts of their professors. Like professors at other arts colleges, the members of the Presidency staff were compelled to prepare their students for the university examinations. But the Presidency professors were also dedicated to enhancing the intellectual qualities of college life. They strove to instill in their students a respect for the standards of excellence and an appreciation for the discipline and skills they would need in later life.[22] Mostly they lectured — tutorials and seminars came much later in the twentieth century. They added personal and informal touches to their lectures, however, by interjecting questions, discussions, and exchange, and by being available for student inquiry and interview both in and after class. Presidency professors groomed their boys for firsts and seconds in the university lists by demanding first-rate work in class assignments and exercises, demonstrations of exactness and fluency in the use of English on essay and composition, and thoughtful answers to the questions on class and college exams. And they often used these as the criteria for admitting students to the university's degree-granting examinations and prize competitions. Of the thirty-two Premchand Roychand studentships, the highest prize in Calcutta University, awarded between 1860 and 1900, Presidency students took twenty-five.[23] The professors' efforts were also reflected in the repeated success of Presidency students on the university examinations, as well as the latters' success in the professions and government service. (See tables 46 and 47.)

The members of the small educated Indian public, who were also the potential political class, were grateful to the Presidency professors for the educational opportunities and results they provided. In consequence, they tended to respect their opinions on the senate and boards of the university. And so long as Presidency was producing a body of competent professionals loyal to the empire, the British authorities, too, were content to leave the professors to themselves, and to allow them to manage and reform the internal life of the college.

In line with their own educational traditions (generally those of the colleges of Oxford and Cambridge), the British professors sought to make the college a community. At Presidency, they created a community in which staff and students might participate in continued traditions of excellence. The effort to reform the institution began slowly: a few attempts at organizing games in the 1870's, a debating club which met intermittently, occasional prize-giving days or gatherings with the old boys.[24] In 1905, the Eden Hindu Hostel was firmly placed under the supervision of the principal, and with that a number of organized activities began to appear. Games were played more often and the boys formed into teams; magazines were issued occasionally and then regularly; clubs and discussion groups were founded and later elaborated.[25] From the hostel, the activities became college-wide, and students had the opportunity to join any number of them. Principal Henry Rosher James set down the ends of his policy in the early years of the twentieth century. "[The college is] an independent commonwealth, which within the limits of the conditions of student-life offers all the elements of complete living. Its end is education for the ultimate purposes of life on a high plane; its means are the common-life in subordination to the interests of all its members. On the one side it is an enlargement of family life, which for the educational purpose is too

Table 46. Presidency College results compared to total results in Calcutta University B.A. examinations.

Year	College/university	Course	Candi-dates ad-mitted	1st	2nd	3rd	Ab-sent	Per-centage passing
1869	Presidency College	–	46	7	13	7	0	59
	Calcutta University[a]	–	128	7	20	23	0	39
1876	Presidency College	–	102	11	9	7	7	28
	Calcutta University[a]	–	179	7	27	8	3	26
1882	Presidency College	Arts	42	3	6	4	0	31
	Calcutta University[a]	Arts	152	2	10	19	7	21
	Presidency College	Sciences	33	3	9	3	1	47
	Calcutta University[a]	Sciences	131	11	24	11	3	36
1886	Presidency College	Arts	46	2	3	27	3	74
	Calcutta University[a]	Arts	252	10	22	172	7	80
	Presidency College	Sciences	34	3	10	13	1	79
	Calcutta University[a]	Sciences	86	0	6	43	1	58
1891	Presidency College	Arts	114	3	29	35	7	63
	Calcutta University[a]	Arts	787	11	58	252	24	42
	Presidency College	Sciences	33	5	16	8	3	97
	Calcutta University[a]	Sciences	148	0	4	50	6	50
1896	Presidency College	Arts	75	4	20	25	4	69
	Calcutta University[a]	Arts	884	0	37	185	44	26
	Presidency College	Sciences	84	6	12	27	3	56
	Calcutta University[a]	Sciences	393	7	26	115	18	39
1901	Presidency College	Arts	94	1	23	23	7	54
	Calcutta University[a]	Arts	1,117	3	33	255	116	29
	Presidency College	Sciences	–[b]	–	–	–	–	–
	Calcutta University[a]	Sciences	–[b]	–	–	–	–	–
1906	Presidency College	Arts	139	3	25	27	5	49
	Calcutta University[a]	Arts	1,217	0	28	232	105	23
	Presidency College	Sciences	111	0	7	31	8	37
	Calcutta University[a]	Sciences	742	0	15	63	76	27

Source: Derived by subtracting the Presidency totals from all the university affiliates and dividing the gross number of examination passes by the number admitted to the examination, less those who failed to attend. They are drawn from the following volumes of the university minutes: University of Calcutta, *Minutes for the Year 1868–69* (Calcutta, 1869), p. 148; *Minutes for the Year 1875–76* (Calcutta, 1876), p. 59; *Minutes for the Year 1881–82* (Calcutta, 1882), pp. 162–163; *Minutes for the Year 1885–86* (Calcutta, 1886), pp. 106–107; *Minutes for the Year 1890–91* (Calcutta, 1891), pp. 114–115; *Minutes for the Year 1895–96* (Calcutta, 1896), pp. 47–48; *Minutes for the Year 1900–01* (Calcutta, 1901), pp. 93–94; *Minutes for the Year 1905–06* (Calcutta, 1906), pp. 285–286.

[a] Data for Calcutta University are exclusive of Presidency College figures.

[b] Page giving science results for the 1901 examinations is missing from the records.

narrow, too concentrated, too closely allied to personal interest; on the other, it is an intensified and more easily comprehended form of the life of the state or commonwealth. It should be at the same time a large family. Its wider aims and interest enlarge and ennoble the narrow intensity of family life. The work and play in common are a mimic representation of

Table 47. Career patterns of Presidency College graduates.

Career	1857–1884 No.	1885–1908 No.	1909–1917 No.
Training abroad[a]	15	90	70
Law:			
Bar	265	415	200
Bench, and other legal			
services for government	150	190	30
Government service in British			
and princely India	90	300	110
Education	80(40)[b]	250(130)[b]	210(65)[b]
Medicine	10 (5)[b]	30 (20)[b]	40(20)[b]
Engineering	2 (2)[b]	15 (10)[b]	10 (5)[b]
Commerce and management	15 (5)[c]	45 (15)[c]	45(15)[c]
Literature and journalism[d]	2	10	3 (1)[b]

Source: Surendrachnandra Majumdar and Gikilnath Dhar, eds., *Presidency College Register* (Calcutta, 1927).

Note: The table takes into account only the careers actually pursued by Presidency College graduates. (There were approximately 675 students who had taken the bachelors degree and reported no further careers during the seventy year period, 370 with the masters degree, and 615 more with the B.A. degree.) Thus, for example, a member of the civil service who had received a B.L. degree and did not pursue a judicial career is included under the government service category, while a member of the civil service who acted as a judge is included under the bench and other legal services category, along with public prosecutors and the like. All figures are rounded off to the nearest multiples of five, except in the obvious instances.

  [a] Includes graduates who received their legal training at the Inns of Court, and thus is the only category which duplicates information found elsewhere on the table.

  [b] The number in the parentheses is the total in British government employment.

  [c] The number in the parentheses is the total managing their own estates.

  [d] Includes only those who indicated no other sources of income.

the life of the state or nation, only in an intense and more concentrated form, comparable, we may fancy, to the life of the city-state of classical or medieval times. It is a working object lesson of the value of disinterestedness and public spirit. It should teach by example the uses of co-operation and the advantage of forming part of an integral whole." [26]

Muir Central College, Allahabad

The history of the Muir Central College in Allahabad is significantly different, in its way a reaction to diverging local conditions and the seeming unsuitability of the Calcutta University syllabus. Unlike Calcutta, which was one of the first centers of British dominion in India, the North-Western Provinces was a relatively late administrative creation. The lieutenant-governorship was not formed until 1834, and contained within its boundaries the last remnants of Moghul rule at Delhi and Agra, as well as the more important centers of the Hindu religion at Banaras and Allahabad. Its capital was located at Agra. The government maintained a small college there, two others at Delhi and Bareilly, and a lightly attended English class at the Sanskrit College in Banaras. These were affiliated to the University of Calcutta after 1857.[27]

In the shock of the Sepoy Mutiny and the slow recovery of the province, all this changed. The Delhi districts were ceded to the Punjab, and the college there fell under the purview of that government's educational department. In 1860, the capital was moved from Agra to Allahabad — one of the few centers in the upper provinces to have resisted the mutineers — and virtually a whole new administrative city was planned. As yet, there were no provisions made for an English college at the new capital. Instead, the provincial educational authorities were straining to meet the exacting demands of the Calcutta University English curriculum. In the heartland of traditional India, Muslims were not coming to the government colleges, while Hindus, unlike their counterparts in Bengal, seemed to respond positively to educational efforts in the vernacular. In consequence, the colleges remained little more than high schools and their showing on university examinations remained poor. In 1868, Bareilly managed to pass only one student in the third division of the first arts degree examination, while Agra could pass only three in the first and second divisions, and at Banaras only four of eleven sent up managed to pass in the third division.[28] By 1869, it was felt that some compromise with the Calcutta system was necessary. The lieutenant-governor, Sir William Muir, expressed the consensus of opinion in the education department.

The system of requiring certain proficiency in English as the condition of University training and University distinctions, is sound and unassailable; but it may be that the condition is pushed too far and made too stringent. By the present rules, no honors in Oriental literature can be secured until the student shall have passed the B. A. Standard. But to produce a beneficial action upon the national mind it is perhaps too much to require so severe a standard in English and in science. The great want of the people is a Vernacular literature: — works in History, Art, and Science, containing sound knowledge, written in an elegant style, and composed on models of thought and expression agreeable to the Native mind. For this end, a body of students is needed who, by the study of the Oriental classics, shall possess the faculty of composing in such a style; and high proficiency in Oriental literature, itself requiring much study, can hardly be looked for in combination with the very high standard in English and in science required for the B. A. Degree. It is therefore a matter for serious consideration whether a greater national benefit would not be secured by offering Honor Degrees in the Oriental languages to students of a certain lower standard in English and in science, than as now by insisting on the pre-requisite of a B. A. Degree.[29]

Sir William went on to suggest that a branch of the university senate be established at Allahabad, and the province's educational needs be met in locally formulated degree requirements. Both the vice-chancellor of the university and the Government of India rejected the idea.[30]

The provincial authorities were not content, and official opinion increasingly favored the establishment of a government college at Allahabad, leading, perhaps, to an independent university in the North-Western Provinces. After a long series of negotiations, a compromise was reached in 1872. The government of India consented to the founding of a government college at Allahabad, and so long as the English requirements of the Calcutta University curriculum were met, the provincial government might use the new institution to promote the development of higher education in the vernacular.[31] When the Muir Central College opened shortly thereafter, it was the task of Muir's first principal, Augustus Harrison, to organize and administer a new province-wide vernacular examination.[32]

By the time Muir moved into its permanent quarters in 1886, however, the vernacular exam was of minor proportions.[33] By then, classes in English had superseded it. Small at first, and composed in large part of young Kashmiris and Bengalis whose fathers had come to Allahabad to find employment in the new city, the classes in English grew as the administrative center, with its networks of courts and subsidiary services, expanded. As local Hindu groups began to take advantage of these increased opportunities, the new middle classes began to send their sons to the English language college, much as their predecessors had done in Bengal two generations before.[34]

Like Presidency, the Muir Central College provided its students with the finest instructional staff in the province, and as the establishment at Allahabad grew, the ones at Bareilly and Agra were reduced. (Eventually the latter were given over to private managers on the advice of the Educational Commission of 1882.)[35] Like his counterpart at Presidency, the Muir principal reaped the benefit: he was usually free to select the best students in the province for admission to the college. By 1883, it had become the second-ranking college in the University of Calcutta, its student body having increased from the meager 13 of 1872 to 105. Among its graduates it numbered fourteen high court pleaders, five holders of the B.L. degree, four of the M.A., and sixteen of the B.A. Only Presidency, which was much larger, surpassed it in university honors and awards: of the 156 honors and awards won between 1877 and 1883, Muir's students took 21 to Presidency's 78.[36]

On the strength of the Muir record, the provincial authorities once again approached the government of India, this time for permission to establish an independent university. The government of India agreed to the proposal, and in 1888, the University of Allahabad was formed.[37] The Muir College was its premier affiliate. In its enhanced position, the North-Western Provinces government treated the college with the same generosity that the Bengal government treated Presidency: budget allocations were slowly increased as the Muir principals repeatedly approached the government for more professors and facilities when new university requirements necessitated them. From the modest curriculum of 1890, which offered courses at the masters level in the fields of English, philosophy, Sanskrit, mathematics, and physical science, Muir expanded to meet the demands of the more sophisticated curriculum of 1920, and offered courses in English, Arabic, Persian, Sanskrit, philosophy, history, economics, physics, chemistry, zoology, and botany at the masters level.[38] In consequence, it continued to draw the best students in the province, and its rate of growth compared favorably with that of Presidency. Its staff of twelve in 1890 had expanded to forty by 1920, while its student body had more than doubled in size to 550.[39] And the Muir staff's success in sending students through the university examinations, and qualifying them for later careers (as the incomplete records show) was equally favorable. (See tables 48 and 49.)

With the support of the government and the educated Indian community, the British professors were left free to enact the same reforms at Muir as their colleagues at Presidency. Because Muir was smaller, they were able to create the same sense of community that existed at Presidency, but earlier and without the organizations needed at the larger Calcutta college. As a student of 1879 recalled, "No visitor, European or Indian, was seen to come and inspect the college. Quiet work was done and there was no display or demonstration — no prize distribution. There was however no lack of prizes. First-Divisioners got a scholarship each and the Principal never failed to give reward to a deserving student out of his own pocket. . . . Limited accommodation — and a limited number of pupils enabled the College to work smoothly — cheaply and effectively like a family — like a happy family." [40] In later years as the college grew, the same extracurricular activities and organizations were elaborated, each guided by an appropriate member of the staff. The first hostels were organized in 1906. In 1907, intramural athletic associations were formed, and clubs, literary societies, and a college magazine followed shortly thereafter.[41] But the English professors' first aims were still to enhance the intellectual aspects and disciplines of college life. Another student recalled the quality of the education he received from Muir's principal, J. G. Jennings, before the institution's conversion to a residential university in 1922: "He was an artist, and he had a great sense of technique, of proportion, of architectonics. He hated loose thought, vague vocabulary, mere showing off. In my first essay on the Lake poets, he cut off three of my last pages, in which I had brought in the minor writers of the school, Lamb, Lloyd, etc., simply saying, 'This is an essay, not a historical treatise.' When he gave me Beta minus at the end, I felt as if the spirit of an essay had been graven on my *tabula rasa* with a stylus of steel. I always got Alpha or Alpha plus from him ever after. He had a Black Book and he noted there what every one of his students did. And he never forgot it. He was very fond of Terminal Examinations and he had three each year for the undergraduates. But we graduates had an option. He left the matter to us. When

Table 48. Muir Central College results compared to total results in the Allahabad University B.A. and B.Sc. examinations.

Year	College/university	Course/ exam	Candi- dates ad- mitted	1st	2nd	3rd	Ab- sent	Per- centage passing
1889	Muir College	Arts	26	1	15	4	1	80
	Allahabad University[a]	Arts	38	0	10	11	1	55
	Muir College	Sciences	4	0	1	0	0	25
	Allahabad University[a]	Sciences	10	1	4	2	0	70
1893	Muir College	Arts	54	2	19	7	1	53
	Allahabad University[a]	Arts	149	3	59	25	1	59
	Muir College	Sciences	14	2	5	2	1	69
	Allahabad University[a]	Sciences	31	1	10	6	0	55
1898[b]	Muir College	B.A.	51	1	21	6	0	55
	Allahabad University[a]	B.A.	274	2	86	57	5	54
1904	Muir College	B.A.	49	0	14	18	1	67
	Allahabad University[a]	B.A.	271	2	58	116	4	66
	Muir College	B.Sc.	13	0	4	6	0	77
	Allahabad University[a]	B.Sc.	6	0	2	2	0	67
1909	Muir College	B.A.	45	1	11	16	0	61
	Allahabad University[a]	B.Sc.	475	1	70	124	12	42
	Muir College	B.Sc.	38	1	10	8	0	50
	Allahabad University[a]	B.Sc.	103	0	6	15	3	21
1915	Muir College	B.A.	58	0	10	15	0	43
	Allahabad University[a]	B.A.	973	1	87	233	19	34
	Muir College	B.Sc.	40	1	6	10	0	43
	Allahabad University[a]	B.Sc.	122	3	17	43	4	53
1920	Muir College	B.A.	79	1	15	32	0	61
	Allahabad University[a]	B.A.	1,313	2	88	382	21	37
	Muir College	B.Sc.	33	4	16	9	0	88
	Allahabad University[a]	B.Sc.	162	2	31	51	4	53

Source: University of Allahabad, *Minutes for the Year 1889* (Allahabad, 1889), p. 95; *Minutes for the Year 1892–93* (Allahabad, 1893), pp. x–xi; *Minutes for the Year 1898–99* (Allahabad, 1899), pp. v–vi; *Minutes for the Year 1903–04* (Allahabad, 1904), pp. vi–ix; *Minutes for the Year 1909* (Allahabad, 1910), pp. vii–xi; *Minutes for the Year 1915* (Allahabad, 1916), pp. xiv–xix; *Minutes for the Year 1920* (Allahabad, 1921), pp. xiv–xvii, xx–xxi.

[a] Data for Allahabad University are exclusive of Muir College figures.

[b] Only one student, from Canning College, Lucknow, appeared for the new B.Sc. degree in this year, and he failed the examination.

we voted for it, he was obviously pleased. When we got back the examined books, the experience really proved valuable for the University examination." [42]

Mohammedan Anglo-Oriental College, Aligarh

The Mohammedan Anglo-Oriental College in Aligarh in the North-Western Provinces was nearly contemporary with the Muir Central College.

Table 49. Career patterns of Muir Central College graduates, 1872–1922.

Career	Number
Law:	
Bar	17
Bench, and other legal services for government	23
Government service in British and princely India	59
Education	61[a]
Medicine	4[b]
Engineering	10[b]
Commerce and management	7[c]

Source: W. H. Wright, *The Muir Central College, Allahabad, Its Origin, Foundation and Completion* (Allahabad, 1886), Appendix 1, *passim;* Jha, *A History of the Muir Central College;* Mehrottra, *University of Allahabad, Seventieth Anniversary Souvenir*, pp. 83–113; University of Allahabad, *Old Students' Who's Who* (Allahabad, 1958).

Note: There is no complete record for the careers of Muir College graduates, and the above has been drawn from varying, and scanty sources. Further, the distribution of information is uneven for the fifty year period, the more complete record covering the very early years. Suffice it to state, however, that the career patterns of the Muir students followed, in general outline, those of the Presidency students.

[a] Thirty of the sixty-one were in British government employment.

[b] In British government employment.

[c] One of the seven managed his own estates.

In 1873, Syed Ahmed (later Sir Syed Ahmed Khan) wished to found an English language school and college with which to regenerate the life of his religious community in India. Disturbed because so few Muslims seemed to be attending the government colleges, he sought to provide the members of his faith with modern learning, while yet assuring them of the continued sanctity of Islam. Like the Hindus in Bengal two generations before him, he thought the solution lay in a community-sponsored institution, offering instruction in secular subjects, without, at the same time, offending the group's religious sensibilities. Unlike the Hindu college, the Muslim college would therefore offer its students instruction in religious subjects. Sir Syed turned to the North-Western Provinces government for financial aid.[43]

The provincial authorities responded generously, agreeing to contribute to the support of the college's secular classes. The original grant of Rs. 350 per month was increased to Rs. 500 in 1878, and renewed again in 1882. It was the largest grant-in-aid accorded to a private institution in the province, and with increases over time, continued to remain so. The lieutenant-governor was named visitor and patron to the college.[44]

The institution's financial position assured, the board of trustees, dominated by Sir Syed, proceeded to draw up its plans. In May 1875, Aligarh's first school classes met, attended by sixty-six Muslim students. They were instructed by seven Indian masters, under the supervision of the college's first headmaster and principal, K. G. Siddons, formerly of the North-Western Provinces education department.[45] Under Siddons, the school was run like any other private institution in the province; it was affiliated to the university at Calcutta and prepared its students for the university examinations. By 1881 when Aligarh was affiliated to the B.A. level, it had 259 students, and the staff had been expanded to include a second European professor and an increased number of Indian assistant professors and masters. Its results until then on university examinations had been respectable: thirty-five of the fifty-six students sent up for the entrance exam and nine of the seventeen sent up for the intermediate exam passed.[46] When Siddons retired from the principalship in 1882–83, there was little to distinguish the M.A.-O. College except for the personality of Sir Syed, the Muslim character of the board of trustees, and the religious training afforded both Sunni and Shia students.

All this changed with the appointment of Theodore Beck to the principalship in 1883. Unlike Siddons, Beck had been specially selected in England for the post, almost directly upon his graduation from Cambridge.[47] He was a young man who brought to his task a sense of dedication and enthusiasm — almost a sense of mission, to which Sir Syed and the board responded. In consequence, Beck was given the freedom to reform the internal life of the college. His model was the British public school and the character of its graduate. "Considering the needs of the country, we should at present I think devote our attention to the active, rather than the contemplative side of human nature, and work more at developing strength of character, a sense of public duty, and patriotism, than at cultivating the imagination, the emotions or the faculty of pure speculation. And thus hope to achieve success, we must reluctantly abandon the cultivation in the majority of our students, of the poetic, artistic, or philosophic temperament, and devote our attention to turning out men who in appearance are neatly dressed and clean, of robust constitution and well-trained muscles, energetic, honest, truthful, public spirited, courteous and modest in manner, loyal to the British government and friendly to individual English men, self-reliant and independent, endowed with common sense, with well-trained intellects, and in some cases scholarly habits." [48]

Reversing the order of priorities at the government colleges, Beck turned first to reorganizing student life at Aligarh. He managed to attract to the staff a number of young Englishmen as dedicated as he, and ready to participate in student activities, associations, and clubs. Theodore Morison, his successor, joined the college in 1889; T. W. Arnold, author of *The Preaching of Islam,* joined in 1888; and Walter Raleigh, later professor of English at Cambridge, joined in 1885.[49] They reformed the hostels into houses, and Aligarh became the first college in India to have a system of student prefects. Games became a required part of daily life, and cricket, tennis, and other teams were formed. The student body was organized into a college-wide union, and a number of clubs and magazines were founded, many of them dealing with aspects of Islamic faith and history.[50]

Beck attempted to disabuse the Aligarh students of their misplaced aristocratic notions and to transform their new sense of corporate loyalties into the wider one of community service. He therefore directed student efforts toward work in the Muslim community. The *Duty* or *Anjuman-al-Farz* was founded to collect college funds for scholarships for poorer students, while other students collected information for the Mohammedan educational census, and still others contributed their labor to local famine relief drives.[51]

Beck and the British staff's goal was to have a regenerated Muslim community make a vital contribution to the empire. Sir Syed supported Beck when the latter stated, "I attach the utmost importance to implanting in the minds of our students a conviction of the inestimable benefits India has derived from the British rule, and to fostering in their hearts a sentiment of loyal devotion to the British Crown." [52] On the one hand, such a conviction was implanted by the relations of mutual confidence and trust which obtained between the European staff and Indian trustees and by the easy and respectful relations the students felt free to assume with their British teachers. On the other hand, it was implanted by the continued demonstrations of support the British government extended to the college authorities: financial aid, official attendance at college functions, and the yearly appearance of the lieutenant-governor as patron of the college at Aligarh's prize-giving day.

During Beck's tenure as principal, Aligarh achieved a respectable showing on the examinations of Allahabad University (to which the college was affiliated after Allahabad's foundation in 1888), but as opposed to the government colleges, its students succeeded in the easier arts courses rather than in the more difficult sciences. The graduates of the smaller college, however, were as successful as the government college graduates in gaining admission to the government services and modern professions. (See tables 50 and 51.)

Theodore Beck died one year after Sir Syed Ahmed Khan, in 1899. The same relation that had existed between Sir Syed and Beck obtained between Sir Syed's son, Justice Syed Mahmood, the new honorary secretary, and Theodore Morison, the new principal; and Morison was able to carry on with Beck's old authority in the college. Syed Mahmood soon resigned from the honorary secretaryship, however, and shortly after, Morison left India in 1905.

Through the nineteenth century, British professors were left relatively free in their colleges; the government was satisfied with the competence of the new professional class being trained in them, and religious communities such as the Muslims were glad of the opportunity to participate once again in the mainstream of a changing Indian life. For the quality of their work, European professors received the approbation of the modern educated Indian community generally; their opinions were respected on the senate and other bodies of the university, and in consequence, the academic organization of the colleges was little interfered with. But could the same relationship, the same trust, exist in the twentieth century, when

Table 50. M.A.-O. College results compared to total results in the Allahabad University B.A. and B.Sc. examinations.

Year	College/university	Course/ exam	Candi- dates ad- mitted	1st	2nd	3rd	Ab- sent	Per- centage passing
1889[a]	M.A.-O. College	Arts	8	0	2	3	0	63
	Allahabad University[b]	Arts	56	1	23	12	2	67
1893[a]	M.A.-O. College	Arts	15	1	7	1	0	60
	Allahabad University[b]	Arts	188	4	71	31	2	57
	M.A.-O. College	Sciences	1	0	1	0	0	100
	Allahabad University[b]	Sciences	44	3	14	8	1	58
1898[a]	M.A.-O. College	Arts	36	1	14	5	0	56
	Allahabad University[b]	Arts	211	3	51	49	3	50
1900[c]	M.A.-O. College	B.A.	30	0	11	12	1	79
	Allahabad University[b]	B.A.	230	4	77	27	6	48

Source: University of Allahabad, *Minutes for the Year 1889* (Allahabad, 1889), p. 95; *Minutes for the Year 1892–93* (Allahabad, 1893), pp. x–xi; *Minutes for the Year 1897–98* (Allahabad, 1898), pp. v–vi; *Minutes for the Year 1899–1900* (Allahabad, 1900), pp. v–vi.
  [a] No M.A.-O. College students took the Sciences examination this year.
  [b] Data for Allahabad University are exclusive of M.A.-O. College figures.
  [c] No M.A.-O. College students took the B.Sc. examination this year.

the bases of Indian politics were changing and the educated public was pushing the Indian university system toward new definitions?

The Decline of Consensus at Presidency:
Government and University Intervention

By the time Henry Rosher James assumed the principalship of Presidency College in 1908, Bengal's new professional public had been effectively radicalized. The partition of the province in 1905 had raised a storm of protest, some violence, and had led the leaders of the Indian public to

Table 51. Career patterns of the M.A.-O. College graduates, 1890–1900.

Career[a]	Number
Law:	
Bar	30
Bench, and other legal services for government	7
Government service in British and princely India	57
Education	27[b]
Engineering	2[c]

Source: Theodore Morison, *The History of the M.A.-O. College, Aligarh, From its Foundation to the Year 1903* (Allahabad, 1903), pp. 68–73.
  [a] Thirty-six students did not list any employment or further education after receiving their B.A. degrees.
  [b] Seven of the twenty-seven were in British government employment.
  [c] In British government employment.

extend the bases of their political appeals and organization. They chose for their platform and rallying point College Square, the intellectual heart of the city, directly opposite Presidency and its hostels. Inevitably, the students were drawn to the meetings, mingled with the crowds, and discussed political events among themselves on quieter evenings. For many, it was a period of romance and exhilaration. Some students joined the more radical organizations, recruiting members for them in the college hostels. The government of India tried to stop the students' activity in 1907 by threatening the disaffiliation of their different colleges from the University of Calcutta.[53] But some students maintained their contacts with radical political organizations after protest ebbed, and the Presidency students at the Eden Hostel were among them.[54]

Although the British eventually reamalgamated the province, the protest left a legacy of distrust in the community, even among its older and more conservative elements. Rather than cooperate easily with the British authorities as they had done before, some members of the public elected to secure control of the institutions afforded them. The University of Calcutta was one such institution. During the vice-chancellorship of Sir Asutosh Mukherji, efforts were made to expand the powers of the university and enhance its central organs with a real teaching authority.

Sir Asutosh was a brahman. As a youth, he had had a brilliant academic career at Presidency, and his exceptional mathematical talents won him the Premchand Roychand studentship, the highest prize in the university. (Later, he was elected to memberships in both the Royal Astronomical Society and the Royal Society of Edinburgh on the strength of his continued mathematic attainments.)[55] After his graduation, he took up the study of law and became one of the most eminent members of the Calcutta bar. When he was appointed to his first vice-chancellorship in 1906, he was justice of the Calcutta high court.[56] Sir Asutosh was the second Indian vice-chancellor of the university. It fell to his administration to enact the reforms called for by the Indian Universities Act of 1904. The purpose of the act was to improve the quality of teaching in the affiliated colleges by strengthening the affiliating powers of the university. Secondarily, it provided for the beginnings of postgraduate teaching in the university proper with the establishment of university professorships.[57] Sir Asutosh emphasized the latter purpose and used his new, more flexibly formulated affiliating powers to subvert the former purpose.

Sir Asutosh, a scholar in his own right, by tradition and achievement, came to feel a great respect for learning. He wished to make the University of Calcutta a great center of scholarship. Moreover, he wished to provide Bengali youth with the opportunity to pursue their studies further, as well as to develop their own scholarly abilities. The expansion of the new research departments of the university was a national and political aim for both Bengal and India. On retiring from the vice-chancellorship in 1914, Sir Asutosh stated in a convocation address: "Let us, therefore, advance the banner of progress in hand, with bold but not unwary steps, drawing confidence and inspiration from the consciousness that so many of the best and truest men of our people are in full sympathy with us; that the rising generation has availed itself with eagerness, nay enthusiasm, of the new opportunities we have created for higher students; that the sparks of the new inextinguishable fire kindled in our midst have already leapt to all parts of India, and that the sister universities are eager to imitate and emulate what we have boldly initiated. I feel that a mighty new spirit has been aroused, a spirit that will not be quenched; and this conviction, indeed, is a deep comfort to me for so many weighty reasons. I thus bid farewell to office and fellow workers, not without anxiety for the future of my University, but yet with a great measure of inward contentment: and — let this be my last word — from the depths of my soul, there rises a fervent prayer for the perennial welfare of our *Alma Mater* — for whom it was given to me to do much and suffer to some extent — and of that greater parental divinity to whom even our University is a mere hand-maiden as it were — my beloved Motherland." [58] During Sir Asutosh's vice-chancellorship, the fulltime staff of the university expanded to include approximately 100 members, and by 1916, there were 1,258 students enrolled in the university's postgraduate classes, as compared to the 326 at Presidency and the 25 at the Scottish Church College (the only other institutions offering advanced instruction in Calcutta).[59]

These policies increased Sir Asutosh's stature in the community as well as his powers for patronage. He was able to elicit substantial donations from Calcutta's wealthier citizens, and invested these in semiautonomous institutes administered by boards controlled by the vice-chancellor rather than the senate. The British professors in the senate protested this new mode of university organization, especially when the University College of Science was planned in 1916.[60] But Sir Asutosh was parliamentarily adept, and pursued his policy of expansion with the support of the Indian members of the senate. He frequently called meetings with little advance notice, or when his opponents were likely to be away, as Messrs. Archbold, Watson, and Biss claimed at a senate meeting in 1914.[61] In 1913, Principal James of Presidency commented upon the procedures which had come to characterize the decisions of the senate. "For the last two years the Senate has been giving their consent to sporadic proposals of this nature without detailed information and without a comprehensive scheme of Post Graduate teaching in the various subjects which the University had undertaken. He thought it would have been more satisfactory if the Senate were supplied with full and detailed information as regards organisation, staff, library and accommodation while they were asked to give their consent to the above proposals [to appoint two lecturers in economics]." [62] James was voted down, as he was a year later when he once again put forward the same suggestion.[63]

The government of Bengal acceded to these innovations, and, to the chagrin of the government of India, repeatedly supported the vice-chancellor's requests for increased financial aid when Indian benefactions did not suffice.[64] Inevitably, these sanctioned extensions of the university's teaching powers impinged upon the postgraduate teaching being conducted in the colleges, raising the whole question of the structure of higher education. British professors found themselves in opposition to Indian aspirations.

James was a senior member of the Indian Educational Service and one of its most respected members. "Most members of the Indian Educational Service, are, I think," stated Sir George Anderson, "in agreement that Mr. James is about the best man in that service on the professorial side. He has written the most helpful book in recent times on the subject of Indian education." [65] A former Queen's scholar at Westminster, James had gone on to win the Westminster scholarship to Christ Church College, Oxford. At Oxford, he took a first in classical moderations and went on to take his greats degree in the first class in 1885. The quality of his examination and a beginning translation of the works of Boethius won him election to a junior tutorship at Christ Church. He joined the Indian Educational Service in 1890 and was appointed to the staff of Patna College. In 1905, he became its principal. Two years later when the Presidency College principalship fell vacant, James was appointed to the post; Sir A. H. Frazer, the lieutenant-governor of Bengal, named him, "the fittest man in the department for the permanent appointment." [66]

Meticulous and exacting, James gave himself up wholeheartedly to all the details of college administration. From the point of view of the secretariat, his inability to delegate authority to subordinates reflected poor executive talents. In 1913, a bureaucrat in the Bengal education department noted that "the duties of the Principal of the college are very heavy, but Mr. James certainly does take a degree of satisfaction in doing with his own hand unimportant matters of which he could be easily relieved by the Steward who is a competent assistant." [67] Many of his students, however, remembered these small efforts on their behalf with gratitude and affection. Writing some years later, Sir Jadunath Sarkar, the historian, recalled James' attempts at "licking raw Indian lads into shape at Patna." He lectured, graded their class exercises, and even remained behind one hot season to catalogue the college library, "removing the books from the shelf himself and writing it out by hand." [68]

Putting much of himself into his work, James hoped, almost yearned, for public recognition. But his efforts went unrewarded. Independent and strong-willed, he persisted in making his case for a stronger educational policy: at the university, in the press, in his own monographs — even when the new governor, Lord Carmichael of Skirling, would have wished otherwise. Taking into account James' uncooperative behavior, the provincial government chose to look outside Bengal for its new director of public instruction. In 1913, W. W. Hornell, an assistant director of examinations at the Board of Education in London, was selected for the directorship.[69] This was too much for the rather austere and reserved James, who by this time was taut and high-strung, his nerves on edge. In an unguarded moment, he penned the following in a letter to Hornell.

You must also be fully aware of the extreme personal injury you have done me. I have, or at least I had, no reason to suppose that you nourished any malice against me, or that it would gratify you to see me brought down. If, however, you do you may have that gratification. Not only am I deprived of a recognition which I had every reason to suppose I had attained, but it is with the greatest difficulty that I can hold to what has long since been in my possession. For reasons strong enough to overcome the hatefulness of it, I force myself to the necessity of such official relations with you as are unavoidable. I pray you to spare me anything beyond that.

I ask you, then, kindly to understand that our relations must be in the strictest sense of official. You have recently written two letters to me. I cannot prevent your writing demi-officially, if you think good, but I must ask you to refrain from addressing me personally by name. That at least you can avoid. I also hope that you will intervene as little as possible in Presidency College affairs. Officially I must endure you as best I can.[70]

From that time, relations between the government and the principal of its most important college were, to say the least, tense.

By any standard, James was a conservative. He believed in the need for empire, Englishmen, and modern education in India. He held the view that India's educational and political goals could be achieved in collegiate communities, organized on autonomous and residential lines. In his book *Education and Statesmanship in India,* he wrote: "When fully developed the sentiment called forth by the institution may be even more powerful in its sway over conduct than the influence of individual teachers. Here a departmental system is to some extent a hindrance, because to a department a college or school is necessarily not a self-contained whole, but one member of a group. Recent tendencies, however, have all been in the direction of giving fuller recognition to the organic unity of the institution and a measure of autonomy is already attained by the colleges within the bounds of the department. It is on this ground as well as on the ground that students living uncared for and insufficiently supervised in "messes" are exposed to dangers, physical and moral, that the immediate prospect of a large provision of hostels in Calcutta is so greatly a matter of congratulation. In order that the full benefit may be realized, it is essential that this provision of hostels should be based on the unity of the college as an institution. This is indeed part of the ideal of the complete residential college, now fully accepted by the University. The members of the college not only study in the same class rooms, but share a social life which extends to all three sides of education, intellectual, physical and moral." [71]

When he was appointed principal, James began to reconstruct the entire

Presidency organization. He wished to absorb student interests in college activities rather than political ones. He therefore proposed that the college's physical plant be expanded to include better residence halls, playing fields, and increased leisure time facilities for Presidency's students. (The government agreed, but was later compelled to postpone the proposed expansion because of the financial shortages caused by World War I.)[72] He also proposed that a student government be formed, so that each student might feel obliged to live up to the responsibilities of the delegation of trust. Thus Presidency became the first government college in India to have a representative student council with the authority to make its own recommendations to the principal. The Bengal government agreed to the suggestion reluctantly.[73]

James also believed that students derived their standards of conduct and probity from the model of their professors' behavior. "Only through the personal influence of the teacher can these great moral results be attained. A high moral tone cannot be communicated to an institution by any rescript, decree or ordinance of State. Rightly devised rules of life will do a great deal, but even these must be informed by the right spirit; a mere lifeless conformity will effect little; even the conformity is sure to be lax without a desire to conform. The right spirit must grow up among the body of students that can be communicated, so far as it is capable of communication, only by the teachers. So the ideals of the teachers and the faithfulness with which they live by them are the real source of moral vitality in school and college." [74] James felt that in the larger Presidency, with its nearly sixty staff members divided into some twelve academic departments, professors' efforts were too easily diffused among the student body of 1,000. To bring the members of the staff in closer touch with the students and coordinate their efforts, James formed an academic council. Composed of the senior British and Indian professors in the college's major departments, it met regularly with the principal to allocate the institution's teaching and extracurricular work. With the consent of the government, the council decided to expand the lecture system to include tutorials, to form special seminars for interested students, and to direct more attention to the students' own academic clubs.[75] James said of its working in 1913: "This at all events has been the policy undeviatingly followed: to devise means of making the College feel and act together, share common aims and interests. The chief instrument has been the College Council, the purpose of which is to keep the different sides and departments of the College in touch. That purpose is, I believe, accomplished, if what has been done is not let go again. Studies are now properly organized and held together through the close co-operation of the teaching staff, subject by subject, and through the apparatus of class exercises, tutorial work, college examinations and seminars." [76] Due to James' initiative, Presidency became the first government college in India to foster a real collegiality.

Like Sir Asutosh, James realized that academic institutions should be

responsive to the needs of the community and informed of the views of
their educated members. To gain the support of the Bengali middle classes
for a reformed Presidency, James suggested that some of its members be
involved in the management of the institution and contribute to the formulation of its educational policies. The Bengal government responded to
the suggestion and in 1909 sanctioned the creation of a governing body
for Presidency. It was composed of the principal, some British and Indian
staff members, Indian representatives of the university and of the legislative council, as well as some government officials. It was empowered as
the institution's final policy-making body, and had the authority to decide
on the allocation of funds within the college, the organization of its academic programs, and significantly, "to deal with all serious breaches of
discipline." [77] Correspondingly, the government consolidated its diverse
budget allocations into a single block grant for the college, also administered by the new governing body.[78] For James, the establishment of a governing body marked the beginning of Presidency's autonomy as an institution of higher learning in Bengal.[79]

Under James' management Presidency had grown, as the director of
public instruction noted, into, "as it were, a small university; it [taught] a
variety of subjects from the matriculation stage right through the M.A.
or M.Sc. examination." [80] Presidency posed the one real challenge to the
success of Sir Asutosh's policies and the university's newly formed postgraduate classes. Of the university's affiliates, it was virtually the only one
that could offer advanced teaching in nearly every subject. And while
Presidency's fees were higher, its teaching was better. In James' time, it
offered smaller classes, tutorial instruction, seminars, and the finest laboratory and library facilities in the province. James made the following
comparison of the origin and quality of the postgraduate instruction available at the two institutions:

The Presidency College organization was also first in the field. Its
classes, as now organized, date from 1908, and have been carried on without any complete break in continuity from a much earlier date, in fact from
the time when definite M.A. *studies* were first instituted under Calcutta
University (that is, 1885). There is thus attaching to the Presidency College classes that very valuable thing, an *academic tradition.*

The organization of the Presidency College classes had not then to be
brought into being for the first time in 1908; it already existed. It has been
carefully modified and improved since. It is based on the principles of (1)
the fitness of the student for the course of studies undertaken; (2) careful
individual training; and (3) such a limitation of numbers as the conserva-
tion of these two principles render necessary.

. . . The problem of what to do with B.A. graduates who wished to take
up an M.A. course of study and could not be received into the Presidency
College and Scottish Churches College classes began to command anxious
attention in 1910. Although the *necessity* for providing higher teaching for

B.A.'s and B.Sc.'s *irrespective of their fitness for it* was not recognized at the Presidency College, the efforts of the University to meet the growing demand for M.A. instruction were sympathetically viewed, and . . . very substantial help . . . was given, voluntarily and gratuitously by members of the Presidency College staff, who delivered courses of lectures to the University classes apart from their work at the Presidency College. . . . At the same time the University organization was acknowledged to be defective. It was confined to lecture-courses; and the class room accommodation was also most inadequate. . . . For the University arrangements were based on large numbers, low fees, and a disregard of standards.[81] (Italics in the original.)

Located just opposite the university's own classrooms, Presidency tended to deter the better students from attending them.

Sir Asutosh sought to eliminate the competition of Presidency through the restriction of all postgraduate teaching in the city of Calcutta to the university. He used his influence in the senate to call into question the quality of the teaching at Presidency. Professor Wordsworth of the Presidency staff noted the following: "Certainly it has long been a cardinal belief among the staff of the Presidency College that there is in university policy a tendency to diminish the prestige, importance and efficiency of the college in the interests of easy administration. I may instance recent inspection reports, in which after a few hours' inspection the inspectors attacked the carefully considered policy of the governing body in the matter of numbers and the combination of subjects permitted; in one of which also they attacked by name, as not fitted for his position, a gentleman of considerable academic distinction and experience, whom one of the inspectors had himself recommended in the highest terms." [82] James protested vigorously. Defeated in the senate, he turned to his own solution. He thought the future lay in the evolution of Presidency from a college to a nonaffiliating university, independent in its own right; otherwise the strengths of its old traditions and new reforms would come to nothing.[83] Both Sir Asutosh and James were seeking educational reform and the reorganization of the Indian university system; the Bengal government had the authority to choose between their differing conceptions of what that system should be.

By 1914, the Bengal government had changed. Sir A. H. Frazer, the lieutenant-governor who had originally brought James to Presidency from Patna, was retired. In 1912, Lord Carmichael of Skirling, whose policy differed from that of Frazer, had been appointed to the newly raised governorship. His aim was to consolidate the position of the British government in the recently reamalgamated Bengal. He decided that this could best be done through a policy of appeasement. Seeking the support of influential allies among the rising Indian political classes, he attempted to recognize loyalty to his regime with concessions in lesser political arenas, one of which was education. In 1913, the Bengal government embarked upon a policy of conciliating Sir Asutosh. In his position as rector of the university, Lord Carmichael acceded to the vice-chancellor's repeated requests for expansion and reform. In March 1916, Lord Carmichael's government found the opportunity to acknowledge the cooperation of the "Tiger of Bengal."

As James' critics were quick to point out, his administration of the college was flawed. He was not inclined, for example, to use the principal's coercive powers arbitrarily, but preferred to rely upon the use of reason. He called the students together once a term to address them, regularly visited their clubs and hostels, and was usually available for student interviews.[84] He met their requests when he could, and explained why when he could not. He attempted to gain the students' trust by listening to their complaints and treating them fairly; he expected the students, and the staff, to reciprocate with the same standards of behavior. The following incident, recounted by the first editor of the college magazine, was typical. "As editor I was faced with a great crisis. My Professor and Tutor Mr. E. F. Oaten who subsequently became Director of Public Instruction, Bengal, had in course of his speech, called certain students of the Eden Hostel "barbarians." I knew my Professor well; he was deeply versed in classical lore and he used the expression "barbarians" in the Greek sense of the term. He was however misunderstood. Our Eden Hostel correspondent strongly protested against the expression used by the Professor, in the columns of the College magazine. The correspondence was published under the authority of the editor. Mr. Oaten got very annoyed and went up to the Principal and asked for the deletion of the offending paragraph. He further demanded an apology from the correspondent. The veteran student-editor, following well-known journalistic etiquette, declined to disclose the name of the correspondent. He declined further to publish an apology. The Principal upheld the liberty of action on the part of the editor. He requested Mr. Oaten, if he chose, to insert a contradiction in the correspondence column." [85] When reason failed, James felt there was little he could do, and situations were often left unresolved — Oaten never inserted the contradiction because, as he put it, "the basic idea was so absurd, that I thought of my students as barbarians, students with whom I spend hours on the cricket field, and whom I in many cases made my friends. It was just too silly." [86] And the student editor continued to enjoy "absolute freedom." [87]

James was also constitutionally minded and conscious of the correctness of due procedures. He always recognized the authority of Presidency's governing body and put consultations with its members before quick, personal decisions, even when situations demanded them. These attitudes may have been to Presidency's ultimate good, but they appeared as a lack of firmness when a small, volatile group of student dissidents disrupted the life of the college.

On 10 January 1916 a number of students had been permitted to leave their classes early to attend a prize-giving day ceremony, at the Hindu and Hare schools on the opposite side of the quadrangle, at which the governor was scheduled to appear.[88] On their way they milled noisily about the corridors chatting among themselves, some in front of Professor Oaten's door. His lecture disturbed, Oaten came out with his arms outstretched, in order to stop the students temporarily and to admonish them for breaking the college's rule of silence in the corridors.[89] Some students thought they had been pushed about. Subhas Chandra Bose (later president of the Indian National Congress and organizer of the Indian National Army), class representative on the Presidency students' consultative committee, formed a student delegation to lodge a complaint with the principal. The principal replied that it was the students' responsibility as gentlemen to approach the history professor themselves. Disturbed by James' seeming lack of sympathy, Bose and his friends organized the students instead. On January 11, the students in the Eden Hostel struck. They were firm in their resolve to stay away from classes and refused to accede to the pleas of their British and Indian professors.[90]

Unknown to the students, James had immediately contacted Professor Oaten and had advised him to discuss the matter with the affronted students. The professor did so the next day, and the dispute seemed to have come to an amicable end. Oaten, however, "sick to death" because the students in the advanced class to whom he had given his "best" had not lived up to the responsibilities of the authority delegated them, told his students that he chose not to lecture to them on that day.[91] With the approval of the governing body, the principal was compelled to intervene again.[92]

One month later, the incident was repeated.[93] A class was dismissed early and noisily passed by Professor Oaten's room. The history professor again came out, and was alleged this time to have grabbed a student by the scruff of the neck. Oaten denied the charge; the student, however, immediately went to the principal's office, where James asked him to set down his complaint in writing and then advised him to consult with his parents if he wished.[94] James also sent a note to Oaten, making arrangements to meet with Professor Oaten later in the day. But a small group of students had already rejected the procedures of delegation and constitutional protest as futile. "Meanwhile about two hours after this incident and shortly before 3 o'clock Mr. Oaten went to the ground floor of the college premises to post a notice on the notice board. He observed a number of students (his own estimate is from 10 to 15) who were assembled near the foot of the staircase. They at once surrounded him, threw him on the floor and brutally assaulted him. Mr. Gilchrist, who was on the first floor, heard a noise and rushed down to help Mr. Oaten, but the assailants disappeared before he could reach the spot."[95] James immediately informed the government of the assault on Professor Oaten and called a meeting of the college's governing body for the next day.

The meeting began at noon. When it was adjourned at 6:30 P.M., James was informed that the Bengal government had, "on its own initiative and without consulting the Governing Body of the college, issued orders closing the college from the afternoon of the 18th February." Responsibility was removed from the hands of Presidency's constituted authorities and given over to an independent committee of enquiry established by the provincial government. "It appeared to Government that the course of events at the college demanded an exhaustive enquiry by an authority free from any such attachment to the institution as might cause it unconsciously to hesitate in exposing the full extent of the evil or to fail to appreciate the necessity which might exist for radical measures of reform; . . . it became the more apparent that while the Governing Body might usefully continue to investigate the circumstances of the assault on Professor Oaten, it was not an authority which could be depended upon to deal with a larger enquiry into the state of discipline in the college with efficiency and weight." [96] Sir Asutosh Mukherji was appointed chairman of the committee of enquiry, and the director of public instruction, W. W. Hornell, was included among its members. James was also named to the committee.

Tired, upset, and feeling that both the institution and his efforts had been betrayed, James demanded an interview with P. C. Lyon, secretary to the Bengal government in the general department and controlling authority in educational affairs. A meeting was arranged for that evening. The exchange between the two men must have been heated, for Lyon claimed to have been "grossly insulted," and James withdrew his name from the planned committee.[97] Sir George Anderson, an educational service officer in Bombay, analyzed the situation. "In any case, it seems clear that in going to see Mr. Lyon, Mr. James had no intention of being abusive or rude. He went for the purpose of discussing the closing of the Eden Hindu Hostel. If he erred, it was in the heat of the moment. Human nature being as it is, such errors are regrettable, but not unpardonable. Moreover, Mr. James had been submitted to a very severe strain. Everybody admits that he was a sympathetic and efficient Principal of a college. Everyone who has been connected with a college knows how tedious is the task of dealing with serious disciplinary cases. Mr. James states that on the day of the interview he had presided over a meeting of the Governing Body of the College which lasted from 12 o'clock till half past six, at the close of which two students were expelled and two rusticated. There can be little wonder that his nerves were all wrong at the time of his interview with Mr. Lyon that evening." [98]

James submitted his formal resignation from the committee two days later, on February 22. "I shall be glad to forward the Committee's enquiry by every means in my power, but seeing that the subject of enquiry is in part, and even mainly, my administration of Presidency College, I hereby lodge an objection against two members, whose names are given in the Resolution under reference, to that of the Hon'ble Sir Ashutosh Mukharji, President of the Committee, and to that of the Hon'ble Mr. W. W. Hornell, Director of Public Instruction, Bengal. I think it should suffice that in a matter in which my good name and reputation are at stake as well as the credit of the Governing Body and of Presidency College, such an objection should have validity on the mere statement. My reason for it, put generally, is that, I do not consider that either of these gentlemen could enter on the work of the Committee free from bias." [99] In reply, the Bengal government released the following public communique on February 24. "We are desired by Government to state that as soon as Mr. James, Principal of the Presidency College, received information of the appointment of the Committee of Enquiry into discipline at Presidency College, with a request that he would serve on the Committee, he paid a visit to the Hon'ble Mr. Lyon, Member of Council in charge of Education, and subjected him to gross personal insult. Mr. James also sent to the Secretary of the Committee, with the request that it should be placed before the Committee, a copy of the letter which he wrote to Government accusing two members of the Committee of bias against himself. The Governor in Council consider that Mr. James has shown himself to be unfit to retain the post of Principal of Presidency College; he has accordingly transferred him from that post, and placed him under suspension pending further orders. Mr. Wordsworth, Inspector of Schools, Presidency Division, has been appointed Principal of the Presidency College." [100]

James stayed on to submit his evidence before Sir Asutosh's committee of enquiry. When the committee finally presented its report, it not only vindicated James, but also suggested that a number of his reforms be instituted at the college on a permanent basis. The members of the committee approved James' reorganization of the college staff into stronger departments and the representation of staff on the academic council, and agreed with him as to the need for extended residential and leisure time facilities for the Presidency students. The report, however, stated little more about academic matters.[101] One year later — within six months of the intended sitting of the Calcutta University Commission in 1917 — all postgraduate teaching in the city of Calcutta was removed to the university's own classrooms. Presidency's principal at the time, William Christopher Wordsworth, offered this comment. "I believe whole heartedly in the value of the collegiate connection for students, and I believe that the Presidency College was doing well its share of the post-graduate work under the old arrangement. It limited its work to its resources, and the work was done with devotion. . . . I signed the report on post-graduate teaching with something of a wrench." [102]

The students' interpretation of Professor Oaten's behavior was the cause of much of the trouble at Presidency, and James' methods of discipline were clearly inadequate to cope with the trouble.[103] Communications between British professors and Indian students broke down as some students confused the personal behavior of one man with the political issues of imperial dominance and racial slur. They followed their elders of a few years before in disregarding the slower methods of constitutional procedures for the more disruptive tactics of agitation and immediate reward. The government used the opportunity to rid itself of an obstinate employee, save its face at Presidency, and give in to Indian demands for an expanded university system under Indian control. The substantive educational questions of the nature of postgraduate study, its quality, and its proper place in the Indian university system had been bypassed in favor of an expedient political policy. The member of the Indian Educational Service who had raised these questions in Bengal was publicly humiliated and retired to England.

Classes resumed at Presidency shortly thereafter, and the college continued its work as the premier affiliate of the university. Future principals were rarely as innovative as James: rarely did they have to confront such challenges. In a redefined educational situation, the members of the staff could usually rely upon the government to provide financial support and to delegate educational authority to professors in a wholly undergraduate institution.[104] Members of the Indian middle classes still sent their sons to Presidency. Even though their support of the British empire might be growing hesitant, they still appreciated the quality of education and the opportunities offered at the government college. Thus, professors in the government colleges were able to carry on with their educational work. It was otherwise for their British colleagues at privately managed Indian institutions.

The Decline of Consensus at M.A.-O.: The Rise of Management and Its External Constituents

William A. J. Archbold succeeded Morison as the principal of the M.A.-O. College in 1905; he was specially recruited for the post in England. After taking his degrees from Cambridge, he had assisted Lord Acton in the organization of the *Cambridge Modern History,* and later had done the same work for the editors of the *Dictionary of National Biography.* When he was appointed to the Aligarh principalship he was nearly forty years of age and had already taught for a period in South Africa.[105] Unlike Beck, he had come to the position in his maturity, and unlike Morison, had come without the prior experience of Aligarh; his experience of education and scholarship had been profounder than that of Beck or Morison.

Like the citizens of Calcutta, the leaders of India's Muslim community were beginning to hold new political aims and aspirations. The change was observed by William S. Marris, the district commissioner, shortly after Archbold's arrival in India. "How far the Aligarh movement has taken on a political colour is plain to any onlooker. The prominence of Aftab Ahmad among the trustees, and of demagogues like Muhammad Ali and Shaukat Ali; the inception of the university movement as a counterblast to the Hindu University scheme; the enlisting of all national leaders like the Aga Khan; its association with the All India Muslim League and All India Muslim Educational Conference — these are all symptoms of one policy. Aligarh is destined to be the focus of all Muhammadan intelligence and activity in India. Begun as a defensive move, it is already acquiring an offensive character. . . . It is an all Indian Muslim and distinctly anti-Hindu movement. It has already lost its reliance on Englishmen and its trust in English methods and ideals. The danger I foresee is that if it is indulged and uncontrolled it will develop rapidly on decidedly anti-English lines." [106]

The college had not yet found its new direction, however, and Archbold was able to establish confident relations with the members of the board of trustees and the honorary secretary, Nawab Mohsin-ul-Mulk. He became the political advisor and confidant of the trustees, if not their ambassador to the British government. In 1906, he drafted the document which a delegation led by the Aga Khan presented to the Viceroy, Lord Minto. It argued the case for reserved Muslim electoral constituencies in India, and the Viceroy gave his consent to the proposal.

But functional alliances among the trustees were changing, and there was no one with the force of personality of Sir Syed to control the trustees. As the activities of the trustees gained more prominence in a politically awakening Muslim community, their activities only brought more attention to themselves and criticism of the administration of the college. Politically, the principal was already associated with the more conservative grouping around the Aga Khan, the group that still dominated at Aligarh. In 1907, an "old boy" complained of the dominant faction in the columns of the Indian *Daily Telegraph*. "In the first place [the trustees] have elected in the majority of cases such people only as were not qualified to give an opinion on matters educational; secondly the system in Aligarh was such that the outside trustees had nothing else to do but to say yes to the proposal sent to them. The 'family party' at Aligarh had the decision of everything. If one dared to disagree, he was a marked man, and was pronounced blind to the interests of the college; thirdly, even those out of the 70 trustees who wanted to take an active and intelligent part in the business of the college were not allowed to do so, unless they were prepared to face the whole of the dominant party, always ready to attack such as questioned their right to manage the affairs of the college. If there was a trustee who refused to accept the dictum of the party in power, he was removed; if there were any senior students who grumbled loudly and made complaints to the authorities, they were turned out bag and baggage; if there were any members of the Central Standing Committee of the Conference who were independent enough to express views antagonistic to the views of the clique, they were publicly insulted and turned out of the room, where the meeting was being held in spite of all the rules and regulations: and the cry for redress up to now has been a cry in the wilderness." [107]

The trustees' greatest source of strength within the community was their control of the college and the opportunities they were therefore able to provide the more ambitious sons of their coreligionists. Increasingly, education was looked upon as being less regenerative and more instrumental than it had been in Sir Syed's day; Marris noted that the trustees were "not thinking of education in itself at all, but of more boys, more subscriptions, more candidates for government employment, more lawyers to fill seats in Council, and more political power generally." [108] To retain their support in the Muslim community, the conservative trustees involved themselves more frequently in campus affairs and student activities. As the director of public instruction commented, a system of "dual control" had grown up, which had "the fatal consequences of undermining the authority of the staff, by setting up the resident Trustees as a court of appeal against [the staff]." [109] Archbold, like James at Presidency, was the victim of his employers' aspirations when the Aligarh students struck in 1907.

In February, the town of Aligarh was celebrating its annual fair, which the students attended in large numbers. A small group of them pushed past a policeman in order to enter an enclave barred to the public. The constable remonstrated with them, and a student, Gulam Husain, assaulted him.[110] The injuries incurred by the constable were minor, but the deputy superintendent of police (DSP) thought the action serious enough to complain to the principal. The next day, Archbold called Gulam Husain to his office and informed him that the DSP contemplated court action; he advised the student to return to his home in the Punjab for three months for the student's own protection. Husain, however, thought he had been suspended. After some negotiations with the deputy superintendent, Archbold changed the student's punishment: Husain was fined twenty-five rupees, told to write a note of apology to the DSP, and required to report to the principal's office every evening. The students thought that an earlier intervention on their part had led to Husain's lighter punishment. "The complaint of the students that the orders about the punishment of Gulam Husain were issued in instalments by the Principal must be due to a misapprehension on their part. The desire of the Principal throughout was to save Gulam Husain from the disagreeable consequences of the latter's alleged assault on the constable." [111]

Some further incidents occurred with the police at the fair on the next day, and the students once again appealed to the principal. Archbold promised to look into the matter, but as at Presidency, communications between British professors and Indian students began to break down. Gulam Husain was confined to his hostel because he had violated his punishment and had earlier left the college grounds. The students thought Archbold had gone back on his word and, like their Hindu counterparts at Calcutta, attributed his supposed action to the racial snobbery of their

British teachers. They called a meeting for the night of February 15 and resolved to consider a student strike.

The situation deteriorated when the proctor, Gardner Brown, and his Indian assistant, Mir Wilayat Hussain, decided to attend the meeting. "Some boys asked Mr. Brown not to come to the meeting as it was private. Mr. Brown in spite of warning did go to the meeting and told the students to disperse within two minutes. This they did not do, but on the contrary used insulting language towards him and Mir Wilayat Hussain, Assistant Proctor, who was suspected of being in league with Mr. Brown. Mr. Towle, another professor was there. He said that certain students even threw missiles and stones at Mr. Brown which the students totally deny. In the meantime the Principal, Mr. Archbold, arrived on the scene. In the beginning the students were respectful to him; they asked him to rescind his order about Gulam Husain. On this being refused, certain offensive words were used towards the Principal." [112] Archbold decided to close the college.

Before the principal actually closed the college, the honorary secretary, Nawab Mohsin-ul-Mulk, intervened to contain the conflict. Without consulting Archbold, he promised the striking students they would be absolved of all guilt and punishment. The students submitted their apology to the principal on the twentieth. Not knowing of the Nawab's promises, Archbold promptly proceeded to take disciplinary action.[113] The students left in a body, the college was closed, and the trustees convened a committee of inquiry to save the reputation of the board in the Muslim community: both the Nawab and Principal Archbold were included among its members.

The committee made few substantial recommendations as to future relations between the British staff and the Muslim trustees; it only suggested that the college principal and the honorary secretary keep in closer touch. Instead of making recommendations, the Muslim members of the committee harkened back to the "golden" days of Beck, Morison, and Sir Syed. "[The students] were accustomed to free, frank, and almost familiar intercourse with the English teachers. Messrs. Beck, Arnold and Morison had accustomed them to such social relations and engendered a belief that the observance of social relations was a distinctive feature of the Mohammedan College and the principal means of promoting the three ideas mentioned above. The want of social intercourse between the staff and the students argued in the minds of the latter a want of sympathy and a departure from the policy of the Great Founder of the College and his no less great coadjutors Messrs. Beck, Arnold and Morison." [114]

But in earlier days, Sir Syed, the trustees, and the members of the British staff had all been taken with the idea of creating a revitalized Islam. Moreover, the British professors possessed a degree of knowledge and educational expertise not yet to be found among the Muslims. Sir Syed and the trustees were dependent upon the British professors. Confident of the latter's dedication to Muslim aspirations, they were willing to delegate educational authority to the British members of the staff. By 1907, the trustees were no longer willing to delegate that authority. In 1909, Archbold resigned over the issue. "My view is that the Principal ought to be the supreme and final authority in the internal affairs of the College. In particular that his authority should be unquestioned as regards discipline, as regards admissions, as regards promotions, as regards the number of hours that the staff ought to teach. He ought to be consulted before negotiations are entered into for engaging new members of the Staff. When I have said this and when I add that I do not consider that a man has the proper authority if he is obliged to refer to someone else before he comes to a decision, it will be at once evident to you how impossible it is for one to work under the present system." [115]

The very success of Beck, Morison and their generation of British professors had changed the situation at the college. Beck had transformed the college into a political instrument designed to produce a new Muslim political elite. As that elite grew in sophistication, some of its members began to question the need for cooperation with the British. The college became the board's means by which to gain support for its conservative position within the community: by offering enhanced admissions rates, easier student controls, and lighter academic standards. In consequence, students at Aligarh, as at Presidency, turned from the educational authority of their teachers to the political authority of their elders. At the same time, a body of educated Muslims was being produced in India, sufficient to meet the teaching needs of an affiliated college. British professors, like Archbold, tended to be too independent to accept the role of "an agent only," in mediating the trustees' relations with the Aligarh student body.[116] And as in Calcutta, pride in the community's accomplishments seemed to justify an increased Muslim staff as aspirations moved toward an independent Muslim university. In reply to Archbold, the members of the board cited the legal rights of the trustees to educational control of the institution. "According to rules 119 & 120 the Hony. Secretary was the chief executive officer of the Trustees and was responsible for management of their affairs. . . . It was also necessary to point out that the post of the Hony. Secretary of the College Trustees was not a ministerial office but so far as its occupant had been regarded as the leader of the community, which looked upon him as their chief representative. Thus, whether as the accredited representative of the governing body of the College or as the leader of the Indian Musalmans, it was the Hony. Secretary of the College that the Chief management and control of the institution was entrusted. For one holding such a responsible position as that of the Hony. Secretary of this College, the desire 'to obtain information in matters' connected with the functions of the Principal, was not only natural and reasonable but absolutely necessary. Whatever might be the scope of the Principal's jurisdiction it could not extend beyond the aims and objects of the College, which it was the duty of the Trustees, through their accredited representative, to guide and control. So far as obtaining more information was concerned every Mohamedan was entitled to ask for it about any part of the management of the College, for, this institution was the property of the whole community." [117]

There were no such disturbances at the Muir Central College in Allahabad, and in 1922, the college was quietly converted into a new, unitary University of Allahabad.

Strains in Autonomy: Professors, Sponsors, and Public Diverge

There were three groups involved in the running of the Indian colleges: British professors, the college sponsors, and the educated Indian public. Professors were brought out to impart modern knowledge, and they saw that as their main role in India. When that role was questioned in 1910, Principal James defended the professors' work. "It will be for some of us a dismal result, if we have to confess that we have been wrong from the beginning; that we never should have attempted to introduce into India knowledge, as knowledge has been understood in Europe since the times of Descartes and Bacon; that we never should have encouraged the study of English literature and European science; and that we should have held fast to traditional learning and pre-Copernical sciences, and have based any more popular education which there was scope for strictly in the vernaculars: that it was a bad policy, and folly little short of a crime to introduce the races and people of Hindustan to the heights and depths of Western speculation, and to the principles that underlie discovery in natural science." [118] Their purpose was to bring the Indian students to a closer understanding of modernity and the assumptions on which it is built. In consequence, they thought that their students would come to appreciate the benefits of British rule in India. James believed that in at least one sense they were right. "Education has certainly not produced in India hatred of all things English; not obviously of English literature, English games, English standards of conduct, English institutions; because the political party which voices the aspirations of the educated classes in India, and is charged with being disaffected or allied with disaffection, is founded on almost slavish imitation of English standards and methods." [119] Professors hoped their students would eventually take their places alongside Europeans, participating together in the administration of the empire. In Britain, these professors would have accomplished their work in independent institutions; in India, they were employees of the government or of Indian communities.

The members of the civil service who composed the government tended to look less to new solutions than to traditional problems. Their perceptions of India were largely the outcome of their early training in the districts. Mindful of the need for decisive leadership in the countryside, they tended to stress the themes of ordered governance and paternal rule. In the cities, their contact with the educated classes was limited, largely restricted to the narrower sphere of official relationships. The government wanted its colleges merely to produce a body of competent professional men and public servants, loyal to the British government.

The sponsoring communities were generally part of the Indian educated public. In the view of that public, modern knowledge was the leaven by which traditional society could be reconstructed to a new and better pattern. They were therefore eager for the spread of western learning and were in a hurry to open up its benefits to ever-increasing numbers of Indian youth. For themselves, this meant the expansion of the educated public, and in a sense, the enlargement of their constituency in British India.

The views of the three groups were not very far apart, and for many years they were able to work together: at Aligarh, at Presidency, and at Muir. But the Indian university had not been endowed with structures to safeguard the working relationships and perpetuate them over time. British professors were not members of autonomous institutions, merely employees in affiliated colleges. The university system worked to separate professors from the knowledge it was their duty to dispense.

A professor's educational authority derives from his relationship to knowledge; he usually knows more in selected intellectual areas than other men. He passes a portion of that knowledge on to students, seeks to protect it from false application, and perhaps tries to elaborate it. In India, professors were not responsible for the content of knowledge. The authority was vested in a senate composed of public men, government officials, and some professors. The senate decided what would be taught, to what degree levels, and with what sophistication, and imposed these decisions upon the members of the teaching community. Moreover, there was no provision made for research or the elaboration of knowledge at its higher levels in the Indian universities. Academic work was entirely restricted to undergraduate and masters teaching, levels at which educated laymen feel competent to judge, contribute, and interfere. Without the safeguards afforded by the boundaries of knowledge and the determination of its contents, the instrumental aspects of education came into prominence in India, and professors came to be looked upon more instrumentally by their employers — some professors, like Beck, Morison, and Arnold at Aligarh, took that role upon themselves.

Through the nineteenth century, the British professors' educational authority derived from their association with the colonial regime and the knowledge that regime brought to India. When a substantial number of Indians educated in the same knowledge emerged in the twentieth century, however, British professors began to lose their authority to Indians who might offer students the same training, but in universities that were not the intellectual dependents of foreign ones. At Aligarh, they began to lose their authority to Muslims who would be more amenable to the trustees' policies. In Calcutta, Indian members of the senate, like the trustees at Aligarh,

pressed the case for lighter standards, lower passes, and easier degree requirements, especially at the postgraduate level. British professors seemed
to deny these aspirations when they argued for honors programs, stiffer
examinations, and more stringent degree requirements. In changed political circumstances, students followed their elders — though not perhaps as
their elders would have wished [120] — and interpreted their professors' actions as anti-Indian. At Presidency and Aligarh they rebelled. For the sake
of loyalty, the provincial governments gave in to Bengal educational demands, and at Aligarh, found a place for Archbold in the Indian Educational Service.

At the Muir Central College, the consensus among British professors,
governors, and the educated Indian public held, and students did not riot.
In Allahabad, the members of the Muir staff were respected and influential
members of the senate. Local politics and the university up to the 1920's
were dominated by men who shared the political persuasions of a Sir Tej
Bahadur Sapru and a younger Moti Lal Nehru. They were convinced of
the worth of the contribution the British had made to life in India, the
values of liberalism, and the soundness of notions of constitutional and
parliamentary procedures. And they considered the questions of examination standards and student numbers to be negotiable. Few British or Indians
questioned the basic purposes and organization of the higher educational
system. Unlike Calcutta, it was a British professor at the university who
protested the weakness of Allahabad in face of the strength of Muir and
the other colleges. In 1917, L. F. Rushbrook-Williams, professor of history
in the university, described the system of higher education in the following way. "It is economically wasteful, on account of its failure to utilize
the available teaching resources in an efficient manner. Not only is the
work of an able teacher at present confined to the college to which he belongs, instead of being at the disposal of the University as a whole; but,
in addition, many College Professors are teaching the same subject in different colleges at the same time. There is thus small opportunity for spe-
cialisation and much waste of energy. . . . The Colleges, dominated by
individual and competing interests, are far too strong as compared to the
University." [121] In 1922, Rushbrook-Williams' criticisms were met with
the conversion of the Allahabad University into a teaching university.

In every society, universities serve instrumental purposes: dispensing
knowledge, qualifying technical and professional men, or perhaps merely
modeling a cultural style. But many universities contain structures within
them which separate the areas of society's legitimate interest in the working of the university from that which pertains to the professor's relation
to his knowledge. That distinction was recognized early in their history
(the segregation of the faculty of theology in the university in the middle
ages) and continues to this day (the contemporary distinction between undergraduate and research-oriented graduate departments). Professors gain
their educational authority from their work at the higher levels, which the

members of society do not usually feel qualified to judge. Because the members of society feel that society might be enriched by the professors' discoveries, they delegate responsibility for the content of knowledge to them and generally restrict their interest to questions of its use, who shall receive it, for what purposes, and the like.

The Indian universities did not have these distinctions built into them. When they were formed, affiliation seemed a cheap and effective method to diffuse modern knowledge in India, and the first attempts at reform did not begin until the twentieth century. Professors were therefore compelled to derive their educational authority from other sources: from their connection to the colonial regime, from the knowledge they brought with them from foreign universities, from the quality of their teaching. When the professors' own purposes in the colleges were more instrumental, they were not able to approximate any of the safeguards of the European institution; that happened at Aligarh. Where they were able to infuse higher academic standards in their undergraduate instruction, they gained the respect of the Indian community and the approbation of government; that happened at Presidency in its restricted role as an affiliated institution, and at Muir. The standard was an elusive one, imported by small groups of professors to a few scattered colleges. Beyond the model of their own teaching, there were no structures in the university to engender habits of restraint and discipline on the part of the public and the government. Without the higher levels of instruction which organize professors in relation to their knowledge and establish them in traditions of learning for learning's own sake, the ambitions of the nonteaching community prevailed. The standards of national pride, public policy, and vocational opportunities prevailed in the nonteaching, undergraduate university in India. These standards continued to prevail in some even after their conversion to teaching, postgraduate institutions; as at Allahabad, Calcutta, and the Aligarh Muslim University.

11 / Parochialism and Cosmopolitanism in University Government: The Environments of Baroda University

Susanne Hoeber Rudolph / Lloyd I. Rudolph

Assisted by Joan Landy Erdman and Janet Guthrie

An Introduction to MS University of Baroda and Its Environment

The Maharaja Sayajirao University of Baroda, or MSU, is representative of India's best universities. It is the only English language university of the seven universities in Gujarat, and concentrates more on opportunity fields — science, technology, medicine, special professional departments — than do the other state universities. Because of its unitary and residential character, it is spared many of the problems that universities with heterogeneous affiliated colleges face.

Located in the prosperous western Indian state of Gujarat, MSU is named after Sayajirao, an enlightened ruler of the former princely state of Baroda. A Mahratta prince known for his intelligent and imaginative reforms, Sayajirao founded an arts and science college in 1881. Other educational institutions were added later.[1] These were consolidated into a university in 1949 just before the maharaja at that time, Sir Pratap Singh, surrendered his powers and agreed to merge his state with the state of Bombay. MSU's initial funding was part of the agreement between Maharaja Sir Pratap Singh and the States Ministry of the government of India under which the maharaja agreed to surrender his powers as ruling prince. Sir Pratap Singh received an annual tax free privy purse of Rs. 2,600,000 and "agreed to set apart the corpus of two State trusts of Rs. 1 crore [ten million rupees] each, the creation of which had been announced by his predecessors."[2] Among the principal beneficiaries of the income from these trusts was to be the new university, realizing thereby the intentions of Maharaja Sayajirao, who in the mid-nineteen twenties had planned for a university at Baroda.

MSU's first vice-chancellor was Hansa Mehta, the vigorous and enter-

The research plan for this study was prepared by the Rudolphs in 1966. Joan Erdman and Janet Guthrie carried on field work in Baroda in 1966–67, conducting some forty-five structured and open-ended interviews with faculty, students, syndics, and administrators, and preparing field notes and memoranda. They also gathered data from Gujarati and English newspapers and from university records and publications. After submitting in advance the draft of this chapter to the interviewees, Lloyd Rudolph conducted re-interviews in November 1969. Lloyd and Susanne Rudolph did so again in February 1971 on the basis of yet another revision. The feedback interviews proved particularly helpful in writing the study. The Rudolphs composed the chapter. We are grateful to Howard Erdman for giving us the benefit of his knowledge of Gujarat and Baroda politics and society. Former Vice-chancellor C. S. Patel very kindly facilitated our research.

prising wife of Jivraj Mehta. (Jivraj Mehta headed the only popular ministry in the princely state of Baroda, and was later chief minister of Gujarat.) Hansa Mehta possessed the imagination, personal force, political skills, and connections to raise funds, recruit a lively, highly qualified faculty, and see to the creation of unusual departments and schools. In a relatively favorable environment, her contribution to launching a university of the first rank was considerable.

MSU lies in a rimland area once ruled by principalities that lay on the trade routes to the Middle East and Africa. Gujarat was open to sea traffic through the port cities of Surat and Cambay until the nineteenth century when Bombay reduced the significance of those ports. Its sons have traded and emigrated abroad, especially to Africa. Gujarat was also the site of some of India's earliest important industrialization, notably the textile industry of the city of Ahmedabad. Gujarat's traditions of economic cosmopolitanism are balanced by a certain cultural parochialism and revivalism. The impact of English culture and education (anglicization) was not as powerful in Gujarat as it was in and around the three great presidency capitals of Calcutta, Bombay, and Madras, nor did the British *raj* generate as large and influential a class of political and cultural collaborators in Gujarat as it did in and around the presidency capitals. Pre-British, local, Hindu and Muslim religious movements have created a diverse tradition. Many Ahmedabadis have managed to become modern industrial entrepreneurs without abandoning the life styles and values of merchant castes in western India and of the Jain and Vaishnavite sects.[3] Gujarat's most famous son, Gandhi, combined some of the state's most conspicuous Hindu and Jain cultural traditions in his simultaneous commitment to radical nationalism, social reform, and cultural revitalization.[4]

In most indicators of development, Gujarat stands high. In 1961, it stood fourth among the states in per capita income and third in the proportion of its population living in districts falling in the top two quartiles of levels of development.[5] The politics of Gujarat have been in the hands of the Congress party, and of a state government, which, although subject to factionalism, until recently maintained a considerable internal stability and effectiveness. The political climate for higher education is affected by the following facts: that the industrial-commercial forces in the state are interested in modern education;[6] that the dominant, formerly agricultural caste in the state, the Patidars, and, increasingly, other groups are eager to see their sons and daughters educated; and that the state's Gandhian traditions and cultural conservatism have endowed it with an enthusiasm for the regional language (Gujarati) or the official language (Hindi) which is uncharacteristic of states of Gujarat's degree of development and rimland location. As elsewhere, the concerns of those interested in a cosmopolitan and high quality education are to some extent at variance with the concerns of those interested in more plentiful and accessible education in the regional language.

MSU, then, is an English speaking university in a state that has favored regional language. It is a unitary university among affiliating ones.[7] It stresses science, technology, and professions where other universities offer mainly B.A.'s and B.Sc.'s. It benefits from the fact that elite consumer demand for English, the key to opportunity professions, is rising even while the political demand increases for regional language. Because qualifying for MSU often depends on having the means to pay for good, private, English language secondary education; and because MSU's education, if declining, remains more desirable than that elsewhere; the university is a conspicuous target for democrat levellers.

MSU's more immediate environment is Baroda, a city of 300,000, formerly capital of the princely state of Baroda. It is rapidly becoming one of west India's most important industrial cities, following immediately behind the Bombay area and the city of Ahmedabad in the number of industrial licenses issued between 1954 and 1961 (greater Bombay, 1071 licenses; Ahmedabad, 110; Thana — the district adjoining Bombay — 106; Baroda, 89).[8] The main industries in the city are chemicals and chemical products; forty-four of Baroda's eighty-nine industrial licenses were issued for drugs and pharmaceuticals, and the city has the largest single share of the ninety-five licenses issued throughout India for drugs and pharmaceuticals.[9] The university lies in the northwest corner of the city, and its institutions there are scattered across almost one-eighth of the city's area. The environment for MSU, the modern and burgeoning industry of Baroda city and its adjoining prosperous environs, stands in marked contrast to the environment surrounding many other Indian universities.

The Framework of Analysis

The government of a university is shaped by the dual influences of its internal and external environments, but it may be more or less independent of one or both of them. The internal environment encompasses the cultural and organizational imprint of the university's founding; the formal structure of the institution; the social, geographic, and cultural composition of its student body; the relative distribution of influence among degree levels of education on the one hand and departments and schools on the other; and the qualifications, reference groups, and values of its various faculties and students.

We think of the external environment as being organized in three concentric circles, local, state, and national-international. The external includes the public and private sources of university funds and the degree of influence on university affairs such sources conventionally exercise: the economic, cultural, and political milieu in which the university is located; the active and potential clients and publics who are served or believe they should be served by the university (such as parents or potential parents of students, state producer interests, and local industries and governments);

public authorities with legal and administrative powers over university affairs; and objective social factors, such as levels of education, wealth, and professionalism in the region or nation. This chapter examines the degree to which and the ways in which the inner and outer environments of MSU affect its government and its organizational life; that is, its policies, leadership, decision-making processes, and goals.

A university's inner and outer environments are linked by two processes, "compression-decompression" and "parochialization-cosmopolitanization." These terms refer to continua whose poles represent parameters for differences of degree. Compression has two dimensions, the physical extent or reach of the university's boundary and the permeability of the boundary. A state of compression (as contrasted with the process) is one in which the university's boundary is both narrow and closed.

Compression describes a primarily physical condition; parochialism and cosmopolitanism describe a primarily ideological condition that has institutional and behavioral aspects. The degree of compression and parochialization (and decompression and cosmopolitanization) is affected by the relationship of the university's inner and outer environments to each other; the more congruent (in physical and qualitative terms) the inner and outer environments, the more parochial and compressed (closed) the institution; the less congruent, the more decompressed (open) and cosmopolitan. We differentiate and operationalize the cosmopolitan end of the continuum into three dimensions; horizontal (or geographic), vertical (or social and cultural), and substantive (the content and quality of education and research).

The goal orientation of a university influences both the type of its leadership and the possibility and nature of cosmopolitanism, particularly substantive cosmopolitanism. In order to explore these relationships we first distinguish four types of goal orientation — cultivation (of knowledge and character), research, training, and service — and then relate them over time to the fate and nature of substantive cosmopolitanism and, later, to four types of leaders; the "politician," the "judge," the "administrator," and the "broker." Goal orientations in turn are affected by the differential impact on university resources and policy of the three dimensions of its outer environment, local, state, and national-international. These relationships, too, are examined.

Three propositions follow from the relationships and associations among these various concepts. The more congruent the two environments, the less likely that a university's government will be differentiated from and independent of its environments, able to defend itself against politicization, and able to use political influence to defend and foster its academic independence and interests. (Conversely, the more incongruent the two environments, the more likely it is that there will be conflict between elements of the university community, for example, faculty, students, administration, and the authorities of one or more of the outer environments.) Although we are prepared to advance and defend these propositions, we are not prepared to reduce university government to its environmental circumstances. University government is not, per se, epiphenomenal, but extraordinary men and conditions are required to enable university governments to transcend environmental circumstances inimical to academic values and cosmopolitanism.

Inner Environment: Structure

MSU is a unitary, residential university. It was not modeled on the paradigm first expressed in the presidency universities at Calcutta, Madras, and Bombay. They were established to serve as examining bodies and to recognize and affiliate colleges across entire presidencies and beyond. A unitary, residential university can be a community, itself the focus of educational activity. The affiliating university served initially (and sometimes even today) as the central office of a dispersed network of potential communities in which educational activity was decentralized. For sixty years affiliating universities did no teaching; gradually after World War I, they began to set up postgraduate departments and to include constituent or university colleges.[10] MSU has been from its founding in 1949 a teaching institution that educates its undergraduate and postgraduate students in constituent and postgraduate departments. Americans used to university-college structures such as Yale or Chicago would find MSU's structure familiar. In India such structures are less common than in the U.S.: in 1965–66, affiliating universities outnumbered unitary universities by better than two to one and students (including preuniversity and postgraduate) enrolled in affiliating colleges outnumbered students enrolled in university departments and colleges by six to one.[11]

The faculty and staff of MSU on the whole attribute the high standing and independence of their university and its relative immunity from the ills afflicting many other universities to MSU's unitary, residential character. Relatively compact and intimate, MSU protects students from some of the worst aspects of the impersonality and anomie that afflict students elsewhere by accommodating them in faculty-led hostels or in local, private housing; by associating them in a variety of curricular and extracurricular activities; and by bringing them into informal touch with their faculty, who live in the university compound in staff quarters. MSU's unitary structure keeps the curriculum and teaching in the hands of the university faculty and makes it easier to protect standards and to strive for excellence. Affiliating universities, MSU faculty believe, are less fortunately placed. First degree (bachelor), and often a large proportion of second and third degree (masters and doctorate), teaching is in the hands of outlying affiliated colleges of varying quality; curriculum is controlled by boards of study usually dominated by affiliated college members who set syllabi attuned to the needs of mediocre teachers out of touch with their disciplines; and university government reflects the aspirations of representatives of local and academic vested interests entrenched in distant colleges. Baroda faculty tend to believe that the university's structure will help to protect them from the parochialism, factionalism, student disorders, decline of standards, and politicization that have subverted many other universities.

Structural factors are important in the life and consciousness of MSU and distinguish it from other universities in Gujarat and India. It is not clear, however, that they are as decisive in warding off evil and encouraging good as teachers and administrators tend to believe. A unitary as opposed to an affiliating university structure is a helpful but not a sufficient condition for university government that can maintain standards and guard autonomy. Environment has proved strong enough to penetrate and adversely affect unitary as well as affiliating universities.

Of the twenty four universities founded up to the time of MSU's creation, seven (including MSU) were residential and unitary. All but one of the residential universities had (in 1966–67) as few or fewer students than MSU (14,200).[12] One fifth of MSU's students resided in hostels while at all but one of the other six unitary universities one fourth to one half resided in hostels.[13] The seven unitary universities have common structural characteristics, strong traditions of academic excellence, and outstanding departments (and in addition, two of them are centrally administered). Yet five of them — Allahabad, Banaras, Aligarh, Lucknow, and Patna — have suffered over the last fifteen years from a combination of educational deterioration, disruptive factionalism, destructive and immobilizing student disorders, and politicization.[14] Of the seven, only Baroda and Annamalai have been spared the kind of subversion that these five have experienced. However important and helpful structural characteristics may be in counteracting adverse environmental influences, they do not explain by themselves the differences between viable and subverted universities.

The structural dimension of a university's inner environment, although analytically distinct, cannot be treated independently of the university's outer environment if the relative success or failure of the university in maintaining itself as a viable educational institution is to be understood and explained. The rising and intense demand for degrees (what Jencks and Riesman call educational certification),[15] the increased consciousness and political capabilities of educational and research consumers, and the paradoxical rapid growth and acute scarcity of publicly and politically supplied resources affect all universities. How these forces in the external environment affect the university, what shape and direction they take, depends in large measure on the economic circumstances, political system, and governmental policies of the state in which the university is located.

Baroda and Annamalai, the two unitary universities that have been relatively free from crisis, are located in rimland states (Gujarat and Tamil Nadu) with high levels of economic and political development and effective stable governments, while the five that have been afflicted with crisis are located in heartland states (Uttar Pradesh and Bihar) with low levels of economic and political development and relatively unstable and ineffective governments. (See chapter 5 for details.)

Between the 1967 and 1971 elections, the governments of Gujarat and Madras were among the most stable and effective in India, and the governments of Uttar Pradesh and Bihar among the least. The former have been among the few states to be ruled by one party governments since 1967 and have not suffered from frequent and destabilizing defections. Coalitions, defections, and changes of government have been the rule in Uttar Pradesh and Bihar since 1967.[16] The 1969 by-election that followed president's rule in the two states, as well as the 1971 parliamentary election, did not produce markedly more stable political alignments or legislative behavior.

There is a marked and revealing contrast in the resource allocations, educational pyramids, and university populations of the four states. Gujarat and Tamil Nadu not only spend a higher proportion of their considerably higher per capita income on education than do Uttar Pradesh and Bihar (see chapter 5, table 20, columns 3, 4 and 6, giving data for 1961) but also have created educational pyramids and university populations more conducive to high quality, high benefit, nonpoliticized university education.

The educational pyramids of Uttar Pradesh and Bihar are top-heavy compared to those in Gujarat and Tamil Nadu, resulting in less efficient organization of the educational system and lower social rate of return (which systematically declines from lower to higher levels of education).[17] Per capita university and school enrollments in Uttar Pradesh and Bihar are larger relative to the primary and middle school enrollments than they are in Gujarat and Tamil Nadu. The contrasting educational pyramids of the four states provide some evidence for the view that educational policy in Gujarat and Tamil Nadu as compared to that in Uttar Pradesh and Bihar is more the product of educational considerations and objectives and less a reflection of the pressures of political demands and influence.

This evidence is re-enforced by the pattern of enrollments at the university level, with Gujarat's and Tamil Nadu's enrollments more concentrated in high cost, high benefit faculties less susceptible to politicization and those in Uttar Pradesh and Bihar concentrated more in low cost, low benefit faculties more susceptible to politicization.[18] Taking arts faculty enrollment as an indicator of low cost, low benefit distribution of the university student population, we find that Gujarat and Tamil Nadu (in 1965–66) had 35.5 and 30.6 percent of total university enrollment in arts degree programs while Uttar Pradesh and Bihar had 42.4 and 52.4 percent in the same programs. Using engineering-technology and medical college enrollments as indicators of high cost, high benefit distribution of the university student population, we find that Gujarat and Tamil Nadu (in 1965–66) had 11.9 and 14 percent of total university enrollment in these two fields of study while in Uttar Pradesh and Bihar the percentages were 3.4 and 8.1.[19] These contrasting indicators reflect pronounced differences in the way educational policy in the two sets of states has been shaped by their respective educational and political systems and has benefited these systems.

For all the differences that exist between rimland and heartland states and between Gujarat and Tamil Nadu, on the one hand, and Uttar Pradesh and Bihar on the other, Gujarat remains a society divided against itself culturally and to an extent territorially in ways that link one side to some of the conditions and forces that dominate Uttar Pradesh and Bihar. Its modern industrialists and progressive farmers wear a pragmatic face and talk about production and profit while its princely traditionalists and cultural revivalists wear a puranic face and talk of the wisdom and achievements of India's ancient civilization. These orientations often overlap in the same social group and even in individuals, sometimes producing the kind of work ethic and cultural revitalization that Gandhi raised to a world historical level. But they also produce debilitating cultural and political contradictions. There is, too, a territorial dimension to Gujarat's two faces and idioms. Kathiawad or Saurashtra are the home of princely traditionalism, Ahmedabad the center of cultural revivalism (and revitalization), Kaira the home of Patidar progressivism, and Ahmedabad and Baroda the centers of modern industrialism.

Inner Environment: Social Composition

We began our investigation of Baroda university with the view, derived from opinions pervasively expressed in interviews with the Baroda faculty, that the university's quality was declining as a result of a process best termed parochialization. We began our analysis by attempting to make both concepts, decline of quality and parochialization, operational, to establish one or more empirical indicators for them, and to measure and test the relationship between them. This effort made us take a more differentiated view of the decline in quality and, because we found parochialization a much more complicated concept than we (and those we interviewed) assumed it to be, made us less confident about the relationship between it and the putative decline in quality.

Our thinking about parochialization and our initial assumption that it was a most useful explanatory concept were shaped by our and other research on British and postindependence India. Since independence, the boundaries of leading traditional structures, especially caste but also village and family, have broadened physically and become more permeable to external influence. Many traditional functions have atrophied or died while new, more modern ones have been added. Such changes in boundary conditions and in functions have been associated with pronounced structural and cultural changes that often contributed to political and social modernization.

Extra-village economic opportunities and new occupations, new sources of political power and influence, and status and reference groups that paralleled or contradicted those found in the sacred world of caste hierarchy and the secular world of land ownership have modified village and family life and transformed the meaning of caste. Decompression and deparochialization have helped to free rural society from many local constraints and definitions of reality.[20]

Our initial assumptions about the causes and consequences of compression and parochialization at MSU led us to hypothesize that they were intimately linked to the causes and consequences of decompression and deparochialization of caste, village, and family. As a result of the modernization of these traditional structures, the boundary of the university seemed to be contracting and becoming less permeable; local needs, issues, and prestige were becoming more relevant and weighty in university life; local and regional reference groups were replacing national and international ones; and academic, intellectual, and professional concerns were being joined or replaced by the need to serve local interests. We thought in short that a certain compression and parochialization of a modern institution such as the university was the price Indian society was paying for expanding the boundaries and reference groups of local and traditional institutions and groups. A more complicated conception of the meanings of cosmopolitanism and parochialism has since obliged us to modify this rather too orderly and symmetrical explanation.

The cosmos is the universe; "cosmopolitanism," says the dictionary, has reference to that which includes all the world. To determine an educational institution's degree of cosmopolitanism or parochialism, we must have reference not only to the students and faculty who make up its inner environment but also to what the institution cultivates, transmits, and creates.

Geographic space is one obvious referent of cosmopolitanism and parochialism. In India one often assumes that geographic spread promotes not only national integration but also cosmopolitanism because it includes students and faculty from different linguistic and cultural areas of that vast and diverse subcontinent. Yet geography is obviously an insufficient referent. Kansas State University, which recruited 84 percent of its students in the fall semester of 1966–67 from within Kansas, reaches further in space than City College of New York for the bulk of its students. Yet the class, ethnic, religious, and cultural heterogeneity of New York City, as well as its greater Cultural (with a capital "C") opportunities, may provide a richer mix than the wide spaces of Kansas. It is not merely the size of a university's catchment basin that tells about its cosmopolitanism but also the variety of fish swimming in that basin.

What is a "national" university by the sole criterion of geographic diversity? In the U.S. in 1938–39, 15 and 16 percent of the students attending state universities and land grant colleges were from out of state compared to 42 and 30 percent of students from out of state in private universities and colleges which were members of or accredited by the Association of American Universities. The Harvard class of 1970 drew 30.6 percent of its students from New England (22.6 from Massachusetts), the University of Chicago class of 1971, 25 percent from Illinois (the next highest states were New York and Pennsylvania), and the University of Sussex, now a strong competitor to "Oxbridge," 21.3 percent from the "South-Eastern Region" of England (the immediately surrounding counties of Kent, Sussex, and Surrey). A recent study done in Germany, which is smaller than India, and has more highly developed communications, a single language, and historical traditions that make movement between universities in the course of a student's career normal, provides yet another norm. It indicates that students tend to come predominantly from the state (*Land*) in which their university is located: the most locally oriented university, Cologne, draws 87 percent of its students from the state in which it lies while Freiburg, the most cosmopolitan, draws only 45 percent from its state. The median of the twelve universities studied falls at 60 percent. The German study also indicates that in most cases the three immediately adjoining districts supply more than half the students, with a median of 55 percent for the twelve universities studied. By these standards, the percentage of MSU's arts and sciences students who are residents of Gujarat (85 and 89 percent respectively in 1965–66) correspond to past and present levels of in-state enrollment in American state universities and colleges, while enrollment in MSU's professional and specialized postgraduate faculties more closely approximate aggregate proportions of the more horizontally parochial contemporary German universities. But horizontal cosmopolitanism is an inadequate and insufficient guide to knowledge about so multidimensioned a concept as cosmopolitanism.[21]

Indeed, geographic diversity may mask class or community homogeneity. "Mere diversity of geographic origins," Jencks and Riesman observe, "will not produce much diversity in . . . outlook and aspiration. . . . When for example, Princeton recruits upper-middle class Protestant suburbanites from outside Baltimore, Chicago, and San Francisco as well as New York, or when Notre Dame recruits the children of white-collar Irish Catholics from all over the country rather than just from Indiana — the result is a very modest increase in diversity" despite the claim that they are "national" universities.[22]

English speaking students from Madras, Bombay, Calcutta, and Delhi attending India's nationally recruited IIT's (Indian Institutes of Technology) display a similar class uniformity, which is also called diversity by virtue of geographic distribution. Yet in India, where the idea of the nation is novel and fragile and faces challenges from linguistic and cultural diversities, horizontal cosmopolitanism, even if it masks class uniformity, is important in maintaining a national society and political community.

Sociocultural variety, by contrast, provides a measure of vertical cosmopolitanism. As educational institutions begin to draw from more limited geographic areas, they may attract a wider social mix by recruiting from more classes, castes, or religious and linguistic communities than they had previously. Such a mix, Jencks and Riesman pointed out in the context of American state and municipal colleges, provides extraordinary educational opportunities, but these are rarely well exploited.

A third measure of an institution's cosmopolitanism — we shall call it substantive cosmopolitanism — has reference to the kind of knowledge it cultivates, transmits, and creates and the kind of intellectual environment that results. This intangible is very difficult to measure when what is defined as knowledge is itself changing.

Factors which lend themselves to the more precise methods of quantitative measurement are horizontal and vertical cosmopolitanism; that they lend themselves to measurement does not assure that they are the most significant factors.

Using this more differentiated notion of cosmopolitanism and parochialism, we hypothesized that there were long range features in the Indian environment operating to reduce horizontal and increase vertical cosmopolitanism. The proliferation of Indian universities has altered educational market conditions both for consumers of education and for seekers of academic jobs. So long as universities were relatively few, they drew students from wide catchment basins. So long as the demand for faculty was modest, staffs had to go far afield in search of jobs. The leap from twenty universities in 1947 to eighty-six universities and "deemed" universities in 1968 and from 437 university-recognized colleges in 1947 to 2572 such colleges in 1966 has meant that students in search of colleges and faculty in search of jobs can often find opportunities near home. That they are likely to favor such opportunities is apparent not only from the data we present below, but also by analogy with the choices expressed by members of a high status and cosmopolitan profession, the Indian Administrative Service. The top men, who are given a choice of postings, normally choose their home states rather than distant ones.[23] The academic professional who is strongly oriented toward his discipline may choose a distant metropolis for the sake of its intellectual advantages, but he represents only a small portion of academic manpower. Sentimental as well as economic factors favor home areas. Given a free market, both faculty and students are more apt to choose a nearby university; with the proliferation of institutions, they are more likely to find one than they were before.

The proliferation of universities and colleges, as well as the great increase in primary and secondary education, has been a precondition for vertical cosmopolitanism. Providing more educational opportunities at the pre-university stage and opening universities in many sub-regions in most states have made higher education a possibility for lower castes, lower classes, and rural communities. New students and faculty come increasingly from backgrounds in which they are the first of their families to have university education.

But the exceedingly rapid proliferation of education at all levels has probably diluted the average quality of secondary preparation of university students and helped to lower the quality of collegiate education. We say probably because, as we point out in our discussion of standards (chapter 4 above), all discussions of quality in education teem with a priori generalizations which have no solid base in rigorous diachronic comparisons.

To test our more complex formulation of cosmopolitanism and parochialism, we turned to MSU. We did not know to what extent it would or would not bear out the hypothesis that horizontal cosmopolitanism was decreasing and vertical cosmopolitanism increasing. The meaning of the MSU findings, in any case, would eventually have to be read in the context of data drawn from other universities which may show different patterns.

While the faculty of MSU believe that their university is declining, becoming less cosmopolitan and more parochial, they believe it is declining from a cosmopolitan standard which is still visible. They consider the decline in recruitment of students from beyond the state an important measure of the university's decline. Our data have not confirmed that such a decline is occurring. As one measure of horizontal and vertical cosmopolitanism, we drew time series data on birthplace, residence, and caste of students from a 10 percent sample of student records in two general and three specialized faculties of the University of Baroda — arts, science, education and psychology (mainly a postgraduate faculty), fine arts, and social work (a postgraduate faculty).[24] We should like to have extracted data as well for urban-rural origins, but locating each residence represented more formidable work than our time and resources allowed.

We found no evidence of a decline in the horizontal cosmopolitanism of students. In fact, the reverse is the case — student origins are slightly more cosmopolitan now than ten or fifteen years ago. The hypothesized (and romanticized) point in the past when Baroda drew a geographically more wide-ranging student body never existed. We also found only a slight increase in vertical cosmopolitanism. The hypothesized recent enrichment of social composition by lower castes never occurred in more than a marginal way. If a decline in horizontal cosmopolitanism and an increase in vertical cosmopolitanism are national trends, as we believe them to be, they were not strongly in evidence at Baroda. Within the interstices of these larger findings, other findings proved of interest.

Since 1955–56, and probably earlier, most MSU students have come from the local, or at least the linguistic, area. Tables 52, 53 and 54 show that in the large bread and butter faculties of arts and science, Gujarat residents or native born were approximately 80 to 90 percent even in the mid-fifties, prior to the great jump in enrollment.[25] This finding is supported by Ramashray Roy's data, which show that 91 percent of the students at Patna College in Bihar in 1936 and in 1963 were from Bihar, although the percentage of students from Patna city climbed from 20 to 50 percent in the same twenty-seven year period.[26] It is quite likely that B.A. degree student bodies in India have never been widely recruited beyond the

Table 52. Birthplace of students in the faculties of arts and science M.S. University of Baroda (percentage).

Birthplace	Year		
	1955/56[a] (N = 107)	1960/61 (N = 145)	1965/66 (N = 190)
Baroda state	44.0	42.0	42.7
Gujarat (excluding Baroda)	46.8	35.9	37.9
Maharashtra	3.8	4.9	5.3
Other Indian states[b]	0.9	2.8	2.1
Africa	0.9	3.5	7.3
Pakistan	1.8	0.6	3.2
Overseas (except Africa)	0.9	–	0.5
Not known	–	10.3	1.0

Source: These figures and those in tables 53–60 represent a 10 percent sample of students in the three-year degree course of the respective faculties, drawn from student records.
    [a] Does not include first-year arts faculty students.
    [b] Andhra, Himachal Pradesh, Bihar, Delhi, Madras, Mysore, and Madhya Pradesh.

political unit in which they are located, and that the assumption of considerable student mobility in the past is unfounded. This impression of mobility may be based on the experience of elite colleges such as St. Stephen's in Delhi or Madras Christian College in Tamil Nadu, which have a cross-regional reputation among the small English speaking elite educated in convent, missionary, and (English) public schools. Or it may be based on the fact that cities like Delhi, Madras, Bombay, and Calcutta attract a cosmopolitan population which is reflected in the enrollment of a college that recruits mainly locally. In the latter case it is the environment, not the institution, that is responsible for the cosmopolitanism of the student body.

We had expected that even a narrow initial base of "outsiders" would

Table 53. Residence of students in the faculty of science M.S. University of Baroda (percentage).

Residence	Year		
	1955/56 (N = 70)	1960/61 (N = 61)	1965/66 (N = 73)
Baroda state	40.0	49.2	46.5
Gujarat (excluding Baroda)	30.0	41.0	42.5
Maharashtra	1.4	4.9	–
Other Indian states	–	1.6	2.7
Africa	–	3.3	5.5
Pakistan	–	–	1.4
Overseas (except Africa)	–	–	1.4
Not known	28.6	–	–

Table 54. Residence of students in the faculty of arts, M.S. University of Baroda (percentage).

	Year		
Residence	1955–56[a] (N = 37)	1960/61 (N = 84)	1965/66 (N = 117)
Baroda state	51.4	77.3	65.8
Gujarat (excluding Baroda)	37.8	16.7	19.6
Maharashtra	2.7	1.2	1.7
Other Indian states[b]	–	1.2	2.6
Africa[c]	–	2.4	7.7
Pakistan	–	–	–
Overseas (except Africa)	–	–	0.9
Not known	8.1	1.2	1.7

[a] Does not include first-year students.
[b] Includes Delhi, Madhya Pradesh, Kerala, Rajasthan.
[c] Uganda, Dar-es-Salam, Kenya, Tanzania.

shrink over time. Contrary to expectations, the figures concerning student residence show, in a rapidly expanding universe, a constant, not increasing, proportion of state (Gujarat) residents between 1955–56 and 1965–66 (tables 53 and 54).[27] However, these *residence* figures understate the diversity of the student body. Baroda students represent a larger variety of birthplaces than they do of residences. The combined figures for arts and science faculties on student birthplace (table 52) show a trend opposite to what might be expected: a 10 percent increase in "foreign" born (non-Gujarati) persons, from 9 percent in 1955–56 to 19 percent in 1965–66. The increasing number of "foreign" born (non-Gujarati), come from a variety of places: Maharashtra, the neighboring state; other Indian States; Africa — the site of large Indian settlements from Gujarat; and Pakistan — presumably refugees. The African students are especially important for the tone of MSU, since the East Africa Gujaratis tend to be much more worldly than the homegrown ones. A delicate and interesting theoretical point, which illustrates the slipperyness of indicators of cosmopolitanism, is whether a Gujarati speaker born in Africa should be counted as contributing more or less to cosmopolitanism than a native Tamil speaker born in Baroda city.

The rather puzzling juxtaposition of a constant proportion of outside residents and an increasing proportion of "foreign" born among MSU students leads back to our discussion of the extent to which geographic reach or the mix within the immediate environment is more determinative of cosmopolitanism. These figures suggest that while MSU's geographic reach has remained relatively static, the content of that reach is in motion: the residents of Gujarat, especially of Baroda city, often come from outside the state, and the university's relatively narrow catchment basin is enriched by migration from outside.

In 1961, 15 percent of Baroda city's population was born outside Gujarat,[28] as opposed to 10 percent of the population of all of Gujarat's urban areas.[29] About 3.5 percent of Baroda city residents were Pakistani refugees, many were born in Maharashtra, and others came from various adjoining states. These figures suggest that a growing industrial center, drawing populations from elsewhere, provides a more diverse geographical mix than residence data alone would imply.[30]

Total "foreign" (by residence or birth) student enrollment in the specialized faculties of the university never exceeds about 25 percent in any faculty. The small postgraduate faculty of education and psychology and the small but significant undergraduate and postgraduate faculty of fine arts, which together accounted for only about 5 percent of MSU's 12,000 students in 1965–66, constitute part of the university's specialized and less conventional postgraduate studies. In education and psychology, out-of-state residents constituted about 11 percent of the student body in 1950–51 and in 1965–66 even though enrollment expanded considerably over the fifteen year period (table 55). In the small and very specialized fine

Table 55. Residence of students, faculty of education and psychology, M.S. University of Baroda (percentage).

Residence	Year			
	1950/51 (N = 27)	1955/56 (N = 34)	1960/61 (N = 38)	1965/66 (N = 42)
Baroda state	22.2	44.2	44.7	42.8
Gujarat (excluding Baroda)	66.6	50.0	47.3	45.3
Maharashtra	3.7	–	2.7	2.4
Other Indian states[a]	7.5	5.8	5.3	9.5
Africa	–	–	–	–
Pakistan	–	–	–	–
Overseas (except Africa)	–	–	–	–
Not known	–	–	–	–

[a] Includes Uttar Pradesh, Assam, and Himachal Pradesh.

arts faculty, one of two in India (the other is at Banaras), about 20 percent of the students were out-of-state residents in 1960 and in 1965 (table 56). We did not draw figures for the large undergraduate and postgraduate faculty of technology and engineering because it is subject to a 25 percent reservation on behalf of out-of-state students. This reservation is related to advice the University Grants Commission attaches to its financial grants to the technical faculties.[31]

The evidence that the proportion of outsiders has not decreased markedly and may even have increased (as measured by birthplace) contradicts what would be expected on the basis of admissions procedures. These discriminate against outside students, those living beyond the ten-mile radius for which MSU has statutory responsibility. Faculty report that out-

Table 56. Residence of students, faculty of fine arts, M.S. University of Baroda (percentage).

	Year	
Residence	1960/61 (N = 25)	1965/66 (N = 32)
Baroda state	52	31.2
Gujarat (excluding Baroda)	28	46.8
Maharashtra	8	9.4
Other Indian states[a]	12	12.6
Africa	–	–
Pakistan	–	–
Overseas (except Africa)	–	–
Not known	–	–

[a] Includes Punjab, Madhya Pradesh, Bengal, Assam, Delhi, Nepal.

siders must have marks approximately ten points higher than those required of applicants from within a ten-mile radius. (If local students are admitted with marks of 55 percent in science, outside students may not be admitted with marks less than 65 percent; arts and commerce, which admit with lower marks, maintain a similar differential.) Yet tables 53 and 54 suggest that the percentage of students from beyond the ten-mile radius increased between 1960 and 1965. Several explanations may account for the discrepancy between expectation and data. It may be that a fairly uniform 10 percent discrimination is a recent phenomenon, not apparent in our 1965 figures. A second possible explanation is that at MSU, an English language institution, outsiders with a good English language education — for example, students from good Bombay schools — have a better chance of admission, even within a scheme of Baroda city preference, than local boys without a good English language education. The trend noted at one IIT, that Bombay boys do well in admissions because of their superior English language education, probably holds at MSU as well.[32]

Faculty familiar with the admissions process believe that the main reason for the present distribution between local residents and outsiders, however, is the pattern of applications (recruitment) rather than any marked preference for locals. For the science and technology faculties, the University Grants Commission's pressure to persuade universities to reserve 25 percent of the seats for outsiders coincides with high demand by outsiders to be admitted. But for the nonspecialized faculties, where most applications are from local residents, only a more aggressive policy of outside recruitment and incentives would be likely to increase the proportion of nonlocals applying.

Vertical cosmopolitanism is increasing slightly by one measure, caste, although patterns differ significantly among faculties. Brahmans and Banias, the traditional literate castes, have retained their proportion in the arts

Table 57. Caste of students in the faculty of arts, M.S. University of Baroda (percentage).

	Year		
	---	---	---
Caste	1955/56[a] (N = 37)	1960/61 (N = 89)	1965/66 (N = 117)
Brahman	29.7	23.8	30.8
Bania	16.2	26.2	16.2
Patidar	18.9	27.4	23.1
Other[b]	35.2	14.3	17.9
Backward classes[c] and castes	–	1.2	9.4
"Hindu" or not given	–	7.1	2.6

[a] Does not include first-year students.
[b] Maratha, Jain, Sikh, Parsi, Muslim, Christian, Rajput, Prabhu, Sindhi, and C.K.P.
[c] Kahwal, Lohana, Kacchia, Vaishar, Tamboli, Kharadi, and scheduled castes.

faculty (table 57); the dominant rural caste, the Patidars, has increased its percentage in the same faculty, as have the backward classes and castes. Their increases have been at the expense of marginal groups, some perhaps from outside the state, including Maratha, Jain, Sikh, Parsi, Muslim, Christian, Rajput, Prabhu, Sindhi, and C.K.P. In the science faculty, on the other hand, the proportions of students from the traditional literate castes and from the Patidars have both declined markedly; their place has been taken by the same marginal castes and sects ("Other") that appear to be declining in arts (table 58). The representation of the backward classes and castes seems to have declined.

One explanation that might cover the differential between these two faculties is that the greater competition for high opportunity science seats favors groups that can afford not only to pay for good, often English lan-

Table 58. Caste of students in the faculty of science, M.S. University of Baroda (percentage).

	Year			
	---	---	---	---
Caste	1951/52 (N = 61)	1955/56 (N = 70)	1960/61 (N = 61)	1965/66 (N = 73)
Brahman	26.3	20.0	29.6	15.1
Bania	27.9	24.3	16.4	21.9
Patidar	31.2	27.1	32.8	23.3
Other[a]	9.8	22.9	13.1	31.5
Backward classes and castes[b]	3.2	5.7	4.9	–
"Hindu" or not given	1.6	–	3.2	8.2

[a] Maratha, Muslim, Christian, Sindhi, Sikh, C.K.P., Jain, Rajput, Parsi. The first three groups are numerically preponderant.
[b] Includes a category given in the records as "Backward Classes and Tribes and Lower Castes."

guage, primary and secondary education for their children but also to inculcate them with the discipline and ambition to do well academically.[33] It is possible that the traditional literate castes and the dominant rural Patidar caste have been less informed and calculating in using family resources and socialization to buy such preliminary education and to instill educational and career goals than have the groups comprising the category "Other." All of the groups in this residual category are characterized by a certain ancient or recent marginality. The category includes: castes and religious minorities that are not an integral part of traditional Gujarat social structure (Christians, Sikhs, Parsis, Sindhis); groups that have traditions of geographic mobility or of special flexibility in relation to new opportunities (Parsis, Sikhs, Muslims — many Gujarat Muslims come from minorities within a minority, that is, they belong to entrepreneurial minority sects within Islam itself); and groups that are refugees or permanently settled "foreigners" in Gujarat (Muslims from Pakistan, Sindhis, Sikhs, Marathas). These groups may have increased their numbers in science by finer sensitivity to new opportunities, the wherewithal to prepare for them, and the transmission of an achievement culture that focuses on academic performance. The decline of the backward castes may be related to their inability to meet the stiff minimum requirements for science seats that apply, at a lower level, to seats reserved for them. On the other hand, the lower standard for arts seats is within reach of prosperous rural castes such as Patidars who lack strong educational traditions and whose established political and economic position may act as a disincentive to the pursuit of academic goals or achievement; it is also within reach of backward castes, for whom seats are reserved.

In the specialized faculties of fine arts and education and of psychology, there has been a slight increase in lower and scheduled castes, from 4 to 9 and 4 to 12 percent respectively (tables 59 and 60). The data are confused by the fact that a large proportion of students, 28 percent and 21 percent

Table 59. Caste of students, faculty of fine arts, M.S. University of Baroda (percentage).

| | Year | |
Caste	1960/61 (N = 25)	1965/66 (N = 32)
Brahman	24	12.5
Bania	–	18.7
Patidar	16	9.4
Other[a]	36	21.8
Backward classes and castes	4	9.4
"Hindu" or not given	20	28.2

[a] Muslim, Christian, Parsi, Maratha, Sikh, Jain.

Table 60. Caste of students, faculty of education and psychology, M.S. University of Baroda (percentage).

	Year	
Caste	1950/51[a] (N = 27)	1965/66[a] (N = 42)
Brahman	37.1	30.9
Bania	14.8	9.6
Patidar	22.2	14.2
Other[b]	18.5	11.9
Backward classes and castes	3.7	11.9
"Hindu" or not given	3.7	21.5

[a] Figures were available for these two years only.
[b] Sikh, Jain, Muslim, Parsi, Christian.

in 1965–66 in fine arts and education respectively, did not give their caste or merely reported "Hindu." This may itself be a sign of the changing ideology concerning caste identities. Those who did not report their caste are probably of higher caste; were they of the backward and scheduled castes, they would sacrifice the advantages of reserved seats by not reporting. (Those capable of sufficiently high academic performance to free them from the need to rely on reserved seats and wishing to abandon their scheduled caste identity may also have listed themselves as "Hindu.")

We do not have time series data about trends with respect to urban-rural background of students or with respect to their parents' education. But B. V. Shah in 1957–58 found MSU very much an urban university in terms of student enrollment, given the fact that 75 percent of the people from Baroda district and adjoining districts lived in rural areas. According to Shah's sample, only 26 percent of MSU's students at that time came from rural areas; that is, from villages below 10,000. Fifty-three percent came from cities of 100,000–500,000.[34] Since Shah's sample excluded non-Gujarati outsiders, who were even more likely to be city people, the urban balance may have been even higher.

We can only speculate about subsequent trends. Less well-educated rural students have gone to Vallabhai Patel and Gujarat universities, both mainly Gujarati language. MSU faculty anticipated that the founding of Saurashtra University and South Gujarat University would drain off additional rural students. It may be that these new universities have allowed Baroda to continue its urban-biased recruitment of the better educated in the face of rising educational demand by rural groups.

In 1957–58, at the time of Shah's study, 64 percent of his sample were the first in their families to finish college. This figure conforms to the findings in 1965–66 of Dr. N. B. Tirtha, professor of education at Osmania. Sixty-one percent of the sample of male students in Osmania's urban colleges were the first in their families to finish college.[35] We expect, but cannot establish, that rural and first generation proportions will increase further.

One significant change in the population of MSU, whose effect on any index of cosmopolitanism is probably positive, is the rise in the proportion of women. This proportion has gone from 10 percent in 1950–51 to slightly less than 30 percent in 1966–67.[36] The women who go to college in India tend to be of higher socioeconomic status than men and bring with them a better education; while rural and modest-status families will struggle to send their boys to college, urban and better-off families often will also send their girls. Hence, even though women students may have had a less adventuresome socialization, they probably are more educated, "cultivated," and sophisticated (and in these senses, cosmopolitan).

The over-all import of these figures, taken together, is that there has been relatively little change in the university's geographic reach for students but that the population within that reach now includes more people born outside of Gujarat, and that the student body includes slightly more members of lower castes than before, mainly in the lesser opportunity faculties. If experienced faculty at Baroda believe there has been a decline in the cosmopolitanism of their students, it is likely that this is due less to the parochialization of MSU recruitment and more to inferior preparation — both linguistically and substantively — among the expanding numbers coming to MSU's faculties at all levels. The "cure" would appear to lie more with stricter admission and examination standards and the improvement of education at the school level than with horizontal or vertical enlargement of the university's recruitment pools.

Although the quantitative data suggest relatively little change in the composition of the student body, the data suggest marked changes in the composition of the faculty. Our data here refer solely to the source of degrees of MSU faculty, which we have taken as indicators of the extent to which MSU recruits teaching and research talent locally, nationally, or internationally. We have been able to gather time series data only on the specialized faculties, which may recruit in a more cosmopolitan fashion than others (table 61).

MSU is increasingly drawing its faculty from its own students. At the same time, however, a large proportion of the faculty hold foreign degrees. Although the percentage of foreign degrees has declined in some faculties, the proportion remains significant.

Because these figures refer to the specialized faculties, one must exercise a certain caution in interpreting them. Home science, helped by Ford Foundation support, is one of the leading faculties in its field in the country. It has been producing its own faculty, a fact that may be related to the lower quality of training provided by the few other home science faculties. To an extent the same may be true of social work. Technology and engineering has drawn faculty from elsewhere but rivalries among

Baroda University   *227*

Table 61. M.S. University of Baroda staff with M.S. University of Baroda and overseas degrees.

Faculty	MSU degrees (%)	Overseas degrees (%)	Number
Home science[a]			
1956–57	35	40	20
1961–62	50	30	30
1966–67	55	29	49
Social work			
1951–52	0	40	15
1956–57	28	33	18
1961–62	57	14	21
1966–67	72	24	25
Technology and engineering			
1951–52	38	9	55
1956–57	33	9	83
1961–62	56	11	164
1966–67	65	15	183
Polytechnic			
1958–59	43	–[b]	21
1960–61	73	–[b]	61
1966–67	90	–[b]	81

Source: The figures are based on the highest degree taken. They were compiled by Janet Guthrie from the *Prospectus* published annually by the university for each faculty.

[a] The first of the four five year intervals has been omitted for Home Science which had not then been founded.

[b] Negligible.

local, regional, and national engineering colleges (IIT's) sometimes make communication and recruitment difficult.[37]

We do not have time sequence figures for the arts faculty, but in 1966–67 44 percent of its teachers held MSU degrees, 30 percent held Bombay University degrees, and most of the remainder held degrees from other Indian universities. Foreign degrees were sparse — less than 5 percent. These figures make the arts faculty less local in composition than the more specialized faculties. The main explanation is that those arts faculty members who received their advanced degrees prior to the university's founding in 1949 had to acquire them elsewhere, but few if any universities in India were producing advanced degree holders for specialized faculties at that time.

Although the prevalence of foreign degrees makes it evident that in the specialized and professional faculties MSU continues to look well beyond its own borders, the pressures toward localization in faculty recruitment are considerable. The main reason for the trend toward localization, the rise of many new universities throughout the country and the changed geographic parameters of the academic market that it is producing, has already been cited. Another reason given by some faculty is that MSU failed to revise its salary scales when other universities raised theirs, enabling other universities to recruit faculty away from MSU by high bidding. Such recruitment is said to have affected outside faculty more than those who had local roots because the economic advantages of a higher salary would not be so marked for local people with nearby family-based resources. We have not been able to confirm this hypothesis in detail, but it makes sense a priori. By 1968–69, localization of faculty could be measured by the fact that twenty-five of forty-four professors (60 percent) were Gujaratis.

Some of those who influence MSU appointments believe it is to the advantage of the university to appoint local people to the faculty. Several of the nonacademic syndics (trustees) hold this view. One told us, "Members of the selection committees prefer the local man if all else is equal. They feel that if he is a local man he will stay . . . whereas an outsider might decide to return to his home place when he was experienced." And another echoed virtually the same argument: "If they appoint an outsider he may stay . . . for a few years and then when experienced and most useful will go back to his home town."

Conventional opinion at the university holds that the university may more easily lose its investment in training faculty when they are mobile outsiders, a point of view which, among other things, increases faculty immobility and institutional dependence by giving a higher priority to teaching experience than to research and publication and by rewarding institutional commitment more than professional commitment.

The selection procedures at Baroda have tended to favor local applicants, at least at the lower levels and possibly at the higher ones as well. Selection for readers and professors is made by a statutory committee or board which must include, in addition to the vice-chancellor, pro-vice-chancellor, dean of the relevant faculty, and head of the relevant department, four experts in the relevant subject, at least two from outside the university.[38] These boards meet in Bombay in order to be conveniently located for outside experts and in order to escape local pressures and canvassing. Higher posts are advertised on a nation-wide basis and attract outside applications. There has been some criticism of appointment procedures even at this level, as when, in a banking and commerce department appointment, a local banker and syndic was asked to serve as an expert. The main pressures toward localization have come from the selection committees for lecturers and assistant lecturers, which until recently lacked the outside experts found on the statutory selection committees for readers and professors. Until recently, lecturer and assistant lecturer committees included nonacademic syndics whose connections with the community were stronger than their understanding of the professional subjects for which they selected candidates. Thakorbhai V. Patel, the most conspicuous politician among the syndics, served on these committees for more than a decade. Some of the syndics were known to canvass local people about lecturer appointments. Notices for lecturer posts are not nationally advertised; limited to Gujarati newspapers, such notices normally attract only local applicants. One faculty member claimed, in what was probably an overstatement, "It is these obviously unobtrusive assistant lecturers who, in course of time are mostly promoted to be Head of the departments and whose entry into the academic line is not always strictly on academic considerations." [39]

Nonacademic syndics and some academic or administrative ones with strong ties to local interests often display little understanding or appreciation for professional certification of academics by academics, either because the reasons for such certification are not recognized or because faculty members at MSU are not thought capable of such professional judgment. An influential syndic gave us his judgment concerning teachers. "They are all gold seekers; they are not interested in intellectual matters or in academic matters; all that interests them is whether or not they will get promoted. A lecturer is only interested in becoming a reader, a reader in becoming a professor, a professor in becoming a dean, a dean in becoming a member of the syndicate, so that he will have a chance to become the pro vice chancellor and ultimately vice chancellor. Of course, there are a few exceptions, thank goodness! But this is the general pattern. They have no real interest in academic matters of the students; they are only interested in themselves and their finances. They do as little as possible as far as these matters are concerned; but they will make enormous efforts to forward themselves by being in with the right people."

A similar view, probably from a similar source, though leavened by the perspectives of comparative education, was expressed in a series of articles on MSU in the *Western Times*. One article held that if academics plead for certification by academic professionals and oppose lay intervention in selection, it must be for reasons of monopoly. "Does Mr. R. T. Leuva [who proposed that experts sit on lecturer selection committees], who is 'shocked' at the Syndicate's powers to choose the teacher, advocate a 'closed shop' policy? Any one who knows even a little of what is happening in the teaching profession today would think twice before suggesting . . . that teachers themselves should select their colleagues. . . . That growing realization that university affairs are of vital concern to the community is reflected in the fact that in the Cantons of Switzerland, entire community elects its teachers [sic]. . . . This may not be ideally suited to India. But that the society must have its say is amply clear." [40]

Despite such populist views among some syndics, faculty pressure from heads of departments in the arts faculty and others led a vice-chancellor's committee, set up to consider the university's founding act, to recommend in 1969 that two experts, one an outsider, be appointed to selection committees for lecturers. The committee resisted extending the principle to selection committees for assistant lecturers.[41] The recommendations have not yet eventuated in a new act.

It is likely that over time the trend toward local candidates and appointments at the lower levels of the faculty will affect the higher levels. Even a conscientious selection board which means to keep some eye on the national academic market and professional standards will have to keep in mind the importance of internal promotion in order to keep up morale and hope in the lower ranks. If the pool from which such promotions are made is mainly local, the more cosmopolitan quality now characteristic of higher level faculty will be affected. In the faculty of engineering and technology, for example, twenty-one of the professors and readers have non-MSU qualifications, eleven have studied at MSU and then added outside qualifications, and three have MSU qualifications only.[42] But those with non-MSU qualifications are professors, while the tendency is for readers to be MSU students who have added outside qualifications. If these readers in due course replace a substantial number of the present professors, the engineering and technology faculty will gradually become locally and internally recruited.

How should one judge the process of present and potential localization of the faculty? From the point of view of standards, there is no reason to believe that in most fields MSU products are inferior to those of other Indian universities. In certain specialized faculties they are probably better. Furthermore, because many professors have additional, often foreign, qualifications, MSU men are being exposed to non-Baroda influences, both intellectual and social, as part of their training. Nevertheless, there is a potential hazard in the situation we have described. As faculty are increasingly recruited from the immediate vicinity, the life of the university and that of the community begin to overlap, and the educational goals and purposes of the former are likely to be swamped by the concerns, demands, and relationships prevailing in the latter. It is this process of increasing congruence that heightens compression. The problem of university autonomy can be formulated in social terms by saying that there must be enough incongruence between the administration, faculty, and students of an educational institution and its local environment to insure that the concerns of all do not coincide.

Inner Environment: Substantive Cosmopolitanism

Our investigation of faculty qualifications and the social and geographic composition of the student body neglects many features which constitute the spirit and quality of the university. Neither of these indicators focuses on the patent rather than latent functions of the university, the organization of knowledge in faculties and departments or the quality of teaching and research.

It is difficult to specify precisely what "substantive cosmopolitanism" in a university might consist of. But an attempt can be made in the context of four broad orientations that have characterized Indian and other universities: cultivation of knowledge and of character (as in Weber's usage of the phrase and as expressed in the English collegiate model); research by independent scholars that adds to knowledge (German university model); training for the professions and for the occupational needs of society; service to state (or national) producer interests, governments, and education consumers (the U.S. land-grant university model).

We are uneasy about too romanitic or purist a view of The University (in capitals) as the seat of a universal intellectual ideal and the guardian of ultimate concerns, partly because real universities have often served parochial interests, calling them cosmopolitan, and partly because no real university has ever devoted itself to cultivation (including guardianship) of knowledge and research to the exclusion of training and service. Yet we would argue that the first two orientations (perhaps without the "character" dimension in these less morally confident days) are essential for the cosmopolitan claims proper to a university. (Even these orientations could presumably be "parochial" in content.) The normative conception of a university requires these orientations, even while the empirical reality often does without them. That does not mean the other two orientations cannot be present as well in an institution calling itself a university. But where they alone exist or dominate, it becomes difficult to distinguish the university from a training or applied research institute or a Lok Sevak Sangh (Community Service Club).

MSU's greatest emphasis over the years has been on the third orientation, training for the professional and occupational needs of society. Its strength has vested in the quality of its professional schools, and its cosmopolitanism in the pioneering of new professional fields — home science, social work — before they were fashionable. Furthermore, MSU has focused on the high opportunity or high standard professional fields. It has stressed professional training as against the humdrum and devalued B.A. and B.Sc. programs which today constitute the bulk of most Indian university teaching.

Table 62 shows that the largest single faculty is technology and engineering, high cost and high standard relative to other faculties. Table 63 shows that more than one third of the students are enrolled in high opportunity professional schools or postgraduate programs and another quarter study in ordinary professional and technical programs. Together, these professional and technical courses outweigh the preuniversity and low opportunity first degree programs.

A comparison made in 1963–64 between MSU and the two other Gujarat universities existing at that time showed that enrollment in the low opportunity arts and science programs was much lower at MSU (39 percent) than at the others (Gujarat University, 74 percent; Sardar Patel University, 61 percent).[43]

The tables also show a relatively small percentage of the student body — 19 percent — in the preparatory units. In chapter 3 we discussed the effect

Table 62. Students[a] at M.S. University of Baroda, by faculty, 1968–69.

Faculty	Number	Percentage
Arts	1,351	9.40
Science	1,030	7.10
Education and psychology	250	1.70
Commerce	1,571	11.00
Medicine	635	4.40
Technology and engineering	2,224	15.40
Fine arts	80	0.60
Home science	525	3.60
Social work	_[b]	–
Law	343	2.40
Preparatory unit, arts and commerce	1,693	11.70
Preparatory unit, science	1,072	7.40
Shri M.K. Amin Arts and Science College, Padra	419	2.90
College of Indian Music, Dance and Drama	68	0.50
Baroda Sanskrit Mahavidyalaya	11	0.07
Polytechnic (diploma only)	1,218	8.50
Diploma (nonpolytechnic)	537	3.60
Postgraduate	1,359	9.40
Total	14,386	100.00

Source: The calculations in this table are based on MS University of Baroda, *Twentieth Annual Report, 1968–69* (Baroda, 1969), Appendix 1, p. 188.

[a] The figures given against each faculty are those for undergraduate students only. Diploma course students and postgraduate students have been separately noted.

[b] Postgraduate students only.

on the quality of Indian higher education of the 40 percent national norm for Pre-University Course enrollment, pointing out that because the PUC year more closely approximates school than higher education and because it occupies an enormous proportion of faculty time and talent, it has a debilitating effect on university level education. At MSU the PUC is taken much more seriously than at most other universities and occupies a smaller proportion of student enrollment. Both factors have important consequences for the over-all quality of intellectual life at MSU.

Within MSU's orientation toward training for the professions a shift in a more "democratic" direction is evident. Table 64 shows the emergence of the polytechnic and the law school, both training at a relatively lower standard than some of the other schools, and jointly capturing 15 percent of the enrollments by 1966–67. Commerce, also a more modest standard field, increased its share of enrollment by 5 percent. To the extent that these schools recruited a high proportion of those students who used to go into the B.Sc. in 1950–51, which was then a low resource program including students aiming only for the intermediate degree, they may represent a sensible diversification at the lower levels of training. But they lack the resources to provide education equivalent to MSU's best. Two of these faculties taught students in 1966–67 with less than half the per student ex-

Table 63. Students at M.S. University of Baroda, by faculty, grouped by type.

Faculty	Percentage
High opportunity professional courses	
Education and psychology[a]	1.70
Medicine	4.40
Technology and engineering	15.40
Fine arts	0.60
Home science	3.60
Postgraduate	9.40
	35.10
Ordinary professional courses	
Commerce	11.00
Law	2.40
Polytechnic	8.50
Diploma (nonpolytechnic)	3.60
Music	0.50
Sanskrit	0.07
	26.07
Pre-University and low opportunity degree courses	
Arts	9.40
Science	7.10
Pre-University Course, arts, commerce	11.70
Pre-University Course, science	7.40
Padra	2.90
	38.50

Source: Table 62.
[a] Education would normally be ranked in the second category, but as Baroda has the Center for Advanced Studies in this field, we have ranked it in the first category.

penditure that constitutes the average for MSU students (per student expenditure in the law and commerce faculties was 30 percent of the MSU average), and one, the polytechnic, taught with slightly higher, but still below average (80 percent) resources. No one can quarrel with India's, and Baroda's, need for middle range technical training, but whether a university is the appropriate seat for it is quite another question. Although the orientation to "training," by responding to manpower needs, always overlaps with a service orientation, a shift into or increase in these three fields is less an expression of a university's orientation toward high quality professional training and more a response to increased local demand for easy access to occupational training and educational certification.

The university's orientation toward cultivation of knowledge and character was never primary, but it was a noticeable part of its program in the fifties. Table 64 provides some evidence for a shift away from this orientation. When the university began, the arts degree to a considerable extent

Table 64. Redistribution of enrollments and resource allocations, 1950/51–1966/67.

| Faculty | Faculty enrollment as a percentage of total enrollment | | | | Faculty per student annual expenditure as a ratio of average annual expenditure per student | | | |
| | Percentage | | Rank order | | Ratio | | Rank order | |
	1950/51	1966/67	1950/51	1966/67	1950/51	1966/67	1950/51	1966/67
Arts	6.7	12.2	3	2	2.3:1	0.7:1	4	10
Science	30.6	10.6	1	4	0.7:1	2.6:1	9	5
Education and psychology	4.8	2.9	5	8	1.7:1	2.3:1	5	6
Commerce	4.5	9.8	6	5	0.9:1	0.3:1	10	11
Technology and engineering	21.3	18.8	2	1	1.3:1	1.1:1	6	8
Home science	1.7	4.4	8	6	2.6:1	1.8:1	2	7
Fine arts	1.1	1.6	9	9	4.1:1	2.6:1	1	4
Social work	1.1	0.6	10	10	2.6:1	4.3:1	3	2
Law[a]	–	4.1	–	7	–	0.3:1	–	12
Music, dance, drama	5.5	0.3	4	11	0.7:1	12.1:1	8	1
Sanskrit	3.1	0.1	7	12	1.1:1	3.2:1	7	3
Polytechnic[a]	–	11.0	–	3	–	0.8:1	–	9

Sources: D. M. Desai and S. S. Pandit, *Growth and Development of Maharaja Sayajirao University of Baroda, 1949–1967* (Baroda, 1968), table 13, "Faculty-Wise Enrollment," p. 44; and ibid., table 48, "Per Student Annual Expenditure in Different Faculties of the University," p. 106.
[a] These faculties did not exist in 1950/51.

still had the status it developed in the preindependence era, when it was a vehicle for general cultivation. Enrollment in arts was modest (6.7 percent) and per student annual expenditure relatively high, more than double (2.3:1) the average per student expenditure at the university. By 1966–67, the situation had reversed itself. Arts enrollment had jumped to 12.2 percent and the resources had declined to a ratio of 0.7:1 of average annual per student expenditure. Arts had become, as it is elsewhere in India, an easy access, low resource field, representing a concession to a service orientation that makes education generally available rather than a vehicle for cultivation.

The establishment and activities of the fine arts, music, dance and drama, and Sanskrit faculties, although in one sense specialized professional training within the arts, can also be regarded as an indicator of the viability of the cultivation orientation at MSU. Fine arts has a higher enrollment and lower per capita resources (table 64), music a lower enrollment and remarkably higher per capita resources. (The drop in enrollment and rise in per capita expenditure may be a danger signal rather than a sign of enhanced quality and capability.) The first two faculties represent some of Hansa Mehta's original innovations; both have India-wide reputations.

The decline of the general education program suggests a shift away from the cultivation orientation. MSU in 1953 inaugurated an effort to break through the specialization parameters of education for the first degree by instituting general education courses. These were required of students in the arts, science, commerce, technology and engineering, fine arts, and home science faculties, as well as in the two PUC units. The courses include general surveys in the humanities; human civilization; social, political and economic problems of India; science and its impact on life; and values of life. The university is known for its pioneering of American-style (University of Chicago or Columbia) general education, an effort that in effect placed MSU at the forefront of a movement to replace or modify the British legacy, which limited general education to the first degree in arts or science.[44] The goal of this education is the development of the cultivated, concerned, and critical generalist. Ford Foundation support enabled the program's director, K. S. Yajnik, to visit the U.S. on several occasions to study general education programs. Such support also enabled Professor Richard McKeon of the University of Chicago to advise on the program's organization in its early years.[45] Like general education elsewhere, the program has encountered considerable student scepticism with respect to its "usefulness," and when examinations were made voluntary, students ceased to attend classes.

Science in contrast to arts has improved its standing in the university. In 1951–52, it had 30 percent of the enrollment, but at a low resource level, per student expenditure running lower (70 percent) than average per student expenditure. Abolition of the old intermediate program thinned down the B.Sc. enrollment. By 1966–67, science had fewer students

(10.6 percent) and higher proportionate resources, more than two and a half times the average per student expenditure (table 64). It had become a smaller but relatively more privileged field in the university, to an extent a counter current to the demand for mere accessibility. This development can be counted as a new opportunity for students to cultivate knowledge while escaping the devalued arts field, but to an even greater extent it can be counted as an aspect of training (pre-professional) for the higher opportunity science fields.

Some indicators show a shift away from an orientation toward research. Research is now less pursued and less funded than it was in the early years of the university. A purely quantitative count of the number of research projects taken up in each faculty over successive five-year periods shows a decline in all faculties except medicine, technology and engineering, and home science (science remains steady). This is true in spite of a staff increase in every faculty.[46] Expenditure on research as a percentage of total expenditure has always been sufficiently low to make a serious research orientation doubtful. In spite of increased resources, however, expenditure on research, which was 3.6, 2.3 and 2.2 percent of total expenditure in the years 1954–55 to 1956–57, had fallen to .9 and .7 percent of total expenditure in 1965–66 and 1966–67.[47]

Another index of research orientation, however, shows an increase over the years. For the three-year period 1952–53 to 1954–55, there were 3.6 Ph.D.'s per ten thousand students, for the five-year period 1955–56 to 1959–60, 13.7 Ph.D.'s per ten thousand, and for the six-year period 1960–61 to 1965–66, 18 per ten thousand.[48] This compares with a national norm in the period 1960–61 to 1963–64 of 8 Ph.D.'s per ten thousand enrolled students.[49] This does not, of course, tell us about the relative quality of these Ph.D.'s.

Another positive index for research orientation is the student distribution by levels. In a growing universe, the postgraduate program at Baroda accounted for a slightly larger proportion of total students in 1966–67 (10 percent) than in 1950–51 (9 percent).[50]

There are some indicators of university quality whose variation affects university performance regardless of goal orientation. Annual per student expenditure has declined. Such expenditure rose slightly from Rs. 682.8 in 1949–50 to Rs. 717.1 in 1966–67; at constant prices, however, this amounted to a decline to Rs. 466.05.[51] The staff-student ratios remained steady for the university as a whole between 1952–53 and 1966–67 (1:15.7 and 1:15.4) but declined markedly from the improved position established in the mid-fifties (1:13.7). The situation of specific faculties differs. Among the large faculties, science, technology, and medicine have improved their positions (science, 1:22 to 1:7) while the positions of arts and commerce have worsened (arts, 1:14 to 1:18; commerce, 1:31 to 1:49). The polytechnic faculty-student ratio deteriorated sharply between 1965–66 and 1966–67 (from 1:10.6 to 1:15.8).[52]

Other intangibles, the precise weight of which it is difficult to assess, include the relatively conspicuous nature of some MSU departments which have attracted foreign and government of India support or collaboration (Ford Foundation aid to the home sciences and general education; University of Michigan assistance to education and psychology and recognition of that department by the UGC as an advanced center qualifying for special assistance; WHO and University of Edinburgh collaboration with the medical college). Other intangibles include a high level of institutional self-consciousness and self-study.[53]

The overall conclusions from this evidence seem to be that while MSU has continued to focus on training for the professions, it has also responded to the consumer demand for easy access professional and occupational training at more modest standards. The first two goals, research and cultivation of knowledge and character, which we posited as essential ingredients of a university which claimed substantive cosmopolitanism, were never first among MSU's goals. Cultivation and research have been weakened to some extent by a decline in the resources allocated to them. Despite this decline some indicators of research remain positive although the overall impact of research remains limited. Despite the continuing influence of cultivation and research, training for professions and jobs and its related orientation, service to the community, are the university's principal goals.

In many ways, MSU has more to recommend it academically than many other universities in India. At the same time, academic and intellectual values do not enjoy a teaching and research environment that enables them to be the decisive factors in university policies, leadership, and decisions. Academic self-confidence enables members of a university to distinguish between those outside pressures that are benign and those that are not. Academic self-confidence at MSU is sufficiently strong to resist blatant forms of infiltration and appropriation but not strong enough to identify, much less resist, more subtle claims made in the name of service, social needs, or historical necessity.

The Vice-Chancellor and Politics at MSU: An Empirical Standard of Judgment

Three elements of the university's organization — the senate, the syndicate, and the vice-chancellor — are, by virtue of their function or composition, formally and directly involved with forces in the university's external environment. Of the three, the vice-chancellor is most continuously and conspicuously engaged in such relationships. He plays a dual role; as a spokesman for the university to the publics outside, and as a principal interpreter to the university of the manifest concerns of such publics. His position is both strategic and vulnerable: strategic for managing the interplay of purposes and interests from within and without in ways that preserve or enhance cosmopolitanism, independence, and educational capability; vulnerable because he is exposed to those pressures that result in parochialization and politicization.

The word "politics" has on the whole a negative connotation in India, as well as in some other countries. This connotation is undiscriminating and ill-informed. By focusing on the partisan, opportunistic, and self-serving aspects of politics, it ignores the constructive and creative consequences of the politician's role in using political resources and skill to gain desirable ends. The word assumes an even more sinister meaning when it is used in connection with education. We have pointed out earlier in this volume that it deserves this sinister meaning when and where educational goals and processes are clearly subordinated to or appropriated by political ones. Harold Gould's chapter analyzes how and to what degree such results can occur. But political resources, skills, and influence are essential to the internal management and external relations of a university. In many instances where politics enters into education, motivations are by no means clear cut or easily discernible and the relationship between intention and consequence is not always consistent. One observer's self-serving or partisan politician may turn out to be another observer's patron of learning. We attempted to construct some standards of judgment that avoid abstract moralism because they are related to the needs and requirements of particular institutions and to the context of at least one university.

When our respondents at MSU used the word "politician" in a negative sense, as they usually did, what they had in mind was a man who used the educational structure as a political resource, that is, to benefit personal, partisan, or factional fortunes. There was general agreement that politics in the sense of furthering party interest was not really an issue at MSU. In this sense MSU presents a sharp contrast to the picture that has been drawn in earlier chapters for school education in Faizabad district or primary education in Rajasthan. But there was also general agreement that people used the university for personal advancement, a charge which is harder to deal with — is the department chairman who succeeds in finding ample funds for science subjects self-interested, as an embittered humanist might claim, or is he advancing science? At MSU, at least, it was assumed that educational goals might be subordinated to personal and group rather than party interest, although it was also believed that the personal and group interests could find their home in a party.

We disaggregated the backgrounds of likely candidates for the office of vice-chancellor in order to understand the meaning particular vice-chancellors might give to their office. We think of four analytic types of vice-chancellors, each of which is associated with a certain kind of recruitment, skill, and expected benefit: (1) the "politician," whose connection with a party, faction, or political leader promises strong support for university interests from government and some of its publics; (2) the "judge," whose reputation for fairness and concern for the public interest suggest that formal rationality and procedural legitimacy will be maximized in the government of the university; (3) the "administrator" (he might be a distinguished civilian or an experienced educationist), whose command of bureaucratic processes, influential connections, and skill in dealing with officials promises organizational leadership and access to outside support; and (4) the "broker" (often an administrator-professor from within the university), whose skill in bargaining and sensitivity to and knowledge of competing forces suggests that conflicts will be avoided and interests reconciled. A residual category which goes beyond these would contain the "leader," whose vision of the needs and possibilities of the educational enterprise and command of some of the qualities associated with the other types promises institutional independence, reform, and creativity.

Earlier we identified four broad orientations that have characterized Indian and other universities: cultivation of knowledge and of character; research; training for the professions; and service to producer interests, governments, and education consumers. The role of a vice-chancellor can be fruitfully assessed in the context of interactions between the possible types of leaders and such university orientations. These interactions provide another conceptualization, in addition to parochialism and cosmopolitanism, of the relationship between the inner and outer environments. Because MSU's orientation has changed over time, affecting the tasks of its vice-chancellors, at least some of the problems we originally conceived of as "politicization" turned out to represent conflicts inside and outside the university over its orientation.

Only one of the four vice-chancellors came to the university as something of a professional politician. Mrs. Hansa Mehta, the first vice-chancellor, had been president of the Bombay Pradesh Congress Committee, member of the legislative council in 1937 and 1940, and a member of the constituent assembly between 1947 and 1950. Bombay presidency, where Mrs. Mehta was active in nationalist and democratic roles, adjoined the princely state of Baroda where her husband, Dr. Jivraj Mehta, was prime minister. She was appointed for a three-year term prior to the demise of Baroda state and the termination of her husband's government there. Her subsequent effectiveness suggests that the fruits of a type 1 (politician) appointment (and one based on kinship at that) are not invariably sour.

Although Mrs. Mehta explicitly resigned her membership in the Congress party when she became vice-chancellor because she believed the vice-chancellor should be nonpartisan, she retained, through her husband, a better than indirect connection to the party. As prime minister of Baroda at the time of its integration into India, her husband assumed a more cooperative and nationalist role than the prince of Baroda, who considered reopening the accession of the princely order to the government of India. Jivraj Mehta's relations with national and Gujarat Congress party leaders were, in consequence, cordial. He was an influential member of the senate in MSU's early years. When Bombay was divided into the states of Maharashtra and Gujarat in 1960, he became chief minister of the latter.

His appointment to this post suggests that his influence in party life was considerable earlier on, when his wife was vice-chancellor.[54]

Hansa Mehta had considerable administrative talent and influence (type 3). She understood the possibilities of legislation and administrative regulations both within the university and in the university's relations to state and national educational agencies; and had enough personal influence to persuade others to interpret legislation and rules in favorable ways. (Her understanding of legislative and administrative possibilities was evidenced in her opening statement on "Financial and Business Administration of Universities" at the Vice Chancellors Conference on University Education convened by the ministry of education in 1957.[55]

Hansa Mehta avoided the role of political broker (type 4). Rather than compromising and aggregating the demands of various interests within the university, or developing a sharp sensitivity to demands from below or outside, she acted like a law-giver shaping a young institution, and built the university's structure and spirit during its critical formative years. At that time, what some faculty thought of as her authoritarian manner caused little trouble, partly because people valued her capacity to lead and build while the university was young, partly because influence in the university's governing bodies, notably the syndicate, was not yet valued by prominent figures in the Baroda community; and partly because the authoritative style common to public figures in the pre-independence period, especially in princely states, was more tolerated than it is now.

Although Hansa Mehta's identity "objectively" included her role as a professional politician, faculty do not remember her as a "politician." Instead, "she protected the University from politics," as one faculty member put it. The apparent anomaly is a function partly of Mrs. Mehta's character and motivation. She used her political access and influence to further educational goals rather than the reverse. It is also a function of the changing meaning of politics in India. The nationalist movement included a substantial number of persons who were more liberal and nationalist than populist and leveling in their political orientation. Prior to the enormous postindependence explosion in political consciousness and participation, it was easier to formulate public policy generally and educational policy specifically free of political pressures. To be a vice-chancellor then did not require the elaborate effort that it does now to establish one's policies and mobilize the support of proliferating and increasingly organized and active constituencies, including faculties and students.

Finally, Mrs. Mehta undoubtedly provided leadership by making educational innovations that went beyond the demands made on her by either the university community or the state of Bombay.

Neither of the other two vice-chancellors at MSU have been professional politicians in the sense in which Mrs. Mehta was. Yet both are seen in the university as more political. The designation refers mainly to a broker (type 4) who manages demands made by groups and interests in the university and the community. There is some question, however, whether Dr. Jyotindra Mehta possessed one of the qualities of the broker vice-chancellor under increasingly democratic conditions, sensitivity to demands from below.

Jyotindra Mehta seems to have been chosen vice-chancellor at least in part in the expectation that he would provide the benefits associated with an administrative leader (type 3). He spent most of his career as an "educationist," a word frequently employed in India to convey a combination of roles: a professionally qualified man who teaches, does a certain amount of research and writing, and expects his career to be crowned by recognition in eminent and influential positions of educational authority rather than by renown in the more abstract world of intellectuals and scholars. (The ambitions and motivations associated with such a career are critical for keeping up the supply of institutional managers; Irene Gilbert, in her chapter on the Indian Educational Service — chapter 13 below — suggests the origins of a culturally patterned career ladder with administrative authority as its apex.) Dr. Mehta was professor of history at Elphinstone College, Bombay, from 1920 to 1922. In 1931 he became principal of Baroda College, and thereafter commissioner of education of Baroda state — a post in which he was influential in shaping the statutes of MSU. Subsequently he became director of public instruction for the state of Bombay, the most influential position in a state's educational service. He moved into noneducational administration as chairman of the public service commission during the time of the short-lived state of Saurashtra, which has since become part of Gujarat. He is related to Hansa and Jivraj Mehta. Like Hansa Mehta, he is remembered as a man who cared for academic values. When Dr. Mehta became vice-chancellor in the late fifties, Gujarat and Bombay were still one, and his position as former director of public instruction provided lines of influence and connection. These lines continued when Jivraj Mehta, husband of former vice-chancellor Hansa Mehta, became chief minister of the new state of Gujarat, although Jivraj's idea of financial control was more detailed than some university people thought good. When he ceased to be chief minister, the Gujarat government sought closer control of the university, a development Dr. Mehta and his successor resisted.

Dr. Jyotindra Mehta's position at MSU was comparable to that of George III. Dr. Mehta hoped to govern in the traditional manner (Mrs. Mehta's), more as king than as king-in-parliament. During his first term, there was very little dissent from the guidance he gave the syndicate. But finding university authorities increasingly obstreperous with the emergence in the syndicate of persons strong in the community, and experiencing a decline of the rather automatic acceptance previously given the vice-chancellor's views and wishes, he was obliged, like George III, to mobilize forces to protect his authority. This step, like George III's organization of loyalist forces to combat radical ones, constituted recognition of the existence and legitimacy of a more conflictual politics. The vice-chancellor now had to involve himself in a political process within the university, a process that drew him into the very internal politics that Dr. Mehta had been anxious to do without. In 1963, two city syndics, Thakorbhai Patel and Nanalal Choksi, both at various times mayors of Baroda, organized to elect a different vice-chancellor who, Dr. Mehta feared, would be excessively responsive to them. The political environment in which these events occurred was affected when, in September 1963, Balwantray Mehta replaced Dr. Jivraj Mehta — friend and protector of MSU — as chief minister. Dr. Mehta hoped to stop the attempt to elect a new vice-chancellor by revising the statutes to allow a vice-chancellor (himself) to occupy his office for more than the sanctioned two terms. In this effort he had the backing of the central government's education minister, M. C. Chagla. The effort, however, failed, and Dr. Mehta did not retain his position in the syndicate after leaving the vice-chancellorship. The term of Jyotindra Mehta proved a watershed. The shift from the politics of deference and command to the politics of opinion and mobilization proved irreversible; the relatively peaceful and benevolent autocracy of Hansa Mehta is no longer a viable alternative at MSU. The question has now become whether brokers can be found who are also educational leaders.

Dr. C. S. Patel, the former pro-vice-chancellor, succeeded Dr. Mehta in 1964 after a bitter battle for the position, and was re-elected in 1967, to a second term. He took his Ph.D. in chemistry at Leeds University in 1930, began his academic career as a lecturer, and in time became professor of chemical technology and dye house superintendent at Kalabhavan Technical Institute (an educational institution of the former princely state of Baroda which has since been absorbed into MSU). From 1941 to 1949, he was director of the institute and an industrial chemist, key roles in a city dominated by the chemical industry. In 1950, he joined MSU as professor of chemistry and served as dean of the science faculty until 1953, when he became pro-vice-chancellor.

C. S. Patel's career reflected a growing tendency at MSU to connect the technological and scientific faculties more closely with Baroda's growing industries. Something of a broker, he saw service as an important part of the university's orientation. "We are part of the community we are catering to. Many courses like social work and the specialized industrial courses run by the University would not have been possible without the help of the local industries and others." [56]

C. S. Patel elicited none of the strong feelings that Jyotindra Mehta did; his faculty and syndicate saw his style as reconciliatory, a quality about which feelings were mixed. By comparison with his autocratic predecessors, he was milder, more easygoing, and more responsive — although it was apparent even in his case that the vice-chancellor's opinions and initiatives still won compliance. Some believe that having been pro-vice-chancellor under two strong vice-chancellors, Dr. Patel was accustomed to holding second position, with the result that he was too easily influenced by others, notably syndicate politicians. Others interpreted his role as responsive, accommodating, and appropriate to the "multiversity" functions MSU now serves.

The selection of Nasarvanji K. Vakil, a retired Gujarat high court judge, with relatively little controversy in March 1970 reflected a dominant preference for the consensual values and disinterested leadership associated with type 2 (judge) vice-chancellors. It also reflected a reaction against the prevailing stress on community relations.

The faculty, particularly the Baroda University Teachers Association (BUTA), in the discussions and deliberations that preceded N. K. Vakil's election, stressed the importance of choosing a vice-chancellor who favored academic as against service values and who was independent of the community. The chief minister of Gujarat and the chief justice of Gujarat were said to be concerned to protect MSU's academic standing. The leading candidates frequently mentioned in the press and organized discussions beforehand were mostly natives of Gujarat who had achieved distinction in the larger, more cosmopolitan national setting: I. G. Patel, special secretary for economic affairs in the finance ministry; the late J. J. Anjaria, deputy governor of the economically powerful and politically influential Reserve Bank of India; and Vakil, who was then a member of the Communal Riot Inquiry Committee appointed to look into the disasterous Hindu-Muslim riots of September 1969 in Ahmedabad (and elsewhere in Gujarat). When the name of Ishwarbhai Patel, vice-chancellor of neighboring Sardar Vallabhai Patel University, was mentioned early in February as a candidate favored by influential members of the syndicate with close ties to city and state publics, "his name had to be dropped," Loksatta reported, "due to objections by most university teachers." [57]

Among the attributes that marked off N. K. Vakil was his apparent capacity for disinterestedness. Not only was he a high court judge thought worthy of sitting on so sensitive a panel as one charged with investigating large scale, bloody Hindu-Muslim riots, but he was also from a marginal community, the Parsis, Zoroastrians who immigrated from Persia to India in the eighth century. A tiny minority of several hundred thousand, the Parsis as a community are highly educated and well-to-do but not politically powerful in Gujarat. N. K. Vakil conducted the affairs of the Parsi Panchayat (a Parsi community organization) with assets running over thirty million rupees and played a leading role for thirty-five years in the Surat Public Education Society (a community organization in the field of education).

Though he had the support of some important political figures at the state level, Vakil's selection was perceived as one that would, by comparison with more partisan possibilities, provide the university with fair, disinterested, and consensually based leadership. "It is a pleasure to welcome Nasar Vanji Vakil as new VC," Champaklal Shah wrote in Loksatta on March 5, the day it became clear that he would be the next vice-chancellor. "It is understood that his selection is consented to by all. Not a word has been uttered against his choice till today. Hence it is hoped that he will improve the polluted atmosphere both inside and outside MSU." [58]

The typology of educational leaders can be used to assess MSU's vice-chancellors in a way that relates their orientations and performance to an empirical standard of judgment. No one at MSU alleges, as some Uttar Pradesh University faculty allege, that their vice-chancellors are an extreme version of type 1, party or factional allies of the government of the day. Nor does anyone at MSU allege, as some faculty at Kurukshetra have of their former vice-chancellor, since then education minister of Haryana state and aspiring to become chief minister, that the university and the office of vice-chancellor were used to further the political ambitions of an incumbent vice-chancellor. From such perspectives as these, Hansa Mehta's political position and connections had the reverse effect; she used her connections while she was vice-chancellor to assure that the flow of benefits and influence were heavily in favor of education.

In interviews with us and in press reports, university faculty and members of the governing bodies revealed attitudes favorable to type 2 (judge) and type 3 (administrator) and unfavorable, if not antipathetic, to type 4 (broker). There was fairly broad agreement that an effective vice-chancellor must be fair and possess administrative skills and an ability to deal with elected and appointed officials, qualities most clearly associated with types 2 and 3. Most thought that the three former vice-chancellors demonstrated these qualities in varying measure. There was much less support for the necessity or legitimacy of a vice-chancellor being a broker (type 4). Since the careers of Jyotindra Mehta and C. S. Patel involved elements of the broker role, reluctantly and unwillingly in Mehta's case, more affirmatively and willingly in Patel's, a gap seems to have opened between academic attitudes toward university leadership and the imperatives and behavior associated with the role.

Faculty members who discussed with us the sort of person they thought would make a good vice-chancellor frequently mentioned a high court judge and directly or by implication contrasted what they saw as his virtues with the difficulties attending the broker type of vice-chancellor. What they wanted was someone who would be fair and impartial but not necessarily democratically representative or responsive. The judge was seen as representing the interests of the university per se, rather than as acting as a common denominator of the most vociferous pressure groups within or without. Procedural rationality, such as that to which a high court judge was dedicated, would, many thought, produce a commonly perceived and accepted substantive rationality, and allow him to transcend (or escape) the pressures of specific interests on university government and policies and to avoid the conflicts that competition for influence and resources engenders. These views, whether realistic or not, played an important role in the choice of the fourth vice-chancellor.

Conflict cannot, however, easily or for long be avoided. Its appearance brings to the foreground the possibility of coping with conflict by performing the functions of a broker. If universities are not to be organized in terms of procedurally legitimized conflict (on the model of legally prescribed collective bargaining in good faith between employers and unions, or on the model of competitive parties with one or several governing and the others for a time in loyal opposition), they will require some brokerage functions to satisfy or integrate the conflicting claims of their diverse interests and publics. Vice-chancellors cannot easily or often avoid the brokerage role. Even when educational communities were more hospitable to autocratic vice-chancellors, the more effective vice-chancellors leavened their direction of university affairs with attention to the voices that spoke from below, outside, and above. Today, paying attention to such voices is less a matter of grace than of necessity; a vice-chancellor who tries to lead his university without being responsive to faculty, community, and governmental opinion and interests risks being overrun by them.

At the same time, a vice-chancellor who is merely a broker, bringing natural harmony out of competing interests, recognizes no hierarchy of interest. Since all pressures are equal in his eye, he can not act to preserve those values that are unique to a university as against those that are demanded by various constituencies both internal and external. The efforts of the distinguished economist, K. N. Raj, to provide leadership transcending brokerage at what is probably India's best university, Delhi, provide a telling cautionary tale. He gave up partly in despair and partly in disgust when teacher and student organizations tried to force him into a broker role exclusively. Taking the position that not all interests and forces are equally worthy, he feared that successful conciliation and brokerage would compromise the goals of a great university.[59]

The choice of N. K. Vakil as vice-chancellor suggests that the university's movement toward congruence with its outer environment (compression) may be slowed. He is not, as were the two other nominees of the syndicate and the three previous vice-chancellors, intimately connected with lay community or political interests in the city and state; at least those in the university who canvassed his name and supported his election (particularly BUTA) did not consider him to be so connected. But the type of leadership he provides as vice-chancellor will be affected not only by the trajectory of historical forces that brought him to the post but also by the conditions and circumstances of the university's existence. And these continue to include a strong service orientation reflected in the allocation of resources and prestige within the university and the nature of support to the university from outside. The brokerage role and a service orientation, we have argued, tend to go together. If we are right, Vakil, who was selected because he could bring to university leadership the attributes of the judge and, to a lesser extent, the administrator, will also have to play the broker role. It remains to be seen whether he does it in a way that preserves the vigor and independence of educational purposes and leaves adequate scope for the other types of leadership implied in his selection.

Leadership Selection and Autonomy

The structure of Indian universities corresponds more to the bureaucratic paradigm of a hierarchical command organization than to the model of a loose federation of self-governing departments and faculties united in a common institution. In consequence, even though departments are more self-governing and autonomous at MSU than at some other universities, the role of the vice-chancellor, as head of the hierarchy, is significant both for the institution's internal life and its external relations. The selection of the vice-chancellor is a critical issue in university government. At MSU, the formal arrangement for selection is an election contest, confined to the university, among three competitors for the post. The actual arrangement is uncontested consensus on a single candidate nominated within the university. The avoidance of contest and the confinement of selection to university circles are related features that have probably helped protect Baroda against the sort of state intervention that a later chapter on Osmania documents.[60]

The reasons for the divergence between statute and practice reveal some of MSU's strengths. A major rationale for the principle of election by the senate is that this assures university autonomy. The main reason given for avoiding elections in practice is that they disrupt university life. Appointment by the chancellor, a common alternative method of selection, gives the decisive voice in most states to the state government. Because the chancellor is often the governor of the state, he is expected to act with the advice of the state ministry of education, although there is some feeling that in choosing a vice-chancellor he should act independently. At MSU, unlike at Osmania, government control through the chancellor was not an issue when we studied the university, since the former Maharaja of Baroda, not the state governor, was chancellor.[61]

Normally, the syndicate nominates three persons for the position of vice-chancellor (a procedure designed to meet the formalities of the statutes), two of whom resign before the senate meets to elect the vice-chancellor. In the early years of the university it was feared that election would undermine the vice-chancellor, who should have unanimous support. Although this feeling is no longer so strong, and some believe that the senate should have a real choice, others continue to favor consensualism. A sharply contested election, many of those we interviewed believed, produces bitterness and disruptive conflict that can weaken and even destroy the educational life of a university. A contest adversely affects the vice-chancellor's subsequent relations with those faculty and deans who are known to have opposed him; it may also make him too dependent on his supporters. Because a contested election requires campaigning and other efforts, it diverts faculty attention and energies from the educational process. Furthermore, where professional and intellectual authority is weak and administrative and organizational authority strong, winning may become an overwhelming preoccupation since so much depends on the outcome.

A contrary argument has been made by D. C. Pavate, a former vice-chancellor of Karnatak University, and an educational entrepreneur of considerable skill. He argues that contested elections oblige a vice-chancellor to cultivate the support and cooperation of his faculty. "I maintain it is useless to have a Vice Chancellor who does not pull his weight in the Syndicate, the Academic Council, and the Senate. . . . It is difficult for a nominated person to carry out projects. On the other hand, an elected Vice Chancellor does have authority behind him." [62]

Pavate's argument holds especially in contexts where those whose good will the vice-chancellor must keep are amenable to appeals on behalf of educational goals. Where the professional commitments of faculties are low and their connections to political and community goals high, a vice-chancellor may not be able to command support without compromising educational goals. In such contexts, it may be impossible for a vice-chancellor to be an educational leader.

At the time of our study, MSU's ritual election of the vice-chancellor helped keep the selection process within the university but avoided the travail of contested elections. [63]

Political and Academic Interests in Governing Bodies

The composition and functions of the syndicate and senate are at the center of university government, highly salient to the university's relationship to the community and potentially important in the process of university politicization. Our interviews revealed the belief (expressed also about student and faculty composition) that these governing bodies were both more local and more parochial (compressed) than they had been in the past, and that as a consequence the university was more susceptible to outside political influence. This belief, however, was more a product of subjective inferences than of objective changes. University and Baroda city affairs have always been congruent. At the time of our study, seventy of ninety-seven senators were residents of Baroda city, [64] but the composition of the syndicate and the senate was no more local in the mid-sixties than it had been in the early fifties. Both bodies have always been mainly controlled by Baroda city and district residents. If there is an increase in parochialism and politicization, as MSU faculty believe, the explanation lies elsewhere than in a change in senate and syndicate composition.

When Baroda was a princely state, the structure of power was relatively simple and overlapping. Power was restricted to a few persons, and its exercise on the whole was unproblematic. As the university's first vice-chancellor, Hansa Mehta profited from remnants of the political culture of a princely state which respected hierarchical authority (what we have called in Rajasthan the *hukum* culture). But democratization and political competition overtook Baroda city and the university in the course of the fifties, dissolving the attitudes of princely India in a sea of participation and mobility. Admissions and services at MSU increased, as did conflict over the disposition of the university's resources. Jivraj Mehta, prime minister of the state of Baroda when the university was created, had an extremely important voice in university affairs. His influence in the university was less contested, however, than the influence in the sixties of Baroda city mayors Nanalal Choksi and Dr. Thakorbhai Patel. Today, there is more competition for influence and control, and politics is partisan, not autocratic. Whether the university is more subject to political influence and appropriation today than before, as those we interviewed generally believed, is not so easily determined.

There seems little doubt, however, that there is more democracy and conflict in its internal government. Increasingly, all decisions in the university are contested. The election of members of both the senate and the syndicate has been affected. The election of faculty representatives is no longer a formality decided in the dean's office. As one MSU syndic described the trend: "It is now necessary to meet people on the senate and be nice to them if you are to be elected. Jyotindra Mehta was not elected to the syndicate because he refused to do this — he was used to having influence and did not realize election campaigning was necessary. He thought his service would be enough. . . . I went to talk with a lot of people before the election and got their votes. People are more likely to vote for a person they have met and talked to." The former mayor of Baroda accounted for his temporary loss of a syndicate seat by saying, "I was in the villages and could not go and get the votes that year." The organization of BUTA in December 1966, under the leadership of Raojibhai Patel, was welcomed among many faculty as a means to challenge the hitherto uncontested and administration-dominated voice of the senate and syndicate. While it represents opinion among both senior and junior faculty, younger faculty hope, through it, to increase their strength in university affairs.

On the one hand the increasing meaningfulness of the election process and the increasing conflict imply an opening up and leveling of hierarchical authority in the university, where collegiality has often been blocked by age and status grading. But these processes do not invariably benefit academic values. Political competition tends to politicize everyone and to reallocate the faculty energy from teaching and research to university government and politics. A talented scholar who left MSU believed that people who wanted to do their own work there found that academic politicians could make things difficult for them professionally if they did not defend their own interests. But to defend them resulted in neglect of their proper work in favor of politics. There is also a possibility that teacher-politicians, like some administrators, will abandon specifically academic values in favor of political brokerage and reconciliation, becoming intent on "reconciling" even those elements which are specifically anti-academic.[65]

The syndicate, MSU's leading decision-making body, in 1967 consisted of seven university people and eight outsiders.[66] It would be misleading to suppose that the university representatives are more clearly academic than some of the outsiders. The most notable political figure on the syndicate was a faculty member, Dr. Thakorbhai Patel, dean of the faculty of medicine. As president of the Baroda city Congress party committee; deputy mayor and subsequently mayor of Baroda city; director of Kalpana Clinic, a private hospital; and first chairman of the Baroda dairy, he combined academic, political, and private business roles in an enormously energetic career. University people tended to think of him less as one of themselves than as a man of public affairs. He had made himself extremely valuable to the university as a successful spokesman for it with the state government, particularly in financial matters. Because he was thought to be influential, faculty turned to him to exercise that influence in their behalf, sometimes even in minor matters such as leave. Prior to his election as mayor, his name came up most frequently as prospective vice-chancellor. Anyone familiar with the swashbuckling style and political skill in handling a state legislature of John Hannah as president of Michigan State University might recognize in Thakorbhai Patel a Gujarati variant of the same type. It is not a style that generally commends itself to academic intellectuals, but in a democratic era it is an important and useful one in American and Indian public universities.

The academic members of the syndicate are said to be too diffident in articulating their views, preferring to go along with the vice-chancellor's views and opinions. This may be because they are normally in agreement with those views; it may also bear out the fear, expressed in connection with the composition of the syndicate of Andhra University (see chapter 12, below), that faculty representatives are unduly dependent on the vice-chancellor. (One would need to sit in such meetings in order to form an opinion on this matter.) The academic syndics in 1966–67 consisted, in addition to vice-chancellor C. S. Patel and pro-vice-chancellor P. J. Madan, of the dean of the faculty of arts, V. Y. Kantak, a professor of English; the dean of the faculty of medicine, Dr. Thakorbhai Patel; the dean of the faculty of technology and engineering, Prof. L. B. Shah; the dean of the faculty of law, Prof. H. C. Dholakia; and the chairman of the department of chemistry, Prof. S. M. Sethna. Representation among the academic syndics was weighted toward the professional subjects. This weighted representation reflects the balance of power among the university faculties in financing and status.

Four of the outsiders can be ranked with Thakorbhai Patel as significant politicians in the city of Baroda. Nanalal Choksi, like Patel from an old Baroda district family, was mayor of the city of Baroda and a leading Congress party member when we began our research. He was defeated for the Lok Sabha (parliament) seat for Baroda city while we were there, and subsequently yielded the mayoralty position to Patel. C. C. Mehta became chairman of the Baroda city Congress party committee. These three were Congress party members, while two other members of the syndicate were prominent in the conservative Swatantra party. One of these was Nanubhai Amin, director of Jyoti Engineering, an independent firm spun off by Alembic Chemicals, one of Baroda's leading industries. Brother of Raminbhai Amin, director of Alembic and former chairman of the Federation of Indian Chambers of Commerce and Industry, he was a reluctant public figure who was said to have been persuaded to join the Baroda syndicate to save it from politicization. Although a prominent political figure, N. Amin was more oriented toward professional than political goals in his relation to the university. The other Swatantra figure was P. C. Hathi, a lawyer who handled much of the university's business.[67]

Other outsiders were less explicitly political. They included K. G. Badlani, director of education of Gujarat state, who is a statutory member of the syndicate by virtue of his office; Amar Patel, a woman with a home economics degree from Howard University in the U.S. who is generally believed to have been elected because she is Thakorbhai Patel's nephew's wife (he campaigned vigorously for her in the senate); J. S. Parikh, manager of the bank of Baroda, which helped MSU substantially in its financial crisis in 1967–68; and Dr. C. B. Patel, an officer of the joint public-private Gujarat state fertilizer company.

The involvement of politically interested persons in the syndicate is widely deplored among MSU faculty. However, no one claims that political figures explicitly further their party viewpoint in the syndicate. It is generally understood, for example, that one of the important Congress party members on the syndicate does not share the Gujarat state Congress party's strongly held view that English must be replaced as the regional language in education. No one claims that syndics in the same party necessarily act together. N. Amin and P. C. Hathi, both of the Swatantra party, ended up on different sides of the debate in the summer of 1967 over whether to revise the university statutes.[68] In the numerous claims that Patel and Choksi have acted "politically," there was no implication that either of them sought to annex MSU to the interests of a faction in the state or municipal government. The political interests were seen as personal, as one leading politician not on the syndicate told us: "When I say [that the University is being politicized], I do not mean party politics — that would be fine — what I do mean is that it is dominated by individual politicians who hope by dominating the syndicate to enhance their own prestige. Here there is no ideological-political discussion, merely a personal power struggle. They just use the syndicate as a platform for their own personal gain. In England in a similar situation you might get a heated dispute between a Labour and a Conservative member of an educational committee on the merits of the public school versus the community school or something like that. . . . These are not to promote party ideals but their own interests."

Many of those we interviewed held theories about the formation or existence of groups in the syndicate, but our inquiries produced descriptions of so many different and shifting forms of alignment that none of these group theories seemed very satisfactory. There was, for example, a theory of the emergence of a "Patidar group," implying solidarity along caste lines. We were told that the earlier dominance of the mercantile and bureaucratic caste which the Mehtas represented had now been superseded by the dominance of the Patidars, represented by the Patels. It is probably true that the Patidars, the dominant agricultural caste in Gujarat, important in cotton, tobacco and dairying, are increasingly taking on urban importance which is reflected in the significance of Patels in many roles and offices. This increased importance, however, does not necessarily represent a supersession of other castes. The Patidars appear now to have been added to the urban elites of Baroda, and this is reflected in the university. No evidence for joint action among the four Patels on the syndicate was offered, except possibly between Thakorbhai Patel and his niece, an alliance better explained on kin lines.

A more likely explanation of Patel influence is that T. V. Patel, a dynamic and energetic person, has been able, with the support of like-minded lay elements and university administrators interested in close relations with the town, and in the absence of vigorous counterefforts by either the academic elements on the syndicate or by differently inclined lay elements, to persuade the syndicate of his view on most issues. In American state universities, presidents and deans who understand reality as seen by state legislatures often command support in similar ways. The academics at MSU, as at some American state universities, at once recognized and resented that some of this realism is necessary for their institution's survival. Their dilemma, not well understood by vigorous lay syndics, is that mobilizing counterefforts is at the same time necessary to and destructive of the academic concerns they espouse.

The suspicion of lay influence and of syndicate power has produced some constitutional proposals. When the revisions of the university act were under consideration in 1969, some argued for raising the proportion of teachers in the syndicate; others argued for an academic council consisting of teachers only, to which certain decisions now taken by the syndicate could be referred. The academic council, which has drawn criticism in other universities for undermining departmental innovativeness, was seen at MSU as a possible counterweight to excessive lay influence in the syndicate, and as a way of removing decisions on politically loaded issues such as language of instruction or examination standards from that more community-oriented body.[69] A demand from faculty members that the number of teachers on the syndicate be increased relative to the lay element was met by a minuscule concession from the Vice-Chancellor's Committee of 1969, raising the number of teachers, including deans, from five to seven in a syndicate increased from fifteen to seventeen.[70] This committee's recommendations have not, however, been implemented so far.

Although the senate is formally "the supreme governing body and authority of the university," the syndicate, as the "executive authority of the university," performs all of the senate's significant functions, and its recommendations form the basis of most senate actions. It is by no means easy to assess the extent to which the syndicate's decisions reflect academic or nonacademic perspectives. By virtue of its power to choose the three candidates from which the vice-chancellor is selected, the syndicate is in a position to select the vice-chancellor.[71] This power is insignificant at the end of the first term of a vice-chancellor because a second term has become conventional. The syndicate did, however, oppose Jyotindra Mehta's attempt to extend his own term beyond two by change of statute, and selected C. S. Patel, so it would be incorrect to think of syndics as dependent in this function on the incumbent vice-chancellor.

The syndicate plays a critical role in the making of the university's financial and academic decisions, notably decisions about appointments and establishment of new departments, establishment of new courses, allocation of research funds, language of instruction, and size of the university. If there are "academic" or "political" ways to take these decisions, academicians and town people cannot be clearly identified with either alternative. Insiders and outsiders do not divide consistently on policy issues such as regional language or expansion. An industrialist and a professor of engineering might both favor English, while an orientalist and a city lawyer might both favor regional language. Younger faculty in search of senior posts and election-minded syndics may both favor expansion. Nor are there clear town-gown divisions on the exercise of academic discretion. A technologically minded administrator and a city official might both favor close town-university relations. Politically oriented syndics do try to influence the extent to which Baroda city and Baroda district applicants get preference at MSU, but they sometimes do so with the collaboration of deans who are eager for the syndics' support of a new course or appointment, or who have a distaste for argument.

There has been a shift of influence over the university's financial affairs to the syndicate, and notably to a committee of its more politically knowledgable members. The previous vice-chancellor, Jyotindra Mehta, on the whole conducted relations with the state government independently of the syndicate. The state government's attempt to exercise detailed control over finances led to a considerable deficit, and a committee consisting of Thakorbhai Patel, N. D. Choksi and Nanubhai Amin was set up to advise the vice-chancellor in financial affairs. Everyone in the university, including the vice-chancellor, credited Patel with an important role in the university's financial relations with government, a role which evidently increased both the indispensability and the power of Patel.

The syndicate is said to have only minor influence in "strictly" academic decisions. As is apparent from previous remarks, not only are there many exceptions, but also certain general policy issues, such as medium of instruction, size of the university, and questions of affiliation have the most profound academic implications. For example, the preparatory, or first, year of the university is organized in 125 student sections. Operationally, expansion is carried out by adding new sections, a decision which lies with the syndics. The syndics influence the appointment of lecturers, who constituted 293 of Baroda's 713 faculty members in 1966. Its members on the selection committee were pictured as being influenced by local opinion with respect to these selections. There were relatively few stories of syndic intervention at other appointment levels, those of reader and professor, although there were some.

Grades are also affected by the decisions of the syndics. In 1969, 70 percent of those sitting for the final exams of the PUC course failed. One must assume that this rate of failure is related to an excessively generous admissions process of the sort which has also been known at some American state universities, leading to similar rates of attrition. The political pressures which led to more generous admission at MSU also operated at subsequent points. Student agitation, which was viewed sympathetically by many affected parents, led to a syndicate meeting which allotted "grace marks" so that only 50 percent failed. Those who failed even with the extra marks were allowed to enter classes pending a second try at the same examination in October 1969.[72]

With respect to courses and new departments, the recommendations of the boards of study, the board of visitors, and the registrar tend to be ratified, but there are exceptions. A discussion in the syndicate concerning new courses in sociology followed when the department suggested a new course in research methods with an academic orientation. Some city syndics thought Baroda needed persons trained in community development, and suggested a paper in that area. They also suggested that the sociology department might take responsibility for training people in propaganda methods. The suggestion that MSU start training petroleum geologists when Gujarat state began to drill for oil is of the same order. On the one hand, too instrumental an orientation, whether proposed by syndics or the university departments themselves, may weaken more theoretical academic effort. On the other hand, it was in part because of the results of relevant research, such as the Babcock fat test, that the University of Wisconsin convinced the state legislature to let it build some great academic departments. Steering between applied and pure research and training poses a delicate problem.

Other decisions in which the requirements of the university and those of its environment have been in conflict concerned the establishment of a law faculty at MSU and the affiliation of new colleges. Hansa Mehta had given rather little importance to the law faculty, keeping it under the arts faculty. She was influenced by the fact that law faculties in India have declined in quality relative to other faculties, and tend to attract students who cannot qualify for the high opportunity professions. Since then, pressures from the town have reversed Mrs. Mehta's policy, winning an independent status for the law faculty. She also resisted the affiliation of a new college at Padra, because it would dilute MSU's status as a residential university. Padra was incorporated as a "constituent college" under Jyotindra Mehta. The chief minister at that time, Balwantray Mehta, pressed by the state legislator from Padra, favored the affiliation.

Although these decisions may have strengthened the service as against the academic functions of the university, it is not apparent that they have divided academic from nonacademic syndics. On many issues on which the syndicate has been too responsive to the political pressures of the community, it has acted with at least the passive consent of the academics, and, in recent times, the active consent of the administrators.

It is likely that a real division among syndics could give the senate greater importance than it now has. Academics constitute more than half of the senate, outweighing the non-academics. The academic membership consists of present and past vice-chancellors at MSU, vice-chancellors of other Gujarat universities, deans and heads of schools at MSU, and representatives elected by the various faculties.[73] The nonacademic membership consists especially of civil servants and judges (twelve), some of whom are required by statute to be members of the senate and some of whom are appointed by the government, which has the right to appoint twenty-five members. The remainder of the nonacademic membership are professional people from Baroda, some elected by special statute-designated constituencies, some elected as representatives of the registered graduates of MSU. Almost all of them live in Baroda city. The annual meetings are not normally marked by sharp debate. The meetings which we witnessed in 1967 and 1968 were on the whole mild and orderly affairs, conducted mainly in Gujarati. With the exception of a few critical and hortatory outbursts, they were more informational and ceremonial than divisive.

The potential for controversy in the senate was illustrated, however, by a requisition in the summer of 1967 for a special meeting of the senate that August. The senate would be asked to appoint a select committee to amend the statutes of the university. Members of the requisition group included former vice-chancellors Jyotindra Mehta and Hansa Mehta. They were among those proposed for the select committee. The requisition was interpreted as an effort by those who believe the present syndicate is political to counteract its influence. N. Choksi and T. V. Patel were not associated with the move. The requisitioners plainly meant to weaken the syndicate.

They proposed setting up an academic council which would dilute the syndics' academic authority; reducing the number of nominees of the Gujarat government — a move which would, in the short run, weaken the vice-chancellor who recommends these nominations, but would provide a long run security against the possibility of government packing the senate; and taking the nomination of vice-chancellor candidates out of the hands of the syndics and placing it in those of a high court judge, the minister for education, and the vice-chancellor — a move which might have weakened the syndics and strengthened the government.

A symposium sponsored by the university in April 1967, bringing together university teachers and administrators, had already responded to requisitionist pressure by foreshadowing changes in the university act.[74] The requisitionists' subsequent move in the senate was pre-empted by the vice-chancellor, who offered to establish a committee to reconsider the act. His initiative eventuated in the vice-chancellor's committee that reported in 1969. The committee did not include the persons proposed by the requisitionists,[75] nor did it include any of the vigorous critics of expansion, affiliation, and the influence of lay interests in the university, except for B. B. Yodh (who was unable to serve). BUTA mounted a massive effort to influence the committee report. Its recommendations were conveyed to the committee through BUTA president Raojibhai Patel in December 1967.[76] BUTA pressed for provisions that would diminish lay and increase teacher influence. Among teachers it sought to increase the power of junior faculty. The effort to influence the report on the whole failed, but it indirectly affected the elections to the syndicate held in December 1969, when BUTA-backed candidates did well. This victory in turn probably influenced the outcome of the vice-chancellor election in 1970.

The final committee report generally stressed the importance of lay influence and of responsiveness to democratic and welfare demands from city and state. "While taking every necessary precaution to ensure within it the entry of students with adequate scholastic attainment, [the modern university] constantly endeavors to enlarge its numbers in response to the manpower needs of the rapidly developing Indian economy." [77]

In summary, the senate and syndicate of MSU at the time of our investigation as often took a public and political as an academic view of issues. But MSU was then relatively free of intimate involvement with the partisan politics of the state. The politically oriented syndics had connections with their state counterparts, but did not allow these connections to subsume MSU to the interests of party factions, as had happened in Uttar Pradesh, or to annex MSU to the jurisdiction of the state ministry of education, as had been attempted at Osmania. The problem of politicization was defined by the degree to which MSU should be generous in its admissions standards for Baroda city, the extent to which it should be responsive to the claims made on it by the producer and municipal interests of the city, and the amount of political influence that some lay and academic individuals might gain for themselves and their friends by a judicious use of the resources and posts (faculty, student, administrative) of the university.

Public Policy Issues at MSU

As has been suggested before, major policy issues at MSU raise the question of how far the university should be responsive to the demands of its outer environments, particularly the local community, and how far it should be responsive to general notions of cultivation and scholarship which may or may not mesh with the felt requirements of the outer environments. Relating to the community has two dimensions: the public demand for more, and more accessible, education; and the university's relevance to its technological, social, and economic needs. The first dimension is expressed in the policy problems of expansion and language of instruction; the second is expressed in MSU's responsiveness to industrial and governmental needs in the city. On both dimensions, the community tends to demand relevance.

Expansion is a major policy issue on which the interests of university and government, or the claims of academic values and democratic social mobility, may clash. When we started interviewing at MSU in 1966, the university had about 12,000 students; at the end of 1966–67, it had 14,000 and further growth was expected. The student population had grown between 1961 and 1965–66 by 30 percent (from 9,000 to 12,000), while the staff had grown by less than 20 percent (from 588 to 713).[78] Officials at MSU envisioned a 15,000 limit on expansion; they hoped they had refuted an argument by the state that MSU should expand to 30,000 students. One high university official thought the Gujarat government might press the university to go to 20,000, and that MSU "might have to do this." In 1968–69, however, expansion virtually stopped for the first time in six years.[79]

Baroda is under pressure either to expand or to affiliate new colleges established within its ten-mile radius. With some exceptions, unitary universities in India not only tend to be smaller than affiliating universities (whose size is continuously swelled by new colleges seeking affiliation), but also tend to have better control over the quality of education. The prospect that new colleges formed to take care of the growing demand for higher education in Baroda city will be affiliated to MSU is a threat, therefore, not only to the size of the institution but also to its standards and ultimately to the quality of its administration.

MSU has staved off pressure for expansion partly by stressing its special status as a residential, teaching university. But its statutes threaten that principle: MSU's jurisdiction runs to a ten-mile radius, and colleges within that area may press for affiliation, thus altering the teaching nature of MSU.[80] Although the new college of Padra was integrated as a constituent, not an affiliated, college, allowing the university closer control over it, admission marks were about ten points below those at MSU proper. The danger is the same as that which has become real at Delhi University, where twelve inferior affiliating colleges created by the Delhi municipal corporation and to an extent under the political control of the corporation, threaten in turn to influence standards through the colleges' role on academic and governing bodies of the university.[81]

The Vice-Chancellor's Committee of 1969, pressed to maintain the unitary character of the university, rejected the representations, declared expansion inevitable, and cited the need for a university to "honour its social obligations and . . . to function like other institutions of democracy, in the welfare of society." [82] It hoped to maintain standards under conditions of affiliation by imposing stringent criteria for faculty and student qualification. The present example and evidence from Delhi University suggest that this will not be effective.

City of Baroda interests have vigorously pressed the university to expand and to ease admissions standards for Baroda students. In 1959–1960 the municipal corporation gave the university two lakh (200,000) rupees to expand classroom space. There has been an informal convention that the corporation should have representation on the syndicate — which it has had in mayors Choksi and Patel. The municipality in 1966–67 expressed its interest in "a second seat," which it did not get. One can imagine a circular process, with municipal councilors on the syndicate on the one hand helping MSU financially but on the other requiring responsiveness in terms of admissions (quantity and quality).

The worst thing that could happen to MSU on the "expansion front" — and some administrators fear it may happen — is to be obliged to affiliate not only in the ten-mile radius, but also beyond, in rural Baroda district or the low literacy Panchmahal area. The colleges that would be founded in these areas, Baroda administrators believe, would "strangle standards."

Positions on expansion do not divide neatly between inside (academic) and outside (lay) interests any more than on other issues. Expansion requires more faculty in the higher reaches as well as in the lower, and raises hopes for advancement. Expansion sometimes takes the form of fission in old departments, so that new professorial posts are created, and readers in the old departments can hope for upgrading to professor. Administrators of an entrepreneurial frame of mind may welcome expansion because it increases the finances and real estate available to the institution. When Mayor Choksi in 1964 pursuaded the heads of science departments to expand admissions from 450 (which they had desired in 1963) to 1000, they explained their consent partly on the ground that they were apprehensive of public opinion in Baroda.

A certain amount of expansion has taken place by the establishment of new fields, departments, and levels of education (i.e. postgraduate). Such expansion may signify differentiation and upgrading. The MSU syndicate and senate in 1967 sanctioned sixty-eight new faculty positions, of which thirty-five were professorial and readership posts. Most of these posts resulted from the creation of new departments or the development into departments of what were previously subunits of other departments (for example: introduction of a postgraduate course in engineering; a three-year degree course in electrical engineering; development of an architecture department; postgraduate teaching and research in home sciences).[83] Only a careful quantitative and qualitative review over time could establish to what extent expansion is of the innovative type — new departments — and to what extent it is merely quantitative — expansion in bread-and-butter fields like arts and sciences.

The major ideological and political reason for expansion is the equalization of opportunity. To some extent, educational expansion at MSU meets this goal. However, parallel with the educational socialism which increased admissions implies, there is at MSU, as at other universities, a countervailing free market educational sector that preserves plutocratic access to intensive if not high quality education. This countervailing plutocratic trend is most noticeable in the high opportunity medical and engineering faculties and is organized around private coaching. Students are admitted to the medical college and the technical and engineering faculties after taking exams given at the end of the preparatory science year that precedes the normal three-year degree or professional course. Top students in the preparatory science exam have the advantage in admission to the engineering and medical faculties. For a fee, some lecturers in the science faculty give private coaching beyond the normal college teaching to groups of students. The groups may contain about ten students; a lecturer might have two classes of ten or so. Some students pay as much as Rs. 150 per month, which supplies a large salary increment for assistant, junior, and senior lecturers whose monthly pay in 1967 ranged from Rs. 400 to Rs. 800.[84] Some of this money may find its way to the examiner to make sure that preparatory students will do well. The tuition system affects all faculties, but its economic advantages are highest in the preparatory science faculty. The advantages of dual sectors, one socialist and one free market, to teachers are such that lecturers are said to turn down readerships which make tuition difficult. The actual prevalence of the tuition system is difficult to determine because its instances cannot be counted and because informal reports probably exaggerate both the numbers and the gains.

Except for the bribery of examiners, the tuition system at Baroda as well as at other Indian universities is considered a normal, if faintly irregular, part of the academic scene. There is some unease, however: a committee headed by Dr. I. S. Gulati investigated the problem for the Baroda University Teachers Association.[85] Its existence made teachers more vulnerable to the contemptuous view of their craft held by a few of the syndics. The existence of the tuition system suggests that while democratization and expansion work to increase teacher-student ratios and to decrease the attention that teachers can give to students, in the countervailing free market it is still possible to buy intensive education. The function of free market educational supplements is unofficially to preserve to the economically privileged some special attention while the goal of more equal access to higher education is officially pursued.

Language of instruction is another major political issue in Gujarat. The Gujarat government has been notably fierce in its encouragement of regional language instruction in schools that receive government funds. In 1965 the Gujarat Pradesh Congress party commitee executive suspended a prominent Congress party member for three years because he had criticized party and state government policy stipulating that institutions receiving government aid could teach English from the eighth standard only. The Ahmedabad municipal election in November 1964 turned in part on the question of English in schools, and it became apparent that Congress party members were deeply divided on the issue.[86] It is striking that, until recently, MSU has been pressed relatively little by the state government to alter its status as the only English language university in the state. Earlier in MSU's history, in 1956, when nationalism and the enthusiasm for Hindi as the official language were still high, the senate of MSU voted to change from English to Hindi as the language of instruction. (An alternative motion that Gujarati should be the language gathered only four votes in a senate with approximately ninety members.) But the motion to change the language of instruction remained a dead letter.[87] In the 1960's, Jyotindra Mehta exerted himself at the capital to block the government effort to insist on Gujarati.

There is a general feeling among MSU faculty that incoming students are now more poorly prepared in English than were students some years ago (which is not surprising for those who start English in the eighth standard) and that they cannot be taught successfully in English alone. Particularly in the preparatory unit, faculty often lecture in English but conduct question periods in Gujarati. The science and technology faculties are more heavily dependent on English than are other faculties. A senior faculty member in the faculty of engineering and technology predicts that English would have to remain the language of instruction for another decade to satisfy the requirements of his department. He was an examiner at Gujarat University, a Gujarati language university, where students have an option of English or Gujarati for their technology and engineering exams. He said that he had yet to see a paper which was not answered in English. His view was shared by an outside examiner from Southern Gujarat University's regional engineering college. The syndics on the whole, as well as most of the deans with whom we spoke, either believe that English will remain for some time, or that it should. Even those syndics most sensitive to political pressures in Baroda city and outside tend to favor English on the ground that Gujarat is an important industrial and commercial state and must have one university to train persons to handle its relations with the world community.

The efforts of former education minister Triguna Sen to establish as national policy the adoption of regional language in five years affected opinion at MSU. The pressures from Sen began in the spring and summer of 1967. Re-interviews in the fall of 1967 and the spring of 1968 showed increasing pessimism at MSU concerning the prospects for English. Although no one had changed his view that English was important to MSU's special mission, a number of senior officials said that if the state insisted on the use of a regional language, the university would of course have to comply. One powerful syndic, who in an earlier interview had expressed himself strongly in favor of English, said that he believed Baroda "would have to move with the country." He added, however, with Tolstoyan insight: "Ours is sometimes an inefficient country; it may be that if we wait, nothing will happen."

Some of our final interviews were conducted during the reverberation of former education minister M. C. Chagla's resignation in the fall of 1967 from the central cabinet in protest against Sen's policy, and the recommendation of the Inter-University Board (an association of vice-chancellors) that the decision should be left to university discretion. These interviews made it more apparent than anything else to us that national policy-making, although not always effective, can change the climate of opinion in marginal ways that can swing a closely balanced policy division from one side to the other.

It is difficult to anticipate the consequences for the university of responsiveness to industrial and governmental needs. In the Indian context, where excessively formalistic education is often criticized for being neither academic nor relevant, some connection with local problems may well lend reality to the educational experience. On the other hand, much depends on the tone and quality of the relationship: on whether the university is merely dotting the "i's" and crossing the "t's" of the local production process (producing hybrid seed in Iowa; testing concrete for the public works department in Gujarat), or whether its professionals are increasing knowledge while serving local producer and municipal interests. American land-grant colleges, at least until World War II, drifted toward the first possibility; presumably some institutions in India will wish to adopt such a self-definition. Some American universities serve both tendencies, with more or less conflict. It is unclear whether MSU has explicitly asked itself what tendencies it can serve or means to serve.

Interests within the university are apt to be divided on these issues. At MSU, the professional schools, which dominate the university (see table 62), have a greater interest in responsiveness to the community than those faculties concerned with postgraduate or general (B.A. and B.Sc.) education. The heads of departments in the arts faculty at MSU were most articulate in criticizing lay influence in the syndicate and other bodies, although some heads of professional schools — law and commerce — also favored arrangements that would somewhat weaken the lay element.[88] Many arts faculty members do not see their concerns as substantially furthered by such responsiveness. Thus a program to improve municipal services in Baroda, which would involve collaboration between MSU and the Baroda Community Council, drew criticism because some department chairmen saw it as committing the research time of their faculty members without compensating the faculties in time or money. Agreement on the program had been reached between MSU, the Baroda Community Council, and the Ford Foundation — which would provide experts only — under the leadership of Thakorbhai Patel in his roles as university syndic and mayor of Baroda. In the absence of provisions for additional resources some faculty saw this agreement as an example of university resources being appropriated by municipal interests.

On the other hand, the dean of the engineering and technology faculty saw his department's close collaboration with local industries, particularly for the purposes of "sandwich courses" (on the job training), as strengthening his faculty's educational capabilities. His best students received better training and access to better jobs in the new courses, and university and industry alike benefited from the technical collaboration between the science and technology faculty and local plants. Similarly, the school of architecture viewed positively its involvement in a development plan for Baroda. Collaboration has two aspects: the university acts as a sort of minor CSIR (Council of Scientific and Industrial Research — a government-financed applied research operation) for industry, and industry provides training opportunities and provides technical apparatus to the university.[89] For example, the public health engineering section has helped the Baroda municipal corporation and several major chemical firms (Jyoti Ltd., Sarabhai Chemicals, Alembic Chemicals) design processes for treating wastes; the highway engineering section has designed mixes for Baroda roads; the mechanical engineering department has helped Hindusthan Machine Tools survey the application, tooling, control and storage systems of machine tools; applied mechanics has tested many thousands of welded joints during the construction of the Gujarat refinery; electrical engineering has run tests for the Gujarat electricity board; the department of architecture has prepared a development plan for Baroda city which has influenced the master plan for the town, and has prepared a scheme for slum eradication; the V. T. Krishnamachari Institute for Rural Development has trained welfare officers and *panchayati raj* office bearers and secretaries for the government of Gujarat; and the department of social work has placed its students in the community for practical training.

Much of this collaboration brings returns: Jyoti Ltd. has donated machine tools and materials worth Rs. 65,000 to the mechanical engineering department; the Gujarat electricity board sends engineers to lecture to the electrical engineering department and to familiarize students with the Gujarat grid; and the Gujarat oil refinery and Gujarat state fertilizer enterprise provide facilities for practical training during vacations. In April 1969 the faculty of engineering and technology began a series of sandwich courses involving in-service training at various Baroda and Gujarat industries, beginning with syndic Nanubhai Amin's Jyoti, Ltd.

It is likely that these close relations not only help close the gap between university education and practical employment — a gap frequently deplored in India — but also put students in touch with potential future employers, a matter of the greatest interest to both. These efforts are evidently viewed positively by many in the university and in the town. It is also evident that such efforts rest on a conception of university education as primarily applied professional training. They do not necessarily appeal to the less professional faculties concerned with general education and research. Many of these efforts represent an urban equivalent of the American land-grant college's extension efforts, which are apt to command more admiration among "applied" than "pure" academicians and to orient the university toward training and service rather than cultivation and creation of knowledge.

Differential Impact of the University's Outer Environments

MSU's outer environment has at least three dimensions which we conceptualize as three concentric circles, each having a differential impact on MSU's financial, social, cultural, and intellectual milieu. These circles are identified with Baroda city, Gujarat state, and national and international agencies, particularly those (such as the UGC and the Ford Foundation) active in financing new educational ventures. We now turn to the relevance of these dimensions of the outer environment for MSU's future.

Throughout this chapter, we have referred to the considerable overlap between the life of Baroda city and MSU. Although, contrary to our expectations and the conventional wisdom among university people, the student body had not become notably more "Baroda city" in origins (birth or residence) over the fifteen-year time span covered by our investigation, the university is very much a city affair. Syndics and members of the senate are overwhelmingly Barodans; faculty are increasingly locally recruited. The administrators of the university explicitly see themselves in a comradely and cooperative relationship with the city, its government, and its industries. Strong mutual ties are created by the considerable interchange of technical, scientific, and social scientific talent between city and university; the significant role on the syndicate of city officials, party politicians, and industrialists; the university's statutory obligation to colleges in the ten-mile radius and its informal sense of obligation to Baroda highschool students; and the Baroda municipal corporation's (modest) subventions to the university budget. As the list of relationships suggests, the connection has benign and harmful possibilities, depending on which university goals are thought most important.

In 1969 an agreement was concluded between the city corporation and the university syndicate to transfer some university land to the city, at nominal cost, for the purpose of widening a street.[90] The explosion which followed — student riots and some faculty protest — took everyone concerned by surprise. Although the world-wide atmosphere of student protest (Herbert Marcuse's *One Dimensional Man* was referred to in student literature) and the political partisanship of some student leaders may have played a role, the transfer became a symbol for the latent discontents about university-town relations. As an issue, it was much less important, but much more concrete, than large issues such as admission or expansion. The riots were protesting alleged exploitation of the university by the city. Thakorbhai Patel, as mayor, syndic, and moving spirit in the transfer, found himself made an example of the relationship's least positive aspects. Although the issues involved were complex — how much was the university land worth? would the university benefit or suffer from the transfer? — their symbolic meaning was not.

Some in the university, notably the vice-chancellor, C. S. Patel, argued that the relationship to the city was valuable because it had made many things possible that MSU could not ordinarily have. "I envisage a day when the corporation would bear the major part of the university's financial needs," he told the *Western Times,* in a statement that may be too sanguine about municipal finance.[91]

MSU sees itself and is seen as having a special tie to the city dimension of its outer environment. Such a relationship has clear consequences for its inner environment (student and faculty recruitment; programs of study; research; membership of governing bodies) and thus for its government. Pressures not of a strictly academic or educational nature are more likely to come from the city than from the state and beyond. On the other hand, the city's relative cosmopolitanism and growing industrial sector make many of its demands less damaging (or more constructive) to a professionally oriented university than comparable local pressures on universities located in rural, less economically developed environments. At Osmania University, by contrast (see chapter 12, below), the university's explicit and special responsibility for its backward Telengana hinterland has generated powerful environmental pressures that run counter to the cosmopolitanism of its immediate Hyderabad city environment. Even more clear are the powerful effects, detailed in its 1958 and 1969 inquiry reports, that eastern Uttar Pradesh and western Bihar have had on Banaras Hindu University (detailed in the reports of the 1958 and 1969 inquiries into the university).

C. S. Patel's expectation that the university in the future may come to depend more on the city implies its present dependence on Gujarat state and the national government. The state and national government agencies and environments, together with the cosmopolitan features of the city environment, give MSU considerable potential maneuverability in its relationship to the parochializing aspects of its local environment.

The relationship between MSU and the government of Gujarat is affected by the fact that higher education in Gujarat state constitutes a system in which MSU is only a part. The system is not formalized by legislative act and explicit bureaucratic structure as it is, say, in California. Gujarat, unlike Andhra state (discussed in the Osmania University study below), has not yet insisted on uniform acts for all its universities, and institutional diversity remains formally possible. The state has seven universities, ranging from the tiny (472 students in 1968–69) "deemed" university, Gujarat Vidyapith, to the 60,000 student Gujarat University. Three of these have been founded since 1966. None has the academic standing of MSU.

The Gujarat universities affect each other in numerous ways some of which depend on direct governmental intervention. Lecturers and readers in older universities often welcome the establishment of new ones that increase the pool of professorships and readerships. MSU has lost good faculty to the new institutions. On the other hand, students transferring from the newer universities to MSU postgraduate departments are often handicapped by their preparation in Gujarati language. It is believed that because of their language training only MSU graduates, not the graduates of other Gujarat universities, can qualify for admission to foreign degree programs and scholarships. Some faculty hope, however, that the establishment of new universities will relieve pressure on MSU to admit rural and other students with moderate secondary preparation, and indeed relieve the pressure on MSU for expansion, thus affecting the student body positively. At the same time, many worry about how MSU will manage in the competition for funds as more state-supported universities open. MSU's future will be affected by whether there is a division of functions between MSU and the newcomers, with MSU falling heir to its traditional role as the English language institution with a special responsibility for professional education. There are contrary pressures toward homogenization of the university system, which would deprive MSU of the competitive advantage that it derives from English language and the special role of its professional departments.

Periodic conferences of the vice-chancellors of Gujarat's seven universities have acted as a clearing house among the vice-chancellors on certain common problems, such as the state government's response to the demand for a "dearness" allowance [cost of living allowance] for university staff. The vice-chancellors are potentially a countervailing power to arbitrary action by the state government, as they were when the government of Gujarat insisted that Gujarat University affiliate six colleges, which it was reluctant to do. Although conditions among the universities are sufficiently diverse that their interests will not always be common, such conferences may prove useful in some cases.

MSU, like all universities in India except those supported by the national government, is heavily dependent on the state government for its finances. In the 1960's the state government contributed between 30 and 40 percent of MSU's income, with another 7 to 10 percent coming from the University Grants Commission and some 50 percent from the university's own fees and income.[92] The state's contribution in the sixties represented a decline from the 40 to 50 percent supplied prior to 1960–61, when the financing came from Bombay state. MSU has fared less well since the division on linguistic lines of Bombay into two states, Gujarat and Maharashtra.[93]

The dependence on state grants is presumably enough to lay the basis for substantial government direction of university affairs. But subvention does not necessarily mean intervention. The extent to which a state government is willing and able to intervene in a university's affairs depends on the government, the university, the current state of public opinion, and the conventions that have grown up to govern relations among them. In India, government aid to schools and colleges is the normal state of affairs. As in England, where University Grants Commission financing of universities is not presumed to imply intervention, government aid is not in itself regarded as a threat to university autonomy. The different states have developed different conventions. Gujarat state's conventions with respect to MSU, if not with respect to other state universities, are sufficiently self-restrained to guarantee considerable autonomy. Senior officers at MSU believed that "there is a lot of understanding between MSU and the Gujarat government. Even a change in the ruling party of Gujarat would make no difference to MSU."

In its relations to MSU the state has not duplicated the intervention of some other states, states such as Andhra, which passed legislation (subsequently declared unconstitutional) to replace the vice-chancellor of Osmania University and which proposed the exclusion of all academics from the syndicate because of their dependence on the vice-chancellor; or Uttar Pradesh, which legislated qualifications for teachers appointed to the universities of Allahabad and Lucknow; or Bihar and Madhya Pradesh, which vested authority to recruit university teachers in the state public service commission (this is true only for the medical college at MSU). But the enormous new demands on the educational system are straining old conventions, and the present situation is no guarantee for the future.

The government of Gujarat is now considering uniform legislation for all seven of the state's universities. Such legislation is thought desirable because it would simplify government procedures and minimize areas of discretion that might prove politically awkward. Whether it is desirable for universities, whose differing needs and capabilities require differential treatment, is quite another question. The trend is in line with developments throughout India, and with the just and unimaginative bureaucratic paradigm of Anglo-Indian university administration discussed in chapter 2 above. However, the prospect of such standardization is not a live issue at MSU, nor is standardization seen as potentially damaging.

Faculty and officials of MSU like to point out that the government's right to nominate twenty-five of the ninety-seven members of MSU's senate is always exercised on the recommendation of the vice-chancellor. On one occasion the government of Gujarat is said to have raised a question about a vice-chancellor's suggestion for a nomination, and to have retreated when the vice-chancellor held his ground. The Vice-Chancellor's Committee of 1969 recommended that the number nominated by government be reduced from twenty-five to twenty,[94] a modest reduction in potential influence.

When the Gujarat government has not provided adequate or timely support in the past, MSU officers have attributed such behavior to financial stringencies rather than to any unfriendliness toward the university. For example, University Grants Commission moneys are usually seed moneys (development grants) representing commitments which the respective states have to pick up after an initial period of five years. The UGC gave MSU moneys for engineering and technology, with the agreement of the Gujarat government that it would step in at expiration of the grant and assume financial support. It did not. The Gujarat government has not been the only state government to fail to honor such a commitment.[95] The state government provides matching funds to universities for approved developmental schemes, D. M. Desai noted, "to the extent possible after meeting all its obligations for elementary and secondary education." [96] In 1970, the committee of vice-chancellors of Gujarat universities asked the state government to take full responsibility for supporting UGC initiated programs. Influenced by the improved financial position in 1970, they were hopeful government would henceforth meet its commitments.

When Gujarat state was formed, and Dr. Jivraj Mehta, husband of MSU's first vice-chancellor, became its first chief minister, Gujarat provisionally took over the custom of triennial block grants from Bombay state. In September 1963, after a bitter factional fight, Jivraj Mehta was succeeded by Balwantray Mehta. The new Gujarat government inaugurated fresh financial procedures, allocating money by heads of expenditure, a measure designed to assure more detailed control of expenditure than was possible under the system of block grants. The new and old vice-chancellors, C. S. Patel and Jyotindra Mehta, both resisted this new departure. Government also refused to make available funds required for certain projects whose five-year UGC grants were expiring, arguing that it had not approved those projects. In consequence, the state contribution to the budget plummeted in 1963–64 to the lowest absolute figure since 1957–58, and to the lowest percentage of the university budget ever (24 percent).[97] In subsequent years, government was persuaded to restore informal block grants. However, deficits smaller than that of 1963–64 continued. The 1965 war with Pakistan and the food shortages of 1966–67 created financial stringencies which affected university finance as it did so many other areas of national life.

In 1967–68, MSU's considerable deficit was not covered by government, but by an overdraft on the Bank of Baroda.[98] By 1968, government finances were sufficiently improved that a committee consisting of vice-chancellor C. S. Patel, Syndic Thakorbhai Patel, and the chancellor, the Maharaja of Baroda, persuaded the state government to cover the deficit.[99]

It is not clear for how long or to what degree the government of Gujarat will be willing or able to maintain MSU's high quality education for relatively better off English speakers. In November 1969, when a number of leading university administrators were re-interviewed, they again expressed confidence that the government of Gujarat would continue to provide, within the resources available, the kind of support MSU needs to maintain its distinctive character and mission. They cited the agreement between the state government and all Gujarat universities on a three-year block grant with a 3.5 percent annual escalator as evidence for their confidence. The end of expansion at MSU in 1968–69 is of considerable significance to the university's ability to maintain its standards; not every university in India is in a position to relate admissions to available resources.

The problems likely to arise from MSU's relation to the state dimension of its outer environment are different from those that arise from its relation to the city dimension of that environment. Given present trends, lay interests, publics, and political ambitions at the state level are less likely to be of importance than they are at the city level. MSU has not become an issue in the state's partisan politics as Osmania did for a time in Andhra Pradesh and as Uttar Pradesh universities have been repeatedly over the past fifteen years. The problems that are likely to arise in MSU's relation to the state government are of a different order. The government of Gujarat may be tempted to impress a common bureaucratic standard on all its universities with respect to structure, funding, or language (as governments have done in other states). This may happen if the effort to cope with the competing demands of present and new universities leads the state government to believe that for reasons of political prudence (or expediency) treating all alike (in ways that count MSU's "extras" against her) is the best policy. A leading educational planner cautioned us against believing that legislatively imposed uniformity will necessarily result in *de facto* financial or educational uniformity among the units involved. The experience of so integrated a state system as California's, where substantial differences in funding and in academic standards exist among the nine university campuses, suggests that there is considerable merit in this caution.[100] Nevertheless it is not clear that MSU will be able to remain the Berkeley of the Gujarat system if a policy of legislative uniformity and integration is adopted.

National and international interest in and support for educational programs at MSU have been especially important for innovation and excellence. The university's ability to attract such attention and help has been important in its identity and self-esteem (as well as a source of inner tension). In 1968, MSU was one of the fifteen universities (out of a total in 1968 of eighty-six universities or "deemed" universities) to have special UGC support for an advanced center (in education).[101] For some years its home sciences and social work departments were unique in the country and supplied founding faculty to new departments elsewhere. Its fine arts and its music, drama, and dance faculties similarly were unique and had national reputations. MSU has been especially favored over the years by the Ford Foundation, which has extended help to its home science department and to general education, and by the World Health Organization, which has contributed to strengthening its medical school. However vital such support from the national and international dimension of MSU's outer environment is for maintaining a desire for excellence and connections with professional reference groups, the conditions for attracting such support cannot be created or sustained unless the state government is prepared to maintain a university of national standing. The three dimensions of the outer environment are interlinked; they can reinforce each other (on the analogy of a vicious or beneficial circle) in ways that contribute to or detract from educational goals and creativity.

Conclusion

Our research began with the hypothesis that a general process of compression and parochialization was affecting the quality of education and the government of the Maharaja Sayajirao University of Baroda. We hypothesized that the university's outer environment, represented by community, regional, and populist pressures, was transforming its inner environment. The growing congruence (compression and parochialization) between the university's outer and inner environment was bringing about changes in the goal orientation of university government, shifting its emphasis from cultivation of knowledge and scholarly research toward training for professions and occupations and toward service to local producer and civic interests. Growing congruence and shifts in goal orientation, in turn, were affecting requirements for university leadership (the office of the vice-chancellor) by strengthening the need for the functions and skills associated with the broker role.

In order to investigate these relationships we examined various indicators of a putative parochialism-cosmopolitanism continuum and sought to relate the findings to the policies and behavior of university officials and governing bodies. Certain changes in the university's inner environment that we expected would help to explain educational and governmental changes — more modest class and caste backgrounds of the students, more local geographic origins of students, the localization of faculty training and recruitment — either had not occurred, had occurred only marginally, or had more complex meanings and ambiguous effects than we had anticipated. Data showing parochialization were clearer with respect to faculty than to students. At the same time certain factors in the university's outer environment not directly connected with changes in its inner environment proved to be important variables in explaining changes in educational quality, goal orientation, and university government. Most obvious was the effect of rapid expansion. In addition to the entrepreneurial skills required to expand, the increase in organizational scale that resulted from expansion enhanced the scope of and the need for management. The result was to strengthen administrative authority and values within the university. Expansion also played a major part in spreading resources more thinly; per capita expenditure showed a marked decline (in constant prices) while the student-teacher ratio showed a discernible though less precipitous downward drift. At the disaggregated level, expansion as a process also involved marked shifts in the distribution of prestige and resources among the teaching and research units of the university (for example, the sharp decline in the per capita resources available to the arts faculty; the growth of low-resource-per-capita professional training; and the proportional decline in the already meager resources for research). These shifts had some bearing on changes in over-all organizational orientation from cultivation and scholarship to training and service.

Another facet of expansion was the rise of new universities. The new Gujarat universities, opened (or recognized) in 1950, 1955, 1963, 1966, and 1968, emphasized by contrast MSU's special mission of English language education for a relatively cosmopolitan, well-off student body, and may have affected its inner environment by draining off Gujarati language educated, less affluent, and less able students from MSU's Gujarat recruitment pool.

The proportion of MSU's budget that the state government has been able and willing to supply declined with the multiplication of universities. Although this proportion fluctuated over the years since 1949, it was appreciably higher before division of Bombay state in 1960–61. The division brought a change in parameters from an average over the twelve "Bombay years" (1949–50 to 1960–61) of 47 percent to an average over the six "Gujarat years" (1961–62 to 1966–67) of 35 percent. Within the six Gujarat years, which saw the creation of new universities and the expansion of enrollments, the drift was downward, from 40 percent in 1961–62 to 35 percent in 1966–67.

Rapid institutional growth affects the relative balance between scholarly and administrative values in an educational organization. By placing a premium on the production and management tasks of the university, growth is apt to favor administrative power. If it does, it reinforces those historical forces in Indian higher education that have allocated higher rewards and status to administration than to scholarship. Three present or former MSU faculty members put the problem this way: "Within our universities a bureaucratic class has arisen which is not confined to the administration alone. It includes those teachers who specialize in university administration and assume accordingly the characteristics of professional bureaucrats. . . . Those outside [this group] aspire either to 'rise' and become part of it or to receive the favours of those within it." [102]

Some academic bureaucrats have been the institution builders that academic expansion requires, others merely bearers of the *raj*'s bureaucratic imprint. How many of them have appreciated and supported academic values, professional concerns, or teaching requirements is a question whose answer can be only partially suggested by the evidence of this book.

One sociologist suggests that "professionals are the organization group closest to the goals of [universities], while administrators are closer to values such as economy, balanced budget, efficiency — what can be referred to as instrumental values." [103] But if a professional scholar's values are closer to the goals of a university than an academic administrator's are, his loyalties, commitments, and reference groups are unlikely to be. According to another proposition, the scholar's "standing as a competent professional cannot be validated by members of his own organization, since they are not knowledgeable about it. . . . The expert is more likely than others to esteem the good opinion of professional peers elsewhere; he is disposed to seek recognition and acceptance from 'outsiders'." [104] Herein lies an important contradiction in the organizational structure and values of a university; those who occupy roles whose values are at best neutral and sometimes inimical to the university's values (that is, administrators) are most likely, for reasons of self-interest and reference-group recognition, to be committed to the university as an institution, while those in roles whose values are most congruent with the university's (that is, scholars) are least likely, for the same reasons, to be committed to the university.

This contradiction in university organization is not fully operative in Indian higher education because of the considerable imbalance between administrative and scholarly values, with the former usually dominant. And administrators have not always (in India or elsewhere) acted in ways consistent with the administrative values of their roles, or if they have, they have interpreted those values as requiring (for whatever reasons) a defense of academic or scholarly interests. Thus, in so far as MSU has preserved its standing as one of India's better universities, it has done so on the basis of administrative rather than scholarly leadership. Although two of its four vice-chancellors were former professors, they made their reputations in public life or educational administration rather than in scholarship. D. S. Reddi, the "hero" of Osmania's struggle for autonomy in 1965–66 (see chapter 12), was an educational administrator. At Delhi University, India's best, three eminent scholars resigned before their first terms as vice-chancellor expired while C. D. Deshmukh, an eminent civil servant (Indian Civil Service) and former cabinet minister, stayed the course for two terms and strengthened the university.

The contradiction between the values associated with administrative roles and those associated with scholarly roles in university organizations takes the following form in India: administrators sometimes defend academic values but they cannot always or easily be relied upon to do so, while scholars have great difficulty providing academic leadership or representing academic values in the governing and faculty bodies of the university. Teachers find that the production tasks of training students undermine their scholarly vocation; that they are unsupported by institutionalized scholarly authority because professional associations and reference groups have little influence; that departments headed by a single professor-administrator strengthen hierarchical and command relationships more than they do peer and professional relationships; and that defending and promoting academic values in university government can overwhelm the "real" work of teaching and research. (Professor K. N. Raj, in his resignation statement, expressed one side of this dilemma when he observed that "the future of Delhi University depends . . . largely on how far teachers are prepared to . . . involve themselves actively in neutralizing the elements within and outside [the university] which apparently do not care for the academic values and purposes which this University has stood for.")[105] It is generally true of university organizations that a scholar's "standing as a competent professional can not be validated by members of his own organization, since they are not knowledgeable about it." In India, it cannot be easily validated by "peers elsewhere" either. The academic market place in economic and status as well as in achievement terms plays too marginal a role in university decisions for policy and personnel to counteract the influence of administrative values and institutional commitment within and demands for certification and service from without.

Under such circumstances, institutional commitment and service which strengthen administrative values and authority more than scholarly values become dominant not only in the government but also in the professional life of the university. When the institutional loyalty of scholars displaces their professional commitment; when administrative values and authority dominate scholarly values; and when parochialism drives out cosmopolitanism, as in many Indian universities today, it becomes extremely difficult to maintain the viability of the university as an organization devoted to the cultivation of knowledge and scholarly contributions to knowledge.

Among the principal causes of this state of affairs at MSU (and elsewhere) has been the differential weight with which the university's various environments influence its goals. Baroda city has been the main source of demands for articulation with local producer and municipal interests and for "easy access." Gujarat state has been a significant source of pressure for use of the regional language rather than English and for expansion of colleges and universities in the face of declining per capita resources. The central government, particularly the University Grants Commission, and international agencies have been the principal source of activity and support designed to strengthen the university's capacity to perform academically. If MSU, and Indian universities generally, are to preserve some measure of cosmopolitanism, the influence of this third dimension of their outer environment will have to be strengthened.

In the face of continued parochialization and expansion, the influence of the national and international dimension of the outer environment can help to upgrade Indian universities professionally and to differentiate them in qualitative terms. Academic professionals will have to be paid more relative to other professionals if universities are to make up the ground lost as a result of expansion and inflation and if, more importantly, universities are to attract a better share of the available talent. The UGC programs providing for advanced centers and clusters of advanced centers provide a ready means for professional upgrading through symbolic and financial means. Student as well as faculty talent can be more systematically concentrated by extending the practice, established by the IIT's, of using a national examination to select students for some masters and doctoral degree programs (for example those at advanced centers). The result will be some degree of inequality among departments, colleges, and universities. The legitimization and funding of the aristocratic values that a visible hierarchy of talent and achievement implies in the face of the powerful current of populist leveling that is running in India today[106] may not be beyond the wisdom and skill of India's national political leadership.

12 / The Problem of Autonomy: The Osmania University Case

Carolyn M. Elliott

Autonomy Revisited

On 25 November 1965, the Andhra Pradesh legislature passed identical amendments to the acts governing the state's three universities. As a result, one of the three, Osmania, feared for its independence. Under the new legislation, the governor, as chancellor of Osmania, Andhra, and Sri Venkateswara universities, and acting on the advice of the Andhra Pradesh government, would directly appoint the vice-chancellor of each university, rather than choose him from a panel submitted by the university. The government of Andhra Pradesh would also have authority to give mandatory instructions to the universities regarding major educational policy. P. V. Narasimha Rao, the law minister who piloted the amendment bills through the legislature, defended them by arguing that autonomy was not a fundamental right, that a university should not grow in isolation into an "ivory tower," and that autonomy should have relevance to the dictates of the times.[1] Challenged in the name of autonomy by the university community and its ally, the central government, the government of Andhra Pradesh gave ground in a second amendment bill, modifying the first bill but legislating new authority to dismiss Osmania's popular and effective vice-chancellor, D. S. Reddi. Action under this legislation was declared invalid by the supreme court of India, reversing the decision of the Andhra high court.

The controversy became a national issue; newspapers carried detailed accounts of several confrontations; the prime minister discussed it in parliament; ultimately the supreme court intervened. In Hyderabad, the Osmania senate organized an action committee that led a mass demonstration and strike. The entire university community — faculty, students, employees — was mobilized in a remarkable display of unity.

The conflict between the government of Andhra Pradesh and Osmania

I wish to express my gratitude to D. S. Reddi, former vice-chancellor of Osmania University; Ravada Satyanarayana, vice-chancellor of Osmania University; P. V. Narasimha Rao, chief minister, government of Andhra Pradesh; B. P. R. Vithal, secretary for planning, government of Andhra Pradesh; Rasheeduddin Khan, professor of Political Science, Nehru University; Gautham Mathur, professor of Economics, Osmania University; A. D. Bhogle, reader in French, Osmania University; P. V. Rajagopal, principal, Secunderabad College of Osmania University; Sudarshun, principal, New Science College; Amrik Singh, secretary, Inter-University Board; and many others for extensive interviews expressing their different points of view, and for making available several documents on the issue. Responsibility for the analysis remains my own.

University provided the occasion for a nation-wide debate that raised basic issues regarding the nature of the university in a democratic society. Patterns of university autonomy based on British models are being challenged by radical changes in the environment, composition, and purposes of universities. As is being increasingly recognized in the United States as well as in India, the university plays a role of great political significance because of its critical relationship to values and opportunities. When politically influential elites find the university no longer in touch with these central concerns, they are likely to question the relevancy of the university's relationship to its environment, and to raise issues of autonomy and control.

Osmania's environment has changed from one dominated by an urban culture to one dominated by rural concerns. The urban culture of Hyderabad city incorporates a number of caste, linguistic, and religious communities that have connections to many cities throughout India, but few roots in the surrounding Telengana villages. The university has remained part of this urban culture while political power has shifted to predominantly Telugu speaking rural areas. The sensitivity of rural representatives to the university's aloofness from their concerns provided the basis for the antagonism raised during the autonomy conflict.

This conflict could not have arisen, however, without changes in the nature of the university. Government regulation had been considered normal under an earlier princely regime. The Osmania case demonstrates how the university's development as a separate institution with its own vital interests and values helps to generate a propensity to resist incursions from "outside." Osmania evolved from a small, Urdu language university closely allied to the dynastic interests of the princely state of Hyderabad into a large, English language, academically sophisticated university set in the diverse, complex society and popular, competitive politics of Andhra Pradesh. Its new-found ambition for development and its sense of influence focused in the office of the vice-chancellor. It is in this dual context, the institutionalization of the university and the changing political environment, that the autonomy issue of Osmania must be understood.

Osmania was the first modern university in India to use an Indian language of instruction. Urdu, the language used, was the aristocratic language of the Muslim court of Hyderabad, the largest of India's princely states. As a result of the administrative reforms carried out in the nineteenth century by prime minister Sir Salar Jung, the Hyderabad aristocratic culture lost its central place in the administration of the state to modern administrators from northern India. In 1918 the Hyderabad interests convinced the nizam to found a university which they viewed as a means to reinvigorate Hyderabad Urdu culture and, more specifically, to regain access for native Hyderabadis to administrative posts in the state.[2] The university's Urdu emphasis served primarily to acculturate aspirants to an urban ruling class; it did not meet the educational needs of the 89 percent of the population of princely Hyderabad who were Telugu, Marathi, or Kannada speakers. The university was no more concerned with the needs of villagers than were the English language universities of British India.

Osmania's environment changed significantly with the coming of independence and the subsequent reorganization of states. Hyderabad's Muslim rulers were replaced in 1949 by centrally appointed administrators, following a police action in which government of India troops marched on the city to force the state's accession to the Indian union.[3] In 1952, after the first general election, the appointed cabinet was replaced by a Congress party ministry predominantly responsible to Hindu interests. Finally, in 1956 the multi-lingual state was divided into three portions according to the majority language of the various districts; the nine Telugu speaking districts, called Telengana and including Hyderabad city, were joined to Telugu speaking Andhra state to form Andhra Pradesh. This merger brought many new Telugu speakers to Hyderabad city, the new capital, where a state government with no previous connection to the old Hyderabad culture or to the university took up residence. The influx of Telugu speakers provided a further dimension to the conflict at Osmania: what might have been a simple cleavage between a Hyderabad city Urdu cultural elite and Telugu speaking democratic politicians from the hinterland was mitigated by the division among the Telugu speakers between those from the Telengana districts and those from former Andhra state. Those from the Telengana area of old Hyderabad were much more attached to the traditions of Osmania than were the newcomers from Andhra.

University Relations with Hyderabad State

The university enjoyed a close and unproblematic relationship with the princely state throughout the periods of the nizam's rule and the appointed Congress party ministry of pre-merger Hyderabad. The university was established by a royal fiat and made a department of the nizam's government. Because the nizam was proud of his creation, the university prospered under government direction. On ample lands just outside the city, a beautiful campus was constructed. Devoted to the purposes of the state, the university had little contact with universities elsewhere in India. Students were drawn entirely from within the state. Recruitment of faculty was restricted by the use of Urdu to local personnel and those drawn from Urdu speaking areas of northern India, from which many government personnel were also recruited. The university's government reflected its close relationship to the state government. The board of governors, called the syndicate, was appointed by the state ministry, and the minister for education was exofficio vice-chancellor. Most of Osmania's vice-chancellors had held other positions in government and were from families closely associated with the nizam's regime. The last but one before independence,

Ali Yawar Jung (later ambassador to the USSR, the U.S., and several other countries), came from government to the university and then returned to government as home secretary.

During this period there was little conflict between the university and its governors.[4] Most matters were handled informally among persons who knew each other as members of the small ruling elite of the state. Cultural life in the state was centered in Hyderabad city, the city elites moved in small arenas, and they met often. Hindu faculty at the university were part of these circles. They were drawn primarily from the cosmopolitan population of the city, spoke Urdu, and had few village connections. Therefore relations between the Hindus on the faculty and Muslim governors were relatively free of communal overtones or tensions.[5]

The most dramatic change brought by independence was the change in language of instruction from Urdu to English. In the short run, many faculty were forced to teach in a language with which they were unfamiliar; ultimately, because the university could recruit faculty from other universities in India, competitive standards for university appointments were raised. Yet the change was not overtly resisted, for it brought a breath of fresh air to a faculty that felt increasingly restricted by dependence on out-of-date translations. Furthermore, English had been a required subject for all students since the founding of the university.

Politically, it is significant that the change was not brought about by the popular, predominantly Hindu government, but rather by a Muslim vice-chancellor, Nawab Ali Yawar Jung, who had earlier served as vice-chancellor under the nizam. He sensed the importance of the change and worked to ease the transition.[6] His position vis-à-vis the Muslim community was helped by the prevailing mood of discouragement in that community.[7] Extremist leadership had promised strong resistance to incorporation into the Indian union, but in the end it vacillated, and then launched civil disorder that led to a forcible takeover by the central government.[8] After this experience Hyderabad Muslims had neither the will nor the political means to protest the university's new policy.

University involvement in politics was rare before the late fifties. Until the amalgamation of the Telengana area of Hyderabad with Andhra state in 1957, political issues relating to the university were settled without much conflict. But issues which would become political in the future were emerging. The issue of university expansion was related to the larger question of reorienting the university toward its backward Telengana hinterland. During the nizam's regime the affiliation of private colleges had been prohibited. Consequently at the time of independence there were only three colleges outside Hyderabad city, and these were two-year intermediate institutions whose students had to come to Osmania to complete a bachelors degree.[9] A vast expansion seemed necessary and not all of it could be undertaken by government. In 1950, the vice-chancellor allowed private colleges to affiliate with Osmania. Subsequently, the Congress party education minister vigorously encouraged the founding of private colleges with a tacit understanding from the vice-chancellor that the new colleges would be given time to meet university standards for affiliation.[10] Later, the government established a series of colleges in the districts that soon became part of Andhra Pradesh, thereby committing the new Andhra Pradesh government to a high level of expenditure on education in the Telengana area of old Hyderabad.

Another emerging political issue was that of the guarantees given to Telengana students when the Telugu portions of Hyderabad state were amalgamated in 1957 into Andhra Pradesh. Under an agreement reached between political leaders of the two regions to be joined, a Telengana committee was established to protect the interests of Telengana personnel who might suffer in competition with the more qualified personnel from the Andhra districts formerly in Madras. This committee, composed of all legislators from Telengana constituencies, was empowered to recommend such modifications in pending legislation as might be necessary for the application of that legislation to the Telengana region.[11] One of these matters was the regulation of admissions to the public institutions of higher education in the Telengana region, which, under an informal gentleman's agreement, were to be restricted to Telengana students.[12] Thus, a committee of the legislature, the Telegana committee, was empowered to give directions to the university on admissions policy.[13] The university has persuaded the committee to relax its central over admissions somewhat, but has not yet pressed hard for the abolition of such control.

One reason there has been little conflict between the committee and the university is that the university has generally agreed with the committee's policy. University teachers themselves had looked forward to some change in the language of instruction. Similarly, in the matter of expansion it was difficult to question in principle that in a state with 21 percent literacy an increase in educational facilities was desirable. Many university teachers were as concerned as the politicians to protect the interests of Telengana students in admissions, and tended to agree with the committee regarding the need for safeguards against encroachment by Andhra students.

Cooperation between the university and political leaders was facilitated by the frequent intermingling of university and political personnel in Hyderabad, which continued as it had under the nizam. The ruling Congress party leaders were urban high caste founders of the party who had been born or raised in Hyderabad and who shared the university's culture. When issues affecting the university did arise, they dealt with them informally. This pattern of close interaction was strengthened by direct participation of politicians in university affairs. The education minister of Hyderabad sat on the syndicate, not ex officio, but because he had been elected from a graduates' constituency. The university was the subordinate partner, however, in this interaction. Because several members of the syndicate had strong ties to the ruling Congress party, the politicians' views rather than the vice-chancellor's tended to dominate university decisions. The university's responsiveness to the government continued for a decade after independence, for little had yet happened to make it conscious of itself as an institution with a purpose, an identity, and interests separate from those of government.

When the political elite suddenly expanded with the amalgamation of Telengana and Andhra in 1957, the system of personal interactions could no longer be sustained. The amalgamation had provoked great controversy, leaving Telengana politicians divided. Furthermore, there was no trusted intermediary who could work among both Telengana leaders and the Andhra newcomers. Because of these circumstances the appointment of the next vice-chancellor, Dr. D. S. Reddi, which took place soon after the amalgamation, brought great strain. The Andhra politicians who had assumed leadership of the state made the appointment on the basis of their own political perspectives and needs. Against the resistance of Telengana leaders, they used the Osmania appointment to accommodate a former director of public instruction from their region. Doing so helped ease a possible conflict over a vice-chancellor's post in one of the Andhra universities. No mediator was able to unite all Telengana politicians behind D. S. Reddi. The Telengana politicians who did accept the appointment probably did so on caste grounds, for both the candidate and the negotiating politicians were of the same Reddy caste. One of the dissatisfied Telengana leaders, also a Reddy but from an opposing Congress party faction, took the issue to the university arena and mobilized opposition. Students demonstrated and burned the new vice-chancellor in effigy — a swift politicization of university affairs. The mobilization of opposition significantly expanded the political channels between the university and its political environment. The personal interactions of Hyderabad courtly politics were replaced by the group affinities of popular, competitive politics.

Patterns of Influence and Constraint within Osmania

The balance of power between Osmania University and the state has been directly related to the power of the vice-chancellor within the university. The focus of internal power has shifted from the university syndicate to the vice-chancellor. When the syndicate contained men of power in government or party circles, the vice-chancellor exercised little control over university policy; as the vice-chancellor became stronger, he played the major role in the syndicate's deliberations. The development of the office of the vice-chancellor has been crucial to the articulation of the institutional distinctiveness of the university, for it has been the vice-chancellors, not the syndicate, who have been sensitive to the distinct goals and needs of the university. The increase in the power of the vice-chancellor was made possible by a systemic change, an expansion of the university's environment that gave university personnel more access to levels of power and influence outside the state. The early postindependence vice-chancellors, however, did not exploit the potential of the newly constituted university environment. Not until D. S. Reddi assumed office in 1957 did a vice-chancellor use the available sources of influence and power within and without the university to self-consciously assert the interests of the university as an independent institution.[14]

The imprint of the *raj* on higher education and a legacy of the Indian Educational Service are expressed in Reddi's career. He came to the vice-chancellorship after many years of government service as director of public instruction (DPI) in Madras. As DPI he had administrative responsibility for government colleges. His experience with universities was confined to his student years at Madras University, where he received an M.A., and at Oxford, where he took a diploma in anthropology. His longstanding attachment to government continued during his career at Osmania.[15] Reddi was proud that there were no quarrels between the university and the government before the 1965–66 crisis. On such policy matters as new courses of instruction and new colleges, the university agreed to government requests. Following government initiative, it established a new course to train officials for responsibilities in *panchayat raj,* a new pattern of decentralized, popularly elected local government inaugurated in Andhra Pradesh in 1959. And in the matter of admissions to government colleges, the question of final authority did not arise because disagreement was so slight. Reddi found his relationship with government prior to the crisis to be one of reciprocity and mutuality, with little pressure from government, even in the potentially troublesome matters of appointments and examinations.[16]

This mutually satisfactory arrangement was not above criticism by several faculty members who found instances when Reddi did not, in their view, adequately defend university interests. Some were disturbed that he had not resisted the Telengana committee's restrictions on admissions. Others were critical of his willingness to raise student fees under governmental pressure to bring them to the level of the other universities, despite the backwardness of the Telengana region that Osmania serves. In both instances, it was not clear that Reddi had alternatives, or, if he did, whether his choice had avoided unpleasant confrontations. In neither instance did Reddi reveal a propensity to assert his own authority or raise the issue of university autonomy.

Given the circumstances of his career and his incumbency as vice-chancellor, it is ironic that Reddi should have become the heroic defender of university autonomy. There were, however, several important elements in Reddi's handling of university matters that made his stand possible, once external challenges were identified and resisted. Most significantly, he was able to win the loyalty of the faculty by fair-minded, efficient administration. Teachers soon saw that he displayed no regional favoritism in promotions and recruitment, which removed a great source of tension. Furthermore, Reddi showed astute political skill in his relations with professors and members of the syndicate. He sensed which persons would be most valuable to him and brought them into his confidence, forming an inner circle of loyal supporters. Among these was a college principal known for his careful work in drafting schemes, preparing budgets, and doing necessary committee work. Another was an articulate young reader who effectively advocated the vice-chancellor's policies in the governing bodies of the university. These choices showed Reddi's ability to identify important political roles and find persons appropriate to them — the mark of a good leader and administrator. Furthermore, the longer he remained in office, the more he could draw upon the support of those who owed their appointments to him. Several faculty members were appointed after an all-India search, and had no local ties in Hyderabad; others were internally promoted after Reddi secured appropriations for second professorial chairs in several departments. Most appointments made under his aegis were good ones that raised the quality of the faculty and expanded the number of higher positions, a nice instance of wise policy that made good politics.

His handling of the syndicate was similarly astute. In consultations with individual syndicate members Reddi presented his ideas and developed supporting arguments. His programs were subsequently presented by syndicate members and approval secured without active intervention by the university administration.[17] Reddi claims not to have encountered difficulty even when he brought politicians on the syndicate into the consultations; indeed, they were often very useful in carrying his wishes to the ministry. Reddi by no means sought to avoid politics: the delegations of professors and students who went to the chief minister of Andhra Pradesh to argue for his reappointment in 1964 are thought to have gone with his approval. An experienced national observer of universities noted that Reddi dealt effectively with politicians, had friends among them, met them often, and worked with them for the university. He decided cases on merit most of the time, but when necessary, in the greater interest of the university, he was not unmindful of political factors as well.[18] In this he showed a sense of priorities which seems to have redounded to the benefit of the university and to have helped him continue as vice-chancellor.

His internal position was strengthened by his remarkable success as an educational entrepreneur in attracting new programs to the university. In Delhi his urbanity and sophistication helped him to gain the confidence of University Grants Commission (UGC) and foreign aid officials. He was known for well-prepared proposals and for arguing his case well. Through careful building of contacts he secured new professorships for several departments, won the competition for an American Studies Center, started French and German language programs staffed with foreign instructors and won recognition as a center of advanced study for the astronomy department, to list only a few accomplishments.[19] This entrepreneurship strengthened his political position in at least two ways. First, expansion of the university provided more funds and positions for allocation within the university and, more importantly, demonstrated his ability to serve the university well and increase its stature. Second, Reddi's Delhi contacts proved important for rallying national support when it became necessary to do so. The variety and weight of institutional support that he was able to mobilize is a fascinating and revealing part of the 1965–66 "autonomy" crisis.

Finally, D. S. Reddi's position was enhanced by his relationship with politicians in the non-Telengana areas of Andhra state. In contrast to the previous two vice-chancellors, Reddi had long-standing ties of kinship, caste, and friendship with important leaders in that area. It was the strength of these ties that enabled him to gain the vice-chancellorship. Caste ties had helped also to make him more acceptable to Telengana politicians than another candidate of a minority caste. After his appointment, D. S. Reddi maintained his contacts with the politicians who aided him in attaining his position. His reputation throughout Andhra Pradesh Congress party circles as a sounding board and adviser on strategies in state politics had given him an independent source of power to use in dealing with government and the chief minister on behalf of the university. When Reddi's friends were friends of chief minister Sanjiva Reddy, it undoubtedly helped the position of the university. But when the state Congress party leadership split into factions, Reddi's identification with one group helped to exacerbate the university's conflict with the government. Reddi's independence, based on his influence in the university and with the national government, led state politicians to become actively concerned about limiting the university's growing assertiveness.

Legal constraints establish the channels within which controversies involving the university take place and the norms of such conflict. The Andhra Pradesh legislature created the university through the Osmania University Act of 1959. The legislature retained the power to amend the university's constitution at any time by ordinary enactment. It was the attempt to amend this act that provoked the controversy between Osmania and the government. The most important sections of the 1959 act as they affected the controversy were those governing the selection of the vice-chancellor and the composition of the governing bodies of the university. The selection of Osmania's vice-chancellor was to take place according to the common Delhi pattern in which the syndicate selects two persons to a nominating panel and the chancellor (in Andhra Pradesh the governor) selects one. This panel then proposes three candidates to the chancellor (governor) who makes the final decision. State governors are appointed by the president of India. They are constitutionally bound to exercise their functions on the advice of the elected ministry; whether this applies to the governor's role as chancellor was at issue in 1965–66.[20]

The 1959 act of the Andhra Pradesh legislature did not alter the unique feature of Osmania's government, established from the time of its founding by the nizam — the inclusion of all professors and all principals of constituent and affiliated colleges on the policy-making body, the senate. This made the senate larger than in many universities and gave it a greater proportion of academic representation, 80 of 134 members.

In addition to determining the composition of university governing bodies, the 1959 act provided for two important substantive constraints on university autonomy. One is an inspection and inquiry clause which gives the government the right to make an inspection into any matter connected with the university, and to issue directives if the advice tendered after the inspection is not adopted within a specified time. Procedures for the inquiry are provided: that the university be given notice, that it be represented, and that the syndicate be given a chance to respond before the government tenders its advice. It was the absence of these procedures in the University Amendment Acts of 1965 which aroused opposition. The inquiry clause in the 1959 act has never been applied to Osmania University but has been used for an inquiry into Andhra University (Waltair) affairs.

Secondly, the university act specifically provides for restrictions on admissions to accommodate Telengana students. In making regulations for admissions, the academic council, the body of academics responsible for courses, admissions, and examinations, is instructed to give effect to the recommendations of the Telengana committee. At the behest of the committee, the academic council laid down restrictions not only on admissions from outside Telengana but also on the number of urban students admitted to professional schools.[21]

The university is also constrained by legislation in the form of authorization and appropriation of funds. Sixty-four percent of the university's non-developmental expenditure in its 1966–67 budget was funded by the state government. These funds are usually negotiated for a five-year period and paid annually as a block grant, a procedure modeled on that of the British and Indian University Grants Commissions.[22] Thus the legislature does not discuss specific items of the university budget in making the grant, as is the case in twenty-four U.S. states, where line expenditures are reviewed by state legislatures. Government does, however, influence crucial questions of university salaries and student fees by the amount it sanctions in block and annual grants and, because of their effect on university employees, by the salaries and "dearness allowances" [cost-of-living allowances] it sanctions for state employees.

Emergence of Conflict: University Amendment Acts of 1965

Patterns of accommodation between university and state were challenged dramatically in 1965 when the government sought to pass legislation which the three Andhra universities, particularly Osmania, considered inimical to their institutional autonomy. The events that precipitated

Osmania's conflict with the government arose in the context of a quarrel between the government and another of the state's vice-chancellors, Dr. A. L. Narayana of Andhra University. When a judicial probe into his alleged corruption and nepotism did not result in a recommendation that he be removed, the government had no legal means to dismiss him.[23] Meanwhile the government had grown more determined to remove him, for public criticism was increasing.[24] In this situation, the government felt that it must have adequate means to remove vice-chancellors. Political leaders reasoned that even supreme court judges could be removed by specific procedures, yet no procedures existed for the removal of vice-chancellors. The vice-chancellors of the other two universities shared this view because Andhra University affairs harmed the public image of vice-chancellors. In the course of regular consultations the vice-chancellors created a committee to consider procedures for removal and appointment, which, in due course, recommended that the existing procedures be changed.

The government had other reasons as well for amending the university acts. The panel system for nominating vice-chancellors provided an opportunity for incumbent vice-chancellors to secure their own re-election by influencing the choice of members for the nominating panel.[25] An able or self-serving vice-chancellor was usually able to assume a powerful position in the university syndicate and thus secure the selection of persons known to be sympathetic to his goals and interests. The chancellor, who made the final choice, retained the option of refusing the nominations and requesting a new set of names but had never done so. On several occasions the government felt its choice was unfairly restricted by the university's role in the panel system. In 1964 when D. S. Reddi was given a third term, the other nominees had been K. P. S. Menon, an eminent diplomat with no interest in the job, and a brahman from outside the state who was unlikely to win support from the Reddy-dominated state ministry. The government, in the person of the governor, was hesitant to reappoint D. S. Reddi, but it had no real alternative.

On the other hand the government was definitely opposed to election of the vice-chancellor by the university senate (as at Baroda and Allahabad), for it feared outside political interference (as happens in cooperative societies, *panchayat raj* institutions, and other formally self-governing bodies). As one state minister candidly declared: "We are at the stage in Indian society now that the politicians are everywhere and they just cannot keep off, for these institutions become a base of support for them." [26]

In preparation for proposing amendments to the university acts, the chief minister, Brahmananda Reddy, convened a conference of vice-chancellors, educationists, UGC representatives, and state politicians interested in education.[27] Legislators at the conference proposed making university governing bodies more democratic by increasing the number of elected representatives of university graduates on the senate and reducing the representation of academic personnel from almost two-thirds to half. They also wished to secure at least one elected politician on the syndicate, either an MLA (member of the legislative assembly) or MP (member of parliament), to be elected by the senate.[28] On the issue of the vice-chancellor's appointment, the conference opted for government appointment to avoid the extramural politics of an electoral procedure. No mention was made in the final report of the issue of removing a vice-chancellor.

Nine months later, in the summer of 1965, three bills were introduced into the two houses of the Andhra Pradesh legislature amending the separate acts of the three state universities. The single most important provision in the acts was the change in the manner and term of appointment of the vice-chancellor, as recommended by the conference. The government's motivation seems to have been not so much desire for control over the post as discomfort with both of the other available systems for filling the post.[29]

Secondly, the bill provided for the removal of the vice-chancellor. As first written, it placed on the vice-chancellor the burden of proof against removal and gave him virtually no procedural safeguards.[30]

The third significant provision was the alteration of the composition of the university syndicate and senate according to the conference recommendations. By cutting university representation on the senate to 50 percent, the provision necessitated the introduction of some principle of representation for university professors and college principals, all of whom had previously sat on the senate.

As the bills emerged from the education department of the government secretariat, more drastic changes were included. The number of government officials on the sixteen-member syndicate was increased from two to four. These provisions also grew out of the situation at Andhra University; the official in charge of drafting the bills for the government had served as registrar in Andhra University where he apparently became convinced that persons outside the control of the vice-chancellor were needed to counterbalance the vice-chancellor's powerful position. Finally, the act reserved a seat for an MLA or MP on the syndicate, no longer requiring election from the university senate in competition with other members for such a seat. This provision also was a response to problems at another university where politicians in the senate had long complained that the vice-chancellor allowed them no voice in its affairs.

The immediate response of the legislature was to send the three bills to a joint select committee for further consideration. In that committee the bill reached its most extreme position, and included many clauses inserted by individual committee members that the government later withdrew.[31] Academic representation in the senate was to be further reduced from 50 percent to 40 percent; academic persons were to be prohibited from contesting for the syndicate on the ground that the syndicate dealt with personnel matters in which "employees" should not participate;[32] and, in a clause reflecting the provincial pride of rural politicians, experts consulted on a professorial candidate's competence were to be drawn from within the state. These clauses were the first to be withdrawn when pressure was brought from university and central government sources, and they were not included in the final act. They suggest, however, the mistrust and low regard in which some legislators held academics and intellectuals.[33]

The most important modification the joint select committee made in the bill was the insertion of a clause empowering the government to issue policy directives to be followed by the university. No one questioned the right of the legislature to issue such directives; the granting of this right to government without the procedural safeguards provided in the existing act was unprecedented, however. Though suggested by a legislator concerned with the language of instruction, the subsequent incorporation of this clause does not seem to have been directly related to the language issue. The language of university education had not been an issue in Andhra politics; the university's policy of "delaying" the linguistic transition from English to Telugu was not sufficiently different from government policy to require the directives clause.[34] As the dispute progressed the issue of language of instruction became more central to the chief minister's argument in favor of giving government the authority to issue policy directives to the university.[35] The use of the issue of language policy,[36] however, appears to have been primarily a means for the chief minister to reach the larger problem of insuring university responsiveness to society.

The procedure for appointing the vice-chancellor drew the most severe criticism: appointment by the chancellor really constituted appointment by government. The recent appointment to two posts on semiautonomous bodies of a defeated exminister and a former minister debarred from contesting elections because of corrupt practices raised the fear that university posts would also be used to accommodate unemployed members of the ruling group. Even with good appointments, government responsibility for the appointment would make the vice-chancellor undesirably dependent on government authorities.[37] In the face of these anticipated dangers, a proposal that the senate elect the vice-chancellor gained support among the bill's opponents.

Another major issue was that of representation on the senate and syndicate, a matter of special interest to the Osmania professors, all of whom sat in the senate. Faculty members objected to greater representation of political and government personnel on both bodies, fearing "groupism, intrigue, corruption and nepotism," and vehemently protested being reduced to the status of employees by the prohibition against their sitting on the syndicate.[38] Finally, some objected to the greatly increased representation of graduates on the university bodies, arguing that this would provide another channel for political control of the university. As evidence they pointed to the Osmania University Graduates Association which has provided substantial support to the veteran Congress party politician (now president of the separatist Telengana *samiti*) who has headed it for many years.[39]

In Delhi, the removal clause aroused most concern. Critics argued that government already had the power under the general clauses act to dismiss any person it had appointed.[40] They feared that further specifying the procedures for dismissal would weaken if not destroy the vice-chancellor's authority by affecting his independence in office and by discouraging good men from accepting the post. At the time of these discussions, there was no precedent for removing vice-chancellors and considerable doubt existed about whether and how it could be done. According to influential spokesmen among the vice-chancellors, this very vagueness, supported by convention, gave vice-chancellors more protection than specific favorable procedures. These spokesmen compared vice-chancellors to judges, arguing that judges, for whom removal procedures are specified, occupy an exalted, independent position which society has agreed to protect, while university autonomy is less well established and more vulnerable to encroachments.[41]

These objections were intensified by the harsh nature of the original removal clause in the 1965 acts.[42] When this clause was modified after discussion with the universities and the central government, objections subsided. Current legal opinion is that the amended clause is a good law, protecting the vice-chancellor more than the general clauses act because it makes provision for an inquiry and for representation.[43] Now that the courts have upheld the right of the appointing authority to dismiss a vice-chancellor, as they did in the dismissal of the vice-chancellor of Kurukshetra University, the formal specification of procedure will protect the university more than convention.

The directives clause further aroused all-India opinion. Friends of the university argued that the government already possessed the power to implement major policy changes through the legislature and that legislative pressures would ensure that the university remained responsible to the public. The attempt of the government to short circuit the legislature could only mean that it desired to step beyond policy directives to more active intervention in daily administration. Not only would government decide the content of policy directives, it would also be the sole judge of what was to be defined as a policy matter, strengthening the possibilities for political interference. Others raised the fundamental question of the government's right to issue policy directives at all. Proposing self-government, they argued that the university was composed of representatives from a broad spectrum of society who were aware of public needs; therefore the university community should have the freedom, within certain broad limits, to determine educational policy.

In the ruling Congress party there was opposition to the amendment acts, though it was not openly articulated. Opponents of the bill claim that many Congress party members would have preferred its defeat but could not state their views because of the government's firm position.[44] Passage of the bills did not represent a general political feeling against the universities. Rather, because few Congress party members felt strongly enough committed to the universities to oppose the bill effectively, the few persons who pushed the bill were able to win out. The universities did not have many enemies but neither did they have many powerful friends willing to take political risks on their behalf.

University opposition was ultimately more effective than that of political parties. In late October 1965, a group of professors went to the chief minister of Andhra Pradesh to explain their misgivings and inquire about his intentions. This meeting went badly. The teachers came away convinced that the chief minister had no understanding of a university's need for autonomy nor any appreciation for its capacity to govern itself, while the chief minister interpreted their questions as a demand for university sovereignty within the sovereignty of the state. Two assurances did result from this meeting. The chief minister declared that he wished to have academic men share in the government of the university and that he would entertain the possibility of compromise on any matter except that of the appointment of the vice-chancellor. Then the revenue minister, who had previously been a member of the university syndicate, met the delegation to assure them that government had no intention of using the bill in the way the teachers feared it would be used.[45]

The effect of these assurances was destroyed the next day, however, when the joint select committee, under the chairmanship of the chief minister, decided to further reduce faculty representation on the senate and to eliminate faculty entirely from the syndicate. In consequence the university senate devoted the major part of its next meeting to consideration of possible actions. A large number of persons spoke against the bill, including several members of the legislature who were also senate members. This meeting was widely reported in the press, and the reports were accompanied by several editorials echoing the protests of the university against lack of consultation and undue haste. After prolonged discussion the senate resolved to request that the bill be deferred and empowered a committee of fourteen to take action. Among those on the committee were two MP's, one MLA, principals, and professors. This senate committee, in collaboration with representatives of the Osmania University Teacher's Association, met the chancellor, cabinet ministers, chairman of the Telengana committee and the secretary of the joint select committee. It could not, however, obtain permission to appear before the joint select committee.

Discouraged by this failure and further alarmed by the insertion of the directives clauses into the bill, a group of professors sought to mobilize higher authorities. They approached the chairman of the Inter-University Board, an advisory body representing most Indian universities.[46] Although the IUB has no official or statutory standing, its status as a "club of the vice-chancellors" gives its voice considerable weight in government educational circles. Sir C. P. Ramaswamy Iyer, the IUB's chairman in 1965, sent a telegram to the chief minister asking him to defer action until a standing committee of the IUB could meet and give its views. Copies of this telegram were sent to the prime minister, the government education minister, and the chairman of the University Grants Commission.

A small group of professors also went to Delhi to plead their case directly. The president and vice president of India offered their sympathy, but declared themselves constitutionally unable to interfere with state legislation. The education minister, M. C. Chagla, gave the strongest support, promising to do all that he could. He wrote to the chief minister of Andhra Pradesh asking for a reply to a letter written earlier requesting that the bill be deferred until state and central government authorities could discuss the matter.[47] Presumably he also consulted with the prime minister, Lal Bahadur Shastri, because the next day the prime minister telephoned the chief minister asking for postponement of the legislation until the IUB could meet and discuss the all-India implications of the bill.

Despite these moves, the state government announced that the bills would be discussed in the legislature on 22 November 1965. Dismayed by its lack of success in securing a postponement, this group of professors organized a meeting of deans, professors, and principals of university colleges to plan further resistance. This meeting was heated and dramatic. There was much discussion, all condemning the government but a good bit of it questioning the wisdom of extreme stands in the light of the university's dependence on the government. The resisters won the day, convincing the gathering to sign a statement of noncooperation in which each signatory pledged to resign from the university senate and from all university administrative duties if nine obnoxious provisions were not withdrawn from the bill. The vice-chancellor sent his support, declaring that he would resign his office if government did not pay heed to their requests.[48] With this endorsement, a group of thirty went directly to the chief minister's house unannounced and demanded a hearing. It was agreed, however, to hold back the statement until further negotiations were attempted.

The chief minister was quite reasonable. He explained his stand and then agreed to discuss the matter further with a smaller group of professors on the following day. At that meeting he made important concessions which were inserted in the bill then pending in the legislature. The provision forbidding academic representation on the syndicate was changed; the provision limiting faculty selection committees to Andhra personnel was deleted; and the procedure for removal of the vice-chancellor was changed by a provision that a high court judge be included in the panel of inquiry required by the procedure. Finally, and most important for the subsequent dispute, the chief minister is said to have assured the teachers that passage of the act did not imply an intention to cut short the term of the existing vice-chancellor.[49] Later he modified the bill further in response to the assembly debate, replacing the very general directives clause, which had aroused much public criticism, with a clause providing for instructions in three specified areas, language of instruction, postgraduate centers, and the pattern of education.[50]

It is difficult to know how much university pressure had to do with these concessions. The law minister of Andhra Pradesh, who was piloting the bills, stated that the government resented Chagla's interference and his taking the issue to the prime minister.[51] The chief minister told the vice-chancellor that he suspected ulterior motives in the university's agitation, particularly in the protest of Class Four university employees (attendants and lab technicians) who had staged a demonstration.[52] In general he dismissed the opposition as coming only from university circles and as being "understandable when old patterns are done away with," thereby undercutting the substantive content of the criticism.[53] Yet the threat of the vice-chancellor's resignation and the professors' noncooperation was one which could not be taken lightly. The chief minister found himself being held responsible for designs on Osmania's autonomy that were far beyond his intentions; he was said to harbor personal motives. As the opposition mounted, however, his priorities became apparent; on the issue of the vice-chancellor he was not willing to move.

Leaders of the university opposition noted the concessions, but wished to press further on the issues of the appointment of the vice-chancellor, the curtailed representation of professors, and the directives clause. When the university senate gathered in an emergency meeting in late November to consider the concessions, its members were uncertain about continuing the agitation. After much debate, the senate decided that the major issues remained unsettled, and a unanimous resolution was passed to continue the opposition.

The University's Political Resources

The next initiative for a change in the amending acts came from outside Andhra Pradesh. The standing committee of the Inter-University Board met and decided that the removal and directives clauses constituted infringements of university autonomy. Therefore they announced to the press that they would raise before the full board the question of disaffiliating all three Andhra universities from the IUB.[54] The *Hindustan Times* gave this news banner headlines throughout India and there was a spate of editorial comment that warned the Andhra government to change the legislation before the February IUB meeting if it wanted to avoid gravely endangering higher education in the state.

Just what disaffiliation would mean is unclear for it has never happened to an Indian university.[55] In the main it would mean a loss of standing within the university community. The chief minister in his reply in the legislative council to the IUB's threat, observed: "We are not aware of the Board's powers in this regard," ignoring the issue of reputation and stressing instead the lack of authority or resources, an interpretation the press noted.[56]

At this point the central government became much more directly involved. When the matter was brought up in parliament, the education minister, M. C. Chagla, announced that the Andhra chief minister, Brahmananda Reddy, had ignored requests from the central government not to proceed with legislation which "constituted a serious violation of university autonomy." [57] Explicitly recognizing the IUB threat, he cautioned the state government that disaffiliation would further arouse students and teachers to oppose the Andhra government. Later Prime Minister Shastri intervened in the parliament discussions to say that he would ask Chagla to meet the chief minister to try to arrive at a compromise. The next day Shastri again intervened to say that he had just received an assurance by phone from the chief minister that the state would not proceed to secure the governor's assent to the amending acts until after the chief minister had talked with the government education minister.

The controversy not only had become more bitter, but also now involved issues which were more political — system level differences, constitutional issues, issues affecting national interests and authorities. Most dramatic was the polarization between the central government and the state of Andhra. Lined up against the state were the government education minister, the chairman of the Inter-University Board, the University Grants Commission, and most of the national press.[58] Facing this array, the chief minister declared that changing the bill meant "bowing to Delhi," and declared he would do so only on one condition, that all states agreed to a uniform pattern of university government.[59] Later in the week he dismissed his earlier assurances to the prime minister, saying that there was no need for discussion with the government education minister because no changes were being contemplated.[60]

Why had the dispute reached such an impasse? Clearly the chief minister felt that he was being misrepresented by central authorities and the national press.[61] Everything he said about his intentions was called into question, and he saw no recourse except to stand firm on a "states rights" position. He felt most abused by Chagla, whom he accused of not reading the bill carefully before publicly expressing an opinion.[62] These remarks suggest a degree of personal antagonism which would have made negotiation difficult.

The conflict was exacerbated and made more personal on 8 December 1965, when D. S. Reddi released a statement. Reddi had so far abstained from speaking publicly on the issue, although he had advised the professors on their efforts. Angry and arrogant in tone, his statement impugned the motives of the politicians and accused the state government of failing to understand the purpose of a university. In obvious reference to his own position as vice-chancellor, he asked "whether the government [had] an intention of removing an existing vice-chancellor who [had] not found favor with them for not being very accommodating or of appointing a particular individual in a resulting vacancy." [63] Why did Reddi now inject this issue into the controversy? [64] It appears he was convinced from the beginning that the chief minister continued to resent the circumstances and bargains that accompanied his initial appointment as vice-chancellor in 1957 [65] and wanted to replace him. His wariness was increased by changes in state Congress party politics that found his close friends in a faction opposed to the chief minister.

D. S. Reddi's statement served as a direct challenge to the chief minister, who responded immediately in what the press termed an "outburst." He chided the vice-chancellor for making derogatory remarks about the nation's leadership and asked him to make amends.[66] This exchange marked a turning point in the dispute. General issues of autonomy became less prominent and the specific matter of the vice-chancellor's tenure became more prominent. At the same time, the central government increased its pressure on the government of Andhra to substantially modify if not withdraw the amendment bills that still awaited the governor's signature. Prime Minister Shastri, in widely publicized remarks to a convocation at Allahabad, reminded the chief minister of his promise to consult with the central government. "It would be a good thing if the measures affecting education were taken by states in consultation with the center. This would not mean any erosion of states' autonomy in the administration of education, but certainly ensure a certain uniformity in the national education field." [67] A week later it was announced that the chief minister had invited representatives of the UGC and the government education ministry to discuss the bill.[68] A few days later, V. K. R. V. Rao, then the education member of the planning commission, used the occasion of a convocation address at Osmania to note the delay in the governor's assent to the bill and to speculate about the effect of public protest on the chief minister's views.[69]

These events seemed to indicate that the pressure from the central government would produce a negotiated settlement. Talks were held. The chief minister agreed to change the legislation by introducing new amending legislation at the next session of the legislature rather than by recommitting the existing bills. Acknowledging that the directives clause provided no procedural guarantees to the university, he agreed to withdraw it. These assurances might have ended the issue. Indeed, many at the university urged that efforts to resist the legislation be abandoned in the interest of future peace with the government.

The leaders of the university delegation remained wary, however. Prime Minister Shastri died in Tashkent in January 1966, and the resulting confusion in Delhi diverted attention from the Andhra case. Because the assurances of the chief minister to introduce new amending legislation had been given to Shastri personally, they were not necessarily valid after his death. No information was available from government circles about the bill to be introduced in the next session of the legislature. Sensing the increasing animosity between the chief minister and D. S. Reddi, some predicted an effort would be made to remove the vice-chancellor.

At this juncture, some Osmania professors asked the new prime minister, Mrs. Indira Gandhi, to intervene. They were much less successful than they had been with Shastri, for Mrs. Gandhi was busy preparing to go abroad. She did, however, instruct Dinesh Singh, a member of the developing "kitchen cabinet," to ask the chief minister to delay the legislation. The chief minister would not be dissuaded. He found the efforts of the central government puzzling: it first convinced him to introduce new legislation to correct bad features of the old, then suddenly asked him to delay. Having made plans, he now would not change them.

The second amendment bill, introduced in the March budget session of the legislature, confirmed all the fears of the university leaders. It contained not only the two promised amendments, but also another which appeared directly aimed at the Osmania vice-chancellor: the terms of the sitting vice-chancellors were to cease within ninety days of enactment. An ulterior purpose was made more obvious by the fact that the term of one of the other vice-chancellors was about to expire in any case; furthermore, there was a provision declaring that terms of the other university governing bodies would not be affected by the legislation. The new amendment bill was passed by the Congress party majority and signed into law on 17 May 1966. Immediately thereafter the chief minister announced that he would appoint new vice-chancellors to all three Andhra universities by the beginning of the new academic year in July.[70] This was the chief minister's response to D. S. Reddi's December challenge. The conflict was now openly a personal one, and the nature of the struggle shifted.

The first round of the contest between Osmania and the government of Andhra, particularly its chief minister, Brahmananda Reddy, was clearly won by the university. The chief minister had been forced to amend the amending legislation soon after its enactment. Critical to this outcome were the impressive political resources the university was able to mobilize. Calling attention to these resources does not imply that the conflict was merely a power struggle; the substance of the issues was of primary importance. But what was remarkable about the university's opposition was the powerful way in which it could force recognition of its cause. University leaders were aware of this. An economics professor who participated in several of the delegations to Delhi, put the case this way: "The success of the university teachers has come as a surprise to those immature politicians who, thinking of the simplified slogan 'one man, one vote,' seem to consider university teachers as political non-entities. . . . However, in all democratic countries the scholars and men of learning form an estate by themselves which cannot easily be trifled with. For one thing, the mere fact that they have accessibility (direct as well as through their well-wishers among the political influential persons) to the highest authorities in the country, invests them with a privilege which is denied to many." [71]

The formal structure of the university must be counted among its resources for action. Other chapters in this volume point out how permeable educational institutions can be to outside influence.[72] At Osmania, by contrast, the majority position of academics on the senate helped that body to speak unanimously in support of resistance, adding moral weight to the university's position in state and national public opinion. This was important during the first phase of the conflict, and even more so during the second, when the senate voted to continue recognition of D. S. Reddi as vice-chancellor despite the chief minister's appointment of a replacement. Seldom was the senate as a body involved in the conflict; the active work of representing the university's case was done by an *ad hoc* body of the senate, a committee of professors, with some advice from the vice-chancellor. However, the ability of the professors to go to Delhi on the authority of the senate of the university, which had constituted them as a committee of fourteen and given them a mandate, undoubtedly added to their case.

In the national arena, the Inter-University Board was important. Its head, Sir C. P. Ramaswamy Iyer, was a respected national leader whose views received widespread attention in the national press. He placed the prestige of the IUB behind the issue of university autonomy by threatening to disaffiliate Andhra Pradesh universities. He also put his sixteen years of experience as vice-chancellor of various Indian universities behind this issue. After the second amendment bill (to be discussed below) became law in February 1966, he again wrote to the chief minister urging reconsideration of the act on the grounds of its conflict with common justice and equity. This letter also was released to the press and received national coverage.

Amrik Singh, secretary of the Inter-University Board, also helped. Frankly a "trade unionist by sentiment," Singh immediately saw the all-India implications of the legislation and pledged his support to Osmania. Throughout the controversy, he served as a consultant to the professors and the vice-chancellor, helped them to arrange interviews and secure publicity, and devoted an entire issue of his journal, the *Journal of University Education,* to the problem. Finally, the IUB lent institutional support, bringing the matter to the attention of its member vice-chancellors at IUB meetings.

Direct appeals to college and university faculty members throughout India resulted in additional useful publicity. The professors enlisted the support of the All-India English Teacher's Conference, which passed a resolution supporting the cause of the teachers in safeguarding autonomy and academic freedom. Teachers of Bombay University, under the auspices of the Congress for Cultural Freedom, passed a resolution requesting the governor of Andhra Pradesh to refuse his assent to the acts.[73] Later, teachers at Lucknow University passed a resolution congratulating the Osmania teachers on their "bold stand . . . in defense of university autonomy." [74] Finally, the issue was raised by prominent speakers at two important academic occasions: by supreme court Chief Justice G. B. Gajendragadkar at the Lucknow University convocation and Vice-Chancellor D. R. Gadgil of Bombay University at the National Convention of University and College Teachers at Lucknow University. These events called more attention to the national consequences of the legislation, spurring the central government to intervene.

Cultural affinities between the professors and the elite in the central government added to the professors' persuasiveness. Most university professors are members of a cultural elite that encompasses upper level civil servants, judges, and some of the central ministers. This elite is relatively cosmopolitan in its attitude and connections as a result of having been educated abroad and in institutions of all-India stature. In talking together they can draw upon common symbols, including that of the British university, which provided them with a model for autonomy. State politicians appear to them provincial and suspect, concerned with patronage and power, and without an understanding, much less an appreciation, of the values of university life and freedom.

The Court Cases

The second phase of the dispute was even more tense and dramatic than the first. The issue was simplified; attention focused on preserving the vice-chancellor in office rather than on fine points of legislation. Action in this phase was more restricted to Hyderabad, and the university fared less well. Many of the political resources it could mobilize on the general substantive issue of autonomy were not available for a personal conflict. The first phase had demonstrated the capacity of the Indian federal system to modify state initiatives on matters of principle, but for the personal conflict of the second phase, action stronger than persuasion was required. The vice-chancellor turned to the courts and the university organized for direct action.

The second amendment act, passed in March 1966 and signed by the governor in May, provided for the removal of D. S. Reddi from office in ninety days, abrogating his contract and denying him the procedures to appeal his removal that the first amendment act had established. The amendment act clearly raised constitutional issues that could be contested in court. D. S. Reddi chose for his lawyer Narsa Raju, a former advocate general of Andhra Pradesh whose previous conflicts with the chief minister had led to his resignation from that post. The case was argued in the high court of Andhra Pradesh for thirty-one days, the longest hearing to that date.

The high court rejected Reddi's arguments. It ruled that the act did not deprive the vice-chancellor of his constitutional right to property because the office of vice-chancellor could not be considered personal property. Reddi had argued that the act was motivated by personal animosity aroused by the vice-chancellor's opposition to the first amendment act, but the court held that motives cannot be attributed to a legislative body and that neither the chief minister nor any nonlegislative authority should be mistaken for the legislature. Most crucial was the question of procedures for removal. Reddi argued that he was denied use of the procedures set forth in the unamended act, and that such denial constituted discriminatory use of legislative powers. The court, however, ruled that the second amendment act provided for cessation of term of office, not removal from office, a matter of policy which the legislature could change from time to time. The policy at issue was in line with the purposes of the act, the limitation of a vice-chancellor's tenure to six years. Since D. S. Reddi had already served more than six years, there was reason to differentiate him from subsequent vice-chancellors who would be able to appeal through the removal procedures.[75]

When D. S. Reddi's writ petition was struck down by the high court on 13 October 1967, he appealed to the supreme court. Without considering the other arguments, it decided in his favor on the grounds of discrimination. There was, the supreme court held, no intelligible difference in the circumstances of D. S. Reddi and future vice-chancellors that had a rational relation to the object sought to be achieved by the statute. The powers and duties of vice-chancellor had not changed; the fact that he was appointed through a different method and had already held office for seven years did not justify discriminatory treatment.[76] Therefore the act violated article fourteen of the Constitution providing for equality before the law.

Direct Action: Faculty, Students, and University Employees

The university began to mobilize while it awaited the high court's judgment. A hurried meeting, attended by seventy-five teachers, passed a resolution urging the government not to appoint a new vice-chancellor even if the judgment went against D. S. Reddi; in the event that the government did so, the teachers would refuse to cooperate. To enforce this decision, they collected letters of resignation to be held in abeyance pending negotiation with the government. The Osmania University Teachers' Association (OUTA), which had not previously taken an active interest in university government nor been previously involved in the conflict over D. S. Reddi's tenure as vice-chancellor, formed a council of action which took the noncooperation resolution to the chancellor (governor). He tried to assuage them by suggesting that the post might be offered to the senior university professor. This professor was a powerful, determined man, known for his courage in conflict against authorities. He declared that he would refuse the post under the prevailing conditions, setting the mood for the others to do the same. Subsequently, he was elected president of OUTA and became the leader of the struggle.

With the announcement of the high court judgment on 13 October 1966, the professors' position was bleak. The judgment legally ended Reddi's stay in office, and news was received that a new vice-chancellor would be appointed any day. The OUTA president asked a former chief minister of the state, who often acted as a mediator in political quarrels, to intervene, but the present chief minister would not listen to further discussion. With diplomatic channels exhausted, the OUTA president made public the offer of the vice-chancellor's post, declared his refusal, and began to mobilize the teachers.[77] An emergency meeting of OUTA, called for October 15, passed a remarkable resolution: each member promised to donate 1 percent of his salary for three months to fund the autonomy struggle.

The teachers' action council was a fascinating arena for the working out of political conflicts among the teachers. Behind the unanimity of the resolution to donate salaries were many differing opinions of the struggle and the personalities leading it. The most significant division until this time had been between professors and teachers (reader and lecturer ranks). Almost all the action had been carried on by a small group of professors and principals working at higher levels. Teachers had not been antagonistic, but simply uninvolved. The OUTA general body had not met since the year before because many members felt that they had little to lose by the new legislation — they had little representation on university bodies anyway.

The professors had also been divided. A group of moderates had urged that the senate recognize the two major concessions by the government, arguing that because the remaining issues had as much to do with the man as the office the university should not unnecessarily antagonize government. The senior professor, who subsequently led the fight, refused at an earlier stage to sign the public appeal for retention of the vice-chancellor, arguing that the appeal insulted the university by making it appear to be dependent on one man. Others did sign the appeal, but argued against extreme means of protest. Throughout the second phase of the struggle, they were anxious that the teachers' activities emphasize the constitutional issues rather than personal loyalty to the vice-chancellor — though to the public and the government, these were inevitably tied together.

The social composition of this moderate group was significant. Prominent were three Andhras who had supported D. S. Reddi when he first became vice-chancellor in the face of opposition from many Telengana teachers. These Andhra faculty members sought to maintain tolerable relations with the Andhra government, possibly because they felt culturally sympathetic with the Andhra chief minister and his government.

The professorial group in the forefront of the struggle was less tied to the surrounding Telugu culture. Among this group were two Muslims, one a member of an old Hyderabad family, the other from northern India. Another professor in this group had joined the university as an economics professor only two years before, after an assignment in Paris. Several brahmans from Hyderabad city or outside the state were also involved. By background and career they shared the values of the national elite culture which upheld the ideal of university autonomy from local pressures. They also had little standing in the emerging rural environment of the university and looked to the vice-chancellor for support for their interests and academic needs.

Many of the younger teachers now also joined in the struggle. The new OUTA president, who had won the respect of teachers through his earlier conflicts with university administration, was instrumental in recruiting many of them. Others saw the occasion as an opportunity to bargain with the professors for more democratic relations within the university and joined the council to bring forward their demands. Such teachers had no strong loyalty to the vice-chancellor, the symbol of a hierarchy they opposed, but they became strongly opposed to what they regarded as the dictatorial methods of the government. They joined the most committed group of the council, and two were made its secretaries.

The problem of internal autonomy, as these young teachers called the issue of internal democratization, had been raised before in the form of a demand for regular meetings of the full staff of teaching departments, but it had never received much support.[78] With considerable political skill these young teachers formed a subcommittee of OUTA under the chairmanship of a senior professor to discuss the issue and make recommendations.[79] This committee observed that "a teacher subject to humiliation is an unfit instrument for autonomy," and suggested changes in university administration. It proposed the rotation of deanships among the professors and, quoting the observation of the Education Commission, 1964–1966, about "the temptation to oligarchy of senior professors," recommended that committees of teachers be set up to assist department heads in their administration. It asked them to take the advice of such committees on teaching and research programs, timetables, subject assignments, and allocation of examination work. Furthermore, all adverse comments about a teacher's work were to be conveyed to the teacher concerned, instead of only being noted on his confidential record. These proposals, if implemented, would have brought great changes in university norms and administration.

The first meetings of the OUTA action council were given over to tiresome trials of strength among these groups. Finally one of the most respected moderates, the principal of the science college, made a suggestion that galvanized the group to action — to test the commitment of the teachers to the issue, the action council would call for all teachers to join in a mass casual leave on the next day.[80] The call was a marked success. More than 90 percent of the teachers of the university and its constituent colleges refrained from holding classes or attending college; the vice-chancellor supported them, saying that the move was consistent with the dignity of their office.[81]

Without plan, the mass casual leave demonstration took place on the same day that the government appointed a new vice-chancellor of Osmania University, Dr. Narsimha Rao, principal of Guntur Medical College.[82] When the faculty heard of the appointment, they were stunned. At a large gathering of teachers, only two persons recognized his name, for he had never been mentioned as a possible candidate. The teachers immediately passed a resolution urging him not to accept the office.[83] The next day, 28 October 1966, was the most dramatic of the conflict. The new vice-chancellor was to take office, having just arrived from Guntur under police escort. Because students were demonstrating on the university campus, he was advised not to come to the university. Instead the governor requested that the university registrar bring the official papers to the governor's house, so that Narsimha Rao could take office there. Having heard through university circles that the registrar would comply, students surrounded his office and prevented him from doing so. The governor sent a police escort, but it was unable to enter the premises of the arts college where the registrar was being kept. Then the students led the registrar away to one of their cars, "kidnapping" him for the day so that he could not hand over papers to the new vice-chancellor. He was returned at six o'clock in the evening.

Meanwhile the university senate met to express its support for the vice-chancellor. At the start of the meeting, the vice-chancellor announced that the registrar had received a message from the governor announcing that he, D. S. Reddi, was no longer vice-chancellor because Narsimha Rao had just been invested with office without benefit of official papers. The chancellor had asked that he not preside over the senate meeting. But then D. S. Reddi followed with an announcement of a supreme court injunction restraining the new vice-chancellor from assuming office. With this news, the senate voted unanimously to express their confidence in D. S. Reddi.[84] At this point, Osmania officially had two vice-chancellors.

The university continued its political pressure. The Council for University Autonomy, successor to the OUTA action council formed earlier, sent telegrams to a large number of central authorities and political leaders requesting their intervention.[85] Then they authorized the president of the council to write a personal letter to Narsimha Rao asking him to step down, stating that they could not cooperate with any vice-chancellor "appointed in disregard of the mode of appointment which [they advocated] as a fundamental right of university members." [86]

And the agitation continued. The president of the Council for University Autonomy issued a direct appeal to all teachers to continue their strike for one more day; when the council met subsequently, it decided to continue the strike for a third day. At that meeting, it called upon professors of Osmania and educationists throughout the country to refuse any offer of the vice-chancellorship of Andhra's third university, Sri Venkateswara University, which was to be announced any day. Furthermore, they passed a resolution of appreciation for the students' spontaneous reaction of support, complimenting them on their sense of discipline despite many provocations.[87]

Students were deeply involved during the four days of the strike. As soon as they heard the new vice-chancellor had been appointed, they went around the city urging students in university and affiliated colleges to strike. When the bus service to the university was cancelled to prevent demonstrations, they commandeered trucks to take students to the campus some eight miles from the city.

For the leaders who came forward from the student community, the strike provided an arena in which they could test political skills which they hoped to develop into a career. The leader of the students supporting the vice-chancellor was from a rich peasant family in Telengana. Many members of his family have been active in politics; his brother is now an MLA, an uncle is a member of the legislative council, and another uncle is a former MLA. In 1965–66 all were opposing the chief minister because of factional conflicts in their district.[88] The leader of the students supporting the state government was a former president of the university-wide union, subsequently president of the Andhra Youth Congress, the student wing of the Congress party. He also was from a rich peasant family and planned a political career, though as a strong supporter of the chief minister.

As it did for the teachers, the autonomy issue provided a vehicle for the students to elaborate other issues which concerned them as an academic interest group. They presented eleven demands to the chief minister, encompassing a wide range of issues of which university autonomy was only one: food ration cards for city students; police not to enter the campus unless requested; retention of previous regulations for exams; bus concessions for evening college students; and abolition of the rank of third class in postgraduate examinations. And in sympathy with the concurrent student strike elsewhere in Andhra they inserted a demand that the central government award the fifth public sector steel plant to Andhra Pradesh rather than to Madras or Mysore.

Once in motion, the strike attracted many outside the university with little interest in the autonomy issue. Many high school students joined the demonstrations, forcing the closing of the schools. An American student observer commented that it was the high school students who caused most of the violence: "for them the strike had merely set the stage for a momentary outcry against social oppressions." [89]

Were the students instigated by the "teacher-politicians" who are so frequently blamed for student strikes in India? There was a previous history of student involvement in university politics at Osmania: a group of student leaders had gone to the governor to urge the vice-chancellor's reappointment in 1964, probably at the suggestion of others in the university. Now students and teachers worked along parallel lines, though OUTA was not formally identified with student activities. Liaison was maintained by two of the young militant teachers who advised the students of the teachers' decisions. In this situation the collaboration between teachers and students may have helped responsible student leaders control what could have become a much more explosive situation. In the larger context, however, mobilization of students may have contributed to problems of indiscipline. The teachers at Osmania recognized that students did things that teachers could not do, such as "kidnapping" the registrar. To the extent that students later felt the vice-chancellor beholden to them for his continuation in office, university administration could suffer. Indeed, there has been some complaint that students have become bolder in their personal demands, making daily administration more difficult.[90]

University employees offered support by abstaining from work. Class Four employees, the peons and lab assistants, were the most active. They had been the first to launch a public demonstration in 1965 when amending bills were initially considered. With a long history of pressure against the vice-chancellor over pay scales, the Class Four Employees Union claimed that it was acting in support of autonomy rather than on behalf of the vice-chancellor personally. To Class Four employees autonomy meant better working conditions than those they anticipated under tighter government control.[91] Despite this dissociation, however, their support for the vice-chancellor at a time when it was not at all certain that he would be retained — the supreme court had not yet made a decision — was a measure of the vice-chancellor's ability to mobilize his university.

The strike was called off after four days when students, in marked contrast to the teachers, succeeded in negotiating with the chief minister. They demanded a conference to discuss changes in the act and threatened a hunger strike to be conducted in front of the government secretariat. The chief minister was so annoyed with the students initially that he refused to contemplate any concessions or to allow teachers at the discussions. Eventually, he met some of the student demands (for ration cards and bus concessions) and offered to convene a conference to discuss the report of the Education Commission, 1964–1966, with the possibility of changing the act if an all-India policy were developed. With these "concessions" in hand, the strike was called off and the supreme court verdict awaited.

Personal and Factional Dimensions of the Conflict

How did the issue of university autonomy gain so much support at Osmania? [92] In the immediate context, the catalytic agent was the appointment of the new vice-chancellor. Teachers were insulted by the disdain shown to their interests, preferences, and "right" to participate, and alarmed by the implications of a government appointment when the issue was before the courts. Furthermore, they resented the appointment of a

nonentity. Because Narsimha Rao was a nonentity, they could only conclude that the appointment was made on personal grounds to spite D. S.
Reddi and please politicians in the chief minister's home district.[93] Leaders
of the teachers admit that the appointment of either a Telengana man or a
more eminent educationist might have split their ranks.[94]

Much credit also must be given to the vice-chancellor's political success
in the university. From the object of active antagonism, he had become a
focal point of loyalty through wise use of the many powers of the vice-
chancellor. He had increased this loyalty through his handling of the pay
scales for teachers and staff employees. Class Three and Four employees
had been demanding that the pay scales granted in 1961 be made retroactive to 1958, giving them large amounts of arrears; this demand was met
in principle in February 1966, though only a portion of the amount was
paid because of financial stringency. The teachers also had been asking that
their scales be raised to those recommended by the UGC during the third
plan period, eliminating the differential between teachers in constituent colleges and those teaching on the university campus. The vice-chancellor had
previously granted the increased scales to all those holding Ph.D. degrees;
he later granted the increased scales to all teachers.[95]

The conflict gained intensity because of several other issues. One of the
most immediate causes was the personal animosity that developed between
the chief minister and the vice-chancellor. Both were proud independent-
minded men from families that have long participated in rural politics as
members of the dominant caste of Andhra, the Reddis. Such families are
known for their willingness to pursue conflicts over status and power, even
to the extent of large material loss. D. S. Reddi showed his determination
at the time of his first appointment to secure what he believed due to him.
The autonomy issue engaged these men in a similar manner. The chief
minister saw the vice-chancellor as an arrogant man asserting independence
in an institution "as though it were his own." [96] Similarly, the vice-
chancellor took the contest as a prestige issue that had to be fought through
successfully even though doing so involved a financial loss as a result of
expensive litigation.[97]

Many in Hyderabad believe that university actions regarding the chief
minister's nephew crystallized this antagonism. One incident involved the
nephew's attempt to transfer from a district medical college to one of the
university medical colleges. It is said that the vice-chancellor was inclined
to permit the transfer, but that the syndicate, in comparing the boy's case
with those of forty-five others also requesting transfers, could find no
ground for making an exception. He was therefore refused the transfer,
which may have annoyed the chief minister. However, no action followed
directly from this incident, which occurred a year before the autonomy
issue.

A second incident concerning the same student occurred after the autonomy issue arose. The boy's paper was marked incorrectly, giving him a

first class grade when he had done poorly on the examination. After the marks were published, the matter was brought to the syndicate and an inquiry commission established. After investigation the syndicate decided that nothing could be done to the student, but that the lecturer would be deprived of his examinership.

Undoubtedly these incidents contributed to some ill feeling. The first incident showed what politicians may have felt was arrogance, the university refusing to adjust its standards to political realities, even in small matters.[98] With so many important public and political reasons for the chief minister's opposition to Reddi, however, it is difficult to believe that this incident itself motivated that opposition.

The second incident appears to be more a result than a cause of the autonomy struggle. There have been many cases of upgrading student examinations, presumably due to influence exercised on the grader, that have not received the public notice that this case did. The vice-chancellor took a long time to bring the case to syndicate notice, possibly in order to conduct his own investigation before making such an allegation about an important examination. But his action delayed the inquiry until after the marks had been published, therefore making the matter more public. The university acted properly in the issue, but it did not seek channels which would have prevented embarrassing publicity.

That the incidents are believed to have played a crucial role in the struggle is in itself instructive about political attitudes. Though there were strong public and factional reasons for the conflict between the chief minister and Reddi, many people personalized the issue. The proclivity to discount institutional ties and constraints in favor of personal ones as explanations of political events is common in Indian politics.

Underpinning the personal conflict was the increasing factional split within the Congress Party. Andhra politics had been dominated by a curious alliance between the former chief minister, Sanjiva Reddy, and his follower Brahmananda Reddy. Though Sanjiva Reddy was soon taken into the central cabinet, he was able for a time to maintain his control over state politics. Soon, however, an increasing strain between the central and state leaders, brought on by a series of small incidents in which the chief minister failed to consult the central minister, resulted in mistrust. D. S. Reddi had a long-standing association with one of the ministers associated with Sanjiva Reddy. Through him he had come to know many of Sanjiva Reddy's group as well, and had entertained them during their stay in Hyderabad. Therefore when Andhra politics split into factions, D. S. Reddi was immediately associated with the dissident group opposing the chief minister. This does not mean that the vice-chancellor participated in the factional maneuvering; he had never directly taken positions in state politics. His association with the dissidents, however, served to accentuate the symbolic importance of the university conflict by relating it directly to the factional struggle for ascendance in the Congress party.[99]

The conflict was intensified by the absence of mediators respected by both sides but identified with neither. At the central level, the IUB, the UGC, and the education minister were clearly aligned with the university. Within the university the politician members of the senate and syndicate were equally identified with the university's position, which they upheld firmly in public speeches denouncing the government. Their position resulted from their long-standing identification with the university as graduates and as members of Hyderabad's elite families; their feelings as Telengana politicians confronting an Andhra chief minister who appeared to be operating with little respect for revered Hyderabad institutions; and their political alignment with the leader of the Telengana dissidents against the chief minister. From the university side the only possible mediator was an old brahman Congress party leader from Hyderabad, a member of parliament (Lok Sabha) and a widely known philanthropist. As a member of the older Congress party generation which now wields little power in the state party, he was not identified with any group in state politics. Though strongly identified with the university on the autonomy issue, he was able to gain an interview with the chief minister at a time when no one else could do so. Without political support to provide sanction for his efforts, however, he could do little.

Nor could the government contribute any mediators. Civil servants most concerned with education were themselves too closely identified with one of the parties. The director of higher education had a long-standing association with the vice-chancellor, who had helped him attain his directorship. On the other hand, the director of public instruction was the author of the government bill and not trusted by the university.

The only persons with sufficient stature and independence to mediate were the two prime ministers and the former chief minister of Hyderabad state, B. Ramakrishna Rao. Through Shastri, the chief minister had agreed to introduce new amending legislation that incorporated changes suggested by central government authorities. Through the offices of Ramakrishna Rao, the teachers agreed to call off their strike on the understanding that a conference would be held. But this happened only after the conflict had run its course and the "second" vice-chancellor had been prevented from assuming office by supreme court injunction.

Without mediators the conflict was conducted almost entirely in public. Throughout the dispute university senate meetings were well covered in the press, and leaders from both sides used the press to talk to each other. Informal channels which were available, such as the office of the director of public instruction, were used primarily for passing along information, rather than for effecting a settlement.

University Budget Crisis

With the supreme court verdict the Andhra Pradesh government dropped its efforts to unseat D. S. Reddi and allowed his term to run its course. Meanwhile the university autonomy dispute shifted from the appointment issue to the question of finance. On 31 August 1967, D. S. Reddi announced that the university would face closure within six months if the government did not pay it rupees seventy lakhs (Rs. 700,000), the balance due it as a result of the increase in the block grant for the two financial years after 1966–67.[100] Government made no provision in its budget for payment of such a sum, and compounded the university's financial crisis by releasing its funds in monthly installments, a practice that did not take into account the disproportionately large expenditure of funds that occurs at the beginning of the academic year.[101] The university was forced to rescind half of its pay increases to employees and to raise tuition and examination fees, moves that risked alienating two important constituencies within the university. Even with these adjustments, the vice-chancellor feared that reserves and interest from the endowments fund might not be sufficient to meet expenditures for more than six months.

The university saw these difficulties as a direct result of the conflict with government over autonomy. Clearly the conflict was a sensitive issue in government circles; the government's defeat was public and decisive. Whether the government's actions were vindictive, however, must be considered in the larger context of state finances. The Andhra Pradesh government was in financial straits. Its overdrafts on the reserve bank were being called in by the central government and its commitment to enhance the dearness allowances of state employees would cost an estimated rupees ten crores per year.[102] Its difficulty was compounded by the temporary loss of revenue that followed invalidation by the supreme court of the Land Revenue Act of 1967. The state had to cut back drastically on its plan expenditures. It retrenched more than a thousand young engineers on public works projects, decreed a 10 percent cut in expenditure for education at all levels, and reduced outlays for rural development by large amounts. In this context, the university's current grant (the old block grant), minus a 10 percent cut, plus half of the increment requested, was probably in line with the stringency in other areas. At the same time, there may have been some vindictive postponement of decisions on university financing. The university budget was not decided in 1966, when its previous five-year grant expired, even though the state was not then in a financial crisis. Subsequently, the university shared the financial suffering of the state.[103] The issue of finance is a very serious one, for it highlights the dependence of the university on government resources, another means for limiting university autonomy.[104]

Autonomy in Perspective

Though D. S. Reddi was allowed to complete his term, the new procedures were used to choose his successor. By then circumstances had changed, and all of Telengana was engrossed in a conflict over separation of the region from Andhra Pradesh. In an attempt to mollify separatist

opinion the leader of the Council for University Autonomy, Ravada Satyanarayana, was chosen vice-chancellor. In these circumstances the university accepted what must be considered a political appointment, though
Satyanarayan had many qualifications that might have won him the post
under other circumstances as well.[105]

Osmania did not change fundamentally, even though the autonomy dispute lasted more than one year and had so dramatic a climax. It is not
likely that the professors could be rallied again for such an issue if there
were not strong backing again by a vice-chancellor, and the demand for
internal autonomy has only now, three years later, begun to make progress.
The personal ground on which the autonomy dispute was conducted led
many to interpret it as a struggle for power and prestige between individuals, the chief minister and the vice-chancellor. Yet to reduce the issues
to the personal level would be to ignore the fundamental divergences underlying the conflict which enabled each side to gather such support and
made mediation so difficult. It is the articulation of these divergences between goals, between elites, and between purpose and performance which
makes the Osmania case an incisive revelation of the tensions inherent in
modernization.

In the debate surrounding the conflict fundamental views of university
autonomy were articulated. One side argued that liberty depends on the
university having autonomy as a matter of right.[106] Assimilating the university into the theory of checks and balances, it argued that universities
must have the same independent standing as the judiciary if liberty is to
be preserved. Constitutional sanctity is especially necessary during the difficult stages of development, when "the backwardness of economy, con-
tinuance of quasi-traditional institutions and social obscurantism, . . .
leads to an inchoate situation resulting among other things in the emergence
of a certain type of political elite, and the first-phase spectacle of faction-
ridden and personality-oriented 'tug-of-war' politics. . . . Faced with such
a political reality it becomes almost imperative for centers of culture and
learning, like the universities, to take necessary precautions in resisting
political influence and control." [107]

The purpose of autonomy is not, however, to isolate the university from
the public. Indeed, this side argued that the university is as true a representative of the general will as the legislature. As an institution creating
knowledge and values, it acts as a trustee of the nation, not only of its
present but also of its future. In this role it must act as a critic of current
actions, seeking to educate public opinion and to change it. "Autonomous
universities are the watchmen of the democratic community." [108]

An alternate view links autonomy more directly with the university's
contribution to democracy and development. This is the view of the model
act committee, which argued that "a university needs autonomy if it is to
discharge properly its functions and obligations to society and play an effective part in the development and progress of the country." [109] This

formulation takes the interpretation and defense of autonomy out of the hands of the university as a self-governing institution and places autonomy in the charge of public authority responsible to the people. It makes the university's autonomy contingent on its fulfilling certain functions deemed necessary by the society as articulated by its government.

Arguing from this position, some socialists have suggested that a planned society devoted to rapid change cannot allow universities the independence they were allegedly given in an older, presumably more stable British society. Surrounded by poverty and backwardness, India's leaders must concentrate their efforts for change, mobilizing all institutions for service to social goals.[110] Thus A. D. Bhogle of Osmania argued: "The fact is, emerging countries have a logic all their own. . . . There is no need to protect the university from the popular will and the state, for these are the prime movers in our social dynamics. Instead of resisting popular and governmental intervention, the universities must try to improve the quality of these interventions. This it [sic] can do by a more vigorous participation by the academics in the social life of the country." [111] Though less explicitly socialist in his orientation, the chief minister made a similar argument in justifying the legislation to education minister Chagla. "While no one disputed the need for giving complete autonomy to the universities in their internal matters and day-to-day administration, I think no one can seriously argue that this autonomy should be absolute covering every item of major educational policy with which the aspirations of the people as also their future are inextricably interlinked." [112]

Even when the universities are not asked to be quite so socially responsive as this view implies, they must prove themselves worthy of autonomy or suffer restrictions on it. If they become, for example, political rotten boroughs for self-serving caste groups then autonomy has little meaning. Pluralists who endorse voluntary associations as the foundations of democracy and liberty assume that they can provide just and orderly self-government that contributes to public good, but such associations may not be capable of doing either. There are many instances of maladministration in Indian universities, of which that at Andhra university was only one example. The public does not have great confidence in universities, nor do university administrators have confidence in the integrity of their teachers, as the resistance to internal examinations suggests.

Pluralists also assume that the ordering of society rests on a consensus of what constitutes the public good, shared by all such voluntary associations and public authorities. Whether this consensus exists in India, divided as it is by communal, regional, and other cleavages that seem to have little common ground, is hard to ascertain. The university argues that it represents the whole society, yet to the rural-based politicians of Andhra it appears to be an interest group dedicated to maintaining the position of an urban cultural elite. The conflict over goals represents a new era in Osmania's history, a history distinguished in the earlier period by the felicitous relations between university and state. Only as goals diverged — as rural peasants began to demand democratization of modern institutions and the university gained a sense of institutional distinctiveness from its new windows on the English-speaking world — did the question of autonomy arise.[113] Osmania's demand for autonomy was reinforced by the support of the central government, whose own goals of nation-building aroused its concern for Osmania's future. In 1951 Prime Minister Nehru sought to make Osmania a national (that is, centrally administered and financed) Hindi-speaking university. In the autonomy controversy of 1965–66 the central government intervened on the side of universalism against the provincialism of state politicians.[114]

The university's contribution to societal goals is problematic, however the goals be conceived. Some societal demands made on Indian universities do appear to be deleterious to more "academic" goals. But is the Indian university contributing to the goals of social uplift in ways which are consonant with its talents, and is it upholding the academic standards under which it takes shelter? [115] Osmania's record on the language of instruction issue is perhaps instructive. The university has not, on the one hand, resisted the goals espoused by state political leaders, but it has not, on the other, developed plans which would smooth the changeover to Telugu language, nor has it initiated a translation program to provide texts in Telugu. There is some redirection toward more social relevance at Osmania. To cite only two examples, the geography department is pursuing a comprehensive study of metropolitan Hyderabad, and the political science department is engaged in a long-term study of electoral trends in the city. Such projects are consonant with the academic skills and interests of a university faculty, yet they clearly also contribute to public concerns.

Divergence in goals has been accentuated by the differing social composition of university and political elites. The distance of university representatives from their political environment goes beyond the isolation from daily concerns that scholars usually desire, resented though that is in many societies. Profound differences in cultural and social backgrounds separate scholars from those in power. The university faculty draws heavily on groups in Hyderabad that have lost political influence to rising peasant groups.[116] Reinforcing the differences in social composition is the resentment by Hyderabadis of the wealthier Andhras whom the Hyderabadis see as unequal competition for jobs and services. Also, the new faculty are more attuned to the modern national culture of foreign-trained intellectuals, the press, and the national leaders to whom they appeal for support against provincialism[117] than to the needs of the Telugu people in the university's hinterland.[118]

The cleavage between political and university elite helps to explain why so few public organizations in the state offered support to Osmania. With the exception of the Communist members, MLA's from Telengana did not speak out in Osmania's defense, nor did the graduates' association or the

administrators of the college which is supported by the graduates' association. More noticeable was the failure of the other two universities in the
state to come forward. Though they also were affected by the first of the
amendment acts, including the directives clause, they had neither the strong
vice-chancellor nor the faculty will to resist. These two universities are
much closer to their political and social environment than is Osmania.
More of their faculty have strong loyalties to values and interests outside
the university, providing crosscutting cleavages that preclude or mitigate
conflict with the environment over academic issues. In contrast, Osmania's
separation from its social and political milieu made it more conscious of
its autonomy and more willing to fight for it.

Public support for the university's academic goals and processes might be
augmented by development of better institutional mechanisms for relating
the university to its environment. The graduates' association is concerned
primarily with sponsoring a public exhibition to finance a college but does
not otherwise participate in the university activities. More significantly, the
senate of the university does not provide a link with the environment. Its
twice-yearly meetings sometimes last only an hour and cannot be an effective forum for discussion. Vice-chancellors have become adept in per-
suading university senates to adopt their policies, but they have neglected
to persuade public representatives in the senate to defend university policies
in public arenas. Conversely, public representatives on the senate rarely
criticize university policies from within and when they do they often feel
uncomfortable because such criticism is too readily taken as political interference.[119] The result is to deprive the university of channels for hearing lay criticism from within.

Like so many other roles in the university, that of representing the public has fallen on the shoulders of the vice-chancellor. At Osmania, D. S.
Reddi was most effective, partly because his own strong ties to the surrounding society enabled him to maintain an independent position vis-à-vis
public men. Yet it was these same ties that inadvertently involved the university in the quarrels of state factional politics. Perhaps the solution is
greater attention to development of institutional channels that would do
for the university what the vice-chancellor has done personally through
his own leadership. Indian universities today are too dependent on the
wisdom and skill of their vice-chancellors; it is this circumstance that made
D. S. Reddi's tenure so large an issue at Osmania.

Government also might profit from rethinking the issues of the conflict.
Its haste in pushing through amending legislation and its refusal to consult
the university until pressed by threats and higher authorities deflected support from the quite tenable changes it sought to make. Originally the government wished to correct widely recognized shortcomings in university
governance. Yet the manner in which the government pursued university
reform created the impression that it had ulterior purposes. Government's
proposals for removing vice-chancellors and giving directives showed little

sense of fair procedure because they neglected accepted canons of representation of parties in a dispute. The effort to replace D. S. Reddi with a nonentity wounded the pride of academics who identified themselves with the university's leadership. These actions did not necessarily indicate malicious intent, as many government critics charged, but they did highlight the importance of respect for conventions and procedure in administrative and political life in maintaining a workable relationship between the educational and political systems in India.

Part IV / *Professional Constraints on Politicization of Education*

Introduction to Part IV

The relationship between education and politics is affected by the professionalization of learning. Professionalism creates mediating structures and communities — professional organizations and "colleagues" — and mediating ideologies — rational and irrational beliefs in the virtues of professionalism — that interpose their own goals and standards between those of the educational and political systems. Professionalism as an identity, ideology, and institutional arrangement can provide reference points for faculty members and constrain partisan, nepotic, and group considerations in appointments and resource allocations. To the extent that professional standards and interests are socially respected, they can influence extrauniversity persons and institutions upon which the university is dependent (for example, state governments and community associations that manage education). Professional standards, interests, and ideology can protect education against politicization. But professional influences are not invariably benign. They can lead to overspecialization, trained incapacity, monopolistic practices, and the appropriation of educational goals and resources. In India, however, these dangers are still largely in the future; professionalization augurs educational benefits more than it does liabilities.

Historically, professional learning in higher education has had a number of meanings. One meaning, quite old in Europe and embodied in professional schools, views knowledge instrumentally, as a device for conveying the technique of the literate crafts, notably law and medicine. A second meaning is specialized education directed to research and the advancement of knowledge "for its own sake"; this meaning had its strongest specific expression in German university education in the nineteenth century, as libraries, museums, and laboratories grew up to serve expanding intellectual frontiers. Both aspects of professionalization may mediate between the political and educational systems if they convince politicians and educators that the criteria and standards they represent are important.

Many of the arrangements in India which are hospitable to politicizing education are also found in the United States, where publicly governed and financed institutions also operate in the context of democratic politics. In the United States, in fact, state universities not only receive their moneys from state governments, as is to a considerable extent true in India, but must justify their budgets annually before the state legislature, a development that has been resisted in India.[1] But the historical development of professionalization in America[2] — the political strength of professional interest groups, the wide belief in the mystique of professional learning, the strength of the German model of specialized learning — alters the picture. The American universities — as distinct from American colleges — established at the end of the nineteenth century (Johns Hopkins, Chicago, Brown, Clark, and Harvard) incorporated German patterns of disciplinary professionalism. These patterns were strengthened by the emergence of powerful professional associations for the various disciplines, allied with journals, meetings, "markets," and other communication networks.[3] The idea of professional learning and status has been popularized with sufficient success that state legislators who vote appropriations are obliged to consider not merely whether the state university admits enough local residents and services state producer interests but also whether it can attract professors distinguished enough to raise the institution's position in the departmental rankings compiled by professional associations.[4] The national reputation of state educational institutions has become an item in local chauvinism and in the demand schedule of local voters.[5]

India also founds and funds the bulk of its higher educational institutions through public means and operates them in the context of a democratic politics. In India, however, political pressures meet with less counter pressure from well-established professional disciplines than in the U.S. This tends to make Indian higher education more vulnerable to partisan social and political infiltration and appropriation.

It is significant for the role of professionalization in Indian university education that the nation's modern educational transplant came from Britain rather than from, say, Germany. English universities avoided the impact of professionalization, both in the sense of training for the learned crafts (law and medicine) and in the sense of research and *Wissenschaft,* longer than did those on the continent. The domination of the university scene by Oxford and Cambridge meant the rule of classical scholarship and literary culture,[6] which were inimical to useful and specialized professional training. Scientific and technological learning were suspect because of their association with trade and were considered to be contaminated by their connection with industry and profit. Systematic and applied knowledge threatened the more diffuse and humanistic generalist style favored for gentlemen. Science and technology and, later, the social sciences, occupied the lower rungs of the intellectual status ladder.[7] Such learning was for second rate minds inept at classical education, although an energetic school reformer like Thring at Uppingham could allow that one might find competent teachers to teach "extra subjects" (botany, natural history, physical sciences, chemistry) as "filling-up work." [8] Proper training in law, engineering, medicine, accountancy, and architecture remained a matter of private arrangement rather than systematic courses of university study through much of the century, even after qualifying examinations were established for many of these fields.[9] Students of law or medicine or architecture would seek out an eminent practitioner and train under him.[10] In consequence, the mainstays of English higher education were relatively insulated from professional influence until the twentieth century.

The University of London provided the structural but not the cultural model for Indian higher education. It placed some emphasis on professional training — King's College had a Department of Engineering in 1838, both King's and University College provided medical education — but such emphasis was not carried over to Indian universities.[11] Irene Gilbert's account of the Indian Educational Service shows us, rather, a service whose members, due to internal and external constraints, often created institutions modeled on the English universities Matthew Arnold described: "where the youth of the upper classes prolong to a very great age, and under some very admirable influences, their school education. . . . They are in fact still schools." [12]

Leading sectors for professionalization in the U.S. and Europe were science and technology. Because the mystique of science and technology is often as powerful as that of democracy, it is capable of legitimizing abstract knowledge and elite higher education in the face of democratic impatience with "useless" learning and meritocratic admission standards. For these reasons, the presence of a strong scientific and technological sector in universities can be significant for the maintenance of the professional idea. In this respect too, however, India has to an extent followed Britain in placing much of its scientific effort in specialized independent research institutes outside the universities. The twenty-nine national laboratories and institutes established under the Council of Scientific and Industrial Research, for example, command facilities and research talent which, were they located in the universities, could strengthen professionalism. This aspect of university organization not only weakens university research and teaching and its capacity to serve society in direct and obvious ways, but also weakens the university's capacity to resist politicizing pressure and appropriation by depriving it of the protections of professional authority.

Finally, as the Education Commission, 1964–1966, pointed out, 40 percent of the students enrolled in Indian colleges are enrolled in the pre-university course or its equivalent.[13] These courses and, according to the commission, the courses leading to the first degree (B.A., B.Sc., B.Comm.) are often the intellectual and academic equivalents of high school education in "advanced" countries.[14] Such education does not command the respect given to specialized expertise. It is not beyond the reach of laymen and politicians, who may feel competent to form judgments on the nature of the education imparted and to intervene in the educational process. Because Indian colleges and universities perform high school functions, many persons are recruited whose expert knowledge suffices for this level of teaching only, and the more advanced professional knowledge of others who teach at these levels is rendered purposeless. In either case, the significance of specialized knowledge is diminished and professional authority accordingly downgraded.

In her chapter on the Indian Educational Service, Irene Gilbert illuminates obstacles in the early growth of professionalization of higher education. The service was formed in 1896 to increase the number and quality of able young Englishmen available to teach in the new government colleges. The conditions of service, it was hoped, would offer attractions similar to those of the Indian Civil Service, which had become a desirable career capable of commanding superior talent.

To an extent, the IES accomplished this purpose by improving the status of college teachers, regulating their benefits, promotions, and pay. But there was much in the structure which was inhospitable to the creation of academic professionalism, especially in the broader sense of research, publication, and the advancement of knowledge through institutionalized specialization. From the beginning, the service suffered from a confusion between administrative roles on the one hand and teaching and intellectual ones on the other. Its members were expected to serve both as college teachers and as administrators in colleges and in the provincial departments of public instruction. As college teachers, most emphasized the "school" goals of character building through extracurricular as well as curricular activities and through serving as models for the young men they taught. Nor was specialization required or emphasized; quite the contrary. The role of teacher was not the significant one for promotion, prestige, and pay. The grading of posts available for staffing by members of the service made administrative jobs the most senior, lucrative, and desirable. To achieve them was the culmination of a man's career. An appropriate analogy would be that the administrators in the New York City department of education and professors at Columbia University not only shared the same career ladder but also that most Columbia professors aspired to be superintendent of education in the city or state of New York, or perhaps United States commissioner of education, as the highest measure of personal success.

In consequence, the status expectations of the service were skewed in favor of administration and moral education (including manners and style) rather than research. The bureaucratic paradigm on which the service was formulated and the "school" dimension of collegiate education militated against academic professionalization in other respects. Seniority and institutional contributions counted more than professional contributions and those who made them were often promoted to a government department that could use their skill or knowledge. Professors were obliged to meet administrative requirements for office work — for example, knowledge of the vernaculars, which were not then used in higher education — but were not obliged to meet professional requirements — particularly publication — which could have served as incentives for intellectual production and as a means to connect teachers to professional (as well as institutional) colleagues. If teachers did publish, and they did, it was despite the structure of incentives.

Until 1916, when postgraduate research degrees were introduced at Calcutta, Indian universities were not postgraduate teaching and research institutions, even though masters degrees began to be awarded in the 1870's. Prior to 1916, and for some time afterward, most remained primarily examining bodies, designed to test boys educated in a variety of colleges. This circumstance further constrained the members of the service. Those experienced in English university teaching were shocked by the limitations of the examination system and by the set syllabi. Irene Gilbert quotes W. W. Hornell, a member of the Service, who noted in 1914: "[A professor] has practically no say in what he shall teach. His business is to train for certain examinations, over which he has neither influence nor control." Irene Gilbert points out that "the curriculum used in his college was legislated in the university senate, the books used in his courses required by the university boards of study, and his teaching always indirectly subject to decisions of the university's board of examiners." When one considers that better paid and more secure teachers from England, armed no doubt with some imperial *hubris,* did not revolt against this system, it becomes less surprising that Indian academics have been so long willing to put up with it.

The IES professors did not specialize. They taught various subjects, "lecturing continuously on basic topics at unsophisticated levels of scholarship." [15] There was a tendency, heightened by the strong administrative, as against professional, incentives in the service, to value contributions to the institutional life more highly than external repute.[16]

Irene Gilbert believes that the reforms contemplated for the Indian Educational Service in 1924 — to shear it of some of its bureaucratic features; to separate administrative and teaching functions — would have strengthened its contributions to the scholarly dimensions of higher education. But these reforms were forestalled with the abolition of the IES in 1924. Although the IES shaped the intellect and character of generations of India's professional and political classes, it did not further the institutionalization of professional standards and ideology in Indian higher education.

Professionalism may insulate the educational system from the political when its criteria — intellectual formulations and research; the qualifications required in a particular discipline or profession — command respect both inside and outside academia. But not every nominally professional association is primarily committed to the creation and application of relevant knowledge and skills. Professional associations may, for example, be more interested in protecting or enhancing their members' economic interest.

Paul Brass analyzes the struggle of three professional medical groups — the modern medical practitioners; the traditional Ayurveds; and the proponents of a "mixed medicine" — to influence the standards of their profession through the curricula of colleges and the giving and recognition of degrees. In a way, his study illustrates the potential of professionalization. These professional bodies, instead of standing as mediating structures and cultures between education and politics, use politics as an entree into the educational system. The demand for Ayurvedic medical training arises not only from a belief in a special theory and method of healing but also from the demand to create medical colleges that is made by those who cannot qualify for the "modern" ones. If we measure the relative professional standing of Ayurvedic and modern medicine in India by the preferences of consumers and students who apply to study, the professional authority of modern medicine is higher.[17] Ayurvedic interests have attempted to establish professional authority equivalent to that of modern medicine, or at least to win the economic fruits of such standing by having state governments and the national government officially declare Ayurvedic educational institutions equivalent to modern medical colleges. The Ayurvedic profession, rather than resisting political interference in professional matters, welcomes it as a principal means to professional respectability and benefits.

Paul Brass' study, like Carolyn Elliott's study of Osmania, suggests the relevance of different political system levels and their interrelationship for educational policy by examining the struggle among the three professional groups as they prod ministries and policy makers at the state and national levels to define professional standards in ways congenial to their particular outlook and economic interest. His account of competing power and policy structures, reaching from senior national ministers with rival notions of correct medical procedure through competing medical interest groups seeking to impose their visions of science on national and state governments; to the ministries of different states, some committed to one vision of medical professionalism and some to another, gives one of the first glimpses students of Indian politics have had of the way an interest can aggregate support vertically through layers of the federal system.[18]

The conflict that Paul Brass' study describes is not over the direct conversion of educational institutions into political resources. The conflict is over the definition of the public interest in medical education, a conflict that involves, among other things, judgments by public authorities on questions of scientific knowledge and professional legitimacy. Its outcome will affect profoundly not only the pattern of resource allocation by the states as well as the national government but also the quantity, quality, and "availability" of medical service in India.

13 / The Organization of the Academic Profession in India: The Indian Educational Services, 1864–1924

Irene A. Gilbert

The Indian Educational Service (1896–1924), by combining administrative and teaching responsibilities in one public organization, expressed and in turn profoundly influenced the structure and culture of academic life in India. The government of India in 1864 had established in each province "superior" graded educational departments and separate "inferior" ungraded ones. These organizations were reformed in 1896 into the Indian Educational Service and Provincial Educational Services.[1] The members of the superior service (from 1864) were employed in the British-administered provinces of India and Burma, occupying the highest positions in their systems of public education. Some served in administrative capacities, inspecting and overseeing primary, Indian language schools and higher, English language secondary schools; others served occasionally as headmasters in the higher schools and training colleges. The greater number of them, however, served as principals and professors in the English language colleges and oriental institutes maintained by the provincial governments.

Originally most members of the superior service were British, but by the 1920's the balance had altered, and nearly half were Indian. In the inferior services, Indians predominated. The younger members of the inferior service were employed in the system's lesser positions as deputy inspectors, high school masters, and assistant professors. Senior members held positions as inspectors, professors, and occasionally as principals.

Educational authority passed into Indian hands after the Montagu-Chelmsford reforms of 1919 established at the provincial level the principle and practice of dyarchy. In 1924, with the abolition of the Indian Educational Service, the distinction between superior and inferior service membership was eliminated, positions in the superior service were incorporated in the provincial cadres, and provincial educational services were rapidly "Indianized" when English recruitment halted.

The professors in the service taught in colleges, not universities. The universities established at Calcutta, Bombay, and Madras in 1857 were modeled on the early University of London, an affiliating university that examined and granted degrees but did not teach or support research. The Indian university was composed of educational policy-making and administrative bodies only. University bodies determined the degree requirements of affiliating colleges, what courses would be taught throughout the university, and what books would be used in particular courses.[2] Furthermore, the university tested the preparations of the students in the system, and indirectly the work of the professors who taught them, by holding degree-granting examinations at three two-year stages in the student's career: at the matriculation or entrance examination (and in this way, the university also controlled the content of the high school curriculum); at the first arts or intermediate examination; and at the B.A. and B.Sc. examinations. Although the universities were not research institutions, postgraduate instruction was inaugurated in the 1870's by introducing a fourth and final examination stage for the M.A. and M.Sc. degrees.

Members of the Indian Educational Service were employed at a small number of arts colleges maintained by the provincial governments. Each provincial government maintained a model or "premier" college attached to the local university.[3] The purpose of the premier colleges was twofold. First, they were to provide the teaching and training standards of the university, acting as a model for the other affiliated colleges and especially their staffs to emulate. Second, they were to function as elite colleges, admitting the best students in the province, giving them the best training possible, and preparing them for eventual responsibilities in the government services and new professions. Thus, the role of educational service professors in British India was crucial: they were to set professional standards in higher education and to help create modern professional elites intellectually and morally prepared to man the modern professions and to assume the highest positions available under the British *raj*. This chapter examines how IES professors pursued these goals within a service whose origins, structure, and culture were not always compatible with them, and indicates the legacies that the IES left for higher education in independent India.

The Civil Service Paradigm in Educational Employment

The service organization was not an unusual one in British India. It was the policy of the British government in India to import its professional talent from home. Doctors, engineers, and some barristers, along with professors, were hired in Great Britain. The professions in India were organized into a series of official departments commonly known as the uncovenanted services, such as the medical service, the public works department for the engineering service, and the smaller judicial service.[4] Staffs for the government's medical colleges were drawn from the medical service and were responsible for their curricula. Members of the public works department staffed the government engineering colleges and high court justices supervised the teaching of law.[5] Such courses of study were arranged to fulfill the requirements of service membership. In the absence of alternative standards provided in Britain by professional or qualifying associations, qualifying for admission to the various government services came to provide the measure of professional competence in India.[6]

Only gradually were Indians admitted to the uncovenanted services, and then at subordinate service levels. The distinction between the races, however, did not reflect upon the professional ability of a service member, British or Indian, as demonstrations of professional competence were the *sine qua non* of admission to service employment. It reflected, instead, the segregation of positions which carried administrative and policy responsibilities from those which did not; the former were reserved for Europeans.[7] For those Indians who did not care to join the uncovenanted services, the government legislated equivalent standards on the advice of the different services' European members. Thus, the colonial government became both the dispenser of professional knowledge and the custodian of professional standards. It acted through the technical services. Could the same structure work for the academic profession?

Prior to the establishment in 1854 of departments of public instruction in the five Indian provinces, the provincial governments had employed professors on an individual and *ad hoc* basis.[8] They were hired as needed, in England or in India, and their salaries varied from province to province. In the North-Western Provinces, for example, a European professor began at Rs. 350 a month, and might rise to Rs. 600 if promoted to the Banaras principalship; in Bengal, on the other hand, salaries ranged from Rs. 380 a month for an assistant professor to Rs. 1,300 for the principal of the Presidency College, and in Bombay, the Elphinstone College principal received an equivalent amount, but only because he also served as educational inspector of the presidency division.[9]

Professors continued to be employed on the same terms after 1857, even though the establishment of universities had enhanced the responsibility and scope of their work. The university curriculum led to a general expansion of the course of study offered at each college and a standardization of its content at a higher level of sophistication.[10] The nub of the problem was set down by William S. Atkinson, the director of public instruction in Bengal in 1864. "The establishment and maintenance of the Government Colleges, and still more the foundation of the University of Calcutta, with the avowed object of encouraging emulation and marking and honoring successful study, afford convincing proof that the Government are determined to make effectual provision for securing a high standard of liberal education as well as the knowledge and training that fit men for employment in the various active professions for life. These objects cannot be secured without the aid of highly cultivated instructors. . . . Now such men are not likely to come out to India on Rupees 400 a month." [11]

Further, the enactment of the Northcote-Trevelyan reforms in 1854 placed new competing demands on the sources of likely government college professors. Before competitive examinations for the civil service were established in 1854, civil servants were recruited directly from the public and grammar schools and trained at the East India Company's college at

Haileybury. With the reforms, candidates to the examination were admitted at a later age, and drawn from the colleges at Oxford and Cambridge Universities, from Edinburgh, from the new University of London, and from Trinity College at Dublin. The colleges had been irregular sources of recruitment for the government colleges in India and the new reforms seemed to close them off; or at least, as Atkinson thought, if a university man was inclined to serve in India, "the attractions of power and political usefulness [would] always tempt the more aspiring minds into the Civil Service." Atkinson concluded that educational appointments in India offered "only a bare subsistence, with the slenderest prospects of any future promotion." He added, "I do not think we need wonder that men with trained intellects prefer to struggle (if there is to be a struggle) at Home within the reach of the sympathy of their friends." [12]

Atkinson was in charge of the largest educational department in India, that of Bengal. It maintained seven arts colleges and employed twenty-seven men, eighteen of them professors and principals.[13] To run the department "in unimpaired efficiency," Atkinson suggested modeling educational employment in Bengal on the employment system in other government services.[14] Positions in the department were to be graded and members of the department promoted from one grade to another as vacancies occurred. Their salaries were to be increased accordingly, from a new starting rate of Rs. 500 a month to an enhanced eventual maximum of Rs. 1,500, excluding the director's salary of Rs. 2,000–2,500, which was to remain outside the grades. Within each grade, salaries were to be increased automatically for the first five years and promotion was to remain a matter of seniority. Between the grades, promotion was to be at the discretion of the provincial government, decided on the basis of both individual merit and seniority of service.[15] Atkinson's proposed reorganization of the department of public administration was as follows: director, starting rate of Rs. 2,000, rising by increments of Rs. 100 to a maximum of Rs. 2,500; first grade, Rs. 1,250, by increments of Rs. 50 to Rs. 1,500; second grade, Rs. 1,000, by Rs. 50 to Rs. 1,250; third grade, Rs. 750, by Rs. 50 to Rs. 1,000; and fourth grade, Rs. 500, by Rs. 50 to Rs. 750.[16] He also suggested that the positions in the three higher grades be distributed among the six principals, five inspectors, and five Presidency professors; the lowest grade would be filled entirely by government college professors.[17]

The Government of India approved the plan, and with the sanction of the secretary of state, the Bengal department was graded in 1865.[18] At a cost of Rs. 25,350 per month, the government of Bengal appointed one inspector and one principal (of Presidency) in the first grade; two principals, two inspectors, and two Presidency professors in the second; three principals, two inspectors, and five professors in the third; and seventeen professors in the fourth. No Indians were among the first appointments.[19]

The Bombay government maintained the second largest educational establishment — two arts colleges with a total staff of two principals and eight professors, five educational inspectors, and the provincial director. Sir Alexander Grant, principal of the Elphinstone College and director of public instruction in Bombay, faced the same problems of recruitment[20] that Atkinson faced in Bengal and came to a similar conclusion: "It is, I think, impossible to deny that, from the nature of the conditions above stated, the Educational Service in this Presidency is a very poor, precarious, and, in fact, miserable sphere, into which one can hardly dare to advise any young man of ability and cultivation to enter." [21] Like Atkinson, Sir Alexander wanted to reform the department into a service. His proposals for the reorganization of the Bombay department were put up in 1867 and were more far-reaching than Atkinson's. Rather than divide the members of the department among grades, Grant thought to divide them among categories appropriate to their different educational tasks. The categories were parallel rather than hierarchic, and each related to the other in logical fashion. Furthermore, Sir Alexander sought to eliminate unnecessary competition among the members of the department for positions of seniority and higher salaries by establishing automatic increments within each category. Sir Alexander's suggestions were as follows: director, Rs. 2,500 (without increment); principal, starting rate of Rs. 500, rising by increments of Rs. 50 to Rs. 1,500; professor, Rs. 500, rising by increments of Rs. 50 to Rs. 1,200; educational inspectors, Rs. 500, by Rs. 50 to Rs. 1,500; and high school masters, Rs. 500, by Rs. 50 to Rs. 800. As different talents and experience were required of inspectors in the vernacular language school system and principals in the English language colleges, the mastership was envisioned as a period of training for the inspectorship, and the professorship a period of training for the principalship. But Sir Alexander allowed that individual masters and professors could be promoted to higher positions before the maxima in their respective categories were reached. He also expected that the high school masters would be university men.[22]

Although the Bombay government supported the proposals, the government of India advised the secretary of state in London to reject them.[23] The Bengal government had already given effect to Atkinson's less expensive plan, and the members of the departments of public instruction in the North-Western Provinces and the Punjab were beginning to press the government of India to sanction a similar reorganization in their own provinces so that they would have the opportunity to benefit from the new increased salary scales as well.[24] A unitary system for all of India seemed the easier one to manage, and the secretary of state acted upon the advice of the government of India. In 1869, the Duke of Argyll sanctioned the establishment of graded educational departments in all the Indian provinces, including Bombay.[25]

The governments in Bombay, the North-Western Provinces, and the Punjab reorganized their departments almost immediately. In Madras, the government chose to wait until 1881 when the provincial authorities felt that the presidency's revenues could finally afford the added expenditure.[26] The distribution of educational personnel in India and the varied costs to all the provincial governments for maintaining graded departments in 1879 are shown in table 65.

Table 65. Distribution of educational personnel, 1879.

Province	D.P.I.	Grade I	Grade II	Grade III	Grade IV	Total	Monthly cost of graded departments (Rs.)
Bengal	1	2	5	12	18 [a]	38	28,300
Bombay	1	2	4	5	6	18	17,825
Madras	1	1	2	6	5 [a]	15	12,200
North-Western Provinces	1	1 [a]	4	3	6	15	15,450
Punjab	1	–	2	3	3	9	9,900
Central Provinces	1 [b]	–	–	2	1	4	4,100
British Burma	–	–	1 [c]	1	–	2	2,250
Assam	–	–	1 [c]	–	–	1	1,050
Total	6	6	19	32	39	102	91,075

Source: Government of India, *Proceedings in the Home Department, Education Branch*, A-June 1879, nos. 16–40.

These figures were actually gathered by the government of India in 1879, and although the members of the Madras department were divided among four grades, their pay scales were still slightly less than the all-India averages. There was also at that time an Indian director of public instruction in the ceded districts of Hyderabad; he was a second grade officer in the Bombay department, receiving Rs. 1,000 a month.

[a] Vacant positions included.

[b] Official title, inspector-general of education.

[c] Served as director of public instruction, and recruited from the Bengal cadre.

The grading served its purpose. As time passed, there were fewer professors without university degrees than there had been in earlier days. At first, the provincial authorities were able to hire university men in India. But as the structure of the Indian government became more bureaucratized, there were fewer career opportunities for the unemployed university graduate in India, and less came out to seek them. Increasingly, recruitment for the government colleges was carried out by the secretary of state in London, who had the complete monopoly of Indian educational appointments in Britain. Acting through local intermediaries, both at the major universities and the board of education in Whitehall, the staff of the India Office was able to locate graduates fresh from the universities or younger men with teaching experience at colleges, public schools, or grammar schools. The prospect of an adequate salary and eventual promotion proved sufficient to attract to a teaching career in India specialized honors graduates with first or second class degrees. They were still hired on an *ad hoc* basis, either as vacancies occurred or the size of the provincial cadres expanded.[27]

But as Sir Alexander Grant had implicitly foreseen, the graded structure was an inappropriate one for a department of public instruction and worked to hasten the unnecessary bureaucratization of the educational service. In the larger departments where the lower grades had been expanded to meet increased educational demands, the higher grades were not proportionately enlarged. Thus later appointees were compelled to spend long periods in the lower grades, in many cases far longer than the five years allotted for automatic increments. In Bengal, for example, there were thirty positions in the third and fourth grades, all filled by professors in 1879, and only seven in the first and second grades (excluding the directorship), and these were reserved for inspectors and college principals. The balance was more even in Bombay where the cadre's seventeen positions were divided into six positions in the higher grades and eleven in the lower, but the distribution of offices was largely the same. In the smaller departments, on the other hand, the higher positions remained unfilled. The one first grade position in the North-Western Provinces was sanctioned only as a long-term vacancy, and in the Punjab there had been no first grade sanctioned for the department.[28] The situation naturally created discontent. To avoid contention for the rare vacancy, governments often found it easier to make their promotions on the basis of seniority rather than merit. As in any bureaucracy, there were likely to be protests if it were otherwise.

More to Sir Alexander's point, however, the graded structure tended to confuse the administrative and teaching functions of the department of public instruction and to divert ambitions from teaching. Although the departments were staffed mostly by college professors, the departments' tasks were primarily administrative; that is, to organize and oversee the province's vernacular language school system.[29] In consequence, provincial governments were likely to prefer the administrative experience of the inspector to the teaching experience of the professor (or principal) when making their selections for the directorship. There were few inspectorships and they were largely concentrated in the higher grades (alongside the principalships). Some professors and principals questioned a system which affected their chances for ultimate promotion.[30] Kenneth Deighton, principal of the Agra College in the North-Western Provinces, compared the qualities needed by the incumbents of the two offices.

But neither in the administrative, nor in the inspectional duties of his office, is there any demand for great talent or much learning. . . . The Inspector does little more than gather information, and throw it into shape; supervise the work of his Deputies, make the inferior appointments; dispense punishment for offenders, and rewards for good service; check accounts;

and listen to petitions. His more properly inspectional function is that of examining schools. None of these, however, affects anything higher than the training stage for the University matriculation; of which a large majority of them are mainly vernacular and, therefore of a lower class.

The case is widely different with a Principal of a College. On the one hand, the administrative functions are less important, or, rather, less laborious than those of an Inspector; on the other, his position as a teacher requires in him a trained intellect, ripe scholarship, and literary tastes. In the earlier days of the Department, there was less need of such abilities and requirements; but the expansion of the Calcutta University in granting Honour Degrees in various branches of learning, has materially altered the conditions of fitness requisite in the Head of an affiliated Institution. An Inspector, on the contrary, now finds a narrower field for the display of a power to organize and originate than when the education of the masses was yet in its infancy. . . . For an appointment of this nature no officer ought to find any difficulty in qualifying himself. For the duties of a Principalship, the fit and proper persons will be comparatively few.[31]

Gottlieb Wilhelm Leitner, principal of the Lahore Government College in the Punjab, carried Deighton's argument to its logical conclusion: "The men who have left their mark on Indian education have been Principals rather than Inspectors. . . . It is neither just nor expedient to confine promotion to the Directorship to *one* Class," that of inspectors.[32] In 1879, there were only two department heads who had once been principals, and one of them, Chatfield in Bombay, had served as an inspector immediately before his appointment to the directorship.[33] By 1887, there were no principals serving as directors, and the discontent among the members of the departments had grown.

Formation of the Indian Educational Service
and the Provincial Educational Service

In an effort to deal with these problems and remove the discontent, the government of India decided to reorganize the service. Acting on the recommendations of the Public Service Commission, 1888, the government of India entered into a long series of discussions with the provincial governments. In 1896, the secretary of state sanctioned the formation of the Indian Educational Service. Like the other superior or "Imperial" services, the new educational service was an entirely European one, and all the more remunerative positions in the departments of public instruction were reserved to its members.[34] The old grades were officially abolished, and a structure approximating Sir Alexander Grant's earlier suggestions was instituted. In place of the third and fourth grades, members of the new IES were now assured guaranteed annual increments of fifty rupees for ten rather than five years, until salary maxima of Rs. 1,000 a month were reached. New recruits still took up their appointments at salaries of Rs.

500 a month. The first and second grades gave way to junior and senior allowances, paying the same scales (Rs. 1,000, rising by Rs. 50 to Rs. 1,250; and Rs. 1,250, rising by Rs. 50 to Rs. 1,500 respectively), and largely attached to the same positions. To add some flexibility to the new system, a small proportion of the allowances was made independent of the cadres' major inspectorships and principalships.[35] But Sir Alexander's main point was still unmet: the distinction between teaching and administrative functions remained confused on a consolidated departmental list. Essentially, the IES was merely a new form of the old graded structure. The distribution of the new service's members (excluding the directors) among the major Indian provinces, as compared to the old, is shown in table 66.

The reorganization's major innovation, enacted on the advice of the Public Service Commission, was a new level of service: the Provincial Educational Service, composed of Indian personnel. On the one hand, the new PES secured the status of the majority of the Indian employees of the departments of public instruction by bringing them into a parallel, if inferior, service. Previously, they had been retained as high school masters, deputy inspectors, or assistant professors on a fairly unregulated basis which varied from province to province. Now, they were brought into a regular graded structure on salaries ranging from Rs. 150 to Rs. 700 a month, with larger increments in higher positions.[36] On the other hand, the PES reduced the status of the small number of Indians who had worked alongside British colleagues as professors or inspectors in the old graded departments.

The provincial education departments had provided opportunities for a few Indians to gain appointments in the same service as Englishmen, and from 1881, when the salaries of Indians in all the government services were generally reduced, at two-thirds the European wage scale.[37] Now, Indians were to do the same work with less status as well as less remuneration. Moreover, the reform came at a time when more Indians had the same intellectual qualifications as Englishmen.[38] With the institution of the Indian and provincial services, the meaning of academic achievement and its rewards in career terms were further confused with the issues of race and imperial dominance.

Like its predecessor, the IES succeeded in its major purpose: the salary scales it offered sufficed to attract British university graduates to the teaching career in India. They were still recruited by the authorities in London on an *ad hoc* basis as provincial cadres expanded and vacancies occurred. They were probably better qualified on the whole than the recruits of an earlier generation, having taken their degrees either at improved provincial universities or at an Oxford and Cambridge which had been consistently reformed during the latter half of the nineteenth century.[39]

In 1910 efforts were made to improve the recruitment process (one of Sir Alexander Grant's original suggestions) by giving responsibility for

Table 66. Distribution of educational personnel, 1896.

Province	Graded educational departments					Indian educational service				
	Grade I	Grade II	Grades III and IV	Total	Monthly cost (Rs.)	Senior allowance	Junior allowance	Incremental scale	Total	Monthly cost (Rs.)
Bengal:	2	6	31	39	33,681	2	3	21	26	22,333
Madras:	1	2	13	16	13,381	2	2	10	14	12,499
Bombay:	2	3	10	15	14,450	2	3	9	14	12,733
North-Western Provinces:	1	4	7	12	11,233	1	2	8	11	9,683
Punjab:	–	2	6	8	7,083	1	1	5	7	6,250
Central Provinces:	1[a]	1	2	4	3,665	1	1	2	4	4,840
Total:	7	18	69	94	83,493	9	12	55	76	78,338

Source: Government of India, *Selections from the Records of the Government of India, Home Department, No. CCCLVIII, Home Department Serial No. 24, Papers Relating to the Re-organization of the Educational Service in India from 1891–1897* (Calcutta, 1897).

Note: The cadres of the new IES were reduced in size because of the projected elimination of Indian-filled positions from the cadres and a planned withdrawal of government from the support of district colleges. Burma was not included in the reforms at this time. I have rounded the figures to the nearest rupee, eliminating *paisaa* and *annaas* in the calculation.

[a] Serving as inspector-general of education.

selection of personnel to a special committee of the board of education. The board of education in London started to admit third class graduates with teaching certificates to serve as headmasters in India, prior to their eventual promotion to inspectorships. Headmasters were correspondingly included on the IES provincial lists, still consolidated ones.[40] By 1914, there were 170 graduates from British or continental universities in the Indian Educational Service: thirty-three of forty-two members in Bengal, twenty-eight of thirty-one in Bombay, twenty-eight of thirty-two in Madras, twelve of fifteen in the Punjab, and ten of fourteen in the Central Provinces. In the United Provinces (earlier the North-Western Provinces), Burma, Bihar and Orissa, and Assam, all the members of the provincial cadres were university men (twenty-five, fifteen, fourteen, and five respectively).[41]

Similarly, as a result of the reform of 1896 more Indians with the training or stature of European professors joined the PES, whose members were locally recruited, often on the advice of directors of public instruction and government college principals:[42] Dr. P. C. Ray of Presidency in Bengal, who took his doctorate at Edinburgh and had an international reputation for his research in chemistry; B. M. Sen, professor of mathematics at Dacca, who had been a second Smith's prizeman at Cambridge; Jadu Nath Sarkar, a graduate of the University of Calcutta on the staff of the Ravenshaw College at Cuttack in Bihar and Orissa, who was winning scholarly acclaim for his investigations in the area of Moghul history; and Samuel Sathianadhan, an Indian Christian teaching at Presidency College in Madras, who was a graduate of Cambridge.[43]

But the new structure did not solve the old problems, which persisted into the twentieth century. Although salaries had been made steadily incremental to the old third grade maxima, the junior and senior allowances allocated each province proved to be as proportionately insufficient as the earlier first and second grade positions. Cadres expanded, and IES men found themselves often waiting long periods before their promotions to the allowance levels. As prices rose and the rupee declined in value, complaints from the cadres increased. Provincial governments were finally compelled to grant individual allowances to service members by way of temporary relief.[44]

The administrative complexion of the service grew more pronounced with the passage of time, as provincial governments elaborated plans for the expansion of vernacular education in the twentieth century. In the United Provinces, the director, Claude de la Fosse, had been an inspector for many years; in Burma, James Covernton, the director, was an inspector imported from the Bombay cadre; in Bengal, the Presidency principal, George Kuchler, had been made to serve as an inspector before his promotion to the directorship, and the provincial government found his executive abilities so wanting that they decided to bring out a man from England to succeed him.[45] Promotions based on seniority rather than merit and a failure to distinguish structurally between teaching and administrative functions continued to characterize the bureaucratic side of the educational service after the reform.

The IES and the Charge of Racial Exclusion

The reforms of 1896 also made the educational service vulnerable to charges of racism. As the new Indian elite gained confidence in its abilities, sought more political freedom, and took pride in the modern intellectual achievements of Indians, they began to demand membership in the Indian Educational Service. In part, it was a matter of economics. With the return to India of increasing numbers of young men trained abroad, the feeling grew that these young Indians should hold teaching posts in government colleges. In a difficult employment situation, the limitations on opportunities that European professors represented was resented. When another commission on the public services met in 1914, the Indian witnesses presented a whole series of subsidiary arguments on that theme to the commissioners: many Indians had taken better European degrees; Indian professors could communicate more effectively with their Indian students than men of British origin could; the high cost of bringing a European professor out to India was prohibitive and detrimental to the economic development of the country.[46] The crux of the matter, however, was status, the recognition of Indian achievement which appointment to the IES would confer. In public discussions and press comments there were a growing number of statements such as the following, which appeared in a July 1914 number of the *Amrita Bazar Patrika,* Calcutta: "The Editor remarks that it is sad that the Government should refuse a scholar like Mr. Bhupati Sen an appointment in the Indian Educational Service, while scores of indifferent men are imported almost every three months from the United Kingdom into the service for no better qualifications than the possession of a white skin. Mr. Sen is the second Smith's Prizeman of the year, and any Englishman in this position would have his fame and fortune made in England. The Indian who now seeks admission into this facsimile of the Indian Civil Service is asked to wait till the Public Service Commission completes its labours. No such difficulty, however, stands in the way of British candidates. The Indian Educational Service is their birthright." [47]

Teaching in India was becoming more subject to public scrutiny as the pressure for Indian admission to the superior service continued to grow. This pressure increased greatly after 1914, when the members of the provincial service began to officiate in the reserved IES positions of Europeans fighting in the war. Indians were demonstrating their teaching ability in the imperial service, but still without the recognition the educated Indian public thought was their due.[48]

The public services commission headed by Lord Islington met to consider all these problems, and in 1916 presented its recommendations to the secretary of state and the government of India. The government of India was not able to act upon them until after the war, when salaries in the incremental scale were immediately raised to Rs. 1,250 a month, and the junior and senior allowances converted to two new selection grades, carrying salaries of Rs. 1,250, rising by Rs. 50 to Rs. 1,500, and Rs. 1,500, rising by Rs. 50 to Rs. 1,750 respectively. At the same time, recruitment to the IES was opened to both Indians and Britons, whether resident in India or the British Isles.[49] The Islington Commission had originally recommended that only one-third of the positions in the expanded IES cadres be reserved to Indians, but when the secretary of state gave his retroactive sanction to the reforms in 1922, the provincial cadres were quickly being filled with Europeans and Indians holding the same qualifications, at an even ratio, as table 67 shows.

Table 67. Europeans and Indians in the Indian Educational Service.

Province	Europeans	Indians	Total
Bengal	34	33	67
Madras	27	27	54
Bombay	23	23	46
United Provinces	24	23	47
Punjab	19	17	36
Bihar and Orissa	17	17	34
Central Provinces	16	16	32
Assam	7	5	12
North-West Frontier Province	4	1	5
Total	171	162	333

Sources: Government of India, *Proceedings in the Department of Education and Health, Education Branch*, A-October 1922, nos. 1–3, and Great Britain, Royal Commission on the Public Services in India, *Report of the Commissioners*, vol. 1 (London, 1916), pp. 114–118

The increase in the size of the cadres was accounted for by the transfer of positions from the provincial to the Indian service cadres. The incumbents of these positions, however, were not named to the higher service unless their qualifications or experience entitled them to the promotion.[50]

From these major reforms, a series of subsidiary reforms emerged. Starting salaries in the superior service were reduced to Rs. 350 a month, or Rs. 50 a month above a received provincial service salary for those appointed in India; it remained at Rs. 500 a month for those appointed in England whether they were British or Indian.[51] Pay-by-age scales were legislated so that older men, perhaps with some specialized academic experience, could be appointed at higher salary levels appropriate to their years.[52] Flexibility in the terms of educational service employment was further enhanced by the drawing up of more liberal retirement rules and proportionate pension plans.[53] Potentially most significant for the future autonomy of the academic profession was the belated decision to give effect to Sir Alexander Grant's proposal of 1867 to divide the service into two parallel branches, administrative and teaching.[54]

Yet within two years of its final enactment, the reorganization came to nothing. In 1924, at the recommendation of the Lee Commission on the superior civil services in India, recruitment to the Indian Educational Service ceased. With the institution of dyarchy under the Montagu-Chelmsford reforms, education became a provincial subject under the control of Indian ministers. An all-India educational service, whose members' positions were protected by the secretary of state, seemed out of place under these political circumstances.[55]

The IES was abolished when it had been reformed to its greatest potentiality: the administrative function separated from the academic; Indian and British professors established as equals; and, following the expansion of postgraduate teaching in the Indian universities, terms of service made flexible enough to attract research scholars to India without committing them to an Indian career. Had the service continued, it might have laid the basis for the emergence of a confident academic profession in India, just as the continued existence of a reformed Indian Civil Service led to the creation of a competent administrative class in the postindependence years. (At the same time that it recommended the abolition of the IES, the Lee Commission recommended the rapid "Indianization" of the civil service.) Instead, for most of its eighty year history, the IES retained many of the features of a bureaucratic organization in which seniority of service and administrative talents rather than intellectual quality were recognized and rewarded. Yet the legitimacy of the service was rarely questioned by the educated Indian public, whose members in 1924 were seeking entry into its higher grades rather than its abolition. Other highly bureaucratized academic services, such as those in France and Germany, have carried out their academic functions successfully. In India, however, there were special circumstances, including the colonial regime, the university structure, and the orientation of the service's members, that strengthened the bureaucratic at the expense of the academic component of the IES.

Civil Service Rules as Constraints on Academic Performance

British professors in India did not gain the respect and approbation of their own (Anglo-Indian) community as did professors in Europe; instead, they were an intellectually isolated group. Members of the police, engineering, and other uncovenanted services typically lacked university degrees or had graduated from the technical or professional institutes in Britain. Members of the Indian Educational Service, like members of the Indian Civil Service (ICS), were university graduates.[56] The academic qualifications of IES officers separated them from the other uncovenanted services, yet the latter were accorded an equal rank on the lists of precedence. At the same time, the uncovenanted service rank of IES members placed them in an inferior status in relation to the only other group in the British official class who shared the same educational experience, the ICS officers.[57] Bureaucratic norms so permeated the outlook and behavior of the Anglo-Indian community that such official judgments carried over into informal ones. The result was that the valuation placed on the professor's work and on the quality of his degree was different than it would have been in Britain. This fact was noted by J. G. Covernton, the Bombay director, when he sought to account for the complaints which perennially arose from the new recruits to the service. "Allowances must be made for young men fresh from the univerities where they have done well, better very likely than many of those whom they find the chances of a competitive examination have placed in a superior position in this country. Allowances, too, must be made for the fact that whereas in England a police officer, a local magistrate, a collector of revenue does not necessarily rank in popular estimation and actual status before a professor, a schoolmaster, or an inspector of schools, the new arrival finds the position here quite different from that in England." [58] For Covernton, there was only one solution for both British and Indian professors alike: "the sensible educational officer settles down to his work and tries to realize its interests and possibilities." [59]

But professors were subordinates in a larger governmental structure. The members of the civil service received their first intensive training in the rural districts, and after being promoted to collectorships still in the *mofussil* (country districts), were perhaps promoted to offices in the provincial government secretariat. As generalist administrators, they thought in terms of the needs of all the services rather than the peculiarities of one, and their conceptions of those needs were often tempered by their own early experiences of rural India. In consequence, they frequently legislated rules for the educational service which were inappropriate to a professor's requirements, and seemed to prevent him from settling down to his work. Members of the service were, for example, liable to transfer. In this way Professor J. A. Cunningham was transferred from the Presidency College to a Bengal inspectorship, just after he had reorganized the chemistry laboratory and had begun joint researches with Professor P. C. Ray.[60] Also, professors were expected to learn the vernacular language of their province within two years of their arrival in India — their promotions and salary increments were dependent upon their doing so — though most of their work was in the cities, and in English.[61] The same Professor Cunningham protested this stricture and its cost to his teaching time. "For I have the honour to submit that any knowledge of the vernacular which I could by the neglect of other and far more rational and useful demands upon my time and energy, have acquired in two years would be no real help whatever to the principal part of my legitimate duties in Calcutta. . . . I am able to assert, therefore, without the smallest fear of contradiction, that my whole time has been very fully occupied since my arrival in India with work for which I was, I repeat with apologies, in some degree specially fitted. Such has been the pressure of this work, becoming daily overwhelming, that I can further assure you that while myself subscribing to four scientific journals in English, French and German, and having a standing order with my Cambridge bookseller to supply me with all new books dealing in any one of those languages, with my own special subject of Physical Chemistry, yet I have read not a single scientific paper and only small portions of a few of those books, during the last six months. Now I submit that it would be far more in the real interests of higher education in this country that I, and others in a similar position to mine, should have leisure enough to read these books and papers than that we should cram up a smattering of Bengali or any vernacular language." [62]

Cunningham was eventually exempted.[63] His case, however, demonstrates the effects of the confusion of teaching and administrative functions in the structure of the IES. Professors were liable to transfer to an inspectorship where the language requirement was a sensible one from the point of view of the secretariat: an inspector's effectiveness depended in large part on his ability to examine students in the vernacular and communicate with their teachers.

The Structure of Universities and Professional Performance

Not only the rules of the service, but also the structure of the university, constrained professors in their tasks. To men with European educational experience, the universities seemed hardly to be universities at all. The senate was largely a public forum of nominated members, many ill-equipped to discuss the range of educational issues that body had the authority to decide. The senate's executive arm, the smaller syndicate, dealt mainly with the details of university examinations and administration, reporting now and then to its parent body. There were some colleges near the university but most were dispersed over extended geographic areas. Affiliated colleges were often run to different purposes by the bodies (missionary, private, or governmental) which managed them. The ties of common location, purpose, and activity which bound together the colleges at Oxford and Cambridge were lacking. Nor were there the ties created by shared participation in strong, discipline-oriented departments, such as those coming to characterize academic life at the University of London, the older provincial universities, and the more recently formed newer ones. W. W. Hornell, the Bengal director in 1914, recalled his surprise as a college professor newly arrived in India. "Let us take then the case first of all of a young Englishman who having had a successful career at the University, and having done some stimulating teaching work for two or three years makes up his mind to accept an appointment in the Indian Educational Service. If the opening which he accepts is on the teaching side of the Service, it must be realized that which he is offered is a Professorship or Chair in some subject at a University College. No amount of explanation in London by those who know the facts will ever make him grasp the vast difference between the work he will be called upon to do and the conditions under which he will be called upon to do it, with anything that he has ever associated with University teaching in England, especially with the tenure of a professorship. . . . In the great majority of cases such an officer has got to adjust himself to an environment of which he had previously no conception. Moreover, he finds himself part of a gigantic examination system. He has practically no say in what he shall teach. His business is to train for certain examinations, over which he has neither influence nor control, students whose careers in after life depend, to an extent absolutely unknown in most walks of life in Great Britain, on their success in these examinations." [64]

With Covernton, Hornell agreed that the new professor, "probably [settled] down and having determined to make the best of it [did] really useful though unostentatious work," but the Bengal director added as an afterthought that the new professor was probably always conscious of the pressure of a system which [was] practically external not only to himself but also practically to the college of which he [was] a member." [65] The curriculum used in his college was legislated in the university senate, the books used in his courses were required by the university's boards of study, and his teaching was always indirectly subject to the decisions of the university's boards of examiners.[66] Nevertheless, despite the dual constraints imposed by governmental regulations and university dominance, most of the members of the service made their college work the touchstone of their educational careers in India.

In part, the concentration on college work was explained by the educational service's members' own university training. They were not research specialists in the contemporary sense, but prepared to lecture broadly in any one of a number of related subjects, as the university curriculum required. The model was thoughtfully set down in 1888 by Sir Alfred Croft, the greatest of the Bengal directors. "For the teaching of English literature there is no better preparation than the study of the Latin and Greek classics. When to that knowledge the professor has added, by private study, a survey of the field of English literature and an acquaintance with grammar and forms of Early English speech, he is fully equipped for his duties, and is a specialist in the highest sense: much more fully equipped, I maintain, and much more of a specialist, than if his studies had been confined to English literature and the English language. So again, there is no better preparation for teaching history and philosophy than the philosophical and historical course which a student at Oxford gets through in reading *in literis humanioribus;* and it is men who have been so trained that are commonly selected to teach these subjects in the colleges of Bengal." [67]

Significantly, the professional Orientalists, who not infrequently came out with definite scholarly purposes and specialized German training, thought in much the same way about their teaching work in India. Charles H. Tawney, principal of the Calcutta Presidency College, felt obliged to defend the integrity of the educational service from the criticisms of his fellow Orientalists abroad. "So when Dr. Garbe in the *Deutsche Revue* characterizes the administration of Public Instruction in India as thoroughly rotten (durchaus korrupt), and proceeds to say that he fears his readers will scarcely believe him when he comes to give a detailed account of it, apparently because Dr. Thibaut is set to teach various subjects besides Sanskrit, he no doubt hits a blot in our Indian system, but perhaps rather overlooks the difficulty of administering a department so limited in number as ours. It is owing to our not being specialists that we are able to do the work we do. . . . I myself have been compelled to teach more than one subject." [68]

At the same time, the members of the service were not unaware of the latest educational trends in Europe, of the increasing specialization in modern university life in Germany, and the similar reforms being enacted in the British university system. But the Indian university structure provided little place for increased specialization. The Indian universities were transformed into unitary, departmental institutions only in the 1920's at the same time that the IES was undergoing its last period of reform. In consequence, the government college staffs were still bound to teach a wide-ranging syllabus at the undergraduate and masters levels until well into the twentieth century. As Sir Alfred Croft noted in 1888, under these conditions, specialists of the newer sort just would not come to India.[69] Some thirty years later, a young specialist, L. F. Rushbrook-Williams, attached to the University of Allahabad, elaborated upon the constraints of the university system. Reflecting upon his experiences as a professor of Moghul history at Allahabad, Rushbrook-Williams wrote in a "Draft Minute on Indian University Organisation from the Teaching Point of View": "How can one or two Professors, able and hardworking though they may be, give their students the same teaching, as a properly organised staff of specialists? Instead of sitting at the feet of a number of experts, each thoroughly acquainted with a particular branch of knowledge, the Indian student has to content himself with the lectures of two or three unfortunate Professors, who have to cover so much ground that they cannot possibly attain to a standard of even modern efficiency in every direction. And yet the capacity for specialization and the taste for it, are *there*. Organise these scattered teachers into a centralised department; divide up the subject among them so that each is responsible for a single branch of knowledge; and without engaging a single extra professor, an efficient teaching instrument will be produced" [70] (italics in the original).

Although lecturing continuously on basic topics at unsophisticated levels of scholarship might easily have led service members to lose interest in teaching, few government college professors seem to have done so — even in the service's later years when the pressures for specialization grew. In part, they maintained interest because of the ideas and commitments most members of the service carried to India from their own educational experience. For most, the wider purposes of education were served by the moral training and character building of the young that resulted from close association of teacher, tutor, and student in a closed educational milieu.[71] These were the ideas bequeathed to generations of British educators by Dr. Thomas Arnold of Rugby and his son Matthew. The younger Arnold's *Culture and Anarchy* might have been called the "bible" of the educational service and this passage its motto: "culture [is] a pursuit of our total perfection by means of getting to know, on all the matters which most concern us, the best which has been thought and said in the world." [72]

With their Indian colleagues in the provincial services, British principals and professors sought to cultivate less official relationships, hoping in this way to overcome the distinctions created by differences in type and conditions of service.[73] Their aims were neither social nor intimate: British and Indian professors usually went their separate ways after college hours. Nor were they markedly professional: there were few shared intellectual endeavors within a common discipline. Their concern was to enhance the college's sense of community. They brought with them to India the traditions of the British common room. The proprieties and courtesies observed by gentlemen in such a setting came to characterize the broader patterns of staff relations. In particular, judgments about work and the quality of contributions to college life, as well as the adjustments made by a number of varying personalities to one another, determined individual relationships. At Presidency, for example, where both Indians and Englishmen participated in the formulation of the institution's academic policy, Sir J. C. Bose, whose scientific stature was international, was criticized by his colleagues for neglecting his duties to the college. The director of public instruction described the situation: "Dr. Bose has of late years been so absorbed in his scientific investigations that he has lost touch with the other duties ordinarily devolving upon a college professor of science, and there can be little doubt that the direction of the physical laboratory must, if it is to prove a success, be placed in the hands of a professor more specially qualified for the task." [74] The principal described the situation as "impossible." [75] P. C. Ray, on the other hand, whose scientific reputation also spread beyond India, earned the special respect of his colleagues because of his efforts to put the chemistry laboratories of Presidency on a sounder and more advanced footing. Dr. Bose was in the IES; P. C. Ray was in the PES. In the end, Indian professors came to hold the same views as their British colleagues. At the premier government colleges, participation in college life came to be one with participation in a tradition of corporate academic excellence — as it is still today at the remaining premier colleges; Presidency in Calcutta and Madras, Elphinstone in Bombay, and the Lahore Government College in Pakistan.

Conclusion: The IES and Academic Professionalism in India

In the smaller world of the Indian government college, the organization of the educational service was undoubtedly a success. It brought to India men whose training and ideas converged with the ends of Indian college education: to train a class of Indians qualified to fill posts in the administration, courts, and colleges as civil servants, magistrates, and professors. For the most part, government college graduates filled such posts as their professors would have wished, with probity and professional competence.[76] Moreover, in the microcosm of the college, the dedication of the service's members to teaching was emulated by Indian officers. In the graded service, in the provincial service, and later as equals in the IES, Indians with the stature of Ramkrishna Gopal Bhandarkar and Ganganatha Jha in Sanskrit, Sir Jadu Nath Sarkar in history, and Sir J. C. Coyajee in economics joined Britishers at the colleges. After 1924 many less eminent men who were as dedicated carried on in the tradition of the IES in the expanded provincial cadres.[77] Despite status differences created by different service membership and the daily manifestation of those differences in separate commons rooms, private rooms for IES men, and annual dinners for superior service officers, a gentlemanly style helped make credible and worthy to Indians the academic values of Oxford and Cambridge graduates.[78]

But from the larger point of view, was the service structure the appropriate model for the organization of the academic profession in India? It is a question one would hardly ask about some of the other professions in India. The practice of medicine is, for example, so well established that, as Brass demonstrates in chapter 14, the practitioners and would-be practitioners of Ayurveda are seeking the same standing as practitioners of modern medicine by emulating the symbols, knowledge, and procedures of the modern profession.[79]

Medical knowledge, or knowledge in the field of engineering, is based upon a systematic and principled methodology which all the members of the profession must master before taking up their various specialties. All members of the profession therefore undergo the same preliminary training: doctors are required to learn the principles of physiology, bacteriology, and pharmacology; engineers, those of mechanics and other related sciences. The techniques of the two professions emerge logically from these bodies of knowledge, and can be applied in a variety of institutional situations: in a surgery or hospital, at a dam or canal site, in a professional or technical college, and even in an administrative office, assigning others to any one of these institutions and supervising the execution of their skills. The members of the medical and engineering services were obliged to serve in all these situations, and though there were distinctions of status among Britons and Indians, the professional competence of any member could be measured against easily ascertainable objective standards derived from the same bodies of knowledge. As such, the standards could be applied to other Indian professionals with the same training who were practicing outside the two services.

None of these characteristics holds for the academic profession. There is no systematic methodology for the art of teaching, and the members of the profession share no common body of knowledge. They come to the profession with diverse preparations, and according to the British system, with specialties taken up at the very beginning of their university careers. There are, in consequence, no easily agreed upon criteria by which to measure the standard of a professor's work. Today such criteria are emerging with the growing emphasis placed on disciplinary professionalism, on methods of research, and on contributions to knowledge; that is, on the demonstrations of intellectual and professional competence that professors demand of one another in order to determine their different capabilities and standing. These notions of professional competence were not widespread in nineteenth century India or Britain. In their absence, the service structure did not readily lend itself to the diffusion of standards of professional competence and achievement in Indian higher education. Indian professors were judged instead by the success of their students on the university examinations.

The service structure followed logically upon the decision to import professors. The initial decision grew out of Indian demands for increased western knowledge. In the 1820's, Rammohun Roy expressed the hopes of reform-minded Indians for English education: "We were filled with sanguine hopes that [a] sum would be laid out in employing European gentlemen of talent and education to instruct the natives of India in Mathematics, Natural Philosophy, Chemistry, Anatomy, and other useful sciences which the nations of Europe have carried to a degree of perfection that have raised them above the inhabitants of other parts of the world. . . . [We] looked forward with pleasing hope to the dawn of knowledge thus promised to the rising generation." [80] The British government eventually responded to the demands expressed by Roy. In time, pressures to form a service arose from the educators themselves. Teaching work in India committed professors to lifelong careers, as "Indian experience in educational matters had no value whatsoever in the English market." [81] The British authorities in India were therefore faced with the problem of drawing relatively young men out to the subcontinent and making an academic career in the government colleges seem attractive. At the suggestion of the director of public instruction in Bengal, the government of India formed the graded educational service in 1864, with its promises of adequate salaries — sometimes more than could have been expected for the equivalent work at home — guaranteed increments, and eventual promotions.

As succeeding public service commissions pointed out, the service retained a bureaucratic character for most of its life in India. Emphases were placed on incremental salaries, promotions, and advancement on the basis of seniority rather than on academic or scholarly achievement. Within the department, the positions of principals and professors were regarded as inferior. So long as inspectorships were included alongside principalships in the proportionately few superior grades and high allowance levels, professors' ambitions were likely to be diverted from teaching to administration. This tendency was enhanced by the emphasis civil servants gave to administrative rather than academic talents and by the series of rules that were legislated to foster administrative talents. Administrative experience and ability were usually the prerequisites for appointment as director of public instruction. The directorship was out of the question for Indians. They were also excluded during the period of the PES from all the education department's higher offices. British and Indian professors alike came to feel that their profession was not regarded by the authorities and by society at large as a worthy one. If educated Indians could, they chose careers in the administrative services or the law over those in the teaching profession.[82]

The association with government did lead to the creation of a modern academic profession and the possibility of an honorable and respected career. Under colonial rule, the government is an agent, and often the legitimator, of change in the traditional society. Those who want political, social, or intellectual reform often ally themselves with the colonial authorities or seek to move them toward policies of change. It was the citizens of Calcutta who prompted the British government to import professors in the 1820's. By spending the money to bring out graduates from the finer British universities, establishing them in superior colleges, and ultimately associating them with its own authority, the British government demonstrated at an early date that modern knowledge was difficult to obtain and its cultivation deserving of special treatment. The service was the example. With its image before them, graduates of Indian universities began to consider teaching in affiliated colleges a worthy career.[83]

The bureaucratic aspects of the service coincided with the situation of most Indian college professors. The majority of the professors in India (excluding the missionaries) were "in service" to the governing committees of particular private colleges. The security, both financial and otherwise, of a bureaucratic organization helped to enhance the value of an academic career in the eyes of these professors. The continued dependence upon bureaucratic rights and status within the university was also related to the genetic imprint of university founding in India[84] and to the style of scholarship brought out to India in the nineteenth century.

The educational service members' idea of scholarship centered, for the most part, on notions of cultivation of an individual's intellect and sensibility that found institutional expression in the life of the college. To sustain the idea and practice of scholarship required sustained personal contacts between members of the service and incipient and active Indian members of the academic profession. Universities did not provide such opportunities. Unlike British universities, Indian universities were not for some time allowed to support professorial chairs.[85] Nor were they empowered to promote joint intellectual or teaching programs among their affiliated colleges, even where the colleges were clustered together in a provincial capital or major district headquarters. Universities provided for only intermittent contacts among professors of different colleges. Such specific business purposes as drawing up a syllabus by a board of study, settling a question on an examination board, or perhaps fixing a new degree requirement at the annual gathering of the senate brought professors into contact, but little else did so. Because professors remained isolated in their colleges, the influence of government college professors was, for the most part, confined to their own educational communities.

Their success there has been emphasized. The places and prizes taken by government college students on university examination lists, and the later eminence attained by many of them as lawyers, doctors, civil servants, and scholars, all attest to the service professors' success. So too does the persistence of their colleges as institutions of relative academic excellence in independent India and Pakistan.

Another aspect of their success is more difficult to gauge. The Indian Civil Service brought British notions of law and justice, progress and constitutional government to India, but its members were distant figures whose contact with educated Indians was confined to the narrow orbit of official relations. Indians in government colleges experienced a different, less distant relationship with British values and practice in the close relations between government college professors and their pupils. To what extent did the professors' vivid and near representation of a new way of life create in the government college students a deep regard for courts, colleges, and parliaments? No precise answer can be given to such a question. That such modern institutions took root and flourished in India is in part due to the commitment of government college graduates and to the quality of their work. The professors who prepared them for their eventual responsibilities in administrative, professional, and political office added a layer to India's rich cultural heritage.

14 / The Politics of Ayurvedic Education: A Case Study of Revivalism and Modernization in India

Paul R. Brass

The movement to revive, restore, and develop Ayurveda, India's ancient system of medicine, a major revivalist movement in modern Indian history, has largely been ignored by contemporary social scientists.[1] Yet this movement has struck deep and permanent roots throughout the Indian subcontinent, led to a great development of educational institutions, governmental organizations, and professional interest groups, and acquired powerful political support throughout the political system. The Ayurvedic movement provides those interested in problems of political development in former colonial societies with an extremely interesting case of an attempt by a traditionalistic interest group[2] to legitimize itself and achieve recognition and status in a modernizing society through the establishment of educational institutions, through internal professionalization, and through government patronage. The Ayurvedic revival provides an example of the professionalization of an indigenous medical system which parallels the system of modern professional medicine and draws its inspiration from the particular traditions of ancient Indian science rather than from the cosmopolitan traditions of the world system of modern medical science.[3] The attempt to achieve legitimacy and recognition for Ayurvedic students and practitioners through professionalization has in turn raised for policy-makers a serious problem of establishing satisfactory educational and professional standards suited to the needs of modernization and development in a society where nationalist sentiment demands the revival and restoration of an ancient culture as a value for its own sake.

To formulate the problem in terms of the relationship between the political system and the educational system, the Ayurvedic movement may be seen as an educational interest group which has attempted to acquire

Research for this case study was carried out in India during 1966–67 with the assistance of grants provided by the American Institute of Indian Studies and the American Council of Learned Societies. It would be impossible to acknowledge the help of all those who gave me their time and provided me with the materials for this study. However, I cannot fail to acknowledge the extraordinary kindness shown to me by Dr. G. S. Pendse, Dr. C. Dwarkanath, Pandit Shiv Sharma, Mr. Tilak Ram Sharma, and Kaviraj Ashutosh Majumdar.

Lloyd and Susanne Rudolph provided invaluable assistance in the preparation and revision of this manuscript. Charles Leslie commented extensively on the entire manuscript and his very helpful criticisms have been taken into account during revision at several places in the text.

The subject discussed here is a controversial one, on which people who assisted me hold different viewpoints. The responsibility for the statements and opinions expressed in this chapter is entirely mine.

legitimacy and professional status through political methods. In this attempt, professionalization has been used partly as a mechanism to develop uniform standards considered desirable in themselves, but also very largely as a political instrument to create an organized body of practitioners able to apply political pressure upon the state and central governments to influence public policy relating to Ayurveda and simultaneously to counteract the influence of the organized modern medical profession, which has been viewed as an entrenched and hostile force. However, the attempts to achieve legitimacy have been hindered by the inability of the Ayurvedic institutions to attract students dedicated to the study of Ayurveda. The attempts to acquire professional status have been hindered by internal conflict within the Ayurvedic movement. In consequence, the advocates of Ayurvedic education have had to seek support among political leaders in the legislatures and in the state and central governments. Ultimately, the success of the movement has depended less on the proven value of the system of education provided in Ayurvedic institutions than upon the ability of prominent leaders in the movement to identify the goals of Ayurvedic education with a form of indigenous modernization adapted more to the needs and cultural values of India than to borrowed international standards. The consequence has been the creation of a large and entrenched educational establishment producing hundreds of graduates annually who are qualified neither in Ayurvedic nor in modern medicine but who demand the status and privileges of modern medical graduates. Thus, the Ayurvedic movement presents an unusual case of penetration of the political system by educational interests who have failed to establish a viable educational structure and who make use of the political system to maintain themselves.

The Nature and History of Ayurveda

The importance of Ayurveda as an ancient and well-developed medical system has been recognized by only a few western medical historians.[4] Until recently, western histories of the development of medical science have completely ignored the existence of Ayurveda.[5] Yet there is no doubt that Ayurveda as taught and practiced in ancient India was at least as well-developed as any other ancient system of medicine. At the same time, Ayurveda, like other ancient systems of medicine, belongs to a prescientific age in which scientific methods of analysis, investigation, and treatment were developed but were never completely freed from superstition, religion, and astrology.

The basic principles of the Ayurvedic system have no relation to most of the discoveries of modern medical science. For example, the Ayurvedic explanation of health and disease is based upon a humoral theory of constitutional balance and imbalance among various elements in the bodily system and does not accept the germ theory of disease. It also lays much greater stress upon the individuality of man, whereas modern medical discoveries have been made and applied on the assumption that most men have a great deal in common and that the same symptoms can usually be treated effectively in the same way.[6] Nevertheless, there is a widespread belief in India that Ayurvedic remedies are effective in the treatment of many bodily disorders, a belief which has been confirmed by modern medical practitioners in India who find certain Ayurvedic drugs useful in their practice.

In any discussion of the Ayurvedic revivalist movement, it is essential to distinguish between the traditional systems of Indian medicine still practiced in some areas of contemporary India and the ancient medical science revealed in the classic Sanskrit texts.[7] Attitudes of revivalist leaders toward contemporary traditional medicine are frequently ambivalent. As with all revivalist movements, part of the ideology of the Ayurvedic movement is that contemporary traditional practices reflect a long period of decadence. Contemporary practitioners may know some Ayurvedic remedies but they do not have a theoretical knowledge of the ancient science. Moreover, it is frequently noted that contemporary Ayurvedic physicians tend to treat their knowledge as private lore rather than as universal science to be made available for all. Consequently, while revivalist leaders have great respect for the truly competent traditional physicians,[8] for their abilities to heal and some of their methods of healing, and for the traditional guru-disciple (or pupilage) system of teaching, the primary orientation of the supporters of Ayurveda is toward the revival, restoration, and further development of the ancient science rather than to the maintenance of contemporary traditional practices. Although many of the leaders in the Ayurvedic movement have acquired their knowledge of Ayurveda by traditional methods (from a guru) and wish to maintain as much of the traditional method of teaching as possible, the primary thrust of the Ayurvedic movement over the last forty years has been toward the building of modern educational institutions for which the historical precedent is the classical system of university education in India as it is believed to have existed in the ancient universities of Nalanda and Taxila.[9]

Revivalist movements in modern South Asian history, which have usually been religious movements,[10] tend to share certain common features. There is first a recognition that contemporary traditional practices do not reflect the highest achievements of the ancient civilization. Second, there is the belief that the decline of indigenous culture, science, and religion is in great measure attributable to their suppression during long periods of foreign rule and the imposition of alien cultures. The third feature follows logically from the second; that is, the demand for state patronage from the new nationalist regimes for the restoration of indigenous values. The consequence of these attitudes is the development of a political orientation on the part of revivalist leaders, of a demand for governmental interference in areas from which most modern secular states have either tended to remove themselves or in which they have been prevented from imposing political criteria by the existence of independent interest and professional organizations.

These common features of revivalist movements are apparent in the Ayurvedic movement. All the proponents of Ayurveda in contemporary India share a belief — not unsupported by objective evidence — in the pristine excellence and scientific character of Ayurveda as revealed in the ancient classics of the science. It is noted that the ancient science was a complete system of medicine comprising eight branches of medical science, including surgery.[11] This great science, however, suffered with the general decline of ancient Indian civilization and the subsequent imposition of first Muslim, then British, rule. Two important consequences flowed from these developments. One was the gradual decline of Ayurveda, especially in the knowledge of surgery and other specialties, until only general practitioners were left.[12] The other was the introduction of alien medical systems — first the Muslim Unani system[13] and then, most importantly, the western system of medicine.

The controversy between Orientalists and Anglicists[14] in the early period of British rule affected British attitudes toward the remnants of the Ayurvedic tradition which they found in Bengal. In 1822, the School of Native Doctors was established in Calcutta in which both Ayurvedic and western medical subjects were taught. However, in 1835 the School was abolished and replaced by a modern medical college on the grounds that the basic principles of the two systems of medicine were incompatible and could not be combined.[15] It is worth noting that this decision was taken in the year of Macaulay's Minute on Education, which is a landmark in the ultimate victory of the Anglicists over the Orientalists in determining the pattern of higher education in India for the next century.[16]

From this period onward, the western medical system became firmly established in British India and asserted its supremacy at least in India's urban centers. The Ayurvedic system, however, continued to receive government patronage in some of the princely states, where either prominent *vaidyas* (Ayurvedic physicians) carried on instruction through the traditional guru-disciple system or, in some cases, Ayurvedic colleges were established.[17] The revivalist movement in British-ruled India asserted itself in 1907 with the establishment of a professional interest group of indigenous practitioners known as the All-India Ayurveda Mahasammelan (Ayurvedic Congress), which is still the leading organization of *vaidyas* in India. The revivalist movement first received political support in the Indian National Congress, which passed annual resolutions from 1920 onwards demanding government patronage for Ayurveda.[18] With the gradual development of representative institutions in the British-ruled provinces and the increasing entry of Indians into the executive councils and legislatures in the provinces, the provincial governments began to grant assistance to Sanskrit Mahavidyalayas imparting instruction in Ayurveda and to help in establishing new Ayurvedic educational institutions. In this period also, a number of state governments passed acts of legislation regulating indigenous practitioners and establishing government institutions for this purpose, usually known as boards of Indian medicine. Each of the provinces also had either branches of the Ayurvedic Congress or independent provincial organizations of the *vaidyas* and *hakims* (Unani physicians) to represent the needs and demands of the indigenous practitioners before the provincial governments. Thus, even before independence, the Ayurvedic movement had entrenched itself in the provincial political and educational systems. Before independence, there were already more than sixty recognized Ayurvedic colleges or Mahavidyalayas spread over the country.[19] In addition, boards of Indian medicine had already been established in Bombay, Madras, and West Bengal and one was about to be established in Uttar Pradesh.[20]

The leaders of the Ayurvedic movement viewed the achievement of independence as the dawn of their own emancipation and began to make increasingly vociferous demands for full-fledged support to Ayurveda on the part of both the central and state governments. The response of the central government was disheartening to many Ayurvedists. As in other areas of central government policy, the reaction of the central government was the appointment of a succession of committees, a process which has continued up to the present.[21] Initially, the central government was reluctant to grant significant support, but it was gradually won over by continued political pressure to a policy of granting support for research and postgraduate training in indigenous systems of medicine.[22] In July 1956, the Central Institute of Research in Indigenous Systems of Medicine and the Post-Graduate Training Centre for Ayurveda began functioning at Jamnagar in what is now Gujarat state. Similar institutions were established later at Banaras and Trivandrum. At the governmental level, an honorary adviser on indigenous systems of medicine was appointed in the ministry of health in 1956. Later, on the recommendation of the Udupa Committee,[23] a Central Council for Ayurvedic Research was established to promote scientific research on drugs and medicinal plants and literary research on the theories and principles of Ayurveda. In the planning commission, a panel on Ayurveda was established to recommend policies and programs to be included in the five-year plans. In the third plan, Rs. 9.3 crores in a total health plan of Rs. 341.9 crores were allocated for the development of indigenous systems of medicine, including Ayurveda, Unani, Siddha, Yoga, homeopathy, and nature cure.[24] The steps taken by the central government have, however, fallen far short of the hopes and expectations of many of the leading advocates of Ayurveda, who have demanded equality with, if not preeminence over, the modern medical system, the establishment of a central council of Ayurveda under the control of Ayurvedists to establish uniform educational and professional standards, and greatly increased allocations of funds for the development of Ayurveda.

In the states, the progress of Ayurveda has varied considerably. There has been a notable increase in the number of Ayurvedic colleges, which in 1964 numbered ninety-five in the country as a whole;[25] boards of Indian medicine have been established in most of the states; separate directors of Ayurveda have been established in a majority of the states; and in Rajasthan and Kerala there are separate ministries for Ayurveda. In addition, thousands of Ayurvedic and Unani dispensaries have been set up by state and local governments throughout the country. Nevertheless, the response of most of the state governments has not come up to the hopes of many Ayurvedic leaders. The proportion of the total medical budget devoted to Ayurveda has varied from less than 1 percent in West Bengal to more than 13 percent in Kerala.[26] In general, the states which have been devoting the greatest attention to Ayurveda are Rajasthan, Kerala, Uttar Pradesh, Punjab, and Gujarat; the least responsive state governments have been those in West Bengal, Madras, and Bihar. Although there is some correlation between a state's general modernity, progress in economic development, and spread of modern medicine and its response to Ayurveda, there is great variation even among the more modern and progressive states, not all of which have been unresponsive to Ayurveda (for example, Kerala, Gujarat, and Punjab), and among the less developed states, not all of which have been more receptive to Ayurveda (for example, Bihar, whose support for Ayurveda has been minimal). There are other important variables which account for these variations — the general strength of the revivalist tradition (which, for example, may account for the strong response to Ayurveda in Gujarat); the administrative performance and financial position of the state government (which accounts for the minimal support for Ayurveda in administratively weak Bihar); the success of the Ayurvedic movement in entrenching itself strongly in some states even before independence (as in Uttar Pradesh); and the existence of a strong and continuous Ayurvedic medical tradition and a large number of indigenous practitioners (as in Kerala or, outside India, in Ceylon). In short, there is no simple and immediate explanation for the strength or weakness of the Ayurvedic movement in each state, but rather, as in all things Indian, great regional variation. Nor is there any basis for the assumption that the gradual spread of modern medicine will inevitably supplant Ayurveda in each state. Modern medical administrators in the two most progressive states — Madras and Punjab — have asserted that the indigenous systems will have a permanent place in the provision of medical relief with or without state patronage.[27]

The consequences of three quarters of a century of efforts to revive and restore Ayurveda have been to create in the Indian subcontinent a dual system of institutions of medical education and medical relief and a dual administrative structure to administer them.[28] Table 68 summarizes some of the available data on medical institutions in India, both modern and Ayurvedic, showing the number of practitioners, colleges, annual student

Table 68. Comparative status of the modern and Ayurvedic systems of medicine in India.

Status indicators	Modern (No.)	Ayurvedic (No.)
Practitioners	108,240 [a]	116,865 [b]
Colleges	85 [c]	95 [d]
Annual admissions (students)	11,500 [c]	1,375 [e]
Hospitals and dispensaries	12,600 [e]	5,471 [b]
Rupees crores allocated for education, training and research in third plan [f]	56.3	9.8

[a] *Times of India*, June 13, 1967, citing survey conducted by the Institute of Applied Manpower Research.

[b] *Bulletin* of the Council of State Boards and Faculties of Indian Medicine, 1, no. 1 (December 1962), p. 34. The comparison between the numbers of modern and Ayurvedic practitioners is not an exact one since the Ayurvedic figure has been inflated by the inclusion of practitioners who have not been institutionally trained. The figure for institutionally trained Ayurvedic practitioners is probably closer to 30,000.

[c] Government of India, Planning Commission, *Annual Plan, 1966–67*, p. 79.

[d] Government of India, Ministry of Information, *India 1964* (Delhi, 1964), pp. 474–475.

[e] Government of India, Planning Commission, *Third Five Year Plan* (Delhi, 1961), p. 652. Although the number of Ayurvedic colleges is comparable to the number of modern medical colleges, there is a great discrepancy in the number of students admitted annually to the two types of institutions. The reason is that there is very wide variation in the size and facilities of the Ayurvedic colleges, which may be tiny Sanskrit colleges teaching the Ayurvedic *shastras* to seven or eight students or colleges of the integrated type serving several hundred students. In a tour of twenty-seven Ayurvedic institutions in India and Ceylon, Charles Leslie found that "many of them had no facilities other than a house, and that they had no students or very few students." Letter of March 13, 1968.

[f] Government of India, Planning Commission, *Third Five Year Plan* (Delhi, 1961), p. 651. The total health plan was 341.8 crores. In the figures listed above, other health plan expenditures (such as for water supply and sanitation, primary health units, control of communicable diseases, and family planning) have been excluded.

admissions, hospitals, and dispensaries. Although the state and central governments are more heavily committed to the modern system of medicine, the Ayurvedic system must be considered a fully entrenched component of the medical, educational, and administrative structure of the country.

Charles Leslie has pointed out that, although there are dual systems of professional medicine in India, there are also important connections between the two systems.[29] The most direct connection is through the dominant system of Ayurvedic institutional training itself, in which both Ayurvedic and modern medical subjects are taught. Second, practitioners of Ayurvedic medicine frequently use modern medicines and modern medical practitioners make use of some traditional remedies. Third, many fully qualified modern medical doctors and scientists are among the leading supporters of both research and training in Ayurveda.[30] Fourth, the sons and grandsons of many of the most prominent leaders of the Ayurvedic movement have become modern medical doctors.[31] Fifth, most people in India from villagers to sophisticated urban intellectuals do not make ideo-

logical distinctions between the two systems of medicine, but use which-
ever system is readily available and which they consider effective for their
ailments. Many people will use modern medicine for acute diseases and
Ayurvedic medicine for minor problems and chronic illnesses.[32] Moreover,
many Ayurvedic physicians claim that modern medical men refer to them
patients with diseases considered incurable or not subject to treatment by
modern medicine. Finally, it is important to keep in mind that both systems
are institutionalized forms of medicine, primarily urban and professional in
orientation, training, and practice.

The simultaneous existence in a poor developing country of two massive
systems of medical education and medical administration, developing side
by side in the urban areas, must give pause to those analysts of the process
of modernization who argue that all the developing countries are engaged
in a process of westernization or "acculturation" [33] toward a more or less
uniform set of goals. The history of the Ayurvedic movement presents an
example of a dual approach to the question of modernization in a society
engaged simultaneously in a process of technological development and cultural revivalism. This dual approach is reflected not merely in the ambivalent
attitudes of the modernizing elite but in the creation of dual structures giving institutional and bureaucratic form and expression to those ambivalent
attitudes and to opposing conceptions of the nature of the modernization
process as it applies to India. The ambivalence and duality of approach
toward Indian medical development are clearly demonstrated in the relations between the advocates of the two systems of medicine and in the
internal efforts of Ayurvedists to establish uniform educational and professional standards.

*Conflict over the National System of Medicine: The Struggle for
Government Support and for Equality with Modern Medicine*

Although the Ayurvedic movement succeeded in establishing a large
network of educational institutions throughout the subcontinent even before independence, it did not succeed in establishing uniform educational
and professional standards. The courses of training, the degrees awarded,
the professional opportunities available to graduates, and the methods of
practice followed by graduates varied from state to state and from institution to institution within the same state. Moreover, the modern medical
system occupied a clear position of superiority in government allocations,
in educational standards, and in the extent of professionalization.[34] In order
to change the balance between the two systems, after independence the
leaders of the Ayurvedic movement adopted the political strategy of demanding full state support for Ayurveda. One of the main tactics in this
political strategy was to identify Ayurveda with nationalism, national independence, and national aspirations. In other words, the strategy of the
Ayurvedic leaders was to confront the leadership of independent India with

political demands which had nothing to do with educational or scientific standards.

Specifically, immediately after independence the demand was made that the political emancipation of the country should be followed by the emancipation of Ayurveda through wholehearted government patronage and the declaration by the government that henceforth Ayurveda would be the national system of treatment. Those "allopaths" (practitioners of modern medicine)[35] who opposed this demand were asked, like the British, to "quit India." [36] Ayurveda was described as the Indian system of treatment and opposition to it was castigated as an insult to "the Indian people, the Indian culture, the Indian health and the *vaidyas* of the country." [37] The lack of response from the central government to Ayurvedic demands and the opposition of modern medical men brought forth comments such as this: "In face of the statements made by the Father of the Nation, our National Government is bent upon making us slaves of modern civilization resting on apparatuses, instruments, injections and inventions. Taking advantage of the stand which the Indian Government has taken, Dr. Chamanlal, President of the All India Medical Council exclaimed loudly at the Allahabad Session of the council, 'that large amounts of money were being wasted in starting Ayurvedic and Unani Colleges and Hospitals and in maintaining them.' Our advice to Dr. Chaman Lal [sic] is to leave our country and to proceed to England with the foreign pathy [sic] which he so dearly hugs to his bossom [sic]. We love that system of treatment which has been so near and dear to Mahatma Gandhi. We are out for that system of treatment which wants to keep us healthy independently of drugs and medicines. We shall accept only that system of treatment the promulgators of which ask the Government to turn out of the land those physicians and surgeons who aim at collecting and amassing money. There is now no place in the country for those medical practitioners who have squeezed crores of rupees out of the life blood of millions of our poor countrymen and have dignified themselves with Degrees and Knighthood." [38]

The extreme Ayurvedic argument, based on an appeal to nationalist sentiment, has had two important additional elements. First, it has been argued that Ayurveda is the only system of medicine suited to the habits, diet, and climate of the Indian people and that, perforce, the modern system is a foreign system not suited to Indians. Second, it has been argued that modern medicine, in any case, has failed to penetrate effectively the rural areas and is not likely to do so in the foreseeable future and that the vast bulk of the population still depends upon the indigenous systems of treatment. Therefore, it is argued, Ayurveda deserves full state patronage for both cultural and practical reasons.

The reply of the modern medical men has been that there can be no such thing as an Indian or a foreign system of treatment, that modern medicine is not tied to any culture, but is universal. It is also argued that India cannot hold on to a system of treatment which is out of date simply for sentimental and nationalistic reasons. Moreover, it is claimed that rural people are entitled to the same care as urban people and that they prefer modern medical treatment when they can get it. It is pointed out that most of the Ayurvedic practitioners make use — or misuse — of modern drugs and instruments themselves. It is argued, therefore, that modern medical relief of the highest standard should be extended as rapidly as possible throughout the countryside.

The arguments of the extreme proponents of pure Ayurveda and pure allopathy have so far not been based on a realistic assessment of the prospects of either system of medicine. Pure Ayurveda cannot possibly cope with the major public health needs of rural India — the control and cure of infectious and communicable diseases. Moreover, for the last forty years, the system of medical education in Ayurveda which has been predominant in most of the Ayurvedic colleges has been an integrated or mixed system,[39] in which both Ayurvedic and modern medical subjects are taught. Both the pure Ayurvedists and the pure allopaths agree that this system has produced practitioners of medicine unqualified in either system, making use of dangerous drugs of which they have inadequate knowledge.

On the other hand, the penetration of modern medicine into the countryside has been so slow that there is no real prospect of providing medical relief in the rural areas of India of a standard approaching that of the developed countries or of India's own urban centers for generations to come. The overwhelming proportion of medical colleges, hospitals, research institutes, and modern medical practitioners remain concentrated in India's urban centers. The latest survey of medical manpower in India reveals that nearly 68 percent of the total number of doctors in the country practice in urban areas. At the end of 1964, it was estimated that there were 108,737 doctors in India, which would mean 73,941 in the urban sector and 34,796 in the rural sector. Taking India's current total population at approximately 500 million with an 80 percent to 20 percent rural-urban ratio, one arrives at an approximate doctor-population ratio of 1 to 1350 for the urban areas and 1 to 11,500 for the rural areas. When one considers that, of the total of 108,737 doctors, only 57,571 hold M.B.B.S. degrees, the rest being Licentiates, and that the more qualified doctors are in private urban practice, then the true dimensions of the paucity of effective modern medical relief in the Indian countryside become apparent.[40]

The extension of modern medical relief to the countryside has so far made minimal progress, on the one hand because of the unwillingness of modern practitioners to live in the rural areas, which lack amenities and educational facilities for themselves and their families, and on the other hand, because of the unwillingness or inability of the state governments to provide sufficient incentives to make rural practice worthwhile. Spokesmen for the Ayurvedic movement frequently argue that Ayurveda is the traditional form of medical relief for the vast masses of rural India and note the failure of modern medicine to penetrate the countryside. In fact, how-ever, neither of the professionalized forms of medicine have spread widely in the rural areas, where people have to depend upon a diverse assortment of allopaths, *vaidyas, hakims,* homeopaths, "biochemists," practitioners of yoga and nature cure, witch doctors, and outright quacks.

Between the extreme positions of the proponents of pure Ayurveda and pure allopathy, there has been a middle position which advocates the de-velopment of a national system of medicine that would integrate and syn-thesize the best elements of both systems.[41] It has been argued by the sup-porters of the integrated system of Ayurvedic training and practice that some knowledge of modern medicine is necessary to supplement the gaps in Ayurveda and to make it possible for indigenous practitioners to provide effective medical relief in the rural areas. There have also been modern medical men who believe that modern medicine may be able to benefit from an absorption of those aspects of Ayurvedic treatment which have been proved effective through scientific and clinical research.

However, the obstacles to effective integration of the two systems of medicine have so far proved insurmountable. Given the fundamental dif-ferences in the basic principles of the two systems, it is not surprising that the first obstacle has been controversy over the terms on which integration should take place. The Chopra Committee de-emphasized the differences in the fundamentals of the two systems and argued for mutual cross-fertilization leading to an ultimate synthesis.[42] Many modern medical men, however, view integration as a process of absorbing into modern medical science whatever is of proven value in Ayurveda, which has meant in prac-tice simply that they are willing to make use of any Ayurvedic drugs which have been proved effective. On the other side, many supporters of Ayurveda have argued that Indian medicine should incorporate whatever is of proven value in modern medicine while maintaining its distinct char-acter and its fundamental theories.

Thus, the *Journal of Ayurveda* announced its support for a scheme of integration which "would preserve that unique characteristic of Indian Culture throughout the ages which has enabled it to go on assimilating the valuable and significant features of other cultures; while it has remained all the time fundamentally rooted in its own cultural excellences. It would build upon these [sic] most valuable and foundational knowledge of Pan-chabhuta, Tridosha and other theories which are basic and vital to Indian Medicine." [43] On the other hand, the report of the Mudaliar Committee argued as follows: "An integration of Modern Medicine and Ayurveda is eminently desirable and all steps toward achieving that end should be pro-moted. Such integration should result in the development of a system of medical knowledge and practice based on all the best that is available in Modern Medicine and in Ayurveda. To us the idea of a concurrent devel-opment and maintenance of different systems of medicine for all time is unacceptable. . . . A synthesis of the type that we envisage will . . . be through the incorporation in Modern Medicine of all that can be tested scientifically and proved to be useful in the Ayurvedic system." [44]

The government of India has been faced over the last two decades with two series of reports, published under its own auspices, that reflect different viewpoints. The Chopra and Udupa Committees have emphasized the desirability of ultimate integration and synthesis. The Bhore Committee Report of 1946 touched only briefly on the indigenous systems of medicine[45] and recommended the rapid extension of modern scientific medicine throughout the country. The Mudaliar Committee Report of 1961 proposed support for *shuddha* (pure) Ayurveda rather than the concurrent system of training, and recommended ultimate absorption of whatever was useful from Ayurveda into modern scientific medicine.

The central government has made substantive concessions on the recommendations of the Ayurvedic committee reports, but has adhered to the ideology of the reports prepared by the modern medical committees. The response of the central government to the Chopra Committee recommendations was almost wholly negative. The government of India felt that integration of the two systems of medicine was not possible because of the fundamental differences in their underlying principles, but said that research should be carried out to discover what is useful in the indigenous systems. The government declared unequivocally that "the Central and Provincial Governments should decide that modern scientific medicine should continue to be the basis for the development of the National Health Services in the country." [46] The central government has not so far departed from this stand, but it has gradually adopted a policy of supporting research and postgraduate training in Ayurveda and any attempts by Ayurvedists themselves to define and establish uniform educational and professional standards. A form of central government recognition was given to the indigenous systems of medicine even before the Chopra Committee report in a resolution passed by the First Health Ministers' Conference[47] in 1946 "that provision should be made for training and research in the indigenous systems and that practitioners of these systems should be utilized in State health programs." [48] The varied response of the state governments to this recommendation has been mentioned above. Although a few states have given considerable support to the indigenous systems, no state government has yet declared Ayurveda as the state system of medicine, nor has any effective integration anywhere taken place.

During the first two decades after independence, the central and state governments in India followed a policy of denying Ayurveda the status of the national system of medicine but encouraging and supporting scientific research relating to Ayurveda and providing employment to the graduates of the Ayurvedic colleges in the state health services in order to extend some form of medical relief to the countryside. However, it has been a major grievance of the Ayurvedic students and graduates that they have been employed only in inferior positions in the state health services at salaries far below those given to graduates of modern medical colleges. In consequence, the students in Ayurvedic colleges throughout India have engaged in strikes, agitations, and demonstrations during the last decade demanding equality in status and pay with the graduates of the modern medical colleges. Moreover, in their efforts to improve their life prospects, the Ayurvedic students have made demands which have threatened the viability of the entire structure of Ayurvedic education built up in India during the last forty years. One of the main methods used by student leaders to rectify the imbalance between themselves and the modern medical graduates has been to demand a condensed M.B.B.S. course after graduating from the Ayurvedic colleges. This demand has intensified the conflict with the modern medical profession and has forced policy-makers to reconsider the utility of maintaining the Ayurvedic colleges at all.

Student demands have played a decisive role in the development of attitudes and policies toward Ayurvedic education in recent years. In most states Ayurvedic graduates spend as much or nearly as much time in training as do modern medical graduates, but when they come out they are poorly paid and suffer from handicaps to their practice and insults to their prestige.[49] There is a widespread feeling, however, that the vast majority of the students are failures in secondary school who have not been able to gain admission to a modern medical school or to some other modern professional school and who have gone to the Ayurvedic colleges as a last resort.[50] The obvious inequalities in the status and pay of the Ayurvedic graduates compared to their modern medical counterparts have created the conditions for student demands. The inferior caliber of the students has created a justification for the rejection of their demands.

Student agitations have not been confined to the poorest institutions, but have affected even the best. By most accounts, the College of Integrated Medicine in Madras was the preeminent institution teaching indigenous medicine in India. Founded in 1925 as the Government School of Indian Medicine, it was converted into a College of Indian Medicine in 1947. Until 1955, the method of concurrent teaching was followed in the college in which roughly 60 percent of the course was Ayurvedic in content and 40 percent was modern. However, in 1955, under the instructions of a health minister unsympathetic to Ayurveda, the curriculum began to shift toward a greater emphasis on modern subjects until, by 1958, the curriculum was about 80 percent modern. Although the students were, therefore, taking a predominantly modern medical course, they were not offered the same status and pay in the Madras health services as the graduates of modern medical colleges. In 1959, the students of the college struck, demanding equality in status and pay with the M.B.B.S. graduates. The Madras government refused to concede the main demands, but offered the students the choice of giving up their integrated course and taking a wholly modern course leading to a D.M. & S. (Diploma in Medicine and Surgery) degree or going back to the college. It is reported that "every student without exception opted for the D.M. & S." The Madras government then acceded to the wishes of the students and converted the College of Integrated Medicine into a modern medical college.[51]

Student demands for equality with modern medical graduates or for the condensed M.B.B.S. course reflect not only a desire for increased emoluments, but also in many places a rejection of the Ayurvedic curriculum itself as it has been taught. For example, in February and March 1958 the students of the Lucknow Ayurvedic College in Uttar Pradesh struck on the same issues which arose in Madras. In addition to demands for equality in emoluments and conditions of practice after graduation, the students in Lucknow demanded fundamental changes in the curriculum — demanding that "the allopathic department [of the Lucknow Ayurvedic College] should be made as complete with material as is the Medical College" and "only such subjects from Ayurveda should be taught as are desired by the students." [52] The response of the Uttar Pradesh government to the student demands was, however, different from that of the Madras government. The Uttar Pradesh government responded to the strike by pointing out that the college had been founded for the purpose of promoting the study of Ayurveda; that the place of Ayurveda in the curriculum would, therefore, have to remain predominant; and that "no resolution . . . opposed to this basic policy would ever be acceptable." [53] Instead of closing down the college, the Uttar Pradesh government increased the emphasis on courses in Ayurveda. Over the years, concessions granting increases in status and pay were made. However, the Uttar Pradesh policy was ultimately no more successful than the Madras policy. In 1967 the students of the Lucknow Ayurvedic College again struck for the same demands. This time, the Uttar Pradesh government responded as the Madras government had done earlier and closed down the college. The college was, however, re-opened after intervention by a committee of citizens and student guardians on the undertaking that the students would end their agitation and resume their studies.[54]

The student strikes in Madras and Lucknow are but two examples of a widespread condition in the indigenous medical colleges throughout India. In the period 1958 through 1964, there were at least fifty-five strikes or other demonstrations in the indigenous medical institutions of India, affecting thirty-four Ayurvedic and four Unani institutions.[55] In a period of seven years, then, more than 40 percent of the indigenous medical institutions experienced incidents of student indiscipline. Forty-one of the fifty-five strikes were focused upon issues relating to student demands for equality with modern medical graduates, for employment, and for modernization and improvement of college facilities and curricula.[56] The most persistently repeated demand in these strikes was for equalization of the pay scales of indigenous medical graduates in government service with the pay scales of modern medical graduates. Other frequently recurring demands on the issue of equality were demands to upgrade or change the name of the degrees granted in the indigenous institutions from inferior diplomas or traditional-sounding degrees such as Ayurvedacharya to degrees bearing English titles similar to and equal in status with the M.B.B.S. degree; demands to permit indigenous medical graduates to be registered as medical practitioners and to practice modern medicine in their states; and demands for equal privileges in the Army Medical Corps.

The student strikes reflect a widespread sense of dissatisfaction among the Ayurvedic students throughout the country, involving in many cases a rejection of the more traditional Ayurvedic curriculum and a desire for more modern subjects and facilities. Interviews and discussions with Ayurvedic college students indicate, however, that the basic underlying issue for the students is less an ideological confrontation between modernity and tradition than a desire for economic opportunity and improvement in their life prospects.

The demand of the Ayurvedic students for equality in status and pay has met with partial success. Many state governments have created new medical positions for the Ayurvedic graduates and have increased their pay scales. In Gujarat, the pay scales of the modern and Ayurvedic graduates have been equalized. However, the demand for a condensed M.B.B.S. course has foundered on the opposition of the modern medical profession. The modern medical argument has been that this demand is nothing but an attempt by people who have failed to gain admission to modern medical colleges to get an M.B.B.S. degree through the back door.

The Medical Council of India, which regulates educational standards in the modern medical colleges, has insisted that Ayurvedic graduates must pass the entrance examinations and go through the full four-year course before they can take the M.B.B.S. degree. The only concession the Medical Council has been willing to make is to permit graduates of Ayurvedic colleges to take a condensed licentiate course in modern medicine provided that the Ayurvedic institutions from which the graduates come agree to terminate the integrated course. In other words, the Medical Council of India has offered a minor concession in return for a promise to abolish the integrated system of Ayurvedic education.

The stand of the Medical Council of India reflects a continued insistence on the part of many representatives of the modern medical profession on maintaining the purity and separateness of modern medicine. From this standpoint, modern medical men have found it possible to give support to pure Ayurveda but not to the integrated or concurrent system. The concurrent system of training represents a threat not only to the ideal standards of the modern medical profession, but also to the economic status of the modern medical graduates, since the integrated graduates frequently provide the same kind (if not quality) of treatment to their patients at lower fees.

Although the central and state governments continue to provide support and have made some concessions, the Ayurvedic movement has achieved neither its maximum demand for a declaration of Ayurveda as the national system of medicine, nor the more modest demand for equality in status and pay. In the meantime, the viability of the entire Ayurvedic educational structure has been thrown into doubt by the demands of the students for an M.B.B.S. degree.

Two questions arise logically out of the failure of the Ayurvedic movement to achieve its main demands: why have the demands been refused, given the existence of widespread sympathy for Ayurveda among the intellectual and political elite of the country; and why do the state and central governments continue to provide significant support to the system of Ayurvedic education and research without conceding the main demands? Part of the answer to the first question has already been given: the Ayurvedic movement has been unable to overcome the opposition of the relatively more powerful modern medical interest group. The failures of the Ayurvedic movement, however, are as much attributable to internal conflict within the movement on educational and professional goals as to external conflict with the modern medical profession. The answer to the second question is that, despite external opposition and internal conflict, the leaders of the Ayurvedic movement have gained the support of powerful political leaders and control over a segment of health administration in the states.

Conflict within the Ayurvedic Movement: Controversy over Uniform Educational and Professional Standards

It is universally recognized by leaders of all shades of opinion in the Ayurvedic movement that Ayurvedic education and practice can be placed on a sound footing only if uniform educational standards are established for the Ayurvedic institutions and professional standards are established for the graduates. However, the main obstacles to the achievement of uniform educational and professional standards have not come from the opposition of the modern medical men but from internal divisions among Ayurvedists themselves. Ayurvedists agree that educational standardization and professionalization are the instruments for achieving a viable modern structure of Ayurvedic education and practice. Profound disagreement exists on the content of the curriculum and, hence, on the qualifications necessary for professional status. These disagreements have been articulated by powerful interest organizations, whose leaders have sought to settle the issues through the political system by acquiring decisive political support and by establishing political structures which would impose uniformity on a divided movement. The result has been not uniformity but the transference of the divisions in the Ayurvedic movement into government itself.

Superficially, the conflict between the two wings of the Ayurvedic movement appears to be between those who favor modernization in the curriculum and those who favor reliance on ancient texts. Moreover, at times, the leaders of the two wings of the movement have been trapped into taking positions in which they do not fully believe. However, the basic conflict within the Ayurvedic movement is between two modernizing wings — one of which favors complete integration with modern medicine and the other of which favors permanent separation from modern medicine.

For the last forty years, the dominant form of Ayurvedic education has been the integrated or concurrent system; that is, a course of studies which includes both Ayurvedic and modern medical subjects in varying proportions, depending on the institution, the time, and the place. This course was designed to train students in the fundamental principles of Ayurveda while simultaneously providing them with a knowledge of modern medicine sufficient to enable them to play a role in public health activities. It is nearly universally recognized even within the Ayurvedic movement that this system of training has been a dismal failure which has produced practitioners qualified in neither system of medicine. The consequence has been the increasing strength in the last decade, under the leadership of the Ayurvedic Congress, of a movement to abolish the integrated system and replace it with a curriculum of *shuddha* Ayurvedic studies, in which modern medical subjects, if taught at all, will be taught only for comparative purposes. The supporters of the integrated system, rebuffed in their efforts at effective integration with the modern medical colleges and having a large vested interest in the network of integrated institutions and their products, have been forced to defend a system in which they do not fully believe. In addition, there is considerable difference of opinion among the supporters of the integrated system as to how much Ayurveda and how much modern medicine should be taught. Some people believe that the integrated colleges should teach primarily modern medicine, with Ayurvedic subjects as a supplement, whereas others feel that the reverse should be the case. The result is that there is great variation in the curriculum from institution to institution and frequent changes in the curricula of individual Ayurvedic colleges.

Since 1952, the divisions in the Ayurvedic movement at the national level have been expressed primarily through two interest organizations — the Ayurvedic Congress, led and dominated by Pandit Shiv Sharma, and the Council of State Boards and Faculties of Indian Systems of Medicine.[57] The Ayurvedic Congress was founded in 1907. The Council was founded in 1952 after a split in the Ayurvedic Congress. The Council immediately became a formidable rival to the older, parent organization. Whereas the Ayurvedic Congress is a voluntary interest organization of individual practitioners and of local, provincial Ayurvedic associations, the Council is a semi-official agency whose members include the heads of the Ayurvedic colleges, the members of the state faculties and boards of Indian medicine, and the directors of Ayurveda in the health administrations of the several states. The Ayurvedic Congress is the representative of the *shuddha* Ayurvedic school, whereas the Council represents the integrated viewpoint. It holds "that integrated education will enable a scientific approach to the study of the Ayurvedic and Unani systems paving the way for the much needed research, fill up the gaps left in the systems especially in the fields of surgery and obstetrics and enable these physicians to give the best of both the systems to the people according to the needs and exigencies of practice." [58] The viewpoint of the Congress is:

So far as the integrated system of education is concerned, it is absolutely unsuited to Ayurveda; it is not only unsuited, it is harmful as well. . . .
   The basic principles of Ayurveda and modern science are so very different that it is very difficult to integrate the necessary parts of one with those of the other, if not impossible. . . .
   It is the result of this propaganda in favor of an ill-advised integrated system that the learned men of Ayurveda were compelled to prefix the word "pure" before Ayurveda. . . . For students of Ayurveda, it is necessary that a course of study, which is basically of Ayurvedic subjects, should be prescribed. For this, it would be proper to present modern science only on the basic principles of Ayurveda.[59]

The conflict between these two interest organizations has been a major obstacle to the establishment of educational uniformity and professional standards. Although leaders of both interest groups have agreed that the primary need of Ayurvedic education and practice is the establishment of a central council of Indian medicine[60] which would regulate educational and professional standards for the indigenous systems of medicine in the same way that the Medical Council of India does for modern medicine, each has been fearful of the consequences if its rival should gain control of such a council. And although both interest groups would like to see professional standards established to eliminate widespread quackery from Ayurvedic practice, the standards of one group would disqualify the practitioners of the other.
   In 1955 the Central Council of Health recommended the appointment of a committee by the Government of India "to formulate a uniform policy in respect of the education and regulation of the practice of Vaidyas, Hakims and Homeopaths." [61] The committee, known as the Dave Committee, submitted its report in the following year. The report recommended the adoption of a uniform pattern of Ayurvedic education throughout India and prepared a model syllabus for an integrated course. To implement its recommendations and maintain control over educational standards, the Dave Committee further recommended the establishment of a central council of Ayurvedic and Unani systems of medicine.
   The report of the Dave Committee and its recommendations brought the internal controversy in the Ayurvedic movement to a head, for it was immediately apparent that the appointment of such a council with powers to regulate teaching in the Ayurvedic colleges would determine the issue

between the advocates of the *shuddha* and integrated systems of teaching. The recommendations of that committee were never implemented because of the existence of a stalemate in the Ayurvedic movement on this issue. In the meantime, conditions in the integrated colleges began to deteriorate and student unrest began to spread in the Ayurvedic colleges throughout the country.

In the years following the report of the Dave Committee, two circumstances combined to shift the emphasis of central government policy from the integrated system to the *shuddha* system. On the one hand, there was increasingly outspoken recognition that the integrated system had failed. Simultaneously, the advocates of *shuddha* Ayurveda recruited powerful political support in the central government, winning to their cause two powerful central ministers, Morarji Desai and Gulzarilal Nanda. As a result, the stalemate in the Ayurvedic movement reached the central government itself. The health minister, Dr. Sushila Nayar, and the honorary adviser in indigenous systems of medicine, Dr. Dwarkanath, supported the integrated cause. At the same time, Gulzarilal Nanda was made chairman of the panel on Ayurveda of the planning commission, and Pandit Shiv Sharma, president of the Ayurvedic Congress, was made honorary adviser on Ayurveda to the planning commission. In October 1962, at the Central Council of Health annual meeting, the advocates of *shuddha* Ayurveda won their first major concession. Under the leadership of Mohanlal Vyas, health minister of Gujarat state, the following resolution was passed: "In so far as the practice of Ayurveda is concerned, it should be developed, as the Planning Commission have urged, on purely Ayurvedic lines, involving deep and intense study of the Classical Ayurvedic literature including its materia medica and pharmacy. Subjects of Modern Medicine in any form or language should not be included in the course." [62] In response to this resolution, the health ministry appointed still another committee, under the chairmanship of Mohanlal Vyas, whose main term of reference was "to draw up a curriculum and syllabus of study in pure (unmixed) Ayurveda extending to over four years, which should not include any subject of modern medicine or allied sciences in any form or language." [63]

The report of the Vyas Committee is a document of exceptional interest to students of the modernization process in developing societies. Noting that the integrated system had failed to produce graduates with a deep knowledge of Ayurveda but had instead created further demands for allopathic training by the students themselves, the committee argued that this problem arose not only from defects in the system of integrated teaching, but also from the precollege training, which did not require sufficient knowledge of Sanskrit as a qualification for admission. In order to place Ayurvedic training on a proper footing, the committee recommended a course of pure Ayurvedic training with a good knowledge of Sanskrit as a prerequisite for admission. The committee was undismayed by the knowledge that there would be few students in the country with both the requisite knowledge of Sanskrit and the desire for pure Ayurvedic training. The committee declared that government support for the integrated system had "caused a famine of proficient Vaidyas in the country" and that the aim of the government should now be "to nurture and develop Ayurveda and to produce Vaidyas of high quality." [64]

The committee denied, however, the clear directive in its terms of reference that the course of pure Ayurvedic training should not include "any subject of modern medicine or allied sciences in any form or language." It declared that the pure Ayurvedic course should have "the benefit of equipment or the methods used by other systems of medicine," that "some knowledge of comparative medicine and, particularly, its fundamentals in their relationship to Ayurveda, must be made available to the students," and that, "in the study of anatomy the Ayurvedic coll[e]ges should continue the practice of employing the present day methods of dissection of dead bodies." [65] It also declared that it was not practical to revive the traditional guru-disciple or pupilage system of Ayurvedic teaching.

In justification of these recommendations, the committee presented practical reasons as well as arguments concerning the meaning of modernity and the meaning of science — arguments of considerable interest to students of modernization. On the practical side, it argued, as the proponents of integration have been arguing for the last forty years, that modern methods would have to replace ancient methods where the latter had fallen into disuse (as in the dissection of dead bodies). A practical, but sophistic, argument was also adduced that modern medical drugs often produce side-effects more serious than the diseases which they are supposed to cure and that the Ayurvedic practitioners must have sufficient knowledge of modern medicine to deal with such cases.

The committee felt that the terms "modernity" and "science" could not be the sole property of the western or allopathic system of medicine and that the latter two terms — western and allopathic — should preferably be used to describe modern scientific medicine. The committee denied the validity of chronological considerations and invoked the universality of scientific truth in defense of its argument: "If the chronological considerations are to decide the application of the terms 'modern' and 'ancient,' homeopathy is far more modern than Ayurveda and allopathy. And since, *consistent with its fundamental principles,* no system of medicine can ever be morally debarred from drawing upon any other branch of science, . . . unless one denies the universal nature of scientific truths, the word 'modern' too, cannot be reserved in the opinion of the Committee for any one medical science" (emphasis added).[66]

The italicized phrase in the above quotation holds the key to the meaning of modernity and science for the proponents of *shuddha* Ayurveda and, in fact, for many revivalists in the Ayurvedic movement as a whole. For the believers in Ayurveda, modernization means the adoption of the techniques of practice, the methods of teaching, and the means of organization of whatever system is most advanced. The pursuit of scientific truth means the maintenance of the fundamental principles and theories of the existing body of knowledge and the integration into it of any discoveries made by other systems which do not contradict those principles and theories.[67] Every western schoolboy has been taught that if science means anything at all it means the constant questioning and testing of fundamental principles and theories and that the history of science is replete with examples of the overthrow of theories which had been accepted for centuries. For the Ayurvedic revivalist, the last point is the most curious, for he cannot understand how westerners can have such unshakeable faith in a system which produces no constant truths. Ayurvedists who accept the metaphysical basis of Ayurveda argue that science is truth and truth is nothing if it is not eternal. Any theory of the modernization process which assumes that one of its end products must be the widespread acceptance of the premises of western science must confront the widespread acceptance of the premises of the Ayurvedic revivalists among the most modern of Indian intellectuals and among powerful policy makers in the state and central governments.

Ultimately, the government of India and the state health ministers accepted the recommendations of the Vyas Committee, if not its philosophy. A special meeting of the Central Council of Health held in New Delhi in April 1963 recommended the introduction of the *shuddha* Ayurvedic course into all Ayurvedic colleges in the academic year 1963–64. To supervise the implementation of the *shuddha* Ayurvedic curriculum, the Central Board of Shuddha Ayurvedic Education was established, composed of the members of the Vyas Committee.

There is little doubt that the acceptance by the government of India of the recommendations of the Vyas Committee amounted to a submission to political pressure. The policy which Dr. Nayar attempted to follow during her tenure in the health ministry was one of encouraging scientific research on the principles and practice of Ayurveda. Her closest advisers, including the honorary adviser on indigenous systems of medicine and the members of the Central Council of Ayurvedic Research, ultimately developed the view that the Ayurvedic colleges ought to be converted into modern medical colleges in which Ayurveda would be introduced at the end of a four-year course and in which the teaching of Ayurveda would be closely related to the results of contemporary research in indigenous medicine. From the point of view of a modern scientific outlook, this policy was unexceptionable.

Pandit Shiv Sharma and his associates succeeded, however, in convincing central government ministers far more powerful than Dr. Nayar that government policy was "killing Ayurveda in the name of Ayurveda." And, because student agitations were bringing matters to a head, the health ministry succumbed to the political pressure. The moves to abolish the integrated system of education and replace it with the *shuddha* system were actively encouraged by the modern medical profession. Thus, government policy toward *shuddha* Ayurveda was the result of successful interest group influence over educational policy formulation. The interests of the purist wing of a medical revivalist movement and the interests of the modern medical profession in controlling standards and eliminating potential professional rivals combined to determine government policy.

In India, however, it is often a long way from policy to practice. For one thing, it is clear from the report of the Vyas Committee analyzed above that the concept of *shuddha* Ayurveda does not exclude modern medicine entirely. Second, because health is a state subject, the recommendations of the Central Council of Health and of the central government are not binding upon the state governments. Third, there have been reports of student resistance to the *shuddha* curriculum in places where the integrated course had previously been taught and of low enrollments in new *shuddha* institutions.[68] Consequently, the decision of the central government has by no means settled the issues of Ayurvedic education and practice in India. Rather, it has widened the split in the movement and has encouraged further interest group conflict between the two wings of the Ayurvedic movement, thus making professionalization as impossible to achieve as a satisfactory educational policy.

Ayurvedists of both the pure and integrated schools share a desire for the establishment of standards and structures which will modernize and professionalize the practice of Ayurvedic medicine. There is universal agreement that standards must be established for the practice of Ayurveda, that the qualified practitioners should be registered by the state governments, that uniform national standards must be developed which would permit interstate registration, and that the practice of Ayurvedic medicine by unqualified and unregistered practitioners must at some point be ended. There is also general agreement that unethical practices such as the use of secret remedies, the tendency to advertise in the press promising cures for everything from the common cold to cancer, and the awarding of "half-baked professional degrees" must be stopped.[69] There is also agreement on the structures which must be established or strengthened at both the central and provincial governmental levels to achieve these ends — a central council of Ayurveda, separate directorates of Ayurveda and effective boards of Indian medicine in the states, and, most important, the control of these institutions by Ayurvedists themselves. It has been pointed out above that present difficulties of the Ayurvedic movement in establishing such structures and making them effective does not lie in the unsympathetic attitudes of the central and state governments, but in the failure of the Ayurvedists to agree amongst themselves on the goals to be pursued and the standards to be established.

This disagreement has intensified to such an extent that the organizations and institutions representing the two wings of the movement have been attempting to disqualify each other from professional standing. The viewpoint of the *shuddha* Ayurvedists toward the professional standing of the integrated graduates was stated clearly in the Vyas Committee report:

"the term 'qualified' or 'highly qualified' Vaidya does not include graduates of the mixed Ayurveda and allopathy the discontinuation of whose further production is the specific aim of the present syllabus." [70] From the integrated side, several measures have been taken to oppose the *shuddha* Ayurvedists. First, the Council of State Boards and Faculties has advised the state governments not to implement the recommendations of the Central Council of Health with regard to the *shuddha* Ayurvedic course. Second, the Council of State Boards and Faculties has demanded that a statutory central council of Indian medicine should be established which would be composed of "representatives of the University Faculties, Statutory Faculties, recognized educational institutions and Directorates of Indian Medicine" or, in other words, a central council which would be dominated by the supporters of the integrated wing and which would "put an end to all these controversies." [71] Third, several of the state boards of Indian medicine have attempted to withdraw recognition from institutions awarding *shuddha* Ayurvedic degrees. Most notably, recognition has been withdrawn by several state boards from the All-India Ayurveda Vidyapith, which is a private examining body of the Ayurvedic Congress and the preeminent institution in India awarding degrees in the *shuddha* Ayurvedic course.[72]

For the time being, therefore, the movement for professionalization of Ayurvedic education and practice has been subordinated to the internal controversy within the Ayurvedic movement over the standards to be adopted. The problems of professionalization of Ayurveda are greater than those faced by the modern medical practitioners, who have simply appealed to international standards and have imposed those standards upon the country, simultaneously resisting all efforts by politicians to provide for shorter requirements for medical degrees to meet the immediate need of the country for more rapid extension of medical relief to the countryside. Thus, the modern medical interest group has interposed itself between the politicians and the medical profession as an effective restraint upon political interference in the establishment of educational and professional standards. In this, they have followed the pattern established by medical associations in the U.S. and Great Britain. The movement for Ayurvedic professionalism has followed an entirely different course. Failing to agree amongst themselves on appropriate standards and torn by a bitter internal ideological controversy,[73] the Ayurvedic interest groups have entered the political arena directly in an effort to win political support for government imposition of professional standards.

Ayurvedists and the Political Process

The influence of the political system on the educational system in India in the sphere of Ayurvedic education has not been benign. Political interference in the establishment of Ayurvedic educational standards, however, has in no way represented an attempt by political leaders to establish political bases or political patronage in education. In Ayurvedic education, the penetration has been in precisely the opposite direction. Educational interests have attempted to penetrate the political system and establish spheres of influence in politics and sources of patronage for the maintenance or establishment of educational structures. This process of penetration has taken place at several levels of the political system and has involved political leaders who are not at all connected with Ayurvedic or any other form of education. Such involvement by noneducationists has been justified on two grounds — the need to provide medical relief to the people by means other than the modern system of medicine and the desirability of preserving an aspect of ancient culture in modern India. By their involvement on behalf of the advocates of *shuddha* Ayurveda, prominent political leaders provided decisive support against the entrenched structure of integrated Ayurvedic education and the policy of the central ministry of health. In the process, competing political forces and institutions have been brought into existence at every level of the political system. Ayurvedic interests have made use of the full spectrum of constitutional political methods — including interest group representation; infiltration into government institutions; the use of politicians to advocate their cause in government, parliament, and the state legislatures; and opposition to government officials who are viewed as opposing their cause. The Ayurvedic interest organizations publish journals containing political propaganda. They also hold annual conferences and foundation-laying ceremonies to which prominent politicians are invited. They present their causes through correspondence with official government institutions and through the sending of deputations to the ministers of health and the directors of Ayurveda. Prominent interest group leaders advise the ministry of health and the planning commission. Copies of important official correspondence and of public statements on issues concerning the Ayurvedic movement are sent to prominent political personalities and well-known political supporters of Ayurveda. Interest group leaders may also be appointed as members of government committees established to prepare reports on Ayurveda.

More important than mere representation, however, is control of government institutions dealing with Ayurveda. The Central Council of Ayurvedic Research (CCAR), for example, was formed on the recommendation of the Udupa Committee, which favored integration. The CCAR has been composed predominantly of supporters of the integrated school and has included modern medical scientists interested in carrying on scientific research on Indian medicinal plants. Control over the CCAR has meant control over the allocation of funds to research institutes. The CCAR has acted as an interest group supporting the integrated cause. A report of a subcommittee on Ayurvedic education of the CCAR gave its approval for continuation of the integrated system of training, with certain improvements.[74]

On the other hand, by achieving representation on the planning commission panel on Ayurveda and the support of Gulzarilal Nanda, the supporters of *shuddha* Ayurveda effectively neutralized the influence of the ministry of health and the CCAR. It was in the planning commission panel meetings of 1962 that the decision was taken to give government support for a course in *shuddha* Ayurveda. This decision was followed by the resolution of the Central Council of Health in 1963 supporting *shuddha* Ayurveda and by the appointment of the *Shuddha* Ayurvedic Education Board, with Mohanlal Vyas as chairman, Anant Tripathi Sharma, a former president of the Ayurvedic Congress as one of the members, and Pandit Shiv Sharma as member-secretary.

In the states, the principals and heads of the Ayurvedic colleges act as interest groups before state planning committees. Here the integrated colleges are clearly in a superior position, but a vigorous principal devoted to or converted to *shuddha* Ayurveda may succeed in receiving state support for a change in the curriculum. Such an attempt has been made, for example, by Pandit Krti Sharma, the brother of Shiv Sharma and the principal of the Punjab Government Ayurvedic College at Patiala.[75]

Another important arena of conflict between the *shuddha* and integrated Ayurvedists is the boards of Indian medicine in the states. These boards have two important powers — registration of *vaidyas* and recognition of institutions and degrees. Given the refusal of the two wings of the Ayurvedic movement to recognize the qualifications of each other's graduates, the power of registration is of considerable importance. The same is true of the power to recognize or refuse recognition to institutions and degrees. It was mentioned above that the Ayurveda Vidyapith, a *shuddha* Ayurvedic degree-granting body associated with the Ayurvedic Congress, has been engaged in a struggle with the boards of Indian medicine in several of the states, which have either refused to recognize or have withdrawn recognition from the degrees granted by the Vidyapith. Many of the boards conduct elections from an electorate composed of practicing *vaidyas*. The provincial *vaidya sammelans* (associations) contest these elections in an effort to gain control over the boards.[76]

The Ayurvedic interest groups also use the parliamentary and electoral arenas to present their case. In their confrontation with the health ministry, the leaders of the Ayurvedic Congress launched a "Dr. Sushila Nayar Hatao" (Get Rid of Dr. Sushila Nayar) campaign, which filled the pages of the Ayurvedic Congress journal month after month during 1966 and 1967. During the 1967 elections, the Ayurvedic Congress urged the *vaidyas* of the country to proceed to Jhansi, Dr. Nayar's constituency, to work for her defeat. A local *vaidya* ran against her with the support of the Ayurvedic Congress, but was defeated.

In the parliament, during the question periods and during the debates on the demands for grants by the health ministry, many members of parliament have supported the demands of Ayurvedic practitioners for increased pay and status and for increased allocations for indigenous medicine in the health plans. One of the past presidents of the Ayurvedic Congress has been a member of parliament since 1957 and has introduced into the Lok Sabha a bill for the establishment of an Ayurvedic medical council. Pandit Shiv Sharma was elected to the Lok Sabha in the 1967 elections with the support of the Rajmata of Gwalior and the Jan Sangh. The Jan Sangh election manifesto for 1967 included a statement demanding support for Ayurveda as the national system of medicine.[77] Other parties, including the Communists, have supported the demands of Ayurvedic students in the state assemblies.

Most important for the cause of *shuddha* Ayurveda, however, has been the support which the Ayurvedic Congress has won from some of the most powerful national leaders of the Congress party. The roster of prominent politicians who have actively supported the cause of *shuddha* Ayurveda includes Morarji Desai (former deputy prime minister of India), Gulzarilal Nanda (former home minister in the government of India), U. N. Dhebar (former president of the Indian National Congress), Mohanlal Vyas (former health minister of Gujarat state), Dinesh Singh (former minister for commerce in the government of India), and Dr. Sampurnanand (former chief minister of Uttar Pradesh and exgovernor of Rajasthan). For the most part, the support given by these political leaders has been based on noneducational criteria. Morarji Desai has based his support simply on his belief that in India "the cause of the people can be served better through Ayurveda than through any other system of medicine." [78] Other politicians have been outspoken in identifying the cause of Ayurveda with national sentiment. Mohanlal Vyas, for example, has declared, "Ayurveda is essentially a part of our ancient culture and our rich heritage. It is a way of life." [79] Dr. Sampurnanand went so far as to see the exclusive extension of modern medicine to the countryside as an evil to be combatted. He characterized the primary health unit scheme of the government of India which "visualises that the whole country will be covered by a network of . . . units which will invariably include a [modern] doctor" as a scheme for the "murder" of Ayurveda.[80]

Through the support of such prominent politicians, the supporters of *shuddha* Ayurveda neutralized the policies of the central health ministry and established alternative governmental structures of support. On the integrated side, lines of policy formulation and implementation between the health ministry and the integrated colleges and research institutes in the country were developed in which the key interests and institutions were the honorary adviser on indigenous systems of medicine in the ministry of health, the Central Council of Ayurvedic Research, the Council of State Boards and Faculties of Indian Medicine, and the two states of Uttar Pradesh and Maharashtra, where the integrated system has been dominant (see figure 3). This structure of influence and control supporting the cause of integration has been paralleled by an alternative structure in which there has been a similar pattern of cooperation among semi-governmental institutions and advisory bodies, interest groups, and state governments. This alternative structure of policy formulation received its main support in the central government from Morarji Desai and Gulzarilal Nanda and had its apex in the planning commission where a panel on Ayurveda was established in which Gulzarilal Nanda was the chairman for a time and Pandit Shiv Sharma was honorary adviser to the planning commission. The panel on Ayurveda became the instrument of the views of the Ayurvedic Congress, which achieved its strongest political support in the state of Gujarat. It was in consequence of decisions made by the planning commission panel, sanctioned by the Central Council of Health, that the Central Shuddha Ayurvedic Education Board was established.

How long this state of affairs will continue remains problematical. Given the nature of India's federal system, it is likely that both viewpoints in the Ayurvedic movement will continue to receive support for the indefinite future from different state governments. Political intervention has not solved the controversy, but has rather provided the institutional basis in government itself for a permanent division in the Ayurvedic movement.

Conclusion: Ayurvedic Education and Modernization in India

The politicization of Ayurvedic education has been caused very largely by the nature of the Ayurvedic movement itself. As a revivalist movement, it has tended from the beginning to be strongly oriented toward politics. Its spokesmen argued that alien rule led to the suppression of indigenous

Support for integrated medicine	Support for *shuddha* Ayurveda
Health Ministry	Morarji Desai – Gulzarilal Nanda
Honorary Adviser	Planning Commission (Panel on Ayurveda) Chairman: Gulzarilal Nanda Honorary Adviser: Pt. Shiv Sharma; Central Council of Health
Central Council of Ayurvedic Research	Central Board of Shuddha Ayurvedic Education
Council of State Boards and Faculties of Indian Medicine; National Medical Association	Ayurvedic Congress
Uttar Pradesh Maharashtra, and other states	Gujarat

Figure 3. Structure of support, integrated medicine and *shuddha* Ayurveda.

medical knowledge and practice and that the patronage of the national government was necessary for their revival. The leaders of the Ayurvedic movement adopted modern methods of organization and political strategy to achieve their ends, including interest group formation and internal professionalization. In a direct confrontation with Ayurvedic interests, the modern medical profession was able to maintain its preeminence because it was more firmly entrenched, more cohesively organized, and able to refer to international standards to support its predominance. In contrast, the Ayurvedic movement was weakened by the poor quality of its educational institutions, the inferior caliber of the students, and the failure of the movement to provide satisfactory economic opportunities for Ayurvedic graduates. The movement was also divided ideologically on the best means to revive the ancient knowledge while simultaneously engaging in modernization.

External opposition and internal divisions notwithstanding, however, the Ayurvedic movement has operated in a sympathetic political environment in which concrete achievements have not been necessary to win political support. The proponents of *shuddha* Ayurveda won the patronage of powerful political leaders and thereby brought about a change in government policy toward Ayurvedic education in India. This policy change involved the government of India in the political arbitration of an educational controversy. Ayurvedic educationists proved unable to evolve a viable educational structure and to formulate acceptable uniform educational and professional standards. Government was asked not to give educationists the statutory power to enforce standards generated by the educationists themselves, but to choose between competing standards. In making its choice, government was guided neither by educational criteria nor by criteria oriented toward satisfying the medical needs of the country. The decision to adopt a curriculum of *shuddha* Ayurvedic studies was ultimately related primarily to the political influence brought to bear on the key decision-makers.

The controversy concerning Ayurvedic education in India has implications which go beyond the specific question of the relationship between the educational and political systems in a developing society. The ability of the Ayurvedic movement to create a large educational establishment teaching an ancient system of medicine in a modernizing society and to win political support at the highest levels of government for its ends suggests some conclusions about the nature of the process of modernization in India.

The impact of colonialism upon a society with an ancient and glorious cultural tradition, particularly the efforts to modernize a traditional society under colonial auspices, produces on the one hand ambivalence toward the process of modernization among the westernized and on the other traditionalistic — or better "modernistic" — revivalism among those most devoted to the ancient culture. It has been argued that the ambivalent attitudes of modernizing elites in developing countries toward the process of modernization tend to produce ineffective political and administrative leadership.[81] At the same time, it is claimed that, however ineffective and slow, the process of modernization is irresistible in developing countries and that the modernization process is a process of acculturation to a world culture of science and technology.[82]

It has also become conventional to view the tensions facing developing societies as deriving from a fundamental dichotomy between a modernizing elite and traditional social forces. This dichotomous characterization of the development process does not pay sufficient attention to the importance of revivalist movements which are neither traditional nor modern in the conventional terminology, but are rather "traditionalistic," promoting and making use of traditional symbols and values while engaging in technological and organizational modernization. It is precisely this latter process which is taking place in the Ayurvedic movement and which has produced not a confrontation between a modernizing elite and a traditional elite but an internal conflict within the modernizing elite, reflecting different conceptions about the nature of the modernizing process.

The history of the Ayurvedic movement demonstrates that there are important interests in Indian society, supported by powerful political leaders, who, with considerable sophistication, reject the notion that modernization must mean westernization or acculturation to any other culture. There are two approaches to modernization in Indian society and politics —one emphasizing the introduction of the most advanced techniques of western science as well as the premises of that science and the other insisting that the techniques can be accepted but not the scientific or cultural premises. It is important to recognize that both these approaches favor modernization in technology, in the development of educational and professional standards, and in principles of organization. In other words, a process of dual modernization is taking place in Indian medical education and practice which is reflected in the creation of a dual political and administrative structure. This dual structure cannot be dismissed as a temporary and ephemeral phenomenon which will wither away as the modernization of India proceeds. Nor can the Ayurvedic half of it, at least, be easily viewed as moving in the direction of acculturation to a world medical culture.

There is ambivalence as well as duality in India's medical politics, however. This ambivalence has affected the proponents of integration more than other interests. With the pure Ayurvedists, the proponents of integration share the desire to revive India's ancient medical culture for its own sake, but they also believe that this must be done by the application of methods of modern scientific investigation to Ayurvedic principles, theories and remedies. They view the outcome of the application of such methods with an open, if anxious, mind. In principle at least and to some extent in practice, however, many supporters of integration have adopted the attitude, associated with modern scientific method, of willingness to question fundamental theories.

This ambivalence has also affected their attitudes toward the proper system of Ayurvedic education, with viewpoints among the integrationists ranging across a broad spectrum, from those who favor the abolition of the integrated colleges and the introduction of a few courses in Ayurveda into the modern medical colleges to those who come close to the pure Ayurvedic position in demanding a predominant emphasis on Ayurveda in the integrated curriculum. However ambivalent the integrationists may be, they also would reject the idea that they are engaged merely in a process of acculturation to a world medical culture. What they demand is an integrated system of medicine, drawing the best from both the western and Indian systems of medicine and oriented to specifically Indian climatic, dietetic, and health conditions. What they oppose is "blindly following and copying the methods followed by the United Kingdom and the United States of America." [83]

The development of such a national system of medicine has been prevented by both the *shuddha* Ayurvedists and the *shuddha* allopaths. The former have insisted upon the development of Ayurveda at all costs and the latter have insisted upon adherence to international professional standards at all costs. The cost to India's medical development has been the failure to provide effective medical relief to the rural areas. The maintenance of *shuddha* allopathy has predominantly benefited India's urban residents. The failure to develop adequate educational and professional standards in the Ayurvedic colleges has meant the production of thousands of new, poorly qualified practitioners, if not quacks, providing a low quality of medical relief to both urban and rural residents. Thus, dual modernization in India is a wasteful process which, in the medical sphere, has not provided effective medical development in the rural areas of the country. In the politics of medical education and development in India, the question of how to make the best use of the country's available medical resources to extend effective medical relief to the countryside has been subordinated to the demands for both modern professionalism and traditionalistic revivalism.

Notes

1. Studying Education and Politics

1. Edward Shils' "The Academic Profession in India," *Minerva,* vol. 7, no. 3 (Spring, 1969), appeared after chapters 1 and 2, which cover the same ground but with a rather different perspective, were first written. We have benefitted from this and other of Professor Shils' published work on higher education in India, and from the opportunity to discuss some of our work on the same subject with him and other members of the Committee for the Comparative Study of New Nations, University of Chicago.

2. See H. Sharp, *Selections from Educational Records, Part I, 1781–1839* (Calcutta, 1920) for Minute of February 2, 1835. For an account of the confrontation between orientalism and Macaulay's perspective, see David Kopf, *British Orientalism and the Bengal Renaissance* (California, 1969).

3. T. H. Marshall, *Class, Citizenship and Social Development* (New York, 1965), chap. 4. See also Ernest Barker, *The Development of Public Services in Western Europe 1660–1930* (Hamden, 1966), chap. 5; Brian Simon, *Studies in the History of Education* (London, 1960); and Richard Hofstadter and Wilson Smith, *Documentary History of Education in America* (Chicago, 1961).

4. Henri Taine, *Les Origines de la France Contemporaine, Le Regime Moderne* (Paris, 1894), pp. 184–186.

5. Ibid., pp. 156–160. See also Henry W. Ehrmann, *Politics in France* (Boston, 1968), pp. 65–74.

6. For the military dimension of educational policy in France and Germany in the nineteenth century, see Ernest Barker, *Public Services in Western Europe,* pp. 79–93. On civilizing and ruling the lower classes, see Robert Webb, *The British Working Class Reader (1790–1848)* (London, 1955). See also Reinhard Bendix, *Work and Authority; Ideologies of Management in the Course of Industrialization* (New York, 1956) for a somewhat different emphasis, one that stresses ideology but does not exclude education in explaining how industrial "masters" came to rule industrial workers. In Western Europe and the United States education, unlike ideology, was subject to state intervention and control. In Russia, particularly under Soviet rule, both education and ideology came under state supervision.

7. For a pioneering critique of the disembodied quality of the concepts of capital and labor and of their resultant failure to take account of education's contribution to production, see Theodore Schultz, *The Economic Value of Education* (New York, 1963); see also John Vaizey, *The Economics of Education* (London, 1962) for another early study. Two more recent empirically based studies of the economics of education in India analyze a variety of its dimensions; see H. N. Pandit, *Measurement of Cost Productivity and Efficiency of Education* (New Delhi, 1969) and Mark Blaug, Richard Layard,

and Maureen Woodhall, *The Causes of Graduate Unemployment in India* (London, 1969).

8. Of the forty-four countries with populations of five million or more which gave figures to the United Nations for publication in *Statistical Yearbook, 1967,* twenty spent most on defense and eighteen spent most on education. Of the twenty that spent most on defense, fourteen listed education as their second largest expenditure. See United Nations, *Statistical Yearbook, 1967* (Louvain, 1968).

9. Harold Gould's essay in this volume ("Educational Structures and Political Processes in Faizabad District, Uttar Pradesh") provides a probing analysis of the causes, processes, and consequences of politicization of intercolleges. Robert Gaudino has also distinguished the various uses of educational politics in a useful discussion. See his *The Indian University* (Bombay, 1965), p. 17. For the student dimension of these processes and relationships see Joseph DiBona, "Indiscipline and Student Leadership in an Indian University [Allahabad]" in S. M. Lipset, ed., *Student Politics* (New York, 1967), pp. 372–393. *Report of the Allahabad University Enquiry Committee* (Lucknow, 1953) also throws some light on Allahabad's situation and problems. Particularly revealing of community and kin factionalism within the university and of the university's link with extrauniversity political forces is Government of India, Ministry of Education, *Report of the Banaras Hindu University Enquiry* (Delhi, 1958). For some of the problems of politicization at Aligarh Muslim University, Uttar Pradesh, see Theodore P. Wright, Jr., "Muslim Education at the Crossroads: The Case of Aligarh," *Pacific Affairs* 39, nos. 1 and 2 (Spring–Summer, 1966), pp. 50–63.

There is similar evidence and analysis for Bihar, also a backward state with poor governmental performance. See Amar Kumar Singh, "The University and the Indian Society: The Case of Ranchi University," in Philip G. Altbach, ed., *Turmoil and Transition: Higher Education and Student Politics in India* (Bombay, 1968), where he observes that "for the politicians . . . the University is seen as a colony to be exploited in order to promote their political power" (p. 216) and "the private colleges in rural areas are important sources of political power and control" (p. 218). See also *Report of the University Enquiry Commission, Bihar, on the Working of Patna University, 1966* (Patna, 1966).

10. See Paul Brass, *Factional Politics in an Indian State; The Congress Party in Uttar Pradesh* (Berkeley, 1965), and "Uttar Pradesh" in Myron Weiner, ed., *State Politics in India* (Princeton, 1968).

11. For example, a dispute at Lucknow University over the morals of a dean who was expected to be advanced to vice-chancellor became the center of a Congress party factional struggle as the incipient vice-chancellor's friends in government and an exminister of an opposing faction mobilized faculty and students within the university (DiBona, "Indiscipline and Student Leadership," p. 375, and personal interviews with Lucknow faculty). Amar Kumar Singh analyzes the political dimensions of vice-chancellor appointments as well as the political pressures on and the political behavior of a particular vice-chancellor in "The Case of Ranchi," pp. 209–212. In the newly formed state of Haryana, a former director of public instruction and vice-chancellor (of Kurukshetra University), Hardwari Lal, used his educational connections and "dependents" as political resources in a meteoric career associated with

the extreme political instability that marked the first year (1966–67) of that state's political existence. Another Haryana "educationist," Sher Singh, used his Arya Samaj ("College section") and Jat connections to establish his leadership of the successful movement for a separate Haryana state (the Haryana Prant) and subsequently became a union minister of state for education.

Political pressures on vice-chancellors by parties, government, and organized interests; the political activity of teachers and students; the various dimensions of vice-chancellor selection, particularly nomination versus election; the parochial pressures associated with teacher recruitment and selection; and the political difficulties associated with student admissions are frankly discussed by the vice-chancellors themselves in Government of India, Ministry of Education, *Indian University Admission; Proceedings of the Vice-Chancellors' Conference on University Administration . . . from July 30 to August 1, 1957* (Delhi, 1958). See particularly chap. 3.

12. Joshi's successes at Punjab were followed, however, by notable failure at Banaras Hindu University.

2.   Historical Legacies: The Genetic Imprint in Education

1. For a discussion of the European universities at their founding, see Hastings Rashdell, *The Universities of Europe in the Middle Ages,* edited by S. N. Powicke and A. B. Enden, 3 vols. (London, 1936).

2. On the principle of making salient comparisons that fit into a framework of meaningful alternatives, we stress the non-plebiscitary European and American examples. We are mindful of the French, German, Russian, and Chinese alternatives.

For the impact of medieval constitutional growth ("feudal liberty") on the non-plebiscitary political development of certain European nations, preeminently Britain, see Guido de Ruggiero, *The History of European Liberalism* (Boston, 1959). For the definition of the concept "plebiscitary," the contrasting concept "non-plebiscitary" (that is, representation based on "independent" private associations, local authorities, and other bodies that "mediate" the relationship between central public authority and the subject or citizen), and the use of both concepts in the study of political development, see Reinhard Bendix, *Nation Building and Citizenship* (New York, 1964). J. L. Talmon makes a similar distinction when he contrasts "liberal" and "totalitarian" democracies (pp. 1–3) in his analysis of Jacobin and Babouvist plebiscitarism in France. See his *The Origins of Totalitarian Democracy* (New York, 1960).

3. Particular patterns of government have, of course, changed over the years. German universities today are ultimately governed by the education ministries of the several states. For an account of the evolution of the government of German universities see Helmut Schelsky, *Einsamkeit und Freiheit* (Hamburg, 1963). For a discussion of the weaknesses of university government by the federal states, see pp. 180–182.

4. See Richard Hofstadter and W. P. Metzger, *The Development of Academic Freedom in the United States* (New York, 1955).

5. The recent critiques of the government of Columbia University have rested on the ground that the faculty, to some extent by default, has taken

control of its own affairs less than in other institutions. Archibald Cox, et al., *Crisis at Columbia* (New York, 1968) (the Cox Commission report).

6. For an account of early private enterprise in education, see Syed Nurullah and J. P. Naik, *History of Education in India During the British Period* (Bombay, 1943), pp. 211–213.

7. "In the denominational era a great proportion of the schools in the U.S. that called themselves 'colleges' were in fact not colleges at all, but glorified high schools or academies." Hofstadter and Metzger, *Academic Freedom in the United States,* p. 224.

8. K. S. Vakil and S. Natarajan, *Education in India,* 3rd rev. ed. (Bombay, 1966), p. 69.

9. For Sir Edward's account of the founding meeting, see S. C. Chakravarti, ed., *The Father of Modern India (Commemoration Volume)* (Calcutta, 1935), p. 329, and Iqbal Singh, *Ram Mohan Roy* (Bombay, 1958), pp. 124–128. For references to the events of 1832, see B. T. McCully, *English Education and the Origins of Indian Nationalism* (New York, 1940), p. 22.

10. "Dispatch of the Court of Directors of the East India Company to the Governour General of India in Council" (no. 49, dated 19 July 1854), in J. A. Richey, *Selections From Educational Records,* pt. 2 (Calcutta, 1922; reprinted by offset, New Delhi, 1965), p. 378.

11. Government of India, Calcutta University Commission, 1917–19, *Report* (Calcutta, 1919), vol. 1, pp. 42, 62.

12. Vakil and Natarajan, *Education in India,* p. 73.

13. For the education of Christian gentlemen, see Rupert Wilkinson, *Gentlemanly Power* (London, 1964). The concern with gentlemanly character and style for India is primary in T. D. Macaulay's famous Minute. (See Wm. Theodore de Bary [ed.], *Sources of Indian Tradition* [New York, 1958], pp. 596–601 for a substantial selection.) But Lord Elphinstone, as governor at Bombay, had a more practical as well as "popular" orientation stressing mass and vernacular education. For a discussion, see Nurullah and Naik, *History of Education in India,* pp. 79–83.

14. Abraham Flexner, *Universities, American, English, German* (New York, 1930), pp. 231–232.

15. For a recent discussion of Humboldt's ideas, see Schelsky, *Einsamkeit und Freiheit,* especially pp. 66–70. Schelsky characterizes the university as devoted to "the development of all of man's potentialities to the high point of self-conscious individuality"; it aimed at "education through *wissenschaft* (learning; science)"; it hoped to institutionalize the spirit of investigation (p. 67).

16. Sir Asutosh was vice-chancellor from 1906 until 1914, and again from 1921 to 1923. He effected most of the postgraduate reforms, however, from his position on the senate in the intervening years. John H. Broomfield, *Elite Conflict in a Plural Society: 20th Century Bengal* (California, 1968), pp. 191–192. See also Irene Gilbert, "Autonomy and Consensus under the Raj: Presidency (Calcutta); Muir (Allahabad); M.A.-O. (Aligarh)," chap. 10, this volume.

17. R. D. Mangles, commenting on the draft dispatch before the Court of Directors, cited in Eric Ashby (in association with Mary Anderson), *Universities: British, Indian, African: A Study in the Ecology of Higher Education* (London, 1966), p. 60, fn. 38.

18. Ashby, *Universities*, p. 62.

19. Ibid., p. 140; B. B. Misra, *The Indian Middle Classes* (London, 1961). Before the 1904 reform there were 181 senators, the majority of whom were elected; after it, there were 84, of whom only 20 were elected. Of the 84 senators (fellows of the senate) 43 were Indian and 41 "European." See chart on p. 287 of Misra, *Indian Middle Classes*.

20. Ashby, *Universities*, p. 140. The government of Bengal did not soften the reality of government influence by conventions of self-restraint. In March 1923 Lord Lytton as governor of Bengal wrote a letter warning Sir Asutosh Mukherji, who was running up William Raney Harper-style deficits for postgraduate education in the face of government efforts at retrenchment, that he would not reappoint the vice-chancellor unless his opposition to government policy ceased. Broomfield, *Elite Conflict*, p. 194.

21. Lord Curzon, writing in "Minutes by H. E. Viceroy on University Reform," 23 February 1901. Cited in Ashby, *Universities*, p. 389.

22. "The chief merit of the Universities is that their constitution is leavened by a large admixture of the popular element composed not merely of Indians but Anglo-Indians as well, which serve to soften the severity of action of the official element, so that in the end the course of action generally taken is the right middle course lined between the extremes of leniency and stringency. This is the reason why the public in this country are so anxious to have the jurisdiction of the Universities extended instead of being curtailed." Sir Gooroo Das Banerjee, *The Educational Problem in India*, p. 39, cited in Calcutta University Commission, *Report*, vol. 1, p. 313.

23. Broomfield notes that "educational politics, particularly the politics of Calcutta University, assumed extraordinary importance for the *bhadralok* (gentry) as one of the few avenues of constructive public endeavor open to them in their circumscribed colonial society" (*Elite Conflict*, p. 8). The Calcutta University Commission cited Sir Gooroo Das Banerjee's assertion that "the universities are composed of Indian and European members who have coordinate authority, while in the Government Education Department Indian members occupy only a subordinate position, so that the control exercised by the university is likely to be better adapted to Indian conditions and to be more regardful of Indian requirements than the control of the Education Department." *The Educational Problem in India*, p. 39, cited in Calcutta University Commission, *Report*, vol. 1, pp. 312–313.

24. For development of this view, see Irene Gilbert, chap. 10, this volume. It is perhaps a fault in Sir Eric Ashby's account of Indian educational policy that he does not credit the political nature of Curzon's work. This leads to a certain inconsistency in Sir Eric's valuation, as when he damns the government's failure to exert itself sufficiently in the University of Calcutta (*Universities*, p. 70) but eventually comes to the conclusion that government intervened too much. Broomfield notes that the government of India decided to "teach the 'traditionists' by refusing to confirm the appointment of three men, Abdul Rasul, Dr. Abdulla-al-Mamud Suhrawardy, and K. P. Jayaswal, who had already taken up their posts at the University of Calcutta with the government of Bengal's sanctions. The government of India refused to confirm their appointments on the ground that they had been active in politics and could not be trusted to refrain from expressing anti-British sentiment. The government

had also issued orders aimed at the tightening of official control over schools and colleges in Bengal." Broomfield, *Elite Conflict,* p. 78.

25.   Flexner points out that the conservatism of German universities was to an extent balanced and corrected by government direction. He also suggests that many important academic appointments in Germany were consummated at the initiative of government rather than at the initiative of unimaginative faculty. Flexner, *Universities,* pp. 321–324. For a striking contrast in the role of government with respect to universities in Germany, see *Die Deutsche Universität im dritten Reich, eine Vortragsreihe der Universität München,* unedited collection (Munich, 1966) and Free University of Berlin, *Universitätstage, Nationalsozialismus und die Deutsche Universität* (Berlin, 1966), both collections of essays. An early study along the same lines is the book by Edward Yarnall Hartshorne, Jr., *The German Universities and National Socialism* (London, 1937). For student enforcement of their definition of the public interest, see for example the demand at Kiel by Nazi students that twenty-eight professors be dismissed, and their subsequent attack on three of them, Professors Gerhard Husserl, Kolm, and Rudolf Höber (Hartshorne, *German Universities,* pp. 55–56).

For an analysis of how the ground was prepared for National Socialist penetration and appropriation of German universities, see Fritz Ringer, *The Decline of the German Mandarins; The German Academic Community, 1890–1933* (Cambridge, 1969). For an earlier effort of a similar although more philosophical kind, see Frederic Lilge, *The Abuse of Learning; the Failure of the German University* (New York, 1948).

The controversy between Governor Ronald Reagan and presidents of University of California Clark Kerr and Charles J. Hitch over whether or not the university should charge tuition for "resident" students provides a less dramatic but undoubtedly significant example of a struggle between those within and those without the university to control educational policy and resources. Such a struggle makes evident the extraordinary difficulty of defining the meaning of university autonomy and of identifying the public interest in education. By January 1970, Governor Reagan had succeeded through a series of appointments to the Board of Regents in overcoming that body's opposition to his pro-tuition policy. Because of this shift in the composition of the Regents and because of Reagan-induced budget cuts that brought the university's building program "to a halt" and jeopardized student financial aid and services, President Hitch found himself in a situation which compelled him to take a step he was "very reluctant to take" — in effect to charge tuition for resident students (and to raise substantially the tuition for out-of-state students). *New York Times,* 14 January 1970, and *California Journal,* January 1970, p. 9.

26.   The recommendations of the Gajendragadkar Committee, which investigated the breakdown of order and authority in 1968–69 at Banaras Hindu University (B.H.U.) under Vice-Chancellor J. C. Joshi, included filling not only top administrative posts but also the membership of the various governing and academic bodies by nominations. The implication was clear; B.H.U. had lost its capacity to govern itself. See Government of India, Ministry of Education, *Report of the Banaras Hindu University Inquiry Committee* (Gajendragadkar Committee) (New Delhi, 1969). See particularly pp. 74–82, which detail the degree to which the university had become subject to influence of

contending student factions with connections to organized partisan political interests.

Because B.H.U. is a centrally administered rather than a state-administered university, the nominating authority is the government of India rather than the government of Uttar Pradesh. If the latter had been put in the position of "saving" B.H.U. it is not at all clear that the remedy would have been better than the disease. It is doubtful that even under the direct influence of the government of India (via its nominating party) B.H.U. can be sufficiently freed from the discouraging effects of its eastern Uttar Pradesh environment and its use as an arena for ideological and political partisan struggles.

The response of the United States government to the controversy in the late 1960's over whether or not it or state governments (or both) should assert their legal and administrative authority to reach into campuses in response to student campus protests and disorders seems to point in the opposite direction from the recommendations of the Gajendragadkar Committee. Secretary Robert Finch (Department of Health, Education and Welfare) and President Richard Nixon have held (in the president's words) that the federal government must avoid interference in the "internal affairs of our colleges and universities . . . I am gravely concerned, of course, about the problems of student unrest. At the same time, I have recognized that the enforcement of discipline and maintenance of order . . . is primarily the responsibility of the schools themselves. The Federal Government is ill-fitted to play the role of policeman on our college and university campuses." *New York Times,* 30 December 1969. Some congressmen and state legislatures have taken the opposite view by requiring the withdrawal of financial support to students involved in disorders, often without a requirement of due process (see, for example, Section 706 of a bill appropriating $2.4 billion for the Departments of State, Justice, and Commerce for the fiscal year 1970) and by authorizing police intervention on campuses and providing resources (additional police) to do so. The Nixon administration's cooperation via the Justice Department's Law Enforcement Assistance Division (funded under the omnibus Crime Control and Safe Streets Act of 1968 and intended to provide economic and technical assistance to local and state law enforcement agencies) in breaking the back of a successful student boycott at all-black Mississippi Valley State College may have signaled a change of policy toward campus disorders. *Chicago Sun-Times,* 19 February 1970.

27. This characterization of Mouat's scheme is from Ashby, *Universities,* p. 54.

28. See below, chap. 3, especially note 30.

29. Lee Warner, director of public instruction in the Bombay government, described the Deccan Education Society and the College as follows: "The College wishes to be largely independent of any European elements in its lecture rooms, and to impress upon its students the patriotic sentiments of its independent founders." Cited in E. M. Limaye, compiler, *The History of the Deccan Education Society* (Poona, 1935), p. 52.

30. Madho Prasad, *A Gandhian Patriarch: A Political and Spiritual Biography of Kaka Kalelkar* (Bombay, 1965), pp. 83–84.

31. S. S. Dikshit, *Nationalism and Indian Education* (Delhi, 1966), p. 145.

32. Kashi Vidyapith was started in connection with the civil resistance

movement of the early 1920's, with a generous donation from that philanthropist politician, Shri Shiva Prasad Gupta. Sampurnanand, *Memories and Reflections* (New York, 1964), p. 23.

33. Ibid., p. 38.

34. The Gandhian doctrine of "constructive work" (including education) that legitimized educational entrepreneurship before independence remains strong in the Congress party to this day. "For both the 1957 and 1962 general elections," Ramashray Roy writes, "the Central Election Committee (CEC) issued to the Pradesh Congress Committees (PCC's) circulars which discussed in detail the principles which were to govern the selection of candidates." In addition to being a primary member of two years' standing, a prospective candidate's "past record of service in the areas of constructive work and legislative bodies" were among the most important criteria. The CEC stressed that "the field of constructive work . . . not be interpreted in a rigid narrow sense" and specifically mentioned education as an area that fell within this ambit. Ramashray Roy, *Election Studies: Selection of Congress Candidates* (Bombay, 1967); reprinted from the *Economic and Political Weekly,* 31 December 1966; 7, 14 January and 11, 18 February 1967, pp. 5 and 7; quoted from "Note on Constructive Work" in All-India Congress Committee, *Proceedings of the Meetings of the President and Secretaries of the Pradesh Congress Committees, March 30 to 31, and April 1, 1957* (New Delhi, 1957), appendix 7.

35. For Gould's analysis, see chap. 7. Carolyn Elliott finds that our and Gould's contrast of the ideal goals that characterize foundings and management in the nationalist period with the interested character of such activity after independence is too sharply drawn because it underestimates the admixture of interest and ideology associated with nationalist educational activity in the preindependence period. Personal communication.

36. For a general account of caste associations which considers their educational role, see our *The Modernity of Tradition: Political Development in India* (Chicago, 1967), pt. 1. The role of Brahman, Vaishya, Kayasth, Rajput, Jat, and Ahir foundings is illustrated by the caste colleges of Punjab and Agra universities cited below. The Nair Service Society was founded in 1914 mainly with a view to starting high schools that would allow the community to compete with Syrian Christians whose schools and colleges were giving them social and economic advantages. V. K. S. Nair, "Communal Interest Groups in Kerala," in Donald E. Smith, ed., *South Asian Politics and Religion* (Princeton, 1966), p. 177. Nadar educational activities are discussed by Robert L. Hardgrave, *The Nadars of Tamilnad; The Political Culture of a Community in Change* (Berkeley, 1969), pp. 145–147. The first Nadar college was founded in 1947, and since then the community has established two additional colleges, including one for women, and founded a polytechnic. SNDP, the community organization of the caste, founded Ezhava colleges in the University of Kerala. Dr. B. R. Ambedkar, leader of the Mahars and many other untouchables, founded Siddharta College in 1946; the Mahars founded Milind College in 1951. Eleanore Zelliott, "The Revival of Buddhism in India," *Asia,* 10 (Winter 1968), p. 4. The role of Lingayats and other castes is illustrated in the article by T. N. Madan and B. G. Halbar, below.

37. For a discussion of the origins of these institutions, see Lala Lajpat Rai, *The Arya Samaj* (Lahore, 1932).

38. The DAV School, dedicated to teaching both English and classical Hindu learning, opened on 1 June 1886. In 1888, intermediate classes were opened. See Sri Ram Sharma, *Mahatma Hans Raj, Maker of the Modern Punjab* (Lahore, 1941), pp. 45–56, for an account of the founding. The *gurukula* at Hardwar was founded in 1902. See also Prakash Tandon, *Punjabi Century* (London, 1961).

39. See Charles Heimsath, *Indian Nationalism and Hindu Social Reform* (Princeton, 1964), pp. 296–297 and notes.

40. The Sanathana Dharma Sabha, growing out of the circles surrounding Pandit Din Dayal Sarma, which vigorously attacked the Arya Samaj, was founded in 1895 in Delhi and at Hardwar. Ibid., p. 318.

41. See Irene Gilbert, chap. 10 below. M.A.-O. College was not the only outgrowth of Muslim community efforts. Delhi College (now in Delhi University), founded in 1824, grew out of the Madrasah Ghaziyuddīn (a traditional teaching institution), and gave a secular education to Muslims. M. Mujeeb, *The Indian Muslim* (London, 1967), p. 519. Dar-ul 'Ulūm of De'oband (a movement of Muslim orthodoxy) which developed during the ten years after the mutiny, vigorously resisted English and western culture. Ibid., p. 409, and Zuya-ul Faruqi, *The Deoband School and the Demand for Pakistan* (Bombay, 1963).

42. There were approximately 2500 colleges in 1965–66. There were 129 Christian colleges in 1967. Richard and Nancy Dickinson, *Directory of Information for Christian Colleges in India* (Madras, 1967), p. 129. A reputation for academic excellence and constitutional protection has preserved their importance in the postindependence period.

43. Our account is taken from Government of India, University Grants Commission, *Handbook of Universities in India, 1963* (New Delhi, 1964). We have determined the sectarian or caste community affiliation of management by inspecting the names of the colleges, a somewhat rough and ready method that undoubtedly understates the number of institutions that have such affiliations.

44. For an analysis of the most important example of how this problem has troubled Indian political life and of the terms of its "resolution" circa 1959 see John C. English, "Federalism and the Kerala Education Act (1958)." Seminar paper for Political Science 398, Modern Indian Politics: The New Federalism, Fall Quarter, 1969, The University of Chicago.

3. The Public Interest and Politicization under Conditions of Popular Higher Education

1. See Government of India, Ministry of Education, *Report of the Education Commission, 1964–1966* (Delhi, 1966) (hereafter cited as *Education Commission*), appendix 1, table 9, p. 590, for 1950–51 enrollments. For 1967–68, see Government of India, University Grants Commission, *University Development in India, Basic Facts and Figures, 1967–68* (New Delhi, 1971), table, p. 6. Our totals include preuniversity and intermediate students, who numbered 221,000 in 1950–51 and 829,078 in 1966–67.

Some sense of the Indian rate of growth is provided by comparing it with developments in Britain and the United States. In Britain during the last prewar year (1938–39), 69,000 students were enrolled full time in higher educational institutions. In 1962–63, the year of the Robbins Report on higher education, there were 216,000 enrolled, an increase of 213 percent. Great Britain, Committee on Higher Education, *Higher Education, Report of the Committee Appointed by the Prime Minister under the Chairmanship of Lord Robbins, 1961/63* (Cmnd. 2154, London, 1963) (hereafter cited as *Robbins Report*), table 3, p. 15. In the United States, the number of students enrolled in higher educational institutions increased from almost 2.7 million in 1950 to 5.5 million in 1965, an increase of approximately 100 percent. U.S., Department of Commerce, Bureau of the Census, *Statistical Abstract of the United States,* 88th ed., table 147, p. 109.

The problem of comparisons in educational statistics is a thorny one and perhaps a few qualifying observations are in order. Who should be counted an enrolled student in higher educational institutions? The exclusion of PUC (Pre-University Course) and intermediate students makes sense if the problem is to compare students at comparable academic levels. They are, in fact, students in classes XI and XII, what the Education Commission, 1964–1966, refers to as the higher secondary stage. *Education Commission,* para. 2.20, p. 32. It recommended that all such courses be transferred from the universities and colleges to the schools. *Education Commission,* p. 32. For the variations among the states and union territories with respect to the location of classes XI and XII in relationship to PUC and intermediate courses see bar graphs on pp. 26 and 27, and for a general discussion of the background and nature of the problem, see *Education Commission,* pp. 23–38.

"In international comparison," the commission writes, "it would be wrong to compare our first degrees in arts, commerce or science with the corresponding first degrees of educationally advanced countries. What is really comparable is our second degrees in arts, commerce and science and first degrees in agriculture, engineering and medicine with the first degrees given by universities in the educationally advanced countries." *Education Commission,* p. 302. At the same time, it is also true that as of 1967–68, 37 percent (829,078 of 2.2 million) of the students in institutions classified in the category of higher education were enrolled in PUC and intermediate courses. UGC, *University Development in India, 1967–68,* p. 6. Judged from the perspectives of educational and political sociology rather than that of internationally comparable educational standards, this characteristic of the Indian educational system is of prime significance. Almost all of these students are under the jurisdiction of universities and affiliated colleges and are their responsibilities.

The Uttar Pradesh "Inter-College" is something of an exception. The intermediate colleges of Uttar Pradesh are supervised by the Board of High School and Intermediate Examinations. *Education Commission,* p. 32. In 1967–68 intermediate college enrollment, which is almost entirely located in Uttar Pradesh's inter-colleges, totalled 300,000. UGC, *University Development in India, 1966–67,* appendix 3, p. 270. Uttar Pradesh intermediate students constitute about 30 percent of the 37 percent among students enrolled in universities and colleges who are in pre-degree programs. With the possible exception of the Uttar Pradesh Inter-College, we conclude that classes XI and XII are likely to continue to be sociologically and politically, if not educationally, part of higher education in India.

2. For the count through 1970 see Inter University Board of India and Ceylon, *Universities Handbook; India and Ceylon* (New Delhi, 1971). Nine institutions are "deemed" universities under Section 3 of the University Grants Commission Act. See Government of India, Ministry of Education, *Education in Eighteen Years of Freedom* (Delhi, 1965), p. 10, where the institutions are listed. In addition, there are nine "institutions of national importance" giving postgraduate degrees, including five Indian Institutes of Technology. They can be counted as universities in the same sense that the Massachusetts Institute of Technology or the California Institute of Technology can; that is, they offer advanced degrees in basic science as well as technology and have some training or advanced degrees or both in the humanities and social sciences. For particulars as of 1964 see Government of India, Ministry of Education, *Facilities for Technical Education in India,* vols. 1 and 2 (combined) (New Delhi, 1965). Vol. 2 gives details concerning courses. Also included among "institutions of national importance" are two advanced medical research institutions (New Delhi and Chandigarh), the Indian Statistical Institute (Calcutta), and the Dakshina Bhavat Hindi Prachar Sabha (Madras), which specializes in advanced degrees and research in Hindi.

3. For a listing of Indian universities by date of founding see UGC, *University Development in India, 1967–68,* appendix 10, pp. 318–319.

4. For the number of affiliated colleges in 1947 see Ministry of Education, *Education in Eighteen Years of Freedom,* p. 28; for the number of affiliated colleges in 1967–68, see UGC, *University Development in India, 1967–68,* p. 21.

5. For example, the Education Commission, 1964–1966, expects total enrollment in higher education to be 2.2 million in 1975–76 and 4.16 million in 1985–86. It would like to slow the annual rate of growth of first degree courses in arts, sciences, and commerce from 9 percent (during the first three five-year plans) to 5.3 percent over these two decades by replacing "open-door access" with "selective admissions." In professional education, including engineering, medicine, teaching, and law, it wants to slow the annual growth rate from 10.6 to 7.9 percent but wants to accelerate slightly the annual rate of growth at the postgraduate level from 11 to 11.5 percent. *Education Commission,* pp. 303–304. Events over the past five years (1966–1971) suggest that such projections seriously underestimate actual and potential annual growth rates. However, financial limitations in the seventies may slow the rate of growth experienced in the sixties.

6. See Anil Seal, *The Emergence of Indian Nationalism; Competition and Collaboration in the Later Nineteenth Century* (Cambridge, 1968), pp. 16–22. Seal observes that "when after 1835 the government at last began to set up western-style schools and colleges of its own, it could not cope with the demand" (p. 18). The grants-in-aid system of 1854 was devised in part to cope with this situation but the result was to further accelerate expansion as demand continued to outstrip supply. In the two decades between 1881–82 and 1901–02 the number of colleges in British India increased from 63 to 140 and the number of students in them from 5,442 to 17,148. Seal, *Emergence of Indian Nationalism,* table 3, p. 22.

The demand for places one hundred years ago was more for arts than science seats. Today science and professional college seats, including PUC and intermediate seats that lead to admission to professional colleges and institutes, are in greater demand. As they are today, standards one hundred years ago were less rigorous and degree programs shorter in arts than in sciences, but the pattern of opportunities no longer favors the distinguished arts graduate, as it did then.

7. See Seal, *Indian Nationalism,* chap. 3, and Ellen E. McDonald, "English Education and Social Reform in Late Nineteenth Century Bombay," *Journal of Asian Studies,* 25, no. 3 (May 1966).

8. Government of India, Ministry of Education, *Survey of Living Conditions of University Students* (Delhi, 1961).

9. At least 63.9 percent of India's first degree holders end up in government service (local, state, or national) and a large proportion (70.8 percent as of 1960) earned less than Rs. 300 per month (below Rs. 100, 8.2 percent; Rs. 100 to Rs. 199, 41.6 percent; Rs. 200 to Rs. 299, 21 percent). Government of India, Ministry of Labour and Employment, Directorate General of Employment and Training, *Report on the Pattern of Graduate Employment* (New Delhi, 1963), tables 5 (8), p. 35, and 6 (1), p. 38. The findings are based on an all-India sample survey conducted in 1960 of 1954 graduates. For particulars of the universe and sample, see p. 68 of the report.

The five centrally administered and financed Indian Institutes of Technology (at Madras, Bombay, Delhi, Kanpur, and Kharagpur), probably the most attractive educational institutions in the country, are still filled with able and relatively well-to-do students, but there is official and political pressure to democratize the enrollment. Students are assured of high paid, secure, and prestigious jobs. A common admissions examination insures that the competition is intense and national. The education commission, however, argued for sacrificing standards in order to promote equality when it observed that "as examination marks figure largely as a basis for selection, in most cases, the students admitted [to the IIT's] . . . generally come from urban areas from good schools or from well-to-do homes." A special study of the IIT's (and other technical institutions) revealed that 87.2 percent of the IIT students came from urban areas (12.8 from rural areas); 61.2 percent had parents whose occupation was "service" (7.2 professional, 20.1 business, 4.3 agriculture, and 7.2 others); and 58.7 percent had parents whose income was over Rs. 500 per month (less than Rs. 140, 6.9; Rs. 151 to 300, 13.8; Rs. 301 to 500, 20.6). *Education Commission,* table 6.4, p. 119. These findings are confirmed by A. D. King's "Elite Education and the Economy: IIT Entrance: 1965–70," *Economic and Political Weekly,* 5, no. 35 (August 29, 1970).

King's study of one IIT suggests increasingly elite recruitment: in 1970, 80 percent of entrants came from families earning Rs. 501 and above per month, while 49 percent had come from such backgrounds in 1966—a rise which cannot be wholly accounted for by inflation and rising incomes. He surmises that the change may be due to the decreased opportunities for engineers (a result of the overproduction of engineers), and that the decrease discourages risk-taking among the lower income groups. The Education Commission, 1964–1966, was moved by its findings to observe that "the admission examinations to the institutes of technology are held in English. This gives undue weightage to students from English medium schools to which the rich send their children." See also Government of India, Ministry of Education, Education Commission, "Socio-Economic Background of Students Admitted to Institutions of Professional, Technical, and Vocational Education, 1965," mimeo (New Delhi, 1965), p. 111. The commission favored distributive justice over (class related) merito-cratic criteria, recommending that examinations be held in the regional lan-guages as well as English and that "the best students from each linguistic group should be selected, if necessary, on the basis of a quota related to popu-lation." Those whose English is weak should be given intensive training in English during their first year of study. *Education Commission,* p. 120. It was similarly critical of other technical institutions on distributive grounds: "the rural areas which form 80 percent of the total population, get only 41.4 percent of the seats in . . . [Institutes of Technology, Regional Engineering Colleges and Engineering Colleges, Medical Colleges, Agricultural Colleges, Polytechnics, and Industrial Training Institutions]. Families with an income of less than Rs. 150 per month, who again form about 80 percent of the total population, get 50.5 percent of the total seats available." *Education Commis-sion,* p. 120. The same evidence, given different expectations, could be inter-preted as indicative of surprising mobility opportunities.

10. *Hindustan Times,* 6 June 1967. The ministry of education has a more direct concern for the University of Delhi since it is one of four centrally ad-ministered universities that get their operating as well as their development funds from the University Grants Commission. As of 1962, the University of Delhi governed forty-nine colleges (including constituent professional, and affiliated colleges) and thirty-six postgraduate teaching departments. Inter University Board, *Universities Handbook,* pp. 251–257.

11. *Hindu* (Madras), 16 June 1967.

12. See Government of India, Election Commission, *Report on the First General Elections in India, 1952, Statistical,* vol. 2, pp. 9 and 188, and *Report on the Fourth General Elections in India, Statistical,* vol. 2, pp. 18 and 118. The percentage voting in parliamentary and state assembly elections in 1952 was 45.7 and 45, respectively, in 1967 61.33 and 61.43. In the U.S. presidential elections of 1960 and 1964, voting participation was 64 and 63 percent respec-tively. In the national elections for the U.S. House of Representatives in 1960, 1962, 1964, and 1966 the voting percentages were 59.6, 46.7, 58.7 and 46.8. India's parliamentary system precludes voting for a national political office such as the U.S. presidency. In this sense, it is important to compare U.S. and Indian voting participation in legislative elections. In 1967, Indian participa-tion in elections for both parliament and state assemblies (over 61 percent) exceeded American participation in the election for the House of Representa-tives (below 60 percent). The U.S. participation data can be found in U.S., *Statistical Abstract of the United States* 88th. ed. (Washington, 1967). For a more generalized analysis of American voting patterns and levels see Walter Dean Burnham, "The Changing Shape of the American Political Universe," *American Political Science Review,* 59 (1965) and "Party Systems and the Political Process," in W. N. Chambers and W. D. Burnham, *The American Party Systems; Stages of Political Development* (New York, 1967).

13. "One of the major reforms we envisage," the Education Commission, 1964–1966, stated, "is to vocationalize higher secondary education and to raise the enrollment in vocational courses [in classes XI and XII] to 50 percent of total enrollment." "It is fundamental . . . that such courses . . . be pre-dominately terminal." *Education Commission,* pp. 173 and 371.

Between 1950–51 and 1965–66, the proportion of students in secondary education classes VIII–X to the relevant age cohort expanded from 6.5 to 19.1 percent and those in classes XI–XII from 1.9 to 7 percent while the proportion of students in these classes enrolled in vocational education declined from 3.1 to 2.2 and from 44.2 to 40.3 respectively. *Education Commission,* tables 7.6 and 7.7, pp. 167 and 172. The figures for 1965–66 were estimated in the secretariat of the commission.

There are six principal institutions for technical and vocational education in India. (1) Polytechnics (admission after matriculation; that is, the senior school leaving certificate after class X), of which there were 370 in 1964, offering three year diploma programs in such fields as civil, mechanical, electrical, and chemical engineering. Government of India, Ministry of Education, *Facilities for Technical Education in India* (New Delhi, 1965). (2) Indian Institutes of Technology (IIT's) (admission at sixteen until 1966, thereafter at fifteen; matriculation required for training in twelve of the trades offered, and middle school (class VII) pass for the remaining thirty-nine), of which there were 356 in 1966, with a total intake of 113,000. (3) Junior technical schools (JTS's) (admission at fourteen with a pass from class VIII; in fact, most applicants are matriculates), of which there were 103 in 1966, with an intake capacity of 18,000. JTS's require a three- or four-year course that combines general education with technical training and workshop practice. The Education Commission, 1964–1966, recommended that the JTS's be renamed technical high schools. (4) The technical, commercial, and agricultural streams of multipurpose secondary schools. (5) Technical high schools, mostly in the area of the old Bombay state. (6) Private and government trade schools. *Education Commission,* p. 371.

14. Government of India, Ministry of Education, Education Commission, "Evidence Led before the Education Commission; Professional, Vocational & Technical Education," supplementary vol. 4-B, mimeo (New Delhi, 1966), p. 3.

15. "Despite repeated exhortation," the Education Commission, 1964–1966, observed, "it is unfortunately still widely felt that vocational education at the school level is an inferior form of education, fit only for those who fail in general education and the last choice of parents and students." *Education Commission,* p. 369. See chap. 15, particularly pp. 369–376, and Education Commission, "Professional, Vocational & Technical Education" for detailed analyses of these problems.

The Education Commission, 1964–1966, cited a planning commission study that showed, inter alia, that "a significant percentage of those passing out [of junior technical schools] do not enter employment but rejoin the educational stream, either in polytechnics or PUC courses" (p. 372). This phenomenon may mean that the graduates could not find "suitable" jobs rather than that they did not wish to use their training.

16. Government of India, *Pattern of Graduate Employment,* table 5 (4), p. 30; *Education Commission,* p. 373. The commission found India's "pyramid of trained manpower . . . top heavy." India's ratio of engineers to technicians was 1 to 1.4 while the ratios in "advanced industrialized countries" ranged from 1 to 3 to 1 to 6. *Education Commission,* p. 373.

17. See, for example, Subbiah Kannapan, "The Economics of Structuring an Industrial Labour Force: Some Reflections on the Commitment Problem,"

British Journal of Industrial Relations 4, no. 3 (November 1966), where he observes that "there can be no quarrel with the argument that the main bottleneck in industrial development is the supply of 'skilled' labour. The real problem is the determination of what is 'skilled' and what is 'unskilled.' " Technical proficiency may or may not be available to employers but may in any case be much less important to them than "intangible, but ignored, abilities which go to make up a skill" (p. 403). "The discipline of the formal educational environment seemed to be far more important than generally recognized, and the specific subject matter a good deal less." Kannapan, personal communication, 14 August 1968. See also Anna Bezanson, "Skill," *The Quarterly Journal of Economics* (August 1922), pp. 626–645.

18. Government of India, *Pattern of Graduate Employment,* table 5 (8), p. 35.

19. Philip J. Foster has cogently presented the "vocational school fallacy in development planning" and attacked the "myth" that it is white collar aspirations that dull or kill vocational aspirations. "In the initial stages," he writes, technical and vocational instruction is the cart rather than the horse in economic growth, and its development depends upon real and perceived opportunities in the economy." Philip J. Foster, "The Vocational School Fallacy in Development Planning," in C. Arnold Anderson and Mary Jean Bowman, eds., *Education and Economic Development* (Chicago, 1966), p. 153.

In relating economic development (as measured by growth in per capita income) to changes in occupational structure, James G. Scoville finds that "professional [including technical] and clerical workers possess the highest growth rate projections for the developing regions" and, "in the early stages of economic growth, they have extremely high income elasticities." James G. Scoville, "The Occupational Structure of Employment, 1960–1980," paper for the Inter-Regional Seminar on Long-term Economic Projections for the World Economy, Elsinore, 14–27 August 1966, pp. 34, 20.

Scoville's projections further suggest that with respect to "net requirements" (that is, policies concerned with education, training, retraining, and labor mobility), the professional (especially technicians) and clerical categories will grow fastest (219 and 68 percent respectively between 1960–70 and 1970–1980). Such expansions should "have primary relevance to the educational systems of the countries involved" (p. 35, table 11).

20. Total educational expenditure per capita has grown from Rs. 3.2 in 1950–51 to Rs. 12.1 in 1965–66 and total educational expenditure as a percentage of national income expanded from 1.2 in 1950–51 to 2.9 in 1965–66. *Education Commission,* table 19.1, p. 465.

In 1962–63, Great Britain spent 4.8 percent of its gross national product on education and in 1960–61 France, Germany, and the U.S.S.R. spent 3.4, 3, and 4.4 percent respectively. *Robbins Report* (appendix 5), *Higher Education in Other Countries* (Cmnd 2154-V), table 5, p. 17, col. 2. These figures are hardly precise or strictly comparable but do give some notion of magnitudes and relationships.

21. *Hindu Weekly Review,* 24 June 1968. "It is stated," the *Hindu Weekly Review* reported, "that the Education Ministry's draft policy has the support of an influential section of the Cabinet. The Planning Commission also would appear to concur with the proposals." By comparison, defense expenditures

constituted 3.15 percent of gross national product in 1967–68 and were expected to drop below 3 percent in 1968–69. Actual figures (provisional) for defense expenditure for 1968–69 were Rs. 1015 crores or $1,353 billion. *India News,* 7 June 1968, p. 6.

22. Government of India, Ministry of Education, Education Commission, *Inequalities in Educational Development (States and Districts),* mimeo (New Delhi, 1966), table 2, p. 12. Assam, Jammu and Kashmir, and Orissa, whose backward road systems pose problems for economic development and national security, spend more on public works than education. Government of India, Ministry of Information and Broadcasting, Publications Division, *India, 1966* (Delhi, 1966), chap. 16, pp. 394–473.

23. Indirect includes direction and inspection, buildings, scholarships, hostels, and miscellaneous.

24. *Education Commission,* table 19.4, p. 468.

25. Assuming that "recurring expenditure on education" and "direct and indirect expenditure on education" are comparable, the next highest after India would be the United States with 27 percent followed by Brazil (20 percent), Pakistan (19.6 percent), Ghana (17.2 percent), and Yugoslavia (16.1 percent). Among the more highly industrialized nations (in addition to the U.S.A.) the percentages were: United Kingdom, 14.1; U.S.S.R., 13.3; West Germany, 13.2; Japan, 13.1; and France, 8.3. These figures are taken from *Education Commission,* table 19.6 and 19.5 (Japan only), p. 469. All figures except those for Japan were compiled by the commission's study team from documents available in the UNESCO Secretariat, Paris. The Japanese figure was taken by the commission from Japan, Ministry of Education, *Japan's Growth and Education* (Tokyo, 1963), table 10.

26. Funds from local authorities dropped from 10.9 to 6.3; fees dropped from 20.4 to 15.3; and other sources from 11.6 to 7.2 percent in the same period. *Education Commission,* table 19.8, p. 471.

27. Robert Ulich observes that "English universities were virtually self-supporting until World War I, as were some of the richly endowed higher institutions in other countries. Today . . . most countries subsidize their universities completely." *The Education of Nations; A Comparison in Historical Perspective,* rev. ed. (Cambridge, Mass., 1967), pp. 338–339. In 1953–54, British universities drew 5.9 percent of their income from endowments, donations, and subscriptions. Fees accounted for another 12 percent, bringing the total from private sources to 17.9 percent. Government of India, Ministry of Education, *University Administration in India* (Delhi, 1958), p. 46.

By 1957–58, the proportion of income available in the United States to universities and colleges (public and private) from endowment earnings had dropped to 4.8 percent. Income from private gifts and grants contributed 8.6 percent, bringing the total proportion of "private" support to 13.4 percent of total income. When tuition and fees were added (25 percent), the proportion of private support rose to 38.4 percent. In *private* higher education institutions (whose income in 1957–58 represented 42 percent of total income available to higher education), the proportions from private sources were higher: endowment earnings 10.5 percent; private gifts and grants, 16.1 percent; tuition and fees, 41.9 percent; for an over-all proportion of 67.5 percent. Harold A.

Haswell, *Higher Education in the United States*, UNESCO, Educational Studies and Documents, no. 47 (n.d.).

28. For an important analysis of this controversy and recent tendencies toward congruence of the public and private sectors, see Christopher Jencks and David Riesman, *The Academic Revolution* (New York, 1968), chap. 7. Lawrence R. Veysey, *The Emergence of the American University* (Chicago, 1965) provides a brilliant account of the heyday of such controversies.

29. See Brian Simon, *Studies in the History of Education* (London, 1960).

30. See *Education Commission,* table 18.1, p. 446 for these and other proportions. In 1960–61 there were 1,751 affiliated colleges of all kinds of which 1,140 were managed by private bodies and 611 were managed by government (national, state, or district or municipal board). Of these, 809 colleges were arts, science, or arts and science (general education) colleges, 640 being privately and 169 being government managed; 755 were colleges for professional education (mainly engineering and medicine), 363 being privately and 392 being government managed; and 187 were colleges for special education (music, dancing, fine arts, oriental studies, sociology, etc.), 137 being privately and 50 being government managed. These calculations are based on data found in Government of India, Ministry of Education, *Education in India, 1960–61,* vol. 2, *All India Tables and Appendices* (Delhi, 1966), table III, p. 6.

Education Commission, table 18.1, p. 446, reports that in 1960–61 institutions for higher general education were 78.8 percent privately managed; colleges for professional education were 49.8 percent privately managed; and colleges for special education were 74.9 percent privately managed. The low proportion of professional colleges privately managed (and founded) is presumably a function of their high cost.

31. The breakdown of expenditure on all universities and colleges, both private and public, by sources, in 1961 was: 53.1 percent government funds; .4 percent local boards funds; 34.8 percent fees; and 11.7 percent other sources (endowments, gifts, etc.). Government of India, Ministry of Education, *Education in India, 1960–61,* vol. 2 (Delhi, 1966), table 157, p. 310. Since this figure lumps together private and government colleges, it does not give a full picture. Such a picture would have to be pieced together out of the grant-in-aid policies of various states. However, the pattern in Madras suggests that the 45 percent figure may not be far off. There, the recurring grant-in-aid is "two-thirds of the [government] approved net cost of maintenance of the college — the net cost being the excess of approved expenditure . . . over the fee income calculated at the [government] standard rate." (Fees cover about one-third of expenditure so that government pays for 2/3 of 2/3, or 4/9 — 44 percent — of expenditure.) Non-recurring grants for building and equipment are available on a 50/50 basis. Government of Madras, Department of Education, *General Education in the Madras State* (Madras, 1966), pp. 60–61.

32. See Harold Gould, "Educational Structures and Political Processes in Faizabad District, Uttar Pradesh," in this volume.

33. J. P. Naik, "The Role and Problems of Private Enterprise in Education," in I.S.S.-Feres Consultation of Principals of Christian Colleges, Tambram, 1967, *The Christian College and National Development* (Madras, 1967), p. 129.

34.   For an editorial on these events by Amrik Singh, Secretary of the Inter-University Board of India and Ceylon, see *University News* (New Delhi),
July 1967, p. 1. Vice-Chancellor Joshi's statement appears in the same issue,
pp. 8–9. By 1969, the government view had been accepted by at least one of the
vice-chancellors who had signed the 1967 statement, Dr. C. S. Patel of Baroda
University. Interview, November 22, 1969.

35.   See *Times of India* (Delhi), 18 September 1970, for the rejected nominations. Swarup Singh replaced K. N. Raj as vice-chancellor in January 1971.
Statesman (New Delhi), 7 January 1971. The dismissal in January 1970 of
Javeed Alam from his lecture's post at Salwan College helped to precipitate
university action. Alam, a Muslim, had married a Hindu. The Hindu governing committee allegedly acted for this reason. For Education Minister
V. K. R. V. Rao's statement in parliament on the Alam dismissal see *Statesman,* 21 November 1971. For the amendment of the university statutes in May
1971 see *Times of India,* 17 May 1971. Other reforms included having principals of colleges share their authority with elected teacher councils; rotating
the chairman of postgraduate departments every three years and electing him
from a panel of the professors and readers; and having departmental chairmen
share their powers with departmental councils.

36.   For the data on PUC and intermediate students, see chap. 3, note 1,
above.

High school teachers "have less charisma, on the average, than professors . . . ," Amitai Etzioni argues, "not only because they have less professional training, their knowledge is considered less forbidding and their roles
involve communication of knowledge rather than its creation or application,
but also because they are in more frequent, continuous and close contact with
their 'subordinates'." *A Comparative Analysis of Complex Organizations* (New
York, 1961), p. 220, fn. 32.

37.   See *New York Times,* 20 December 1969, "Regents Endorse Open
Admissions," and two editorials, "Sense on Open Admissions," 16 October
1969 (dealing with the majority and minority reports of the City University's
Commission on Open Admissions) and "Faculty Independence at C.U.," 16
December 1969, which attacks the administration of City University for proposing to deprive academic departments of their right to elect their chairmen
because such a policy, particularly in the context of the pressures generated by
the open admissions policy, would undermine an essential of academic self-
government.

The second batch of freshmen admitted under the open admission program
included 59 and 56 percent who required remedial mathematics and reading
respectively. Students numbered over 200,000 and faculty over 16,000 (*New
York Times,* 12 September 1971).

The conflict between utilitarian and professional goals in universities is
developed by Amitai Etzioni. "In direct contrast to utilitarian organizations,
the development of charisma in top administrative positions is dysfunctional
for [colleges and universities]," Etzioni observes. "It gives the administrator
additional power, which may be used to overemphasize values such as economy, efficiency, and instrumental expansion, while direct service of the professional goals of the organization is neglected. It tends to introduce lay interference with professional decisions and goal-related activities — for example,

in the recruitment and promotion of personnel — which is likely to inhibit the organization's pursuit of its dominant goal." Etzioni goes on to observe (in a footnote) that "in organizations owned and managed by public representatives [such as universities] in which professionals enter as private entrepreneurs, the administrators may have to force some professional norms on the professionals. But, in general, professionals are the organization group closest to the goals of these organizations, while administrators are closer to values such as economy, balanced budget, efficiency — what can be referred to as instrumental values." Etzioni, *Complex Organizations,* p. 220. For additional observations on this point see Amitai Etzioni, "Authority Structure and Organizational Effectiveness," *Administrative Sciences Quarterly,* 4 (1959), pp. 43–67.

38.   For the quotations from the first conference of vice-chancellors see Government of India, Ministry of Education, *Indian University Administration; Proceedings of the Vice-Chancellors' Conference . . . July 30 to August 1, 1957* (Delhi, 1958), pp. 25, 29, 31, 37, and 38.

39.   Government of India, Ministry of Education, *Proceedings of the Vice-Chancellors' Conference, June 15–16, 1960* (Delhi, 1961), pp. 24–25.

40.   For a detailed description of such activities see Government of India, Ministry of Education, *Educational Activities of the Government* (Delhi, 1963). Eighteen ministries or departments are active in the educational field.

41.   Government of India, University Grants Commission, *Centres of Advanced Study in Indian Universities* (New Delhi, 1964).

42.   Government of India, Ministry of Education, *Conference of Vice Chancellors, 1967,* p. 47.

43.   Recent years have seen continuing spurts of university foundings: 1966 — Kanpur, Meerut, Madurai, Saurashtra, South Gujarat; 1967 — Berhampur, Sambalpur; and 1968–69, Awadesh Pratap Singh University, Rewa; K. S. Darbhanga University; Maharashtra Agricultural University; University of Calicut; Nehru University, New Delhi; Guru Nanak University, Amritsar.

4.   Outputs: "Standards" in Democratized Higher Education

1.   See Lloyd I. Rudolph and Susanne Hoeber Rudolph, "Student Politics and National Politics in India," *Economic and Political Weekly,* vol. 6, no. 31 (31 July 1971), for an empirical examination of the levels and causes of student unrest.

2.   Government of India, *Report of the Calcutta University Commission, 1917–1919* (Calcutta, 1919), vol. 1, pt. 1, p. 327.

3.   Cited in ibid., pp. 327–328.

4.   Ibid., p. 331.

5.   Government of India, Ministry of Education, *Report of the Education Commission, 1964–1966* (Delhi, 1966), p. 42. "The holders of the first degree of our universities in arts and science are now generally equated with matriculates in the important universities of western countries and are eligible for admission only to the first year of their first degree course."

6.   In 1952–53, the enrollment was 512,000 students, including the figures for the Intermediate Boards. Government of India, University Grants Commission, *University Development in India, Basic Facts and Figures, 1962–63*

(New Delhi, 1963), p. 72. The figure for 1964–65, including Intermediate Boards, was 1,528,227. Government of India, University Grants Commission, *University Development in India, Basic Facts and Figures, 1964–5* (New Delhi, 1966), p. 24.

7. UGC, *University Development in India, 1964–5,* p. 63.

8. These levels cover the years X to XII.

9. For increased rates of failure at some bachelor level exams, see chap. 4, table 14, this volume. The increased first degree (bachelor) enrollment has been associated with a small increase in "wastage," the inability of the enrolled to pass the bachelor level exams.

10. UCG, *University Development in India, 1964–65,* p. 149.

11. Personal communication from Donald Rosenthal, and Government of India, *Report of the Education Commission, 1964–66,* p. 310.

12. See chap. 4, table 6, this volume.

13. Admissions to the arts programs in the three-year degree courses fell between 1957 and 1961 from 47 percent to 24 percent, while admissions in science rose from 53 percent to 76 percent. K. C. K. E. Raja, "The Changing University," *Educational Quarterly* (India), 14, no. 56 (December 1962), p. 219. See also *Hindu Weekly Review,* 6 July 1964.

It was estimated that there were 70,000 unemployed engineers in 1969. Institute of Applied Manpower Research, New Delhi, "Employment Outlook for Engineers, 1969–70" IAMR Working Paper no. 11 (1969), cited in A. D. King, "Elite Education and the Economy," *Economic and Political Weekly,* 5, no. 35 (29 August 1970). The IIT figures are from the same article.

14. UGC, *University Development in India, 1964–65,* p. 149.

15. Government of India, Ministry of Education, *Education in Eighteen Years of Freedom* (Delhi, 1965), p. 28. For example, M.A.'s in chemistry have gone from 930 in the period 1941–1945 to 3,634 in 1956–1960. Government of India, University Grants Commission, *Chemistry in Indian Universities* (New Delhi, 1963), p. 7.

16. See A. D. King, "The IIT Graduate: 1970; Aspirations, Expectations, and Ambitions," *Economic and Political Weekly,* 5, no. 36 (5 September 1970), for a picture of the dim view among IIT students of arts, which are seen as having no future.

17. UGC, *University Development in India, 1964–65,* pp. 155, 156, 159, 166, 172, and 175.

18. Of the twenty-five universities that awarded 165 degrees in economics, Agra awarded 62, Bombay 24, Delhi and Poona, 12 each, Calcutta and Rajasthan 6 each, Mysore, Nagpur, and Vikram 4 each, Banaras, Punjab and Saugar 3 each, and others, 20.

Of eighteen universities that awarded 112 degrees in political science (or politics), Agra awarded 26, Saugar 19, Delhi 17, Allahabad and Rajasthan 6 each, Bombay 4, Aligarh, Madras, Patna and the Indian School of International Studies 3 each, and others, 11.

Of the twenty-five universities that awarded 96 Ph.D.'s in history, Patna awarded 15, Rajasthan 13, Agra 10, Calcutta and Delhi 7 each, Bombay and Punjab 6 each, Lucknow and the Indian School of International Studies 4 each, Aligarh and Gauhati 3 each, and others, 18.

Nine universities awarded 45 Ph.D.'s in psychology. Six were awarded by Banaras, 5 each by Agra, Aligarh, Baroda, Lucknow and Madras, 3 each by Mysore and Gujarat, and 8 by others.

Eight universities granted 28 Ph.D.'s in geography. Thirteen were awarded by Agra, 7 by Banaras, 2 each by Calcutta and Patna, and 4 by others.

One university, Lucknow, awarded 4 Ph.D.'s in anthropology.

The Indian School of International Studies (ISIS) awarded 2 Ph.D.'s in international relations and Punjab awarded 1 in public administration. UGC, *University Development in India, 1964–5,* p. 150.

19. The following universities had set up independent departments of political science by 1947: Lucknow (1921), Allahabad (1922), Banaras (1929), University of the Punjab (1936), Madras (1937), Nagpur (1946), and Saugar (1946).

As of 1967 there were thirty-six departments teaching political science in universities and an additional sixty-nine affiliated colleges providing postgraduate instruction. Government of India, University Grants Commission, *Political Science in Indian Universities* (New Delhi, 1967), pp. 4–9.

See also G. N. Sarma, "The Growth of Political Science in India," in S. P. Aiyar and Usha Mehta, *Essays on Indian Federalism* (Bombay, 1965), pp. xxi–xxxiv.

20. See Government of India, University Grants Commission, *Sociology in Indian Universities* (New Delhi, 1966), p. 5 and the more recent product of a seminar at the University of Rajasthan, T. K. N. Unnithan, Yogendra Singh, Narendra Singh, and Indra Deva, eds., *Sociology for India* (New Delhi, 1967).

21. Annamalai (1953), Baroda (1951), Osmania (1946), Delhi (1959), Gujarat (1964), Patna (1951), Agra (1956), Poona (no date), Rajasthan (no date). See UGC, *Sociology in Indian Universities,* pp. 4–5. Only inspection would reveal how many departments, due to the close alliance of anthropology and sociology in India, are what Americans would call social anthropology and how many sociology. For a discussion of sociology in India by two foreign observers see Marshall B. Clinard and Joseph W. Elder, "Sociology in India: A Study in the Sociology of Knowledge," *American Sociological Review,* 30, no. 4 (August 1965), pp. 581–587, and the important response to this by Imtiaz Ahmad, "Note on Sociology in India," *The American Sociologist,* 1, no. 6 (November 1966).

For some Indian views of the development of this field see M. N. Srinivas, Y. B. Damle, S. Shahani, and Andre Beteille, "Caste: A Trend Report and Bibliography," *Current Sociology,* 8, no. 3 (1959).

22. For these developments, see Department of Sociology (University of Delhi), *Annual Report: 1968–9* (Delhi, 1969).

23. UGC, *Sociology in Indian Universities,* p. 6. See also Bernard S. Cohn, "Notes on the History of the Study of Indian Society and Culture," in Milton Singer and Bernard S. Cohn, eds., *Structure and Change in Indian Society* (Chicago, 1968).

24. Edward Shils, *The Intellectual Between Tradition and Modernity: The Indian Case* (The Hague, 1961).

25. Edward Shils noted this shift in the paper he gave at the conference on "Social Structure and Social Change in India," University of Chicago, June

5, 1965. For the problem of academic colonialism see *Seminar,* no. 112 (December 1968), number on "Academic Colonialism," and the *New York Times* report on it dated 12 January 1969.

26.   Together Hindi and Sanskrit accounted for 472 (34 percent) of all arts degrees and surpassed the total number of Ph.D.'s in all other Indian languages and literatures (including English with 62 Ph.D.'s) by 264 degrees. Two hundred eight Ph.D. degrees were awarded in eighteen Indian languages and literatures (including English) other than Hindi and Sanskrit in the period 1960–61 to 1963–64. See chap. 4, table 7, this volume.

Among the non-social science arts degrees, Hindi was by far the most numerous with 329 Ph.D.'s (24 percent of all arts degrees). Eight universities granted 273 of these degrees (Agra, 88; Saugar, 38; Lucknow, 37; Allahabad and Rajasthan, 27 each; Banaras, 20; and Delhi and Punjab 18 each). The remaining 56 degrees were divided among thirteen other universities. Sanskrit ranked second with 143 degrees, five universities granting 74 (Agra, 29; Banaras, 14; Calcutta, 12; Bombay, 10; and Delhi, 9) and nineteen other universities granting the remaining 69.

27.   Government of India, *Report of the Education Commission, 1964–1966,* p. 309.

28.   The 1966–67 Presidency College strike at Calcutta was organized initially by students in the Eden hostel, whose first demands dealt in part with hostel living conditions. See Jayabrata Bhattacharjee, "Presidency College; Tradition and Legend in the Troubled Sixties," prepared for the Conference on Education and Politics in India, New Delhi, 28–30 June 1967 (mimeo).

29.   See Irene Gilbert's "Autonomy and Consensus under the Raj: Presidency (Calcutta); Muir (Allahabad); M.A.-O. (Aligarh)," chap. 10 of this volume.

30.   A recent study by Raj Narain, professor of psychology and philosophy at Lucknow University, attempts to clarify the term "standards" by undertaking a content analysis of responses to a questionnaire by interviewees at Lucknow and Madras and by correspondents in India and abroad (how or why these particular respondents were selected is not clarified), and of newspaper references from the *National Herald.* See his *Falling Educational Standards; an Analysis* (Agra, 1970). The analysis takes as its main evidence those commonly held views which we tend to regard as rhetorical obstacles to a serious examination of "real" data, a perspective at which the Narain study arrives in its conclusion, when it calls for, inter alia, "comparing the percentages of passes." Such data is presented in chap. 4, table 14, this volume.

5.   Regional Patterns of Education

1.   See Anil Seal, *The Emergence of Indian Nationalism; Competition and Collaboration in the Later Nineteenth Century* (Cambridge, 1968), chaps. 2 and 3.

2.   Ibid., pp. 57–59.

3.   In 1879–80, 80 percent of the undergraduates and 70 percent of high school boys were from the Tamil districts; 10 percent and 14 percent were from the Telugu districts. Ibid., p. 104.

4.   Efforts by CABE (Central Advisory Board for Education) to shape

policy in this area are discussed in chap. 6 of this volume. See also William Richter, "National Politics and Educational Language Policy" (typescript), which is devoted entirely to national policy with respect to medium of instruction.

5. See note 3 above.

6. Seal, *Indian Nationalism*, p. 104.

7. Ibid., p. 104.

8. In consequence of substantial pressure to convert education from English to regional language in the universities, the Madras government announced in 1959 that it would allow B.A. students to study for their degree in Tamil beginning in 1963–64. (They did not, it may be noted, recommend a switchover for the B.Sc.) *Asian Recorder, 1959* (New Delhi), p. 2,631. In pursuance of this intention, the Madras government experimentally introduced Tamil as the language of instruction in the city of Coimbatore's colleges. Student response to this opportunity was notably unenthusiastic (*Times of India* [New Delhi], 19 October 1962), and in 1963 the government announced that it would not effect the proposed switchover. Instead, the government proposed to offer Tamil as an optional language if a specified number (ten to fifteen) demanded it (*Express* [New Delhi], 5 April 1963). Such sections were opened in the Government Arts College and Queen Mary's College of Madras city, and the Government Arts College at Kumbakonam, for the humanities (*Educational India*, 29, nos. 11 and 12 [May–June 1963], p. 390). These trends have been strengthened since 1967 when a DMK government assumed office. It too has tried to strengthen Tamil language collegiate education by, among other policies, reserving certain government jobs for Tamil language graduates. It is too early, however, to judge what success it will have in this effort.

9. See Janet Guthrie, "Shiv Sena; Opportunism or Nationalism," paper for Sociology 350, "Political Sociology," University of Chicago, Winter Quarter, 1969, and Mohan Ram, *Hindi Against India, The Meaning of the D.M.K.* (New Delhi, 1968).

10. Government of India, Department of Commercial Intelligence and Statistics, *Statistical Abstract for British India, for the years 1920–21 and 1939–40* (Delhi, 1941).

11. Government of India, Official Language Commission, *Report of the Official Language Commission, 1956* (New Delhi, 1957), p. 456.

12. Except in Saurashtra. Ibid., p. 459.

13. J. P. Naik, "The Role and Problems of Private Enterprise in Education," in I.S.S.-Feres Consultation of Principals of Christian Colleges, Tambram, 1967, *The Christian College and National Development* (Madras, 1967), p. 129.

14. See V. K. S. Nayar, "Communal Interest Groups in Kerala," in Donald Eugene Smith, ed., *South Asian Politics and Religion* (Princeton, 1966), pp. 176–190. See also Lloyd I. Rudolph and Susanne Hoeber Rudolph, *The Modernity of Tradition; Political Development in India* (Chicago, 1967), pp. 71–76 for an analysis of Kerala politics that helps to explain this pattern of allocation.

15. See chap. 3, this volume.

16. See chap. 5, table 15, this volume.

17. For the 1949–50 to 1958–59 data, see George Rosen, *Democracy and Economic Change in India* (Berkeley, 1966), table E3, p. 307. The rank order

of the states after Rajasthan in growth per capita was: (2) Madhya Pradesh (also a poor state with a better than average rate of investment in education); (3) Punjab; (4) Madras; (5) Bihar; (6) Bombay; (7) Andhra; (8) West Bengal; (9) Mysore; (10) Uttar Pradesh; (11) Orissa; (12) Kerala; (13) Assam. For the 1960–61 to 1967–68 data, see Marshall Bouton, "Economic Development, Regionalism and Political Stability in a Federal State," paper for Political Science 398, "Modern Indian Politics," University of Chicago, Fall Quarter, 1969, table 15, p. 48. Bouton's table is derived from figures published in Indian Institute of Public Opinion, *Quarterly Economic Report*, 15, no. 4 (April 1969).

18. For the industrialization of Ahmedabad, Gujarat, see Kenneth L. Gillion, *Ahmedabad; A Study in Indian Urban History* (Berkeley, 1968), especially pp. 99–100 for the origins of technical education in Ahmedabad. Aspects of industrialization in Madras are analyzed by James J. Berna in *Industrial Entrepreneurship in Madras State* (Bombay, 1960), and Milton Singer, "The Indian Joint Family in Modern Industry," in Bernard S. Cohn and Milton Singer, eds., *Structure and Change in Indian Society* (Chicago, 1968), pp. 423–452. Other important recent studies of industrialization include George Rosen, *Industrial Change in India; Industrial Growth, Capital Requirements, and Technological Change, 1937–1955* (Bombay, 1959), which focuses on the cement, paper, cotton textile, sugar, and iron and steel industries in prepartition Bombay, and Morris David Morris, *The Emergence of an Industrial Labor Force in India; A Study of the Bombay Cotton Mills, 1854–1947* (Berkeley, 1966).

19. See Richard P. Taub, *Bureaucrats Under Stress; Administrators and Administration in an Indian State* (Berkeley, 1969), pp. 116–118 and tables 11 and 12.

6. National Educational Policy in a Federal Context:
    A Proximate Goal

1. *Constitution of India,* Seventh Schedule, details the legislative authority involved.

2. Nine had been so declared as of 1966. *Constitution of India,* List 1, Item 63. Under section 3 of the University Grants Commission Act the following institutions were "deemed to be universities" for the purposes of central grants by the government of India: Indian Agricultural Research Institute, New Delhi; Indian Institute of Science, Bangalore; Indian School of International Studies, New Delhi; Gurukul Kangri Vishvavidyalaya, Hardwar; Jamia Millia Islamia, New Delhi; Gujarat Vidyapith, Ahmedabad; Kashi Vidyapith, Varanasi; Tata Institute of Social Sciences, Bombay; and Birla Institute of Science and Technology, Pilani. Government of India, Ministry of Education, *Education in Eighteen Years of Freedom* (Delhi, 1965), p. 10.

3. *Constitution of India,* List 1, Item 64.

4. Other institutions administered by the ministry of education include the School of Planning and Architecture, New Delhi; the Indian School of Mines, Dhanbad; the National Institute for Training in Industrial Engineering, Bom-

bay; the All-India Institutes of Management at Calcutta and Ahmedabad; and the Lakshmibai College of Physical Education, Gwalior.

5. *Constitution of India,* List 1, Items 65 and 66.

6. For example, the All-India Council for Technical Education, through its four regional committees and seven boards of technical studies, provides policy and technical guidance to the national and state governments. The University Grants Commission grants for technical education are given on its recommendation. The National Council of Educational Research and Training, together with its various research and training institutions, provides new ideas and encourages experiments in the field of education.

7. The case is reported in *All India Reporter,* 1963, sc. 703. For an account of the case see David S. Lelyveld, "Education, Language and the Courts, The Gujarat University Case." Background paper for the Conference on Education and Politics, India International Centre, New Delhi, June 28, 29, and 30, 1967; and Indian Law Institute, for Government of India, Ministry of Education, Education Commission, "Major Trends in Law Cases on Education, Decided by the Supreme Court of India and All High Courts (1960–1964)," mimeo (New Delhi, 1966), vol. 1, pp. 2–10.

8. For the state authority, see *Constitution of India,* Entry 11, List II (state list), Seventh Schedule.

9. The Indian Law Institute study (see note 7 above) observed that the states have "exclusive jurisdiction to prescribe medium of instruction in primary and secondary stages" and "may indicate medium of instruction in higher education"; where doing so has an impact on coordination and determination of standards, the central government only has the authority to act. In making such a determination the quality of reading material and "the facility of teaching and understanding" in a particular language are supposed to be taken into consideration.

10. Government of India, Ministry of Education, *Report of the Committee of Members of Parliament on Higher Education* (Delhi, 1964), p. 13.

11. Government of India, Ministry of Education, *Report of the Education Commission, 1964–1966* (Delhi, 1966), p. 453.

12. J. P. Naik, *Educational Planning in India* (Bombay, 1965), p. 2.

13. The report of Sir John Sargent, educational commissioner to the government of India, 1944, was the first comprehensive plan for educational development. For a history and critique of educational planning by the man who took a leading role in the research and perspectives represented by *Report of the Education Commission, 1964–1966,* see Naik, *Educational Planning in India,* pp. 8–10. The report of 1948 is to be found in Government of India, University Education Commission, *The Report of the University Education Commission,* 3 vols. (Delhi, 1951); that of 1964–1966 in Government of India, *Report of the Education Commission, 1964–1966.*

14. For a picture of the alternatives between rhetorical agreement and actual resistance, see Government of India, Ministry of Education, *Proceedings of the 28th Meeting of the Central Advisory Board of Education,* and subsequent *Proceedings* through the 32nd meeting, especially *Proceedings,* 29th meeting, appendix A; "Statement Issued by the Chief Ministers Conference (1960) Regarding Education, Medium of Instruction and Script," pp. 34–40,

and "Steps to Be Taken to Implement . . . ," pp. 55–66. The following report conveys some sense of the difficulties of gaining compliance for the three-language formula, which was to an extent resisted by Madras, which did not wish to adopt Hindi, and by Hindi area states, which did not wish to adopt a South Indian language and were not particularly enthusiastic about English either. "The Committee noted with satisfaction," wrote CABE's committee to implement the three-language formula, "the decision of the Madras government to make Hindi an examination subject in which the marks secured, though not yet counting for eligibility for university courses of study [i.e. not compulsory for university admission] will be taken into account for moderation [i.e. to improve chances of admission], and the decision of the U.P. government to make English a compulsory subject of study at the school stage and to make increasingly greater provisions for teaching other modern Indian languages in addition to Sanskrit in the school curriculum." Government of India, Ministry of Education, *Proceedings of the 30th Meeting of the Central Advisory Board of Education* (Delhi, 1964), p. 296. The Uttar Pradesh decision making English compulsory was reversed after the 1967 election by the coalition government headed by Charan Singh. Bihar and Madhya Pradesh, but not Rajasthan, also dropped English as a compulsory subject for university admission. See *Asian Recorder, 1967* (New Delhi), p. 7734.

15. See Government of India, *Report of the Education Commission, 1964–1966*, pp. 35–38 for problems of reorganizing the structure of education.

16. Seventeen of eighty-nine universities and institutions "deemed" universities in India and Ceylon were not members of the IUB in 1969. Inter-University Board of India and Ceylon, *Universities Handbook, 1969* (New Delhi, 1969).

17. For the number of universities and institutions deemed universities in 1966 as well as the number of affiliated colleges see Government of India, *Report of the Education Commission, 1964–1966*, p. 298. For particulars concerning the universities see Government of India, Education Ministry, University Grants Commission, *Handbook of Universities in India, 1963* (New Delhi, 1964). We have estimated the number of teachers by projecting the 7 to 8 percent annual increase reported in *India 1966*, table 35, p. 71, to 1965–66. Enrollment figures are from Government of India, *Report of the Education Commission, 1964–1966*, table 9, p. 590.

18. Government of India, *Report of the Education Commission, 1964–1966*, chap. 13.

19. Ibid., pp. 343–344.

20. In calculating the UGC's proportion of expenditure on higher education, we have used the totals of plan (development) expenditures, excluding nonplan (maintenance) expenditure on the ground that the latter, most of which supports the proportionally small national sector in higher education, does not directly affect innovation, standards, or growth. Unless and until the national sector is expanded under UGC auspices, UGC nonplan (maintenance) expenditures will not substantially affect educational policy or growth. See chap. 6, note 35, this volume, for the legal distinction between maintenance and developmental grants. In 1960–61, UGC plan expenditure was Rs. 5.5 crores ($7.15 million). Government of India, Estimates Committee (1965–66), *Hundred and Second Report (Third Lok Sabha)*; *Ministry of Education, Uni-*

versity Grants Commission (New Delhi, 1966), p. 42. Direct and indirect central government expenditure on higher education in 1960–61 amounted to Rs. 20.23 crores ($26.3 million).

Direct government of India expenditure on higher education in 1960–61 was Rs. 9.2 crores ($11.96 million). See Government of India, *Report of the Education Commission, 1964–1966,* table 19.16, p. 493. Indirect government of India expenditure on higher education in 1960–61 was approximately Rs. 11.03 crores ($14.3 million). We have calculated the government of India's indirect expenditure on higher education by using the proportions given in table 19.3, Government of India, *Report of the Education Commission, 1964– 1966,* table 19.3, "Indirect Expenditure at School and University Stages," p. 468. In 1965–66, 80 percent of the expenditure on hostels and 50 percent of the expenditure on miscellaneous was allocated to higher education. We have applied these proportions to the amounts given under the same heads in Government of India, *Report of the Education Commission, 1964–1966,* table 19.16, "Educational Expenditure Through Central Funds by Objects (1950–51 to 1960–61)," p. 493.

21. For a description of the origin, organization, and functions of the University Grants Commission, see Government of India, *Hundred and Second Report (Third Lok Sabha),* chap. I, Introductory, pp. 1–22, particularly pp. 1–13. For a brief account of the 1968 legislation, see *Hindu Weekly Review,* August 12, 1968. The Education Commission, 1964–1966, had resisted the recommendation to exclude vice-chancellors, which came from the Government of India, *Report of the Committee of Members of Parliament on Higher Education,* p. 45. See Government of India, *Report of the Education Commission, 1964–1966,* p. 344. For a knowledgeable analysis of the 1968 legislation see Amrik Singh, "The Reconstituted UGC," *Economic and Political Weekly,* 5, no. 33 (August 15, 1970).

22. Singh, "The Reconstituted UGC," p. 8. The legislation of 1968 was designed to "streamline" the UGC so that it coud cope more readily with its expanding burdens. Three members may now be fulltime; previously only the chairman was. The legislation also reduced the term of members from six to three years to "facilitate rotation," and it increased membership from nine to twelve, a move in accord with the recommendation of a parliamentary committee, but which may convert an efficient body into a more ceremonial one.

23. Personal communication, April 1968.

24. Government of India, Ministry of Education, *University Grants Commission, Some Facts and Figures* (New Delhi, 1966), p. 2. A private member's amendment to the University Grants Commission Act of 1968, which would have blocked central aid to universities set up without UGC approval, was not accepted by the government. *Hindu Weekly Review,* August 12, 1968.

25. The following were founded without or against UGC advice through 1966: Varanaseya Sanskrit Vidyalaya; Marathwada University; K. S. Darbhanga Sanskrit Vidyalaya; U. P. Agricultural University; Udaipur University (as an agricultural university); Andhra Pradesh Agricultural University; Bhagalpur University; Punjab Agricultural University, Ludhiana; Rabindra Bharati, Calcutta; Orissa University of Agriculture and Technology; University of Agricultural Sciences, Bangalore; Jawahar Lal Nehru Krishi Visvavidyalaya, Jabalpur; Indira Kala Visvavidyalaya; Gorakhpur University; Jabalpur University; Ku-

rukshetra University; and Vikram University, Ujjain. List compiled from the following reports: Government of India, *Hundred and Second Report* (*Third Lok Sabha*), pp. 30–31; Government of India, University Grants Commission, *Report of the University Grants Commission, April 1958–March 1959* (New Delhi, 1960), p. 2; and UGC, *Report, April 1957–March 1958*, p. 1.

26.   Government of India, University Grants Commission, *Report of the University Grants Commission, 1964–5* (New Delhi, 1966), p. 19.

27.   The opinion of state political forces with respect to educational foundings cannot be easily disregarded. The battle over whether a new university in Gujarat should be located at Rajkot or Bhavnagar led to resignations from the Gujarat Congress parliamentary party which nearly toppled the ministry. A massive agitation which led to the replacement of the Kerala Communist government in 1959 was occasioned by the Kerala education bill which sought to provide state control over privately managed schools. The immediate cause bringing the powerful Nair Service Society (NSS) into the agitation was government refusal to permit the NSS to found an engineering college in Palghat District, a stronghold of Communist party electoral strength. V. K. S. Nair, "Communal Interest Groups in Kerala," in D. E. Smith, ed., *Religion and Politics in South Asia* (Princeton, 1966), p. 180.

28.   Since its founding, the UGC has been empowered to disburse funds to universities "as it may deem necessary for the development of such universities." Government of India, *University Grants Commission, Some Facts and Figures,* pp. 1–2. It could presumably argue that development of universities in line with UGC responsibility for maintaining standards requires limitation of university growth unless state governments are prepared to allocate enough resources to such universities to meet certain basic requirements.

29.   Government of India, *Hundred and Second Report* (*Third Lok Sabha*), p. 31.

30.   Ibid., pp. 9–10.

31.   Ibid., p. 10.

32.   Government of India, University Grants Commission, *University Development in India, Basic Facts and Figures, 1966–7* (New Delhi, 1969), p. 246. See Government of India, *Report of the Education Commission, 1964–1966,* p. 309, for a discussion of conditions in colleges with less than 100 students. In the same year, five colleges "died," suggesting some expire prior to disaffiliation.

33.   "In practice, there has grown up a system of provisional or temporary recognition as a method of nursing schools to efficiency. As the main reason why a school desires recognition is that it may present its pupils at the matriculation examination, and as this privilege is granted by temporary recognition, and a temporary recognition may be renewed year after year, the promotion of efficiency is not necessarily secured by this means." Testimony of Mr. W. C. Wordsworth before the Commission. Government of India, *Report of the Calcutta University Commission, 1917–1919* (Calcutta, 1919), vol. 1, pt. 1, p. 307.

34.   Government of India, *Report of the Education Commission, 1964–1966,* pp. 344–345.

35.   Ibid., p. 345. Again, it should be noted that D. S. Kothari headed both organizations, and, in this sense, was speaking to and judging himself.

36.   The University Grants Commission Act of 1956 empowered the commission to make grants for "maintenance and development" of central universities (those founded by an act of the central legislature), but only for the "development" of all other universities. See provisions of the act in Government of India, *University Grants Commission, Some Facts and Figures,* pp. 1–2. For an interpretation of these provisions by the attorney general of India, see Government of India, *Hundred and Second Report (Third Lok Sabha),* pp. 191–192. Under the University Grants Commission Act of 1968, the commission was authorized to make expenditures for maintenance in special cases.

37.   Ibid., p. 58. The pay scale enhancements are discussed in Government of India, Ministry of Education, University Grants Commission, *Development Programmes Sponsored by the U.G.C.* (New Delhi, 1964), pp. 18–19.

38.   Government of India, *Hundred and Second Report (Third Lok Sabha),* pp. 55–56.

39.   New legislation obliging states to take UGC advice with respect to foundings if they want to qualify for federal funds may be desirable. Although such legislation would mean that the UGC would lose its capacity to influence all types of institutions for the better, it would also mean that it could productively concentrate its funds. Inspection by UGC teams could indeed, as the Education Commission, 1964–1966, suggests, be more vigorously pursued. If UGC inspection teams are clearly academically, not politically, motivated and represent professional rather than bureaucratic authority, they need not be seen as any more of a threat to autonomy than are the inspection teams of American regional accreditation organizations. Although the latter also neither impose a very rigorous standard nor intervene in the details of university life, they help to insure minimum standards.

40.   Government of India, University Grants Commission, *Centres of Advanced Study in Indian Universities* (New Delhi, 1964). Twenty-six centers were established in 1964, fifteen in science (three in physics; two in chemistry; two in botany; two in zoology; two in geology; three in mathematics; and one other) and eleven in humanities and social sciences (three in economics; one in history; three in philosophy; one in Sanskrit; two in linguistics; and one in education). In 1968, the UGC approved a twenty-seventh center by agreeing to support sociology at Delhi University.

"The scheme," the UGC wrote in inaugurating it, "is intended to encourage the pursuit of 'Excellence' and team work in studies and research and to accelerate the realisation of 'International Standards' in specific fields. With this object in view it is proposed to give active support and substantial assistance to promising departments in the universities carefully selected on the basis of quality and extent of work already done by them, their reputation and contribution to research, and their potentiality for further development." Government of India, *Report of the Education Commission, 1964–1966,* pp. 279–284. For a more recent, quasi-official interpretation of the policy see D. S. Kothari, *Education, Science and National Development* (Bombay, 1970), chap. 6, "University Matters, and Centres of Excellence," particularly pp. 63–67.

41.   Government of India, *Report of the Education Commission, 1964–1966,* p. 280.

42.   Government of India, Ministry of Education, *Report of the Committee of Members of Parliament on Education, 1967* (Delhi, 1967), p. 1.

43. Government of India, Ministry of Education, *Conference of Vice-Chancellors, 1967* (New Delhi, 1968), pp. 47 and 42.

44. Government of India, *Hundred and Second Report* (*Third Lok Sabha*), p. 69.

45. Government of India, *Report of the Education Commission, 1964–1966,* p. 283; Government of India, *Report of the Committee of Members of Parliament on Education, 1967,* p. 16.

Introduction to Part II

1. See chap. 3, note 33.

2. Latter-day versions of these memoirs, good reading for those who wish to remind themselves about the quality of life in English private entrepreneurial education, are George Orwell's "Such, Such Were the Joys" in *Shooting an Elephant and Other Essays* (New York, 1950), and *The Clergyman's Daughter* (New York, 1960).

3. See chap. 5, table 23 and its note for the basis of this ranking.

4. The problematic relations between politics and education in California, where such indicators would be very high indeed, provides at least a cautionary example, reminding us that universe indicators may not always be useful in specific cases or that very high indicators (as against high) may be associated with outputs not unlike those associated with low measures of key independent variables.

5. See Government of India, Ministry of Education, *Report of the Education Commission, 1964–1966* (Delhi, 1966). "In spite of the offer of Central assistance, only five States have implemented the proposal so far, while the others have either not accepted it at all, or having decided to accept it in the first instance, have gone back on their earlier decision. Only about 25 percent of the total number of secondary schools in the country were converted to the higher secondary pattern by the end of the third plan. Many of these conversions are purely notional. . . . No uniform pattern of school and college classes has emerged as a result of the reorganization and there is almost as great a variety of patterns today as there was when the scheme of reorganization was first launched" (pp. 24–25). Table 2.1, page 25 of the report presents this variety in organized form.

6. For the problems Uttar Pradesh's categories raise in ascertaining total enrollment in higher education, see chap. 3, note 1, this volume.

7. Government of India, *Report of the Education Commission, 1964–1966,* p. 251.

8. There is a considerable literature that relates the problem of learning by the children of poor and subject classes and cultures to the organization of government and the policies pursued by it. The three main solutions to the problem are: integration, which involves the assimilation of the subjected in the culture of the dominant; more resources, including a more equitable distribution of those presently allocated to education and the allocation of larger proportions of public resources to education; and the decentralization of power over education in ways that enable local communities to control it in the center cities (as well as in the suburbs). An important document for this ongoing

debate is the Coleman Report (U.S., Commission on Civil Rights, *Racial Isolation in the Public Schools,* vol. 1 (Report) and vol. 2 (Appendices) (Washington, 1967). Although the report has been subject to a variety of interpretations (see for example Christopher Jencks, "A Reappraisal of the Most Controversial Educational Document of Our Time," *New York Times Magazine,* 10 August 1969), Coleman has maintained, "School integration is vital not merely for some vague, generalized social purposes, but because it is the most consistent mechanism for improving the quality of education of disadvantaged children." See the *New York Times,* 9 March 1970. Whether or not integration is the best way to enable disadvantaged blacks to learn, it seems increasingly clear that for the foreseeable future integration is a political failure. See for example David Rogers, *110 Livingston Street; Politics and Bureaucracy in the New York City School System* (New York, 1969), and the *New York Times,* 8 March 1970.

For alternate views that stress the relationship of power to "the quality of education of disadvantaged children" see Herbert J. Gans, "We Won't End the Urban Crisis until We End 'Majority Rule,' " *New York Times Magazine,* 3 August 1969 and Jason Epstein, "The Politics of School Decentralization," "The Brooklyn Dodgers," and "The Issue at Ocean Hill," in the *New York Review of Books,* 6 June, 10 October, and 21 November 1968. Gans advocates political reform ("pluralistic democracy") that will enable poor and subjected minorities to become majorities in their own subjected bailiwicks; Epstein argues that "the children will not learn . . . until a substantial shift of power has taken place within the city."

9.   The supreme court handed down its judgment on May 22, 1958.

10.   Government of India, Committee on Plan Projects, *Report of the Team for the Study of Community Projects and National Extension Service,* 3 vols. (New Delhi, November 1957). Balvantray Mehta, head of the study team, was a Gandhian, an important leader in the Praja Mandal (States' Peoples Freedom Movement) and, later, chief minister of Gujarat. He died tragically in an air crash during the Indo-Pakistan war of 1965.

11.   Government of India, *Report of the Education Commission, 1964–1966,* p. 52, for example, where government and local authority schools are criticized for average performance, below that of the best private schools, in spite of many advantages; for isolation from and indifference to their communities; and for complacency and lethargy resulting from "over-security" of service rules.

12.   See Government of India, Ministry of Education, *Report . . . on . . . The Administration of Primary Education* (Delhi, 1948), pp. 113–114, and Government of India, Ministry of Education, *Report of the Committee on the Relationship between State Governments and Local Bodies in the Administration of Primary Education* (Delhi, 1954), p. 111.

13.   In 1969 there were 5,265 community development blocks (at various "stages") covering 566,900 villages and over 400 million people. See Government of India, Ministry of Information and Broadcasting, *India, 1969; A Reference Annual* (New Delhi, 1969), table 126, p. 257. For the experimental origins of community development in India, see Richard L. Park and McKim Marriott, eds., *Pilot Project India* (Berkeley, 1958). For an excellent micro-study of community development in operation, see S. C. Dube, *India's Chang-*

ing Villages (London, 1958). For a comprehensive analysis of the two pro-grams, including an extensive bibliography, see S. C. Jain, *Community Development and Panchayat Raj in India* (Bombay, 1967).

14. For the Jacobins of the national convention period, see Robert J. Vignery, *The French Revolution and the Schools; Educational Policies of the Mountain, 1792–1794* (Madison, Wisconsin, 1965). The Common School or Public School movement is described and analyzed in Lawrence A. Cremin, *The American Common School* (New York, 1951). Aspects of Maoist edu-cational populism, particularly as it was expressed in the red-expert contra-diction, are admirably analyzed in Mitchell Meisner, "Revolution and Mod-ernization: The Three Revolutionary Movements for Class Struggle, Production Struggle, and Scientific Experiments," M.A. paper, Department of Political Science, University of Chicago, 1968. For the official proposal to decentralize the New York school system, see Mayor's Advisory Panel on Decentralization of the New York City Schools, McGeorge Bundy, Chairman, *Reconnection for Learning; a Community School System for New York City* (November 9, 1967). For a critical but sympathetic analysis of the Bundy Report, see Rogers, *110 Livingston Street,* pp. 475–486. See also Maurice Berube and Marilyn Gittell, eds., *Confrontation at Ocean Hill-Brownsville; The New York School Strikes of 1968* (New York, 1969).

15. See Narain, "Rural Local Politics and Primary School Management," chap. 9, this volume, note 1, for his and other studies that make recommen-dations for reform.

16. For the progressive education movement see Lawrence A. Cremin, *The Transformation of the School; Progressivism in American Education, 1876–1957* (New York, 1961). The leading critic of the progressive education estab-lishment probably was Arthur E. Bestor. See his *Educational Wastelands: The Retreat from Learning in Our Public Schools* (Urbana, Illinois, 1953), and *The Restoration of Learning* (New York, 1955), which incorporates a good bit of *Educational Wastelands.* In the postsputnik era, the most popular critic of education along these lines was Admiral Himan G. Rickover. See his *Education and Freedom* (New York, 1959).

17. Marilyn Gittell, *Participants and Participation; A Study of School Policy in New York City* (New York, 1967), p. 57.

"In New York City," Jason Epstein reports, "nearly 50,000 children in the third grade, about 60 percent of the total, read so poorly that according to the Board of Education, 'their success in the higher grades is highly unlikely.' . . . Their failure to learn to read marks the first of a series of failures whose cumulative effect must be devastating and permanent." In 1967, only 700 of 30,000 academic diplomas awarded to graduates of the city high schools went to Negroes. Jason Epstein, "The Politics of School Decentralization," *New York Review of Books,* 6 June 1968, p. 29.

18. Mario D. Fantini, in his foreword to Marilyn Gittell's *Participants and Participation,* pp. vii–viii. Fantini, a Ford Foundation official, was execu-tive secretary of the 1967 Mayor's [Local Advi]sory Panel on Decentrali-zation of the New York City Schools. [Bu]ndy, Ford Foundation president, was the panel's chairman.

19. See George Rosen, *Democracy and Economic Change in India* (Berke-ley, 1966), table E3, p. 307.

20. See, for example, William Munroe Newton, *History of Barnard, 1761–1927* (Vermont Historical Society, 1928), vol. 1, pp. 199–209.

21. See chap. 5, this volume, for other dimensions that help explain Rajasthan's rapid rate of growth.

22. It is in the interest of the opposition to build a record against the government in legislative debates. The opposition is therefore likely to emphasize negative features of local management of primary education.

7. Educational Structures and Political Processes in Faizabad District, Uttar Pradesh

1. J. P. Naik, "The Role and Problems of Private Enterprise in Education," in I.S.S.-Feres Consultation of Principals of Christian Colleges, Tambram, 1967, *The Christian College and National Development* (Madras, 1967), pp. 124–125.

2. Personal communication, March 29, 1967.

3. Government of India, Ministry of Education, *Report of the Education Commission 1964–1966* (New Delhi, 1967).

4. An unambiguously negative view of primary and secondary education by an observer whose concerns are with quality judged by professional standards is to be found in an article by Edward Shils, "On the Improvement of Indian Higher Education," in A. B. Shah, ed., *Education, Scientific Policy and Developing Societies* (Bombay, 1967). "The students are ill-prepared by their secondary schools for work at the level of higher education. They come increasingly from families with little background; their vocabularies are limited; their capacity for assiduous application to their studies is untrained. They have had little experience of independent study; they have learnt by unthinking memorization and their curiosity has not been encouraged."

5. Anil Seal, *The Emergence of Indian Nationalism; Competition and Collaboration in the Later Nineteenth Century* (Cambridge, 1968), p. 18.

6. Ibid., p. 20, quoted by Seal from Government of India, Home Department (Education), Resolution of the Government of India on State Aided Education (18 June 1888). Home Department Proceedings (Education), P.P. 1888, 77, pp. 375–386.

7. Seal, *Emergence of Indian Nationalism,* p. 21.

8. A large, intradistrict subdivision employed for administrative and judicial purposes. Faizabad district has four *tehsils*.

9. See H. A. Gould as follows: "Traditionalism and Modernism in U.P.: Faizabad Constituency," *Economic Weekly,* August 18, 1962, pp. 1342–1350 (reprinted in Myron Weiner and Rajni Kothari, eds., *Indian Voting Behaviour* [Calcutta, 1965]); "The Incident of the Fish: A Sociological View of Contemporary Politics," in Robert F. Sakai, ed., *Studies on Asia* (Lincoln, Nebraska, 1963); "Religion and Politics in a U.P. Constituency," in Donald E. Smith, ed., *South Asian Politics and Religion* (Princeton, 1966); and "Changing Political Behavior in Rural Indian Society," *Economic and Political Weekly,* Special Number, Bombay, July 1968.

10. See the Rudolphs' observation in "Regional Patterns of Education," chap. 5, this volume. "Uttar Pradesh and Bihar, which rank ninth and fifteenth with respect to per capita income and eleventh and twelfth with respect to per

capita expenditure on education, tie for fourth position with respect to secondary school enrollment."

11. Higher secondary schools take the student through the eleventh year of education. Intercolleges are institutions which take the student up through his intermediate arts degree, which comes three years after higher secondary school or, in other words, at the fourteenth year of education. Obtaining the intermediate arts degree, then, is roughly equivalent to completing junior college in the United States. The Education Commission, 1964–1966, has recommended that in states such as Uttar Pradesh, where higher secondary education now extends to the eleventh year, an extra year be added prior to commencement of matriculation.

12. For more details on these aspects of Uttar Pradesh politics, see Paul Brass, *Factional Politics in an Indian State: the Congress Party in Uttar Pradesh* (Berkeley, 1965).

13. About $350 to $400. (The exchange rate at the time of this writing is Rs. 7.5 = $1.)

14. Susanne Rudolph points out in a private communication, "It is well to keep in mind that the conditions for founding and maintaining institutions are probably less onerous in U.P. than in at least some other states with stronger administrative and political traditions. Thus Madras State required that all private aided schools opened after 1948–9 provide an endowment of Rs. 35,000 (Rs. 15,000 for the middle school stage, Rs. 20,000 for the high school stage). Schools opened since 1965–6 must provide Rs. 70,000 of endowment. Nor are these requirements easy to circumvent." She cites Government of Madras, Department of Education, *General Education in the Madras State* (Madras, 1966), p. 16.

15. Interview, 12 March 1967.

16. A middle-range peasant caste variously ranked as "Vaisya" or "Touchable Sudra" in the local culture.

17. See Brass, *Factional Politics in an Indian State.*

18. A Punjabi business caste widely distributed throughout India.

19. See Brass, *Factional Politics in an Indian State.*

20. The name indicates that he is of the Ahir caste, which like Jai Ram Varma's Kurmi caste is in the backward classification of castes.

21. For a useful study of the manner in which Congress tickets are apportioned, see Rameshray Roy, *Economic and Political Weekly,* 31 December 1966; 7, 14 January, 11, 18 February 1967.

22. The Legislative Council, the second legislative or upper house in Uttar Pradesh, is equivalent in structure to the *Rajya Sabha* in Delhi and the House of Lords in England.

23. Prior to 1967, many of the constituencies in Faizabad district had other names and slightly different boundaries. For simplicity's sake, however, I have used the current names only. Further precision is unnecessary for the purposes of this chapter.

24. For the best account of the ideological and factional differences between the Gandhians and the socialists in Uttar Pradesh, see Paul Brass, *Factional Politics in an Indian State.*

25. Most of his support among Muslims was generated by the *Majlis-e-Mushawarat.* The *Majlis-e-Mushawarat* is an organisation which came into

being prior to the 1967 general elections for the purpose of representing Muslim interests in India through political action. The *Majlis* is a political pressure group whose purpose is to induce Muslims to cast their votes in elections for candidates of any party who subscribe in fact or in principal to the "People's Manifesto" which the organization has issued. In the words of the "Manifesto": *"We decided that the Muslims should give up weeping and wailing and should try to regain their lost energies and strive for a change in the prevailing conditions"* (p. 3, italics in the original).

26. Joseph R. Gusfield, "Equality and Development: Education and Social Segmentation in Modern India," forthcoming in a volume based on papers prepared for the Comparative Education Conference, University of California, Berkeley, California (March 25–27, 1966), ms. p. 8.

27. See T. N. Madan's and B. G. Halbar's contribution to this volume for a more detailed discussion of this matter.

28. Joseph R. Gusfield, "Equality and Development: Education and Social Segmentation in Modern India," ms. p. 41.

8. Caste and Community in the Private
   and Public Education of Mysore State

1. Government of India, Ministry of Education, *Report of the Education Commission, 1964–1966* (New Delhi, 1966), p. 18.

2. C. Arnold Anderson, "The Modernization of Education" in Myron Weiner, ed., *Modernization: The Dynamics of Growth* (Washington, D.C., 1966), p. 78.

3. See D. N. Majumdar and T. N. Madan, *An Introduction to Social Anthropology* (Bombay, 1956), pp. 137–140.

4. See Robert Redfield, *The Primitive World and Its Transformation* (Ithaca, 1953), and *Peasant Society and Culture* (Chicago, 1956).

5. "Particularism" and "universalism" are used throughout this paper in the sense bestowed upon these terms by Parsons and his colleagues. See Talcott Parsons and Edward A. Shils, eds., *Toward a General Theory of Action* (Cambridge, Mass., 1952), p. 82.

6. See A. L. Mudaliar, *Education in India* (Bombay, 1960) and R. K. Mookerji, *Ancient Indian Education: Brahmanical and Buddhist* (London, 1951).

7. K. S. Vakil and S. Natarajan, *Education in India* (Bombay, 1966), p. 96.

8. Syed Nurullah and J. P. Naik, *A History of Education in India (During the British Period)* (Bombay, 1951), p. 164.

9. Vakil and Natarajan, *Education in India*, p. 143.

10. Ibid., pp. 137, 140–141.

11. Writes B. B. Misra in *The Indian Middle Classes: Their Growth in Modern Times* (Bombay, 1961), p. 283: "The Government thus adopted a policy of *laissez-faire* in education. As a result, educational expenditure, especially on government secondary and primary schools, registered a marked decline. In about three years local taxation and popular endowments took over nearly three-fourths of the burden. Encouraged by this result, the Government reaffirmed its policy 'to avoid entering into competition with private enterprise'.

It declared that its duty was to pioneer the way; 'but, having shown the way, it recognizes no responsibility to do for people what people can and ought to do for themselves' (Government of India, Education Department, Education in India, *Quinquennial Review, 1886–1904*)."

12.   Nurullah and Naik, *A History of Education in India,* p. 260.

13.   See J. P. Naik, *The Status of Private Enterprise in Indian Education (in the Post-Independence Period)*, mimeo. (New Delhi, 1965), p. 12.

14.   The senior author was at that time teaching at the Karnatak University, Dharwar, and therefore Dharwar district was chosen primarily for reasons of convenience. Belgaum district was included in the study at a later stage when the authors became aware of the importance of the Karnatak Liberal Education Society which has its headquarters in Belgaum city.

15.   Postgraduate institutions were excluded according to the terms of the grant from the National Council of Educational Research and Training.

16.   Lingayats, also known as the followers of *Virashaivism,* are a sect whose Hindu status is being debated among themselves. Non-Lingayats regard them as Hindus, however. The founder of the sect, Basava (A.D. 1132–1168), was born a Brahman. See Hardekar Manjappa, *Basava: The Dimension of Universal Man* (Dharwar, 1966). They are the most numerous community in the state of Mysore (about 20 percent of the population), and dominate its politics. Their rather weak rivals are the Vokkaligas, a Hindu peasant caste, who constitute about 14 percent of the total population. See M. N. Srinivas, *Caste in Modern India and Other Essays* (Bombay, 1962), pp. 32–34.

17.   Interview schedules were the principal instrument employed to gather data. In addition, records and reports of various kinds were studied. These included prospectuses of educational societies, annual reports, minutes of meetings, pay bills, admission and school attendance registers, audited statements of accounts, annual statistical returns, and personal staff files.

18.   For Mysore state, particularly the old Mysore areas, see G. S. Halappa, *History of the Freedom Movement in Karnatak,* vol. 2 (Bangalore, 1964), and also, Government of Mysore, *Report of the Educational Survey in Mysore State, 1958, pt. 1* (Bangalore, 1961). D. C. Pavate's *Memoirs of an Educational Administrator* (New Delhi, 1965) contains many insightful observations on the former Bombay Presidency.

19.   Government of India, *Report of the Education Commission 1964–1966,* p. 251.

20.   For details of the data and the sources, see B. G. Halbar and T. N. Madan, "Caste and Educational Institutions in Mysore State," mimeo. (Dharwar, 1966), pp. 137–143.

21.   The facts and figures are taken from Government of Mysore, *Handbook on Education 1964–65* (Bangalore, 1965).

22.   A revised grants-in-aid code was announced in June 1967, following the government's decision to make secondary education free beginning in the academic year 1966–67.

23.   Source: unpublished statistics made available by the Office of the Director of Public Instruction in Mysore, Bangalore. There are four universities in Mysore state, one each at Mysore, Dharwar, Bangalore, and Hebbal. The last of these is an agricultural university.

24.   Cf. Government of India, *Report of the Education Commission 1964–*

66, p. 253: "Their [private educational institutions] main assets are: strong ties with the local community on whom they depend for support. . . . Their main weaknesses are two: a precarious financial position . . . , and, very often, a bad and even unscrupulous management."

25. See Lloyd I. and Susanne H. Rudolph, "The Political Role of India's Caste Associations," *Pacific Affairs,* 33, no. 1 (1960), pp. 5–22, and T. N. Madan, "The Changing Political Functions of Caste in India" in B. Singh and V. B. Singh, eds., *Social and Economic Change* (Bombay, 1967), pp. 208–225.

26. For the manner in which managements of educational societies are constituted, see chap. 7 in this volume.

27. Government of India, *Census of India, 1931, Mysore State,* vol. 25, pt. II, table 14.

28. The proportion of Marathas in the population of Belgaum city is considerably higher than in the district as a whole and is partly responsible for the border dispute between the states of Maharashtra and Mysore.

29. See Pavate, *Memoirs of an Educational Administrator,* pp. 118–132.

30. Data on the religion and caste of members of the management and teaching staff are not maintained by any of the educational societies or their institutions, and had to be collected through interviews.

Similar data on students are also not available, and had to be looked up in admission registers and application forms. There is a ban now on the mention of caste in any application or other records, unless statutorily obligatory or administratively essential, as in the case of the so-called backward classes, scheduled castes, and scheduled tribes. In view of these new laws, it may be difficult in future to conduct research on all aspects of the interaction between educational institutions and their social environment. Luckily the present study was conducted during the transitional period, just when data on caste were beginning to be left out of records.

For comprehensive statistical tables on the composition of managements, staff and students, see Halbar and Madan, *Caste and Educational Institutions in Mysore State,* pp. 91–136.

31. Of the 156 private institutions studied by us, only 19 (12 percent) are located in rural areas (17 in Dharwar and 2 in Mysore). The smaller number of educational institutions in rural areas as compared to urban areas limits the choices open to entrants.

32. See chap. 7, this volume.

33. Personal communication from Professor M. N. Srinivas.

34. Anderson, "The Modernization of Education," p. 76.

35. See C. Arnold Anderson and Mary Jean Bowman, eds., *Education and Economic Development* (London, 1966).

36. See, for example, Philip J. Foster, *Education and Social Change in Ghana* (London, 1965), and Hans W. Weiler, ed., *Education and Politics in Nigeria* (London, 1965).

37. M. N. Srinivas, *Social Change in Modern India* (Bombay, 1966), p. 140.

38. Susanne H. Rudolph, "Transcript, Conference on Politics and Education," New Delhi, June 28–30, 1967, discussion on draft of the present paper by T. N. Madan and B. G. Halbar, mimeo., pp. 17–18: "Now it is the same

sort of development that we discover as we look at caste in politics. The meaning of caste today is different from what caste meant in the political system of traditional villages. . . . What it meant to some extent was that . . . people were related to one another as superiors and inferiors. The caste structures that move into politics tend to be groups of peers horizontally organized, and in that sense quite a different cultural construct."

39.   Glynn Wood, who knows the old Mysore region better than we, writes in a personal communication to the senior author: "The situation has deteriorated from the Brahman point of view so that domination is hardly apt. When one considers that well over half of all university students in princely Mysore in 1945 were Brahman, it is not surprising that large numbers have turned up on the staff of the public (educational) institutions. However, it should be noted that the position of the Brahman on the staff of these institutions since World War II has not been particularly happy. While Brahmans have been hired because of the general lack of qualified persons in other communities, as you point out about the Lingayat institutions in Mysore district, positions of power and prestige (department chairmanships and principalships) have almost invariably gone to the non-Brahman."

40.   See Lloyd I. Rudolph, "Transcript, Conference on Politics and Education," p. 12: "You want everyone to be equal citizens and use the educational system for this purpose, and you want citizens to have the freedom to associate, educate, etc. as they like. These objectives come into conflict. And this is what is in conflict in Mysore."

41.   Thus, itself unable to satisfy the demand for higher technical education, the government is unable to prevent even such undesirable practices as the realization of the "capitation fee" from students who are admitted to private engineering and medical colleges. Though the government has fixed a ceiling of Rs. 5,000 per seat, we were told by some responsible informants that the usual practice is to charge between Rs. 10,000 and Rs. 20,000. The student, however, is given a receipt for Rs. 5,000 only and the balance is credited to the revenues of the management under "Miscellaneous Receipts." Part of the capitation fee, often running into four figures, is thus a kind of graft.

During the financial years 1964–65 and 1965–66 direct government expenditure on education was 19.7 and 23 percent respectively of the total estimated expenditure on revenue account.

42.   The recommendations of the Education Commission, 1964–1966, are not clear on the policy to be adopted, as may be seen from the following quotation in which recommendations (a) and (b) are contradictory.

"*The Role of Private Enterprise.* (1) The future role of private enterprise in education should be broadly on the following principles; (a) as most private enterprise has played an important role in the development of education in modern India, the State should make all possible use of the assistance that can come from the private sector for the development of education. (b) The State has now rightly assumed full responsibility to provide all the needed educational facilities and private enterprise can, therefore, have only a limited and minor role." Government of India, *Report of the Education Commission 1964–1966,* p. 667.

9. Rural Local Politics and Primary School Management

1. This chapter is a trend analysis in the specific context of Rajasthan. The analysis is based on the following sources: *Panchayati Raj* Research Project, Department of Economics and Public Administration, University of Rajasthan, "Report on the Management of Primary Schools under *Panchayati Raj,* a Study in the Jaipur District," mimeo. (Jaipur, 1967); cited hereafter as "The Jaipur District Report"; Cell of Applied Research in Rural Politics and Administration, Department of Political Science, University of Rajasthan, "An Opinion Survey Report on the Management of Primary Schools under *Panchayati Raj,* a Study in the Jhalawar District," mimeo. (Jaipur, 1967); referred to henceforth as "The Jhalawar District Opinion Survey"; Government of Rajasthan, *The Report of Rajasthan State Primary Education Committee* (Jaipur, 1965); henceforth cited as *Naik Committee Report,* after the name of its chairman, J. P. Naik; Government of Rajasthan, *Report of the Study Team on Panchayati Raj* (Jaipur, 1964), popularly known as *Sadiq Ali Committee Report,* after the name of its chairman, and hereafter cited as such; a content analysis of *Rajasthan Legislative Assembly Proceedings,* hereafter referred to as *RLAP;* and a set of select informal but intensive interviews.

2. *Panchayati raj* was introduced in Rajasthan in November 1959. As an institutionalized mechanism of rural local government, it treats the block as the key unit of decentralization and has a three-tier institutional structure which consists of: the *panchayat* at the village level with its members (*panchas*) elected on a ward basis and its chairman or head (*sarpanch*) elected by all the adult residents of the *panchayat,* both on the basis of universal adult franchise; the *panchayat samiti* at the block level with the *sarpanchas* of the constituent *panchayats* as its ex officio members and its chairman or head (*pradhan*) elected by an electoral college of the *sarpanchas* and *panchas* of its area; and the *zila parishad* at the district level with the *pradhans* of the *panchayat samitis* as its ex officio members and its chairman or head (*pramukh*) elected by an electoral college consisting of all the *sarpanchas, pradhans,* members of the state legislative assembly (MLA), and members of parliament (MP) of the area. The block development officer (B.D.O.), popularly known as *Vikas Adhikari* (in charge of development) is the administrative officer attached to the *panchayat samiti.*

3. See table 40. We have made very rough extrapolations of the 1965 figures given there.

4. *RLAP,* 1, no. 21 (June 12, 1967) (Barkatulla Khan, minister for education). The quotations have been translated from Hindi.

For further details see *Naik Committee Report,* pp. 56–58. The "Jaipur District Report" (with which I was associated as deputy director of the project) earlier reported on similar lines, stating:

The transfer of the management of primary schools to the Panchayati Raj institutions has meant:

i) Mobilisation of local leadership in boosting up the cause of primary education and consequently the increase in the primary schools and the raising of local resources to a limited extent;

ii) Organization of a better system of on the spot supervision and control; and

iii) Facilities to teachers in terms of regular and more convenient payment of salaries, better access to authorities and quicker redress of difficulties (p. 23).

5. For the governor's speech, see *RLAP,* 1, no. 3 (4 May 1967), pp. 59–60. For data on primary school attendance in 1965–66, see Government of India, Ministry of Education, *Report of the Education Commission, 1964–1966* (Delhi, 1966), table 9, p. 590.

6. *RLAP,* 1, no. 21 (12 June 1967) (Barkatulla Khan, Minister for Education).

7. *RLAP,* 9, no. 20 (22 March 1966) (Bhairon Singh, Jan Sangh), pp. 4447–4456.

The difficulty in enrolling children from the poor and subjected is partially explained by the persistence of "untouchability" in village India. The commissioner for scheduled castes and tribes in his report covering 1966–67, noted, "untouchability persists in Gram Panchayats." For a summary of the report by a staff correspondent, see the *Statesman* (Delhi), 1 July 1968, p. 7.

For an over-all view of the problem see Barbara Ravenell (Joshi), "The Scheduled Castes and Panchayati Raj," M.A. thesis, The University of Chicago, 1965.

8. *Naik Committee Report,* p. 16: "To sum up, the Committee found that the quality of education has been adversely affected during the last 15 years. This is due to several factors. To begin with, there has been an unprecedented expansion of education and a large majority of children in elementary schools belong to the first generation to be educated. The fall in standards due to this social cause cannot probably be helped at this stage of our development. But the deterioration has been also due to a number of avoidable available factors such as the failure to provide adequate buildings and equipment, the non-provision of text books and writing material to all children, the failure to develop an adequate and high quality programme of training elementary teachers, ineffective supervision and the *general demoralization in the ranks of teachers because of transfer of primary schools to Panchayati Raj institutions"* (Emphasis added).

9. *RLAP,* 7, no. 12 (1 March 1965), p. 4543 (Man Singh Mahar, Swatantra).

10. *RLAP,* 8, no. 8 (7 March 1960), p. 1799. The "Jaipur District Report" also noted as early as 1962: "The first and in order of priority certainly the most important problem is how to safeguard the management of primary schools against the baneful effects of politics" (p. 23).

11. The *Statesman* (Delhi), 1 July 1968, p. 5.

12. For an elaboration of the point in the context of rural leadership, see: Iqbal Narain, "Democratic Decentralization and Rural Leadership in India: The Rajasthan Experiment," *Asian Survey,* 4, no. 8 (August 1964), pp. 1013–1022.

13. For an empirical probe of the process of interaction, see Iqbal Narain and Associates, "Political Behaviour in Rural India: The Case of a Panchayat

Election in Rajasthan," *Journal of Commonwealth Political Studies,* 5, no. 2 (July 1967), pp. 109–129.

14. For an empirical discussion of the process, see G. B. Mathur, "Link Politics: A Case Study," in Iqbal Narain, ed., *State Politics in India* (Meerut, 1967), pp. 608–618.

15. *RLAP,* 8, no. 5 (7 March 1960), p. 1799. See also *RLAP,* 1, no. 18 (4 April 1962), pp. 2963–2964 (Laxmi Chand, Jan Sangh), 2972–2975 (Hari Prasad Sharma, Jan Sangh), 3071–3072 (Govind Sahai, Jan Sangh); 4, no. 15 (21 August 1964), pp. 150–152 (Jodh Singh Chauhan, Jan Sangh); 5, no. 38 (4 April 1964), pp. 11–14 (Shrimati Sumitra, Congress); and 9, no. 25 (28 March 1966), p. 108 (Maharawal Laxman Singh, Swatantra).

16. *RLAP,* 3, no. 16 (19 March 1963), pp. 3277–3278 (Govind Singh, Congress). See also *RLAP,* 18, no. 8 (7 March 1960), p. 3302 (Digvijaya Singh, Swatantra); 1, no. 12 (30 March 1962), p. 1674 (Amar Singh, Swatantra); and 7, no. 12 (21 March 1965), p. 4747 (Kedar Nath, Independent), where, after accepting the existence of the phenomenon, the speaker also struck an optimistic note: "The growing awakening among the masses would provide the internal checks which would ensure that the teachers are not used as stooges to fulfil political interests."

17. *RLAP,* 8, no. 8 (7 March 1960). Also see *RLAP,* 10, no. 35 (4 April 1961), p. 8 (Prithvi Raj, Independent); 1, no. 6 (18 March 1962) (Govind Sahai, Jan Sangh); 1, no. 18 (4 April 1962), pp. 2996–3001 (Mathuresh Bihari Mathur, Independent); 3, no. 16 (19 March 1963), pp. 3228–3240, where Jodh Singh of Jan Sangh alleged that Har Lal Chaudhary of Mavali had been transferred nine times within two and a quarter years. See also *RLAP,* 3, no. 16 (19 March 1963), p. 3268 (Shyopat Singh, Communist); and 9, no. 9 (9 March 1966), pp. 1453–1457, where Jai Narain Salodia (Swatantra) pointed out, "The teachers who keep away from politics are transferred to distant places."

18. In the light of the experiences of other state, central, and all-India services, the experience of Rajasthan's primary school teachers with respect to transfers is neither unique nor extraordinary. To politicians, transfer is an immediately effective and legally legitimate means to gain compliance from civil servants.

19. *RLAP,* 1, no. 21 (12 June 1967) (Mahendra Singh, Jan Sangh).

20. Jai Narain Salodia cited the following case, "The newly elected pradhan of Niwai is doing the same. The B.D.O. who resisted the mid-term transfers on the ground that they would harm teaching was transferred. The pradhan then had a free hand in the transfers, which were made on political grounds. The secretary, zila parishad, and the collector were approached to exercise a check. But they too failed and subsequently more transfers were made." *RLAP,* 9, no. 9 (9 March 1966), pp. 1453–1457.

21. *Naik Committee Report,* p. 22. *RLAP,* 1, no. 18 (4 April 1962), pp. 3072–3074 (Pohu Mal, Congress).

22. Interviews with the officers of the education department at the state and district levels and a review of representations made by *Rajasthan Shikshak Sangh* (an all-Rajasthan association of primary school teachers) has led me to draw these conclusions.

23. *RLAP,* 7, no. 12 (10 March 1965), Q. no. 275, pp. 2366–2367.

24. T. H. is the short form of Tazirate Hind (Indian Penal Code). According to Article 342 of the code, whoever wrongfully confines any person shall be punished with imprisonment of up to one year or with a fine of up to Rs. 1000, or both.

25. To fight against mounting corruption the Rajasthan government, on the pattern of the central government, set up a vigilance commission in 1964 to examine the complaints made by the citizens and suggest action against defaulting officers. It is usually a one-man commission, the vigilance commissioner being a person of the status of a high court judge appointed by the state government. The commission, though an independent body, is only advisory in character. It submits an annual report to the state legislature; since its jurisdiction excludes politicians, its importance in fighting corruption is reduced.

26. *RLAP,* 5, no. 20 (18 March 1964), Q. no. 513, 296–298. See also *RLAP,* 8, no. 8 (7 March 1960), p. 1799, where the Jan Sangh leader complained: "The teachers who are used to further the interests of and propagate for the ruling faction, do not care to take the classes. They travel with the pradhan in his jeep and are marked present for that." Also, see *RLAP,* 1, no. 21 (21 June 1967), where Mahendra Singh of the Jan Sangh alleged: "The primary school teachers . . . have to take into account and abide by the wishes not only of the pradhans and the sarpanchas but of their 'yes man' as well. Naturally the teachers find less time to devote to their business. The teachers are also developing a taste for politics. They side with the party in power in order to secure more facilities and to assure less control over irregular opening of the schools."

27. The name of the person who replied on behalf of the government is unavailable.

28. See *RLAP,* 2, no. 2 (22 October 1962), p. 2098, where Shri Man Singh Mahar (Swatantra) said: "The teachers, the poor fellows, have to suffer a lot. Earlier, they had to please only one master, the inspector. But now they have to seek the pleasure of not only the pradhan and the B.D.O., but of all the panchas and sarpanch as well." A more telling observation has been made by the Jan Sangh leader, Bhairon Singh. "Earlier only one, the inspector, was a raja, but now there are too many rajas." *RLAP,* 8, no. 8 (7 March 1960).

29. *RLAP,* 8, no. 8 (7 March 1960). Also, see *RLAP,* 1, no. 26 (24 April 1962), p. 4803, where Ghasi Ram Yadav (Congress) described PR as an irresponsible government within a responsible government.

30. *RLAP,* 8, no. 4 (1 March 1960), p. 793 (Narottam Lal Joshi, Congress).

31. *RLAP,* 1, no. 3 (16 March 1962), pp. 127–128 (Maharawal Laxman Singh, Swatantra); also 1, no. 19 (19 April 1962), p. 3131 (Man Singh Mahar, Swatantra), where the speaker alleges that the teachers were advised to canvass for the Congress candidates in general elections; 7, no. 24 (27 March 1965), p. 6045 (Amar Singh, Swatantra, who found fault with the appointment of teachers as polling officers as they are politically involved); and also p. 6103 (Umrao Singh Dhabaria, Samyukta Socialist Party).

32. *RLAP,* 1, no. 21 (6 June 1967) (Badri Prasad Gupta, Independent). Fateh Singh (Swatantra) also alleged: "The teachers of primary schools along with other teachers had participated in electioneering on behalf of Congress

candidates in Beawar constituency. They travelled in jeeps and organized meetings. Complaints were made against them during the period of electioneering to the Returning Officers, I.O.S., and Director of Education. But no action has been taken against them. Does it mean that higher officials are also a party to it? The teachers openly said that they had instructions from the chief minister and education minister to do so." *RLAP*, 1, no. 21 (6 June 1967).

33. *RLAP*, 3, no. 16 (19 March 1963), p. 3236, where the Jan Sangh MLA alleged: "How manipulation and interference goes on in the samiti schools is evident from the following letter [of a B.D.O. to the head master of a primary school]:

You have not followed the instructions from the office. Neither has the said student been promoted, nor has his character been mentioned as satisfactory. Now this is the last warning. Do in accordance with the instructions.

In case you fail to do that, you will be considered suspended by July 16. You are guilty of that now. The student has already been granted special promotion.

And in spite of that, the teacher has been transferred at 25 miles distance and his increment has been stopped for 2 and a half years."

The details of the case, however, could not be obtained and therefore it could not be verified whether the headmaster was guilty of corrupt practice, which would have invited administrative intervention. The case was quoted on the floor of the house as a case of politico-administrative interference in educational administration.

34. *RLAP*, 4, no. 8 (28 October 1963), p. 79 (Gokul Prasad Sharma, Congress).

35. A militant wing of the Hindu-oriented Jan Sangh party.

36. See the verdict of the *Naik Committee Report:* "Worst of all, political pressures have come into the picture and the inspection of schools is no longer the purely academic function it once was or should always be" (p. 15).

37. Government of India, Ministry of Education, *Report of Fourth National Seminar on Compulsory Primary Education* (New Delhi, 1964), pp. 81–82.

38. *RLAP*, 1, no. 26 (29 April 1962), p. 4803 (Murli Dhar Vyas, PSP).

39. See *RLAP*, 3, no. 12 (3 March 1963), pp. 2258–59, where Man Singh Mahar (Swatantra) makes a plea to close unproductive schools (that is, schools with fewer than forty students) without any party considerations; 4, no. 9 (9 March 1966), p. 1473, where Shankar Lal (Congress) alleges that "the samitis open new schools to take political advantage without considering the number of students; and 1, no. 21 (17 June 1967), where Kedar Nath (Samyukta Socialist Party) calls "the expansion of primary education as totally unplanned and haphazard" because "the schools have been opened on political considerations."

40. *RLAP*, 4, no. 15 (21 October 1964), pp. 123–138 (Umrao Singh Dhabaria, SSP).

41. For example, Murli Dhar Vyas (Praja Socialist Party), citing *Education in Districts of Rajasthan,* pointed out that Rs. 147,600 have been spent

in primary education in Udaipur, the chief minister's home district, while in Bikaner, only Rs. 34,000 have been spent. (*RLAP,* 8, no. 14 [16 March 1960], p. 3009.) The significance of this discrepancy could only be fully determined by investigating the relative populations and previous educational progress in the two districts, which has not been done here. It is generally known that Bikaner state was ahead of Udaipur in education at independence.

42. See the observation of the Naik Committee: "After assessing the situation from every point of view, the Committee feels that, during the last 15 years, the morale of the elementary teachers has been adversely affected, especially after the transfer of primary education to the Panchayat Samitis" (*Naik Committee Report,* p. 13). In this connection, J. P. Naik said elsewhere: "We must realize that the quality of elementary education is just proportional to the morale of the elementary teachers and that this would be the highest in government service and lowest in the service of a local body where every teacher is forced, willy-nilly, to become a pawn in a local political game." J. P. Naik, *Elementary Education in India: The Unfinished Business* (Bombay, 1966), pp. 47–48.

43. For elucidation of the point see *RLAP,* 9, no. 2 (9 March 1966), p. 1489, where Chosar Singh (Swatantra) alleges that the teachers in the *samitis* have become the servants of the *pradhan* and the BDO; and *RLAP,* 1, no. 4 (5 May 1967), p. 106, where Maharawal Laxman Singh (Swatantra) finds "primary schools under the samitis" to be "a mockery of the whole of the eductional system. The teacher who should be given high regard is considered as a servant by the local leaders. This is a tragic situation."

44. For examples of exceptional misbehavior, see *RLAP,* 9, no. 3 (24 October 1960), Q. no. 87, pp 480–488, where Dr. Bahadur Singh (Congress) poses the question of misbehavior of a *sarpanch* and an *upsarpanch* with a woman teacher, which the *panchayat* minister confirms; *RLAP,* 10, no. 10 (20 September 1966), pp. 102–207, where Ramanand Agarwal (Communist Party of India) moves a motion of adjournment on the beating of a teacher in a *panchayat samiti* with the connivance of police and where the government promises an immediate enquiry; and *RLAP,* 9, no. 36 (14 March 1966), pp. 126–127, where a call attention motion is moved on an allegation of a teacher having been badly beaten by a *sarpanch.*

45. *RLAP,* 1, no. 5 (5 June 1967) (Manohar Singh Mehta, Independent). See chap. 9, note 32, this volume.

46. *RLAP,* 14, no. 14 (11 March 1964), pp. 127–130 (Bhairon Singh, Jan Sangh).

47. The latest position with regard to the teachers' grievances was summed up by a spokesman of the Rajasthan Teachers' Association in a press conference and reported in the *Statesman* (Delhi), July 1, 1968.

The teachers were completely fed up with the panchayat samitis which harassed them by transferring them from one place to another. The teachers, he added, had to work for 12 hours a day.

Besides teaching the students in school, they were forced to take up adult literacy classes in the evenings. Also every teacher had to compulsorily deposit money in small savings and if he refused, he was transferred.

Most of the teachers, the spokesman added, were not paid their salaries for three or four months because the panchayat samitis were short of funds. Arrears of pay and allowances amounting to nearly Rs. 50 lakhs had not been paid since 1959, he said.

The spokesman also said that the Association had drawn attention of the department authorities in this connection. According to him, meetings had been called thrice in this connection but nothing had been done.

48.   Eighteen teachers were interviewed; four of these were managing single teacher schools; of these, two were women. In all, thirteen officials and fifty-four elected PR officials were interviewed.

49.   Impression as recorded by our interviewer.

50.   It is interesting to note that two out of five women teachers (already included in the total in table 42) said that they did not know, while one denied involvement and two affirmed it.

51.   Protection against transfer to distant places can be cited as an example. Teachers are sometimes more concerned to cover irregularities than to protect their legitimate interests. For example, teachers do not always stay at the headquarters, as they are required to do under the law. Consequently they often are late in reaching the school. They can live away from headquarters only with the connivance of the elected representatives and block officials.

52.   The question was not put to teachers, as it was rather delicate for them to answer.

53.   Letter No. EDB/P1/III/23742/12/67 (by courtesy of the Jt. Secretary).

54.   *Naik Committee Report,* pp. 115–116.

55.   "Jaipur District Report," appendix 4, which embodies a note on the control of the schools, develops the idea of the autonomous managerial pattern.

In order to insulate the school management from political influences, the Panchayat Samiti might be relieved of all their administrative responsibilities in matters of school management. As we have separate Nyaya Panchayat so we could have separate school Panchayat also. While suggesting this, it is certainly not the intention to take education away from the hands of the representatives of the local community. The local community would still be in the overall control of it, because it will elect members of the school Panchayat or school Panchayat Samiti. This will have two-fold advantages:

(i)   The local community will have a tendency to elect people who are interested in education since they are to administer only schools and nothing else.

(ii)   As has been the experience elsewhere in such an election, politics is likely to have only a secondary role to play. The suitability of the persons concerned will be a primary consideration for the present day Panchayat and Panchayat Samiti election. This is just the other way at present.

Thus for educational purposes the community will have a separate chain of institutions — School Panchayat, School Panchayat Samiti, and School Zila Parishad, etc.

On average a School Panchayat should have three members, School Panchayat Samiti might have five to seven members, and School Zila Parishad might have 15–20 members. The small numbers will ensure integrity and efficiency. In a Panchayat area it might not be difficult to select three good persons who are really interested in providing good educational system. If larger number of persons are to be elected at this level, standards must of necessity be lowered.

At all the levels that this could be provided for at least ⅓ of total membership should come from teachers. In these school Boards ⅓ members should be elected by the local community, another ⅓ should be nominated from amongst the persons employed in these educational institutions as teachers.

These bodies will be separate statutory bodies and should not be subordinate to the Panchayat or Panchayat Samiti, otherwise their very purpose is likely to be defeated. Their term of office may be two years. Normal practice should be that they are not paid for serving on the Boards. However, a small fee to meet the out of pocket expenses might be admissible.

56. Naik, *Elementary Education in India,* p. 48.

57. The cross reference is to an earlier recommendation which reads:

The remaining persons should not be elected members of the Municipality and should have any one or more of the following qualifications:

(1) A Graduate of a University (or a person with an equivalent qualification) with three years standing;
(2) A teacher in a college with not less than two years experience;
(3) A Headmaster of a Secondary School with five years experience or an Assistant Master in the Secondary School with 10 years experience;
(4) The Headmaster of a Primary/Middle School with 15 years experience or a primary/middle school teacher with 20 years experience; and
(5) A retired officer of the Education Department in the State.

58. *Naik Committee Report,* pp. 118–119.

10.   Autonomy and Consensus under the Raj:
       Presidency (Calcutta); Muir (Allahabad); M.A.-O. (Aligarh)

1. The description which follows is based on the enabling acts of the three older universities; the later universities were founded on the same pattern. James Alexander Richey, ed., *Selections from Educational Records, pt. 2, 1840–1859* (Calcutta, 1922), pp. 408–423.

2. The office of rector of the Calcutta University was later created for the lieutenant-governor of Bengal. For the particular histories of the five universities, see Pramathanath Banerjee, ed., *Hundred Years of the University of Calcutta* (Calcutta, 1957); S. R. Dongerkerry, *A History of the University of Bombay, 1857–1957* (Bombay, 1957); University of Madras, *History of Higher Education in South India,* vol. 1, *University of Madras, 1857–1957* (Madras, 1957); K. K. Mehrottra, ed., *Seventieth Anniversary Souvenir, University of Allahabad* (Allahabad, 1957); J. Bruce, *A History of the Punjab University* (Lahore, 1933).

3. The bachelors degree was required for admission to the university law classes, and the first arts degree usually required for admission to the medical college.

4. This was an intermediate examination taken after the first two of four years devoted to the bachelors degree.

5. The same was true for the masters in the anglo-vernacular high schools, who taught the university curriculum and prepared students for the university matriculation or college entrance examination.

6. *Presidency College, Calcutta, Centenary Volume, 1955* (Alipore, West Bengal, 1956), pp. 1–3 (no author given).

7. Banerjee, *Hundred Years of the University of Calcutta*, pp. 10–11.

8. *Presidency College, Calcutta, Centenary Volume*, pp. 1–3.

9. Ibid., p. 4.

10. Ibid.

11. India Office, *Notes to Public Despatches to Bengal and India*, vol. 35, despatch dated 12 September, 1854, no. 62 Public (Educational).

12. *Presidency College, Calcutta, Centenary Volume*, pp. 15, 22, 23.

13. John Eliot, Presidency College, *Annual Report for the Year Ending 31 March 1893* (without publishing information), in the Presidency College Library; W. C. Wordsworth, *Quinquennial Report on the Presidency College and the Attached Institutions for the Quinquennium ending 31st March 1917* (Calcutta, 1918).

14. The only other affiliates which offered masters degree courses were the colleges at Dacca and Gauhati (both government colleges), in English, and the Scottish Church College in Calcutta and the Victoria College in Cooch Behar, in philosophy. Government of India, *Proceedings in the Education Department*, Deposit-November 1916, no. 19.

15. Calcutta University Commission, 1917–19, *Report*, vol. 1, pt. 1, *Analysis of Present Conditions* (Calcutta, 1919), p. 414.

16. Government of Bengal, *Proceedings in the General Department, Education Branch*, A-22, May 1869, nos. 25–31.

17. Government of India, *Proceedings in the Home Department, Education Branch*, A-14, August 1869, nos. 19–22.

18. Ibid.

19. From the principals' annual reports, on file in the Presidency College Library.

20. James Sutcliffe, *Presidency College, Annual Report for 1872–73*, and Alexander Pedler, *Presidency College, Annual Report for the Year Ending 31 March 1896* (without publishing information), both on file in the Presidency College Library; Wordsworth, *Quinquennial Report on the Presidency College*.

21. Rs. 12 was the tuition fee through most of the nineteenth century, supplemented by a scholarship program financed by the Bengal government.

22. The following is drawn from information gathered from interviews, memoires, and reminiscences of government college students and professors.

23. *Presidency College, Calcutta, Centenary Volume*, p. 18.

24. *Presidency College Magazine, Silver Jubilee Number*, 25, no. 2 (March 1939).

25. *Presidency College Magazine*, 2, no. 2 (September 1915), pp. 126–134.

26. Henry Rosher James, *Problems of Higher Education in India* (Calcutta, 1916), pp. 78–79.

27. Premanath Banerjee, ed., *Hundred Years of the University of Calcutta, Supplement* (Calcutta, 1957), p. 1.

28. University of Calcutta, *Minutes for the Year, 1868–69* (Calcutta, 1869), pp. 146–147.

29. Government of the North-Western Provinces, *Proceedings in the General Department*, A-November 1870, nos. 17–23.

30. Ibid.

31. Government of the North-Western Provinces, *Proceedings in the Education Department*, A-November 1872, nos. 29–47.

32. Government of the North-Western Provinces, *Proceedings in the Education Department*, A-November 1873, no. 8.

33. There is no mention of the vernacular examinations in the provincial education records in connection with the Muir Central College after 1884; the examinations may have been transferred to a different set of institutional auspices.

34. This is largely an educated guess. The university records, including the Muir records, were destroyed in 1960 for want of storage space; nor were the Muir principals' annual reports reprinted in the North-Western Provinces gazette until well into the twentieth century. The information is drawn from impressions based upon settlement patterns and social patterns in Allahabad, some family histories, and a number of interviews which seemed to confirm these impressions.

35. Government of India, Indian Education Commission, *Report of the Indian Education Commission* (Calcutta, 1883), pp. 585–602 ("Recommendations").

36. Government of the North-Western Provinces, *Proceedings in the Education Department*, B-February 1884, nos. 1–4.

37. Government of the North-Western Provinces, *Proceedings in the Education Department*, A-September 1887, nos. 1–62.

38. University of Allahabad, *Calendar for the Year 1893–94* (Allahabad, 1894), pp. 155–157; *Calendar for the Year 1920* (Allahabad, 1920), pp. 417–421; *Minutes for the Year 1890* (Allahabad, 1890), p. 95; *Minutes for the Year 1920* (Allahabad, 1921), pp. v, xi.

39. Amaranatha Jha, ed., *A History of the Muir Central College, 1872–1922* (Allahabad, 1936), pp. 111–47.

40. Jha, *A History of the Muir Central College*, p. 17.

41. Ibid., pp. 129–147.

42. Mehrottra, *Seventieth Anniversary Souvenir, University of Allahabad*, p. 98.

43. Government of the North-Western Provinces, *Proceedings in the Education Department*, A-June 1873, nos. 29–41.

44. Government of the North-Western Provinces, *Proceedings in the Education Department*, A-June 1873, nos. 29–41; B-January 1879, no. 1; A-January 1883, nos. 3–9.

45. The day was Queen Victoria's birthday. Theodore Morison, *The History of the M.A.-O. College, Aligarh, From its Foundation to the Year 1903* (Allahabad, 1903), pp. 60, 62.

46. Ibid., pp. 25, 65, 66, 67.

47. *Times* (London), 7 September 1899, p. 8.

48. Theodore Beck, *The Principal's Annual Report for 1895–96* (Aligarh, 1896), pp. 2–3.

49. Arnold later joined the Indian Educational Service in the Punjab, and Morison went on to become a member of the secretary of state's India council in England. During Beck's time, a total of twelve British professors joined the Aligarh staff for varying periods; Morison, *History of the M.A.-O. College, Aligarh,* p. 67.

50. Letter from Theodore Beck to Sir Syed Ahmad Khan, dated March 19, 1896; in the Azad Library, Aligarh Muslim University.

51. File in the record room, council house, Lucknow, marked only File no. 40 of 1918, a block file in the education department relating to Aligarh.

52. Theodore Beck to Sir Syed Ahmad Khan, 19 March 1896.

53. Government of India, *Proceedings in the Home Department, Education Branch,* A-June 1907, nos. 76–79.

54. Interviews, especially with Mr. Nirmal Chandra Bhattacharyea, Calcutta, May 1967.

55. N. K. Sinha, *Asutosh Mookerjee, A Biographical Study* (Calcutta, 1966), pp. 7–8. I have used the spelling used in the government records, and found most often in the contemporary press.

56. Sir Asutosh was vice-chancellor from 1906 to 1914, and again from 1921 to 1924, but during the intervening years, he was still the controlling force in the formulation of university policy. Sinha states, "The two Indian Vice-Chancellors had walked in the footsteps of Sir Asutosh Mookerjee and his ascendency in university affairs was never shaken." A commentator in the *Times of London* was less polite, calling him a "virtual dictator." Sinha, *Asutosh Mookerjee,* pp. 6, 7, 32, 121; *Times* (London), June 3, 1931, p. 11.

57. The act was based on the recommendations of the Raleigh commission of 1902; see Government of India, Indian Universities Commission, *Report of the Indian Universities Commission* (Simla, 1902).

58. Banerjee, *Hundred Years of the University of Calcutta,* pp. 248–249.

59. Government of India, *Proceedings in the Education Department,* A-January 1917, nos. 41–45.

60. University of Calcutta, *Minutes for the Year 1916, Senate and the Faculties* (Calcutta, 1917), pp. 93–109.

61. University of Calcutta, *Minutes for the Year 1914,* pt. 1 (Calcutta, 1915), pp. 200–229.

62. University of Calcutta, *Minutes for the Year 1913,* pt. 5 (Calcutta, 1914), p. 1818.

63. Ibid., p. 1819, and University of Calcutta, *Minutes for the Year 1914,* pt. 3 (Calcutta, 1915), pp. 572–574.

64. Government of India, *Proceedings in the Education Department,* A-March 1914, nos. 26–32.

65. The book was *Education and Statesmanship in India, 1797 to 1910* (Calcutta, 1910). Government of India, *Proceedings in the Education Department,* A-November 1916, nos. 4–6.

66. From James' service history published annually by the Bengal government, and the *Times* (London), June 3, 1931, p. 11; William Christopher

Wordsworth, "Principal Henry Rosher James," *Presidency College Magazine,* 25, no. 2 (March 1939), p. 117; Government of Bengal, *Proceedings in the General Department, Education Branch,* B-December 1907, nos. 7–13.

67. Government of Bengal, *Proceedings in the General Department, Education Branch,* A-November 1913, no. 24.

68. *Presidency College Magazine,* 38, no. 1 (September 1953), pp. 15–20.

69. Hornell was a retired member of the Bengal education department.

70. Government of India, *Proceedings in the Education Department,* Deposit-April 1914, no. 21.

71. James, *Education and Statesmanship in India,* p. 139.

72. James, "Progress, 1906–1916," *Presidency College Magazine,* 3, no. 3 (January 1917), pp. 179–189; Government of Bengal, *Proceedings in the General Department, Education Branch,* A-May 1910, nos. 28–9.

73. The students' consultative committee was formed in 1913 to bring the students and principal in closer touch with one another. Wordsworth, *Quinquennial Report on the Presidency College,* p. 4; Government of Bengal, *Proceedings in the General Department, Education Branch,* A-November 1913, no. 24.

74. James, *Education and Statesmanship in India,* pp. 137–138.

75. Government of Bengal, *Proceedings in the General Department, Education Branch,* A-November 1913, no. 24.

76. Henry Rosher James, *Report on the Presidency College and the Attached Institutions for the Year 1912–13* (Calcutta, 1914), pp. 5–6.

77. Government of Bengal, *Proceedings in the General Department, Education Branch,* A-March 1909, nos. 51–54.

78. Ibid.

79. Henry Rosher James, *Report on the Presidency College for the Quinquennium and Year Ending 31 March 1912* (Calcutta, 1913), pp. 11–12.

80. Government of Bengal, *Proceedings in the General Department, Education Branch,* A-March 1915, nos. 1–3.

81. University of Calcutta, *Minutes of the Year 1917, Part V* (Calcutta, 1918), pp. 1840–1871.

82. Calcutta University Commission, 1917–19, *Report,* vol. 7, *Evidence and Documents, General Memoranda and Oral Evidence,* p. 435.

83. Calcutta University Commission, 1917–19, *Report,* vol. 10, p. 416.

84. Government of Bengal, *Proceedings in the General Department, Education Branch,* A-November 1913, no. 24.

85. The word actually used by Oaten was "barbaroi" which, as he explained to the students, meant non-Greek speaking. *Presidency College Magazine,* 25, no. 2 (March 1939), p. 116; Edward Farley Oaten, *My Memories of India* (unpublished manuscript, Archives, Centre of South Asian Studies, Cambridge University), p. 42.

86. Oaten did not recall the incident concerning the correspondence described by P. N. Banerjee, the student editor, but in a recent interview he presumed that if he had been annoyed it would have been because the editor apparently expected him "to enter into a correspondence on a very serious accusation with an anonymous contributor." Oaten, *My Memories of India,* pp. 42–43; interview with Mr. E. F. Oaten, Walton on Thames, Surrey, England, 26, 27 February 1969.

87. *Presidency College Magazine,* 25, no. 2 (March 1939), p. 116.

88. Government of India, *Proceedings in the Education Department,* A-June 1916, nos. 122–27.

89. Oaten, *My Memories of India,* p. 43.

90. Government of India, *Proceedings in the Education Department,* A-June 1916, nos. 122–27.

91. Interview with Mr. E. F. Oaten, Walton on Thames, Surrey, England, 26, 27 February 1969; Oaten, *My Memories of India,* p. 45.

92. Government of India, *Proceedings in the Education Department,* A-June 1916, nos. 122–27.

93. Oaten had no recollection of the second incident, and it is not mentioned in his *My Memories of India.* In a personal letter, however, he recalled, "I suffered repeated infringements of the rule about noise in the corridors. . . . The Committee referred only to two incidents that had been brought to their notice. This was natural, as on the other occasions there were no incidents. . . . The fact [was] that I was intolerably provoked, quite possibly by the political element in the College, the result being frequent disturbance of my lectures." Letter from Mr. E. F. Oaten, dated 24 March 1969.

94. Oaten, *My Memories of India,* pp. 43–45; interview with Mr. P. K. Basu, the student who claimed to have been assaulted by Oaten. Mr. Basu described Principal James' treatment of him as fair and courteous throughout. Calcutta, May 1967.

95. Government of India, *Proceedings in the Education Department,* A-June 1916, nos. 122–27.

96. Ibid.

97. Ibid.

98. Government of India, *Proceedings in the Education Department,* A-November 1916, nos. 4–5.

99. Ibid.

100. Eventually, on condition of a public apology, the Bengal government agreed to retract the suspension, and place the fifty-four year old James on long leave preparatory to retirement. Government of India, *Proceedings in the Education Department,* A-June 1916, nos. 122–27; A-November 1916, nos. 4–6.

101. Government of India, *Proceedings in the Education Department,* A-June 1916, nos. 122–27.

102. Calcutta University Commission, 1917–19, *Report,* vol. 7, p. 229.

103. The charges against Oaten were never proved. When the college reopened in July of 1916, he returned to find an amicable situation, and taught there for two and one-half months. In mid-September, because the war in Europe had depleted the Indian Army of British officers, he was given a commission in Probyn's Horse, an elite Indian Cavalry regiment, and served for two and one-half years on the North-West Frontier and in the Punjab. He returned to Bengal in April of 1919 as principal of the Hughli College, and eventually rose to be director of public instruction in Bengal in 1924. Government of India, *Proceedings in the Education Department,* A-June 1916, nos. 122–127.

104. The masters students enrolled at Presidency took their courses at the university after 1917.

105. The *Times* (London), 16 June 1947; *The Muir Central College Magazine*, 5, no. 1 (September 1918), p. 2.

106. Marris eventually rose to become governor of the United Provinces. File in the record room, council house, Lucknow, marked only File no. 40 of 1918, a block file in the education department relating to Aligarh.

107. Government of the United Provinces, *Selections from the Native Newspapers Published in the United Provinces, Received up to the 16th February 1907* (without page number or publishing information).

108. Government of the United Provinces, File no. 40 of 1918.

109. Ibid.

110. The following narrative is a reconstruction drawn largely from Committee of Inquiry, *Report of the Committee of Inquiry at Aligarh* (Aligarh, 1907), pp. 7–17.

111. Ibid., p. 17.

112. From the Lucknow *Advocate* of March 7, 1907; Government of the United Provinces, *Selections from the Native Newspapers Published in the United Provinces, Received up to the 16th March, 1907* (without page number or publishing information).

113. Archbold revoked his rustication order for six students when he was informed of the Nawab's promise, but by that time the students had already left the college. Committee of Inquiry, *Report of the Committee of Inquiry at Aligarh*, p. 17.

114. Ibid., p. 11.

115. A place was found for Archbold in the Indian Educational Service as principal of the government college at Dacca. Collection of printed papers in the Azad Library, Aligarh Muslim University, Dated 25 March 1909.

116. Government of the United Provinces, File no. 40 of 1918.

117. *Minutes of the Proceedings of a Consultation Meeting of the Trustees,* held on the 24th, 25th, and 29th of April 1909 at the house of the Hon'ble Nawab Sir Faiyez Ali Khan Bahadur, Aligarh, p. 1 (in the collection of the Azad Library, Aligarh Muslim University).

118. James, *Education and Statesmanship in India,* pp. 83–84.

119. Ibid., pp. 121–122.

120. Sir Asutosh opposed Chittaranjan Das in the early 1920's when the latter called upon the Calcutta University students to leave their classrooms for political action. Sir Asutosh told the students to stay in their classrooms.

121. Government of India, *Proceedings in the Education Department,* B-October 1917, no. 112.

11. Parochialism and Cosmopolitanism in University Government: The Environments of Baroda University

1. These included the Central Library, the Oriental Institute (1927), the Kalabhavan (Polytechnic), the College of Indian Music, Dance and Dramatics (1881), the Baroda Sanskrit Mahavidyalaya (1915), the Pratap Singh College of Commerce and Economics (1942), and the Secondary Teachers Training College (1935). See Maharaja Sayajirao University of Baroda, *Thirteenth Annual Report, 1961–62* (Baroda, 1962). Other sources of university history are the records of the K. M. Munshi Committee, Government of Baroda, *Re-*

port of the Baroda University Committee (Baroda, 1948); Saraswati S. Pandit, "A Study of the Development of the Maharaja Sayajirao University of Baroda (1949–1965)," M. Ed. Dissertation, MS University of Baroda, 1966; and Government of Baroda, *The Report of the Baroda University Commission* (Baroda, 1927), the report of an earlier, aborted attempt to establish a university.

2. The university's founding preceded by a year the "derecognition" of the last ruling maharaja for attempting, in a manner characteristic of the energy, if not the prudence, of his line, to create a combination of princes who might reconsider accession to the Indian union. V. P. Menon, *The Story of the Integration of the Indian States* (Calcutta, 1956), pp. 425–430. Menon quotes Baroda's contention that the merger agreement (to accede to India) "was with the Dominion Government and not its successors," that is, the Republic of India (p. 427). Menon also discusses the other causes of Baroda's loss of recognition.

3. For the industrial development of Ahmedabad, including the traditional quality of its merchants, see K. L. O. Gillion, *Ahmedabad: A Study on Indian Urban History* (Berkeley, 1968).

4. See Lloyd I. Rudolph and Susanne Hoeber Rudolph, *The Modernity of Tradition, Political Development in India* (Chicago, 1967), pt. 2, "The Traditional Roots of Charisma: Gandhi."

5. See chap. 5, table 20, this volume.

6. For the partisan commitments and ideological orientations of Baroda's industrial elite see Howard L. Erdman, "Political Attitudes of Baroda Industrialists," in the "Review of Management" section of the *Economic and Political Weekly,* 4, no. 29 (29 November 1969), pp. M 117-M 122.

7. Gujarat Vidyapith is the other exception.

8. The other districts in west India (Gujarat, Maharashtra, Rajasthan, and Madhya Pradesh) with high license rates are Poona, eighty-one; Surat, fifty-one; Jamnagar, twenty-eight; Rajkot, twenty-three; Bhavnagar, twenty-two; Kaira, twenty-two. No other west Indian district tops twenty. See Government of India, *Census of India, 1961, General Report on India,* vol. 1, pt. 1A (i), "Levels of Regional Development in India," and table 15, "Industrial Licenses Issued between January, 1953 and March, 1961, under the Industries (Development and Regulation) Act, Classified by Major Industrial Groups and by District to which Issued," (no page).

9. Ibid., p. 298.

10. Of the 2572 university-recognized colleges in 1965–66, 163 were university colleges. One hundred of 163 were associated with 27 affiliating universities and 63 with unitary universities. There were 1,327 university teaching departments functioning in 1965–66, 766 associated with 56 affiliating universities (an average of 13.6 per university) and 561 associated with 18 unitary universities (an average of 31.2 per university). These calculations are based on Government of India, University Grants Commission, *University Development in India; Basic Facts and Figures, 1965–66* (New Delhi, 1968), appendix 1(c), "University Colleges," pp. 225–226, appendix 1(d), "Affiliated Colleges," pp. 227–228, and appendix 2(a) "University-wise Distribution of Teaching Departments," pp. 229–230, read together with table 2, "Location, Year of Establishment, Type and Territorial Jurisdiction of Universities as on 1, 7, 1966."

11. There were twenty unitary and forty-four affiliating or federal universities in 1966. See UGC, *University Development in India, 1965–66,* table 3. Enrollment figures are given in appendix 4(b) and (c), pp. 236 and 237. The respective totals are 207, 558, and 1,281,215.

12. Lucknow had 17,528 students in 1966–67. See Government of India, University Grants Commission, *University Development in India; Basic Facts and Figures, 1966–67* (New Delhi, 1969), table 7, "University Enrollment," p. 27.

13. Ibid., pp. 189–190. Lucknow with 18.3 percent had fewer than one fifth.

14. See Joseph DiBona, *Change and Conflict in the Indian University* (Durham, N.C., 1969), and Philip Altbach, ed., *Turmoil and Transition: Higher Education and Student Politics in India* (Bombay, 1968).

15. Christopher Jencks and David Riesman, *The Academic Revolution* (Garden City, N.Y., 1969), pp. 61–64.

16. For a detailed analysis of this period see Subhash Kashyap, *Politics of Defection; A Study of State Politics in India* (New Delhi, 1969).

Tamil Nadu and Gujarat are among the eight (of sixteen, excluding Nagaland) states that have been governed by the same party or coalition since March 1967, when governments were formed after the fourth general election. Bihar and Uttar Pradesh are the most and next most unstable among the remaining eight with seven governments and two spells of presidential rule, and five governments and two spells of presidents rule respectively. There was a change of government in the technical sense in Tamil Nadu when M. Karunanidhi became chief minister in February 1969, after the death of C. N. Annadurai. We are indebted for this information to Vraj Mohan Sinha, "The Challenges of 1970's for Public Administration," a paper presented at the Annual Conference of the Indian Institute of Public Administration, New Delhi, 24 October 1970, cyclostyled, appendix 1.

17. See chap. 5, table 20, columns 2, 4, and 6, this volume. For the social rates of return to education, see Amartya Sen, "The Crisis in Indian Education," (The Lal Bahadur Shastri Memorial Lectures, delivered March 10 and 11, 1970), cyclostyled.

Sen also argues that enrollment data based on education ministry reporting is likely to be substantially inflated and cites census data for 1961 that show primary school enrollment in Uttar Pradesh and Bihar not only to be the lowest in the country but also at about *half* the level shown in chap. 5, table 20, column 2; that is, they had 30 and 29 percent respectively of the relevant age group (six to eleven years) enrolled compared to a national average for 1960–61 (based on education ministry figures) of 62.8 percent.

In 1965, university enrollments per million were, Gujarat, 3,990; Tamil Nadu, 2,800; Uttar Pradesh, 4,614; and Bihar, 2,437. UGC, *University Development in India, 1965–66,* table 13, "University Enrollment and Population," p. 38. We have not used the summary measures of university enrollment in chap. 5, table 2, column 10, this volume, because the Uttar Pradesh figures do not include students enrolled under the Uttar Pradesh Board of High School and Intermediate Education, which has jurisdiction over intermediate education (classes XI and XII). Of the 374,447 university enrolled students in Uttar Pradesh in 1965–66, 240,000 (approximately two-thirds) were under the Board. This proportion holds for the 1960–61 data, raising the figure in chap. 5, table 20, column 10, this volume, from 1.5 to 4.5. For enrollments under the Uttar Pradesh Board, see UGC, *University Development in India, 1965–66,* appendix 3, "Enrollment Statistics Relating to Intermediate Board, U.P., 1963–64, 1964–65, 1965–66," pp. 232–234.

18. The higher benefits that accrue to engineering and medical as against arts education are both individual and collective (social). We recognize the difficulties involved in establishing how and to whom or to what benefits accrue at the collective levels. Incomes of engineers and doctors are higher than those of arts graduates, and we assume here that their potential contribution to "productivity" under favorable conditions of employment and of economic growth is higher too. Under the conditions of unemployment for engineers and even doctors that characterized the Indian economy in the late 1960's, it is a wasteful investment from a social if not from a political point of view to subsidize at the margin such expensive professional education. But the failure of government policy to expand production and welfare at rates that absorb the output of engineers and doctors is as much the "cause" of such waste as is the pressure of political demand to provide access to seats that yield high private benefits.

19. Calculations based on UGC, *University Development in India, 1965–66,* table 21, "State-wise and Faculty-wise Distribution of Enrollment," p. 93. On a per million basis, the figures for arts faculty enrollment in 1965–66 were: Gujarat, 1,417; Tamil Nadu, 856; Uttar Pradesh, 1,954; and Bihar, 1,277. Per million enrollment for engineering and technology and for medicine in 1965–66 was: Gujarat, 476; Tamil Nadu, 391; Uttar Pradesh, 156; and Bihar, 197. Gujarat's higher per million enrollment in arts than Bihar's is a reflection of Gujarat's over-all higher enrollment levels, and of the fact that Bihar's educational pyramid is not as top-heavy as that in Uttar Pradesh. Although Gujarat has more B.A.s per million enrolled than does Bihar it also has more than twice as many engineering and technology and medical students enrolled (476 to 197).

20. For an extended version of this argument and a survey of the relevant literature, see Rudolph and Rudolph, *The Modernity of Tradition,* especially pt. 1, "Traditional Structures and Modern Politics: Caste."

21. These data are drawn from Kansas State University, "Enrollment by State and Protectorate, Fall Semester, 1966–67," mimeo. (n.d.), kindly supplied to us by William Richter; U.S., Office of Education, *Residence and Migration of College Students* (Washington, D.C., 1939), table B, p. 6; *Report of the President of Harvard College and Reports of Departments, 1965–66* (Cambridge, 1967), table 9 of the report of the Admission and Scholarship Committee; University of Chicago, Director of Admissions and Aid, "A Biographical Sketch of the Class of 1971," (Chicago, 1971, mimeo.), p. 2; The University of Sussex, "Admissions: Annual Statistical Report (Shortened Version), 1964–65," (Sussex, n.d., mimeo.), table 13, p. 12, kindly supplied to us by Professor Anthony Low; and Clemens Geissler, *Hochschulstandorte, Hochschulbesuch* (Hanover, 1965), tables 26.1 to 26.14, pp. 42–55, kindly supplied to us by Mrs. Paul Fischer.

22. Christopher Jencks and David Riesman, *The Academic Revolution* (Garden City, 1968), pp. 179–180.

23.   Interviews with IAS probationers studying at the National Academy of Administration, Mussoorie, November 1962.

24.   The records were made available due to the courtesy of officials of the various faculties and the support extended to the research by the vice-chancellor.

25.   Until 1956–57, average annual growth at MSU was 300 students; since then, the average annual growth has been 700–800.

26.   The figures, based on a one-fifth sample of students admitted to the B.A. program, are thirty-one Bihar students out of the sample of thirty-four in 1936 and sixty-three out of sixty-nine in 1963. For the city of Patna, the figures are seven of thirty-four in 1936 and thirty-five of sixty-nine in 1963. Personal communication from Ramashray Roy.

27.   Table 54 (arts faculty) shows a slight decline in Baroda and Gujarat residents from 88 percent to 85 percent of all students between 1955–56 and 1965–66. There may even have been more residents in 1955–56; 8 percent failed to give residence. The science figures (table 53) are inconclusive because of the high percentage (28 percent) unknown in 1955–56. If we use the arts records as guidance and predict on the basis of their distribution, these unknowns are locals. But we cannot with certainty allocate the science unknowns anywhere. It would not be proper to conclude, however, that the number of local residents has been rising.

28.   Of the city's 284,705 residents, 43,999 were born out of state or out of India. Government of India, *Census of India, 1961,* vol. 5, "Gujarat," pt. 2 C, cultural and migration tables, pp. 410 and 616.

29.   Of Gujarat's 5,316,624 urban dwellers, 500,187 were born out of state or out of India. Ibid., pp. 218–221.

30.   Discussion of a preliminary version of this chapter at the Sociology Seminar, Delhi School of Economics, Summer 1967, first drew our attention to this point. The seminar included a number of distinguished ex-Barodans. We are specifically indebted to Arvind Shah.

31.   This appears to be one area in which UGC advice, which, as we have suggested in the introduction, is not always adhered to, appears to be taken seriously. MSU of Baroda, Faculty of Technology and Engineering, *Prospectus, 1966–67* (Baroda, 1966), p. 26.

32.   For the pattern at IIT's, see A. D. King, "Elite Education and the Economy: IIT Entrance, 1965–70," *Economic and Political Weekly* (Bombay), 5, no. 35 (29 August 1970).

33.   The preparatory science course, which is a precondition for entrance to the Science B.Sc. course at Baroda, requires that the Senior School Leaving Certificate exam of Gujarat, or its equivalent, be passed with English, physics, chemistry, algebra, and geometry as subjects. It is likely that high standard English language public (private) schools provide better training in these fields than do state schools. See MSU of Baroda, Prep Unit, *Prospectus, 1965–66* (Baroda, 1965), p. 3.

34.   B. V. Shah, *Social Change and College Students of Gujarat* (Baroda, 1964), p. 18.

35.   United Nations, *Patterns of Social Requirement and Occupational Choice in an Apex Educational Institution,* typescript (UNESCO Research

Centre, New Delhi, 1965–6), table 3, p. 9A. Rural colleges may well show different figures. In Osmania's rural affiliates, 89 percent of the students were the first in their families to go to college. See table 7, p. 15.

36.   D. M. Desai and S. S. Pandit, *Growth and Development of Maharaja Sayajirao University of Baroda, 1949–1967* (Baroda, 1968), p. 27.

37.   W. S. Titus, writing about "Warning Signals from IITs" in the *Hindustan Times* of 26 September 1970, reports that fear of mutual talent grabbing discourages contacts and communication among the five IIT's, and between them and regional engineering and local colleges.

38.   Baroda Act XVII of 1949, chap. 7, Article 48. MSU of Baroda, *The Handbook 1961*, pt. 2 (corrected up to 1 February 1961) (Baroda, 1961), p. 31.

39.   MSU of Baroda, *The Report of the Vice-Chancellor's Committee on the Amendment of the Maharaja Sayajirao University of Baroda Act* (Baroda, 1969), letter from N. Chaudhuri, Dean, Fine Arts Faculty, p. 63.

40.   *Western Times* (Ahmedabad), 31 August 1969.

41.   MSU of Baroda, *Report of the Vice-Chancellor's Committee*, p. 45.

42.   MSU of Baroda, Faculty of Technology and Engineering, *Prospectus, 1966–67* (Baroda, 1966), pp. 1–10.

43.   D. M. Desai, "Enrollment Trend and Behaviour in Higher Education in the Gujarat State," *Education and Psychology Review* (Baroda), 6, no. 1 (January 1966), p. 14.

44.   The ethos and aspiration of the movement are well represented in MSU of Baroda, General Education Centre, *Report of the Regional Seminar on General Education* (December 10 to 14, 1963). This seminar may represent the crest of the wave as far as the general education movement in India is concerned.

45.   For some of the program's difficulties in its early years see MSU of Baroda, Department of General Education, *General Education Annual Report, 1957–58* (Baroda, 1958), pp. 140–153. Some of the difficulties mentioned there (for example, the need for synopses to provide students with reading material preparatory to discussion and lecture classes on "great books") have been alleviated by the production of syllabi or selections by the General Education Centre on such topics as "Comparative Study of Epic Eastern and Western with Reference to Homer, Vyasa and Valmiki."

46.   Desai and Pandit, *Growth and Development,* table 39, p.92.

47.   Ibid., table 40, p. 93.

48.   The calculations are based on ibid., table 10, p. 40 and table 44, p. 101. In each case we have related the number of Ph.D.s in a given period to cumulative annual enrollments in the same period.

49.   For the total Ph.D. production in the period 1960–61 to 1963–64, see chap. 4, tables 2 and 4, this volume. For enrollments during this period, see Government of India, *India, 1969,* table 33, p. 66.

50.   Desai and Pandit, *Growth and Development,* table 11, p. 41.

51.   The figure for per student cost comes from ibid., table 47, p. 105. The calculation of real prices is based on a conversion ratio derived from the statement of 1966–67 values at 1948–49 prices, adopted by the Economic Survey of 1968–69, cited in Government of India, *India, 1969,* p. 160.

52. Desai and Pandit, *Growth and Development,* table 32, p. 68. The figures for science are partly accounted for by the abolition in the mid-1950's of the old intermediate course, which had a large number of science students.

53. These efforts, in part a consequence of the presence of the faculty of education and psychology, its department of educational administration, and the Centre of Advanced Study in Education (CASE) include: D. M. Desai, *Vital Statistics of the Growth and Development of the Maharaja Sayajirao University of Baroda (1949–50 to 1966–67),* (Baroda, 1967); A. S. Patel, *Problem of Student Unrest and Indiscipline; a Symposium Report* (Baroda, 1967); D. M. Desai, *Some Problems of Education in the Gujarat State* (Baroda, 1967); P. J. Madan and A. S. Patel, eds., *Report of the Symposium on University Administration* (Baroda, 1968).

54. The biographical facts come partly from *curriculum vitae* of the vice-chancellors made available to us by the vice-chancellor's office, and partly from interviews. For an apt discussion of vice-chancellors see Robert Gaudino, *The Indian University* (Bombay, 1965), pp. 173–182.

55. Government of India, Ministry of Education, *Indian University Administration* (Delhi, 1958), pp. 43–48.

56. *Western Times* (Ahmedabad), 30 August 1969.

57. *Loksatta* (Baroda), 21 February 1970.

58. Champaklal Shah went on to thank the chief minister of Gujarat, Hitendra Desai, the chief justice of the Gujarat high court, P. M. Bhagvati, and the chancellor of MSU, the (ex) Gaekwad of Baroda, Fatehsingh Rao, "for the interest they have taken and for smoothing the road of selection of the new vice-chancellor." The array of persons thanked suggests that external procedures and voices were involved in the canvassing and selection processes.

59. K. N. Raj's public letter submitted at the time of his resignation is an essay on the problems of the Indian university and the vice-chancellor's role. "The University and Its Future; an Open Letter to the Teachers of the University," mimeo. (Delhi, 6 October 1970).

60. For a thoughtful discussion of problems concerning vice-chancellor roles, see D. M. Desai, "Some Recent Thinking on the Role and Appointment of Vice Chancellors and Pro-Vice-Chancellors in Indian Universities," in Madan and Patel, eds., *Report of the Symposium on University Administration,* pp. 42–47. See also Baroda Act No. XVII of 1949, Clauses 10(1) and (2), 12(1); and MSU of Baroda, *The Handbook, 1961,* pt. 2, pp. 8 and 9.

61. The subsequently reversed derecognition of the princes by ordinance in 1970 did not affect the chancellorship of Baroda. In November, the university senate voted that the Maharaja of Baroda should continue in view of the services rendered by him and his family to the university. Although the maharaja served as health minister in the government of Gujarat after March 1967, he did not hold the same constitutional position as a governor acting as chancellor.

62. Government of India, *Indian University Administration,* p. 39.

63. In 1967 and 1968, a substantial number of Baroda faculty began to favor, and the vice-chancellors committee supported, a more complex process of selection. It would have removed election from the senate and asked the government (or governor) of Gujarat to choose from a panel of three formu-

lated by a committee composed of nominees of the state government, of the vice-chancellors of Gujarat, and of the senate.

64. "Members of the Senate, MS University of Baroda," Baroda, no date, mimeo.

65. K. N. Raj at Delhi believed that the elected teacher members of Delhi's academic council, who asked for a review of the case of students he had rusticated, were asking him to pursue a brokerage function inimical to academic work.

66. MSU of Baroda, *The Handbook, 1961*, pt. 2, pp. 15 and 16.

67. For an account of Patel's election as president of the city Congress committee, see *Loksatta* (Baroda), 27 March 1967; for Amin's and Hathi's roles in the Baroda municipal election which was due in 1967 but held in 1968, see *Loksatta* (Baroda), 18 March 1967.

68. *Swatantra Sarjan* (Baroda), 20 August 1967, and miscellaneous interviews.

69. The heads of departments in the arts faculty favored an academic council, to deal with "courses of studies, medium of instruction, tutorial system, methods of examination." MSU of Baroda, *Report of the Vice-Chancellor's Committee, 1969*, p. 59. The academic council was also favored by the symposium on university administration held in April 1967. Madan and Patel, eds., *Symposium on University Administration*, p. 87.

70. MSU of Baroda, *Report of the Vice-Chancellor's Committee, 1969*, pp. 33 and 53.

71. MSU of Baroda, *The Handbook, 1961*, pt. 2, p. 11.

72. Interviews and *Western Times* (Ahmedabad), 31 August 1969.

73. MSU of Baroda, *The Handbook, 1961*, pt. 2, p. 11–13, and official lists of the senate.

74. Madan and Patel, eds., *Symposium on University Administration*.

75. MSU of Baroda, *Report of the Vice-Chancellor's Committee, 1969*, pp. 1–2.

76. Baroda University Teachers' Association, untitled leaflet (Baroda, 1969).

77. Ibid., p. 7. The committee did not recommend an academic council, although both the symposium and heads of departments in the arts faculty favored it. The committee recommended a minuscule increase in teacher representation on the expanded syndicate, from five to seven in a syndicate increased from fifteen to seventeen. It defended the principle of state nomination of senate members, but recommended that nominated members be reduced from twenty-five to twenty members.

78. MSU of Baroda, *Seventeenth Annual Report, 1965–66* (Baroda, 1966), p. 173. We have also consulted *Ninth Annual Report*, p. 7; *Eleventh Annual Report*, p. 7; *Fourteenth Annual Report*, p. 7. The exact figure for 1965–66 was 11,629.

79. MSU of Baroda, *Twentieth Annual Report, 1968–69* (Baroda, 1969), p. 3. The growth in this year was 1.1 percent.

80. MSU of Baroda, *The Handbook, 1961*, p. 39.

81. See K. N. Raj, "The University and Its Future."

82. MSU of Baroda, *Report of the Vice-Chancellor's Committee, 1969*, p. 13.

83. MSU of Baroda, *Statement of Business, Senate Meeting, 31 March 1967* (Baroda, 1967), pp. 6–7.

84. MSU of Baroda, *Budget Estimates for 1967–68* (Baroda, 1967). (Submitted to the Senate 31 March 1967.)

85. *Western Times* (Ahmedabad), 31 August 1969.

86. *Link* (Delhi), 7 February 1965; 14 March 1965; 21 March 1965.

87. *Loksatta* (Baroda), 2 May 1956.

88. For the opinion of heads of arts faculty departments, see MSU of Baroda, *Report of the Vice-Chancellor's Committee, 1969,* pp. 57–60.

89. See MSU of Baroda, Faculty of Technology and Engineering, *Synopsis of Research and Development Projects in Collaboration with Industries* (Baroda, 1969).

90. The syndicate voted on April 19, 1969, to give 300,000 square feet of university land to the Baroda municipal corporation, at nominal cost, "for the purpose of widening of the roads necessary for development, and improvement of traffic facilities on the road in and around the university campus." Copy of the resolution published in *Emester* (Baroda), 15 August 1969.

91. *Western Times* (Ahmedabad), 30 August 1969.

92. The proportions for 1965–66 were 40 percent, state government; 7 percent, UGC; and 53 percent, universities own income from fees and endowments, mostly the former. MSU of Baroda, *Budget Estimates for 1967–68,* pp. 2 and 4, "Actuals," 1965–66.

93. Desai and Pandit, *Growth and Development,* table 56, "Block Grants of the State Government to the Baroda University," p. 116.

94. MSU of Baroda, *Report of the Vice-Chancellor's Committee, 1969,* p. 28.

95. The university's budget memorandum suggests the nature of the three-cornered relationship between the UGC, MSU, and the state government. MSU of Baroda, *Budget Estimates for 1967–68,* p. 146.

96. Desai and Pandit, *Growth and Development,* p. 117.

97. Desai and Pandit, *Growth and Development,* table 56, p. 116. The average percentage of state contributions from 1961–62 to 1966–67, the terminal date of the table, was 35.

98. MSU of Baroda, *Budget Estimates for 1967–68,* p. 141.

99. The details are the result of interviews, and may be verified in MSU of Baroda, *Budget Estimates for 1967–68,* p. 146.

100. An interview with chancellor William McGill (now president of Columbia) in November 1969 confirmed what is apparent from budget allocations and manifest differences in size, distribution, and quality of faculty and students, particularly at the postgraduate level. Such differences arise, in California's case at least, from differential treatment by the president's office and by the regents rather than from the legislature.

101. The UGC, to be sure, has also been significant for bread and butter matters. Its role in "development expenditures" — the buildings for the departments — has been crucial. From 1953 to 1967 it contributed 71 percent to such university construction. See Desai and Pandit, *Growth and Development.* The calculations are based on figures in table 1, p. 22.

102. I. P. Desai, R. F. Kothari, and I. S. Gulati, "Our Universities," *Seminar* (Bombay), March 1960, p. 13.

103.   Amitai Etzioni, *A Comparative Analysis of Complex Organizations* (New York, 1961), p. 220.

104.   Alvin W. Gouldner, "Cosmopolitans and Locals: Towards an Analysis of Latent Social Roles," *Administrative Sciences Quarterly*, 2 (1957), p. 288.

105.   Raj, "The University and Its Future," pp. 23–24.

106.   In response to the recommendation of the Education Commission, 1964–1966, that selective admission be adopted for higher secondary and undergraduate institutions, the parliamentary committee that reviewed its report argued that "every effort should be made to provide admissions to institutions of higher education to all eligible students who desire to study further." Government of India, *Report of the Committee of Members of Parliament on Education, 1967: National Policy on Education* (New Delhi, 1967), p. iv.

12.   The Problem of Autonomy: The Osmania University Case

1.   *Asian Recorder*, 1965 (New Delhi), p. 6826.

2.   The historical part of this study has benefitted greatly from comments and sources supplied by Karen Leonard. In her Ph.D. dissertation she traces the rise of feelings of native Hyderabadis against the influx of outsiders, the *mulki* movement, of which the founding of the university was an expression. For this background see her "The Kayasths of Hyderabad City; Their Internal History and Their Role in Politics and Society from 1850 to 1900," Ph.D. thesis, Department of History, University of Wisconsin, 1969.

3.   For further information on this period, see Arthur Lothian, *Kingdoms of Yesterday* (London, 1951) and V. P. Menon, *The Story of the Integration of the Indian States* (Bombay, 1956), chap. 19.

4.   Whether this lack of conflict meant that there were no undesirable informal consequences of government control — patronage appointments, admission of favored students, intervention in teaching curricula — or that these practices were an accepted part of Osmania and so did not become issues is not known. Nostalgic teachers looking from the present dispute into the past argue that the university then had more freedom, but I am dubious.

5.   The major exception to the general calm was the Vande Mataram movement, in which Hindu students went on strike for the right to sing nationalist prayers in the university hostels and were suspended from the university.

6.   Jung personally opposed English as a medium of instruction except for medicine and engineering. He secured Nehru's approval for a plan to convert Osmania into a centrally administered Hindi language university; since spoken Hindi is very similar to spoken Urdu, this would have effectively maintained the position of Urdu and Urdu speakers in the university. The plan was dropped, however, because of opposition from the new political leaders in the state who feared that a central university would not serve the educational needs of the surrounding region.

7.   The fact that Jung was appointed vice-chancellor even though he had served the old regime is an indication of his preeminence. One of the few men in the state with an Oxford degree, he was a good choice to guide Osmania in its transition.

8. See Menon, *Integration,* chaps. 17–19, and Susan G. Hadden, "The Telangana Revolt, 1946–1951; The Failure of a People's National Liberation Struggle in India," M.A. paper, The University of Chicago, Spring Quarter 1968.

9. Government of Hyderabad, Department of Statistics and Census, *Statistical Yearbook, 1941–1945* (Hyderabad, 1946), p. 194.

10. The procedure for affiliation is as follows: the founders of the college make an application to the university for affiliation. (Affiliation means that the university agrees to examine and grant university degrees to students of the college.) In response to this request, the university sends out an inquiry committee, chosen by the syndicate, to examine the college facilities and make recommendations of improvements to be undertaken before affiliation. In almost all cases, the college is affiliated immediately after making a promise to fulfill the conditions. If the college does not comply, the university may disaffiliate the college, but has never done so.

11. Government of India, Ministry of Home Affairs, *Andhra Pradesh Regional Committee Order, 1958* (Delhi, 1958), schedule 1, clause 4.

12. "Gentleman's Agreement," Telengana Mahasabha, typescript, 1958, point 3. This was an agreement between eight prominent ministers and chief ministers of the two regions; it has no legal status but is expected to be honored. The same document also assured that revenue surpluses from Telengana would be spent only in the region, and that government service posts would be reserved for Telengana personnel wherever qualified people were available. Failure to observe these provisions generated grievances which erupted in 1969 in a movement to separate Telengana from the state. The employment issue caused much concern among university students, who initiated the movement.

13. This includes admission into all postgraduate courses, except those recognized and funded by the UGC as all-India centers, of which there is one at Osmania. The UGC's potential influence through other grants has not been used on this issue.

14. Inter-University Board secretary Amrik Singh agreed that the personality and skills of the vice-chancellor are the most important factors in university administration. Interview, New Delhi, August 1967.

15. The identification with administration is, in part, a legacy of the Indian Educational Service, and, in part, a manifestation of the "genetic imprint" that British rule and British founding of Indian universities left on Indian higher education. See chaps. 2 and 13, this volume.

16. Interview, Hyderabad, September 1967.

17. A former member of the syndicate and admirer of D. S. Reddi's astuteness declared he did not remember an occasion when the syndicate opposed the wishes of the vice-chancellor. Interview, Hyderabad, September 1962. This does not mean, however, that Reddi dominated faculty and other syndicate members. Many faculty appreciated his willingness to adopt ideas suggested by them.

18. Interview, New Delhi, August 1967.

19. Osmania is the only Indian university, excepting the Delhi School of Economics, with four professorships in economics.

20. See *Constitution of India,* Article 163.

21. Seventy percent of the seats in professional schools are reserved for

students from *outside* Hyderabad city. Osmania University, "Rules of Admission," mimeo. (Hyderabad, 1968), p. 26.

22.   Regarding the UGC in Britain see Robert O. Berdahl, "British Universities and the State: A Contrast with the American Scene," appendix B of Malcolm Moos and Francis O'Rourke, *The Campus and the State* (Baltimore: 1959), pp. 339–370. For the functioning of the UGC in India, see chap. 6, this volume.

23.   It had been alleged in political and educational circles throughout the state that vice-chancellor Dr. A. L. Narayana favored his relatives in hiring staff and interfered in examination results to benefit friends able to help him with control of the university administration.

24.   The text of the report had been serialized in the daily newspapers. An exacerbating factor in this case was the resentment of the increasing brahman population of the university, strengthened by the appointment of Narayana's relatives. Many of the ministers, who were predominantly Reddis, were from Andhra, where antagonism between brahmans and non-brahmans arose during the nationalist movement. At about this time the vice-chancellor of Andhra's third university, Sri Venkateswara University, also was becoming known for favoritism toward his caste, the Naidu community. Thus both universities raised caste issues which aggravated the politicians' distrust of educationists.

25.   For a general discussion of this and other dimensions of vice-chancellor selection, see chap. 11 and pt. 3, "Editors' Introduction," this volume.

26.   Interview with P. V. Narsimha Rao, minister of law during the conflict, Hyderabad, August 1967.

27.   The three vice-chancellors had been having annual meetings since 1962 to discuss matters of common interest with the state education minister, but this was a much larger conference.

28.   Government of Andhra Pradesh, "Report of the Conference of the Chief Minister of Andhra Pradesh with the Vice-Chancellors and Educationists on Collegiate and Secondary Education, October 23 and 24, 1964," mimeo. (Hyderabad).

29.   In a subsequent letter to national education minister, M. C. Chagla, the chief minister noted that the Radhakrishnan report on higher education in 1951 had recommended abolition of the election system because of the embarrassing effects of canvassing. Brahmananda Reddy, "Letter to M. C. Chagla," released to the press and extensively quoted in *Deccan Chronicle* (Hyderabad), 7 December 1965.

30.   By virtue of a five-year contract the Indian vice-chancellor has much more protection than the American university president. When Clark Kerr was dismissed from the presidency of the University of California by the regents at the behest of Governor Ronald Reagan, there were no procedural safeguards available in what was openly recognized as a politically motivated action. Similarly, the dismissal in August 1970 of Texas Dean John R. Silber by regent board chairman Frank C. Erwin Jr. lacked any procedural safeguards.

31.   Because this committee was chaired by the chief minister, it could make significant changes in the bill.

32.   This was reported in "Why We Oppose the Amendment Bill," pamphlet published by the teachers of Osmania University (Hyderabad, November 1965).

33. For similar attitudes in the United States, see Richard Hofstadter, *Anti-Intellectualism in American Life* (New York, 1963).

34. Both D. S. Reddi and the law minister who piloted the bill report that there was no specific reference to future policy issues when the clause was formulated. Government language policy, as outlined in the chief minister's official statement in March 1965, was most concerned with the problem of securing an equitable division of central government posts among different language groups. This suggests that the state government did not intend to press the university for regional language instruction until employment of students trained in regional languages was more secure. Enrollments in courses in languages other than English bear out the chief minister's concern for employment first. In 1966, the university reported that out of 35,640 students, only 110 students were enrolled in Hindi language sections, 92 in Urdu language, and 24 in Telugu. These figures did not represent a significant increase over previous years. "Vice-Chancellor's Report to the Annual Convocation," pamphlet published by Osmania University (Hyderabad, 23 December 1966).

35. Interviews, Hyderabad, August and September 1967.

36. The locus of authority over the language of instruction in higher education has been a subject of national political and judicial debate. See M. C. Chagla's resignation as external affairs minister in September 1967, when national education minister Triguna Sen tried unsuccessfully to bypass university and state authority over language of instruction in an effort to replace English with regional languages within five years. *Asian Recorder,* 1967 (New Delhi), pp. 7930, 7932. Note also the supreme court case denying the state government of Gujarat authority to impose Gujarati as a language of instruction on the ground that doing so touches the maintenance of national standards in education, a subject reserved for the central government. See chap. 6, this volume, regarding Gujarat University case.

37. "Why We Oppose the Amendment Bill."

38. Gautham Mathur, "Autonomy and Osmania University Legislation," unpublished pamphlet (December 1965), p. 41.

39. There were several minor provisions which were disputed, also in the name of autonomy. The clause restricting the choice of outside experts on selection committees to Andhra natives was clearly unworkable and opposed by both university and central government authorities. A clause giving the government control over the service conditions of teachers in affiliated colleges was supported by the university. Thirdly, there were strong objections to the reduction of the vice-chancellor's term to three years, though others suggested that this provided a way of insuring his responsibility which was preferable to a removal clause.

40. Under the Hyderabad general clauses act (Act No. 111 of 1308F) an appointing authority has power to suspend or dismiss, unless otherwise expressly provided. D. S. Reddi, Writ Petition.

41. Interviews with C. D. Deshmukh and Amrik Singh, September and August 1967. Since the initial passage of the acts the procedures for dismissal of a vice-chancellor have been tested in a case in which a vice-chancellor of Kurukshetra University was dismissed. "Freedom and Right," that he had not revealed to the university syndicate. *Delhi,* 10 December 1965, went his compulsory

retirement from government service. He took the case to court, which upheld the syndicate's right to dismiss a vice-chancellor.

42.   D. S. Reddi declared in a meeting of the university senate that the vice-chancellor was not even accorded the protection and dignity given a minor employee of the university. *Indian Express* (Vijayawada), 30 October 1965.

43.   Interview with Narsa Raju, advocate for D. S. Reddi, and former advocate general of Andhra Pradesh, Hyderabad, September 1967.

44.   Several members of the joint select committee were unhappy with the procedures of the committee and with the results they produced. Three members, all non-Congress party members, none Communists, wrote dissenting opinions which raised most of the issues that have been discussed above. Among the spokesmen of political parties, the secretary of the Hyderabad city Communist party was one of the first to speak out in favor of the teachers. His statement represented a reversal of the earlier Communist position as expressed by the state leader, P. Sundarayya, at the 1964 educationists' conference, where he had supported provisions that increased political controls. Communists had been critical of the university for its isolation from society, but found that the government bills pushed intervention, at least by a Congress government, too far.

45.   This sequence of events conforms with that given in Mathur, "Autonomy and Osmania University Legislation."

46.   A few of the new universities have failed to meet the rather modest qualification criteria that IUB inspection committees require, so the IUB membership does not include all universities. See chap. 6, this volume, for details.

47.   *Hindustan Times* (New Delhi), 19 November 1965.

48.   *Statesman* (Calcutta), 22 November 1965.

49.   Mathur, "Autonomy and Osmania University Legislation," p. 50. The vice-chancellor repeated this assurance to an emergency senate meeting the next day; *Daily News* (Hyderabad), 24 November 1965.

50.   The ambiguity of this third area was what most alarmed university protagonists.

51.   *Times of India* (Bombay), 23 November 1965.

52.   The motive alluded to was their demand that recent pay increases be made retroactive, a demand which the union had been making for some time. *Daily News* (Hyderabad), 24 November 1965.

53.   *Deccan Chronicle* (Hyderabad), 22 November 1965.

54.   IUB Chairman, Sir C. P. Ramaswamy Iyer, declared, "The committee felt that vesting of power in the government to give directives or instructions to the university on matters of educational policy was a serious distraction from autonomy."

55.   See chap. 6, this volume, for some discussion of this point.

56.   *Maharastra Times,* 6 December 1965 (translated).

57.   *Patriot* (New Delhi), 8 December 1965.

58.   The press had given wide coverage to a letter from C. P. Ramaswamy Iyer, chairman of the IUB   arshly cri   zed the acts for violating the "university's inherent

59.   *Patriot* (Ne

60. *Indian Express* (Vijayawada), 13 December 1965; *Statesman* (Calcutta), 14 December 1965.

61. His news statements in this period were almost a ritual recitation that his government had no intention of interfering in university autonomy, and that there were reasons for the bills which no one would acknowledge. *Indian Express* (Vijayawada), 6 December 1965.

62. The chief minister said he had a feeling, "that the controversy is a result of subjective attitudes of interested friends." *Times of India* (Bombay), 9 December 1965.

63. D. S. Reddi, press statement, *Statesman* (Calcutta), 9 December 1965.

64. The professors had raised this issue earlier with the chief minister and he had declared that he had no intention of removing Reddi. However, the chief minister had declined to make a public statement to this effect. Meanwhile there were rumors in Hyderabad that the removal of D. S. Reddi had been discussed in the select committee hearings. Ibid.

65. Reddi had been interested in becoming vice-chancellor of Thirupathi University, located in his home region. When chief minister Sanjiva Reddy, of the same region, refused to appoint him, D. S. Reddi decided to contest the post, which was formally filled by election. His family and caste ties in the area enabled him to mobilize a large number of state legislative assembly members on that university's senate. It was to avoid such a contest that the chief minister offered D. S. Reddi the Osmania position.

66. D. S. Reddi had remarked that the government had enough other urgent problems and had unwisely chosen to give priority to a bill which had been condemned unequivocally. *Statesman* (Calcutta), 8 December 1965. For a report of Brahmananda Reddy's reaction, see *Deccan Chronicle* (Hyderabad), 10 December 1965.

67. *Statesman* (Calcutta), 19 December 1965.

68. *Statesman* (Calcutta), 26 December 1965.

69. *Deccan Chronicle* (Hyderabad), 28 December 1965.

70. *Indian Express* (Vijayawada), 19 May 1966.

71. Mathur, "Autonomy and Osmania University Legislation," pp. 13–14.

72. See particularly chaps. 1 and 3, and pt. 2.

73. *Deccan Chronicle* (Hyderabad), 14 December 1965.

74. Mathur, "Autonomy and Osmania University Legislation," p. 27.

75. It is interesting that the attorney general argued on behalf of the state government that the government had always intended to remove the vice-chancellor because he had served more than six years, but had found that it needed new legislation to carry this out. Writ Petition #835 of 1966, in the High Court of Judicature, Andhra Pradesh at Hyderabad, 13 October 1966, p. 98.

76. Supreme Court of India, Civil Appeal No. 2313 of 1966, D. S. Reddi vs. Chancellor, Osmania University and others, pp. 27–28.

77. *Andhra Reporter* (Hyderabad), 22 October 1966.

78. The modesty of the demand suggests the seriousness of the problem. Such problems are not unique to Indian universities; many departments in American universities also do not hold such meetings, and there is no forum in which concerns of junior faculty may be expressed.

79. See "Report of the Committee for Internal Autonomy," Report of a

Sub-committee of the Osmania University Teachers Association, mimeo. (Hyderabad, n.d.).

80. Every teacher has the privilege of taking a specified number of days per year for any purpose he wishes by securing prior permission. This practice is common in many Indian institutions.

81. *Indian Express* (Vijayawada), 28 October 1966.

82. The government could have appointed a new vice-chancellor immediately after the stay was lifted by the high court decision, but refrained for one week while the leave for appeal to the supreme court was being debated. When that week expired on October 27, it announced the appointment.

83. *Indian Express* (Vijayawada), 28 October 1969.

84. The next day the OUTA held a mass meeting which adopted a resolution that "no university could function unless the proper atmosphere was created and maintained. Appointment of the new vice-chancellor in complete disregard of the teachers' wishes was unfortunate and could not be binding on the teachers. 'We do not recognize it,' they said." *Indian Express* (Vijayawada), 30 October 1966.

85. Telegrams were sent to the speaker of parliament, prime minister, home minister, education minister, University Grants Commission, Inter-University Board, Bhupesh Gupta of the Communist party, Madhu Limaye of the Socialist party, N. G. Ranga and Minoo Masani of the Swatantra party, Atul Bihari Vajpayee of the Jan Sangh, Ram Manohar Lohia of the Socialists, C. Setelvad, a respected legal scholar and lawyer, and Sanjiva Reddy, former chief minister of Andhra Pradesh. Copies of the telegrams were shown to me by Manzur Alam, professor of Geography, and head of the Hyderabad Metropolitan Project, Osmania University, September 1967.

86. Letter from Ravada Satyanarayan to Dr. Narsimha Rao, 31 October 1966 (typed). This letter made it clear that the opposition of the Committee for Internal Autonomy rested not on personal grounds, but on the lack of consultation with the university. They urged him not to appeal to judicial sanctions, but to withdraw in the interest of higher education.

87. *Indian Express* (Vijayawada), 31 October 1966.

88. Interview, Hyderabad, September 1967.

89. Robert C. Shaw, "Student Unrest in an Indian University," paper submitted to University of Wisconsin College Year in India Program, 2 April 1967.

90. The phenomenon of university administration being intimidated by student demands has been observed in many different contexts. The situation at Osmania does not appear as serious as elsewhere, but the trend could become serious if authorities do not act to curb it.

91. The president of the Class Four Employees Union declared, "In the university we are able to get many small considerations which we would not get in government service, such as credit when we need it in a hurry, some loans, etc. And within the pay scales, set by the syndicate, there is more room for consideration, for a professor of science has more understanding that a lab attendant has more work and should be raised to a higher pay scale than the government would have." Interview, Hyderabad, September 1967. The much weaker Class Three Employees Union (the non-gazetted officers association), also offered their support by abstaining from work.

92. Framing the question in this manner is not meant to suggest that con-

victions about university autonomy were not of prime importance. Rather, I wish to focus the analysis here on those who entered at the later stage when interests within the university were deciding whether, how, and when to act.

93.   Dr. Narsimha Rao is from Guntur district, the home district of the chief minister.

94.   Government tried to secure the services of Humayun Kabir and C. D. Deshmukh, respected national figures in the education field, and B. Gopal Reddy, a well-liked and cultured former chief minister. When they refused, the chief minister was still committed to making an appointment, very possibly against the wishes of advisers in the education department. It is known that he did not consult the education minister. *Indian Express* (Vijayawada), 22 November 1966.

95.   The situation at Osmania University is different from that at other universities, for Osmania is the only university with constituent colleges outside the university campus which are run directly by the vice-chancellor. At the time of the amalgamation with Andhra the university was allowed to keep these colleges, all but one of which are in the city, as a concession to Telengana people. The UGC scales are recommended pay scales for university, not college, teachers. The UGC agrees to pay the increment for the first five years, providing the state government agrees to take up the burden after that point. Due to Osmania's unique organization, these scales potentially applied to many more teachers than the UGC intended. When the UGC became aware of this, it asked the vice-chancellor to suggest some way of differentiating among teachers. It was therefore decided to amend the new scales on the basis of merit; then from January 1966 they were applied to all. Whether the extension of these scales to the whole body of university teachers was purposely done to mobilize support behind the vice-chancellor is a matter of debate, but the raise does seem to have contributed to the vice-chancellor's support in the university.

96.   This sentiment was expressed by an opposition leader who said that the vice-chancellor seemed to think he was the only man in the state who knew anything about education. Interview, Hyderabad, August 1967.

97.   Though the vice-chancellor argued before the high court that the position should be considered personal property, he spent more money on the supreme court case than he gained in salary by remaining in office.

98.   One thinks, for example, of Harvard's willingness to make special arrangements for scions of old or prominent families and foreign notables, such as the readmission of Edward Kennedy, who had had his "connection severed" for having a friend take an examination for him. The action was not unique, but did at least use discretion in a favorable manner; also the admission of the son of the then chief of staff of the Pakistan army, General Musa, later governor of East Pakistan, at the behest of the Aga Khan, a graduate and benefactor of the university, even though the son did not have strong secondary school credentials. It should be added, however, that these arrangements tend to be limited by the propensity of most faculty not to adjust their standards. The general's son did not survive his first year.

99.   Another channel for transmitting outside politics to the university arena was through the politician members of the syndicate: it was they who urged rejection of the chief minister's nephew's medical school transfer. This need not

suggest that their stand on the university issue was motivated by Congress party factional politics, but it may suggest that their experiences in state politics disinclined them to trust the motives of the chief minister in the university or to allow him any more room than they might have received from him in the state arena.

100. *Hindu* (Madras), 31 August 1967.

101. Increased funds were needed partly in order to grant the same dearness allowance to university employees that the state had given its own employees. This is an example of the escalation of wage demands throughout the country. When central rates were increased, state employees went on strike to have theirs increased, and won their demand just before the 1967 election. The pressure on the university followed. The total wage bill for university employees would increase to more than eighteen lakhs in the following year, 1967–68. Osmania University "Note on the Block Grant of Osmania University," (n.d.).

102. C. V. H. Rao, "Andhra's Unsound Finances," *Economic and Political Weekly,* 1 April 1967, p. 632.

103. The vice-chancellor argued, however, that because university requests are taken into account by the periodic finance commissions that allocate centrally collected revenues to the states, education's share of such funds should be secure rather than subject to arbitrary cuts. The state government held that finance commission allocations are not tied to specific items in the state budget, and that therefore the state government is free to appropriate funds as it deems necessary. For the role of the finance commissions see D. T. Lakdawala, *Union-State Financial Relations* (Bombay, 1967).

104. To the credit of the government the university never before complained of financial limitation, except in such matters as student fee increases. In comparison with many American state universities, Indian universities are much more financially independent. Their grants extend for five years, eliminating the annual waiting period before the state legislature acts which many American state universities must endure. The rhetoric about the need to separate financial controls from academic decision-making in India shows, however, the increasing nervousness of educationists about such control. See Moos and O'Rourke, *The Campus and the State,* particularly chaps. 4, 10, and 11, for an account of the financial relationships of U.S. state universities to state governors and legislators.

105. Some of the roots of the Telengana conflict can be traced back to the Osmania dispute. University faculty complained of the same feeling of misunderstanding and domination by an Andhra-based government, a feeling which later erupted into the separatist movement. This movement was launched by Osmania students who complained that they were not getting their share of jobs, as promised in the agreement which joined Telengana with Andhra. (All government positions in Telengana were to be filled by Telengana personnel. Students complained that many jobs had been given to Andhras; the government rebutted that Andhras had been employed only when no qualified Telengana people were available. The roots of the problem extend far beyond job discrimination, as the similar dilemma over Negro employment in the United States makes clear.) The pride with which student leaders described their role in the Osmania dispute suggests that that organizing experience con-

tributed to their ability to launch the separatist movement. The Telengana movement quickly passed out of student hands, however, as political leaders tapped a number of other grievances and took the movement far beyond the employment issue to a full separatist demand.

106. See Government of India, Ministry of Education, *Report of the Education Commission, 1964–1966,* pp. 326–331, for its view of this issue.

107. Rasheeduddin Khan, "The Concept of University Autonomy," *Journal of University Education,* 4, no. 2 (December 1965), pp. 99–104.

108. Gautham Mathur, "Autonomous Universities in a Democratic Community," *Conspectus,* Quarterly Journal of the India International Center, no. 4 (1966).

109. Model Act, p. 8.

110. Brian Simon, *Studies in the History of Education, 1780–1870* (London, 1960), chap. 4, notes that in a time of similar rapid change in Britain, the parliamentary reports of 1852 on Oxford and Cambridge made arguments similar to those of Osmania's socialists: "the universities were national institutions"; the colleges were "wholly unable to take the necessary steps"; the university was in the hands of a "narrow oligarchy," so that parliament had every right to intervene.

111. A. D. Bhogle, "Autonomy in a Plan-oriented Society," *Journal of University Education,* 4, no. 2 (December 1965), pp. 104–107.

112. Reddy, "Letter to M. C. Chagla."

113. For a comparative analysis, see chap. 10, this volume, where Irene Gilbert shows how Muir Central College was saved the conflict over autonomy to which Presidency was subjected.

114. Theodore P. Wright points out the similarity between Chagla's intervention in a dispute at Aligarh Muslim University and his handling at the same time of the Osmania controversy; in both he upheld secularist cosmopolitan vice-chancellors. It is interesting that the Aligarh vice-chancellor was Ali Yawar Jung, who earlier had piloted Osmania through its transition from Urdu to English and had sought to make it a Hindi-speaking university. Private communication. See Theodore P. Wright, "Muslim Education in India at the Crossroads: The Case of Aligarh," *Pacific Affairs,* 39, nos. 1 and 2 (Spring and Summer 1966), pp. 50–63.

115. Indian universities are not entirely at fault for their failure to engage in research and contribute to knowledge. Much of the financial support for these activities has been given to special research institutes or agencies. This attempt to bypass tradition-bound, politics-ridden universities may have been the quickest way to enable the recently trained sophisticated modern professionals to get on with their work, but it has deprived the universities of crucial reinvigoration. See chaps. 4 and 6, this volume.

116. A representative from the government observed, "Our universities and particularly Osmania have been functioning in isolation, cut away from the social life, aspirations and frustrations, the song and drama of Andhra Pradesh. It has been gloating over its own traditions and living on old laurels, making much of the abused expression, cosmopolitan atmosphere." *Andhra Reporter* (Hyderabad), 8 January 1966.

117. Theodore P. Wright points out that less than half of the university

faculty would be able to teach in Telugu. Many of the Hyderabad Telugus were educated in Urdu and do not even read Telugu. Private communication.

118. The press seems to have been unanimously on the side of the university. Even the Telugu newspapers, which one might expect to be more sympathetic to the Andhra politicians, ran articles upholding the university position.

119. Interview, Hyderabad, August 1967.

Introduction to Part IV

1. See Malcolm Moos and Francis E. Rourke, *The Campus and the State* (Baltimore, 1959), for an overview of financial procedures and relationships. For particulars of state budgets in the U.S. see the annual review by M. M. Chambers for the National Association of State Universities and Land-Grant Colleges entitled "Appropriations of State Tax Funds for Operating Expenses of Higher Education." (Washington, annual, mimeo).

2. See, for example, Everett C. Hughes, *Men and Their Work* (Glencoe, Ill., 1958).

3. For these developments see Laurence R. Veysey, *The Emergence of the American University* (Chicago, 1965); Christopher Jencks and David Riesman, *The Academic Revolution* (Garden City, N.Y., 1969), chaps. 1, 5, and 12; Richard J. Storr, *The Beginnings of Graduate Education in America* (Chicago, 1953), and *Harper's University* (Chicago, 1966); and Theodore Caplow and Reece J. McGee, *The Academic Marketplace* (Garden City, N.Y., 1965).

4. See for example Allan M. Cartter, *An Assessment of Quality in Graduate Education* (Washington, D.C., 1966), sponsored by the American Council on Education.

5. Ronald Reagan's success in running "against" the university when he won the California governorship in 1966, and the firing of Dean John R. Silber, who had raised the level of scholarship and teaching, by Texas Board of Regent's chairman Frank C. Erwin, Jr. in August 1970, qualify but do not contradict this observation. See *New York Times,* 17 August 1970, and *Time,* 10 August 1970.

6. See C. P. Snow, *The Two Cultures* (Cambridge, England, 1959) and the subsequent controversy. For the reception of engineering at Cambridge, see T. J. N. Hilken, *Engineering at Cambridge University, 1783–1965* (Cambridge, 1967). A chair in engineering was established in 1875, and Isaac Milner, "dabbled in" the subject in the late eighteenth century. See Brian Simon, *Studies in the History of Education, 1780–1870* (London, 1960), for an overview of this period. W. J. Reader, *Professional Men, The Rise of the Professional Classes in Nineteenth Century England* (London, 1966), discusses the reports of the Oxford University Commission of 1852, the Cambridge University Commission of 1852, the Public Schools Commission of 1864 (Clarendon Commission), and the Schools Enquiry Commission of 1868 (Taunton Commission). These reports provided the impulse for re-evaluation and reform.

7. See the articles by Tom Burns and A. H. Halsey on the social sciences in British government and higher education together with "commentary" on

them in the *Times Literary Supplement,* 5 March 1970, pp. 249–250, 252, and 257–258. The Burns article details the very recent academic growth of the social sciences in British universities.

8. Reader, *Professional Men,* p. 108.

9. Examinations in medicine were conducted before 1880; examinations in civil engineering began in 1897; examinations in law in 1836–37; in architecture in 1863 (voluntarily) and 1882 (compulsorily); in pharmaceutical fields in 1842; in veterinary science in 1881; in mechanical engineering in 1913; and in insurance in 1850. Geoffrey Millerson, *The Qualifying Associations; A Study in Professionalization* (London, 1964), p. 121.

10. Reader, *Professional Men,* p. 118; Millerson, *The Qualifying Associations,* p. 130.

11. Reader, *Professional Men,* p. 176.

12. Cited in Eric Ashby, in association with Mary Anderson, *Universities: British, Indian, African: A Study in the Ecology of Higher Education* (London, 1966), p. 6.

13. Government of India, Ministry of Education, *Report of the Education Commission, 1964–1966* (Delhi, 1967), p. 32, and section 3. For a discussion of these enrollment figures, see chap. 3, note 1.

14. Government of India, *Report of the Education Commission, 1964–1966,* p. 302.

15. See chap. 13, this volume.

16. For the implications of these circumstances in the light of role theory set in the context of educational institutions, see Alvin W. Gouldner, "Cosmopolitans and Locals: Toward an Analysis of Latent Social Roles—I," *Administrative Sciences Quarterly,* 2, no. 3 (1957–58), pp. 281–306.

17. See T. N. Madan, "Who Chooses Modern Medicine and Why," *Economic and Political Weekly* (Bombay), 13 September 1969 and Charles Leslie, "Modern India's Ancient Medicine," *Trans-Actions,* 6 (June 1969), pp. 46–55, for the appeals and relative standing of modern and traditional medicine. The ambiguity of their standing and relationship is reflected in Madan's empirical finding among his sample in Ghaziabad (about twenty kilometers from Delhi) that although a "four-fifths majority of [his] interviewees have a first preference for allopathy," professionals among them "show the lowest preference for allopathy . . . [combining] various types of treatment more than others . . . on the ground of effectiveness" (p. 1483).

18. For one recent study that does so, see Robert Stern's analysis of the goldsmiths' and jewellers' lobby that emerged in response to the government's effort to regulate trade in and the use of gold, *The Process of Opposition in India; Two Case Studies of How Policy Shapes Politics* (Chicago, 1970).

13. The Organization of the Academic Profession in India: The Indian Educational Services, 1864–1924

1. The terms "superior" and "inferior" are taken from British usage, and were used to mark the difference between higher and lower positions within each government service. The distinction between the elite Indian Civil Service

and the superior services, on the other hand, was marked by the use of the terms "covenanted" and "uncovenanted"; all members of the civil service signed covenants, while members of the other services merely signed agreements.

For the sake of convenience, I have used the term "educational serice" generally, except when referring to particular periods in the service's history.

2. See any one of the standard histories of the Indian universities: Premathanath Banerjee, ed., *Hundred Years of the University of Calcutta* (Calcutta, 1957); S. R. Dongerkerry, *A History of the University of Bombay, 1857–1957* (Bombay, 1957); University of Madras, *History of Higher Education in South India,* vol. 1, *University of Madras, 1857–1957* (Madras, 1957).

3. Many provincial governments also maintained arts colleges in the districts. The premier colleges were usually located in the capital city near the seat of the university, and often served as university buildings for senate and syndicate meetings, examinations centers, and convocation halls until these were built. The district colleges, on the other hand, were smaller, with fewer students and staff, and designed to fill local educational needs where the missionaries or Indian initiative had failed to do so.

4. The government of India brought out barristers from "home" to serve as justices in the high courts and assigned members of the civil service or the Indian-filled judicial service to serve as magistrates in the district courts.

For a fuller discussion of the organization and founding of the uncovenanted services, see H. H. Dodwell, ed., *The Cambridge History of India,* vol. 6, *The Indian Empire, 1858–1918* (Cambridge, 1932), pp. 357–378.

5. After 1857, these responsibilities were vested in the appropriate faculties of the universities, to which many members of the technical services were appointed in their ex officio capacities.

6. The situation thus came to resemble that in France or Germany, where university or *grandes écoles* courses were the means of professional qualification.

7. Dodwell, *The Cambridge History of India,* vol. 6, pp. 357–378.

8. The Punjab government was the exception; it did not contribute to the support of higher education in English until the establishment of the Lahore Government College in 1864.

9. The provincial governments calculated their general establishment costs on a monthly basis. For the sake of convenience, I have used the same method. In the 1850's, the rupee was valued at ten to the British pound, and retained that value through most of the nineteenth century. Government of the North-Western Provinces, *Proceedings in the General Department,* A-September 1865, nos. 145–161; Government of India, *Proceedings in the Home Department, Education Branch,* A-20 December 1862, nos. 14–15; India Office, *Public Letters from Bengal and India,* vol. 47 (1855), Letter from Government of India, dated 13th August 1855, no. 67 (Education).

10. For a detailed outline of the curriculum and syllabi required in the three universities shortly after their founding, see Sir Alexander Grant, *Report by Sir A. Grant, Director of Public Instruction at Bombay, on the note of Mr. A. Monteath on the State of Education in India* (London, 1867).

11. Government of India, *Proceedings in the Home Department, Education Branch,* A-3 June 1864, nos. 1–7.

12. Ibid.

13. Government of India, *Proceedings in the Home Department, Education Branch,* A-20 December 1862, nos. 14–15.

14. Government of India, *Proceedings in the Home Department, Education Branch,* A-3 June 1864, nos. 1–7.

15. Although no permanent increase in salary attached to it, seniority within a grade was important because it opened the way to temporary or acting promotions as vacancies occurred in the higher grades in consequence of their incumbents' leaves or furloughs. According to the rules of uncovenanted service employment, salaries were also increased temporarily. Ibid.

16. Atkinson did not make any suggestions as to pension and leave rules for the members of the educational department, but by the 1870's the same rules that generally obtained for members of the uncovenanted services were adopted. Members of the department were permitted to retire on medical certificate after twelve years' service at one-third their average salary for the preceding five years if they entered the service after the age of twenty-five; after twenty-two years at one-half the average; and without medical certificate, after twenty-seven years, also at one-half the average of their salary for the preceding five years. If they entered service before the age of twenty-five, they were obliged to work fifteen, twenty-five, and thirty years before receiving their respective pensions. Professors, who received yearly vacations, were not permitted the annual one month's privilege leave except in the instance of ill health, but they were permitted furloughs to Europe on full pay after eight years' service. Ibid.; and Government of India, *Proceedings in the Home Department, Education Branch,* A-June 1879, nos. 16–40.

17. Government of India, *Proceedings in the Home Department, Education Branch,* A-3 June 1864, nos. 1–7.

18. The secretary's final, retroactive sanction to the scheme was accorded in November 1865. Government of India, *Proceedings in the Home Department, Education Branch,* A-12 January 1866, no. 7.

19. Government of India, *Proceedings in the Home Department, Education Branch,* A-27 July 1865, nos. 26–31.

20. Sir Alexander's title was not a reflection of his services to India, but was one he inherited as a Scottish baronet. He retired from India in 1868 to become principal of Edinburgh University. The information is drawn from a variety of sources, including the service histories of all officers published annually by the provincial governments, the civil and military list published annually by the India Office, C. E. Buckland's *Dictionary of Indian Biography* (London, 1906), and the different editions of the *Dictionary of National Biography.* Since they are drawn from collated sources, the references to one man are not usually cited. See Government of India, *Proceedings in the Home Department, Education Branch,* A-21 March 1867, nos. 24–25.

21. Government of India, *Proceedings in the Home Department, Education Branch,* A-21 March 1867, nos. 24–25.

22. Ibid.

23. Ibid.

24. Government of the North-Western Provinces, *Proceedings in the General Department,* B-April 1866, no. 86; and, Government of India, *Proceedings in the Home Department, Education Branch,* A-4 November 1871, no. 24.

25. Government of India, *Proceedings in the Home Department, Education Branch,* A-June 1879, nos. 16–40.

26. Government of India, *Proceedings in the Home Department, Education Branch,* A-June 1881, nos. 61–65.

27. Government of India, *Proceedings in the Home Department, Education Branch,* A-16 May 1864, no. 23.

28. Government of India, *Proceedings in the Home Department, Education Branch,* A-June 1879, nos. 16–40.

29. The university was responsible for supervising the work of the colleges; the provincial governments merely staffed and financed their own collegiate institutions. See the standard university histories.

30. Government of India, *Proceedings in the Home Department, Education Branch,* A-June 1879, nos. 16–40.

31. Deighton himself was transferred to an inspectorship in 1884, and completed his career in India in that position. Government of India, *Proceedings in the Home Department, Education Branch,* B-December 1870, nos. 37–39.

32. Leitner was a naturalized British citizen of German origin who had been professor of Arabic at King's College, London, before his appointment to the Lahore principalship in 1864. Ibid.

33. The other, Griffiths in the North-Western Provinces, formerly principal of the Sanskrit College, had officiated from time to time as inspector of the Banaras division. Government of India, *Proceedings in the Home Department, Education Branch,* A-June 1879, nos. 16–40.

34. A general reform of all the European uncovenanted services was enacted at this time, and the services called the imperial or all-India services. Dodwell, *Cambridge History of India,* vol. 6, pp. 357–378.

35. Government of India, *Selections from the Records of the Government of India, Home Department, No. CCCLVIII, Home Department Serial No. 24, Papers relating to the Re-organization of the Educational Service in India from 1891–1897* (Calcutta, 1898), pp. 166–169.

36. Ibid., pp. 179–193.

37. Government of India, *Proceedings in the Home Department, Education Branch,* A-June 1881, nos. 52–58.

38. Indian members of the graded departments were permitted to continue on under the old rules, being promoted to higher positions in the diminished grades at two-thirds the regular pay. Unlike their European colleagues, they were not given the option of joining the IES, even at two-thirds the salary. An exception was later made in the case of J. C. Bose of Presidency College in Bengal, however, who was appointed to the imperial service and knighted for his contribution to science. Government of India, *Proceedings in the Home Department, Education Branch,* A-October 1891, nos. 99–103.

39. For a description of the changes enacted in British higher education at this time generally see the relevant portions of J. W. Adamson, *English Education 1789–1902* (Cambridge, 1964); for the reforms at Oxford and Cambridge in particular, see C. E. Mallet, *A History of the University of Oxford,* vol. 3, *Modern Oxford* (New York, 1928), and D. A. Winstanley, *Later Victorian Cambridge* (Cambridge, 1947).

40. Great Britain, *The India Office List for 1913* (London, 1913), pp. 211–212.

41. The discrepancies arose because some cadres carried positions for which no university training was required; for example, the heads of the Calcutta School of Art in Bengal and the Sir J. J. School in Bombay, as well as the staffs of the princes' corps. Government of India, *Proceedings in the Education Department,* B-May 1914, nos. 172–186.

42. Government of India, *Selections,* pp. 179–193.

43. Sen and Sarkar were both promoted to the IES at a later date, and Sarkar knighted for his contributions to the study of Indian history.

44. The Government of India approved the measure on all-India terms in 1915. Government of India, *Proceedings in the Education Department,* A-February 1915, no. 87–91.

45. De la Fosse was later knighted, and Covernton was called back to Bombay as director some years after. W. W. Hornell, a retired inspector of the IES, was appointed by the Bengal government in 1913 from the board of education, where he had been assistant director of examinations. Government of Bengal, *Proceedings in the General Department, Education Branch,* A-August 1906, nos. 71–78.

46. These themes were all touched upon by the Indian witnesses before the commission. Great Britain, Royal Commission on the Public Services in India, *Evidence,* vol. 20 (London, 1916).

47. Government of Bengal, *Report (Part II) of Indian-Owned English Newspapers in Bengal for the Week Ending Saturday, 1st August 1914,* no. 30 (1914), p. 441.

48. Members of the PES received an acting allowance of Rs. 100 per month for officiating in the higher service.

49. Government of India, *Proceedings in the Department of Education and Health, Education Branch,* A-October 1922, nos. 1–3.

50. Government of India, *Proceedings in the Department of Education and Health, Education Branch,* A-October 1922, nos. 1–3.

51. Government of India, *Proceedings in the Education Department,* A-March 1918, nos. 40–42.

52. Government of India, *Proceedings in the Education Department,* A-May 1920, nos. 7–9.

53. Government of India, *Proceedings in the Department of Education and Health, Education Branch,* B-June 1923, "Notes and Orders," (no proceedings number).

54. Government of India, *Proceedings in the Department of Education and Health, Education Branch,* A-October 1922, nos. 1–3.

55. The members of the service were given the choice of retiring on the new pension plans or remaining on with their positions still guaranteed by the secretary of state. In 1931, the IES positions officially reverted to the provincial cadres, some still filled by British and Indian IES men. Great Britain, *Report of the Royal Commission on the Superior Civil Services in India* (London, 1924), p. 16.

56. The members of the educational service did not, however, seem to have been drawn from quite the same levels of the British middle class as the ICS officers. Fewer of them attended the more prestigious public schools, or belonged to the same great Anglo-Indian families. These are only impressions

based on a preliminary reading of the recruitment records. More precise information will be available after I have had an opportunity to analyze research done in England on the social background of IES officers.

57. The directors of public instruction in the larger provinces were included in the forty-sixth rank of the second class of the warrant of precedence, along with inspectors-general of police and accountants-general; directors in the smaller provinces were in the sixty-seventh rank of the third class, along with inspectors-general of police, comptrollers, deputy auditors-general, and the deputy director of the criminal intelligence department. Members of the civil service, on the other hand, were forty-first in the second class if they had twenty-three years' service, and fifty-sixth in the third class if they had eighteen years. Great Britain, *India Office List 1913,* pp. 194, a, b, and c.

58. Covernton's statement about degrees remains to be measured empirically. Royal Commission on the Public Services in India, *Evidence,* vol. 20, pp. 98–99.

59. Ibid.

60. Cunningham described his work at the college in a petition to the Bengal government. Government of Bengal, *Proceedings in the General Department, Education Branch,* A-May 1908, nos. 10–13.

61. See Great Britain, *India Office List for 1913,* p. 211. It was the same for the earlier period.

62. Government of Bengal, *Proceedings in the General Department, Education Branch,* A-May 1908, nos. 10–13.

63. Ibid.

64. Royal Commission on the Public Services in India, *Evidence,* vol. 20, p. 108.

65. Ibid.

66. Many members of the educational service did serve on these university bodies, but in their individual capacities rather than as the appointed representatives of their particular colleges, which is the main point of Hornell's argument. Ibid.

67. Government of India, *Proceedings in the Home Department, Education Branch,* A-October 1891, nos. 99–103.

68. Ibid. Thibaut was principal of the Muir Central College in Allahabad.

69. Ibid.

70. The minute was prepared for Sir Sankaran Nair, education member of the Imperial Legislative Council. Government of India, *Proceedings in the Education Department,* B-October 1917, no. 112.

71. All these themes are discussed at length in my "Autonomy and Consensus under the Raj: Presidency (Calcutta); Muir (Allahabad); M.A.-O. (Aligarh)," chap. 10, this volume.

72. Matthew Arnold, *Culture and Anarchy, An Essay in Political and Social Criticism* (London, 1903), p. xi.

73. What follows is based on information gathered in interviews with retired Indian members of the Indian Educational Service and the Provincial Educational Service cadres in Bengal, the United Provinces, and the Punjab.

74. Government of Bengal, *Proceedings in the General Department, Education Branch,* B-September 1909, nos. 203–204.

75. Ibid.

76. Tables 47 and 49, chap. 10, this volume, outline the career patterns of Presidency and Muir College graduates.

77. The former president of India, Sarvapelli Radhakrishnan, was also a member of the IES in Madras, but spent most of his time in the service up to 1924 on loan to the new university of Mysore.

78. The classrooms were most often used as private rooms; the annual dinner for superior service officers seems only to have been practiced in the Punjab. Interviews with G. C. Chaterjee and Hrish Candhra. New Delhi, November 1966.

79. See Paul Brass, "The Politics of Ayurvedic Education: A Case Study of Revivalism and Modernization in India," chap. 14, this volume.

80. Banerjee, *Hundred Years of the University of Calcutta*, p. 14.

81. Statement by Sir Alfred Croft in 1888, quoted in Government of India, *Proceedings in the Home Department, Education Branch,* A-October 1891, nos. 99–103.

82. For the career patterns of the Presidency, Muir, and Aligarh college graduates, see chap. 10, this volume. Most chose law.

83. Such graduates were still significantly fewer than those who entered the legal profession or the government services, but that is true in most countries, especially in those that inherit an elitest tradition of public service.

84. See Lloyd I. Rudolph and Susanne Hoeber Rudolph, chap. 2, this volume.

85. University chairs in academic subjects began to be established in 1910; law professorships were created a few years earlier. For the particular dates of their founding at each university, see the standard university histories.

14. The Politics of Ayurvedic Education: A Case Study
    of Revivalism and Modernization in India

1. I am indebted to Charles Leslie for pointing out to me the importance of studying Indian medicine from the viewpoint of social science. See his "Professional and Popular Health Cultures in South Asia: Needed Research in Medical Sociology and Anthropology," in Ward Morehouse, ed., *Understanding Science and Technology in India and Pakistan,* Occasional Publication no. 8, University of the State of New York Foreign Area Materials Center (1967), pp. 27–42, and "The Professionalization of Ayurvedic and Unani Medicine," *Transactions of the New York Academy of Sciences,* series 2, vol. 30, no. 4 (February 1968), pp. 559–572.

2. The term "traditionalistic interest group" is used here to describe an interest which uses traditional symbols and which favors the revival of ancient values, but whose clientele does not necessarily come exclusively or even predominantly from the traditional sectors of contemporary Indian society and whose goals are not necessarily opposed to some forms of modernization.

3. Leslie, "Professional and Popular Health Cultures in South Asia," p. 27. The example is not unique to India. A recently published work by Ralph C. Croizier, *Traditional Medicine in Modern China: Science, Nationalism, and the Tensions of Cultural Change* (Cambridge, 1968) and an unpublished manuscript by Edwin J. Allen, Jr., "Medicine in Communist China," indicate that

there are striking similarities, as well as some differences, in the development of traditional medicine in China.

4.   See, for example, J. Filliozat, *The Classical Doctrine of Indian Medicine: Its Origins and Its Greek Parallels* (Delhi, 1964) and Henry R. Zimmer, *Hindu Medicine* (Baltimore, 1948). For some studies of Ayurvedic medicine by Indian scholars, whose interpretations are frequently sharply at variance with those of western scholars, see C. Dwarkanath, *The Fundamental Principles of Ayurveda* (Mysore, 1953); P. Kutumbiah, *Ancient Indian Medicine* (Bombay, 1962; and Shiv Sharma, *The System of Ayurveda* (Bombay, 1929).

5.   For example, the Oxford history of medicine contains nothing on Ayurveda. See Charles J. Singer and E. Ashworth Underwood, *A Short History of Medicine*, 2d ed. (New York, 1962).

6.   This is an oversimplification, but substantially true. On the relationship between theory and treatment in Ayurveda, see Filliozat, *Classical Doctrine of Indian Medicine*, pp. 29–30 in which he argues that, in practice, Ayurvedic treatment was based on experience, to which the theory was adjusted. Modern medicine also recognizes variations in individual constitutions and in individual reactions to medical treatment, depending upon the general condition of the patient and his sensitivities or allergies to certain drugs.

7.   This distinction was emphasized by Dr. C. Dwarkanath, former adviser in indigenous systems of medicine to the ministry of health in an interview on 17 August 1966: "Now, the kind of medical attention [people] get in the rural areas is from what is called a *traditional* medicine. I'm underscoring the word traditional. This is the opposite of what is called classical medicine. The traditional medicine does not proceed on the well-known principles or theories of the medical classics." Personal interview document IM 3: 14.

8.   The following quotation expresses the mixed feelings of many Ayurvedic revivalist leaders toward the traditional Ayurvedic practitioners. "And now, there are only a very few learned Vaidyas who, inspite [sic] of adverse circumstances are keeping the meagre flame of learning alive, while the practice of the art has fallen into the hands of persons, a great majority of whom have neither fully studied the subject nor are competent enough to minister to the needs of the people." Government of India, Ministry of Health, *Report of the Committee on Indigenous Systems of Medicine,* vol. 1 (Delhi, 1948), p. 3; hereafter referred to as *Chopra Committee Report.*

9.   Government of India, Ministry of Health, *Report of the Committee to Assess and Evaluate the Present Status of Ayurvedic System of Medicine* (Delhi, 1959 [?]), p. 25; hereafter referred to as *Udupa Committee Report.*

10.   For example, see J. N. Farquhar, *Modern Religious Movements in India* (New York, 1915); W. Howard Wriggins, *Ceylon: Dilemmas of a New Nation* (Princeton, 1960), chap. 6, "Religious Revival and Cultural Nationalism."

11.   For descriptions of the eight branches of Indian medicine, see C. Dwarkanath, "The Indian Systems of Medicine," *Indian Express* (Delhi), 30 December 1951 and *Udupa Committee Report*, p. 1.

12.   *Udupa Committee Report*, p. 154.

13.   The Muslim Unani or "Greek" system of medicine is today widely practiced in India by both Muslims and Hindus and is undergoing a process of revival similar to that of the Ayurvedic system.

14. That is, between those who favored imparting education in India according to Indian cultural traditions and through Indian languages (the Orientalists) and those who favored the introduction of western education and its instruction through the English language. H. H. Wilson, a leading Orientalist and Sanskritist in this period published an essay "On the Medical and Surgical Sciences of the Hindus," Oriental Magazine, vol. 1 (February 1823), pp. 207–212; see also Zimmer, *Hindu Medicine,* p. lxxi. Macaulay, the most vitriolic of the Anglicists, attacked the Orientalists for their desire to "teach false history, false astronomy, false medicine"; Thomas Babington Macaulay, "Minute on Education," in William Theodore de Bary (ed.), *Sources of Indian Tradition* (New York, 1958), p. 600.

15. *Udupa Committee Report,* p. 25; Leslie, "The Professionalization of Ayurvedic and Unani Medicine," p. 566.

16. From 1835, which is also the year in which Macaulay became president of the committee of public instruction, "higher education in India became, and has since always remained, education in western knowledge of all kinds"; George Anderson, "Education," in Edward Blunt, ed., *Social Service to India: An Introduction to Some Social and Economic Problems of the Indian People* (London, 1938), p. 247.

17. For example, a government school of Ayurveda was established in Travancore as early as 1887. See Government of India, Ministry of Health, *Report of the Health Survey and Planning Committee* (Delhi, 1962), vol. 1, 454; hereafter referred to as *Mudaliar Committee Report.*

18. *Udupa Committee Report,* p. 2.

19. A list of Ayurvedic colleges and their dates of starting is given in *Udupa Committee Report,* appendix ii, pp. 198–205.

20. Ibid., pp. 149–150.

21. The important reports on Ayurveda published under the auspices of the Ministry of Health of the Government of India are as follows: *Chopra Committee Report* (Delhi, 1948); *Report of the Committee Appointed by the Government of India to Advise Them on the Steps to be Taken to Establish a Research Centre in the Indigenous Systems of Medicine and Other Cognate Matters (Pandit Committee Report)* (Delhi, 1951); *Report of the Committee Appointed by the Government of India to study and report on the question of establishing uniform standards in respect of education and regulation of practice of Vaidyas, Hakims and Homoeopaths* (sic) (*Dave Committee Report*) (Delhi, 1956) (this report was preceded by an interim report with the same title published in the same year); *Udupa Committee Report* (Delhi, 1959 [?]); *Report of the Shuddha Ayurvedic Education Committee (Vyas Committee Report)* (Delhi, 1963). In addition, there have been separate reports on the development of modern medicine (which contain references to the subject of indigenous medicine), Unani, and homeopathy.

22. There are constitutional limitations on the central government's ability to act in the sphere of medicine and public health. Although regulation of the medical profession comes under the concurrent list in the Constitution of India, public health and education are state subjects.

23. *Udupa Committee Report,* p. 109.

24. *Mudaliar Committee Report,* vol. 1, p. 32.

25. Government of India, Ministry of Information, *India 1964* (Delhi,

1964), pp. 474–475. However, see table 68, footnote e, chap. 14, this volume.

26. *Udupa Committee Report,* p. 136.

27. Interviews in Chandigarh on 8 October 1966 and in Madras on 20 January 1967.

28. Leslie, "Professional and Popular Health Cultures in South Asia," p. 27.

29. Ibid., pp. 34–35; "The Professionalization of Ayurvedic and Unani Medicine," p. 563; and a letter to me of 13 March 1968.

30. In this category are, among others, Dr. C. G. Pandit, Dr. K. N. Udupa, and Dr. G. S. Pendse.

31. The son of Pandit Shiv Sharma, president of the Ayurvedic Congress, is a modern medical physician in Canada. The son of Ashutosh Majumdar, president of the Council of State Boards and Faculties of Indian Medicine, has an M.B.B.S. degree and has done postgraduate work in Ayurveda at Banaras.

32. This distinction, which was frequently reported to me in India, has also been noted by Charles Leslie and Harold A. Gould. See Leslie, "Professional and Popular Health Cultures in South Asia," where Gould's article, "The Implications of Technological Change for Folk and Scientific Medicine," *American Anthropologist,* 59, no. 3 (1957), is also cited.

33. The notion of "acculturation" appears in Lucian W. Pye, *Politics, Personality and Nation Building: Burma's Search for Identity* (New Haven, 1962), chap. 1; in his "Democracy, Modernization, and Nation Building," in J. Roland Pennock, ed., *Self-Government in Modernizing Nations* (Englewood Cliffs, N.J., 1964), pp. 13–18; and in his *Aspects of Political Development* (Boston, 1966). The general identification of modernization with westernization is extremely common, if not always explicit, in the theoretical literature of nonarea specialists, but is increasingly spurned by field workers, especially in India. There is a growing gap between the theoretical literature on modernization and development, which grows apace, and empirical research on developing countries, which grows more slowly. One example of this easy identification of modernization and westernization can be found in Alfred Diamant, "Political Development: Approaches to Theory and Strategy," in John D. Montgomery and William J. Siffin, eds., *Approaches to Development: Politics, Administration and Change* (New York, 1966), p. 25. "At this point it should not be necessary to define precisely what is meant by modernization except to say it is the sort of transformation which we have come to know in Europe and North America and in less complete forms in other parts of the world. The details might vary, but there is little disagreement about the types of goals involved." In fact, there is hardly an aspect of Indian development policy making which does not involve fundamental disagreement on the goals of modernization. See Wilfred Cantwell Smith, *Modernization of a Traditional Society* (Bombay, 1965), for a trenchant criticism of "the facile fallacy that 'modernization' and 'westernization' are interchangeable terms."

34. This does not mean, however, that the modern medical profession in India does not have its own problems. The Indian Medical Association is the Indian counterpart of the American Medical Association, but it by no means approaches the AMA in scope of membership coverage and control over education and practice. A constantly recurring problem for the modern medical profession in India has been to ward off attempts by government leaders and

groups oriented both to Ayurvedic and to modern medical practice to reduce the qualifications for medical practice in order to extend medical relief more rapidly to the countryside. A national statutory body to regulate medical education, called the Medical Council of India, was created under the Government of India Medical Council Act of 1938 and the Medical Council has been largely successful in imposing international professional standards in modern Indian medical education. One of the main demands of the Ayurvedic movement has been the establishment of a similar council for indigenous medicine. The demand, for long unmet, largely because of internal conflict in the Ayurvedic movement itself on the standards to be enforced by such a council, was finally conceded in 1969 with the establishment of the Central Council of Indian Medicine and Homeopathy.

35. Most Ayurvedic supporters prefer to use the archaic and incorrect terms "allopaths" and "allopathy" to describe modern medical practitioners and the modern system of medicine, respectively.

36. "Whither Are We Going" (editorial), *Journal of Ayurveda* 2, no. 2 (February 1950), p. 6.

37. Ibid., pp. 1–2.

38. Ibid., pp. 5–6. The invocation of Gandhi's name in the quotation is not justified by Gandhi's own views toward medicine and toward Ayurvedic medicine in particular. Gandhi personally favored nature cure. His advice to Ayurvedic practitioners in 1925 was to imitate the "scientific spirit" of western doctors and to "frankly acknowledge and assimilate that part of Western medicine which they at present do not possess." *Young India,* 11 June 1925, cited in *The Bulletin of the Council of State Boards and Faculties of Indian Medicine,* 2, no. 1 (December 1963), pp. 12–13.

39. The system is also called the concurrent system. Proponents of integration distinguish the ideal of integration of the concepts and methods of modern and Ayurvedic medicine from the merely concurrent or side-by-side teaching of the two systems without any real efforts to reconcile them, which has been the predominant manner of instruction in the Ayurvedic institutions. I am grateful to Dr. G. S. Pendse, who has urged me to make this distinction clear.

40. Figures on medical manpower are from *The Bulletin of the Council of State Boards and Faculties of Indian Medicine,* 4, nos. 8–10 (May and June 1967), p. 14, citing Institute of Applied Manpower Research paper no. 6 (1965), pt. 1.

41. This was the view of both the *Chopra* and *Udupa Committee Reports.*

42. *Chopra Committee Report,* vol. 1, chap. 6.

43. "A Rejoinder to the Editorial of the Journal of Indian Medical Association Published in the Month of June 1949 on the Report of the Chopra Committee," *Journal of Ayurveda,* 2, no. 2 (February 1950), p. 41.

44. *Mudaliar Committee Report,* vol. 1, pp. 456–457.

45. See Government of India, Ministry of Health, *Report of the Health Survey and Development Committee (Bhore Committee Report)* (Delhi, 1946), vol. 1, pp. 455–457, where it is argued that the indigenous systems of medicine are out of date and cannot give the best medical relief available, that modern scientific medicine should be extended throughout the country, and that a chair in the history of medicine should be established at the All-India

Medical Institute for the purpose of investigating the possible contribution of these systems "to the sum total of medical knowledge."

46. *Udupa Committee Report*, p. 5.

47. The annual meeting of the central and state health ministers, now called the Central Council of Health.

48. *Mudaliar Committee Report*, vol. 1, pp. 453–454.

49. The Udupa Committee found that the starting salary for an Ayurvedic graduate in government service in most states ranged between Rs. 60 and Rs. 80 or not much more than the salary of a clerk in a government office. The maximum salaries ranged from Rs. 120 to Rs. 375. These figures compared very unfavorably with those of modern medical graduates who, in the lower grades, began at about Rs. 200 and might reach Rs. 400 and, in the higher grades, would start at Rs. 400 and could reach Rs. 1150 per month. In addition, the Ayurvedic practitioners were found to suffer from various handicaps in their practice, including prohibitions against their right to use modern drugs, and refusal of the central and state governments to recognize medical certificates given by Ayurvedic practitioners or to reimburse government employees for medical expenses incurred by them on Ayurvedic medical treatment. The Udupa Committee was distressed to find that "no organised attempt had been made by the members of the Ayurvedic profession themselves to approach Government to revise their status" and that, "in the circumstances," the Ayurvedic practitioners "resort to malpractices and end up as quacks of modern medical science." To remedy this situation, the Udupa committee recommended that the Ayurvedic practitioners should unite and form a single All-India organization of all Ayurvedic practitioners to professionalize themselves and present their case effectively and that the government should grant equality of pay to the Ayurvedic practitioners in government service. *Udupa Committee Report*, pp. 63, 155, 161, 170.

50. *Udupa Committee Report,* p. 60; interviews with faculty and students at the Government Ayurvedic College, Patiala, 19 October 1966, and at the Tilak Ayurved Mahavidyalaya, Poona, 16 January 1966.

51. Interview in Madras, 21 January 1967. The college is now known as the Government Kilpauck Medical College. The curriculum is wholly modern, but there are three research officers in indigenous medicine in residence on the campus and the Medical College hospital has an Ayurvedic ward.

52. *Ayurveda Sandesh* (Lucknow), 15 March 1958. Translated from the Hindi by Dr. Hori Lal Saxena.

53. Ibid.

54. *National Herald* (Lucknow), 22, 24 September; 11, 12, 22, 23, 24, 26 November; 3 December 1966; 6 January 1967; *Times of India* (Bombay), 27 October 1966; *Statesman* (Delhi), 17 November 1966.

55. The data in this and the following paragraph were derived from the materials on student indiscipline in India compiled by Lloyd and Susanne Rudolph from seven national and regional newspapers and generously provided to me.

56. For the remaining fourteen strikes, the issues were either not made clear in the press reports, were related to internal college politics, or were related to external politics on public issues other than education.

57. A third national organization representing the integrated medical gradu-

ates, but less powerful than the Council, is the National Medical Association. In addition, there are many provincial organizations of *vaidyas* and *hakims*, and many lines of conflict at the state and local level which do not necessarily parallel the grand ideological conflict at the national level. In this chapter, the emphasis has been placed upon ideological conflict and national interest group organizations influencing policy-making at the center. However, this dimension of the conflict is only one among many.

58. *Bulletin,* 1, no. 2 (March 1963), p. 3.

59. Krti Sharma, "Ayurvedic Course of Study," *Ayurveda Mahasammelan Patrika,* 48, no. 1 (January 1961), pp. 13–16. Translated by Dr. Hori Lal Saxena.

60. Such a council, called the Central Council of Indian Medicine and Homeopathy, was formed in 1969, after this manuscript was completed.

61. Interim *Dave Committee Report,* p. 7.

62. *Vyas Committee Report,* p. 16.

63. Ibid., p. 14.

64. Ibid., p. 7.

65. Ibid., pp. 5, 8, 10.

66. Ibid., p. 11.

67. For example, the report mentions as concepts compatible with Ayurveda those of "psychosomatic medicine, infection, immunity, susceptibility, endocrine metabolism," and welcomes Dr. Sheldon, the psychologist and somatotypist as a "neo-Ayurvedist" (ibid., p. 9).

68. Interview in Chandigarh, 8 February 1967; Rudolph data on strikes in the Dayanand Ayurvedic College, Jullundur, from January 6 to 16, 1964, and in the Ayurvedic Degree College, Rohtak, 21 January 1964; unrecorded conversations with Dr. C. Dwarkanath and others on the introduction of the *shuddha* curriculum in Madras.

69. *Udupa Committee Report,* pp. 154, 160, 161.

70. *Vyas Committee Report,* p. 8.

71. Council of State Boards and Faculties of Indian Medicine, *A Case for Ayurvedic and Unani Education and Practice* (memorandum submitted to the prime minister of India, 3 December 1963), p. 4.

72. Information on the question of withdrawal of recognition was drawn from the office files and correspondence of the Ayurvedic Congress.

73. Leslie points out that the inability of the Ayurvedists to acquire the internal agreement and cohesion necessary to achieve true professionalization is not simply an ideological problem. The failure goes deeper and reflects the widespread absence of professional norms among Ayurvedic practitioners and the presence of "spurious elements" interested in promoting personal antagonisms and factional rivalries in the Ayurvedic movement. See his "The Professionalization of Ayurvedic and Unani Medicine."

74. Cited in *Mudaliar Committee Report,* vol. 1, p. 456.

75. Interviews at the Government Ayurvedic College, Patiala, 19 October 1966.

76. In the states, the national ideological conflict between the *shuddha* and integrated causes is much less sharp. Politics in the state boards are more likely to follow lines of local factional cleavage, which may become integrated with the national conflicts but have an independent existence. The situation is similar

to the structure of party politics in India, in which there are "national" parties, regional parties, and independents. For example, in the December 1966 elections to the Board of Indian Medicine in Uttar Pradesh, some of the candidates were backed by the National Medical Association and by the Uttar Pradesh Vaid Sammelan, which is affiliated with the Ayurvedic Congress. One candidate was identified with a regional interest organization called the Ashtang Sanrakshini Sabha. There were also several independents. Interview in Lucknow in December 1966 with the registrar and a member of the Board of Indian Medicine, Uttar Pradesh.

77. "In the sphere of medicine, Bharatiya Jan Sangh is not bound to any particular system. It will encourage them all. Ayurveda . . . will be accorded the status of the national system of medicine." Bharatiya Jan Sangh, *Election Manifesto 1967*, reprinted in R. Chandidas et al. (eds.), *India Votes* (New York, 1968), p. 25.

78. Morarji R. Desai, *Inaugural Address . . . at the 40th All Indian Ayurvedic Congress held at Trivandrum (Travancore-Cochin) on May 22–24, 1955* (Delhi, n.d.), p. 5.

79. Mohanlal P. Vyas, *Problems Relating to Future Development of Ayurveda* (Ahmedabad, 1964), p. 1.

80. Letter of Dr. Sampurnanand to all members of the panel on Ayurveda of the planning commission, Lucknow, 12 July 1960.

81. Pye, *Politics, Personality, and Nation Building,* and *Aspects of Political Development*, p. 13.

82. Pye, "Democracy, Modernization, and Nation-Building."

83. *Udupa Committee Report*, p. 145.

Index

30-vidyapilhs